Economics and the theory of games

This textbook offers a systematic, self-contained account of the main contributions of modern game theory and its applications to economics. Starting with a detailed description of how to model strategic situations, the discussion proceeds by studying basic solution concepts, their main refinements, games played under incomplete information, and repeated games. For each of these theoretical developments, there is a companion set of applications that cover the most representative instances of game-theoretic analysis in economics, e.g., oligopolistic competition, public goods, coordination failures, bargaining, insurance markets, implementation theory, signaling, and auctions. The theory and applications covered in the first part of the book fall under the so-called classical approach to game theory, which is founded on the paradigm of players' unlimited rationality. The second part shifts toward topics that no longer abide by that paradigm. This leads to the study of important topics such as the interplay between evolution and rationality, the behavioral dynamics induced by social learning, and how players might tackle the problem of multiple equilibria.

Fernando Vega-Redondo is currently Professor at the Universidad de Alicante and the Universitat Pompeu Fabra. His recent research has focused on both game theory and learning and other interdisciplinary fields such as evolution and Complex networks. His papers have been published in a wide array of influential journals including *Econometrica, Journal of Economic Theory, International Economic Review, Games and Economic Behavior, Economic Theory, Journal of Theoretical Biology*, and *Physical Review Letters*. Professor Vega-Redondo is author of the book *Evolution, Games and Economic Behavior* and the Spanish-language textbook *Economía y Juegos: Teoría y Aplicaciones*. He has been a visiting scholar at the Indian Statistical Institute; the Institute for Advanced Studies in Vienna; the Hebrew University of Jerusalem; and the Universities of Harvard, California – San Diego, and Boston. He is co-editor of *Spanish Economic Review* and member of the Editorial Board of *Lecture Notes in Economics and Mathematical Systems*. Professor Vega-Redondo received his Ph.D. from the University of Minnesota.

Economics and the theory of games

FERNANDO VEGA-REDONDO

Universidad de Alicante and Universitat
Pompeu Fabra, Spain

CAMBRIDGE
UNIVERSITY PRESS

PUBLISHED BY THE PRESS SYNDICATE OF THE UNIVERSITY OF CAMBRIDGE
The Pitt Building, Trumpington Street, Cambridge, United Kingdom

CAMBRIDGE UNIVERSITY PRESS
The Edinburgh Building, Cambridge CB2 2RU, UK
40 West 20th Street, New York, NY 10011-4211, USA
477 Williamstown Road, Port Melbourne, VIC 3207, Australia
Ruiz de Alarcón 13, 28014 Madrid, Spain
Dock House, The Waterfront, Cape Town 8001, South Africa

http://www.cambridge.org

First published 2003

Printed in the United States of America

Typeface Times 11/13 pt.   *System* LATEX 2_ε [TB]

A catalog record for this book is available from the British Library.

Library of Congress Cataloging in Publication Data available

ISBN 0 521 77251 6 hardback
ISBN 0 521 77590 6 paperback

To Olalla,

who happily entered the game as I was completing the last

stages of this book

Contents

Contents

Preface

The twofold aim of this book is to provide both a wide coverage of modern game theory and a detailed account of many of its economic applications. The book is possibly too extensive to be fully covered in a single course. However, selected parts of it could be used in a variety of alternative courses, by adapting either the focus (e.g., altering the relative emphasis on theory and applications) or the technical difficulty of the discussion (e.g., approaching the more advanced topics less formally). I have written the book with the aim of rendering these different routes to using the book reasonably easy to pursue.

The material is organized in twelve chapters. The first nine of them embody the topics that generally would be included in a standard course of game theory and economic applications. In line with my objective of providing a smooth integration of theory and applications, these nine chapters display a repeated alternation of one and the other. Thus, on the one hand, there are five theory chapters that cover in turn the basic *Theoretical Framework* (Chapter 1), *Strategic-Form Analysis* (Chapter 2), *Refinements of Nash Equilibrium* (Chapter 4), *Incomplete Information* (Chapter 6), and *Repeated Interaction* (Chapter 8). In each of these five chapters, the first part is devoted to "core topics," while the more demanding discussion is gathered next under the heading of "supplementary material." In principle, most of the core topics could be taught at an undergraduate level, whereas the supplementary material typically would be covered only in more advanced (possibly graduate) courses.

Except for Chapter 1, each of the theory chapters has a subsequent companion one centered on applications (i.e., Chapters 3, 5, 7, and 9, respectively). These companion chapters include a thorough discussion of some of the most paradigmatic economic applications that rely on the corresponding theory. They are organized into three blocks or "general themes": *Oligopoly, Mechanism Design*, and *Markets*, with each of them including five different applications (labeled I through V). The study of these applications could be conducted in at least three ways. One possibility, of course, is to discuss them in association with the companion theory. A second option is to cover these applications in separate blocks, each block then being used for a monographic course on the respective topic. Still a third approach is to gather them in terms of comparative difficulty, selecting those applications in each block that are best suited to the target level. To facilitate this route, the harder applications are singled out by adding a star ($*$) to their headings, a general convention that is also used throughout this book in other respects (e.g., to mark those exercises that are somewhat more challenging than the others).

The methodological standpoint adopted in the first nine chapters of the book is the classical one in the discipline – that is, players are assumed to know the game, behave rationally, and believe that others will do so as well. In recent times, however, there has been a strong move among game theorists to consider more realistic scenarios, in which players are assumed subject to limited (typically called "bounded") rationality. The last three chapters of the book are concerned with these developments. Thus, Chapter 10 focuses on the relationship between *evolution and rationality*, Chapter 11 discusses different models of *learning in games*, and Chapter 12 deals with issues of *equilibrium selection*. Some, or all, of these chapters could be used for a specific course on the subject, but they could also serve to complement selectively some of the subjects (either concerning theory or applications) that are studied earlier in the book.

I would like to conclude this brief Preface by thanking the large number of people who have helped me in a variety of different ways to complete this book. First, I must refer to the colleagues and students at the Universidad de Alicante and the Universitat Pompeu Fabra, where I have been teaching different courses on game theory in recent years. Even though they are too numerous to list in detail, it is all too clear to me how their constructive feedback all along has helped to improve the book very substantially. I want to single out, however, the role played by four doctoral students: Dunia López Pintado, Rafael López, Miguel Angel Meléndez Jiménez, and Fernando Luis Valli. They have invested much time and effort in reading the twelve chapters of the book very thoroughly and have provided numerous helpful suggestions. I also want to thank my colleague Giovanni Ponti, who helped me, generously and cheerfully, with the simulations and graphical illustrations of the various learning dynamics studied in Chapter 11. Finally, as always, my deepest sense of gratitude belongs to my family, whose support for my work has always been so generous, even at times when it was a powerful contender for time and attention. The fact that we have nevertheless managed quite well is the essential merit of Mireia, my partner in so many other endeavors.

CHAPTER 1

Theoretical framework

1.1 Introduction and examples

In ordinary language, we speak of a "game" as a (generally amusing) process of interaction that involves a given population of individuals, is subject to some fixed rules, and has a prespecified collection of payoffs associated to every possible outcome. Here, the concept of a game mostly embodies the same idea. However, in contrast to the common use of this term, the kind of interaction to be studied may be far from amusing, as illustrated by the following example.

Consider the game usually known as the prisoner's dilemma (PD). It involves two individuals, labeled 1 and 2, who have been arrested on the suspicion of having committed jointly a certain crime. They are placed in separate cells and each of them is given the option by the prosecutor of providing enough evidence to incriminate the other. If only *one* of them chooses this option (i.e., "defects" on his partner), he is rewarded with freedom while the other individual is condemned to a stiff sentence of twelve years in prison. On the other hand, if both defect on (i.e., incriminate) each other, the available evidence leads to a rather long sentence for both of, say, ten years in prison. Finally, let us assume that if neither of them collaborates with the prosecutor (i.e., they both "cooperate" with each other), there is just basis for a relatively light sentence of one year for each.

The payoff table corresponding to this situation (where payoffs are identified with the *negative* of prison years) is shown in Table 1.1.

Table 1.1: *Prisoner's dilemma*

1 \ 2	D	C
D	$-10, -10$	$0, -12$
C	$-12, 0$	$-1, -1$

What would be your prediction on the most likely outcome of this situation? It seems clear that the prediction must be (D, D) because D is a *dominant strategy*, i.e., it is better than the alternative C, no matter what the other individual might choose to do; and this is so despite the fact that (C, C) would indisputably be a better "agreement" for both. However, unless the agents are somehow able to enforce such an agreement (e.g., through a credible threat of future revenge), they will not be able to achieve that preferred outcome. If both individuals are rational (in the sense of aiming to maximize their *individual* payoffs), choosing D is the only course of action that makes sense under the circumstances described.

It is important to emphasize that the former line of argument continues to apply even if the individuals are *not* isolated in separate cells and may instead communicate with each other. As long as their decisions have to be taken *independently* (e.g., in the prosecutor's office, one by one), the same reasoning applies. No matter what they might have agreed beforehand, when the time comes to implement a decision, the fact that D is a dominant choice should lead both of them to adopt it.

The game just outlined is paradigmatic of many situations of interest. For example, the same qualitative dilemma arises when two firms are sharing a certain market and each one must decide whether to undertake an aggressive or conciliatory price policy (see Chapter 3). Now, we turn to another example with a very different flavor: the so-called battle of the sexes. It involves a certain young couple who have just decided to go out on a date but still have to choose where to meet and what to do on that occasion. They already anticipate the possibilities: they may either attend a basketball game or go shopping. If they decide on the first option, they should meet by the stadium at the time when the game starts. If they decide on the second possibility, they should meet at the entrance of a particular shopping mall at that same time.

Let us assume they have no phone (or e-mail), so a decision must be made at this time. The preferences displayed by each one of them over the different alternatives are as follows. The girl prefers attending the basketball game rather than going shopping, whereas the boy prefers the opposite. In any case, they always prefer doing something together rather than canceling the date. To fix ideas, suppose payoffs are quantified as in Table 1.2.

Table 1.2: *Battle of the sexes*

Girl\Boy	B	S
B	3, 2	1, 1
S	0, 0	2, 3

where B and S are mnemonic for "basketball" and "shopping," respectively, and the pairs of numbers specified quantify the utilities obtained by each individual (first the girl's, second the boy's) for each choice combination. In principle, the couple could "agree" on implementing any pair of choices on the day in question. However, only (B, B) and (S, S) represent robust (or stable) agreements in the sense that if they settle on any of them and each believes that the other side is going to abide by it, both have incentives to follow suit. Each of these agreements will be labeled a *Nash equilibrium* and either of them may be viewed as a sensible prediction for the game. The problem, of course, is that there is an unavoidable multiplicity in the task of singling out *ex ante* which one of the two possible equilibria could (or should) be played. In contrast with the previous PD game, there is no natural basis to favor any one of those outcomes as more likely or robust than the alternative one.

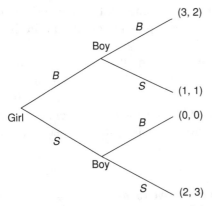

Figure 1.1: Battle of the sexes, sequential version.

Let us now explore a slight variation of the previous story that is not subject to the aforementioned multiplicity problem. On the day set for the date, rather than both individuals being out of reach, it turns out that the boy (only he) is at his home, where he can be contacted by phone. Suppose that the girl knows this and that, initially (i.e., when the plans were drawn), the boy managed to impose the "agreement" that they both would go shopping. The girl, angry at this state of affairs, may still resort to the following course of action: she can arrive at the stadium on the specified day and, shortly before the boy is ready to leave for the shopping mall, use the phone to let him know unambiguously where she is. Assume that it is no longer possible for the girl to reach the shopping mall on time. In this case, she has placed the boy in a difficult position. For, taking as given the fact that the girl is (and will continue to be) at the stadium waiting for him, the boy has no other reasonable option (if he is rational) than to "give in," i.e., go to the stadium and meet the girl there. What has changed in this second scenario that, in contrast to the former one, has led to a single prediction? Simply, the time structure has been modified, turning from one where the decisions were independent and "simultaneous" to one where the decisions are sequential: first the girl, then the boy.

A useful way of representing such a sequential decision process diagrammatically is through what could be called a "multiagent decision tree," as illustrated in Figure 1.1. In this tree, play unfolds from left to right, every intermediate (i.e., nonfinal) node standing for a decision point by one of the agents (the boy or the girl) and a particular history of previous decisions, e.g., what was the girl's choice at the point when it is the boy's turn to choose. On the other hand, every *final* node embodies a complete description of play (i.e., corresponds to one of the four possible outcomes of the game), and therefore has some payoff vector associated to it.

In the present sequential version of the game, it should be clear that the only intuitive outcome is (B, B). It is true that, at the time when the plans for the date are discussed, the boy may threaten to go shopping (i.e., choose S) even if the girl phones him from the stadium on the specified day (i.e., even if she chooses B). However, as explained above, this is *not* a credible threat. Or, in the terminology to be introduced in Chapter 4, such a threat does not belong to a (subgame) "perfect" equilibrium – only (B, B) defines a perfect equilibrium in the present case.

The representation of a game by means of a multiagent decision tree permits an *explicit* description of the order of movement of the different players as well as their information and possible actions at each point in the game. It is called its *extensive-form representation* and provides the most fundamental and complete way of defining any game. The next section formalizes this theoretical construct in a general and rigorous manner.

1.2   Representation of a game in extensive form

1.2.1   *Formalization*

The extensive form of a game requires the description of the following items.

1. *The set of players.* It will be denoted by $N = \{0, 1, 2, \ldots, n\}$, where player 0 represents "Nature." Nature performs every action that is exogenous to the game (whether it rains, some player wins a lottery, etc.). When it has no specific role to play, this fictitious player will be simply eliminated from the description of the game.

2. *The order of events.* It is given by a certain binary relation, R, defined on a set of nodes, K. More precisely, the set K is identified with the *collection of events* that can materialize along the game, whereas the relation R embodies a suitable criterion of *precedence* (not necessarily temporal, possibly only logical) applied to those events.[1] Here, the notion of event is the usual one, i.e., a description of "what is possible" at any given juncture in the game. Thus, in particular, an "elementary event"[2] is to be conceived simply as a sufficient description of a complete path of play, whereas the "sure event" refers to the situation that prevails at the beginning of the game (where still any path of play is attainable). As the players make their choices, the game advances along a decreasing (or nested) sequence of events, with a progressively narrower set of possibilities (i.e., paths of play) becoming attainable. Formally, this is captured through the relation R, which, for any pair of nodes $x, y \in K$, declares that $x R y$ whenever every path of play that is (possible) in y is (possible) as well in x. Thus, for example, if y stands for the event "both agents attend the basketball game" in the sequential battle of the sexes represented in Figure 1.1, the event x given by "the girl attends the basketball game" precedes y. Thus, by writing $x R y$ in this case,

---

[1] A binary relation R on K is defined as some subset of the Cartesian product $K \times K$. If $(x, y) \in R$, then we say that x is related to y and typically write $x R y$.

[2] In the language of traditional decision theory [see, e.g., Savage (1954)], an elementary event is the primitive specification of matters that would correspond to the notion of a "state," i.e., a description of all relevant aspects of the situation at hand. For a formal elaboration of this approach, the reader is referred to the recent (and somewhat technical) book by Ritzberger (2002).

we mean that x logically precedes y in the set of occurrences that underlie the latter event – therefore, if y occurs, so does x as well.

Given the interpretation of R as embodying some notion of precedence, it is natural to postulate that this binary relation is a (strict) partial ordering on K, i.e., it displays the following properties[3]:

Irreflexivity: $\forall x \in K, \neg(x R x)$.

Transitivity: $\forall x, x', x'' \in K, [x R x' \wedge x' R x''] \Rightarrow x R x''$.

Associated to R, it is useful to define a binary relation, P, of *immediate precedence* in the following manner:

$$x P x' \Leftrightarrow [(x R x') \wedge (\nexists x'' : x R x'' \wedge x'' R x')].$$

Correspondingly, we may define the set of immediate predecessors of any given $x \in K$ as follows:

$$P(x) \equiv \{x' \in K : x' P x\}$$

and the set of its immediate successors by

$$P^{-1}(x) = \{x' \in K : x P x'\}.$$

Having interpreted (K, R) as the set of partially ordered events that reflect the unfolding of play in the game, it is useful to postulate that every $y \in K$ *uniquely* defines the set of its preceding events – or, expressing it somewhat differently, that y uniquely induces the chain (or history)[4] of occurrences that give rise to it. In essence, this is equivalent to saying that (K, R) must have the structure of a *tree of events*, thus displaying the following two properties:

(a) There exists a unique root (or initial node) x_0 that has no immediate predecessor ($P(x_0) = \emptyset$) and precedes all other nodes (i.e., $\forall x \neq x_0$, $x_0 R x$). This initial node is to be viewed as the beginning of the game.

(b) For each $\hat{x} \in K$, $\hat{x} \neq x_0$, there exists a unique (finite) path of predecessors $\{x_1, x_2, \ldots, x_r\}$ joining $\hat{x}$ to the root x_0 – i.e., $x_q \in P(x_{q+1})$, for all $q = 0, 1, \ldots, r - 1$, and $x_r \in P(\hat{x})$.

As intended, (a) and (b) permit identifying each node in K with a (unique) particular history of the game – possibly partial and incomplete if it is an intermediate node, or even "empty" if it is the initial x_0. Also note that, from (a) and (b), it follows that every $x \neq x_0$ has a *unique* immediate predecessor (i.e., $P(x)$ is a singleton). Indeed, this is precisely the key feature that allows one to associate to every node the set of its preceding events (i.e., the underlying history) in a univocal fashion. A possible such

---

[3] As customary, we use the symbol $\neg(\cdot)$ to denote the negation of the statement in question, or $\wedge$, $\vee$ to join two statements by "and," "or." An alternative way of expressing negation is by superimposing / on a certain symbol, e.g., $\nexists$ stands for the negation of existence.

[4] Its temporal connotations notwithstanding, the term "history" is typically used in game theory to describe the unfolding of a path of play even when the implied irreversibility does not involve the passage of time. An illustration of this point may be obtained from some of our upcoming examples in Subsection 1.3.2.

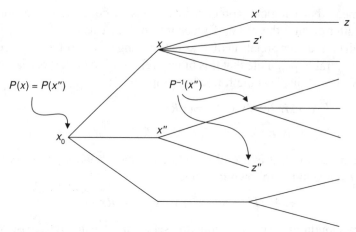

Figure 1.2: Tree of events with $x_0\, P\, x\, P\, x'\, P\, z$; $x_0\, P\, x\, P\, z'$; $x_0\, P\, x''\, P\, z''$.

tree of events is graphically illustrated in Figure 1.2, where the play of the game unfolds from left to right and any two nodes linked by a line segment are taken to be immediately adjacent according to the relation P.

For simplicity, let us posit here that every path of the game reaches a definite end.[5] Denote by $Z \equiv \{x \in K : P^{-1}(x) = \emptyset\}$ the set of final nodes, i.e., those nodes with *no* successors (for example, the nodes z, z', and z'' in Figure 1.2). As explained, the interpretation of any such node is that of a primitive event, a complete history, or simply a *game play*. It is worth emphasizing that every final node includes not only information on the "characteristics" of the final outcome of the game but also describes in full detail its underlying history. To illustrate this point, consider for example the event "wearing the two gloves" resulting from the concatenation of the intermediate events "not wearing any glove" and "wearing just one glove." Then, the two different ways in which one may end up wearing the two gloves (either the right or the left glove first) give rise to two different final nodes, even though they both display the same relevant features.

3. *Order of moves.* The set $K \setminus Z$ of intermediate nodes is partitioned into $n + 1$ subsets $K_0, K_1, \ldots, K_n$. If $x \in K_i$, this simply means that when the event reflected by x materializes, it is player i's turn to take an action. For convenience, it is typically assumed that, if Nature moves in the game, it does so first, thus resolving once and for all any bit of exogenous uncertainty that may affect the course of play. In terms of our previous formalization, this amounts to making $K_0 \subseteq \{x_0\}$ – of course, K_0 is empty if Nature does not have any move in the game.

4. *Available actions.* Let $x \in K_i$ be any node at which some player $i \in N$ moves. The set of actions available to player i at that node is denoted by

---

[5] Some of the game-theoretic models proposed at later points in this book (cf., for example, Subsections 5.2.1 and 8.2) admit the possibility that the game never ends, a case that requires a natural extension of the present formulation. Then, every infinite history must be interpreted as a different "end node," which again embodies a full description of the whole turn of events that underlie it.

$A(x)$. Naturally, the cardinality of $A(x)$ must be identical to that of $P^{-1}(x)$, the set of immediate successors of x. This simply reflects the fact that it is player i who decides how the game proceeds after x along one of the possible ensuing directions. Formally, what is required is that the sets $A(x)$ and $P^{-1}(x)$ be isomorphic, i.e., each immediate successor of x must have a *unique* and *different* action a in the set $A(x)$ associated to it, and *vice versa*.

5. *Information sets.* For every player i, we postulate that her corresponding set of decision nodes K_i can be partitioned into a set H_i of disjoint sets, i.e., $K_i = \bigcup_{h \in H_i} h$ with $h \cap h' = \emptyset$ for all $h, h' \in H_i$ ($h \neq h'$). Each of these sets $h \in H_i$ is called an *information set* and has the following interpretation: player i is unable to discriminate among the nodes in h when choosing an action at any one of them. Intuitively, if player i cannot distinguish between two different nodes $x, x' \in h$, it must be that player i did not observe (or has forgotten – see Section 1.4) the preceding occurrences (choices) on which x and x' differ. Obviously, this interpretation requires that $A(x) = A(x')$ – that is, there must exist the same set of available actions at both x and x'. Otherwise, the inconsistency would arise that player i could in fact distinguish between x and x' on the basis of the different set of actions available at each node (an information that of course player i should have because she is the *decision maker* at both of those nodes).

6. *Payoffs.* Associated with every possible game play (i.e., final node or complete history of the game) there is a certain payoff for each of the different players. Thus, for every one of the final nodes $z \in Z$, we assign an n-dimensional real vector $\pi(z) = (\pi_i(z))_{i=1}^n$, each $\pi_i(z)$ identified as the payoff achieved by player $i = 1, 2, \ldots, n$ if the final node z is reached. These real numbers embody how players evaluate any possible outcome of play and thus reflect every consideration they might deem relevant – pecuniary or not, selfish or altruistic. Payoffs for Nature are not specified since its behavior is postulated exogenously. (Fictitiously, one could simply posit constant payoffs for Nature over all final nodes.)

   Payoff magnitudes are interpreted as von Neumann–Morgenstern utilities and, therefore, we may invoke the well-known theorem of expected utility[6] when evaluating random outcomes. That is, the payoff or utility of a certain "lottery" over possible plays (or final nodes) is identified with its expected payoff, the weights associated with each one of those plays given by their respective *ex ante* probability. This implies that payoffs have a cardinal interpretation (i.e., payoff *differences* have meaning) and embody players' attitude to risk. Formally, it amounts to saying that the specification of the payoffs in the game is unique *only* up to monotone *affine* transformations.[7]

   Finally, note that even though "payoff accounting" is formally performed at the end of the game (i.e., payoffs are associated with final nodes alone),

---

[6] See, e.g., Kreps (1990) for a classical textbook treatment of this topic.

[7] A monotone affine transformation of a utility function $U(\cdot)$ is any function $\tilde{U}(\cdot)$ over the same domain, which may be written as follows: $\tilde{U}(\cdot) = \alpha + \beta U(\cdot)$ for any real numbers α, β, with $\beta > 0$.

this does not rule out that partial payoffs may materialize at intermediate stages. In those cases, the payoff associated with any final node is to be interpreted as the overall evaluation of the whole stream of payoffs earned along the unique history that leads to it.

The above six components define a game in extensive form. Often, we shall rely on a graphical description of matters where

- the unfolding events $x \in K$ induced by players' actions are represented through a tree structure of the sort illustrated in Figure 1.2;
- intermediate nodes are labeled with the index $i \in N$ of the player who takes a decision at that point;
- the edges departing from intermediate nodes $x \in K$ are labeled with the respective actions $a \in A(x)$ leading to each of its different successors in $P^{-1}(x)$;
- the intermediate nodes $\{x \in h\}$ that belong to the same information set h are joined by a dashed line;
- the final nodes $z \in Z$ have real vectors $\pi(z)$ associated with them, expressing the payoffs attained by each player in that game play.

A simple illustration of such a graphical way of describing a game in extensive form is displayed in Figure 1.3.

1.2.2 *Examples*

1.2.2.1 *A simple entry game.* Consider two firms, 1 and 2, involved in the following game. Firm 1 is considering whether to enter the market originally occupied by a single incumbent, firm 2. In deciding what to do (enter (E) or not (N)), firm 1 must anticipate what will be the reaction of the incumbent (fight (F) or concede (C)), a decision the latter will implement only after it learns that firm 1 has entered the market. Assume that the monopoly (or collusive) profits to be derived from the

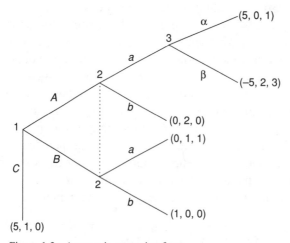

Figure 1.3: A game in extensive form.

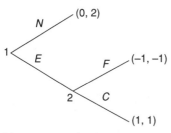

Figure 1.4: A simple entry game, extensive form.

market are given by two million dollars, which firm 2 either can enjoy alone if it remains the sole firm or must share with firm 1 if it concedes entry. On the other hand, if firm 2 fights entry, both firms are assumed to incur a *net* loss of one million dollars because of the reciprocal predatory policies then pursued.

The extensive-form representation of the entry game considered is described in Figure 1.4. In this simple extensive form, each firm has just one information set consisting of only one node. Thus, in both of these information sets, the corresponding firm is fully informed of what has happened at preceding points in the game. With this information at hand, each firm has two possible actions to choose from (N or E for firm 1; F or C for firm 2).

1.2.2.2 *A matching-pennies game.* Consider the following game. Two players simultaneously choose "heads" or "tails." If their choices coincide (i.e., both select heads, or both select tails) player 2 pays a dollar to player 1; in the opposite cases, player 1 pays this amount to player 2.

As explained above, the extensive form is to be conceived as the most basic and complete way of representing a game. However, since an extensive-form representation displays, by construction, a sequential decision structure (i.e., any decision node can belong to only a single agent), one might be tempted to think that it is inherently unsuited to model any simultaneity of choices such as the one proposed here. To resolve this puzzle, the key step is to grasp the appropriate interpretation of the notion of "simultaneity" in a strategic context. In any given game, the fact that certain actions are described as "simultaneous" does not necessarily reflect the idea that they are chosen at the same moment in *real time*. Rather, the only essential requirement in this respect is that at the time when one of the players takes her decision, she does not know any of the "simultaneous" decisions taken by the other players.

To formalize such a notion of simultaneity, we rely on the concept of information set, as formulated in Subsection 1.2.1. This allows us to model the matching-pennies game through *any* of the two extensive-form representations displayed in Figures 1.5 and 1.6 (recall the graphical conventions illustrated in Figure 1.3). In either of these alternative representations, each player has just one information set and two possible actions (heads (H) or tails (T)). However, while in the first representation it is player 1 who "fictitiously" starts the game and then player 2 follows, the second representation has the formal roles of the players reversed. Clearly, both of these

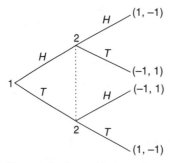

Figure 1.5: A matching-pennies game in extensive form, alternative 1.

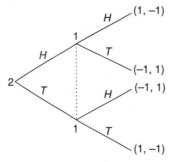

Figure 1.6: A matching-pennies game in extensive form, alternative 2.

alternative extensive-form representations of the game should be viewed by the players as *strategically equivalent*. In both of them, no player is informed of the action played by the opponent, either because she moves first or because she is unable to distinguish between the possible "prior" moves of the other player.

1.2.2.3 *Battle of the sexes.* Along the lines pursued for the previous example, we may return to the battle of the sexes introduced in Section 1.1 and describe the extensive-form representation of its simultaneous version as displayed in Figure 1.7.

Again, the alternative representation of the simultaneous battle of the sexes where the formal roles of the boy and the girl are reversed is strategically equivalent to the one described in Figure 1.7. Of course, this is no longer the case if we consider instead the sequential version of the game where the girl moves first. Such a game has the extensive-form representation described in Figure 1.1. In it, the girl still has only one information set (she moves without knowing the decision her partner will make), but the boy has two information sets (he already knows the decision adopted by the girl at the time he makes his own decision). As explained in our informal discussion of Section 1.1, this sequential version of the game leads to a rather strong strategic position for the girl. It is obvious, however, that the relative strength of the strategic positions is reversed if the roles of the players (i.e., their order of move) is permuted. Thus, in contrast with the simultaneous version, such

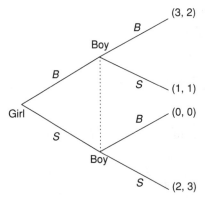

Figure 1.7: Battle of the sexes, simultaneous version; extensive form.

a permutation does not produce strategically equivalent extensive-form games in this case.

1.2.2.4 *The highest-card game.* Two players use a "pack" of three distinct cards, $C \equiv \{h(high), m(medium), l(low)\}$, to participate in the following game. First, player 1 picks a card, sees it, and then decides to either "bet" (B) or "pass" (P). If player 1 bets, then player 2 picks a card out of the two remaining ones, sees it, and chooses as well to either "bet" (B') or "pass" (P'). If both players bet, the player who has the highest card (no ties are possible) receives a hundred dollars from the opponent. On the other hand, if at least one of the players does *not* bet, no payments at all are made.

The extensive-form representation of this game is displayed in Figure 1.8. First, Nature moves at the root of the game (recall Subsection 1.2.1) and chooses one of the six possible card assignments for the two players in the set $D \equiv \{(c_1, c_2) \in C \times C : c_1 \neq c_2\}$. Next, there are three possible information sets for player 1, as she is informed of her own card but *not* of that of the opponent. (Again, we use the convention of joining the nodes included in the same information set by a discontinuous line.) In each of these information sets there are two nodes (those that correspond to the opponent receiving one of the two cards she herself has not received) and the same two choices available (B or P).[8] In case player 1 decides to bet, three further information sets for player 2 follow, each of them reflecting analogous information considerations for this player. If both bet (i.e., choose *B and B'*, respectively), the induced final nodes have a payoff vector that assigns 100 to the player with the highest card and -100 to the opponent. On the other hand, if one of them does not bet (i.e., passes), the corresponding final node has a payoff vector $(0, 0)$ associated with it.

---

[8] Note that, for notational simplicity, the same label (P or B) is attributed to pass or bet in different information sets of player 1. To be fully rigorous, however, we should have different labels in different information sets because their respective actions of passing and betting should be conceived as different in each of them. Of course, the same comment applies to the action labels of player 2 in the subsequent information sets.

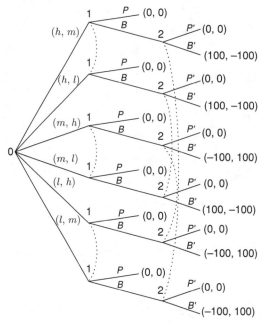

Figure 1.8: The highest-card game, extensive form.

1.3   Representation of a game in strategic form

1.3.1   *Formalization*

Consider a game in extensive form:

$$\Gamma = \left\{ N, \{K_i\}_{i=0}^n, R, \{H_i\}_{i=0}^n, \{A(x)\}_{x \in K \setminus Z}, \left\{ [\pi_i(z)]_{i=1}^n \right\}_{z \in Z} \right\} \quad (1.1)$$

where each of its components has been formally defined in Subsection 1.2.1. All players involved in the game are assumed to be perfectly informed of its underlying structure, i.e., they know each of the components listed in Γ. Therefore, every one of them can precisely identify the different situations in which she might be called upon to play and consider, hypothetically, what her decision would be in every case. In modeling players who can perform *ex ante* such an exhaustive range of hypothetical considerations, we are led to the fundamental notion of *strategy*.

For each player, a strategy in Γ is a *complete* collection of *contingent* choices that prescribe what this player would do in each of the occasions in which she might have to act (i.e., make some decision). Thus, a strategy has to anticipate *every* possible situation in which the player could be asked to play and, for each of them, determine a particular choice among the alternative options available. Obviously, since it is impossible to demand from a player that she make a decision that depends on information she does *not* hold, a strategy must prescribe the *same* action for all the nodes included in any particular information set. Or, rephrasing it somewhat differently, a strategy can make players' decisions contingent only on their respective information sets, *not* on the particular decision nodes (among which they are not always able to discriminate).

A different and complementary perspective on the concept of strategy is to view it as a *sufficient* set of instructions that, if the player were to convey them to some intermediary, would allow the former to leave the game and have the latter act on her behalf. Only if this set of instructions can *never* leave the intermediary at a loss (i.e., not knowing how to proceed in some circumstances), can we say that it properly defines a strategy for the player in question.

To proceed now formally, recall that, for each player $i \in N$, H_i denotes the partition of her respective decision nodes K_i in disjoint informations sets. For any $h \in H_i$ and $x \in h$, consider the simplifying notation $A(h) \equiv A(x)$, and denote $A_i \equiv \bigcup_{h \in H_i} A(h)$. Then, as explained above, a strategy for player i is simply a function

$$s_i : H_i \rightarrow A_i, \tag{1.2}$$

with the requirement that

$$\forall h \in H_i, \ s_i(h) \in A(h), \tag{1.3}$$

i.e., any of the actions selected at given information set h must belong to the corresponding set of available actions $A(h)$.

Note that since any strategy s_i of player $i \in N$ embodies an *exhaustively* contingent plan of choice, every particular *strategy profile* $s \equiv (s_0, s_1, s_2, \ldots, s_n)$ specifying the strategy followed by each one of the $n + 1$ players uniquely induces an associated path of play. Denote by $\zeta(s) \in Z$ the final node representing this path of play. Because all players are taken to be fully informed of the game Γ (i.e., know the different items specified in (1.1)), every player can be assumed to know as well the *mapping* $\zeta : S_0 \times S_1 \times \cdots \times S_n \rightarrow Z$. Therefore, the decision problem faced by each player i can be suitably formulated in the following fashion: choose strategy $s_i \in S_i$ under some anticipation, conjecture, or guess concerning the strategies $s_j \in S_j$ to be chosen by the remaining players $j \neq i$. But then, if players may approach the strategic situation from such an *ex ante* viewpoint (i.e., by focusing on their own and others' plans of action), the same must apply to us, game theorists, who aim to model their behavior. Indeed, this is in essence the perspective adopted by the model of a game that is known as its *strategic (or normal) form representation*, which is denoted by $G(\Gamma)$.[9] It consists of the following list of items:

$$G(\Gamma) = \left\{ N, \{S_i\}_{i=0}^n, \{\pi_i\}_{i=1}^n \right\},$$

where

1. N is the set of players.
2. For each player $i = 1, 2, \ldots, n$, S_i is her strategy space, i.e., the set of possible mappings of the form given by (1.2)–(1.3). Often, if we denote by $|H_i|$ the cardinality of the set H_i, it will be convenient to think of S_i

---

[9] The notation $G(\Gamma)$ responds to the idea that Γ is taken to be the most fundamental representation of the game, whereas $G(\Gamma)$ is conceived as a "derived" representation. Nevertheless, we often find it convenient to formulate a game directly in strategic form, thus dispensing with the explicit detail of its extensive-form structure.

Table 1.3: *A simple entry game,*
strategic form

1 \ 2	F	C
N	0, 2	0, 2
E	−1, −1	1, 1

as contained in the Cartesian product $A_i^{|H_i|}$, a set that is isomorphic to the family of functions of the form (1.2).[10]

3. For each player $i = 1, 2, \ldots, n$,

$$\pi_i : S_0 \times S_1 \times \cdots \times S_n \to \mathbb{R} \tag{1.4}$$

is her payoff function where, abusing former notation, the payoff associated to every strategy profile $s \equiv (s_0, s_1, s_2, \ldots, s_n)$ is identified with the payoff $\pi_i(\zeta(s))$ earned by player i in the final node $z = \zeta(s)$ uniquely induced by those strategies.

The apparent simplicity displayed by the strategic-form representation of a game is somewhat misleading. For if the underlying game is complex (e.g., displays an involved sequential structure), a complete specification of the strategy spaces may become a quite heavy task. Then, the full richness of detail (order of movement, dispersion of information, player asymmetries, etc.), which is *explicitly* described by the representation of the game in extensive form, becomes implicitly "encoded" by a large set of quite complex strategies. To illustrate matters, we now focus on the collection of leading examples introduced in Subsection 1.2.2 and describe for each of them in turn their corresponding strategic form.

1.3.2   *Examples*

1.3.2.1 *A simple entry game (continued).* Consider the entry game whose extensive form is described in Figure 1.4. In this game, both players have only one information set. Therefore, their respective strategy sets can be simply identified with the set of possible actions for each of them. That is, $S_1 = \{N, E\}$ and $S_2 = \{F, C\}$. To complete the specification of the strategic form, one still has to define the players' payoff functions. These may be characterized by a list of payoff pairs $[(\pi_i(s_1, s_2))_{i=1,2}]_{(s_1, s_2) \in S_1 \times S_2}$, as displayed in Table 1.3, where each row and column, respectively, is associated with one of the strategies of individuals 1 and 2.

1.3.2.2 *A matching-pennies game (continued).* Consider now the matching-pennies game whose two equivalent extensive-form representations are described in Figures 1.5 and 1.6. Again in this case, because each player has only one

---

[10] Let the elements of H_i be indexed as $h_1, h_2, \ldots, h_r$. Then, any $y = (y_1, y_2, \ldots, y_r) \in A_i^{|H_i|}$ can be identified with the mapping $s_i(\cdot)$ such that $s_i(h_k) = y_k$. Of course, for such a mapping to qualify as a proper strategy, it has to satisfy (1.3).

Table 1.4: *A matching-pennies game, strategic form*

1 \ 2	H	T
H	1, −1	−1, 1
T	−1, 1	1, −1

Table 1.5: *Battle of the sexes, sequential version; strategic form*

Girl \ Boy	(B, B)	(B, S)	(S, B)	(S, S)
B	3, 2	3, 2	1, 1	1, 1
S	0, 0	2, 3	0, 0	2, 3

information set, her strategies can be identified with the actions available in that single information set. That is, $S_1 = \{H, T\}$, $S_2 = \{H, T\}$ where, for simplicity, we do not distinguish notationally between each player's strategies. Finally, to define the payoff functions, the induced payoff pairs are arranged in Table 1.4 with the aforementioned conventions.

1.3.2.3 *Battle of the sexes (continued).* The simultaneous version of the battle of the sexes (cf. Figure 1.7) is formally analogous to the previous example, its payoffs as given by Table 1.2. On the other hand, its sequential version, whose extensive-form representation is given by Figure 1.1, has the girl displaying one information set and the boy displaying two of them. Thus, for the girl, her strategy set is simply $S_g = \{B, S\}$, whereas for the boy we have $S_b = \{(B, B), (B, S), (S, B), (S, S)\}$. Here (recall Subsection 1.3.1), we view each of the boy's strategies as an element of $\{B, S\}^{|H_b|} = \{B, S\}^2$, with the information sets indexed downward (i.e., the upper one first, the lower one second). With this notational convention, the payoff functions are as indicated in Table 1.5.

An interesting point to note in this case is that the payoff table displays a number of payoff-vector equalities across pairs of different cells. This simply reflects the fact that, given any particular girl's strategy, only that part of the boy's strategy that pertains to the information set induced by the girl's decision is payoff relevant. Therefore, the two different boy's strategies that differ only in the information set *not* reached (given the girl's chosen strategy) lead to the same payoff for both players.

1.3.2.4 *The highest-card game (continued).* Consider the game whose extensive-form representation is described in Figure 1.8. In this game, the players' strategy spaces (including Nature in this case) are as follows:

- *Nature:* $S_0 = \{(c_1, c_2) \in C \times C : c_1 \neq c_2\}$.
- *Player 1:* $S_1 = \{s_1 : C \longrightarrow \{Bet(B), \ Pass(P)\}\} = \{B, P\}^{|C|}$.
- *Player 2:* $S_2 = \{s_2 : C \longrightarrow \{Bet(B'), \ Pass(P')\}\} = \{B', P'\}^{|C|}$.

Table 1.6: *Highest-card game; payoff table when Nature chooses* (m, l)

1 \ 2	(B, B, B)	(B, B, P)	(B, P, B)	$\cdots$	(P, P, P)
(B, B, B)	100, -100	0, 0	100, -100	$\cdots$	0, 0
(B, B, P)	100, -100	0, 0	100, -100	$\cdots$	0, 0
(B, P, B)	0, 0	0, 0	0, 0	$\cdots$	0, 0
$\vdots$					$\vdots$
(P, P, P)	0, 0	0, 0	0, 0	$\cdots$	0, 0

The strategies of players 1 and 2 may now be represented by terns, whose components are, respectively, associated with each of their three information sets (a different one for each of the three cards that may be drawn). Thus, indexing information sets downward on the associated card number received (i.e., starting with the highest card and finishing with the lowest one), we can write:

$$S_1 = \{(B, B, B), (B, B, P), (B, P, B), \ldots, (P, P, P)\}$$

$$S_2 = \{(B', B', B'), (B', B', P'), (B', P', B'), \ldots, (P', P', P')\}.$$

Once the strategy spaces have been determined, to complete the specification of the game's strategic form we just need to list the collection of payoff pairs for players 1 and 2, $[\pi_1(s), \pi_2(s)]$, associated with every possible strategy profile $s = (s_0, s_1, s_2)$. Since the strategy profiles are three-dimensional in the present case, this may be done by specifying the collection of two-dimensional payoff tables involving player 1's and player 2's strategies that is spanned by the *whole range* of possible strategy choices on the part of Nature. In this fashion, for each $s_0 = (c_1, c_2) \in S_0$, we obtain a payoff table analogous to those used in previous examples. Rather than tediously describing all such six payoff tables in detail, let us illustrate matters by focusing on just one particular Nature's choice, say $(c_1, c_2) = (m, l)$. For this case, the induced payoffs (for player 1 and 2) are as described in Table 1.6.

1.4   Mixed extension of a game

The concept of strategy introduced above corresponds to what is usually known as a *pure strategy*, i.e., it prescribes the choice of a specific action at every information set in a *deterministic* fashion. However, as we shall see (cf., e.g., Section 2.4), there are many games of interest where the analysis would be unduly limited if one were to be restricted to pure strategies. In particular, it turns out that, under such a restriction, even the most basic equilibrium notions customarily proposed to study strategic situations are often subject to troublesome problems of nonexistence. This is the main motivation that has led game theorists to extend the deterministic decision framework considered here so far to a more general one that allows for so-called *mixed strategies*. In essence, what this extension provides is the possibility that players may select one of the pure strategies in a random fashion; that is, through an associated (*ex ante* uncertain) lottery whose induced consequences must then be evaluated in expected terms.

Formally, the space of mixed strategies for any player i coincides with the set of probability measures on her space of pure strategies S_i. Assume that $S_i \equiv \{s_{i1}, s_{i2}, \ldots, s_{ir_i}\}$ is a finite set with cardinality $r_i = |S_i|$. Then, player i's space of mixed strategies, denoted by Σ_i, may be simply identified with the $(r_i - 1)$-dimensional simplex $\Delta^{r_i - 1} = \{\sigma_i = (\sigma_{i1}, \sigma_{i2}, \ldots, \sigma_{ir_i}) \in \mathbb{R}^{r_i} : \sigma_{iq} \geq 0$ $(q = 1, 2, \ldots, r_i), \sum_{q=1}^{r_i} \sigma_{iq} = 1\}$, i.e., the set of the r_i-dimensional real vectors whose components are nonnegative and add up to one. Given any $\sigma_i \in \Sigma_i$, its qth component σ_{iq} (sometimes, alternatively denoted by $\sigma_i(s_{iq})$) is interpreted as the probability with which player i actually adopts (*ex post*) the pure strategy s_{iq} when choosing the mixed strategy σ_i.

Once mixed strategies are allowed as a possible object of choice on the part of players, their payoff functions $\pi_i(\cdot)$ in (1.4) must be extended to the full set of mixed-strategy profiles $\Sigma = \Sigma_0 \times \cdots \times \Sigma_n$. Recalling from Subsection 1.2.1 that the payoffs of the game are to be conceived as von Neumann-Morgenstern utilities, this may be done simply by computing the corresponding *expected* payoffs. Thus, abusing previous notation and letting $\pi_i(\cdot)$ denote both expected as well as realized payoffs, the (expected) payoffs $\pi_i(\sigma)$ induced by any given profile of mixed strategies $\sigma = (\sigma_0, \sigma_1, \ldots, \sigma_n) \in \Sigma$ are given by

$$\pi_i(\sigma) = \sum_{q_0, q_1, \ldots, q_n = 1}^{r_0, r_1, \ldots, r_n} \sigma_{0q_0} \sigma_{1q_1} \ldots \sigma_{nq_n} \pi_i \left(s_{0q_0}, s_{1q_1}, \ldots, s_{nq_n} \right). \tag{1.5}$$

Note that

$$\sum_{q_0, q_1, \ldots, q_n = 1}^{r_0, r_1, \ldots, r_n} \sigma_{0q_0} \sigma_{1q_1} \ldots \sigma_{nq_n} = \sum_{q_0=1}^{r_0} \sigma_{0q_0} \left(\sum_{q_1=1}^{r_1} \sigma_{1q_1} \left(\cdots \left(\sum_{q_n=1}^{r_n} \sigma_{nq_n} \right) \cdots \right) \right) = 1$$

so that $[\sigma_{0q_0} \sigma_{1q_1} \cdots \sigma_{nq_n}]_{q_0, q_1, \ldots, q_n = 1}^{r_0, r_1, \ldots, r_n}$ embodies a suitable probability vector, each component $\sigma_{0q_0} \sigma_{1q_1} \cdots \sigma_{nq_n}$ indicating the probability that each of the $n + 1$ players $i = 0, 1, \ldots, n$ happens to select the pure strategy s_{iq_i} thus leading to a pure-strategy profile $(s_{0q_0}, s_{1q_1}, \ldots, s_{nq_n})$. Of course, a crucial implicit assumption underlying this formulation is that the randomization induced by each player's mixed strategy is *stochastically independent* of that performed by any other player.[11] Given any game in strategic form $G = \left\{ N, \{S_i\}_{i=0}^{n}, \{\pi_i\}_{i=1}^{n} \right\}$, the extended framework where players $i \in N$ may use mixed strategies Σ_i and payoff functions $\pi_i(\cdot)$ are defined by (1.5) is known as the *mixed extension of G*.

Heuristically, a mixed strategy reflects a randomization whose induced uncertainty over the alternative plans (i.e., pure strategies) is fully resolved at the beginning of the game. That is, once the particular *deterministic* plan has been chosen, it is maintained unchanged throughout the game. In contrast with this approach, we could also conceive of a situation in which a player may wish to perform an *independent* (ad hoc) randomization when choosing an action at *each* of the information

---

[11] This requirement of stochastic independence across players' choices may be relaxed, as in the concept of correlated equilibrium discussed in Section 2.6.

sets visited along the game. This is the idea that underlies the concept of behavioral strategy.

Formally, a *behavioral strategy* is a function

$$\gamma_i : H_i \longrightarrow \Delta(A_i), \tag{1.6}$$

which for each $h \in H_i$ associates a probability vector $[\gamma_i(h)(a)]_{a \in A_i} \in \Delta(A_i)$ with the following interpretation: for every $a \in A(h)$, $\gamma_i(h)(a)$ is the probability with which player i selects action a at node $x \in h$. Naturally, it must be required that $\gamma_i(h)(\hat{a}) = 0$ if $\hat{a} \notin A(h)$; i.e., the support of $\gamma_i(h)$ is included in $A(h)$. The set of behavioral strategies of player i will be denoted by $\Psi_i \equiv \{\gamma_i : H_i \to \Delta(A_i)\}$, with $\Psi \equiv \Psi_0 \times \Psi_1 \times \cdots \Psi_n$.

In a certain sense, we may view the notion of behavioral strategy as introducing the possibility of "mixing" directly in the extensive form of the game, in contrast with the notion of mixed strategy, which is a concept derived from its strategic form. Clearly, any profile of behavioral strategies $\gamma \in \Psi$ induces a probability measure on the set of possible paths of play and, therefore, on the set of final nodes and corresponding payoffs as well. This allows players to evaluate the performance of any behavioral strategies on the extensive form in the same way they do it for mixed strategies on the strategic form. The parallelism between the two choice constructs (mixed and behavioral strategies) naturally leads to the following question: Might players ever prefer to "mix" (or randomize) in one way over the other? We do not address this question here in any detail other than saying that, under standard conditions, mixed and behavioral strategies are strategically equivalent. That is, under those conditions, players (as well as ourselves, the analysts of the situation) are not limited in any significant way by relying on either of the two approaches to plan (or analyze) strategic behavior. The conditions that have been generically referred to as "standard" always obtain whenever the game displays *perfect recall*, in the sense that players never forget what each of them formerly knew or chose. All our applications and further theoretical developments in this book will have players display perfect recall. However, because of the theoretical and pedagogical interest of the issue, further discussion of it (in particular, a formal definition of perfect recall) is included in the supplementary material of this chapter.

Supplementary material

1.5   Mixed and behavioral strategies

1.5.1   *Formal relationship*

As a preliminary step in contrasting the strategic implications of mixed and behavioral strategies, it is useful to start with the explicit description of a procedure that, given any mixed strategy $\sigma_i \in \Sigma_i$ for some player i, associates a behavioral strategy $\gamma_i \in \Psi_i$ in a univocal and coherent fashion. Intuitively, the behavioral strategy γ_i induced by any mixed strategy σ_i must have, at each information set $h \in H_i$ and

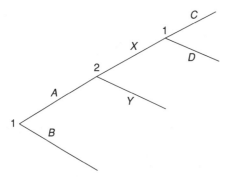

Figure 1.9: Extensive-form structure.

for every $a \in A(h)$, the following equality satisfied:

$$\gamma_i(h)(a) = \Pr_{\sigma_i} [s_i(h) = a \mid h];$$

that is, the probability of choosing a at h must coincide with the probability associated by σ_i to choosing a pure strategy that prescribes a at h (of course, the latter probability computed *conditional* on reaching this information set).

To understand some of the subtle issues that arise in this connection, consider a game with the extensive-form structure represented in Figure 1.9. (Payoffs are not included here because they are immaterial to the argument.) In this game, player 1 has four pure strategies: (A, C), (A, D), (B, C), (B, D). Focus, for example, on the mixed strategy $\tilde{\sigma}_1 = (1/2, 0, 0, 1/2)$ and the second information set of player 1. Within this information set (which is referred to as $\tilde{h}$) the strategy $\tilde{\sigma}_1$ associates with action D a "total" probability equal to

$$\sum_{\{s_1 \in S_1 : s_1(\tilde{h})=D\}} \tilde{\sigma}_1(s_1) = 1/2.$$

However, this is *not* the *conditional* probability of choosing D, provided the information set $\tilde{h}$ is effectively reached. In fact, this probability is *zero* because this information set is reached (given $\tilde{\sigma}_1$) only if player 1 adopts strategy (A, C).

To obtain a suitable formalization of matters, denote by $\hat{S}_i(h)$ the set of pure strategies by player i that are compatible with a certain information set h, i.e., *admit* the possibility that realized play may visit a node in h for *some* profile of the remaining players. (For example, in the game illustrated in Figure 1.9, if $\tilde{h}$ continues to refer to the second information set of player 1, $\hat{S}_1(\tilde{h}) = \{(A, C), (A, D)\}$.) Then, the behavioral strategy associated with any given strategy $\sigma_i \in \Sigma_i$ may be formally constructed as follows:

$$\forall h \in H_i, \ \forall a \in A(h),$$

$$\gamma_i(h)(a) = \frac{\sum_{\{s_i \in \hat{S}_i(h) : s_i(h)=a\}} \sigma_i(s_i)}{\sum_{s_i \in \hat{S}_i(h)} \sigma_i(s_i)} \quad \text{if } \sum_{s_i \in \hat{S}_i(h)} \sigma_i(s_i) > 0;$$

$$\tag{1.7}$$

$$\gamma_i(h)(a) = \sum_{\{s_i \in S_i : s_i(h)=a\}} \sigma_i(s_i) \quad \text{otherwise.}$$

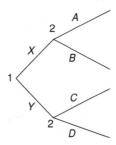

Figure 1.10: Extensive-form structure.

That is, the probability that the behavioral strategy γ_i attributes to playing any action a in some information set h is identified with the *conditional probability* induced by σ_i, as long as such strategy renders it possible that the information set h be reached (i.e., as long as $\sum_{s_i \in \hat{S}_i(h)} \sigma_i(s_i) > 0$). Otherwise, if the strategy σ_i itself rules out that h could be visited, then the contemplated conditional probability is not well defined. In those cases, we follow the somewhat arbitrary procedure of identifying the probability of playing each action a in h with the total probability that (in an essentially irrelevant manner) the strategy σ_i associates with this choice.[12] Note that, by construction, the formulation described in (1.7) guarantees that both σ_i and γ_i induce the same "conditional randomization" over available actions at each information set. From this viewpoint, therefore, both of them reflect the same contingent behavior on each separate information set.

In general, the procedure embodied by (1.7) defines a mapping from mixed to behavioral strategies that, although single-valued and on-to (cf. Exercise 1.9), is *not* injective. That is, generally there will be more than one mixed strategy that induces the *same* behavioral strategy. To illustrate this fact, consider the extensive-form structure displayed in Figure 1.10.

Player 2 has four pure strategies in this game: $(A, C), (A, D), (B, C), (B, D)$. Consider the following two mixed strategies: $\sigma_2 = (1/4, 1/4, 1/4, 1/4)$ and $\sigma_2' = (1/2, 0, 0, 1/2)$. Both generate the same behavioral strategy $\gamma_2 = ((1/2, 1/2), (1/2, 1/2))$, where the first pair corresponds to the probabilities applied in the first information set and the second pair to those applied in the second information set.

As advanced in Section 1.4, the fact that there may well be a common behavioral strategy induced by several different mixed strategies poses no fundamental problem in the analysis of a game if players display *perfect recall*. Under these conditions, it turns out that every behavioral strategy is fully equivalent (from a strategic viewpoint) to *any* of the mixed strategies that induces it. These issues are explained in more detail in Subsection 1.5.2, once the concept of perfect recall has been rigorously defined.

---

[12] There would be other alternative ways of completing the behavioral strategy at information sets that are *not* reachable (with positive probability) given the mixed strategy in question. The particular choice to be made in this respect nevertheless would have no important implication on the analysis of the game. For example, one could associate a uniform conditional probability with each of the actions available in any unreachable information set.

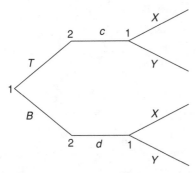

Figure 1.11: Game with perfect recall.

1.5.2 *Perfect recall and strategic equivalence*

A game is said to exhibit perfect recall if, throughout it, players never forget either the actions they previously took or the information they formerly knew. How can one formalize this twin and seemingly vague idea? Relying on the versatile and by now familiar notion of information set, we next provide a transparent and rigorous formalization of it.

Formally, a player i does *not forget* a certain action $a \in A(x)$ adopted at some preceding node $x \in K_i$ if

$$\forall x', x'' (x' \neq x''), \ x = P(x') = P(x''),$$

$$(x' R \hat{x}, \ x'' R \tilde{x}, \ \hat{x} \in K_i, \ \tilde{x} \in K_i) \Rightarrow h(\hat{x}) \neq h(\tilde{x}),$$

where $h(\cdot)$ denotes the information set to which the node in questions belongs.

Analogously, we may now turn to the requirement that any given player i does *not forget* any information she previously knew. This is equivalent to asserting that if a player does *not* hold some particular information at a certain point of the game, she did not hold it before. Formally, it can be described as follows[13]:

$$\forall x, x' \in K_i, \ x' \in h(x), \ [\hat{x} \in K_i, \ \hat{x} R x] \Rightarrow [\exists \tilde{x} \in h(\hat{x}) : \tilde{x} R x'].$$

When a game exhibits perfect recall, mixed and behavioral strategies are strategically equivalent forms of modeling players' behavior. That is, for any player and any particular strategy profile of her opponents (either mixed or behavioral), the probability distribution over paths of play (or final nodes) generated by

   (i) a particular behavioral strategy on the player's part, or
   (ii) any of her mixed strategies that induce that behavioral strategy

are completely identical. In this sense, therefore, players should be indifferent about using one form of strategy or the other in shaping their (random) behavior along the game.

To illustrate the issue, consider the simple games displayed in Figures 1.11 and 1.12. Their extensive-form structure is the same, except that the first displays perfect recall, whereas the second does not.

---

[13] Of course, $\tilde{x}$ may well coincide with $\hat{x}$.

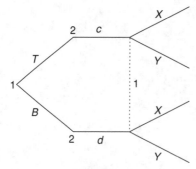

Figure 1.12: Game with imperfect recall.

In the first game, player 1 has eight pure strategies:

$$(T, X, X), \ (T, X, Y), \ (T, Y, X), \ (T, Y, Y), \ (B, X, X),$$
$$(B, X, Y), \ (B, Y, X), \ (B, Y, Y),$$

where, for our present purposes, we find it convenient to abuse notation and identify with the same labels (X and Y) the actions available in each of the two last information sets of player 1. Consider any mixed strategy $\sigma_1 \in \Delta^7$ and let $\gamma_1 \equiv (\gamma_{11}, \gamma_{12}, \gamma_{13}) \in \Delta^1 \times \Delta^1 \times \Delta^1$ be its induced behavioral strategy. It is easy to see that both are equivalent in the above indicated sense. Let us focus, for example, on the probability that the path T-c-X be realized when player 1 adopts strategy $\sigma_1 \in \Sigma_1$. Denoting the first information set of player 1 by h_1 and her second upper one by h_2, that probability is given by

$$\mathrm{Pr}_{\sigma_1}(T\text{-}c\text{-}X) = \mathrm{Pr}_{\sigma_1}\{(s_1(h_1){=}T) \wedge (s_1(h_2){=}X)\}$$
$$= \mathrm{Pr}_{\sigma_1}\{s_1(h_1){=}T\} \times \mathrm{Pr}_{\sigma_1}\{s_1(h_2){=}X \mid s_1(h_1){=}T\}.$$

On the other hand, using (1.7), we have

$$\gamma_{11}(T) = \mathrm{Pr}_{\sigma_1}\{s_1(h_1) = T\}$$
$$\gamma_{12}(X) = \mathrm{Pr}_{\sigma_1}\{s_1(h_2) = X \mid s_1(h_1) = T\},$$

which indicates that player 1 enjoys the same range of possibilities over the final course of play by either using σ_1 or its associated γ_1. That is, even "restricting" to a behavioral strategy such as γ_1 above, player 1 may guarantee that

$$\mathrm{Pr}_{\gamma_1}(T\text{-}c\text{-}X) = \mathrm{Pr}_{\sigma_1}(T\text{-}c\text{-}X).$$

In contrast, consider now the alternative version of the game with imperfect recall displayed in Figure 1.12, where player 1 forgets what action she took in her first information set. In this game, player 1 has only two information sets and the following four pure strategies:

$$(T, X), (T, Y), (B, X), (B, Y).$$

Let us focus on the following mixed strategy $\tilde{\sigma}_1 = (1/2, 0, 0, 1/2)$. It gives rise to the behavioral strategy $\tilde{\gamma}_1 = ((1/2, 1/2), (1/2, 1/2))$, where each of the two vectors in it correspond to the conditional choice probabilities at the two alternative information sets of player 1 in the game. In this case, strategy $\tilde{\gamma}_1$ is no longer equivalent to $\tilde{\sigma}_1$. To see it, note that strategy $\tilde{\sigma}_1$ induces probability $1/2$ for each of the two paths T-c-X and B-d-Y. Instead, $\tilde{\gamma}_1$ induces a uniform probability of $1/4$ over all four possible paths in the game. This different performance obtained with the two types of strategies (mixed and behavioral) is a direct consequence of the lack of perfect recall displayed by player 1 in the second game. By means of strategy $\tilde{\sigma}_1$, this player can *correlate* the actions chosen in her first and second information sets, something that is not feasible (because of "memory failure") when relying on strategy $\tilde{\gamma}_1$.

Kuhn (1953) showed that, as illustrated by our example, the only reason why mixed and behavioral strategies can fail to be equivalent is due to the presence of imperfect recall. This is the content of the next theorem, whose proof is omitted.

Theorem 1.1 (Kuhn, 1953): *In a game with perfect recall, mixed and behavioral strategies are strategically equivalent – i.e., they generate the same set of possibilities (probability measures) over alternative paths of the game.*

1.6 Representation of a game in coalitional form

The two alternative forms of representing a game introduced so far (extensive and normal forms) emphasize the strategic aspects of player interaction. This is the main focus of the so-called *noncooperative game theory* that represents our main concern in this book. In addition to this approach, game theorists have pursued another parallel (and, to a large extent, independent) route, which proceeds under the general heading of *cooperative game theory*. In it, the main focus is not on the strategic interactions of individuals, but on the set of possibilities jointly available to the different coalitions in which they may participate. Given such a range of coalitional possibilities, this alternative cooperative theory is built under the implicit assumption that players must always be able to reach a satisfactory *ex ante* agreement (which has to be efficient) and that this agreement may be enforced by a binding contract. Then, in a nutshell, the essential concern becomes to study what kind of contract will (or should) be signed and how its features are to depend on the coalitional possibilities of each player.

Associated with different possible rules for "signing a contract," the theory has proposed a wide range of different solutions for cooperative games. Some of the most widely used include the following: Shapley value, the core, the nucleolus, the Nash bargaining solution, and the Kalai-Smorodinsky solution. We end this introductory chapter with a simple example used to provide a heuristic explanation of some of the main underlying ideas. The interested reader is referred to other sources (e.g., Myerson, 1991) for a detailed and rigorous discussion of this vast field of inquiry.

Let there be a set of individuals $N = \{1, \ldots, n\}$, $n \geq 2$, to whom the following tempting possibility is offered: a thousand dollars will be freely given to any subgroup of N for which both of the following conditions apply:

(a) it includes a (strict) majority of individuals, and
(b) their members fully agree on a precise form of dividing the money among them.

The coalitional representation of this game is known as its *characteristic function*. This function associates to every possible coalition of individuals (the collection of subsets of N, $\mathcal{P}(N) = \{M : M \subseteq N\}$) a *complete* specification of its range of possibilities (in our example, the different possible money allocations that can be implemented by its members, given the rules of the game).

Consider first the context with $n = 2$. In this case, the characteristic function (in fact, a correspondence) is of the following form[14]:

$$V : \mathcal{P}(N) \rightrightarrows \mathbb{R}_+^2$$

where, under the simplifying assumption that agents' payoffs coincide with their monetary rewards (measured in dollars),[15] we have

$$V(\emptyset) = V(\{1\}) = V(\{2\}) = \{(0, 0)\};$$
$$V(\{1, 2\}) = \left\{ (x_1, x_2) \in \mathbb{R}_+^2 : x_1 + x_2 = 10^3 \right\}.$$

In this situation, fully symmetric, every solution proposed by the theory naturally prescribes a symmetric outcome. For example, the Shapley value assigns to each individual her average marginal contribution in the sequential process of formation of the *grand coalition* N, where every possible order in which this process may be carried out is attributed the same weight. Thus, given that $N = \{1, 2\}$, there are only two possible orders in which the grand coalition can be formed: first player 1, followed by player 2; or vice versa. In the first case (i.e., the order 1-2), the marginal value of player 1 is zero because, when she is the first to enter the process of formation of the grand coalition, she is still short of the strict majority at the point of entry. Instead, in the second case (the order 2-1), her marginal value is the full thousand dollars because it is precisely her participation that allows the resulting coalition to gain a majority. Overall, therefore, her average marginal contribution (i.e., her Shapley value) is $10^3/2 = 1/2 \times 0 + 1/2 \times 10^3$. The argument is symmetric for player 2, who therefore obtains an identical Shapley value.

The approach taken by the alternative solution concept known as the core is very different. Informally, this concept focuses on those agreements that are stable against the possibility of being "blocked" by some coalition. More specifically, an agreement is judged stable in this case when there is *no* coalition that can *guarantee* for itself an outcome that is preferred by *every* member of the coalition to the agreement in question. In the example considered, when N is composed

---

[14] As customary, $\mathbb{R}_+^k$ denotes the nonnegative orthant of the Euclidean space $\mathbb{R}^k$, $k \in \mathbb{N}$. That is, $\mathbb{R}_+^k \equiv \{x = (x_1, x_2, \ldots, x_k) \in \mathbb{R}^k : x_i \geq 0$ for each $i = 1, 2, \ldots, n\}$.

[15] If this were not the case, the possibility sets would have to be formulated in payoff (or utility) space.

of only two agents, it is clear that the core consists of the *whole* set $\{(x_1, x_2) \in:$ $x_1 + x_2 = 10^3\}$. Therefore, the symmetry of the solution is maintained, although now it does not involve a specific allocation but a whole (in fact, the full) set of efficient, nonwasteful, outcomes.

Let us now reconsider the situation with $n = 3$. In this case, the characteristic function

$$V : \mathcal{P}(N) \rightrightarrows \mathbb{R}^3_+$$

is as follows:

$$V(\emptyset) = V(\{1\}) = V(\{2\}) = V(\{3\}) = \{(0, 0, 0)\};$$
$$V(\{i, j\}) = \{(x_1, x_2, x_3) \in \mathbb{R}^3_+ : x_i + x_j = 10^3\}$$
$$(i, j = 1, 2, 3, i \neq j);$$
$$V(\{1, 2, 3\}) = \{(x_1, x_2, x_3) \in \mathbb{R}^3_+ : x_1 + x_2 + x_3 = 10^3\}.$$

The Shapley value reflects again the symmetry of the situation and prescribes that the thousand dollars be divided equally among the three players, i.e., $10^3/3$ for each of them. To see this, consider the six possible sequences of formation of the grand coalition. Among them, each individual has a zero marginal contribution in four of them (specifically, when she occupies either the first or the last position). Instead, when she occupies exactly the second position, her marginal contribution is 10^3. Averaging over all these six possibilities, the indicated conclusion follows.

In contrast to the preceding discussion, it is interesting to note that the core of the game with three players is empty. This responds to the following considerations. Suppose that three individuals sit down at a table to sign a "stable" agreement. If two of them (say players 1 and 2) intend to reach a bilateral agreement that ignores player 3, the latter will react immediately by offering to one of them (say, player 2) an alternative contract that improves what 2 would otherwise receive in the intended contract and still leaves some positive amount for herself. It is clear that this option is always feasible, thus ruling out the existence of strictly bilateral contracts.

And what about stable contracts that are fully trilateral? Do they exist? To see that they do not, observe that any contract among the three individuals in which *all* receive *some* positive amount admits the possibility that two of them improve their part by signing a separate bilateral contract. (Consider, for example, an alternative contract in which any two of the players supplement their initially intended amounts with an equal split of what the other individual would have received according to the original contract.) We may conclude, therefore, that neither bilateral nor trilateral contracts can be stable, which implies that *no* contract is stable. That is, for any coalition that could be formed, there is always an alternative one whose members would benefit by signing a different agreement. In sum, this implies that the core is empty in the context described when $n = 3$. In fact, it is easy to see that the same nonexistence problem persists in this setup for all $n > 3$.

Summary

This preliminary chapter has introduced the basic theoretical framework required to model and analyze general strategic situations. It has presented two alternative ways of representing any given game: the extensive form and the strategic (or normal) form.

The first approach (the extensive form) is the most general, in that it describes *explicitly* the players' order of moves and their available information at each point in the game. It embodies a formal specification of the tree of events, where each of its intermediate nodes has a particular player associated with it who decides how play (i.e., the "branching process") unfolds thereafter. Eventually, a final node is reached that has a corresponding vector of payoffs reflecting how the different players evaluate such a path of play.

In contrast, the strategic form of a game is based on the fundamental notion of strategy. A player's strategy is a contingent plan of action that anticipates *every* possible decision point at which the player may be in the course of game. Given a profile of players' strategies, the path of play is uniquely defined and so is the corresponding outcome and payoffs. In essence, the strategic form of a game is simply a compact description of the situation through the corresponding mapping from strategy profiles to payoffs.

Often, we shall be interested in allowing players to randomize when selecting their strategy. This possibility gives rise to the so-called mixed extension of a game, where (von Neumann-Morgenstern) payoffs associated with mixed strategies are defined in expected terms. If a player's randomization can occur independently at each one of her information sets, the induced plan of (randomized) action is called a behavioral strategy. One can establish the formal relationship between mixed and behavioral strategies. At a strategic level, however, they turn out to be fully equivalent, as long as players display perfect recall (i.e., never forget prior information or their own previous choices).

Finally, we have briefly outlined the sharp change of focus adopted by the branch of game theory that has been labelled "cooperative," as opposed to the noncooperative game theory which is the object of the present book. The implicit assumption of cooperative game theory is that players can jointly enforce (or commit to) the implementation of any outcome and will use this possibility to reach *some* efficient configuration. To illustrate the nature of this approach, we have outlined the implications of two of the most widely used solution concepts (the core and the Shapley value) within a very simple setup.

Exercises

Exercise 1.1: Represent in extensive form the following variations of the example described in Figure 1.8.

  (a) An initial amount has to be paid by both players at the start of the game, which is added to their bet if neither passes or it is received by the player who does *not* pass if one of them passes.

(b) As in (a), with the additional possibility that player 1 may bet after having passed initially, if player 2 bets. In this case, if both players decide to pass (note that now both receive this option), the initial payment is returned to the players.

Exercise 1.2: Two generals, A and B, whose armies are fortified in opposite hills have to decide whether to attack the enemy camped in a valley separating them. For the attack to be successful, General A must receive reinforcements. The arrival of these reinforcements on time has a prior probability of $1/2$ and depends on weather conditions not observed by the generals. They have reached the agreement that if A receives the reinforcements, he will send an emissary to B. They both know, however, that in this case the emissary has only probability $1/3$ of being able to cross the enemy lines. The payoffs have been evaluated as follows. They are equal to 50 for each general in case of victory. If they both refrain from attacking, their payoff is zero. If one attacks and the other does not, the former obtains a payoff of -50 and the latter a payoff of -10. Finally, if both generals attack but are defeated (because A has not received the reinforcements) each of them receives a payoff of -40.

(1) Represent the game described in extensive form.
(2) As in (1), for a modified game where General A now has the possibility of deciding whether to send an emissary, both when reinforcements arrive and when they do not.
(3) As in (1), for a modified game where General A always attacks but sends an emissary only in case he receives reinforcements.
(4) As in (1), for a modified game where General A always sends an emissary but attacks only if he receives reinforcements.
(5) Propose a prediction (perhaps in probabilistic terms) for the outcome of the battle in the latter two cases.

Exercise 1.3: Two individuals have to agree on how to divide 4 dollars. Two divisions are being considered: an even split that would give 2 dollars to each of them, and an asymmetric division that would leave 3 dollars with one of the players (labeled player 1) and one dollar with the other (player 2). The following allocation procedure is considered. First, player 1 has to make a proposal (i.e., one of the previous two possibilities), to which player 2 then has to respond with acceptance or rejection. If the proposal is accepted the 4 dollars are divided accordingly, whereas in the alternative case neither of them receives any money at all. Formulate the situation as a game in extensive form and discuss informally the likelihood of different outcomes.

Exercise 1.4: Consider the game described in Exercise 1.3. Define the players' strategy spaces formally, and specify in detail its strategic-form representation.

Exercise 1.5: Consider three individuals involved in the following situation. There is a certain good, originally in possession of individual 1, that may end reaching individual 3. However, individuals 1 and 3 are not in direct contact so that, if the first individual wants to send the good to individual 3, she must count on individual 2 to pass it on. At each stage, both individual 1 and individual 2 (for the latter, only if she receives the good from 1) may decide to pass the good or keep it. Eventually, individual 3 knows only whether she has received the good or not (i.e., if she does not receive the good, she does not know who has kept it). On the basis of that information, she has to decide whether to punish individual 1, individual 2, or either of them. Assume that the good has a valuation equal to 2 dollars for any of the three individuals and that the punishment inflicted by individual 3 on either 1 or 2 is quantified to have a monetary value of 3 dollars (which is subtracted from the payoffs of the punished party but does not affect either of the other two). Formulate the situation as a three-player game and represent it in extensive form.

Exercise 1.6: Consider the game described in Exercise 1.5. Specify the players' strategy spaces and provide a precise definition of its strategic-form representation.

Exercise 1.7: Let there be two individuals, 1 and 2, who play the traditional rock-scissors-paper $(R$-S-$P)$ game: R beats S, S beats P, and P beats R. Suppose that "beating the opponent" amounts to receiving one dollar from her, whereas if both individuals choose the same action no payment is made.

1. Represent the game in extensive and strategic forms. What would be your prediction on the strategy used by each player?
2. Consider now the following variation of the previous game: the order of movement is sequential (first one of them, then the other), each of the two possibilities being chosen with equal probability (say, by tossing a fair coin) at the beginning of the game.
   (a) Represent the game in extensive and strategic forms.
   (b) Propose a prediction for the strategy that will be played by each player.
   (c) Suppose that one of the individuals is given the option of choosing whether to play first or second in the sequential game. Which option will she prefer?

Exercise 1.8*: Consider the game represented in Figure 1.11 and suppose that player 1 uses a mixed strategy σ_1 that assigns an equal weight of $1/3$ to the three following pure strategies: $(T, X, Y), (T, Y, Y), (B, X, X)$, where the first component refers to her first information set, the second one to the information set that follows action T, and the third one to the information set that follows B. Determine the behavioral strategy associated with σ_1. Consider now the mixed strategy σ_1' that associates an equal weight of $1/2$ to the strategies (T, X, Y) and (T, Y, Y). Determine the behavioral strategy associated with σ_1'.

Exercise 1.9*: Prove that the mapping from mixed to behavioral strategies is on-to, i.e., given any behavioral strategy γ_i, there is a mixed strategy, σ_i, that gives rise to the former through the application of (1.7).

Exercise 1.10*: Consider the game with imperfect recall represented in Figure 1.12. In your view, what is the most natural concept of "stochastic plan of action": that embodied by a mixed or a behavioral strategy? Justify your answer.

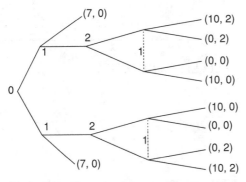

Figure 1.13: Extensive-form game.

Exercise 1.11*: Consider the extensive-form game with perfect recall represented in Figure 1.13, at which Nature moves first with two equiprobable choices.

Propose and justify a prediction for this game. Alternatively, propose and justify a prediction for the game with imperfect recall obtained from the original game by integrating the last two information sets of player 1 into a single one.

Exercise 1.12*: There are $2n + 1$ individuals with a single glove each, n of them having a right-hand glove and the remaining $n + 1$ having a left-hand one. Suppose a trader in gloves offers to pay 10 dollars for each complementary pair of gloves that is delivered to her. Modeling the situation as a cooperative game, specify its characteristic function and determine its core. (Recall from Section 1.6 that the core coincides with the set of "stable agreements" that may be signed by the agents.)

CHAPTER 2

Strategic-form analysis: theory

2.1 Dominance and iterative dominance

Consider again the prisoner's dilemma game introduced in the previous chapter (Table 1.1). It will be recalled that, in this game, D is the best strategy for each player, independently of what her opponent does. In other words, C is a dominated strategy, which led us to predict that both players would choose D instead when playing the game.

The use of such payoff-dominance criteria becomes much more interesting when it is applied iteratively. Consider the following bilateral game in strategic form, where no player has a dominant (i.e., uniformly best) strategy:

Table 2.1: *A strategic-form game with no dominant strategies*

1 \ 2	A	B	C
X	2, 7	2, 0	2, 2
Y	7, 0	1, 1	3, 2
Z	4, 1	0, 4	1, 3

First, we observe that player 1's strategy Y gives her a payoff higher than that of strategy Z, irrespectively of the strategy chosen by player 2. That is, strategy Y dominates strategy Z (sometimes the qualifier "strongly" will be added). Thus, assuming that player 1 is rational (i.e., aims at maximizing her payoffs), we can guarantee that she will never use strategy Z. But if player 2 reasons along these same lines, she may discard the possibility that 1 adopts Z. And once this is done, the relevant game to be considered is reduced to:

1 \ 2	A	B	C
X	2, 7	2, 0	2, 2
Y	7, 0	1, 1	3, 2

In this modified game, it is now player 2 who has a dominated strategy: strategy B, which is dominated by strategy C. Therefore, if player 1 knows that 2 is rational, she will rule out that 2 might play B. Note the important point that, when player 1 reasons on the reduced game (rather than on the original one), she is implicitly relying on the belief that player 2 knows that 1 (i.e., herself) is rational. Once B is discarded, the game becomes:

1 \ 2	A	C
X	2, 7	2, 2
Y	7, 0	3, 2

On the basis of this new payoff table, player 1 has a new dominated strategy, X, which becomes dominated by strategy Y. Therefore, if 2 knows that 1 reasons on the basis of this table, she can rule out that 1 will adopt X. Again, note that in supposing that 1 reasons on the latter payoff table, it is implicit that 1 knows that 2 knows that 1 is rational. Once X is discarded, 2 confronts the following table:

1 \ 2	A	C
Y	7, 0	3, 2

which will of course lead 2 to choosing C, because this is the strategy that entails her highest payoff. Overall, therefore, we reach the conclusion that only the profile (Y, C) may (or should) be played, because it is the unique outcome that survives the whole series of aforementioned rationality-based considerations.

The former discussion can be summarized in a somewhat more systematic fashion through the following chain of (roughly) "nested" statements. First, if

(a) player 1 is rational,

it can be ruled out that player 1 might choose strategy Z. Next, if

(b) player 2 is rational and she knows (a),

it can be asserted that player 2 will not play B. Next, if

(c) player 1 is rational and she knows (b),

it can be ensured that player 1 will not play X. Finally, if

(d) player 2 is rational and she knows (c),

it can be guaranteed that player 2 will not play A. Thus, to reach the prediction that the profile (Y, C) will be played it is enough that

   (i) players 1 and 2 are rational,
   (ii) players 1 and 2 know that both are rational,
   (iii) players 1 and 2 know that both know that both are rational,
   (iv) players 1 and 2 know that both know that both know that both are rational.

The *unbounded* chain of assertions obtained by extrapolating (i)–(iv) *ad infinitum* defines what is labeled *common knowledge of rationality* (Aumann, 1976). Thus, common knowledge of rationality refers to a state of affairs where players' rationality is not only known but is also known to be known at any higher level. That is, it is known at the "second level" (which pertains to what players know about the opponent's knowledge); it is known at the "third level" (which concerns each player's knowledge about what the opponent knows about what she herself knows), etc.

Traditionally, common knowledge of rationality has been an implicit (or even explicit)[16] axiom on players' understanding of the situation that has been used to motivate most of the solution concepts proposed for the analysis of games. As in the previous considerations, "rationality" may be *minimally* identified with "not playing dominated strategies." Alternatively, one could identify it with the (stronger) condition that players should choose a "best response to some beliefs" about what their opponents will play. But then one would have to face the delicate issue of what beliefs are admissible and, most importantly, whether they should be consistent across the different players (see Sections 2.2 and 2.7). Here, we choose to ignore for the moment these problems and insist that common knowledge of rationality (in the minimal sense of eschewing dominated behavior) should provide the *sole basis* for players' analysis of the game.

Under these circumstances, each player should reason about the game in a fully separate and independent manner. The "mental process" thus induced, which was illustrated by the example above, is now formalized precisely. To this end, we first define and discuss the notion of payoff dominance that underlies the resulting iterative process. Let $G = \{N, \{S_i\}_{i=1}^n, \{\pi_i\}_{i=1}^n\}$ be any game in strategic form.[17]

Definition 2.1: *The strategy $s_i \in S_i$ of player i is (strongly)[18] dominated if there exists some $\tilde{\sigma}_i \in \Sigma_i$ such that*

$$\forall s_{-i} \in S_{-i} \equiv S_1 \times \cdots \times S_{i-1} \times S_{i+1} \times \cdots \times S_n,$$

$$\pi_i(\tilde{\sigma}_i, s_{-i}) > \pi_i(s_i, s_{-i}). \tag{2.1}$$

The above concept focuses on *pure* dominated strategies but allows players to rely on *mixed* strategies to evaluate payoff dominance. It is easy to see, however, that if some pure strategy is dominated, so is any mixed strategy that assigns to that pure strategy any positive probability (cf. Exercise 2.1). That is, if $s_i \in S_i$ is dominated and $\sigma_i \in \Sigma_i$ has $\sigma_i(s_i) > 0$, then there exists some alternative $\sigma_i' \in \Sigma_i$ such that

$$\forall s_{-i} \in S_{-i} \equiv S_1 \times \cdots \times S_{i-1} \times S_{i+1} \times \cdots \times S_n,$$

$$\pi_i(\sigma_i', s_{-i}) > \pi_i(\sigma_i, s_{-i}).$$

---

[16] There is a branch of the literature that studies the epistemic basis of game-theoretic solution concepts. Its aim is to develop formal models of players' reasoning in order to study the implications of alternative assumptions on what players know and how they use that knowledge. See, for example, Aumann (1987), Tan and Werlang (1988), or the more informal discussion in Binmore and Brandenburger (1990).

[17] Throughout this chapter, we shall dispense with an explicit consideration of Nature as a distinct player since it has no important role to play in the issues discussed here.

[18] Typically, we shall dispense with the qualifier "strongly," unless we want to underscore the contrast between the present concept of payoff dominance and some other weaker notions (cf., for example, Definition 4.9).

Of course, the converse is not true, which implies that the set of dominated mixed strategies is never smaller (and generally larger) than the set of mixed strategies whose support[19] contains some dominated pure strategies.

Further elaborating on the contrast between pure and mixed strategies concerning issues of payoff domination, it is natural to wonder about the relationship between the concept presented in Definition 2.1 and the following two, seemingly stronger, versions.

Definition 2.1′: *The strategy* $s_i \in S_i$ *of player i is* dominated (alternative 1) *if there exists some* $\tilde{\sigma}_i \in \Sigma_i$ *such that*

$$\forall \sigma_{-i} \in \Sigma_{-i} \equiv \Sigma_1 \times \cdots \times \Sigma_{i-1} \times \Sigma_{i+1} \times \cdots \times \Sigma_n,$$

$$\pi_i(\tilde{\sigma}_i, \sigma_{-i}) > \pi_i(s_i, \sigma_{-i}). \tag{2.2}$$

Definition 2.1″: *The strategy* $s_i \in S_i$ *of player i is* dominated (alternative 2) *if there exists some* $\tilde{s}_i \in S_i$ *such that*

$$\forall s_{-i} \in S_{-i} \equiv S_1 \times \cdots \times S_{i-1} \times S_{i+1} \times \cdots \times S_n,$$

$$\pi_i(\tilde{s}_i, s_{-i}) > \pi_i(s_i, s_{-i}). \tag{2.3}$$

Clearly, the notions of domination reflected by Definitions 2.1′ and 2.1″ are *at least* as demanding as that embodied by Definition 2.1. In other words, if pure strategy s_i is dominated according to either of those two latter alternatives, it is dominated as well in terms of the former notion. This is a simple consequence of the following two facts. First, the collection of inequalities contemplated in (2.2) subsumes those in (2.1); second, the pure strategy $\tilde{s}_i$ considered in (2.3) can be viewed as a degenerate mixed strategy in (2.1).

However, concerning the first alternative (Definition 2.1′), it turns out that, in fact, (2.2) is *not* really stronger than (2.1). To see this note that we can write:

$$\pi_i(s_i, \sigma_{-i}) = \sum_{s_{-i} \in S_{-i}} \pi_i(s_i, s_{-i}) [\sigma_1(s_1) \cdots \sigma_{i-1}(s_{i-1}) \sigma_{i+1}(s_{i+1}) \cdots \sigma_n(s_n)].$$

Thus, if (2.1) applies, i.e., there exists some $\tilde{\sigma}_i$ such that $\pi_i(\tilde{\sigma}_i, s_{-i}) > \pi_i(s_i, s_{-i})$ for *every* $s_{-i} \in S_{-i}$, we must also have

$$\sum_{s_{-i} \in S_{-i}} \pi_i(\tilde{\sigma}_i, s_{-i}) [\sigma_1(s_1) \cdots \sigma_{i-1}(s_{i-1}) \sigma_{i+1}(s_{i+1}) \cdots \sigma_n(s_n)]$$

$$> \sum_{s_{-i} \in S_{-i}} \pi_i(s_i, s_{-i}) [\sigma_1(s_1) \cdots \sigma_{i-1}(s_{i-1}) \sigma_{i+1}(s_{i+1}) \cdots \sigma_n(s_n)],$$

or

$$\pi_i(\tilde{\sigma}_i, \sigma_{-i}) > \pi_i(s_i, \sigma_{-i})$$

for *every* $\sigma_{-i} \in \Sigma_{-i}$; i.e., (2.2) holds as well. We conclude, therefore, that (2.1) and (2.2) are in fact equivalent requirements.

---

[19] Since a mixed strategy defines a probability vector (or measure) over the set of pure strategies, the support of any such mixed strategy is given by the set of pure strategies that display positive weight.

Turning next to Definition 2.1″, we now show that this second alternative criterion of domination is indeed *substantially stronger* than that embodied by Definition 2.1. To confirm this point, simply consider a game whose strategic form has payoffs for player 1 given by the following table (the payoffs of player 2 are immaterial for the discussion):

1 \ 2	A	B
X	1, *	1, *
Y	3, *	0, *
Z	0, *	3, *

In this game, none of the pure strategies of player 1 is dominated by an alternative pure strategy. However, it is clear that the mixed strategy $\sigma_1 = (0, 1/2, 1/2)$ dominates the pure strategy X: it guarantees a larger expected payoff than X, independently of the strategy adopted by player 2. We conclude, therefore, that requiring payoff domination in terms of a *pure* strategy may, in general, reduce significantly the set of strategies (pure or mixed) that qualify as "dominated." Reciprocally, of course, it follows that the set of a player's strategies that are undominated is typically larger when one insists that payoff domination materializes through "dominating" pure strategies (Definition 2.1″) than when it may take place through mixed strategies (Definition 2.1).

To conclude this section, we are now in a position to provide a general formalization of the iterative process of strategy elimination based on payoff-dominance considerations which was illustrated by our opening example. This process unfolds along a sequence of iterations $q = 0, 1, 2, \ldots$. At the start, one makes $S_i^0 = S_i$ and $\Sigma_i^0 = \Sigma_i$, i.e., all pure and mixed strategies are available at the beginning of the process. Then, for $q \geq 1$, one defines

$$S_i^q = \left\{ s_i \in S_i^{q-1} : \neg \left(\exists \sigma_i \in \Sigma_i^{q-1} : \forall s_{-i} \in S_{-i}^{q-1}, \pi_i(\sigma_i, s_{-i}) > \pi_i(s_i, s_{-i}) \right) \right\}$$

(2.4)

$$\Sigma_i^q = \left\{ \sigma_i \in \Sigma_i^{q-1} : \mathbf{supp}\, (\sigma_i) \subseteq S_i^q \right\},$$

(2.5)

where, as customary, $\mathbf{supp}\, (\sigma_i)$ stands for the support of the mixed strategy, i.e., the set of those pure strategies to which σ_i assigns positive weight (cf. Footnote 19). Thus, at each stage of the process, every player is taken to eliminate from her strategy set all those mixed strategies whose support includes "currently dominated" (pure) strategies, where the set of opponents' strategies that are judged admissible (or possible) at that stage include only those that have not been eliminated so far in previous stages.

Note that, by construction, the chain of undominated strategy sets prevailing at each stage defines a nonincreasing sequence, i.e., $S_i^q \supseteq S_i^{q+1}$ for every q and each $i \in N$. Therefore, the set of strategies eventually surviving the indefinite process of elimination,

$$S_i^\infty = \lim_{q \to \infty} S_i^q = \bigcap_{q=0}^\infty S_i^q, \tag{2.6}$$

is well defined. If we restrict attention to finite games (i.e., games with a finite number of players and finite strategy spaces), such an elimination process must necessarily finish in a finite number of iterations (see Part (a) of Exercise 2.2). Moreover, it is clear that $S_i^\infty \neq \emptyset$ for every $i = 1, 2, \ldots, n$ because there must always be at least one undominated strategy in every round of elimination.[20] When each S_i^∞ is a singleton, the game in question is called *dominance solvable*. In this case, iterative elimination of dominated strategies gives rise to a unique strategy profile s^*, i.e., $S_1^\infty \times \cdots \times S_n^\infty = \{s^*\}$. A simple example of a dominance-solvable game is provided by the one described in Table 2.1, where an iterative elimination of dominated strategies was found to yield a unique outcome.

2.2 Nash equilibrium

2.2.1 *Formalization and discussion*

As explained in Section 2.1, dominance-solvable games admit a very transparent and clear-cut analysis, based on quite uncontroversial postulates: players eschew dominated strategies and it is common knowledge that everyone does so. Unfortunately, few games of interest qualify as dominance solvable, thus allowing for such a straightforward approach.

Consider, for example, the simple games *battle of the sexes* and *matching pennies*, which were described in Subsection 1.2.2. In neither of these games is there a player with a dominated strategy. Therefore, the process of iterative elimination formulated above cannot have any "bite," leaving the strategy sets of both players unaffected. That is, any of their strategies is consistent with common knowledge of rationality, when rationality is understood in the weak sense of leading players to avoid dominated strategies.

As advanced, however, the postulate of rationality can be understood in the stronger sense of having players maximize their respective expected payoff on the basis of some expectations (or beliefs) about what their opponents will do. If, holding this view of rationality, it is further postulated that the underlying expectations have to be accurate (sometimes, misleadingly labeled as "rational"), the key theoretical concept known as Nash equilibrium arises. It embodies the two following requirements:

(1) Players' strategies must be a best response (i.e., should maximize their respective payoffs), given some well-defined beliefs about the strategies adopted by the opponents.

---

[20] More formally, note that payoff domination defines a strict partial ordering and, therefore, the maximal set is always well defined and nonempty.

(2) The beliefs held by each player must be an accurate *ex ante* prediction of the strategies actually played by the opponents.

Given conditions (1) and (2), it is natural to raise the basic question of how players should be conceived to achieve, in general, the consistency between optimality and beliefs required at every Nash equilibrium. Is there any simple "algorithmic" process (e.g., an iterative procedure such as the one described in Section 2.1) by which players may hope to attain such an equilibrium? Unfortunately, there are not very good answers to this crucial issue. Three possible routes for addressing it are now outlined in turn.

One way of understanding that players may end up playing a Nash equilibrium is to invoke the power of players' reasoning in analyzing the situation. Suppose that (rational) players are perfectly informed of all relevant details of the game and, in particular, can count on the assumption that rationality is common knowledge. Then, if their analysis of the game aims at identifying *logically coherent* outcomes of play, they will find that, indeed, only Nash equilibria qualify as such. That is, only a Nash equilibrium reconciles a definite prediction of play with rationality and common knowledge thereof. If players were to predict some other, nonequilibrium, kind of play, there would always be a player who (trusting the prediction as it pertains to others) would nevertheless fail to play her part in it. Thus, unless limited reasoning capabilities prevent them from identifying the contradiction embodied by nonequilibrium behavior (something that is implicitly ruled out in this approach), they should never predict or play anything other than some Nash equilibrium.

The former approach exhibits major shortcomings. Not only does it ignore the possibility that no Nash equilibrium might exist (a problem discussed at some length in Subsection 2.2.3 and Section 2.4) but, typically more important, the possibility that several of them could *coexist*. In the latter case, the following obvious question arises: How will agents coordinate their actions on one particular (the same) equilibrium?

To illustrate matters, consider the battle of the sexes (Table 1.2). Both strategy profiles (B, B) and (S, S) satisfy (1) and (2). In view of this, one might suggest that, in the presence of such equilibrium ambiguity, players (the boy and the girl in this case) should discuss matters in advance and eventually reach an agreement about what particular Nash equilibrium to play. This approach, however, amounts to embedding the original game (which allowed for no explicit communication) into a larger one where communication is possible. But then, "talking" (sending messages) becomes in itself a new strategic component of the problem, and its analysis should be carried out strategically as well. The threat of an infinite (unbounded) regress becomes apparent: possibly, the new enlarged game exhibits equilibrium multiplicity as well, and further communication procedures should then be habilitated to resolve it. Thus, in the end, one may well find that an explicit modeling of communication does not prove to be an effective or practical way of addressing the problem in many cases.

It could be argued, however, that it is not necessary to model communication *explicitly* to have it exert a useful role in tackling equilibrium multiplicity. The battle of the sexes again illustrates the weakness of this point. In this game, as in many others, the complete *ex ante symmetry* of the situation implies that any informal appeal to player's implicit communication can hardly be of any help in understanding equilibrium play. Any argument that could be informally used to support, say, (B, B) could be used to suggest that (S, S) should (or will be) played instead.

A second route for motivating Nash equilibrium play adopts a very different perspective. It espouses the viewpoint that the concern of game theory is *not* to understand *how* players will reach an agreement on play but to help them (or us, the analysts) identify the consistent, robust, or otherwise appealing possibilities at their disposal. A somewhat related stand suggests that players often face passively some given pattern of play that has been proposed by external agents (tradition, a planner, or a mediator), and the role of game theory simply is to check out the coherence of the proposals. The implicit idea here is that any solution concept (e.g., Nash equilibrium) is to be conceived as an analytical tool in the hands of "society," helping it to evaluate what patterns of play are incentive compatible and can thus be actually implemented. Of course, a natural criticism to this approach is that, in essence, it "solves" the problem by simply assuming it away. If tradition, say, plays such an important role in equilibrium determination, any history-free model of strategic situations is crucially incomplete.

Finally, a third way of tackling the problem partly elaborates on the latter point concerning the potential importance of "history." It views any Nash equilibrium as the limit outcome of some genuine process of adjustment taking place in real (rather than virtual) time. That is, instead of formulating a tâtonnement process that models agents' hypothetical reasoning (e.g., the iterative procedure considered in Section 2.1), it conceives the adjustment dynamics as having tangible payoff consequences at every point in time. Two possibilities along these lines are studied in later chapters. First, in Chapter 10, we focus on evolutionary dynamics that reflect considerations akin to those of biological natural selection and happen to select undominated (i.e., "rational," sometimes even equilibrium) behavior in the long run. Second, in Chapters 11 and 12, we study population-based models of learning that, under certain circumstances, turn out to lead agents toward playing some Nash equilibrium in the long run. Even though neither of these approaches is free of theoretical problems, they prove successful in some important cases where other approaches fail to provide satisfactory answers.

We now formalize the concept of Nash equilibrium. In contrast with other more "refined" concepts (see Chapter 4), it is defined on the strategic form of a game; i.e., it requires only information contained in a more compact representation of the situation.

Definition 2.2 (Nash, 1951): *Given a game G in strategic form, the profile $s^* \equiv (s_1^*, s_2^*, \ldots, s_n^*)$ is called a* Nash equilibrium *if $\forall i = 1, 2, \ldots, n, \forall s_i \in S_i,$* $\pi_i(s^*) \geq \pi_i(s_i, s_{-i}^*).$

It is easy to verify that, in any given strategic-form game G, every Nash equilibrium must involve only strategies that survive the iterative elimination of

Table 2.2: *A strategic-form game with a unique Nash equilibrium*

1 \ 2	A	B	C
A	1, 1	1, 0	1, 0
B	0, 1	2, −2	−2, 2
C	0, 1	−2, 2	2, −2

dominated strategies. Thus, in particular, if the game is dominance solvable and $\{s^*\} = S_1^\infty \times \cdots \times S_n^\infty$, then s^* is the unique candidate to being a Nash equilibrium of the game (see Exercise 2.5). In this general sense, therefore, the concept of Nash equilibrium can be said to embody behavioral requirements that are at least as stringent as those reflected by the approach based on payoff dominance. This in turn implies that the predictions derived from the former must always be at least as sharp as (i.e., a subset of) those induced by the latter. To illustrate that the latter conclusion generally holds *strictly*, consider the strategic-form (symmetric) game described in Table 2.2. This game has no dominated strategy and, therefore, $S_i^\infty = \{A, B, C\}$; i.e., it includes all three possible strategies for each $i = 1, 2$. In contrast, it is straightforward to see (cf. Exercise 2.6) that it has a *unique* Nash equilibrium given by (A, A).

The previous example notwithstanding, it is important to bear in mind that uniqueness of Nash equilibrium is not a feature to be expected for general games. Indeed, in many cases of interest (recall our former discussion of the battle of the sexes), one should expect that several strategic configurations satisfy the optimality and consistency conditions underlying the concept of Nash equilibrium, all of them being therefore "valid predictions" for the game. But, of course, polar to such disturbing problems of equilibrium multiplicity, there is the even more basic issue of *equilibrium existence*. When can the existence of *some* Nash equilibrium be guaranteed? Unfortunately, even the simplest games can pose insurmountable problems of nonexistence if, as in Definition 2.2, we restrict to pure strategy profiles.

By way of illustration, consider for example the matching-pennies game described in Table 1.4 (see also Subsection 2.2.2 for a formal analysis of it). In this game, for each of the four possible profiles of pure strategies, there is always a player who benefits from a unilateral deviation. Thus, none of them may qualify as a Nash equilibrium of the game. Intuitively, the problem is that, given the fully opposite interests of players (that is, if one gains the other loses), accuracy of prediction and individual optimality cannot be reconciled when players' strategies are deterministic or pure. Given this state of affairs, it seems natural to try to tackle the problem by allowing for the possibility that players can "hide" their action through a stochastic (i.e., mixed) strategy. Indeed, suppose that both players were to choose each of their two pure strategies (heads or tails) with equal probability. Then, even if each player would know that this is the case (i.e., beliefs are correct concerning the mixed strategy played by the opponent), neither of them could improve by deviating from such a mixed strategy. This happens because both pure strategies (and thus any mixed strategy) induce the same expected payoff. In a natural sense, therefore, this provides accuracy of *ex ante* beliefs and individual optimality, as required by the notion of Nash equilibrium.

How can one generalize the Nash equilibrium concept to allow players to rely on mixed strategies? Clearly, this must involve modeling the game through its mixed extension, as explained in Section 1.4. Within such an enlarged framework, the former notion of Nash equilibrium (cf. Definition 2.2) can be readily reformulated as follows.

Definition 2.3: *Given the mixed extension of a game G in strategic form, the profile* $\sigma^* \equiv (\sigma_1^*, \sigma_2^*, \ldots, \sigma_n^*)$ *is called a* Nash equilibrium *if* $\forall i = 1, 2, \ldots, n$, $\forall \sigma_i \in \Sigma_i, \pi_i(\sigma^*) \geq \pi_i(\sigma_i, \sigma_{-i}^*)$.

To gain a complementary perspective on the notion of Nash equilibrium, it is useful to restate matters in terms of what are known as the players' best-response correspondences. For each player i, her "best-response" correspondence

$$\rho_i : \Sigma_{-i} \rightrightarrows \Sigma_i$$

is defined as follows:

$$\rho_i(\sigma_{-i}) = \{\sigma_i \in \Sigma_i : \pi_i(\sigma_i, \sigma_{-i}) \geq \pi_i(\tilde{\sigma}_i, \sigma_{-i}), \forall \tilde{\sigma}_i \in \Sigma_i\}. \tag{2.7}$$

That is, for each player i and any $\sigma_{-i} \in \Sigma_{-i}$, $\rho_i(\sigma_{-i})$ consists of all those (mixed) strategies for player i that maximize her expected payoffs when the profile of opponents' strategies is σ_{-i}. Then, if we define[21]

$$\rho : \Sigma \rightrightarrows \Sigma \tag{2.8}$$

as the Cartesian product of those correspondences, $\rho \equiv \rho_1 \times \rho_2 \times \cdots \times \rho_n$, the concept of Nash equilibrium can be simply recast as follows.

Definition 2.3′: *Given the mixed extension of a game G in strategic form, the profile* $\sigma^* \equiv (\sigma_1^*, \sigma_2^*, \ldots, \sigma_n^*)$ *is called a* Nash equilibrium *if* $\sigma^* \in \rho(\sigma^*)$, *i.e.*, $\forall i = 1, 2, \ldots, n, \sigma_i^* \in \rho_i(\sigma_{-i}^*)$.

Obviously, the formulation of Nash equilibrium presented in Definition 2.3 is equivalent to that introduced in Definition 2.3′. Verbally, the latter one merely redefines a Nash equilibrium as a (mixed-) strategy profile where every player's strategy is an (expected) best response to all others' strategies. This alternative way of presenting the concept underscores the fact that a Nash equilibrium may be identified with a *fixed point* of ρ in the space of mixed-strategy profiles. Such a reformulation of the concept of Nash equilibrium will turn out useful in two respects: first, to facilitate the computation of equilibria in specific games (cf. Subsection 2.2.2); second, to prove a general existence result (cf. Section 2.4).

---

[21] Note that, even though each separate ρ_i has been defined on the respective Σ_{-i}, the product correspondence ρ must be defined on the whole space of mixed-strategy profiles Σ.

Table 2.3: *A simple entry game, strategic form*

1\\ 2	F	C
N	0, 2	0, 2
E	−1, −1	1, 1

2.2.2 Examples

Now, for the sake of illustration, we turn to three of the games already considered in Chapter 1, computing explicitly for each of them their corresponding Nash equilibria.

2.2.2.1 *A simple entry game.* Consider the game described in Subsection 1.2.2.1, whose strategic-form representation is recalled in Table 2.3.

Our first task is to determine the best-response correspondences ρ_i, $i = 1, 2$, as given by (2.7). For notational simplicity, represent any mixed strategy $\sigma_1 = (\sigma_{1N}, \sigma_{1E})$ of player 1 by $\sigma_{1N} \in [0, 1]$ – the weight associated with pure strategy N – since $\sigma_{1E} = 1 - \sigma_{1N}$. Similarly, any mixed strategy $\sigma_2 = (\sigma_{2F}, \sigma_{2C})$ of player 2 is represented by $\sigma_{2F} \in [0, 1]$ – the weight of pure strategy F – with $\sigma_{2C} = 1 - \sigma_{2F}$. Then, each player i's best-response correspondence can be defined as a one-dimensional mapping $\rho_i : [0, 1] \rightrightarrows [0, 1]$. For player 1, it is immediate to compute that

$$\pi_1(N, (\sigma_{2F}, 1 - \sigma_{2F})) \gtrless \pi_1(E, (\sigma_{2F}, 1 - \sigma_{2F})) \Leftrightarrow \sigma_{2F} \gtrless \frac{1}{2}$$

and, therefore,

$$\rho_1(\sigma_{2F}) = \begin{cases} 0 & \text{if } \sigma_{2F} < \frac{1}{2} \\ [0, 1] & \text{if } \sigma_{2F} = \frac{1}{2} \\ 1 & \text{if } \sigma_{2F} > \frac{1}{2}. \end{cases}$$

On the other hand, for player 2 we have

$$\sigma_{1N} < 1 \Rightarrow \pi_2(F, (\sigma_{1N}, 1 - \sigma_{1N})) < \pi_2(C, (\sigma_{1N}, 1 - \sigma_{1N}))$$
$$\sigma_{1N} = 1 \Rightarrow \pi_2(F, (\sigma_{1N}, 1 - \sigma_{1N})) = \pi_2(C, (\sigma_{1N}, 1 - \sigma_{1N})),$$

which implies that

$$\rho_2(\sigma_{1N}) = \begin{cases} 0 & \text{if } \sigma_{1N} < 1 \\ [0, 1] & \text{if } \sigma_{1N} = 1. \end{cases}$$

From Definition 2.3', a Nash equilibrium is a pair of mixed strategies $\sigma^* = [(\sigma_{1N}^*, 1 - \sigma_{1N}^*), (\sigma_{2F}^*, 1 - \sigma_{2F}^*)]$ such that

$$\sigma_{1N}^* \in \rho_1(\sigma_{2F}^*)$$
$$\sigma_{2F}^* \in \rho_2(\sigma_{1N}^*).$$

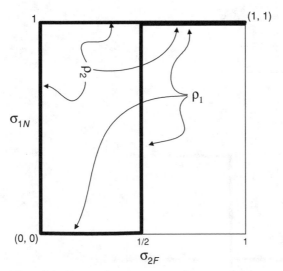

Figure 2.1: Best-response correspondences, a simple entry game.

An easy way of identifying those equilibrium configurations is to plot the two best-response correspondences on the same $\sigma_{2F} - \sigma_{1N}$ plane (with, say, ρ_2 "rotated" $90°$) and look for points of intersection. This is done in Figure 2.1.

Mere inspection of Figure 2.1 indicates that there are two kinds of Nash equilibria in the game. On the one hand, there is the pure-strategy equilibrium $[(0, 1), (0, 1)]$ (i.e., the pure-strategy pair (E, C)), which corresponds to the intersection between the best-response correspondences that occurs at the origin $(0, 0)$. It reflects a situation where firm 1 decides to enter the market under the (correct) anticipation that firm 2 will concede entry. On the other hand, there is the *component* of Nash equilibria

$$\mathcal{C} \equiv \{[(\sigma_{1N}, \sigma_{1E}), (\sigma_{2F}, \sigma_{2C})] : \sigma_{1N} = 1, \ \sigma_{2F} \geq 1/2\},$$

where the potential entrant (firm 1) is deterred from actual entry by firm 2's "threat" of fighting entry (i.e., choosing F) with high enough probability (larger than $1/2$). As explained in Chapter 4, such a threat is not a credible one, which casts doubt on the robustness of those equilibria when tested against natural refinement criteria.

2.2.2.2 *A matching-pennies game.* Consider now the matching-pennies game, whose strategic form is recalled in Table 2.4.

As explained in Subsection 2.2.1, no pure-strategy equilibrium exists in this game. There, we also suggested that if players could rely on mixed strategies, they might be able to tackle the problem of equilibrium existence satisfactorily. Now, we explore this idea formally, again relying on a detailed analysis of the players' best-response correspondences. Denote their mixed strategies by $\sigma_i = (\sigma_{iH}, \sigma_{iT})$, $i = 1, 2$, and identify each possible such strategy by its weight σ_{iH} on the pure strategy H (with $\sigma_{iT} = 1 - \sigma_{iH}$). Relying on this notation, the best-response correspondence

Table 2.4: *A matching-pennies game, strategic form*

1\2	H	T
H	1, −1	−1, 1
T	−1, 1	1, −1

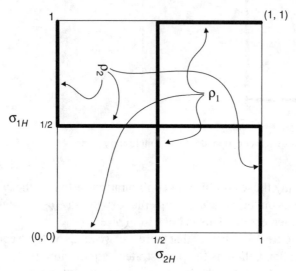

Figure 2.2: Best-response correspondences; a matching-pennies game.

of player 1 is easily seen to be of the following form:

$$\rho_1(\sigma_{2H}) = \begin{cases} 0 & \text{if } \sigma_{2H} < \frac{1}{2} \\ [0, 1] & \text{if } \sigma_{2H} = \frac{1}{2} \\ 1 & \text{if } \sigma_{2H} > \frac{1}{2} \end{cases}$$

and that of player 2 is as follows:

$$\rho_2(\sigma_{1H}) = \begin{cases} 1 & \text{if } \sigma_{1H} < \frac{1}{2} \\ [0, 1] & \text{if } \sigma_{1H} = \frac{1}{2} \\ 0 & \text{if } \sigma_{1H} > \frac{1}{2}. \end{cases}$$

Combining again $\rho_1(\cdot)$ and $\rho_2(\cdot)$ into a single diagram (see Figure 2.2), it becomes immediately apparent that the unique (mixed-strategy) Nash equilibrium of the game has $\sigma_i^* = (1/2, 1/2)$ for each $i = 1, 2$.

When each player i chooses the mixed strategy $\sigma_i^* = (1/2, 1/2)$, the optimality and consistency required by Nash equilibrium are jointly met. For, under the assumption that the opponent will indeed play in this fashion, both players are indifferent concerning the two possible *pure* strategies. Thus, they are indifferent as well among all mixed strategies and, in particular, they find the one that attributes

Table 2.5: *Battle of the sexes*

1 \ 2	B	S
B	3, 2	1, 1
S	0, 0	2, 3

an equal probability to each pure strategy as good as any other. In a sense, one may interpret this equilibrium as reflecting a decision by each player to attach payoff-irrelevant noise to her action in order to "strategically control" the uncertainty faced by her opponent. As we shall see in further examples, this is an interpretation that often can be attributed to equilibria involving mixed strategies.

2.2.2.3 *Battle of the sexes.* Finally, we reconsider the battle of the sexes, whose strategic form is recalled in Table 2.5.

This game has the two pure-strategy Nash equilibria already discussed at some length: (B, B) and (S, S). Are there any more (mixed-strategy) equilibria in this game? To answer this question, we turn to specifying the best-response correspondences of players 1 (the girl) and 2 (the boy). With the same notational conventions as before (here mixed strategies are parametrized by the probability σ_{iB} of choosing B), those correspondences may be defined as follows:

$$\rho_1(\sigma_{2B}) = \begin{cases} 0 & \text{if } \sigma_{2B} < \frac{1}{4} \\ [0, 1] & \text{if } \sigma_{2B} = \frac{1}{4} \\ 1 & \text{if } \sigma_{2B} > \frac{1}{4} \end{cases}$$

$$\rho_2(\sigma_{1B}) = \begin{cases} 0 & \text{if } \sigma_{1B} < \frac{3}{4} \\ [0, 1] & \text{if } \sigma_{1B} = \frac{3}{4} \\ 1 & \text{if } \sigma_{1B} > \frac{3}{4}. \end{cases}$$

The best-response correspondences are represented diagrammatically in Figure 2.3. The two vertices of intersection, $(0, 0)$ and $(1, 1)$, correspond to the two pure-strategy Nash equilibria of the game, (S, S) and (B, B), respectively. On the other hand, Figure 2.3 also shows that there exists a third mixed-strategy Nash equilibrium, $\sigma^* = (\sigma_1^*, \sigma_2^*) = ((3/4, 1/4), (1/4, 3/4))$. In the latter equilibrium, players behave asymmetrically, each of them placing a larger weight of $3/4$ on the pure strategy they would prefer to coordinate on (B for 1, S for 2).

2.2.3 *Existence: informal discussion*

Going beyond the simple examples considered above, one may naturally wonder whether the existence of some Nash equilibrium may be guaranteed under reasonably general conditions. If one restricts consideration to *finite* games, the following positive answer can be provided:

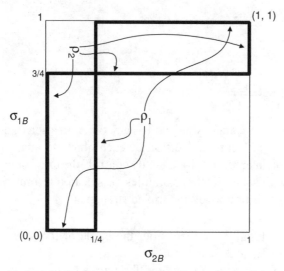

Figure 2.3: Best-response correspondences, battle of the sexes.

In every game where there is *any* finite number of players and these players have only a finite number of pure strategies available, some Nash equilibrium (possibly in mixed strategies) always exists.

This result is formally stated and proven in the Section 2.4 (cf. Theorem 2.2) as part of the Supplementary Material of this chapter.

The previous result does not apply to many economic applications that require formulating strategic situations as an *infinite* game. Often, the game arising in these applications involves only a finite number of players, but the strategy spaces are infinite (typically, with the cardinality of the continuum). This happens, for example, when the strategies pertain to the choice of some price or quantity, as in many models of oligopolistic competition (cf. Subsection 3.1.1 or 3.1.2). In those cases, the problem of equilibrium existence becomes mathematically more sophisticated and has to deal with a number of technical issues. In particular, compactness of the pure-strategy spaces must be required and the payoff functions are to be either continuous or at least have the extent of their discontinuuity somewhat limited. A more detailed discussion of these issues is postponed to Section 2.4.

Sometimes, the intuitive appeal of mixed strategies is criticized because of their seeming lack of realism. Specifically, it is argued that, in economically relevant strategic contexts, one seldom observes agents resorting to stochastic decision mechanisms: the decision rules used may be quite complex but should usually be conceived as deterministic. Naturally, these misgivings arise more forcefully in connection with infinite games, where a mixed strategy (rather than being a straightforward probability *vector*) is instead a probability *measure* belonging to an infinite-dimensional space.

Even though, as discussed in Section 6.5, there are reasonable arguments justifying mixed strategies as a useful theoretical construct (in particular, as a suitable description of agents' *perceptions* on the opponents' play), it is still worthwhile having conditions under which a game can be ensured to have pure-strategy Nash equilibria. As it turns out, the existence of a Nash equilibrium involving only pure strategies can be guaranteed in many infinite games (e.g., when the pure-strategy set is a compact real interval of, say, quantities or prices) if each player's payoff function is continuous and quasi-concave (the latter, only with respect to her own strategy). This is the content of Theorem 2.4, whose formal statement may be found in Section 2.4.

2.3   Zero-sum bilateral games

There is an important class of noncooperative games that, in the bilateral case with just two players, admit a much more exhaustive analysis than is possible for other kinds of games. They are the so-called *zero-sum games*, sometimes also referred to as *strictly competitive games*.[22] This class includes some of the games that ordinarily are thought as such in the customary use of the term (bridge, chess, a tennis match). Another simple example of a zero-sum game is the by now familiar one of matching pennies.

The interest for this kind of game is threefold. First, there are historical reasons. The original research on game theory focused, to a great extent, on this context. Later on, as the discipline turned toward social and economic applications, the rigidly noncooperative nature of these games was often found inappropriate to model the strategic problems arising in those contexts. In economic relationships, there is typically a mixture of cooperation and competitive dimensions, both playing an essential part in how players perceive and analyze the situation. Indeed, it is this mixture that underlies much of what makes most of the strategic problems in economic environments interesting (e.g., the tension between selfish interest and social efficiency in public-good allocation problems – cf. Section 3.2).

Second, an additional reason for studying zero-sum games resides in the fact that, in the analysis of these games, we find an especially transparent illustration of some of the key concepts underlying later developments for "varying-sum" games (e.g., the maximin or minimax values in the study of repeated games – cf. Chapter 9). In this sense, therefore, their analysis has not only a historical but also a useful pedagogical value.

Finally, a third motivation for the study of zero-sum games is derived from considerations of esthetic value and theoretical elegance. For, as we shall see, the approach to bilateral zero-sum games developed by John von Neumann and others during the early part of the twentieth century is a masterful piece of mathematical analysis. Furthermore, with the concourse of modern tools and results (e.g., the guaranteed existence of Nash equilibrium, not yet available at that time), it is surprisingly accessible as well.

Zero-sum games are just a special case of constant-sum games, the latter being simply defined as those games in which the sum of players' payoffs remains constant

---

[22] Some authors use the term "strictly competitive game" to refer to the wider class of games where players display opposite interests concerning any pair of alternative profiles of *pure* strategies. The problem with this categorization is that it does not guarantee that such opposing interests are "inherited" by the set of mixed-strategy profiles (cf. Remark 2.1).

across *every* possible strategy profile. It is easy to verify, however, that there is no real loss of generality in focusing attention on the case where the "constant sum" is identically equal to zero (see Exercise 2.11). There is, of course, significant loss of generality in constraining to bilateral games (i.e., those with just two players). This is nevertheless the context we mostly focus on here because, as explained below, it represents the only one where the zero-sum condition allows for a truly sharp analysis. Bilateral zero-sum games are defined as follows.

Definition 2.4: *A bilateral game in strategic form $G = \{\{1, 2\}, \{S_1, S_2\}, \{\pi_1, \pi_2\}\}$ is said to be* zero sum *if it satisfies $\pi_1(s) + \pi_2(s) = 0$ for all $s \in S$.*

Remark 2.1: *Zero-sum condition and mixed strategies*

Note that the zero-sum condition contemplated for pure-strategy profiles extends without any loss of generality to the set of mixed-strategy profiles. That is, one may equivalently reformulate the zero-sum condition as follows: $\forall \sigma \in \Sigma, \ \pi_1(\sigma) + \pi_2(\sigma) = 0$. ♦

Let G be a bilateral and finite zero-sum game. For each pair of strategies, $s_{1j} \in S_1$, $s_{2k} \in S_2$, denote by $a_{jk} \equiv \pi_1(s_{1j}, s_{2k})$ and $b_{jk} \equiv \pi_2(s_{1j}, s_{2k})$ the payoffs associated with each respective player. Since the game is zero-sum, we must obviously have that $b_{jk} = -a_{jk}$. Therefore, the game admits a compact but sufficient representation through a matrix A of dimension $r_1 \times r_2$, i.e., (cardinality of S_1) × (cardinality of S_2), a typical entry a_{jk} $(j = 1, \ldots, r_1; \ k = 1, \ldots, r_2)$ representing the payoff to player 1 associated to the strategic profile (s_{1j}, s_{2k}). Similarly, given any mixed-strategy profile $(\sigma_1, \sigma_2) \in \Delta^{r_1-1} \times \Delta^{r_2-1}$, we have

$$\pi_1(\sigma_1, \sigma_2) = -\pi_2(\sigma_1, \sigma_2) = \sigma_1 A \sigma_2,$$

where σ_1 is interpreted as a row vector and σ_2 as a column vector.

Since both players have opposite interests in the game, while player 1 will aim at maximizing the expression $\sigma_1 A \sigma_2$, player 2 will try to minimize it. Two specific values for this expression enjoy special relevance: the *maximin* and the *minimax*. They are explained in turn.

Heuristically, the *maximin* is the maximum payoff that player 1 would obtain if 2 could react (optimally) to every strategy on her (i.e., 1's) part by minimizing 1's payoff. In a sense, this value corresponds to the payoff that 1 should expect if she were extremely pessimistic over 2's ability to anticipate her own actions. Formally, it is equal to

$$v_1 \equiv \max_{\sigma_1 \in \Sigma_1} \min_{\sigma_2 \in \Sigma_2} \sigma_1 A \sigma_2, \tag{2.9}$$

where we are allowing both players to rely on mixed strategies.

Symmetrically, the *minimax* is defined to embody an analogous "pessimistic" interpretation for player 2, i.e.,

$$v_2 \equiv \min_{\sigma_2 \in \Sigma_2} \max_{\sigma_1 \in \Sigma_1} \sigma_1 A \sigma_2. \tag{2.10}$$

The fundamental result for bilateral zero-sum games is contained in the following theorem.

Theorem 2.1 (von Neumann, 1928): *Let G be a bilateral and finite zero-sum game. Then*

(i) There exists some $v^* \in \mathbb{R}$ such that $v_1 = v_2 = v^*$.

(ii) For every Nash equilibrium (σ_1^*, σ_2^*), $\sigma_1^* A \sigma_2^* = v^*$.

Proof: We prove first that $v_2 \geq v_1$. Given any $\sigma_1 \in \Sigma_1$ and $\sigma_2 \in \Sigma_2$, we obviously have

$$\min_{\sigma_2' \in \Sigma_2} \sigma_1 A \sigma_2' \leq \sigma_1 A \sigma_2. \tag{2.11}$$

Then, applying the operator $\max_{\sigma_1 \in \Sigma_1}$ to both sides of the preceding inequality, it follows that

$$v_1 = \max_{\sigma_1 \in \Sigma_1} \min_{\sigma_2' \in \Sigma_2} \sigma_1 A \sigma_2' \leq \max_{\sigma_1 \in \Sigma_1} \sigma_1 A \sigma_2 \tag{2.12}$$

for any *given* $\sigma_2 \in \Sigma_2$. Therefore, applying now the operator $\min_{\sigma_2 \in \Sigma_2}$ to both sides of (2.12), we obtain

$$v_1 \leq \min_{\sigma_2 \in \Sigma_2} \max_{\sigma_1 \in \Sigma_1} \sigma_1 A \sigma_2 = v_2,$$

which proves the desired inequality $v_2 \geq v_1$.

We now show that $v_1 \geq v_2$.[23] Let (σ_1^*, σ_2^*) be a Nash equilibrium of G (an equilibrium always exists, by Theorem 2.2 below – recall Subsection 2.2.3). From the definition of Nash equilibrium we know

$$\sigma_1^* A \sigma_2^* \geq \sigma_1 A \sigma_2^*, \quad \forall \sigma_1 \in \Sigma_1 \tag{2.13}$$

$$\sigma_1^* A \sigma_2^* \leq \sigma_1^* A \sigma_2, \quad \forall \sigma_2 \in \Sigma_2. \tag{2.14}$$

On the other hand,

$$v_1 = \max_{\sigma_1 \in \Sigma_1} \min_{\sigma_2 \in \Sigma_2} \sigma_1 A \sigma_2$$

$$\geq \min_{\sigma_2 \in \Sigma_2} \sigma_1^* A \sigma_2.$$

Because, by (2.14),

$$\min_{\sigma_2 \in \Sigma_2} \sigma_1^* A \sigma_2 = \sigma_1^* A \sigma_2^*,$$

it follows that

$$v_1 \geq \sigma_1^* A \sigma_2^*.$$

In view of (2.13), we then have

$$\sigma_1^* A \sigma_2^* = \max_{\sigma_1 \in \Sigma_1} \sigma_1 A \sigma_2^*$$

---

[23] In von Neuman's original approach, this was the difficult part of the proof because, as mentioned, he could not rely at that time on an existence result for Nash equilibrium. Our present proof is drastically simplified by invoking such a result.

and therefore

$$v_1 \geq \max_{\sigma_1 \in \Sigma_1} \sigma_1 A \, \sigma_2^*$$

$$\geq \min_{\sigma_2 \in \Sigma_2} \max_{\sigma_1 \in \Sigma_1} \sigma_1 A \, \sigma_2 = v_2.$$

Combining $v_2 \geq v_1$ and $v_1 \geq v_2$ we obtain part (i) of the theorem, i.e., $v_1 = v_2 = v^*$. Part (ii) is an immediate consequence of this equality. ■

By part (i) of Theorem 2.1, the *maximin* and *minimax* of a bilateral and finite zero-sum game always coincide. Then, along the lines of our former motivation of these payoffs, one could interpret part (ii) as indicating that the most pessimistic expectations of the two players are *simultaneously* confirmed at *any* Nash equilibrium (σ_1^*, σ_2^*). That is, each player i obtains the best payoff consistent with "perfect anticipation" by her opponent. For player 1 this means that

$$\pi_1(\sigma_1^*, \sigma_2^*) = \max_{\sigma_1 \in \Sigma_1} \min_{\sigma_2 \in \Sigma_2} \sigma_1 A \, \sigma_2 = v^* \tag{2.15}$$

and for player 2

$$\pi_2(\sigma_1^*, \sigma_2^*) = - \min_{\sigma_2 \in \Sigma_2} \max_{\sigma_1 \in \Sigma_1} \sigma_1 A \, \sigma_2 = -v^*. \tag{2.16}$$

The common v^* present in each of these expressions is called the *value* of the game. Note that the clear-cut and rather startling twin conclusion embodied by (2.15) and (2.16) implicitly assumes that each player has just a *single* opponent. In fact, it is crucially dependent on this assumption because, as illustrated in Exercise 2.13, the conclusions established by Theorem 2.1 do *not* extend to zero-sum games with more than two players.

We observed above that parlor games in which players may just win or lose are zero-sum. This is also the case if there are monetary bets involved (recall, for example, the stylized card game represented in Figure 1.8), as long as players' von Neumann-Morgenstern utility is *linear* in money – cf. Exercise 2.14. As yet a further example of a zero-sum game, we have the matching-pennies game, whose payoffs are given by Table 2.4. By virtue of Theorem 2.1, we know that the value of this game is equal to the Nash equilibrium payoff

$$v^* = \pi_i(H, (1/2, 1/2)) = \pi_i(T, (1/2, 1/2)) = 0 \quad (1 = 1, 2). \tag{2.17}$$

It is instructive, however, to derive v^* directly, to illustrate the computation of the *maximin* and *minimax*. First, for each strategy of player 1, $\sigma_1 = (\sigma_{1H}, \sigma_{1T})$, define

$$\phi_1(\sigma_{1H}) \equiv \min_{\sigma_{2H} \in [0,1]} \pi_1(\sigma_{1H}, \sigma_{2H}),$$

where, as before, we identify any mixed strategy with the weight it assigns to choosing H. And, analogously, for each strategy $\sigma_2 = (\sigma_{2H}, \sigma_{2T})$ of player 2, define

$$\phi_2(\sigma_{2H}) \equiv \max_{\sigma_{1H} \in [0,1]} \pi_1(\sigma_{1H}, \sigma_{2H})$$

$$= - \min_{\sigma_{1H} \in [0,1]} \pi_2(\sigma_{1H}, \sigma_{2H}),$$

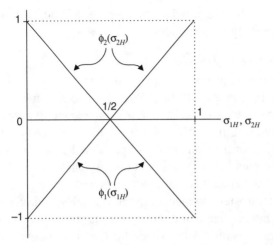

Figure 2.4: The (equilibrium) value of the matching-pennies game.

where the latter equality is simply a consequence of the fact that

$$\pi_2(\sigma_{1H}, \sigma_{2H}) = -\pi_1(\sigma_{1H}, \sigma_{2H})$$

for all σ_{1H} and σ_{2H}. It is immediate to compute that:

$$\phi_1(\sigma_{1H}) = \begin{cases} \pi_1(\sigma_{1H}, H) = 2\sigma_{1H} - 1 & \text{if } \sigma_{1H} < \frac{1}{2} \\ \pi_1(\sigma_{1H}, H) = \pi_1(\sigma_{1H}, T) = 0 & \text{if } \sigma_{1H} = \frac{1}{2} \\ \pi_1(\sigma_{1H}, T) = 1 - 2\sigma_{1H} & \text{if } \sigma_{1H} > \frac{1}{2} \end{cases}$$

and similarly,

$$\phi_2(\sigma_{2H}) = \begin{cases} \pi_1(T, \sigma_{2H}) = 1 - 2\sigma_{2H} & \text{if } \sigma_{2H} < \frac{1}{2} \\ \pi_1(T, \sigma_{2H}) = \pi_1(H, \sigma_{2H}) = 0 & \text{if } \sigma_{2H} = \frac{1}{2} \\ \pi_1(H, \sigma_{2H}) = 2\sigma_{2H} - 1 & \text{if } \sigma_{2H} > \frac{1}{2}. \end{cases}$$

Hence, from (2.9) and (2.10), we have

$$v_1 = \max_{\sigma_{1H} \in [0,1]} \phi_1(\sigma_{1H}) = 0$$

$$v_2 = \min_{\sigma_{2H} \in [0,1]} \phi_2(\sigma_{2H}) = 0,$$

which reconfirms (2.17). A graphic illustration of the approach is presented in Figure 2.4.

Remark 2.2: *Maximin and minimax in general games*

Note that the maximin and minimax values, v_1 and v_2, can always be defined for arbitrary bilateral games (not necessarily zero-sum). The argument by which we concluded in the proof of Theorem 2.1 that $v_2 \geq v_1$ is valid for any bilateral game. However, this is not the case for the reciprocal inequality $v_1 \geq v_2$, which in turn led to the equality of both values – this latter inequality holds only for zero-sum games. ♦

Remark 2.3: *Equilibrium interchangeability*

Theorem 2.1 indicates that, in any bilateral zero-sum game, players always obtain the same equilibrium payoff, the value of the game, at each of the (possibly multiple) Nash equilibria. In fact, it is interesting to note that, to obtain this common equilibrium value, players do not even need to resort to the implicit or explicit coordination usually required in the presence of equilibrium multiplicity – recall for example our discussion of the battle of the sexes in Subsection 2.2.1. In a zero-sum game, each player may select *any* of her equilibrium strategies independently, nevertheless being sure that an equilibrium will materialize if the remaining players behave similarly. This interesting property is often labeled equilibrium interchangeability.[24]

To establish this property, consider any bilateral zero-sum game G and two different Nash equilibria of it, $\hat{\sigma} = (\hat{\sigma}_1, \hat{\sigma}_2)$ and $\tilde{\sigma} = (\tilde{\sigma}_1, \tilde{\sigma}_2)$. By Theorem 2.1, both yield the same payoff for each player, as induced by the value of the game v^*. But then, since both are Nash equilibria, it follows that

$$v^* = \hat{\sigma}_1 A \, \hat{\sigma}_2 \leq \hat{\sigma}_1 A \, \tilde{\sigma}_2 \leq \tilde{\sigma}_1 A \, \tilde{\sigma}_2 = v^*$$

and therefore

$$\hat{\sigma}_1 A \, \tilde{\sigma}_2 = v^* \geq \sigma_1 A \, \tilde{\sigma}_2, \quad \forall \sigma_1 \in \Sigma_1$$

$$\hat{\sigma}_1 A \, \tilde{\sigma}_2 = v^* \leq \hat{\sigma}_1 A \, \sigma_2, \quad \forall \sigma_2 \in \Sigma_2.$$

That is, the profile $(\hat{\sigma}_1, \tilde{\sigma}_2)$ is a Nash equilibrium. Obviously, a similar argument shows that $(\tilde{\sigma}_1, \hat{\sigma}_2)$ is a Nash equilibrium as well. ♦

Supplementary Material

2.4   Nash equilibrium: formal existence results

As advanced, the mixed extension of any *finite* game in strategic form can be guaranteed to have some Nash equilibrium. Here, we formally establish this result, stating as well other existence theorems that apply instead to the alternative class of *infinite*-strategy games.

As it is clear from the formulation of Nash equilibrium presented in Definition 2.3′, this concept embodies the solution of a fixed-point problem for the joint best-response correspondence ρ. Thus, to tackle the existence issue, it is natural to rely on some of the wide variety of fixed-point theorems offered by mathematical analysis. Specifically, we find it useful to invoke the following well-known result (see e.g., Border, 1985).

---

[24] Formally, equilibrium interchangeability implies that the set of equilibrium profiles Σ^* has a Cartesian-product structure, $\Sigma_1^* \times \Sigma_2^*$, where each Σ_i^* is the set of equilibrium strategies of player i.

Kakutani's Fixed-Point Theorem: Let $X \subset \mathbb{R}^m$ ($m \in \mathbb{N}$) be a compact, convex, and nonempty set, and $\varphi : X \rightrightarrows X$ an upper hemicontinuous correspondence[25] with convex and nonempty images (i.e., $\forall x \in X$, $\varphi(x)$ is a nonempty and convex subset of X). Then, the correspondence φ has a fixed point, i.e., there exists some $x^* \in X$ such that $x^* \in \varphi(x^*)$.

Based on this theorem, we may establish the following existence result.

Theorem 2.2 (Nash, 1951): *Every finite game in strategic form – i.e., its mixed extension – has a Nash equilibrium.*

Proof: Consider any finite game and let ρ be its best-response correspondence. To prove the existence of a fixed point of ρ (i.e., a Nash equilibrium), we invoke Kakutani's fixed-point theorem, as stated above. Specifically, we identify X with $\Sigma = \prod_{i=1}^{n} \Delta^{r_i-1}$, φ with ρ, and check that its different hypotheses are satisfied in our case. On the one hand, it is clear that Σ is compact, convex, and nonempty. Moreover, for every $\sigma \in \Sigma$, $\rho(\sigma)$ is also nonempty because each π_i is a continuous function (it is separately linear, or bilinear, in σ_i and σ_{-i}), which implies that its maximum is attained in the compact domain Σ_i. The bilinearity of each π_i also implies the convexity of $\rho(\sigma)$ for any given $\sigma \in \Sigma$. To see this, take any $\sigma', \sigma'' \in \rho(\sigma)$ and denote

$$H \equiv \pi_i(\sigma_i', \sigma_{-i}) = \pi_i(\sigma_i'', \sigma_{-i}) = \max_{\sigma_i \in \Sigma_i} \pi_i(\sigma_i, \sigma_{-i}).$$

Then, for any given $\lambda \in [0, 1]$, we compute

$$\pi_i(\lambda\sigma_i' + (1-\lambda)\sigma_i'', \sigma_{-i}) = \lambda\pi_i(\sigma_i', \sigma_{-i}) + (1-\lambda)\pi_i(\sigma_i'', \sigma_{-i}) = H,$$

which implies that $\lambda\sigma_i' + (1 - \lambda)\sigma_i'' \in \rho(\sigma)$. Finally, the upper hemicontinuity of ρ is a direct consequence of Berge's theorem (cf. Border, 1985), whose line of argument is nevertheless spelled out next for the sake of completeness.

First, note that it is enough to show that every "component" correspondence $\rho_i : \Sigma_{-i} \rightrightarrows \Sigma_i$ ($i = 1, 2, \ldots, n$) is upper hemicontinuous. Consider any such ρ_i and let $\{\sigma_{-i}^q\}_{q=1}^{\infty} \subset \Sigma_{-i}$ be any sequence converging to some σ_{-i}^*. On the other hand, let $\{\sigma_i^q\}_{q=1}^{\infty} \subset \Sigma_i$ be a corresponding sequence of player i's strategies such that $\sigma_i^q \in \rho_i(\sigma_{-i}^q)$ for each $q = 1, 2, \ldots$; i.e.,

$$\forall \sigma_i \in \Sigma_i, \quad \pi_i(\sigma_i^q, \sigma_{-i}^q) \geq \pi_i(\sigma_i, \sigma_{-i}^q). \tag{2.18}$$

Since Σ_i is compact, it can be assumed without loss of generality (taking a subsequence if necessary) that $\lim_{q\to\infty} \sigma_i^q = \sigma_i^*$ for some $\sigma_i^* \in \Sigma_i$. We want to show that

$$\forall \sigma_i \in \Sigma_i, \quad \pi_i(\sigma_i^*, \sigma_{-i}^*) \geq \pi_i(\sigma_i, \sigma_{-i}^*).$$

---

[25] Under the maintained assumption that X is compact, the correspondence $\varphi : X \rightrightarrows X$ is said to be *upper hemicontinuous* if its graph $g(\varphi) \equiv \{(x, y) : x \in X, \ y \in \varphi(x)\}$ is a closed set (in the usual topology). An equivalent requirement is that given any $x^* \in X$ and some sequence $\{x^q\}_{q=1}^{\infty}$ convergent to x^*, every sequence $\{y^q\}_{q=1}^{\infty}$ with $y^q \in \varphi(x^q)$ has a limit point y^* such that $y^* \in \varphi(x^*)$.

In view of the continuity of π_i, this follows immediately from (2.18) by taking limits in q within this expression.   ∎

Since Kakutani's fixed-point theorem only applies to finite-dimensional spaces, the proof of Theorem 2.2 requires that each player's set of pure strategies be finite and, therefore, the corresponding space of mixed strategies be a finite-dimensional simplex. There are, however, many economic applications where players' strategies are best modeled as part of an infinite set, say a continuum of possible outputs, prices, or cost shares. For these contexts, a suitable extension of Kakutani's theorem to infinite-dimensional spaces can still be used to guarantee Nash equilibrium existence in games where the sets of pure strategies are compact (e.g., compact real intervals) and the payoff functions are continuous. The classical result in this respect may be stated as follows.

Theorem 2.3 (Glicksberg, 1952): *Let G be a game in strategic form such that, for each player $i = 1, 2, \ldots, n$, $S_i \subset \mathbb{R}^m$ is compact and $\pi_i : S_1 \times \cdots \times S_n \to \mathbb{R}$ a continuous function. Then, the game G has a Nash equilibrium, possibly in mixed strategies.*[26]

The previous result requires that the payoff functions of all players be continuous, a condition that is unfortunately violated in many applications (cf. the case of Bertrand competition in oligopoly studied in Subsection 3.1.2). It turns out, however, that such a continuity is not strictly required and the assumption may be substantially generalized to fit most of the cases of interest. This was first shown by Dasgupta and Maskin (1986a),[27] who established the existence of Nash equilibrium in mixed strategies when the players' set of pure strategies S_i are compact subsets of a Euclidean space $\mathbb{R}^m$ and, even if some of the payoff functions π_i are discontinuous, they satisfy the following:

1. For any given $s_{-i} \in S_{-i}$, each function $\pi_i(\cdot, s_{-i})$ is a *lower* semi-continuous function of s_i.[28]
2. The sum of players' payoffs, i.e., $\sum_{i \in N} \pi_i(s)$, defines an upper semi-continuous function of the whole pure-strategy profile.[29]
3. For each i, the collection of points in S where the function π_i is discontinuous is included in a subset of S displaying less than full dimension.

---

[26] Here, mixed strategies are Borel probability measures on the corresponding space of pure strategies. Of course, one needs to endow these sets with an appropriate *topology* to have corresponding notions of continuity and compactness well defined. Specifically, this theorem may be proved using the so-called topology of weak convergence (cf. Munkres, 1974) where, roughly, two probability measures are judged "close" if the integrals they induce on any continuous function are close.

[27] For a good discussion of more recent developments concerning equilibrium existence in discontinuous games, the reader may refer to Reny (1999).

[28] Let X be a subset of some Euclidean space. A real function $f : X \to \mathbb{R}$ is lower semi-continuous at some $x^* \in X$ if for any sequence $\{x^q\}_{q=1}^\infty$ convergent to x^*, $\liminf_{q \to \infty} f(x^q) \geq f(x^*)$. In fact, Dasgupta and Maskin (1986a) contemplate a substantially weaker form of lower hemi-continuity that requires the previous inequality to hold only when x^* is approached in a single direction or, even more generally, when one considers some particular convex combination of the limits obtained along different directions.

[29] A function $f : X \to \mathbb{R}$ is upper semi-continuous at some $x^* \in X$ if for any sequence $\{x^q\}_{q=1}^\infty$ convergent to x^*, $\limsup_{q \to \infty} f(x^q) \leq f(x^*)$.

As emphasized, none of the preceding existence results guarantees that there is some Nash equilibrium involving only pure strategies. However, given the misgivings sometimes expressed against the concept of mixed strategy (recall the discussion in Subsection 2.2.3), it is certainly of some interest to wonder under what conditions the existence of a pure-strategy Nash equilibrium may be guaranteed. Within the realm of infinite games, the following result identifies conditions on the payoff functions that ensure the existence of some Nash equilibrium in pure strategies.

Theorem 2.4 (Debreu, 1952; Fan, 1952; Glicksberg, 1952): *Let G be a game in strategic form such that, for each $i = 1, 2, \ldots, n$, $S_i \subset \mathbb{R}^m$ is compact and convex, and the function $\pi_i : S_1 \times \cdots \times S_n \to \mathbb{R}$ is continuous in $s = (s_1, s_2, \ldots, s_n)$ and quasi-concave in s_i.*[30] *Then, the game G has a Nash equilibrium in pure strategies.*

Proof: Exercise 2.10.   ∎

As it turns out, the conditions spelled out in the previous theorem will be found of some relevance in the study of many setups in economics. For example, a paradigmatic case in point is provided by the basic model of Cournot oligopoly studied in Subsection 3.1.1.

2.5   Strong and coalition-proof equilibria

Verbally, a Nash equilibrium may be described as a strategic profile for which there are no profitable unilateral deviations. This concept is based on the implicit assumption that players cannot coordinate on any *joint*, mutually beneficial, change of strategies. In some contexts, however, this assumption might not be reasonable and we would then like to have an equilibrium concept that is sensitive to the possibility of multilateral deviations. Consider, for example, the game in strategic form described in Table 2.6.

This game has two pure-strategy Nash equilibria: (T, L) and (B, R). Even though players might have originally aimed at playing the inefficient equilibrium (B, R), it is reasonable to argue that, if they could reconsider matters, the efficient equilibrium (T, L) would be targeted instead. Certainly, both profiles define robust Nash equilibria and, therefore, from a purely strategic perspective, there are no essential differences between them. In fact, it is precisely because of this comparable standing of the two equilibria that it becomes all the more plausible that players should focus attention on Pareto efficiency, i.e., on achieving the *equilibrium* payoff that they *both* prefer. But then, if this indeed happens, one would expect that only the equilibrium (T, L) might be played.

A first attempt to address these issues was put forward by Aumann (1959), who proposed the concept of *strong equilibrium*. Extending the concept of Nash equilibrium, a strong equilibrium is defined as a strategic profile for which no subset of players has a *joint* deviation that (strictly) benefits *all* of them. Formally, we have the following:

---

[30] The condition that $\pi_i(\cdot)$ be quasi-concave in s_i is simply the requirement that, for *any fixed* $s_{-i} \in S_{-i}$, the function $\pi_i(\cdot, s_{-i})$ be a quasi-concave function of its single argument, s_i.

Table 2.6: *A strategic-form game with two pure-strategy Nash equilibria, one of them efficient*

1 \ 2	L	R
T	2, 2	0, 0
B	0, 0	1, 1

Table 2.7: *A three-player strategic-form game with no strong equilibrium*

1 \ 2	A	B	1 \ 2	A	B
X	0, 0, 10	−5, −5, 0	X	−2, −2, 0	−5, −5, 0
Y	−5, −5, 0	1, 1, 4	Y	−5, −5, 0	−1, −1, 5
3	M			N	

Definition 2.5 (Aumann, 1959): *A strategic profile σ^* is a strong equilibrium if $\forall M \subseteq N$, there is not any $(\sigma_j)_{j \in M}$ such that $\forall j \in M$,*

$$\pi_j((\sigma_j)_{j \in M}, (\sigma_i^*)_{i \in N \setminus M}) > \pi_j(\sigma^*).$$

Obviously, the concept of strong equilibrium is substantially more demanding than that of Nash because it requires immunity against a much wider set of deviations. In particular, since the deviating coalition may coincide with the whole set of players, it follows that every strong equilibrium must be weakly Pareto efficient (i.e., there must not exist any alternative strategic profile preferred by *all* players). Thus, in a terminology that will be profusely used in Chapter 4, the concept of strong equilibrium can be viewed as a quite stringent *refinement* of Nash equilibrium. In fact, it is so demanding a refinement that it fails to exist in many situations of interest, e.g., in those games in which every strategic profile that is efficient in the weak Pareto sense is *not* a Nash equilibrium. This is not a problem in the game described in Table 2.6 – where (T, L) is obviously the unique strong equilibrium – but leads to nonexistence in a simple game such as the by now familiar prisoner's dilemma (cf. Table 1.1).

Furthermore, the concept of strong equilibrium is also subject to a difficult conceptual problem, which may be illustrated through the following example proposed by Bernheim, Peleg, and Whinston (1987). There are three players involved in a game with the strategic form described in Table 2.7 (player 1 selects rows (X or Y), player 2 columns (A or B), and player 3 chooses between boxes (M or N)).

This game has two Nash equilibria. One of them, (X, A, M), Pareto dominates the other one, (Y, B, N). The latter, therefore, cannot be a strong equilibrium in Aumann's sense. Consider, however, the "deviation" on the part of *all* three players from (Y, B, N) to (X, A, M). If players 1 and 2 take indeed as given that player 3 will play M, the same motivation that underlies the notion of strong equilibrium would require that there should be no joint deviation from (X, A) that improves *both* player 1 and player 2. Unfortunately, this is not the case. If player 3 chooses the first payoff table, players 1 and 2 both prefer to play (Y, B), which is a Pareto efficient equilibrium for their induced bilateral game. But then, if player 3 anticipates this joint deviation, she will prefer to choose N rather than M, thus leading the population back to the inefficient equilibrium (Y, B, N).

In view of such conceptual problems afflicting the notion of strong equilibrium, Bernheim, Peleg, and Whinston (1987) propose the concept of *coalition-proof equilibrium*. We only provide a heuristic description of it. Informally, a strategic profile is said to define a coalition-proof equilibrium if it is consistent with the following inductive process.

- First, it must be a Nash equilibrium; i.e., it must be immune to profitable *unilateral* deviations.
- Second, it must not allow for any *bilateral* deviation that is profitable for the two players involved. Such a joint deviation, however, must induce a Nash equilibrium of the bilateral game induced when the remaining players keep their strategies fixed. Otherwise, it is *not* judged a valid deviation.
- Third, it must not allow for profitable trilateral deviations that qualify as *valid*, in the sense that they are themselves immune to further bilateral and unilateral (valid) deviations in the three-player game induced when all other players keep their strategies fixed.
- Proceeding inductively, the former considerations are further iterated for every coalition of size 4, 5, ... And at each such iteration, any joint deviation by a certain coalition is judged valid only if it defines a coalition-proof equilibrium of the game induced when the remaining players keep their respective strategies fixed.

Clearly, the stability criterion embodied by the concept of coalition-proof equilibrium is substantially weaker than that of strong equilibrium: fewer joint deviations are allowed, since some are declared invalid because of their "lack of internal consistency." For example, reconsidering again the prisoner's dilemma, notice that its Nash equilibrium (D, D) does qualify as a coalition-proof equilibrium. For, once the aforementioned internal consistency of deviations is demanded, the joint bilateral deviation to (C, C) is no longer admitted because it is not itself immune to a deviation by the "subcoalition" consisting of just one player.

The previous considerations notwithstanding, the concept of coalition-proof equilibrium has been shown to suffer from the same fundamental problem as strong equilibrium. That is, despite being substantially weaker than the latter, it also fails to exist in many interesting contexts.[31] Because of this very basic problem, the application of coalition-based approaches to the analysis of games has hitherto been restricted to a rather limited set of socioeconomic contexts.

---

[31] An interesting case where a coalition-proof equilibrium always exists is provided by those games where the set $S^\infty \equiv S_1^\infty \times S_2^\infty \times \cdots \times S_n^\infty$ (cf. (2.6)) includes a strategy profile s^* that Pareto dominates (weakly) all other profiles $s \in S^\infty$. Under these circumstances, Moreno and Wooders (1996) prove that s^* is a coalition-proof equilibrium.

Table 2.8: *A strategic-form game with two pure-strategy Nash equilibria*

1 \ 2	A	B
X	5, 1	0, 0
Y	4, 4	1, 5

2.6   Correlated equilibrium

Consider the bilateral game represented in strategic form whose payoffs are displayed in Table 2.8. This game is similar to the battle of the sexes in that it has two Nash equilibria in pure strategies. One of them, (X, A), is that preferred by player 1; on the other hand, player 2 prefers the alternative pure-strategy equilibrium (Y, B). If one insists on implementing a symmetric outcome, there is also a symmetric equilibrium in mixed strategies that provides an identical expected payoff equal to $5/2$ for both players. However, this payoff is inefficient because the profile (Y, A) induces a higher payoff of 4 for each player. This inefficiency can be partly attributed to the *independent* randomization undertaken by the players at the mixed-strategy equilibrium, which unavoidably induces positive probability to the strategy profile (X, B). Conceivably, if players could resort to some suitable coordination mechanism, possibly stochastic, efficiency and symmetry could be restored as some sort of equilibrium outcome in this game.

This is the idea that largely underlies the concept of *correlated equilibrium,* again proposed by Aumann (1974). Suppose that the players decide to adopt the following mechanism of coordination: they toss a coin and, if heads turn out, they play (X, A); if tails comes up instead, they play (Y, B). Since both of these alternative strategy profiles are Nash equilibria, such a "random coordination" on each of them is also an equilibrium. To be more precise, if the players agree to use this mechanism, neither of them will have a unilateral incentive to deviate from its prescriptions. Moreover, the *ex ante (*expected) payoff derived from using it is equal to 3 for each player, thus narrowing significantly the inefficiency gap displayed by the symmetric (mixed-strategy) Nash equilibrium.

Despite the improvement entailed by the contemplated mechanism, its outcome is not yet efficient because the profile (Y, A) still dominates it. Unfortunately, this strategy profile is not an equilibrium and appears, therefore, like too ambitious an objective to be attained. Could the players nevertheless come somewhat closer to its payoffs by going beyond a mere alternation of pure-strategy equilibria? At first sight, the answer would seem negative: if a strategy profile does not define a Nash equilibrium, nothing will make the agents want to play it through independently adopted decisions. This intuitive assertion is indeed essentially true if, in the coordination mechanism used, the signals sent to the players are common for both of them (for example, if these signals are fully public as in the aforementioned flipping of a coin).

Consider, however, the possibility that the mechanism used in the present context may involve sending different (although typically correlated) signals to each player.

Specifically, suppose the mechanism produces one of three *states* chosen from a certain *state space* $\Omega = \{\omega_1, \omega_2, \omega_3\}$ with *equal* prior probability. But once the particular state has materialized, the mechanism does *not* communicate any longer the same signal to both players:

- If ω_1 occurs, player 2 is informed only that the event $U \equiv (\omega_1 \vee \omega_2)$ – i.e., "ω_1 or ω_2" – has turned up, whereas player 1 is precisely informed of the state ω_1.
- If ω_2 takes place, player 1 is informed that the event $V \equiv (\omega_2 \vee \omega_3)$ has occurred, while player 2 continues to receive the information that U has materialized.
- Finally, if ω_3 results, player 1 is informed only of the event V but player 2 is precisely informed about the state ω_3.

More compactly, such an *asymmetric* signaling framework may be described by specifying the informational partition $\mathcal{P}_i$ assigned to each player $i = 1, 2$ as follows:

$$\mathcal{P}_1 = \{\omega_1, V\},$$

$$\mathcal{P}_2 = \{U, \omega_3\}.$$

Assume now that the mechanism "recommends" the following responses to the signals received by each player.

- For player 1: X if ω_1, Y if V;
- For player 2: A if U, B if ω_3.

If the players follow these recommendations, the expected payoff for each of them is $10/3$, which is larger than the payoff of 3 they can obtain by simply randomizing between the two pure-strategy Nash equilibria of the game. Furthermore, it is easy to see that these recommendations will indeed be voluntarily followed by the players, provided they believe the other player will also do so. Let us check it in detail for the cases when ω_2 and ω_3 occur, the instance when ω_1 happens being analogous to that with ω_3.

First, consider the case where ω_2 materializes. Then, player 1 receives the signal V and player 2 the signal U. Given the signal received by player 1, she knows that either ω_2 or ω_3 has occurred and must attribute to each possibility a subjective (posterior) probability of $1/2$. Player 1 also knows that if, in fact, ω_2 has occurred (something she is uncertain of), player 2 will adopt A, whereas she will adopt B if the state that has happened is ω_3 (see the above recommendations). In view of this information, the recommendation to play Y received by player 1 is indeed optimal for her (although not uniquely so). The situation is analogous for player 2: after this player receives the signal U, she will attribute an equal probability of $1/2$ to player 1 adopting either X or Y. In the face of it, the recommendation to play A is indeed optimal for player 2 (again, not uniquely so).

Consider now the case in which the state ω_3 occurs. Then, since player 1 receives the same signal V as before, her posterior probabilities are of course the same ($1/2$

for each possible choice by player 2). Therefore, the proposed recommendation continues to be optimal. Concerning player 2, her posterior subjective probability on player 1's action after receiving the signal ω_3 is now concentrated on Y. Therefore, the recommendation she receives of playing B is optimal as well, because it is a best response to the strategy Y chosen by player 1 in this case.

We now formalize matters. Let G be a finite game in strategic form. A stochastic coordination mechanism of the type discussed involves

(i) a random variable defined on the set Ω (assumed finite) with probabilities $p(\omega)$ for each $\omega \in \Omega$, and

(ii) for each player $i = 1, 2, \ldots n$, a partition $\mathcal{P}_i$ of the set Ω that reflects player i's information on the realization of the underlying random variable.

In this context, a strategy for each player i is given by a function

$$\gamma_i : \Omega \to \Sigma_i,$$

mapping each possible state to an associated mixed-strategy choice,[32] which has to be measurable with respect to $\mathcal{P}_i$. That is, every function γ_i must satisfy

$$\forall e_i \in \mathcal{P}_i, \ \forall \omega, \omega' \in e_i, \quad \gamma_i(\omega) = \gamma_i(\omega').$$

This measurability requirement simply reflects the idea that each player i is informed only about what element of her partition $\mathcal{P}_i$ prevails and, as usual (recall Section 1.2), her strategy can depend only on information she actually has.

Based on a coordination mechanism and corresponding strategies as described, the equilibrium notion proposed is formally defined as follows.

Definition 2.6 (Aumann, 1974): *A strategy profile* $\gamma = (\gamma_1, \ldots, \gamma_n)$ *is said to be a* correlated equilibrium *if* $\forall i = 1, 2, \ldots, n$, $\forall \tilde{\gamma}_i : \Omega \to \Sigma_i$ *that is measurable with respect to* $\mathcal{P}_i$,

$$\sum_{\omega \in \Omega} p(\omega) \pi_i(\gamma(\omega)) \geq \sum_{\omega \in \Omega} p(\omega) \pi_i(\tilde{\gamma}_i(\omega), \gamma_{-i}(\omega)).$$

Remark 2.4: *Conditional payoff maximization*

Note that the preceding definition embodies in essence a collection of independent ("parallel") maximization problems conducted by each individual at every element e_i of her partition $\mathcal{P}_i$ (see Exercise 2.16). That is, the *ex ante* optimality displayed by any player i's strategy at equilibrium requires that the choice it prescribes for every signal e_i maximizes the *ex post* (conditional) payoffs associated with the posterior beliefs $p(\omega \mid e_i)$. ◆

As formulated in Definition 2.6, the concept of correlated equilibrium appears to be quite a cumbersome construct. For, associated with any such equilibrium, it

---

[32] Without loss of generality, strategies in this context could have been postulated to prescribe deterministic choices (i.e., pure strategies in each corresponding S_i of the underlying game). For, if some randomization on choices is required, this may be implemented directly through the (stochastic) mechanism itself.

seems necessary to define *explicitly* the stochastic mechanism (state space, random variable, signals, recommendations) that support it. However, as it turns out, this formal apparatus is largely unnecessary. Instead, one may focus directly on the essential objective achieved by a correlated equilibrium, namely, to provide a (stochastic) pattern of incentive-compatible recommendations.

To see this, let us approach matters in such a "reduced" fashion. Then, all that is needed to define a correlated equilibrium is a *direct* specification of the probabilities with which the mechanism issues the different profiles of player recommendations (i.e., mixed-strategy profiles). And, with this perspective, a correlated equilibrium may be simply reformulated as a probability density over recommendation *profiles* that, once the players are *fully* informed of their *ex ante* probabilities, induce each player to follow her *personal* recommendations in every case. Formally, this approach is embodied by the following alternative definition.

Definition 2.7: *A* correlated equilibrium *is a probability density* $p : \Sigma_1 \times \cdots \times \Sigma_n \to [0, 1]$ *such that* $\forall i = 1, 2, \ldots, n$, $\forall \eta_i : \Sigma_i \to \Sigma_i$,

$$\sum_{\sigma \in \Sigma} p(\sigma) \pi_i(\sigma) \geq \sum_{\sigma \in \Sigma} p(\sigma) \pi_i(\eta_i(\sigma_i), \sigma_{-i}).$$

The above definition may be interpreted as follows. Suppose that every player i *privately* receives a recommendation to play some particular $\sigma_i \in \Sigma_i$ but is fully aware of the probability density $p(\sigma)$ with which every recommendation profile σ is issued by the mechanism. Then, if $p(\cdot)$ is to define a correlated equilibrium, no player i should be able to improve by reacting to some of the recommendations σ_i with a different choice σ_i'. (That is, she must not gain by relying on a mapping $\eta_i(\cdot)$ in Definition 2.7 that is different from the identity.) This alternative equivalent way of defining correlated equilibrium stresses the important idea that the induced recommendations are the only relevant information the mechanism provides to each player i. Thus, any deviating strategy must be measurable with respect to the partition generated by these recommendations, i.e., it should depend only on them.

As a further illustration of the crucial role played by informational asymmetries in the present context, we consider now a somewhat paradoxical example. It illustrates the important idea that, in contrast with what happens in single-agent (and, therefore, nonstrategic) decision contexts, agents involved in genuinely strategic scenarios may end up improving their (equilibrium) payoffs after losing some *ex post* valuable possibilities. This general phenomenon will arise repeatedly throughout this book in a number of different variants (here, the foregone possibilities will concern "information," but in Exercise 2.4 it will involve "utiles," and in Chapter 4 it will pertain to alternative choices).

There are three players, 1, 2, and 3, involved in the strategic-form game described in Table 2.9: the first player selects rows, the second columns, and the third boxes. If we restrict consideration to Nash equilibria in pure strategies, there are just two of them: (Y, A, M) and (X, B, Q). In both of them, every player obtains a payoff of 1. Suppose now that players contemplate introducing a stochastic coordination

Table 2.9: *A three-player strategic-form game with a correlated equilibrium Pareto dominating Nash equilibria*

$_1$\\$^2$	A	B	$_1$\\$^2$	A	B	$_1$\\$^2$	A	B
X	0, 0, 3	0, 0, 0	X	2, 2, 2	0, 0, 0	X	0, 0, 0	1, 1, 1
Y	1, 1, 1	0, 0, 0	Y	0, 0, 0	2, 2, 2	Y	0, 0, 0	0, 0, 3
3	M			N			Q	

mechanism that might allow them to obtain the higher payoff of 2 available in the middle box. As explained, if such a mechanism exists, its details need not be given explicitly. That is, its performance may be compactly summarized through a (stochastic) pattern of incentive-compatible recommendations as formalized by Definition 2.7.

Consider therefore the probability density $p : \Sigma_1 \times \Sigma_2 \times \Sigma_3 \to [0, 1]$, which distributes all positive probability equally over the following two (pure) strategy profiles: (X, A, N) and (Y, B, N). That is,

$$p(X, A, N) = p(Y, B, N) = 1/2. \tag{2.19}$$

Then, if each player is communicated only her respectively recommended strategy (but is aware of the way the whole pattern of recommendations is stochastically chosen), it is immediate to check that such a strategy will be willingly followed in every case. In other words, the probability density $p(\cdot)$ given by (2.19) defines a correlated equilibrium.

Now, suppose player 3 is given the option of modifying the nature of the underlying mechanism, so that she may decide whether to access the recommendations provided to her opponents. Will she want to exercise this option for more information? If, as it is natural to assume, what player 2 decides in this respect will be known by players 1 and 3, the answer must be negative: she will prefer to forego this possibility. For, if she were to accept it, the above set of recommendations would not define a correlated equilibrium any longer. Her opponents would understand that, if player 3 were to trust that others will behave according to these recommendations, she herself will react as follows:

- M when the recommendation to the other players is (X, A);
- Q when the recommendation to the other players is (Y, B).

This, of course, destroys the incentives of players 1 and 2 to behave as recommended, leading to the collapse of the coordination device that allowed *every* player to achieve a payoff equal to 2.

To end our discussion of correlated equilibrium, we address two pending but crucial issues: its existence and its interpretation. Concerning existence, the problem is particularly straightforward in this case. Simply note that every Nash equilibrium of a strategic-form game trivially defines a correlated equilibrium in which players' recommendations are *not* correlated. That is, if $\sigma^* = (\sigma_i^*)_{i=1}^n$ defines a

Nash equilibrium of the game, the pattern of probabilities $p(\cdot)$ given by

$$p(s_1, s_2, \ldots, s_n) = \sigma_1^*(s_1)\sigma_2^*(s_2)\cdots\sigma_n^*(s_n)$$

for each $(s_1, s_2, \ldots, s_n) \in S$ defines a correlated equilibrium. Therefore, we may invoke Theorem 2.2 to assert that, in every finite game, some correlated equilibrium always exists. In general, however, the set of correlated equilibria will be much larger than that of Nash equilibria. This is indeed the case when the Nash equilibrium is not unique, as illustrated by one of our examples. In this case, *any* probability distribution defined over the different Nash equilibria specifies a correlated equilibrium, thus allowing players to achieve any point in the convex hull of the set of Nash equilibrium payoffs.

If the coordination mechanism uses only public signals (or recommendations), such stochastic alternation of Nash equilibria is the only kind of correlated equilibrium that exists. Nevertheless, our examples have also illustrated that players may have access to a much richer set of possibilities if the signals they receive can involve discretional (in particular, asymmetric) degrees of privacy. Under these conditions, there often exist correlated equilibria in which players reach payoff levels that are unattainable through mere convex combinations of Nash equilibria.

Finally, we address the issue of interpretation concerning the notion of correlated equilibrium. In this respect, we can pursue a slight variation on one of the lines used to motivate Nash equilibrium in Subsection 2.2.1. In view of the efficiency gains that can be potentially achieved by correlating actions, we might anticipate that the players involved in a game would often want to go through an initial *communication phase* where they try to agree on some stochastic coordination mechanism. That is, they would try to find and agree on some incentive-compatible pattern of "recommendation probabilities" to guide their subsequent play. If such an agreement were indeed reached, then all that would remain is to design a suitable "machine" that implements it or, if not, trust a fair mediator to carry it out.

In a sense, the kind of interagent communication reflected by this interpretation of correlated equilibrium is not very different from that invoked in Subsection 2.2.1 pertaining to Nash equilibrium. It is therefore subject to the same criticisms that were raised there. In response to such conceptual difficulties, it often has been argued that a satisfactory analysis of strategic situations should not rely on an "equilibrium approach" but proceed instead from more fundamental, individualistic, premises. This is indeed the route described in the following section.

2.7   Rationalizability

When no prior convergence or compatibility of players' expectations is taken for granted, their *independent* analysis of the game must be based exclusively on the assumption of rationality of their opponents; more precisely, on the assumption that rationality (hers and that of her opponents) is *common knowledge*. As explained in Section 2.1, to say that players' rationality *is common knowledge* amounts to asserting that the following *indefinite* chain of statements is true:

(i) every player is rational;
(ii) every player knows that every player is rational;
(iii) every player knows that every player knows that every player is rational;
(iv) every player ..., etc.

Here, we contemplate a notion of rationality that is stronger than that introduced in Section 2.1. Specifically, we postulate the idea of rationality implicitly underlying the concept of Nash equilibrium, in that a player is called rational if she is maximizing her expected payoff on the basis of *some* expectations of what the other players will do. Clearly, this precludes her from playing any dominated strategy (in the sense of Definition 2.1), which indicates that this notion of rationality is indeed stronger than that derived from payoff nondominance.

Suppose, for simplicity, that there are only two players, 1 and 2. If the above chain of statements is true and no player experiences any limitation of her ability to analyze the situation, the strategy chosen by any of them, say player 1, must satisfy the following:

(i)′ By (i), her strategy must be a "best response" to some perceptions (subjective probability measure) of what is the strategy chosen by player 2. These perceptions are called her first-order beliefs.

(ii)′ By (ii), it must be possible to "rationalize" (i.e., provide some foundation for) any first-order beliefs contemplated in (i)′ on the basis of some perception (by 1) of what 2 perceives at her first level and what is a corresponding best response. These perceptions (subjective probability measures by 1 over first-order beliefs by 2) are called player 1's second-order beliefs.

(iii)′ By (iii), it must be possible to rationalize any player 1's second-order beliefs contemplated in (ii)′ on the basis of some third-order perceptions (by 1) on what are player 2's second-order beliefs. These perceptions are called player 1's third-order beliefs.

(iv)′ By (iv), ...

Figure 2.5 illustrates the former process of "rationalizations".

A strategy that fulfills the whole chain of assertions stated above is called *rationalizable*, a concept independently proposed by Bernheim (1984) and Pearce

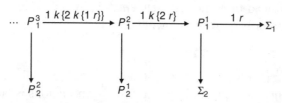

Figure 2.5: Beliefs that reflect "common knowledge of rationality." "jr" ($j = 1, 2$) represents the statement "player j is rational"; "$jk\{\cdot\}$" represents the statement "player j knows $\{\cdot\}$"; P_j^q represents beliefs of order q by player j, defined (i.e., are probability measures) over the set $P_{j'}^{q-1}$ (the beliefs of order $q-1$ by player $j' \neq j$, where $P_j^0 = \Sigma_j$). Downward vertical arrows point to the space where the upper beliefs are defined. Rightward horizontal arrows stand for the consistency requirements higher-order beliefs impose on those of lower order (of the same player) by common knowledge of rationality.

(1984). Next, we present its formal definition, which reflects in a rigorous fashion the considerations embodied by (i)′–(iv)′.

Let $G = \{N, \{S_i\}, \{\pi_i\}\}$ be a finite game in strategic form. Consider, for each player i, the sequence $\{\hat{\Sigma}_i^q\}_{q=0}^{\infty}$ defined as follows:

(a) For $q = 0$, we make $\hat{\Sigma}_i^0 = \Sigma_i$;
(b) $\forall q = 1, 2, \ldots,$

$$\hat{\Sigma}_i^q = \left\{ \sigma_i \in \hat{\Sigma}_i^{q-1} \mid \exists \sigma_{-i} \in \hat{\Sigma}_{-i}^{q-1} : \forall \tilde{\sigma}_i \in \hat{\Sigma}_i^{q-1}, \right.$$
$$\left. \pi_i(\sigma_i, \sigma_{-i}) \geq \pi_i(\tilde{\sigma}_i, \sigma_{-i}) \right\} \tag{2.20}$$

Definition 2.8 (Bernheim, 1984; Pearce, 1984): *For each $i = 1, 2, \ldots, n$, $R_i \equiv \cap_{q=1}^{\infty} \hat{\Sigma}_i^q$ is called the set of* rationalizable strategies. *Furthermore, a strategic profile σ is said to be* rationalizable *if each of its components σ_i is* rationalizable.

The iterative process induced by (a) and (b) above formalizes the chain of heuristic requirements listed above. Thus, for $q = 1$, the process discards all mixed strategies that cannot be rationalized as a best response to some i's first-order beliefs on j's strategy ($j \neq i$). For $q = 2$, the process discards those mixed strategies that cannot be rationalized as a best response to some i's second-order beliefs – or, more precisely, as a best response to some first-order beliefs by i over j's strategy, which are in turn consistent with the rationality of j and some second-order beliefs about what j believes at her first-order level. Proceeding inductively, the requirement that any given player i satisfies an indefinite chain of such considerations is embodied by the demand that her chosen strategy belongs to every $\hat{\Sigma}_i^q$, for $q = 0, 1, 2, \ldots,$ i.e., that it belongs to their intersection $\cap_{q=1}^{\infty} \hat{\Sigma}_i^q$. (Note that we can also think of this intersection as $\lim_{q \to \infty} \hat{\Sigma}_i^q$ because, by construction, $\{\hat{\Sigma}_i^q\}_{q=0}^{\infty}$ is a decreasing sequence, i.e., $\hat{\Sigma}_i^{q+1} \subset \hat{\Sigma}_i^q$ for all q.)

First, we address the issue of existence of rationalizable strategies.

Theorem 2.5 (Bernheim, 1984; Pearce, 1984): *The set $R \equiv R_1 \times R_2 \times \cdots \times R_n \neq \emptyset$.*

Proof: We argue, by induction, that $\{\hat{\Sigma}_i^q\}_{q=0}^{\infty}$ is a sequence of closed and nonempty sets. Therefore, since it is a decreasing sequence, their intersection is nonempty by a well-known result of mathematical analysis (see, for example, Rudin, 1976).

Consider any q and suppose that its associated $\hat{\Sigma}^q = \Pi_{i=1}^n \hat{\Sigma}_i^q$ is nonempty and closed. We need to show that $\hat{\Sigma}^{q+1}$ is also nonempty and closed. On the one hand, it is nonempty because it is the outcome of a set of optimization programs conducted within a compact set. To see that $\hat{\Sigma}^{q+1}$ is closed, it is enough to verify that each $\hat{\Sigma}_i^{q+1}$ is closed, since the Cartesian product of closed sets is itself closed. Thus, choose any given i and consider a convergent sequence $\{\sigma_i^r\} \subset \hat{\Sigma}_i^{q+1}$, with $\sigma_i^r \to \sigma_i^*$. For each r, we have

$$\exists \sigma^r_{-i} \in \hat{\Sigma}^q_{-i} : \forall \tilde{\sigma}_i \in \hat{\Sigma}^q_i, \quad \pi_i \left(\sigma^r_i, \sigma^r_{-i} \right) \geq \pi_i \left(\tilde{\sigma}_i, \sigma^r_{-i} \right).$$

Since $\hat{\Sigma}^q_{-i}$ is a compact set, $\{\sigma^r_{-i}\}$ includes a convergent subsequence. Let $\hat{\sigma}_{-i} \in \hat{\Sigma}^q_{-i}$ be the limit of such a subsequence. This limit must satisfy

$$\pi_i \left(\sigma^*_i, \hat{\sigma}_{-i} \right) \geq \pi_i \left(\tilde{\sigma}_i, \hat{\sigma}_{-i} \right), \quad \forall \tilde{\sigma}_i \in \hat{\Sigma}^q_i,$$

which confirms that $\sigma^*_i \in \hat{\Sigma}^{q+1}_i$. By induction, the proof is complete. ∎

Even though the formal definition of each set R_i displays a potentially unbounded number of iterations, in fact, the process may be completed in a finite number of steps because the underlying game G is assumed finite. This is the content of the next proposition, which is analogous to the similar conclusion found in Section 2.1 for the iterative process of elimination of dominated strategies.

Proposition 2.1: *There exists some $\bar{q} \in \mathbb{N}$ such that $\forall q \geq \bar{q}$, $\forall i = 1, 2, \ldots, n$,* $\hat{\Sigma}^q_i = \hat{\Sigma}^{q+1}_i$.

Proof: See Exercise 2.18. ∎

It is straightforward to check (Exercise 2.19) that every strategy forming part of some Nash equilibrium is rationalizable. Therefore, rationalizability is a concept that generalizes that of Nash equilibrium. Sometimes, it can amount to such a wide generalization that all its predictive power is utterly lost. To illustrate this, consider the battle of the sexes (cf. Table 2.5). The set of rationalizable strategies in this game coincides with the whole set of mixed strategies, i.e., $R_i = \Sigma_i$. Thus, if the boy and girl in this game are allowed no prior coordination possibilities (as implicitly assumed by the notion of rationalizability), *any* strategy profile $\sigma \in \Sigma_1 \times \Sigma_2$ is a possible outcome when players' analysis of the situation is based alone on common knowledge of rationality.

The previous discussion underscores the point that a profile of rationalizable strategies need not define an equilibrium *profile*. However, this still leaves open the question of whether an analogous conclusion should hold as well at the level of each player's individual *strategies*. Specifically, we may ask whether every rationalizable strategy must assign positive weight only to those pure strategies that are played with positive probability at *some* Nash equilibrium. To refute this conjecture, consider the 4×4 bilateral game proposed by Bernheim (1984) whose strategic form is described in Table 2.10 (see also Exercise 2.20).

This game turns out to have a unique Nash equilibrium given by the pure-strategy profile (X, B) (cf. Exercise 2.9). Therefore, we know that the two pure strategies involved in this equilibrium are rationalizable. Are there any other strategies that qualify as such? We now argue that strategies W and Y for player 1, and strategies A and C for player 2, are *all* rationalizable. To see this, consider, for example, strategy W. How can we "rationalize" that player 1 may indeed choose this strategy? – simply, by positing that she holds (point) expectations on player 2 choosing C.

Table 2.10: *A strategic-form game with a unique*
(pure-strategy) Nash equilibrium

1 \ 2	A	B	C	D
W	0, 7	2, 5	7, 0	0, 1
X	5, 2	3, 3	5, 2	0, 1
Y	7, 0	2, 5	0, 7	0, 1
Z	0, 0	0, −2	0, 0	10, −1

And is this choice by 2 rationalizable? – certainly, by supposing that player 2 has expectations concentrated on player 1 choosing Y. And what about the latter strategy? It is enough to assume that player 1 expects player 2 to choose A. And for this choice by player 2? It may be rationalized if player 2 is taken to hold point expectations concentrated on 1 playing W. In this fashion, a "rationalizable cycle" may be constructed that is able to rationalize *ad infinitum* that player 1 might choose W. But, clearly, this cycle can be used to rationalize (*ad infinitum* as well) any of the four pure strategies indicated, if started at the "right point." Thus, we find that all mixed strategies for player 1 with support in her first three strategies – W, X, Y – and those of player 2 with support on her first three – A, B, C – are rationalizable. Formally,

$$R_1 \subset \{\sigma_1 \in \Sigma_1 : \sigma_{1W} + \sigma_{1X} + \sigma_{1Y} = 1\}$$

$$R_2 \subset \{\sigma_2 \in \Sigma_2 : \sigma_{2A} + \sigma_{2B} + \sigma_{2C} = 1\}.$$

In fact, it can be easily shown that the above pair of inclusions hold reciprocally as well (cf. Exercise 2.17), so that those strategies are the only rationalizable strategies in the game considered. In line with our previous discussion, this illustrates the fact that the notion of rationalizability generally embodies much more than mere "equilibrium dis-coordination", i.e., more than just Nash equilibrium strategies played *without* the required players' coordination.

The induction process that defines the set of rationalizable strategies is quite parallel to that contemplated on undominated strategies in Section 2.1. Is there any relationship between them? Clearly, the process of elimination based on the dominance criterion is *not* stronger than that based on discarding suboptimal responses. (As explained above, if a strategy is dominated, it can never be a best response against any strategy profile by the other players.) Can it be strictly weaker? For the bilateral case (i.e., two players), the next result establishes that it cannot.

Theorem 2.6 (Pearce, 1984): *Let $N = \{1, 2\}$. For each player $i = 1, 2$, the set of rationalizable strategies and the set of (mixed) strategies which are iteratively undominated coincide.*

Proof: Denote by Σ_i^q and $\hat{\Sigma}_i^q$ the sets of mixed strategies of player $i = 1, 2$, that survive iteration q in the processes that underlie the concepts of iterative nondominance and rationalizability, respectively. The second one is as defined above (cf. (2.20)). The first one is the set of mixed strategies that assign all positive weight to the following set of pure strategies (cf. Section 2.1):

$$S_i^q = \left\{ s_i \in S_i^{q-1} : \neg \left(\exists \sigma_i \in \Sigma_i^{q-1} : \forall s_{-i} \in S_{-i}^{q-1}, \ \pi_i(\sigma_i, s_{-i}) \right. \right.$$
$$\left. \left. > \pi_i(s_i, s_{-i}) \right) \right\}.$$

We proceed inductively. By construction, $\hat{\Sigma}_i^0 = \Sigma_i^0 = \Sigma_i$. Now suppose that $\hat{\Sigma}_i^q = \Sigma_i^q$ for some q. We shall prove that this implies $\hat{\Sigma}_i^{q+1} = \Sigma_i^{q+1}$.

For each $q = 1, 2, \ldots, i = 1, 2, \sigma_i \in \hat{\Sigma}_i^q$, consider those vectors of the form

$$\rho(\sigma_i) = \left(\pi_i \left(\sigma_i, s_j \right) \right)_{s_j \in S_j^q}$$

whose dimension is equal to the cardinality of S_j^q, denoted by v_j^q. Clearly, the set

$$C_i^q \equiv \left\{ \rho(\sigma_i) : \sigma_i \in \hat{\Sigma}_i^q \right\}$$

is convex. Choose any strategy $s_i \in S_i^{q+1}$. By the definition of S_i^{q+1}, $\rho(s_i)$ must define a boundary point of C_i^q. Therefore, invoking the separating hyperplane theorem (see, e.g., Border, 1985), there exists a v_j^q-dimensional vector μ such that $\forall \tilde{\sigma}_i \in \hat{\Sigma}_i^q$,

$$\mu \cdot \rho(s_i) \geq \mu \cdot \rho(\tilde{\sigma}_i),$$

which may be rewritten as

$$\sum_{s_{jr} \in S_j^q} \mu_r \, \pi_i \left(s_i, s_{jr} \right) \geq \sum_{s_{jr} \in S_j^q} \mu_r \, \pi_i \left(\tilde{\sigma}_i, s_{jr} \right).$$

By choosing

$$\hat{\sigma}_j \left(s_{jr} \right) = \frac{\mu_r}{\sum_{r'} \mu_{r'}}$$

one concludes that s_i is indeed a best response against $\hat{\sigma}_j$, an element of $\Sigma_j^q (= \hat{\Sigma}_j^q)$. Therefore, $s_i \in \hat{\Sigma}_i^{q+1}$, which shows that $\Sigma_i^{q+1} \subseteq \hat{\Sigma}_i^{q+1}$. Since the converse inclusion is immediate, the identity of both sets follow. ∎

Theorem 2.6 indicates that the requirement of rationalizability provides little cutting power in those bilateral games where a payoff-domination criterion alone is by itself of limited predictive use. However, it is important to stress at this point that, if the game involves more than two players, the conclusion does not hold. This is illustrated by the trilateral game whose strategic form is given by Table 2.11 (only the payoffs of player 2 are included, with the first player selecting rows, the second columns, and the third boxes).

Table 2.11: *A three-player strategic form game – only the payoffs of player 2 are specified*

1＼2	a	b	c	1＼2	a	b	c
A	6	10	0	A	6	10	10
B	6	10	10	B	6	0	10
3		M				N	

First, note that the pure strategy a of player 2 is undominated by any alternative (possibly mixed) strategy on her part. That is, for *any* mixed strategy $\hat{\sigma}_2$ of the form $(0, \hat{\sigma}_{2b}, 1 - \hat{\sigma}_{2b})$, $\hat{\sigma}_{2b} \in [0, 1]$, strategy a provides a payoff at least as large as $\hat{\sigma}_2$ for some associated (pure) strategies on her opponents' part. Specifically, if $\hat{\sigma}_2 \leq 1/2$, then

$$\pi_2(a, A, M) = 6 \geq \pi_2(\hat{\sigma}_2; A, M),$$

while if $\hat{\sigma}_2 \geq 1/2$,

$$\pi_2(a, B, N) = 6 \geq \pi_2(\hat{\sigma}_2; B, N).$$

However, there is *no* pair of opponents' strategies for which a is a best response for player 2. To see this simply note that, for any such pair $\sigma_1 = (\sigma_{1A}, \sigma_{1B})$ and $\sigma_3 = (\sigma_{3M}, \sigma_{3N})$, it is impossible to satisfy *simultaneously* the following two conditions:

$$\pi_2(a, \sigma_1, \sigma_3) = 6 \geq \pi_2(b; \sigma_1, \sigma_3) \tag{2.21}$$

$$\pi_2(a, \sigma_1, \sigma_3) = 6 \geq \pi_2(c; \sigma_1, \sigma_3), \tag{2.22}$$

For (2.21) to hold, one must have

$$10(\sigma_{1A} + \sigma_{3M} - \sigma_{1A}\sigma_{3M}) \leq 6$$

whereas for (2.22) it is required that

$$10(1 - \sigma_{1A}\sigma_{3M}) \leq 6.$$

It is straightforward to check that these two requirements are jointly incompatible for any $\sigma_{1A}, \sigma_{3M} \in [0, 1]$. Therefore, no matter the opponents' strategies, there is always an alternative pure strategy (b or c) that provides player 2 with a strictly better payoff. The key issue here is that because player $2's$ opponents (i.e., players 1 and 3) randomize *independently* when carrying out their respective mixed strategies, the space of *feasible* probability vectors over the set $S_1 \times S_3$, which player 2 may use to rationalize strategy a, is *not* the whole of $\Delta^{r_1+r_3-2}$. It is instead restricted to the set of "product probability vectors":

$$\left\{ \begin{array}{l} \mu \in \Delta^{r_1+r_3-2} : \exists \sigma_1 \in \Sigma_1(= \Delta^{r_1-1}), \ \exists \sigma_3 \in \Sigma_3(= \Delta^{r_3-1}) \text{ s.t.} \\ \mu(s_{1j}, s_{3k}) = \sigma_1(s_{1j}) \cdot \sigma_2(s_{3k}) \quad \forall s_{1j} \in S_1, \ \forall s_{3k} \in S_3 \end{array} \right\}.$$

This constraint rules out precisely those subjective probabilities that are needed to sustain as optimal (i.e., "separate," in the proof of Theorem 2.6) the undominated strategy a on the part of player 2.

Summary

This chapter has focused on the main theoretical tools and concepts available for the analysis of games in strategic form. It has started with the most basic notion of payoff dominance, for which we have contemplated a variety of different specific versions. For the standard one, we have formulated an *iterative process of elimination of dominated strategies* that responds to the idea that rationality (in a weak sense) is common knowledge. In some games (those called dominance solvable), this process leads to a unique prediction of play.

Then, we have turned to the concept of *Nash equilibrium*, a central notion in game theory that embodies a joint requirement of individual rationality (in the stronger sense of payoff maximization) and correct ("rational") expectations. Even though it is typically nonunique, at least one can guarantee its existence in every finite game, provided players may use mixed strategies. Nash equilibrium becomes a particularly well-behaved concept for the restricted class of strategic situation known as zero-sum games, the original context studied by the early researchers in game theory. In these games, players' interests are strictly opposed, which turns out to afford a very elegant and clear-cut analysis. In particular, all Nash equilibria provide the same payoff and equilibrium play displays interchangeability, i.e., it does not require any implicit or explicit coordination among players.

The last part of this chapter has discussed a number of different variations (strengthenings or generalizations) on the notion of Nash equilibrium. First, we have briefly focused on the concepts of *strong and coalition-proof equilibria*, which require that the equilibrium configuration be robust to deviations jointly devised by any coalition of players. Unfortunately, both of these notions (even the latter weaker one) happen to be afflicted by acute nonexistence problems. Next, we turned to the concept of *correlated equilibrium*, which allows players to rely on incentive-compatible stochastic coordination mechanisms in choosing their actions. The wider possibilities this affords enlarge substantially the range of payoffs that may be achieved in some games. In particular, payoffs that are larger than those attainable at any Nash equilibrium can be achieved by a carefully designed (in particular, asymmetric) pattern of individual signals.

Finally, we have discussed the notion of *rationalizability*. Its motivation derives from the idea that, unless players explicitly communicate with each other (a possibility that, in any case, would have to be modeled as part of the game), there is no reason to believe they must succeed in coordinating on a particular Nash equilibrium. This suggests that players' analysis of the game should often be based alone on the knowledge of payoffs and the presumption that the opponents are rational maximizers. Then, what arises is an iterative process of *independent* reasoning for each player that has a close parallelism with the iterative elimination of dominated strategies. In fact, they both coincide for bilateral games, which indicates that a wide range of non-Nash behavior should typically qualify as rationalizable.

Exercises

Exercise 2.1: Let $G = \left\{ N, \{S_i\}_{i=1}^n, \{\pi_i\}_{i=1}^n \right\}$ be a game in strategic form. Prove that, for every player $i \in N$, every mixed strategy $\sigma_i \in \Sigma_i$ that assigns positive weight to a pure strategy $s_i \in S_i$ that is dominated is itself dominated in the same sense as indicated in Definition 2.1.

Exercise 2.2:

(a) Show that the iterative process of elimination of dominated strategies defined in Section 2.1 may be completed in a finite number of steps.

(b) Reconsider now this process so that one, and only one, strategy of one, and only one, player is eliminated in each iteration. Prove:

    (i) The resulting process is independent of the order in which the elimination of strategies is carried out if, in any given step of the process, there is more than one dominated strategy.

    (ii) The limit set of this process coincides with the one originally defined in Section 2.1.

Exercise 2.3: Consider the strategic-form game represented by the following payoff table:

	2	A	B
1			
X		100, 2	-1000, 2
Y		99, 3	1000 , 2

What outcome would you predict? Discuss any relevant considerations that might impinge on your prediction.

Exercise 2.4: Consider a simultaneous game with the following payoff table:

	2	A	B
1			
X		1, 3	4, 1
Y		0, 2	3, 4

    (i) Formulate a prediction of play.

    (ii) Suppose now that player 1 has taken away two payoff units ("utiles") if she adopts strategy X. Does your prediction change?

    (iii) Consider now the following second possibility. Player 1 may decide, in an initial stage of the game, whether to have the two utiles mentioned in (ii) removed. Once she has made this decision, both individuals play the resulting game. Represent the full game in both extensive and strategic forms. After finding *all* its *pure-strategy* Nash equilibria, predict some outcome and compare it with (ii).

Exercise 2.5*: Prove that if the game is dominance solvable, it has a unique Nash equilibrium.

Exercise 2.6: Show that the strategic-form game whose payoffs are described in Table 2.2 has (A, A) as its *unique* Nash equilibrium.

Exercise 2.7: Consider the game in strategic form represented by the following payoff table:

	R	S
A	5, 0	0, 4
B	1, 3	2, 0

Compute all its Nash equilibria.

Exercise 2.8: Consider the game in strategic form represented by the following payoff table:

	R	S	T
A	3, 0	2, 2	1, 1
B	4, 4	0, 3	2, 2
C	1, 3	1, 0	0, 2

What strategies survive the iterative elimination of dominated strategies? Compute *all* its Nash equilibria, in pure and mixed strategies.

Exercise 2.9: Show that the game in strategic form described in Table 2.10 has only one Nash equilibrium in pure strategies.

Exercise 2.10*: Prove Theorem 2.4.

Exercise 2.11: Given any bilateral zero-sum game G, show that strategy profile σ is a Nash equilibrium for G if, and only if, it is a Nash equilibrium for the constant-sum game $\tilde{G}$ obtained from G by adding any fixed amount d to the payoffs of *both* players. Is the conclusion affected if the fixed amount, call it now d_i for each $i = 1, 2$, differs between the two players?

Exercise 2.12: Compute the value and equilibrium strategies of the zero-sum games with the following payoff matrices:

$$\begin{pmatrix} 1 & 0 \\ 0 & 1 \end{pmatrix} \qquad \begin{pmatrix} 2 & 3 \\ 1 & 0 \\ 2 & 3 \end{pmatrix} \qquad \begin{pmatrix} 2 & 3 & 1 \\ 1 & 0 & 3 \\ 2 & 3 & 0 \end{pmatrix}$$

Exercise 2.13: Show that the conclusions of Theorem 2.1 do not hold for the following zero-sum trilateral game in strategic form (player 1 chooses rows, player 2 columns, and player 3 boxes):

1 \ 2	X	Y	Z
A	8 , 6	2 , 2	1 , 0
B	4 , 8	12 , 13	7 , 18
C	2 , 8	6 , 18	10 , 23

1 \ 2	X	Y	Z
A	10 , 8	4 , 4	3 , 2
B	6 , 10	14 , 15	9 , 20
C	4 , 10	8 , 20	12 , 25

3   Q   R

Exercise 2.14: Show that, for *any* given specification of players' von Neumann-Morgenstern preferences over "winning" and "losing" (ties are not allowed), chess may be regarded as a zero-sum game. What does this imply for chess tournaments?

Suppose now that there are two players involved in a game of poker who display a *common* von Neumann-Morgenstern utility for money. Is the game zero sum?

Exercise 2.15: Construct a bilateral zero-sum game displaying two, and only two, equilibria in pure strategies where, for each player, the particular strategies played in each case have disjoint supports. Is it possible? Discuss any possible problems.

Exercise 2.16*: State formally and prove the conclusion described in Remark 2.4.

Exercise 2.17*: Show that the *full* sets of rationalizable strategies corresponding to the strategic-form game described in Table 2.10 are as follows:

$$R_1 = \{\sigma_1 \in \Sigma_1 : \sigma_{1W} + \sigma_{1X} + \sigma_{1Y} = 1\}$$
$$R_2 = \{\sigma_2 \in \Sigma_2 : \sigma_{2A} + \sigma_{2B} + \sigma_{2C} = 1\}.$$

Exercise 2.18*: Prove Proposition 2.1.

Exercise 2.19*: Prove that every strategic profile that defines a Nash equilibrium is rationalizable.

Exercise 2.20*: Consider the following assertion: "If a bilateral 3×3 game (i.e., with three strategies per player) has a unique Nash equilibrium, its constituent pure strategies (i.e., those played with positive probability) are the only rationalizable pure strategies." Prove it or show a counterexample.

CHAPTER 3

Strategic-form analysis: applications

3.1 Oligopoly (I): static models

3.1.1 *Cournot model*

The first clear application of modern game-theoretic reasoning to be found in the economic literature appears in Cournot's (1838) discussion of oligopoly. By now, it has probably become the most paradigmatic model of strategic interaction studied in economics. It is just natural, therefore, that Cournot oligopoly should be the first economic application to be presented in this book.

Let there be n firms operating in a certain market for a homogeneous good, where the consumers' aggregate behavior is captured by a demand function

$$F : \mathbb{R}_+ \to \mathbb{R}_+. \tag{3.1}$$

This function specifies, for each $p \in \mathbb{R}_+$, the corresponding total demand for the good, $F(p)$. It will be assumed that the function $F(\cdot)$ satisfies the so-called *law of demand*, i.e., the total quantity demanded in the market is strictly decreasing in the prevailing price. It is therefore an invertible function, with its corresponding inverse being denoted by $P(\cdot)$. (That is, $P(Q) = p \Leftrightarrow F(p) = Q$.)

Identify each of the firms participating in the market with subindex $i \in \{1, 2, \ldots, n\}$. Every firm i displays a respective cost function

$$C_i : \mathbb{R}_+ \to \mathbb{R}_+,$$

assumed increasing, with $C_i(q_i)$ standing for the cost incurred by firm i when it produces output quantity q_i.

In the present Cournot context, the decision of each firm concerns solely its output produced, their respective amounts chosen *independently* (i.e., "simultaneously") by each of them. Given any output vector $q \equiv (q_1, q_2, \ldots, q_n)$ resulting from these independent decisions, the induced aggregate quantity is simply given by $Q \equiv q_1 + q_2 + \cdots + q_n$, which leads to a market-clearing price, $P(Q)$, and the following profits for each firm $i \in \{1, 2, \ldots, n\}$:

$$\pi_i(q) \equiv P(Q)q_i - C_i(q_i). \tag{3.2}$$

Note that the above expression implicitly assumes that all output produced by every firm is sold in the market.

The above elements define a *strategic-form game* among the n firms, where each of them has an identical strategy space, $S_i = \mathbb{R}_+$ (i.e., the set of its possible production decisions), and the payoff functions are identified with the profit functions given in (3.2). In this game, a *(Cournot-)Nash equilibrium* is any vector $q^* \equiv (q_1^*, q_2^*, \ldots q_n^*)$ satisfying, for each $i = 1, 2, \ldots, n$, the following conditions:

$$q_i^* \in \arg \max_{q_i} \pi_i(q_i, q_{-i}^*) \tag{3.3}$$

or equivalently

$$\forall q_i \in \mathbb{R}_+, \quad \pi_i(q^*) \geq \pi_i(q_i, q_{-i}^*),$$

where (q_i, q_{-i}^*) is just the convenient shorthand for the output vector where firm i chooses q_i and the remaining firms $j \neq i$ choose their respective q_j^*.

Let us assume that the function $P(\cdot)$ as well as every $C_i(\cdot)$, $i = 1, 2, \ldots, n$, are differentiable. Then, for the n optimization problems in (3.3) to be simultaneously solved at $(q_1^*, q_2^*, \ldots q_n^*)$, the following first-order necessary conditions (FONC) must hold:

$$P'(Q^*)q_i^* + P(Q^*) - C_i'(q_i^*) \leq 0 \qquad (i = 1, 2, \ldots, n), \tag{3.4}$$

where $Q^* \equiv \sum_{i=1}^n q_i^*$ and the notation $g'(\cdot)$ stands for the derivative of any arbitrary function $g(\cdot)$ of a single variable with respect to its (only) argument. That is, each firm i must have its respective q_i^* satisfy the FONC of its *individual* optimization problem when the other firms are taken to choose their respective equilibrium values q_j^*, $j \neq i$.

Whenever the Nash equilibrium is interior (that is, $q_i^* > 0$ for each $i = 1, 2, \ldots, n$), the weak inequalities in (3.4) must apply with equality. Moreover, provided standard second-order conditions hold (e.g., concavity of every firm's payoff function in its own output), one can ensure that such a system of n equations fully *characterizes* the set of interior Nash equilibria. In what follows, we assume that those second-order conditions are satisfied (cf. Exercise 3.2) and focus on interior equilibria alone. In this case, (3.4) can be rewritten as follows:

$$C_i'(q_i^*) - P(Q^*) = P'(Q^*)q_i^* \qquad (i = 1, 2, \ldots, n). \tag{3.5}$$

Verbally, the above conditions can be described as follows:

> *At equilibrium, the (negative) deviation of each firm's marginal cost from the market price is proportional to its own output, with the proportionality factor (common to all firms) equal to the slope of the demand function.*

To understand the relevance of the previous statement, it must be recalled that, under *perfect competition*, the prevailing price is assumed to be equal to the marginal cost for each firm. In such a competitive setup, firms do *not* conceive themselves as market participants of a significant size and, therefore, each of them takes the price prevailing in the market, say $\bar{p}$, as independent of its behavior. Consequently, each firm i maximizes

$$\widehat{\pi}_i(\bar{p}, q_i) \equiv \bar{p} \, q_i - C_i(q_i)$$

with respect to $q_i \in \mathbb{R}_+$, whose solution $\hat{q}_i(\bar{p})$, if interior, must satisfy the following FONC:

$$C_i'(\hat{q}_i(\bar{p})) = \bar{p}. \tag{3.6}$$

Naturally, the prevailing price $\bar{p}$ must "clear" the market, given the vector of firm outputs $\hat{q}(\bar{p}) \equiv (\hat{q}_1(\bar{p}), \hat{q}_2(\bar{p}), \dots, \hat{q}_n(\bar{p}))$ that solves their respective optimization problems. That is, in a perfectly competitive equilibrium, the following "fixed-point condition" must hold:

$$P\left(\sum_{i=1}^{n} \hat{q}_i(\bar{p})\right) = \bar{p}.$$

Note that an analogous condition of market clearing is also required in the Cournot model, as implicitly embodied by the function $P(\cdot)$ in (3.2).

In a heuristic sense, one can interpret the perfectly competitive scenario as a pseudo-Cournotian context in which every firm *perceives* a totally "elastic" demand function – that is, an *inverse* demand function that is essentially *inelastic* so that the price is not affected by the quantity sold. In this case, (3.6) can be seen as a particular case of (3.5). Of course, if the number of firms is finite and the law of demand holds, this perception is wrong. Only when the number of firms is large enough (and, therefore, the weight of each one of them is relatively insignificant) does a very elastic demand function represent a good approximation of the situation faced by each firm. Only then, that is, may the perfect-competition paradigm represent a suitable strategic model of firm behavior and corresponding market performance.

In view of the former discussion, it is natural to conjecture that any discrepancy between Cournot and perfect competition might be understood in terms of the following two factors:

(a) the elasticity of the demand function (i.e., how sensitive is market demand to price changes);
(b) the extent of market concentration (roughly, how many firms enjoy a significant share of the market).

Focusing, for convenience, on the *inverse* demand function, its elasticity $\lambda(Q)$ (i.e., the "inverse elasticity") is defined in the usual fashion: the relative (marginal) decrease experienced by the market-clearing price for any given relative increase (also marginal) in the quantity sold in the market. That is,

$$\lambda(Q) \equiv \frac{-dP/P}{dQ/Q} = -P'(Q)\frac{Q}{P}.$$

On the other hand, a traditional way of measuring market concentration is given by the so-called *Herfindahl index*. This index is defined over the firms' vector of market shares $\alpha \equiv (\alpha_1, \alpha_2, \ldots, \alpha_n)$, where

$$\alpha_i \equiv \frac{q_i}{Q}$$

represents the fraction of total output produced by each firm $i = 1, 2, \ldots, n$. Given any such vector α, its induced Herfindahl index $H(\alpha)$ is given by

$$H(\alpha) \equiv \sum_{i=1}^{n} (\alpha_i)^2.$$

Observe that, if the number of firms n is kept fixed, the function $H(\cdot)$ obtains its maximum, as desired, when $\alpha_i = 1$ for some firm i. That is, the maximum is attained when the market is "fully concentrated." In contrast, $H(\cdot)$ obtains its minimum when the market output is uniformly distributed among all firms, i.e., all firms display the same market weight and therefore the market is at its "least concentrated" state. Thus, in a meaningful sense, the Herfindahl index does appear to reflect an intuitive measure of market concentration.

To attain a clear-cut relationship between concentration, market elasticity, and deviation from perfect competition, it is useful to rewrite (3.5) in the following way:

$$\frac{P(Q^*) - C_i'(q_i^*)}{P(Q^*)} = -P'(Q^*)\frac{1}{P(Q^*)}q_i^* \qquad (i = 1, 2, \ldots, n). \tag{3.7}$$

The left-hand side of the previous equation expresses, for each firm i, the proportional deviation from the "individual" competitive situation where the firm's marginal cost would coincide with the market equilibrium price. If these relative deviations are added across all firms, each of them weighted by the market share $\alpha_i^* \equiv q_i^*/Q^*$ commanded by the respective firm i in a Cournot-Nash equilibrium $q^* = (q_1^*, q_2^*, \ldots, q_n^*)$, one obtains the so-called Lerner index

$$\mathfrak{L}(q^*) \equiv \sum_{i=1}^{n} \alpha_i^* \frac{P(Q^*) - C_i'(q_i^*)}{P(Q^*)}.$$

This index expresses the weighted-average deviation from perfect competition observed in the Cournot-Nash equilibrium q^*. Adding up the terms in (3.7) and carrying out suitable algebraic manipulations, we have

$$\mathfrak{L}(q^*) = -\sum_{i=1}^{n} \alpha_i^* \frac{q_i^*}{Q^*} Q^* P'(Q^*)\frac{1}{P(Q^*)}$$

$$= -P'(Q^*)\frac{Q^*}{P(Q^*)} \sum_{i=1}^{n} (\alpha_i^*)^2$$

$$= \lambda(Q^*) H(\alpha^*),$$

which is indeed the sought-after relationship. It reflects, very sharply, the two considerations (demand elasticity and market concentration) that were formerly suggested as important to understand the magnitude of any discrepancy between competitive and Cournot equilibria. It indicates, that is, that the average deviation from perfect competition (as given by Lerner's index) is simply the product of the two measures we have proposed to measure each of those two factors (i.e., the inverse-demand elasticity and the Herfindahl index, respectively).

Now, we illustrate the previous developments for a particularly simple duopoly context with linear cost and demand specifications (see Exercise 3.3 for a context with more firms). Let there be two firms, $i = 1, 2$, with identical cost functions:

$$C_i(q_i) = c\, q_i, \quad c > 0. \tag{3.8}$$

Let the demand function be also linear:

$$P(Q) = \max\{M - dQ,\ 0\}, \quad M,\ d > 0. \tag{3.9}$$

For an interior Cournot-Nash equilibrium, the first-order conditions (3.5) are particularized as follows:

$$(M - d(q_1^* + q_2^*)) - c = dq_i^* \quad (i = 1, 2). \tag{3.10}$$

Its solution,

$$q_i^* = \frac{M - c}{3d} \quad (i = 1, 2), \tag{3.11}$$

defines an interior equilibrium, which exists as long as $M > c$.

The above computations may be fruitfully reconsidered by focusing on the firms' best response correspondences (cf. (2.7)), which, in the present oligopoly context, are denoted by $\eta_i(\cdot)$ and receive the customary name of firms' *reaction functions*. For each firm $i = 1, 2$, its $\eta_i(\cdot)$ may be obtained from the first-order condition of its *individual* optimization problem, as this problem is parametrized by each of the hypothetical decisions q_j ($j \neq i$) that may be adopted by i's competitor. For interior configurations, these reaction functions may be implicitly defined by adapting (3.10) as follows:

$$(M - d(\eta_i(q_j) + q_j)) - c = d\eta_i(q_j) \quad (i, j = 1, 2;\ i \neq j).$$

Including as well the boundary points where one of the firms chooses not to produce, they are found, explicitly, to be of the following form:

$$\eta_i(q_j) = \max\left\{0,\ \frac{M - c}{2d} - (1/2)q_j\right\}. \tag{3.12}$$

Thus, for example, the optimal monopoly decisions may be obtained from these functions as follows:

$$q_i^m \equiv \eta_i(0) = \frac{M - c}{2d}, \quad (i = 1, 2),$$

that is, they are simply the optimal reactions of each firm i when the competitor produces no output.

In the present linear context, the reaction functions (3.12) are also linear (for interior configurations). Their intersection obviously defines a Nash equilibrium; that is, a pair of outputs such that, simultaneously, each one of them is a suitable

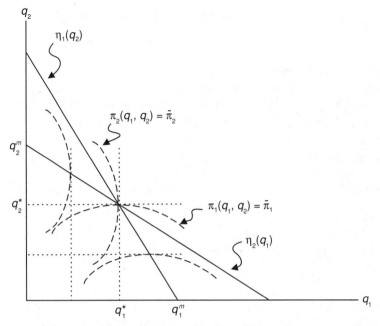

Figure 3.1: Cournot-Nash equilibrium in a linear duopoly.

"reaction" to the other. A graphic illustration of this situation is depicted in Figure 3.1. There, the reaction function of each firm (1 or 2) is identified as the locus of tangency points of its iso-profit curves to the straight lines (horizontal or vertical) associated with each of the outputs (taken as fixed) on the part of the competitor.

In the specific *duopoly* context where the reaction functions are decreasing and intersect only once (of which the linear case discussed above is just a particular case), its Nash equilibrium enjoys a much stronger foundation than the ordinary one discussed in Subsection 2.2.1. For, in this case, the (unique) Nash equilibrium is also the unambiguous prediction resulting from an iterative elimination of dominated strategies (cf. Section 2.1 and Exercise 2.5).

To verify this claim, it is convenient to use the identification of rationalizable and iteratively undominated strategies established by Theorem 2.6.[33] This result allows us to focus on the firms' reaction functions and, at each stage, rely on them to discard those strategies that cannot be "rationalized" as a best response to some of the remaining strategies by the opponent.

Proceeding in this fashion, we can first discard, for each firm $i = 1, 2$, those outputs that exceed the monopoly levels, i.e., those q_i such that

$$q_i > q_i^m \equiv \eta_i(0).$$

These outputs can never be an optimal response to *any* beliefs over the competitor's output – or, diagrammatically, they are not on the reaction function of firm i for any possible output of $j \neq i$. Once we have ruled out those outputs in the intervals

---

[33] This theorem was stated and proven only for games involving a finite set of pure strategies. However, it is extendable to contexts such as the present one where the spaces of pure strategies are infinite (a continuum).

(q_1^m, ∞) and (q_2^m, ∞), we can do the same for those q_i that satisfy

$$0 \leq q_i < \eta_i\left(q_j^m\right) = \eta_i(\eta_j(0)), \qquad (i, j = 1, 2; \ i \neq j),$$

because, having established that firm $j \neq i$ will *not* produce beyond the monopoly output, any q_i that verifies the above inequality cannot be a best response to any admissible belief on the opponent's output. Graphically, what this inequality reflects is simply that, if outputs in the interval (q_j^m, ∞) are not allowed on the part of the opponent, there is *no* output $q_i \in [0, \eta_i(q_j^m))$ that is on the reaction function of firm i. Or, somewhat more precisely,

$$\left[q_i = \eta_i(q_j), \ q_j \leq q_j^m\right] \Rightarrow q_i \in \left[\eta_i\left(q_j^m\right), q_i^m\right]$$

for each $i, j = 1, 2 \ (i \neq j)$. Undertaking one further iteration after the elimination of the intervals (q_i^m, ∞) and $[0, \eta_i(q_j^m))$, it is immediate to check that, for analogous reasons, we can discard outputs q_i that satisfy

$$q_i > \eta_i(\eta_j(\eta_i(0))) \qquad (i, j = 1, 2; \ i \neq j).$$

Proceeding indefinitely along this process, it is clear that, in the limit, only the outputs q_1^* and q_2^* that define the Nash equilibrium remain undiscarded.

More precisely, q_1^* and q_2^* are the only outputs that verify the following conditions:

$$\eta_i(\eta_j(\cdots(\eta_i(\eta_j(0))))) \leq q_i \leq \eta_i(\eta_j(\cdots(\eta_j(\eta_i(0)))))$$
$$(i, j = 1, 2; \ i \neq j).$$

for all (finite) alternate compositions of the reaction functions. The above expression embodies, in a compact fashion, the progressively more stringent series of inequalities induced by each of the iterations of the process. They can be summarized as follows:

- *First iteration:* $q_i \leq \eta_i(0)$;
- *Second iteration:* $q_i \geq \eta_i(\eta_j(0))$;
- *Third iteration:* $q_i \leq \eta_i(\eta_j(\eta_i(0)))$;
- *Fourth iteration:* $q_i \geq \eta_i(\eta_j(\eta_i(\eta_j(0))))$ $\quad \cdots$

This indefinite shrinkage of admissible outputs is illustrated in Figure 3.2 for the linear case formerly considered in Figure 3.1.

3.1.2 *Bertrand model*

Almost half a century after Cournot's work, Bertrand (1883) proposed an alternative model of oligopolistic competition where firms have their prices (instead of outputs) as their decision variable. Again, firms' decisions in this respect are assumed to be simultaneously adopted by all of them.

Let us focus first on the case where, as postulated in Section 3.1.1, the good produced by every firm is homogeneous. Under these circumstances, it is clear that if the market is "transparent to the eyes" of the consumers and frictionless, any

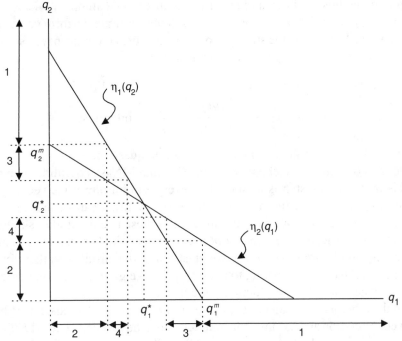

Figure 3.2: Cournot duopoly – iterative elimination of dominated strategies. (The output intervals discarded in iterations 1–4 are spanned by corresponding arrows.)

equilibrium of the induced game must have all *active* firms set the same price – all firms demanding a higher price will enjoy zero demand because consumers will buy the homogeneous good only from those that offer the cheapest price. This gives rise to some especially acute competition among firms that, under quite general conditions, tends to reduce very substantially their profits. In fact, as we shall presently show, there exist paradigmatic conditions in which firms are forced to zero profits at equilibrium, independently of how many of them there are (obviously, as long as there are at least two). Because of its marked contrast with the Cournotian conclusion presented in Section 3.1.1, this state of affairs is often referred to as Bertrand's paradox.

To illustrate this paradox in its starkest form, consider n (≥ 2) firms that confront a continuous and nonincreasing demand function $F(\cdot)$ of the sort described in (3.1) and display linear and identical production costs as given in (3.8) for some common marginal cost $c > 0$. To render the setup interesting, suppose that $F(c) > 0$, i.e., there is positive demand at the price equal to the marginal cost. We posit that each firm i decides on its respective price p_i independently ($i = 1, 2, \ldots, n$), which results in a price vector $p \equiv (p_1, p_2, \ldots, p_n)$ faced by consumers. As explained, because the good is assumed homogeneous (and the information on market conditions perfect), all consumer demand flows to those firms that have set the lowest price.

Given any p, denote $\theta(p) \equiv \min\{p_1, p_2, \ldots, p_n\}$ and let $F(\theta(p))$ be the total demand induced by such a configuration of firm prices. For simplicity, it will be supposed that this total demand is uniformly distributed among all firms that have set the minimum price $\theta(p)$. Formally, this defines a strategic-form game for the n firms, where $S_i = \mathbb{R}_+$ is the strategy space of each firm i and the payoffs associated to any strategy (i.e., price) vector p are as follows:

$$\pi_i(p) = 0 \quad \text{if } p_i > \theta(p)$$

$$= (p_i - c)\frac{F(\theta(p))}{\#\{j \in N : p_j = \theta(p)\}} \quad \text{otherwise,} \tag{3.13}$$

where $\#\{\cdot\}$ stands for the cardinality of the set in question.

Our first objective is to characterize the (Bertrand-)Nash equilibria of this game. In this task, the key step is to show that every equilibrium price vector p^* must satisfy $\theta(p^*) = c$, i.e., the minimum price set by firms can neither be (strictly) higher or lower than c. We now discard each of these two possibilities in turn.

On the one hand, it is clear that $\theta(p^*) < c$ cannot hold. For, in this case, the firms that set the minimum price $\theta(p^*)$ would earn negative profits and therefore could benefit by unilaterally deviating to a higher price – e.g., if they chose a price equal to c, in which case they would make zero profits.

On the other hand, it can not happen that $\theta(p^*) > c$. To see this, let p^* be some such configuration and assume, for simplicity, that the induced demand $F(\theta(p^*)) > 0$. Consider any of the firms, say firm i, which does *not* capture the whole demand $F(\theta(p^*))$. (There must always be at least one firm in this situation, either because its price is higher than $\theta(p^*)$ and therefore its demand is zero, or because it is sharing the total demand $F(\theta(p^*))$ with some other firm whose price is also equal to $\theta(p^*)$.) If firm i were to deviate to a price "infinitesimally lower" than $\theta(p^*)$, say to some $p_i' = \theta(p^*) - \varepsilon$ for some small $\varepsilon > 0$, it would absorb the whole of the induced market demand $F(\theta(p^*) - \varepsilon)$ and obtain profits

$$\pi_i(p_i', p_{-i}^*) = [(\theta(p^*) - \varepsilon - c] F(\theta(p^*) - \varepsilon).$$

Instead, if it does not deviate, its profits are either zero or, if positive, no higher than

$$[\theta(p^*) - c] \frac{F(\theta(p^*))}{2}$$

because, in the latter case, the set $\{j \in N : p_j^* = \theta(p^*)\}$ includes firm i and at least one additional firm. Obviously, if $\varepsilon > 0$ is low enough,

$$\pi_i(p_i', p_{-i}^*) > [\theta(p^*) - c] \frac{F(\theta(p^*))}{2}.$$

Therefore, the deviation toward p_i' would be profitable for firm i, which implies that p^* cannot be a Nash equilibrium.

Since we have ruled out that $\theta(p^*)$ might be higher or lower than c, only a price vector p^* that satisfies the equality $\theta(p^*) = c$ remains a possible equilibrium candidate. In fact, it is straightforward to check (cf. Exercise 3.4) that, if at least two firms set the minimum price in p^*, this price profile defines a Nash equilibrium of the Bertrand game; Bertrand-Nash equilibria p^* can be simply characterized by the following twofold condition:

$$\theta(p^*) = c$$
$$\#\{j \in N : p_j^* = \theta(p^*)\} \geq 2. \tag{3.14}$$

Thus, in equilibrium, all firms in the market (both those that enjoy a positive individual demand as well as those that do not) attain zero profits.

Under price competition, therefore, the Bertrand-Nash equilibrium gives rise to a fully competitive outcome when firms display common and constant marginal costs. This result contrasts sharply with that obtained in the Cournot model under similar cost and demand conditions (cf. Section 3.1.1). This serves to underscore the idea that, as suggested before, competition in prices (i.e., á la Bertrand) typically leads to significantly more aggressive behavior than competition in quantities (à la Cournot), at least under benchmark conditions.[34]

Naturally, the analysis turns out to be much less extreme (i.e., the contrast with Cournot competition less "paradoxical") if the stringent and somewhat unrealistic assumption of good homogeneity is relaxed. Suppose, for example, that each firm is taken to produce a different kind of car, computer, or cooking oil. That is, firms produce different goods, but all of these cover similar consumer needs in a less-than-perfect substitutable manner. Then, if we make the reasonable assumption that consumers' preferences over the range of differentiated goods are not fully homogenous, some potential for variety arises concerning the range of possible goods sold in the market as well as their corresponding prices. It also becomes natural to posit that the specific demand for any particular good should be *gradually* (i.e., continuously) responsive to price changes in *all* prices. Overall, this suggests that, building upon the partially "monopolistic" features brought about by product differentiation, firms might well be able to earn positive profits at equilibrium even under Bertrand (price) competition.

To fix ideas, consider a simple model of oligopolistic competition with differentiated products that involves just two "symmetric" firms with linear costs. Thus, each firm $i = 1, 2$ displays a cost function of the form

$$C_i(q_i) = c\,q_i, \quad c > 0,$$

which specifies the cost at which firm i may produce any given q_i units of its firm-specific (differentiated) good. Concerning the demand side, suppose that each product i (the good produced by firm i) faces an *inverse* (also linear) demand function:

$$P_i(q_1, q_2) = \max\{0, \ M - q_i - bq_j\} \quad (i, j = 1, 2, \ i \neq j), \tag{3.15}$$

where $M > 0$. This formulation embodies the idea that, in general, the demands

---

[34] For other cost and demand scenarios (e.g., when marginal costs are different and/or they are not constant), the conclusions may be much less clear cut. In particular, one may even encounter that Nash equilibria in pure strategies fail to exist due to the abrupt discontinuity induced on the payoff functions by the assumption of good homogeneity (see Exercise 3.5). It can be seen, however, that existence of Bertrand-Nash equilibria in *mixed* strategies always follows from the general existence results discussed in Section 2.4 (in particular, those due to Dasgupta and Maskin (1986a)).

for the goods are not independent nor are both regarded as indistinguishable by consumers. To be more precise, the first consideration (nonindependence) would be captured by the requirement that $b \neq 0$, and the second (not perfect substitutes) would be given by the condition $b \neq 1$. In principle, the sign of b may be positive or negative (see below). However, a natural assumption to make in every case is that $|b| < 1$, i.e., the "direct effect" on the price of good i of a change in q_i (i.e., the quantity of this *same* good being sold) is more important than the "cross effect" induced by the quantity q_j of the alternative good.

Since we are postulating here that the decision variables of firms are their respective prices, the analysis must focus on the induced system of *direct* demand functions whose arguments are precisely these price variables. By inverting (3.15), it is straightforward to find that the corresponding system of demand functions is of the following form:

$$F_i(p_1, p_2) = \max\left\{0, \ \frac{M}{1+b} - \frac{1}{1-b^2}p_i + \frac{b}{1-b^2}p_j\right\}$$

$$(i, j = 1, 2, \ i \neq j). \tag{3.16}$$

Note, from the above expression, that if $b > 0$ the goods are to be conceived as *partial* substitutes; i.e., any increase in the price of one of them rises the demand enjoyed by the other. On the other hand, if $b < 0$, the goods are complements.

In view of (3.16), the payoff functions of the game are as follows:

$$\tilde{\pi}_i(p_1, p_2) = (p_i - c) \max\left\{0, \ \frac{M}{1+b} - \frac{1}{1-b^2}p_i + \frac{b}{1-b^2}p_j\right\}.$$

Therefore, the FONC for an interior (Bertrand-)Nash equilibrium gives rise to the following system of equations:

$$\frac{\partial \tilde{\pi}_i}{\partial p_i}(p_1^*, p_2^*) = \left(\frac{M}{1+b} - \frac{1}{1-b^2}p_i^* + \frac{b}{1-b^2}p_j^*\right) - \frac{1}{1-b^2}(p_i^* - c) = 0$$

for $i, j = 1, 2 \ (i \neq j)$. Relying on the symmetry of the problem, they can be easily solved to yield[35]:

$$p_1^* = p_2^* = \frac{M(1-b)}{2-b} + \frac{c}{2-b}. \tag{3.17}$$

As explained, the parameter b reflects the degree of substitutability (or complementarity) between the two products. In particular, as $b \uparrow 1$, the goods become progressively better substitutes (or, equivalently, the two firms produce goods that are less heterogeneous) and (3.17) tends to (3.14). In the limit, since the equilibrium prices coincide with the (constant) marginal cost, profits are zero for both firms, which was indeed the conclusion already obtained above when full homogeneity was directly assumed. In general, it is easy to show (see Exercise 3.7) that the higher the degree of heterogeneity between the two products (that is, the worse substitutes they are), the higher the equilibrium profits earned by the firms.

---

[35] Note that the second-order conditions for these optimization problems also hold since $\partial^2 \tilde{\pi}_i / \partial p_i^2(p_1, p_2) < 0$ for both $i = 1, 2$.

The strategic model of differentiated-product oligopoly studied here displays an important shortcoming: it imposes *exogenously* on the firms a certain degree of differentiation between their products. In Section 5.3, we undertake a fuller approach to the problem in which price competition is just the last stage of a larger (multiperiod) game where firms themselves must previously determine their extent of product differentiation. This enriches the present analysis quite significantly.

3.2   Mechanism design (I): efficient allocation of public goods

Consider a community of n individuals who have to determine the level x at which a certain public good will be provided to all of them. (For example, they have to decide on the quality of a public transportation system or the resources devoted to running a public school.) The cost of attaining any particular level of the public good has to be financed by individual contributions $(c_i)_{i=1}^{n}$ of a private good – we may think of it as money – where c_i stands for the private contribution of individual i. For simplicity, it is assumed that the "production" of the public good displays constant returns, so that a total contribution $C \equiv \sum_{i=1}^{n} c_i$ may finance a public-good level $x = C$. (Note that, given constant returns, a transformation rate between private and public good equal to one can be simply obtained by a suitable choice of units, e.g., the units in which money is expressed.)

Let $w_i > 0$ be the amount of private good originally held by each individual i. Her preferences over public-good levels and her own contributions are assumed to be represented by a function of the form

$$U_i : \mathbb{R}_+ \times (-\infty, w_i] \to \mathbb{R}$$

that specifies the utility $U_i(x, c_i)$ enjoyed by agent i when the level of public good is x and her individual contribution is c_i. In principle, individual contributions could be negative, which would be interpreted as the receipt of (positive) transfers. Naturally, we postulate that all those functions $U_i(\cdot)$ are increasing in their first arguments and decreasing in the second. It is also convenient to assume that they are jointly differentiable and strictly concave.

As a useful benchmark, we first identify the allocation that would be chosen by a "benevolent planner" whose preferences may be represented by a certain linear combination of the utilities obtained by the different individuals. Denoting by $\alpha = (\alpha_1, \alpha_2, \ldots, \alpha_n)$ the vector of (positive) weights α_i she attributes to each agent $i = 1, 2, \ldots, n$, the planner's decision must be a solution to the following optimization problem,

$$\max \sum_{i=1}^{n} \alpha_i U_i(x, c_i), \tag{3.18}$$

with respect to $\left(x, (c_i)_{i=1}^{n}\right)$, subject to the following constraints:

$$x \leq \sum_{i=1}^{n} c_i, \quad x \geq 0, \quad w_i \geq c_i \quad (i = 1, 2, \ldots, n). \tag{3.19}$$

It is immediate to check that any allocation that solves the above optimization problem must be efficient (i.e., Pareto optimal). In fact, it is well known – see, for example, Varian (1992) – that the concavity of the functions $U_i(\cdot)$ implies that *any* efficient allocation has to be a solution to that problem for an *appropriately chosen* vector of weights α.

Suppose that any allocation $(x^*, (c_i^*)_{i=1}^n)$ that solves the planner's problem is interior, i.e., $x^* > 0$ and $w_i > c_i^* > 0$, $\forall i = 1, 2, \ldots, n$ (see Exercise 3.9). Then, approaching the problem with the usual Lagrangian methods, the following conditions are to hold:

$$\sum_{i=1}^n \alpha_i \frac{\partial U_i(x^*, c_i^*)}{\partial x} - \lambda = 0 \tag{3.20}$$

$$\alpha_i \frac{\partial U_i(x^*, c_i^*)}{\partial c_i} + \lambda = 0 \qquad (i = 1, 2, \ldots, n) \tag{3.21}$$

$$x^* = \sum_{i=1}^n c_i^*, \tag{3.22}$$

where $\lambda > 0$ is the Lagrange multiplier associated with the feasibility constraint (3.22). Using (3.20) and (3.21), we obtain the condition

$$\sum_{i=1}^n -\frac{\frac{\partial U_i(x^*, c_i^*)}{\partial x}}{\frac{\partial U_i(x^*, c_i^*)}{\partial c_i}} \equiv \sum_{i=1}^n \left. \frac{dc_i}{dx} \right|_{U_i(\cdot) = U_i(x^*, c_i^*)} = 1 \tag{3.23}$$

that embodies the essential requirement underlying efficient allocations: the sum, across all individuals, of the marginal *rates of substitution* between the public and private goods (say, between the public good and money) must coincide with the marginal *rate of transformation* at which the latter may be turned into the former. This is the equality known in traditional welfare economics as the *Bowen-Lindahl-Samuelson condition*. In view of our former discussion, this condition can be conceived as characterizing the set of interior and efficient allocations.

With such a characterization of efficiency as a reference point, we now turn to studying the performance of some alternative allocation mechanisms. For the sake of focus, we concentrate on just two of them. The first one reflects what is probably the most natural and intuitive approach to the problem at hand. It simply requests from the consumers that they propose their desired individual contributions to the provision of the public good. Unfortunately, this procedure turns out to display marked inefficiencies. Motivated by this unsatisfactory performance, we then study an alternative "successful" mechanism that guarantees the desired allocation efficiency. This is achieved, however, at the cost of relying on a substantially more abstract formulation, the messages required from the agents being much less intuitive or natural than in the former case.

3.2.1   Subscription mechanism

Consider a context in which each of the individuals $i = 1, 2, \ldots, n$ proposes, in an independent (i.e., "simultaneous") manner, a respective contribution $\xi_i \geq 0$ for the provision of the public good. Given these proposals, every agent i is requested an actual contribution $c_i = \xi_i$ (i.e., equal to her proposal), all these contributions then jointly used to finance a level of public good equal to $\sum_{i=1}^{n} c_i$.

The procedure described defines a strategic-form game in which the strategy space for each individual i is $S_i = [0, w_i]$ and the payoff functions are given by

$$\pi_i(\xi_1, \ldots, \xi_n) = U_i\left(\sum_{j=1}^{n} \xi_j, \xi_i\right) \qquad (i = 1, 2, \ldots, n),$$

for each strategy profile $(\xi_1, \ldots, \xi_n) \in S$. It is straightforward to check that necessary and sufficient conditions for a particular profile $\hat{\xi} = (\hat{\xi}_i)_{i=1}^{n}$ to define a Nash equilibrium are as follows:

$$\frac{\partial U_i(x(\hat{\xi}), \hat{\xi}_i)}{\partial x} + \frac{\partial U_i(x(\hat{\xi}), \hat{\xi}_i)}{\partial c_i} = 0 \qquad (i = 1, 2, \ldots, n), \tag{3.24}$$

where

$$x(\hat{\xi}) \equiv \sum_{i=1}^{n} \hat{\xi}_i. \tag{3.25}$$

Rewriting each of the conditions in (3.24) as follows,

$$-\frac{\frac{\partial U_i(x(\hat{\xi}), \hat{\xi}_i)}{\partial x}}{\frac{\partial U_i(x(\hat{\xi}), \hat{\xi}_i)}{\partial c_i}} = 1 \qquad (i = 1, 2, \ldots, n)$$

and adding them, we obtain

$$\sum_{i=1}^{n} -\frac{\frac{\partial U_i(x(\hat{\xi}), \hat{\xi}_i)}{\partial x}}{\frac{\partial U_i(x(\hat{\xi}), \hat{\xi}_i)}{\partial c_i}} = n. \tag{3.26}$$

Comparing (3.26) and (3.23), we conclude that the first-order conditions that characterize the Nash equilibrium of the subscription mechanism are incompatible (as long as $n \geq 2$) with the Bowen-Lindahl-Samuelson condition. It follows, therefore, that the allocation attained by this mechanism (i.e., at an equilibrium of the induced game) is inefficient.

To show *directly* that the allocation induced by the mechanism

$$\left(\hat{x}, (\hat{c}_i)_{i=1}^{n}\right) \equiv \left(x(\hat{\xi}), (\hat{\xi}_i)_{i=1}^{n}\right)$$

is inefficient, it is enough to find an alternative (feasible) allocation that dominates it in the Pareto sense. Consider, for example, the allocation $(\tilde{x}, (\tilde{c}_i)_{i=1}^{n})$ that, starting from the Nash equilibrium $(\hat{x}, (\hat{c}_i)_{i=1}^{n})$, contemplates a "marginal" increase in the contribution of each individual of the same magnitude, i.e., $\tilde{c}_i - \hat{c}_i = \Delta$ for all $i = 1, 2, \ldots, n$ and some small $\Delta > 0$. Obviously, $\tilde{x} > \hat{x}$. Furthermore, in view of (3.24), the effect of this *joint* change on the utility of *each* individual i may be suitably approximated by

$$\frac{\partial U_i(\hat{x}, \hat{\xi}_i)}{\partial x} n\Delta + \frac{\partial U_i(\hat{x}, \hat{\xi}_i)}{\partial c_i} \Delta = \frac{\partial U_i(\hat{x}, \hat{\xi}_i)}{\partial x} (n-1)\Delta,$$

which is positive because every $U_i(\cdot)$ is increasing in its first argument. Thus, every individual may gain from such a change, which reconfirms the fact that the original Nash allocation is Pareto inefficient. The intuitive reason for this conclusion should be clear: individuals, in a Nash equilibrium, do not take into account the effect of their contribution on the overall utility of all other agents. In essence, they treat the public good as a private good, which entails that their desired contribution to it is inefficiently small. This effect, which is the key strategic feature of public-good allocation problems, is often known in the literature as the free rider problem.

3.2.2   *An efficient mechanism*

In view of the unsatisfactory performance induced by the "natural" subscription mechanism considered in Subsection 3.2.1, one may rightly wonder whether there are other mechanisms, perhaps more complex or less natural, that may tackle the public-good problem successfully. These are the sort of issues addressed by the so-called implementation literature. In general, this literature poses the following kind of questions: Is it possible to design a mechanism that reconciles individual incentives and some (given) standard of social desirability? What criteria of social desirability are consistent with a certain predetermined notion of strategic stability (e.g., Nash equilibrium)? To formulate and answer such questions in a general (and therefore abstract) fashion will be the objective of Section 3.3 below. For the moment, we restrict attention to the present public-good problem and ask for it the following more concrete question: Is there any mechanism guaranteeing that, at any Nash equilibrium of the induced game, the allocation of resources (in particular, the level of public good determined) is efficient? A positive answer was constructively provided by Walker (1981), who proposed the following, rather simple, mechanism.[36]

Each individual sends a message, $m_i \in \mathbb{R}$ (i.e., some real number, positive or negative), in an independent fashion. Given the profile of messages sent $m \equiv (m_1, m_2, \ldots, m_n)$, the mechanism determines a public-good level x as follows:

$$x = \psi(m) \equiv \max \left\{ \frac{\sum_{i=1}^{n} m_i}{n}, 0 \right\}, \tag{3.27}$$

that is, x is made equal to the average of the messages sent, as long as this number is nonnegative; otherwise, it is made equal to zero. On the other hand, the contribution

---

[36] Another similar, but more complicated, mechanism was proposed earlier by Hurwicz (1979).

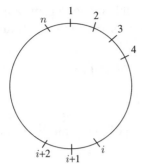

Figure 3.3: Players' arrangement in Walker's mechanism.

of private good, c_i, required from each individual i is determined as follows:

$$c_i = \left(\frac{1}{n} + m_{i+1} - m_{i+2}\right)\psi(m) \qquad (i = 1, 2, \ldots, n), \tag{3.28}$$

where the player indices are normalized to "modulo n" (that is, $n + 1$ is identified with 1, and $n + 2$ with 2, under the implicit assumption that $n \geq 3$).

By way of illustration, we may think of the individuals as being arranged clockwise along a circle, with the individuals indexed 1 and n being adjacent to each other (see Figure 3.3). With this interpretation, agents $i + 1$ and $i + 2$ are simply the two individuals who are closest to i, moving clockwise along the circle.

To have (3.27) and (3.28) represent a suitable basis for constructing a game, the outcome associated with *any* possible message profile must be well defined – in particular, the resulting allocation must be always feasible, both at the individual as well as the aggregate level. First, concerning the requirement of *individual feasibility*, we abstract here from the difficult problems it entails by simply making the following extreme assumption:

$$w_i = \infty \qquad (i = 1, 2, \ldots, n);$$

that is, *no* contribution demanded from an agent may be judged individually unfeasible since the amount of resources (i.e., private good) available to any of them for this purpose is virtually unlimited. On the other hand, pertaining to *aggregate feasibility*, we need to check that, for *any* arbitrary message profile m, the individual contributions are sufficient, in total, to satisfy the input required for the production of the public good. To this end, we add the different expressions in (3.28) for all $i = 1, 2, \ldots, n$ and obtain

$$\sum_{i=1}^{n} c_i = \sum_{i=1}^{n} \left(\frac{1}{n} + m_{i+1} - m_{i+2}\right)\psi(m) = \psi(m) = x. \tag{3.29}$$

This implies that, for any message profile m, the set of individual contributions $(c_i)_{i=1}^{n}$ determined by the mechanism is exactly enough to produce the public-good level x induced by those same messages. That is, the desired aggregate feasibility of the mechanism is guaranteed in every case.

We conclude, therefore, that (3.27) and (3.28) suitably induce a game among the n individuals involved, with respective strategy spaces $S_i = \mathbb{R}$ and payoff functions

$$\pi_i(m_1, \ldots, m_n) = U_i\left(\psi(m), \left(\frac{1}{n} + m_{i+1} - m_{i+2}\right)\psi(m)\right)$$

$$(i = 1, 2, \ldots, n).$$

Let $m^* = (m_1^*, m_2^*, \ldots, m_n^*)$ be a Nash equilibrium of this game,[37] and denote

$$p_i^* \equiv \frac{1}{n} + m_{i+1}^* - m_{i+2}^* \qquad (i = 1, 2, \ldots, n) \tag{3.30}$$

$$x^* \equiv \psi(m^*) \tag{3.31}$$

$$c_i^* \equiv p_i^* x^*. \tag{3.32}$$

We now show that the collection $[(p_i^*)_{i=1}^n, (c_i^*)_{i=1}^n, x^*]$ defines a *Lindahl equilibrium* for the present economic environment.[38] That is, it satisfies the following three conditions:

(a) $\sum_{i=1}^n p_i^* = 1$.
(b) $\sum_{i=1}^n c_i^* = x^*$.
(c) For all $i = 1, 2, \ldots, n$, (x^*, c_i^*) is a solution of the following optimization problem:

$$\max_{c_i, x} U_i(x, c_i) \quad \text{s.t.}$$

$$p_i^* x = c_i \tag{3.33}$$

$$c_i, \, x \geq 0.$$

Condition (a) is satisfied by mere construction. It ensures that the "personalized prices" paid by the different individuals are enough to cover the unit cost of production of the public good. On the other hand, condition (b) is a direct consequence of the aggregate feasibility displayed by the allocation rule (cf. (3.29)), as particularized to the equilibrium message profile m^*. Finally, condition (c) follows from the ensuing argument.

Suppose, for the sake of contradiction, that $[(p_i^*)_{i=1}^n, (c_i^*)_{i=1}^n, x^*]$ does *not* define a Lindahl equilibrium. Then, for some individual $i \in \{1, 2, \ldots, n\}$, there exists a public-good level $\tilde{x} \neq x^*$ such that

$$U_i(\tilde{x}, p_i^* \tilde{x}) > U_i(x^*, p_i^* x^*). \tag{3.34}$$

---

[37] It follows from Exercise 3.12 that, provided there exists a Lindahl equilibrium for the underlying economic environment (see below for a definition), there always exists a Nash equilibrium for the present game.

[38] The reader may refer to Varian (1992) or Mas-Colell et al. (1995) for a discussion of this standard economic notion. It represents the natural public-good counterpart of Walrasian equilibrium. In an only-private-good economy, Walras equilibrium sets (common) equilibrium prices to reconcile individuals' (typically heterogenous) decisions and obtain interagent consistency (market clearing). By contrast, in a public-good economy, Lindahl equilibrium allows for (typically heterogenous or "personalized") prices to reconcile individuals' diverse preferences and achieve interagent consensus (or consistency) in their public-good choices. In either case, the respective equilibrium concept guarantees efficiency under rather weak regularity conditions.

Now choose

$$\tilde{m}_i = n\tilde{x} - \sum_{j \neq i} m_j^*,$$

so that

$$U_i(\tilde{x}, p_i^*\tilde{x}) = U_i\left(\psi(\tilde{m}_i, m_{-i}^*), \left(\frac{1}{n} + m_{i+1}^* - m_{i+2}^*\right) \psi(\tilde{m}_i, m_{-i}^*)\right).$$

Then, since

$$U_i(x^*, p_i^*x^*) = U_i\left(\psi(m_i^*, m_{-i}^*), \left(\frac{1}{n} + m_{i+1}^* - m_{i+2}^*\right) \psi(m_i^*, m_{-i}^*)\right),$$

the inequality (3.34) leads to a contradiction with the hypothesis that $m^* = (m_1^*, m_2^*, \ldots, m_n^*)$ defines a Nash equilibrium of the game.

Once it has been shown that the outcome induced by the Nash equilibrium m^* is a Lindahl allocation, its efficiency merely becomes a direct consequence of a well-known general result that establishes the efficiency of these allocations. In our present simple context, however, we can provide a straightforward proof of this conclusion by relying on the Bowen-Lindahl-Samuelson condition presented in (3.23). Let $[(p_i^*)_{i=1}^n, (c_i^*)_{i=1}^n, x^*]$ be the Lindahl equilibrium induced by m^*, as explained above. For each individual i, the pair (c_i^*, x^*) must be a solution to (3.33). Assuming, for simplicity, that it is an interior solution, the following first-order conditions must hold:

$$-\frac{\frac{\partial U_i(x^*, c_i^*)}{\partial x}}{\frac{\partial U_i(x^*, c_i^*)}{\partial c_i}} = p_i^*$$

for each $i = 1, 2, \ldots, n$. Therefore, in view of (3.30), we have

$$\sum_{i=1}^n -\frac{\frac{\partial U_i(x^*, c_i^*)}{\partial x}}{\frac{\partial U_i(x^*, c_i^*)}{\partial c_i}} = \sum_{i=1}^n p_i^* = 1,$$

which is precisely the Bowen-Lindahl-Samuelson condition.

In sum, we have shown that the Walker mechanism is a successful one, in the sense of being able to tackle effectively the acute free rider problem that impairs the performance of other more naive procedures – e.g., the subscription mechanism studied in Subsection 3.2.1, where individual incentives and efficiency were shown to be incompatible desiderata. The success is achieved, however, at the cost of relying on a somewhat abstract procedure, whose rules and messages lack a direct intuitive interpretation. This may well be judged a significant drawback because, typically, one would expect that intuitive mechanisms prove more readily applicable to real-world allocation problems than those that are less intuitive or transparent. After all, one should not forget that the desired outcome is attained only *at an equilibrium* of the induced game. And, in general, it is reasonable to expect that the plausibility of equilibrium behavior in any given game should hinge on how easily and transparently players understand the strategic situation in which they are involved.

Thus, a broad insight to be gained from contrasting the different procedures studied in this section (i.e., the subscription and the Walker mechanisms) may be formulated as follows. In general, a significant trade-off should be expected between the straightforwardness or intuitive appeal of a mechanism and its effectiveness in addressing "difficult" incentive problems. Analogously, one should also expect a similar trade-off to arise if, rather than being concerned with the difficulty of a particular problem, the aim were to tackle a wide set of different incentive problems with a common or canonical approach. This is indeed the approach undertaken in Subsection 3.3.2 below where, by relying on a single but quite abstract mechanism, all problems that happen to have *some* Nash-compatible solution can be suitably addressed.

3.3   Mechanism design (II): Nash implementation

The "implementation problem" is, in essence, a problem of institutional design. It starts with a collection of agents, a set of possible outcomes, a certain universe of environments, and the specification of a desired collection of outcomes for each of the possible environments (the so-called social choice rule). With these data of the problem in place, the designer (the planner, the society, the theorist, . . .) asks whether a certain institution – a game, with well-specified rules – can be *designed* so that, in every possible environment and for every possible equilibrium of the resulting game, the range of outcomes induced coincides with those that were specified as "desired" under those circumstances.

In general, the answer to this question obviously must depend on what game-theoretic concept of equilibrium is to be used. If the equilibrium notion is either very restrictive (e.g., players must use dominant strategies) or the opposite (e.g., players can use any nondominated strategy), the problem may be quite hard to solve. In the first case (restrictive equilibrium notions), the difficulty is to design a game whose equilibria span the range of desired outcomes (in particular, it may be even difficult to guarantee that an equilibrium exists in some cases). In the second case (unrestrictive equilibrium notions), the problem is quite the opposite: in general, it may be hard to avoid that some of the equilibria end up producing undesired outcomes. In this section, we tread on a sort of middle ground in this respect and focus on the Nash equilibrium concept as our leading game-theoretic tool. Later, we enrich the scope of equilibrium notions to be used (see Sections 5.4 and 7.3.2), an approach that proves effective in enlarging the range of feasible implementation in some cases.

3.3.1   *Formulation of the design problem**

As advanced, the design problem includes the following components.

1. A finite *collection of agents* $N = \{1, 2, \ldots, n\}$.
2. An *outcome space* Ω, sometimes called the set of social states. These are the objects over which the designer and the agents have their respective preferences defined.

3. A *set of environments* $\mathcal{E}$. Each particular environment $e \in \mathcal{E}$ specifies all details that are relevant to the problem. In general, these may include preferences, endowments, exogenous circumstances, etc. However, to simplify the problem, we follow a common practice in this literature and assume that the only variable components of the environment are agents' preferences.

   Specifically, let $\mathcal{U}$ denote the set of von Neumann-Morgenstern utility functions on Ω. Each agent i is supposed to have utility function $U_i(\cdot)$ belonging to some individual subset $\mathcal{U}_i \subset \mathcal{U}$. Thus, as the universe of possible environments, we postulate $\mathcal{E} = \mathcal{U}_1 \times \mathcal{U}_2 \times \cdots \times \mathcal{U}_n$; i.e., any utility profile $U = (U_1, U_2, \ldots, U_n)$ is a valid environment.

4. A *social choice rule (SCR)* $\phi : \mathcal{E} \rightrightarrows \Omega$. This is a correspondence that defines the standard of desired performance. For every environment $e \in \mathcal{E}$, it determines the set of outcomes $\phi(e) \subset \Omega$ that are to be judged as satisfactory or admissible.

The above items define the *data* of the implementation problem. In particular, the set of possible environments $\mathcal{E}$ defines its *scope*, i.e., determines how "universal" (or ambitious) one is in posing the implementation problem. Often, the focus is on so-called *economic environments*. Then, the outcome space Ω is identified with the set of (feasible) allocations and the family of admissible utilities in each $\mathcal{U}_i$ typically are assumed to satisfy the standard conditions of continuity, quasi-concavity, etc.

On the other hand, the nature of the SCR ϕ reflects how "specific" the solution of the implementation problem is required to be. Thus, ϕ could be simply a function specifying a *single* desired outcome for every environment, or it could be a quite thick correspondence allowing for a wide set of different outcomes. For example, in the public-good scenario presented in Section 3.2, the SCR might select a particular Lindahl allocation for every possible preference profile of individuals or allow instead for, say, any efficient allocation.

Concerning now the "unknowns" of the implementation problem, this role is played by the *mechanism* that is to be *designed* so as to attain the desired performance. In this context, a mechanism is identified with what game theorists call a *game form,* here to be considered in its normal or strategic formulation. Heuristically, a game form simply consists of a detailed specification of the "rules of the game," i.e., the strategies available to the players and the mapping from strategies into outcomes. Formally, that is, a *mechanism* (or game form) M is a collection $\{\{S_i\}_{i=1}^n, g\}$ where

- For each $i = 1, 2, \ldots, n$, S_i is agent i's strategy space.
- The function $g : S_1 \times \cdots \times S_n \to \Omega$ specifies the outcome associated to every possible strategy profile. It is called the *outcome function*.

Any such mechanism M by itself does not define a game. To obtain a strategic-form game from it, we need to supplement the rules provided by the mechanism with information on the players' evaluation of the different outcomes, i.e., their utility functions. Let $U = (U_1, U_2, \ldots, U_n)$ be some vector of prevailing utility functions. Then, the pair $\langle M, U \rangle$ defines the game $G \langle M, U \rangle = \{N, \{S_i\}, \{\pi_i\}\}$ where the set

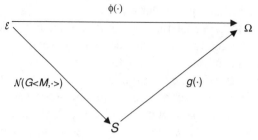

Figure 3.4: Nash implementation problem.

of players is $N = \{1, 2, \ldots, n\}$, their respective strategy spaces S_i are as given by M, and the payoff functions $\pi_i : S_1 \times \cdots \times S_n \to \mathbb{R}$ are defined as follows:

$$\forall s = (s_1, \ldots, s_n) \in S_1 \times \cdots \times S_n, \quad \pi_i(s) = U_i[g(s)].$$

Consider any SCR ϕ, as defined above. The objective is to find some mechanism M so that, for *any* particular utility profile $U \in \mathcal{E}$, the strategic-form game $G \langle M, U \rangle$ has the set of its Nash outcomes coincide with $\phi(U)$. More formally, denote by $\mathcal{N}(G)$ the set of pure-strategy[39] Nash equilibria of the game G. Then, our notion of "satisfactory implementation" is as described in the following definition.

Definition 3.1: *Let $\phi : \mathcal{E} \rightrightarrows \Omega$ be a SCR. Mechanism M is said to* Nash implement *ϕ if for all $U \in \mathcal{E}$, $g(\mathcal{N}(G \langle M, U \rangle)) = \phi(U)$.[40] If some such M exists, ϕ is called* Nash implementable.

The above definition embodies two reciprocal requirements. On the one hand, it demands that every Nash equilibrium of the game produces *only* outcomes that are qualified as admissible by the SCR ϕ. On the other hand, it requires as well that *every* admissible outcome should be attainable at some Nash equilibrium of the induced game. (This is sometimes described as reflecting *unbiasedness* on the part of mechanism). Diagrammatically, such a solution of the implementation problem may be illustrated in Figure 3.4. In terms of this diagram, it may be simply understood as a situation where the functions involved commute; i.e., any of the two "routes" of mapping $\mathcal{E}$ into Ω give rise to an identical correspondence.

As emphasized, what distinguishes the present implementation approach from other branches of economic analysis is that, for an implementation theorist, the allocation problem is tackled from the "designer's point of view" (see Hurwicz, 1972). Thus, a successful mechanism becomes the solution of the problem rather than a datum of it. It is, in a sense, an exercise in *institutional design*, where the wealth of possible mechanisms is explored unrestrained. And the aim is to achieve some twin compatibility: on the one hand, compatibility with a desired standard of

---

[39] Here, the discussion is restricted to Nash equilibria in pure strategies, as in Maskin's (1977) original approach to the problem. This approach, however, can be extended with some difficulty to encompass the possibility of mixed-strategy equilibria as well, as shown in Maskin (1999).

[40] As customary, we use the convention that a correspondence $h : X \rightrightarrows Y$ applied to a set $A \subset X$ consists of all those elements in Y that are in $h(x)$ for some $x \in A$. That is, $h(A) \equiv \bigcup_{x \in A} h(x)$.

performance, as embodied by the prespecified SCR; on the other hand, compatibility with individual incentives, as reflected here by the notion of Nash equilibrium.

3.3.2 *Partial characterization**

We now address the following issue.[41] Suppose we are given some particular SCR ϕ. Can we ascertain whether there is *some* mechanism M that Nash implements it? The key condition in this respect turns out to be what Maskin (1977; see also Maskin, 1999) called *monotonicity*. As we show below, an SCR ϕ must be monotonic if it is to be Nash implementable (i.e., this condition is *necessary* for implementability). But, in fact, this same condition also happens to be *sufficient* if (provided there are at least three agents) it is complemented by a requirement called *no veto power (NVP)*. In effect, this latter requirement happens to be very weak since it will be shown redundant (i.e., always satisfied) in many environments of interest – e.g., economic environments. Thus, in this sense, we can say that monotonicity is a necessary and often sufficient condition for Nash implementability.

Monotonicity is defined as follows.

> **Monotonicity (M)** An SCR ϕ is said to be *monotonic* if the following condition holds. Consider any utility profile U and choose an arbitrary $\omega \in \phi(U)$. Let U' be some other profile and suppose that whenever $U_i(\omega) \geq U_i(\hat{\omega})$ for some alternative outcome $\hat{\omega} \in \Omega$ and any $i \in N$, it also happens that $U_i'(\omega) \geq U_i'(\hat{\omega})$ for that *same i*. Then, it is required that $\omega \in \phi(U')$.

The intuition underlying condition (M) may be understood as follows. Focus on some utility profile and an admissible outcome (according to ϕ) for this profile. Then, if any other profile materializes for which such an outcome is always as good as before for every one (i.e., relative to any other alternative, it never falls in the corresponding bilateral utility comparison), that outcome must also qualify as admissible, according to ϕ, under the new circumstances. In a sense, monotonicity simply captures the natural idea that ϕ must be responsive to individuals' preferences. If the SCR is to be Nash implementable, some such condition would seem unavoidable. Indeed, this is confirmed by the following result.

Theorem 3.1 (Maskin, 1977): *Let ϕ be a Nash implementable SCR. Then, it is monotonic.*

Proof: Because ϕ is assumed Nash implementable, there is some mechanism, say M, that implements it. Let U be any utility profile and choose some $\omega \in \phi(U)$. Then, for some (pure-strategy) profile $s^* \in \mathcal{N}(G \langle M, U \rangle)$, we must have $g(s^*) = \omega$. Consider now any alternative profile U' such that

$$\forall i = 1, 2, \ldots, n, \ \forall \omega' \in \Omega, \quad U_i(\omega) \geq U_i(\omega') \Rightarrow U_i'(\omega) \geq U_i'(\omega').$$

Clearly, $s^* \in \mathcal{N}(G \langle M, U' \rangle)$, which implies (because M implements ϕ) that $\omega \in \phi(U')$. Thus, ϕ is monotonic, as desired. ∎

---

[41] Much of what is done in this subsection is borrowed from Repullo (1987).

How demanding is condition (M)? One quite restrictive implication of it is that any monotonic ϕ can respond *only* to ordinal information (see Exercise 3.14). To see, moreover, that even within the realm of ordinal SCRs, one can find interesting nonmonotonic instances, we now turn to an example that has received quite a lot of attention in the recent implementation literature: the biblically inspired King Solomon's dilemma. This problem is revisited in Section 5.4. There, a multistage mechanism is proposed that (despite the violation of monotonicity) addresses successfully a generalized version of the problem by relying on a natural refinement of the Nash equilibrium concept.

King Solomon faces the problem of deciding to which of two mothers, A or B, to assign a child in dispute. His desire is to give the child to the genuine mother. To extract the true information (that of course both women have, but not the King), he threatens to kill the baby if a consensus is not reached between the two women as to who is the real mother of the child. Formally, we can formulate the problem as follows. There are two possible environments: α and β. In the first one, the true mother is A, whereas in the second it is B. The possible outcomes in which the women have their preferences defined are

a : "the baby is given to A";
b : "the baby is given to B";
c : "the baby is killed".

Given these outcomes, the preferences of each woman in each of the environments are postulated as follows:

- In environment α, woman A has $U_A^\alpha(a) > U_A^\alpha(b) > U_A^\alpha(c)$, whereas woman B has $U_B^\alpha(b) > U_B^\alpha(c) > U_B^\alpha(a)$.
- In environment β, woman A has $U_A^\beta(a) > U_A^\beta(c) > U_A^\beta(b)$, and woman B has $U_B^\beta(b) > U_B^\beta(a) > U_B^\beta(c)$.

These preferences embody the distinctive features of the setup: each woman (true mother or not) prefers to have the child for herself, but the true mother prefers that the baby be given to the other woman rather than killed – the false mother has opposite preferences in this respect. On the other hand, the SCR (that may be conceived as reflecting the "preferences" of King Solomon) is simply given by

$$\phi(\alpha) = a; \quad \phi(\beta) = b.$$

This SCR is *not* monotonic. To see this, focus on environment α and compare its utilities $U_i^\alpha(\cdot)$, $i = A, B$, with those of environment β, $U_i^\beta(\cdot)$. Note, in particular, that outcome a (the selection of ϕ in environment α) is still the most preferred outcome in β for woman A, whereas it rises in the ranking of woman B when switching from α to β. By (M), we should have $\phi(\alpha) = a \in \phi(\beta)$, a contradiction with the fact that $\phi(\beta) = b$. Thus, King Solomon's ϕ is not monotonic, which in view of Theorem 3.1 implies that is *not* Nash implementable either.

In fact, there are also many well-known SCRs defined on economic setups that happen not to be monotonic. For example, the Lindahl (or Walras) rule that assigns to every economic environment its corresponding set of Lindahl (or Walras) allocations, or even the Pareto rule that associates the Pareto optimal (or efficient) allocations, are not monotonic – see Exercise 3.15. In general, one needs to contemplate some regularity (e.g., interiority) conditions, to ensure that condition (M) holds in those traditional cases (cf. Exercise 3.16). Some useful illustration of these matters is provided below when showing the Nash implementability of a Walras SCR in "regular" economies.

Given that monotonicity has been established to represent a *necessary* condition for Nash implementability, the following natural question arises: Is it also *sufficient?* In general, this turns out not to be the case and further conditions are needed. One of them is simply that there should be at least three agents. As will become clear from the constructive proof of Theorem 3.2 below, this is essentially an issue of endowing the design problem with enough "strategic richness" to tackle individual manipulation incentives.

On the other hand, one also needs to extend a bit the notion of "responsiveness to individual preferences" that, as explained above, is the main idea embodied by condition (M). To define the additional condition required, it is convenient to introduce some notation. Given any outcome $\omega \in \Omega$ and utility function $U_i \in \mathcal{U}_i$ let

$$L(\omega, U_i) \equiv \{\omega' \in \Omega : U_i(\omega') \le U_i(\omega)\}. \tag{3.35}$$

That is, $L(\omega, U_i)$ represents what, in traditional microeconomics, would be labeled the *lower-contour set* induced by utility function U_i and outcome ω. With this notation in hand, we formulate the referred additional condition as follows.

No veto power (NVP) An SCR ϕ is said to satisfy *no veto power* if the following condition holds. Given any utility profile U, if there exists some $i \in N$ and $\omega \in \Omega$ such that, for all $j \ne i$, $L(\omega, U_j) = \Omega$, then $\omega \in \phi(U)$.

Condition (NVP) simply posits that, if all but one of the agents agree that a certain outcome is among the best possible in a particular environment, the SCR must include this outcome as well for that environment. Note that this condition holds in any of the typical economic contexts where there exists at least one perfectly divisible commodity everyone desires (i.e., utility functions are strictly increasing in it). In those setups, there is *no* allocation that two different individuals have in their respectively most preferred sets and, consequently, (NVP) holds trivially (i.e., voidly). We are now ready to establish a partial converse to Theorem 3.1.

Theorem 3.2 (Maskin, 1977, 1999): *Assume $n \ge 3$, and let ϕ be an SCR that satisfies (M) and (NVP). Then, ϕ is Nash implementable.*

Proof: The proof is constructive. That is, we shall explicitly describe a mechanism $M = \{\{S_i\}_{i=1}^n, g\}$ that implements any ϕ satisfying the contemplated assumptions. The strategy spaces S_i are identical for each agent i. They are given by $S_i = \mathcal{E} \times \Omega \times \mathbb{N}$, a typical element $s_i = (U^i, \omega^i, k^i)$ specifying a utility *profile* $U^i = (U_1^i, U_2^i, \ldots, U_n^i)$, an outcome ω^i, and a natural number k^i. (Note that a superindex here is used to identify the player whose strategy is being specified and does not refer to players' attributes – e.g., preferences.) Given any strategy profile $s = [(U^i, \omega^i, k^i)]_{i=1}^n$, the prescription induced by the outcome function g depends on which of the two following (exhaustive) possibilities apply:

(†) If there exists some $i \in N$ and $(\hat{U}, \hat{\omega}, \hat{k})$ such that $\hat{\omega} \in \phi(\hat{U})$ and, for all $j \neq i$, $s_j = (\hat{U}, \hat{\omega}, \hat{k})$, then

$$g(s) = \begin{cases} \omega^i & \text{if } \omega^i \in L(\hat{\omega}, \hat{U}_i) \\ \hat{\omega} & \text{otherwise.} \end{cases} \qquad (3.36)$$

(‡) If (†) does not apply, then $g(s) = \omega^i$ where i is chosen among those agents j who chose the highest k^j – say, the player with the lowest index.

We need to show that both $\phi(U) \subset g(\mathcal{N}(G \langle M, U \rangle))$ and $g(\mathcal{N}(G \langle M, U \rangle)) \subset \phi(U)$ hold for all $U \in \mathcal{E}$. First, we address the inclusion $\phi(U) \subset g(\mathcal{N}(G \langle M, U \rangle))$. Choose any $\omega \in \phi(U)$ and consider the strategy profile s where $s_i = (U, \omega, 1)$ for all $i \in N$. To see that s defines a Nash equilibrium of $G \langle M, U \rangle$, note that, by deviating to some $(U^i, \omega^i, k^i) \neq (U, \omega, 1)$, player i can attain ω^i only if $\omega^i \in L(\hat{\omega}, U_i)$ – otherwise, the mechanism prescribes the original ω. Thus, since any outcome $\omega^i \neq \omega$ that is achievable to player i has $U_i(\omega) \geq U_i(\omega^i)$, no unilateral deviation can be profitable.

To prove the converse inclusion $g(\mathcal{N}(G \langle M, U \rangle)) \subset \phi(U)$, consider any arbitrary $s = [(U^i, \omega^i, k^i)]_{i=1}^n \in \mathcal{N}(G \langle M, U \rangle)$. It has to be checked that $g(s) \in \phi(U)$. The argument is now somewhat more involved and needs contemplating three cases.

(a) Suppose that $s_j = (U', \omega, k)$ for all $j \in N$ and assume as well that $\omega \in \phi(U')$. Then, $g(s) = \omega$ from (†). Consider now any given player i and any $\hat{\omega} \in \Omega$ such that $U_i'(\omega) \geq U_i'(\hat{\omega})$. Relying on (†) again, we know that this player i could deviate to some $\hat{s}_i = (\tilde{U}, \hat{\omega}, \tilde{k})$ – arbitrary $\tilde{U}$ and $\tilde{k}$ – and obtain $g(\hat{s}_i, s_{-i}) = \hat{\omega}$. Since this deviation should not be profitable for i because $s \in \mathcal{N}(G \langle M, U \rangle)$, it follows that $U_i(\omega) \geq U_i(\hat{\omega})$. In sum, we conclude that $U_i'(\omega) \geq U_i'(\hat{\omega}) \Rightarrow U_i(\omega) \geq U_i(\hat{\omega})$. By (M), this implies that $\omega \in \phi(U)$, as desired.

(b) Suppose, as before, that $s_j = (U', \omega, k)$ for all $j \in N$ but now assume $\omega \notin \phi(U')$. Then, (‡) applies and any player i could deviate to some $\tilde{s}_i = (\tilde{U}, \tilde{\omega}, \tilde{k})$ with $\tilde{k} > k$ and obtain $g(\tilde{s}_i, s_{-i}) = \tilde{\omega}$. Since the outcome $\tilde{\omega}$ is arbitrary and $s \in \mathcal{N}(G \langle M, U \rangle)$, it follows that $U_i(\omega) \geq U_i(\tilde{\omega})$ for all $i \in N$. Then, (NVP) implies again that $\omega \in \phi(U)$.

(c) Finally, suppose that there are two agents who play different strategies at equilibrium. By necessity, there must be at least $n - 1$ such agents

i for whom the remaining players in $N\setminus\{i\}$ do not all play the same strategy. (Note that this presumes $n \geq 3$.) Each of those $n - 1$ agents could obtain, given the strategies of others, any outcome ω desired by playing a strategy $s_i' = (U, \omega, \tilde{k})$ with $\tilde{k} > k^j$, $j \neq i$. The fact that $s \in \mathcal{N}(G \langle M, U \rangle)$ implies that $U_i(g(s)) \geq U_i(\omega)$ for any $\omega \in \Omega$ and each of the $n - 1$ players considered. By (NVP), this requires that $g(s) \in \phi(U)$.

In view of the fact (a), (b), and (c) are exhaustive contingencies, we conclude that $g(\mathcal{N}(G \langle M, U \rangle)) \subset \phi(U)$, as claimed. ∎

Despite its abstract form, the "universal" mechanism proposed in the constructive proof of Theorem 3.2 is rather intuitive and its main features can be heuristically understood as follows. On the one hand, if agents agree on the prevailing environment as well as on an outcome that is admissible for that environment, the mechanism simply abides by the agents' consensus. The problem, of course, is how to make every such "true and admissible consensus" a Nash equilibrium. To achieve it, the crucial issue is how to deter *unilateral* deviations, the sole criterion of strategic stability embodied by the Nash equilibrium concept. This is precisely the purpose of (3.36), which ensures that no single deviating player may ever gain if indeed the remaining players are agreeing on the *true* environment. Therefore, if a deviation nevertheless occurs, it must be because the other players are "lying" and this fact provides a possibility for the player in question to unveil it in a credible (i.e., incentive-compatible) manner. This is the key feature of the mechanism that deters players from reaching a misleading consensus – or, reciprocally, that ensures that every consensus is genuinely informative of the environment. The only pending point concerns how to rule out that an equilibrium may take place under some sort of disagreement among the players. This is the role played by (‡), which is geared toward discarding that any such possibility could ever become an equilibrium: by granting extreme manipulation possibilities to almost every player in this case, some player will always have something to gain by deviating.

Remark 3.1: *Full information extraction*

> It is interesting to observe that the canonical mechanism proposed in (†) and (‡) demands from the agents all the information they have. That is, agents are not simply asked to reveal their own preferences but they are required to submit the whole (same) information they all share about each other's preferences. Thus, in this mechanism, the implicit assumption of complete information that underlies the Nash equilibrium concept (i.e., that every agent must know all relevant details of the game) is introduced explicitly into the game itself through the players' strategy spaces. ◆

To end with a simple example, consider an exchange economy with perfectly divisible goods, as traditionally considered in general equilibrium theory (see, e.g., Mas-Colell *et al.*, 1995). Specifically, suppose that each agent $i \in \{1, 2, \ldots, n\}$ is endowed with a certain (fixed) amount of every good $k \in \{1, 2, \ldots, m\}$, $y_{ik} \geq 0$, and let $U_i : \mathbb{R}^m_+ \to \mathbb{R}$ stand for player i's utility, defined on her consumption bundles. Furthermore, assume that the set $\mathcal{U}_i$ of permissible utilities is such that, for every profile $(U_1, U_2, \ldots, U_n) \in \mathcal{E} \equiv \mathcal{U}_1 \times \mathcal{U}_2 \times \cdots \times \mathcal{U}_n$, the following conditions are satisfied: (a) the individual utilities are quasi-concave and strictly increasing; (b) the set of Walrasian allocations (i.e., allocations obtained at some Walrasian equilibrium) is both nonempty and *interior*. Now define the Walrasian correspondence $\phi_w : \mathcal{E} \rightrightarrows \Omega$ as the mapping that associates to every $e \in \mathcal{E}$ its corresponding Walrasian allocations. We next show that, if $n \geq 3$, the SCR ϕ_w is Nash implementable.

In view of Theorem 3.2, it is enough to show that conditions (NVP) and (M) are verified. Concerning (NVP), this is obviously the case because utility functions are assumed strictly increasing (recall our previous discussion on this issue). On the other hand, to show that (M) holds, consider any permissible utility profile $U = (U_1, U_2, \ldots, U_n)$ and let $\omega = \left[(x_{ik})_{k=1}^m \right]_{i=1}^n \in \Omega$ be a corresponding Walras allocation, where $x_i \equiv (x_{ik})_{k=1}^m$ stands for the consumption bundle associated to agent i in this allocation. Since ω is part of a Walras equilibrium, there are some associated equilibrium prices $p = (p_1, p_2, \ldots, p_m)$ such that, for every $i \in N$,

$$\forall \tilde{x}_i \in \mathbb{R}^m_+, \quad \sum_{k=1}^m p_k \tilde{x}_{ik} \leq \sum_{k=1}^m p_k y_{ik} \Rightarrow U_i(x_i) \geq U_i(\tilde{x}_i). \tag{3.37}$$

Now, consider some alternative utility profile $U' = (U'_1, U'_2, \ldots, U'_n)$ that verifies the hypothesis of condition (M), relative to U and ω. That is,[42]

$$\forall \hat{\omega} = \left[(\hat{x}_{ik})_{k=1}^m \right]_{i=1}^n \in \Omega, \ \forall i \in N,$$

$$U_i(x_i) \geq U_i(\hat{x}_i) \Rightarrow U'_i(x_i) \geq U'_i(\hat{x}_i). \tag{3.38}$$

We need to show ω is also a Walras allocation for utility profile U'. This demands two conditions. One of them, the *aggregate feasibility* of the allocation,

$$\sum_{i=1}^n x_{ik} = \sum_{i=1}^n y_{ik} \quad (k = 1, 2, \ldots, m),$$

is trivially true because it does not depend on individuals' utilities. For the second condition, i.e., *individual optimality* relative to suitable equilibrium prices, consider the same equilibrium prices p that supported ω above. As a counterpart to (3.37), it needs to be shown that

$$\forall \tilde{x}_i \in \mathbb{R}^m_+, \quad \sum_{k=1}^m p_k \tilde{x}_{ik} \leq \sum_{k=1}^m p_k y_{ik} \Rightarrow U'_i(x_i) \geq U'_i(\tilde{x}_i).$$

But this clearly holds, by virtue of (3.37) and (3.38), which implies that, for each $i \in N$, the lower-contour sets for U_i passing through x_i, $L(\omega, U_i)$, are included in those induced by U'_i, $L(\omega, U'_i)$ – recall (3.35). Note that, as illustrated in

---

[42] Graphically speaking, this condition can be conceived as reflecting a situation in which the indifference curves of each agent i passing through her respective x_i "bend inward" when switching from U_i to U'_i.

Exercises 3.15 and 3.16, this conclusion crucially relies on the fact that the Walrasian allocation is interior (i.e., $x_{ik} > 0$ for every i and all k) and the assumption that every utility function in $\mathcal{U}_i$ is quasi-concave.

3.4 Markets (I): macroeconomic coordination failures*

The use of game theory in economics has not been limited to problems of a microeconomic nature. In the last decades, it has also been applied to the study of a wide variety of macroeconomic phenomena, approached from a strategic perspective. Here, we focus on a simple model inspired by the work of Bryant (1983; see also Bryant, 1994) whose objective is to illustrate in a stylized form the consistency between Keynesian macroeconomic theory and the rationality paradigm espoused by classical game theory.

Consider the following "macroeconomic" context. The economy is segmented into K sectors ($K > 1$), each of them having I individuals ($I > 1$) working in them. All the n ($\equiv K \times I$) individuals in the economy have an identical utility function

$$U : \mathbb{R}_+^2 \to \mathbb{R}, \quad (c_{ik}^1, c_{ik}^2) \to U(c_{ik}^1, c_{ik}^2),$$

where c_{ik}^1 and c_{ik}^2 are the amounts consumed of each of the two goods, 1 and 2, by the individual $i = 1, 2, \ldots, I$ of sector $k = 1, 2, \ldots, K$. It will be posited that $U(\cdot)$ is differentiable, quasi-concave, and strictly increasing in its two arguments. Good 1 is interpreted as leisure and good 2 is conceived as a material consumption good that is produced by means of a collection of intermediate products, as presently described.

Each individual is endowed with a perfectly divisible unit of time that may be directed to one of two uses. On the one hand, she may "consume" it as leisure that, as indicated, is one of the arguments of her utility function. On the other hand, the complementary fraction of time that she devotes to "work" is used to produce (by herself) a certain amount of intermediate good with a constant-returns technology. Thus, without loss of generality, it can be postulated that x_{ik} units of work produce an identical amount z_{ik} of intermediate product, i.e., $z_{ik} = x_{ik}$.

The intermediate products obtained in each separate sector are assumed heterogeneous commodities and used to produce the consumption good (good 2) in fixed proportions, i.e., through a constant-returns technology of the so-called Leontieff type. More specifically, this technology is captured by a production function, $f : \mathbb{R}_+^K \to \mathbb{R}$, that, given the total amounts $z_k \equiv \sum_{i=1}^I z_{ik}$ of intermediate goods produced in each sector k ($k = 1, 2, \ldots, K$), induces a production of good 2 equal to

$$f(z_1, z_2, \ldots, z_K) = \min\{z_1, z_2, \ldots, z_K\}.$$

In this context, the allocation procedure is assumed to be conducted as follows. First, all individuals ik ($i = 1, 2, \ldots, I, k = 1, 2, \ldots, K$) must decide simultaneously how much work to devote to the production of their respective intermediate product. Once these decisions have been adopted, the corresponding amounts produced $z_{ik} (= x_{ik})$ are sent to the "marketplace" where the firms involved in the production of good 2 buy the required intermediate products in a perfectly competitive environment and all their respective markets clear.[43] By Walras law (see Mas-Colell *et al.*, 1995, Ch. 17), the income obtained by individuals in this manner induces an aggregate demand for good 2 that clears its market as well.

The procedure described can be formulated as a strategic-form game among the n individuals, the payoffs earned with each strategy profile $x = ((x_{ik})_{i=1}^{I})_{k=1}^{K} \in [0, 1]^n$ being those anticipated from the induced competitive allocation taking place in the markets for intermediate products. To be precise, let $p(x) \equiv (p_k(x))_{k=1}^{K}$ be the vector of equilibrium prices determined in the intermediate-good markets for each possible strategy profile x, where prices are expressed in terms of good 2 (chosen as the numeraire). Further denote $x_k \equiv \sum_{i=1}^{I} x_{ik}$. Then, by standard arguments in general equilibrium theory (see again Mas-Colell *et al.*, 1995), we know that

$$\left[x_{k'} > \min_{k=1,\ldots,K} \{x_k\} \right] \Rightarrow p_{k'}(x) = 0. \tag{3.39}$$

That is, any good displaying a positive excess supply at equilibrium must have a zero equilibrium price associated with it. On the other hand, whenever there are at least two intermediate products for which demand equals supply, the setup proposed allows for a wide multiplicity of possible equilibrium prices. Specifically, the only further condition (i.e., in addition to (3.39)) that *completely* characterizes the *set* of equilibrium prices is

$$\sum_{k=1}^{K} p_k(x) = 1; \quad p_k(x) \geq 0 \qquad (k = 1, \ldots, K). \tag{3.40}$$

This condition simply reflects the requirement that the price of the consumption good (equal to one, since it is the numeraire) must equal its unit (marginal) cost of production. Thus, to summarize, for a price-formation rule $[p_k(\cdot)]_{k=1}^{K}$ to qualify as valid in the postulated competitive environment, it has only to meet the following two conditions:

(a) It must prescribe a null price for those intermediate products in excess supply.

(b) The (nonnegative) prices of the remaining intermediated products (i.e., those in zero excess supply) are to induce in total an average production cost for the final good, $\sum_{k=1}^{K} p_k(\cdot)$, equal to one.

Given the indeterminacy displayed by (b), some price selection rule is required to close the model. Since the choice made in this respect does not affect the gist of the analysis, we simply postulate the following symmetric formulation:

$$\left[x_{k'} = x_{k''} = \min_{k=1,\ldots,K} \{x_k\} \right] \Rightarrow p_{k'}(x) = p_{k''}(x). \tag{3.41}$$

---

[43] Note that the number of firms producing good 2 is irrelevant because the production technology displays constant returns. Therefore, under perfect competition, the particular way total production is to be distributed among existing firms is indeterminate but also irrelevant.

Consider the price-formation rule $[p_k(\cdot)]_{k=1}^K$ fully specified by (3.39), (3.40), and (3.41). On the basis of it, the strategic-form game may be specified as follows:

- For each player ik, her strategy space is simply $S_{ik} = [0, 1]$, with a typical element of it denoted by x_{ik}.
- Given any strategy profile $x = ((x_{ik})_{i=1}^I)_{k=1}^K \in [0, 1]^n$, the payoff function $\pi_{ik}(\cdot)$ of each agent ik ($i = 1, 2, \ldots, I, k = 1, 2, \ldots, K$) is given by

$$\pi_{ik}(x) = U(1 - x_{ik}, p_k(x) x_{ik}). \tag{3.42}$$

The theoretical framework described aims at formalizing, in a very stylized manner, the frictions and complementarities inherent to modern economies. In particular, its objective is to illustrate that, as argued by traditional Keynesian theory, it is perfectly possible that relatively low-level macroeconomic situations, well below full capacity, may materialize and persist in equilibrium. In a drastic fashion, this is the conclusion established in the following result.

Proposition 3.1: *Consider the game whose payoff functions are given by (3.42), with $[p_k(\cdot)]_{k=1}^K$ defined by (3.39), (3.40), and (3.41). The vector $x^o = (0, 0, \ldots, 0)$ defines its unique Nash equilibrium.*

Proof: It is straightforward to check that $x^o = (0, 0, \ldots, 0)$ is a Nash equilibrium of the game. To prove that it is unique, let x be some *other* Nash equilibrium. First, we show that

$$\forall k, k' = 1, 2, \ldots, K, \quad x_k = x_{k'}. \tag{3.43}$$

Suppose otherwise. Then, there must be some sector $\hat{k}$ such that $x_{\hat{k}} > \min_{k=1,\ldots,K} \{x_k\}$. Therefore, $p_{\hat{k}}(x) = 0$ and, for every individual $i\hat{k}$ ($i = 1, 2, \ldots, I$), her equilibrium consumption bundle is of the form

$$\left(c_{ik}^1, c_{ik}^2\right) = (1 - x_{i\hat{k}}, 0).$$

Since $x_{\hat{k}} > 0$, there exists some $\hat{i}$ such that $x_{\hat{i}\hat{k}} > 0$. For that individual $\hat{i}\hat{k}$, a unilateral deviation to the strategy $\tilde{x}_{\hat{i}\hat{k}} = 0$ provides her with a payoff $U(1, 0)$, which is greater than $U(1 - x_{\hat{i}\hat{k}}, 0)$. This contradicts that x is a Nash equilibrium and therefore proves the above claim.

Now, assume that x satisfies (3.43) and therefore there is some $\theta > 0$ (because $x \neq x^o$) such that $x_k = \theta$ for every $k = 1, 2, \ldots, K$. Then, by (3.41), the payoff obtained by each individual ik' is given by

$$U\left(c_{ik'}^1, c_{ik'}^2\right) = U\left(1 - x_{ik'}, \frac{1}{K} x_{ik'}\right). \tag{3.44}$$

Choose any ik such that $x_{ik} > 0$ and consider any unilateral deviation on her part to $\tilde{x}_{ik} = x_{ik} - \varepsilon$ for some arbitrarily small $\varepsilon > 0$. Denoting by $(\tilde{x}_k)_{k=1}^K$ the sectorial profile resulting from such *unilateral* deviation, we obviously have

$$\tilde{x}_k < \min_{k' \neq k} \tilde{x}_{k'}$$

and consequently

$$p_k(\tilde{x}) = 1; \quad p_{k'}(\tilde{x}) = 0 \quad \forall k' \neq k.$$

Thus, if ε is small enough, the continuity of $U(\cdot)$ implies that

$$U(1 - \tilde{x}_{ik}, \tilde{x}_{ik}) = U(1 - x_{ik} + \varepsilon, x_{ik} - \varepsilon) > U\left(1 - x_{ik}, \frac{1}{K}x_{ik}\right),$$

which indicates that agent ik would benefit from the deviation considered. This yields a contradiction, completing the proof of the result. ∎

Proposition 3.1 reflects a situation in which, despite perfectly flexible prices, the market system is drawn to full collapse and thus becomes incapable of sustaining a positive production level.[44] Of course, this extreme conclusion is a direct consequence of the acute price-manipulation possibilities allowed to the agents in this context. If these possibilities were curtailed somehow, one would expect quite a wide range of allocations might then arise as possible equilibrium outcomes.

To explore the latter point, consider the following (somewhat artificial) variation of the previous framework. As before, individuals decide independently how much intermediate good to produce in their respective sectors. However, once this production is brought to the marketplace, let us now assume that they can irreversibly destroy whatever amount they wish, in response to (or anticipation of) similar behavior of this sort on the part of others. Under these conditions, no agent producing an intermediate good in *zero* excess supply can benefit from unilaterally destroying any of the output she originally brought to the market – any such manipulation attempts will simply be matched by other agents, thus having no final effect on relative prices. Consequently, we now postulate that the payoff function $\pi_{ik}(\cdot)$ of any agent ik satisfies the following condition[45]:

No Price Manipulation (NPM) Let $x = ((x_{ik})_{i=1}^I)_{k=1}^K \in [0, 1]^n$ be any given strategy profile and denote $v \equiv \min_{k=1,\ldots,K} x_k$.

(i) For any sector k' such that $x_{k'} = v$, the payoff obtained by any individual ik' is $\pi_{ik'}(x) = U(1 - x_{ik'}, \frac{1}{K}x_{ik'})$.

(ii) For any sector k'' such that $x_{k''} > v$, the payoff obtained by any individual ik'' is $\pi_{ik''}(x) = U(1 - x_{ik''}, \frac{1}{K}\frac{v}{I})$.

Part (i) of (NPM) simply formalizes the previous idea that no agent can manipulate prices by restricting the supply of the intermediate product she produces. Part (ii), on the other hand, contemplates a "uniform quota" among the agents of any sector whose original production is in excess supply. This latter condition obviously implies that every Nash equilibrium configuration must have the same amounts of each intermediate being produced and the same equilibrium price

---

[44] In fact, the considerations involved are quite reminiscent of those underlying both the prisoner's dilemma (recall Section 1.1) and Bertrand oligopolistic competition (see Section 3.1.2).

[45] Thus, for simplicity, we model this part of the strategic situation in reduced form and have the postulated payoff function reflect the equilibrium outcome prevailing at the marketplace when players may choose to destroy part of what they have brought to it.

$p_k = 1/K$ prevailing for every $k = 1, 2, \ldots, K$ (recall (3.41)). In this respect, therefore, the conclusion is akin to that of Proposition 3.1. The key difference now is that the range of common production levels displayed by each sector at equilibrium typically spans a nondegenerate interval. This is the content of the following result.

Proposition 3.2: *Consider a context as described above where payoff functions satisfy (NPM) and assume there exists some $\theta^* > 0$ such that*[46]:

$$\frac{\frac{\partial U}{\partial c^1}\left(1 - \theta^*, \frac{1}{K}\theta^*\right)}{\frac{\partial U}{\partial c^2}\left(1 - \theta^*, \frac{1}{K}\theta^*\right)} = \frac{1}{K}. \tag{3.45}$$

Then, given any $\theta \in [0, \theta^*]$, every strategic profile x such that

$$x_{ik} = \theta, \qquad \forall i = 1, 2, \ldots, I; \ \forall k = 1, 2, \ldots, K, \tag{3.46}$$

is a Nash equilibrium of the induced game.

Proof: Let x be a strategic profile verifying (3.46). In it, each agent ik obtains a consumption vector

$$\left(c_{ik}^1, c_{ik}^2\right) = \left(1 - \theta, \frac{1}{K}\theta\right), \qquad (i = 1, 2, \ldots, I, k = 1, 2, \ldots, K)$$

with payoffs equal to $U(1 - \theta, \theta/K)$. If individual ik deviated unilaterally and chose instead some $\hat{x}_{ik} > \theta$, she would obtain

$$\left(\hat{c}_{ik}^1, \hat{c}_{ik}^2\right) = \left(1 - \hat{x}_{ik}, \frac{1}{K}\theta\right)$$

whose associated payoffs are obviously worse than (c_{ik}^1, c_{ik}^2), because of the strict monotonicity postulated on $U(\cdot)$.

On the other hand, if agent ik were to choose some $\hat{x}_{ik} < \theta$, her consumption vector would be $(1 - \hat{x}_{ik}, \frac{1}{K}\hat{x}_{ik})$. Since $\theta \leq \theta^*$ (where θ^* is defined in (3.45)), it follows that

$$U\left(1 - \hat{x}_{ik}, \frac{1}{K}\hat{x}_{ik}\right) < U\left(1 - \theta, \frac{1}{K}\theta\right),$$

which completes the argument. ∎

Proposition 3.2 indicates that, in an economy where the decision process is subject to intertemporal frictions and payoffs display substantial complementarities, the materialization of a wide range of different activity levels is compatible with the following classical assumptions:

(i) *rational agents,* i.e., agents who maximize their payoffs in terms of well-defined expectations;

---

[46] The existence of such a positive θ^* requires that the marginal utility of leisure not be too large. If it is large enough, then the situation is as in Proposition 3.1 and the unique equilibrium again involves a zero activity level.

(ii) *rational expectations*, i.e., expectations that are consistent with the (rational) behavior of others;

(iii) *flexible prices*, i.e., endogenous price adjustment toward market clearing.

In the modern macroeconomic literature, such a compatibility has been defended by some authors (see Heller, 1986; Cooper and John, 1988) as a theoretically sound way of providing traditional Keynesian analysis with rigorous microfoundations.

Summary

This chapter has discussed a number of different economic applications where agents' strategic interaction is modeled through a strategic-form game. First, we have dealt with what is perhaps the most paradigmatic application of game theory to economic environments: the one-shot model of oligopoly, where firms are postulated to make their once-and-for-all decisions independently (i.e., simultaneously). Depending on the nature of the strategic variable considered, outputs or prices, two different kinds of oligopolistic competition arise: Cournot and Bertrand competition.

Comparing these two scenarios, Cournot competition tends to be the strategic context where, at Nash equilibria, (a) firms typically obtain higher profits, and (b) the deviation from perfect competition is larger. In particular, we have shown that the average deviation from a perfectly competitive price (i.e., a price that equals firms' marginal cost) increases, at a Cournot-Nash equilibrium, with both market concentration and the inelasticity of demand. In contrast, Bertrand competition tends to place firms in a much more competitive situation. In fact, the market outcome even becomes perfectly competitive (independently of market concentration or demand elasticity) in some benchmark cases – e.g., if the goods are homogenous and marginal costs are constant and identical across firms.

Next, we have entered the field of implementation theory, a vast area of research that aims at exploring the possibilities and limitations of reconciling individual incentives and some standard of social desirability. To break ground, we have started focusing on public-good allocation problems, where strong free-rider inefficiencies have been seen to arise when simple-minded approaches are used, e.g., the natural subscription mechanism. We have concluded, therefore, that a more "creative" approach to the problem is called for, leading the enquiry into the field of mechanism (or institutional) design. In this vein, we have shown that a rather simple and satisfactory solution to the problem is provided by a mechanism proposed by Walker (1981), whose performance was found to display the following regularity: every Nash equilibrium of the induced game results into a Lindahl (and therefore efficient) allocation of the underlying economic environment.

Our following concern has been to cast and study the implementation problem in a more abstract but substantially more general fashion. Specifically, we have asked the question of what sort of desired SCRs (i.e., performance mappings from environments to outcomes) can be implemented successfully through Nash equilibria of suitably constructed mechanisms. Monotonicity of the SCRs (a certain notion of responsiveness to individual preferences) turns out to be the crucial condition in this respect. Not only is it a necessary condition for Nash implementation but (together with an additional weak condition of no veto power) is also sufficient, provided that at least three agents are involved.

Finally, we have proposed a simple strategic model for the study of macroeconomic coordination failures. The main theoretical issue here has been posed as follows. Is it possible to provide a coherent strategic rationale for the Keynesian claim that, despite flexible prices, a market system may become trapped into a low-activity equilibrium? Indeed, we have provided a stylized framework that allows for (in fact, forces) this possibility at the extreme lowest level of zero activity. Its main features are (i) acute production complementarities among intermediate commodities in the production of a final consumption good, and (ii) sequential timing in the production and marketing decisions that entails important allocation irreversibilities. To obtain less drastic conclusions, the problem has been reconsidered within a variation of the original framework that curtails agents' price-manipulation possibilities quite significantly. In this revised setup, the model displays a wide equilibrium multiplicity, which allows for a nondegenerate range of different equilibrium activity levels at which agents may (mis)coordinate.

Exercises

Exercise 3.1: Consider a general model of oligopoly with n identical firms and demand function $F(\cdot)$ that satisfies the law of demand. Show that, if the cost functions are strictly convex, the quantity produced in an oligopolistic market is always lower than that produced in a perfectly competitive context.

Exercise 3.2: Consider again a general model of oligopoly with n identical firms and demand function $F(\cdot)$ that satisfies the law of demand. Postulate additional conditions on both $F(\cdot)$ and the firms' cost functions that guarantee that the first-order necessary conditions for a Nash equilibrium are also sufficient.

Exercise 3.3: In a context with identical linear costs and linear demand, as given by (3.8) and (3.9), consider a model of Cournot competition with n (≥ 3) firms. Compute the Nash equilibrium. What happens as $n \to \infty$?

Exercise 3.4: Show that (3.14) characterizes the set of Bertrand-Nash equilibria of a homogeneous-good oligopoly where firms display common and constant marginal costs.

Exercise 3.5: Consider a context of duopolistic Bertrand competition with a *homogeneous* product and a nonincreasing demand function $F(\cdot)$. Suppose the two firms display zero fixed costs and constant marginal costs, the marginal cost of firm 1, c_1, being lower than that of firm 2, c_2. Let $\hat{p}_1$ be the monopoly price of firm 1 (i.e., the price firm 1 would set if it were alone in the market). Assume that $c_2 < \hat{p}_1$ and

$F(c_2) > 0$. Find the pure-strategy Nash equilibria of the game (there are possibly none) under the following alternative specifications on how the market is divided between them in case of price equality:

1. firm 1 captures the whole market;
2. firm 2 captures the whole market;
3. the two firms divide equally the induced demand.

Exercise 3.6*: Consider again a context of duopolistic competition à la Bertrand with a homogeneous product and demand function $F(\cdot)$, where the total demand is divided equally in case of price equality. Both firms exhibit an identical cost function, $C(\cdot)$, with $C(0) = 0$, $C'(\cdot) > 0$, $C''(\cdot) > 0$. Let p^* be the perfectly competitive price (a scalar) satisfying

$$p^* = C'\left(\frac{1}{2}F(p^*)\right).$$

Prove that the pair (p^*, p^*) defines a Nash equilibrium of the induced game.
Hint: Following Dastidar (1997), define $\hat{q}_i(p)$ as the output that maximizes the profit of firm i when taking price p as given. Then, verify and use that the expression $p\hat{q}_i(p) - C_i(\hat{q}_i(p))$ is increasing in p.

Exercise 3.7: Consider a context of duopolistic competition à la Bertrand with demand functions given by (3.15) where the goods are partial substitutes – i.e., $0 < b < 1$. Show that the higher the degree of substitutability between the goods the lower the equilibrium profits of firms.

Exercise 3.8: Two individuals bargain over the distribution of a "pie" of unit size. Each individual $i \in \{1, 2\}$ introduces in a sealed envelope demand x_i specifying how much she wishes to obtain of it. An outside agent then opens the envelopes and performs the following division.

- If $x_1 + x_2 \leq 1$, she gives to each individual $i = 1, 2$ a portion of the pie equal to $x_i + (1 - x_1 - x_2)/2$ (i.e., what she asks for plus half of the residual pie left after satisfying both individuals' demands).
- If $x_1 + x_2 > 1$, no individual receives any share at all.

Identify all Nash equilibria of the game that involve only pure strategies. Is there any other equilibrium in mixed strategies? If so, specify one of these.

Exercise 3.9: Propose conditions on the data of the planner's optimization problem given by (3.18) and (3.19) that ensure that the corresponding solutions are interior.

Exercise 3.10*: Consider the following variation on the context studied in Section 3.2. A community of individuals faces the decision of whether to finance an *indivisible* public good at cost K. The individuals propose simultaneously their respective contributions ξ_i ($i = 1, 2, \ldots, n$). If the aggregate contribution level $\sum_{i=1}^{n} \xi_i$ is enough to cover the cost K, the public good is provided, and any excess funds are returned to the individuals in equal shares. Otherwise, the public good is not provided and no one has to materialize any actual contribution (i.e., the effective payment is zero for everyone). Suppose, for simplicity, that the preferences displayed by each individual $i = 1, 2, \ldots, n$ admit the representation

$$U_i(x, c_i) = V_i(x) - c_i,$$

where c_i stands for the contribution of the individual in question and x indicates whether the public good is provided ($x = 1$) or not ($x = 0$). Let us also assume that $\sum_{i=1}^{n} (V_i(1) - V_i(0)) - K > 0$ but $V_i(1) - V_i(0) < K$ for each $i = 1, 2, \ldots n$.

Consider now a benevolent planner who can impose in the present context any allocation that respects the "voluntary participation" constraint

$$U_i(x, c_i) \geq U_i(0, 0)$$

and whose utility function (the planner's) is given by a linear combination of agents' utilities according to some positive vector of weights $\alpha = (\alpha_1, \alpha_2, \ldots, \alpha_n)$. Verify the following two claims.

(a) There are Nash equilibria of the induced game whose associated allocation does *not* coincide with a solution of the planner's optimization problem for any weight vector α.

(b) There is *some* Nash equilibrium of the game that *does* coincide with one of those solutions, for suitably chosen weights. Contrast this latter assertion with the conclusion derived in Section 3.2.

Exercise 3.11: A group of fishermen concentrate their activity on a certain restricted area. The fishing returns in that area depend on the total hours worked by the whole group. Thus, letting h_i denote the number of hours worked by each fisherman $i = 1, 2, \ldots, n$ and $H \equiv \sum_{i=1}^{n} h_i$ the total number of hours worked by the group, it is postulated that the *hourly* returns of each of them is given by a concave function of H, $\rho : \mathbb{R}_+ \to \mathbb{R}_+$, with $\lim_{H \to \infty} \rho'(H) = 0$.

On the other hand, each worker i incurs an individual cost (or disutility) per hour worked that is captured by some function of h_i, $c : \mathbb{R}_+ \to \mathbb{R}_+$, which is supposed identical across individuals. It is also assumed that $c(\cdot)$ is convex, increasing, and satisfies $\lim_{h_i \to T} c'(h_i) = \infty$ for some given $T \leq 24$. Overall, the payoffs of each fisherman i are given by a function $U_i(\cdot)$ defined as follows:

$$U_i(h_1, \ldots, h_n) = \rho(H) h_i - c(h_i) \qquad (i = 1, 2, \ldots, n).$$

1. Pose the optimization problem solved by a planner whose objective is to maximize the sum individuals' utilities and characterize the solution.
2. Formulate precisely the strategic-form game in which the fishermen independently decide their work hours. Characterize its Nash equilibria and draw a comparison with the solution to the planner's problem.

Exercise 3.12: We have shown in Section 3.2.2 that all Nash equilibria of Walker's (1981) mechanism lead to Lindahl allocations (that is, allocations obtained at some Lindahl equilibrium under suitable personalized prices). Prove that the reciprocal statement is also true, i.e., every Lindahl allocation may be obtained at some Nash equilibrium of Walker's mechanism.

Exercise 3.13*: Recall the mechanism proposed by Walker (1981) and studied in Section 3.2.2. In contrast with that mechanism, let us now insist that the messages m_i sent by every agent i should admit the interpretation of "amount of public good desired" and, therefore, must be nonnegative for each $i = 1, 2, \ldots, n$.

1. Are all Nash equilibria of the revised mechanism efficient?
2. Is there any efficient equilibrium?

Exercise 3.14: Let ϕ be some Nash-implementable SCR and consider any two utility profiles U and U' such that

$$\forall i = 1, 2 \ldots, n, \forall \omega, \omega' \in \Omega, \qquad U_i(\omega) \geq U_i(\omega') \Leftrightarrow U_i'(\omega) \geq U_i'(\omega').$$

Show that $\phi(U) = \phi(U')$. Discuss the implications of this conclusion.

Exercise 3.15*: Consider a family of simple two-consumer exchange economies, as customarily represented by an "Edgeworth box" (see, e.g., Mas-Colell *et al.*, 1995, Ch. 15B). Show that, *in general*, the Walras SCR that associates with every possible environment (i.e., profile of individual utilities) the allocation obtained at some Walras equilibrium is not monotonic.
Hint: Consider an environment in which the Walras allocation is *not* interior.

Exercise 3.16*: Again in the context of exchange economies, postulate *primitive* conditions on agents' preferences and endowments that restrict the universe of environments in a way that the Pareto SCR (i.e., the rule that associates with each environment its Pareto efficient allocations) becomes Nash implementable. Contrast your answer with the opposite claim made in the text for unrestricted contexts.

Exercise 3.17: Consider the following variation on the model proposed in Section 3.4. There is an additional agent, the government, whose preferences coincide with those of a benevolent planner (recall Section 3.2). It can intervene in the process through fiscal and expenditure policies impinging on the allocation of resources. (The particular details in this respect are left unspecified because they are intended to be personal "modeling choices" in addressing this exercise.) Describe precisely at least two alternative policies on the part of the government – an additional player in this context – that could remedy the equilibrium multiplicity displayed by the original game.

Exercise 3.18: Consider a scenario as described in Section 3.4 but under the following alternative assumption:

$$\frac{\partial U}{\partial c_1}(\cdot) \equiv 0. \tag{3.47}$$

That is, individuals no longer find it costly to work (or, equivalently, leisure is not a relevant argument of their utility function). Explore the effects of this modification on the conclusions stated in Propositions 3.1 and 3.2.

Exercise 3.19*: Within the context studied in Section 3.4, assume there are only two sectors ($K = 2$) but the payoff conditions are as indicated in (NPM). However, in contrast with what was formerly postulated, now suppose that the production decisions concerning sector 2 are adopted *after* those of sector 1. For simplicity, also suppose that the condition (3.47) assumed in Exercise 3.18 holds.

1. Model the situation as an extensive-form game.
2. Specify the Nash equilibria of the induced game. Do some of these equilibria appear more reasonable than others? Return to this issue after having completed Chapter 4.

Refinements of Nash equilibrium: theory

4.1 Introduction

The Nash equilibrium concept is the central theoretical tool most frequently used in the analysis of noncooperative games. As explained in Subsection 2.2.1, it may be conceived as a basic requirement for strategic stability (i.e., a necessary condition) in the sense that any prediction for a game that embodies rational behavior *and* accurate (or rational) expectations must be a Nash equilibrium.

However, given the multiplicity of Nash equilibria encountered in many games of interest, the conditions characterizing this equilibrium often prove insufficient to pin down a unique outcome. Then, what we need are further criteria of strategic stability that, *in addition* to those embodied by the Nash concept, might permit a fruitful (ideally unique) equilibrium selection. In fact, one such possibility has already been considered in Section 2.5. There, it was suggested that, for a strategic configuration to be judged stable, it should be immune not only to unilateral deviations but also to those involving multilateral coalitions. Such a demand, however, turned out to be too stringent since it was shown incompatible with existence even in rather simple games. This is why, by and large, game theory has advanced along this line by proposing further criteria of strategic stability that are strictly *unilateral*, i.e., individual based. This approach has given rise to a wide range of so-called *refinements of Nash equilibrium*, the object of the present chapter.

Our ensuing discussion of this topic is divided into three parts. First, in Sections 4.2–4.4 we present the basic Nash refinements formulated in the *extensive form* of a game. These refinements are designed to rule out what are customarily known as "incredible threats" and represent the core of the present chapter. Then, in Sections 4.5–4.7 (as part of the supplementary material), we present other more advanced refinements that still focus on the extensive form but aim at discarding "untenable perceptions." Finally, in Section 4.8, we discuss some refinement concepts formulated in the *strategic form* of a game and outline their relationship with those defined in the extensive form.

4.2 Refinements excluding "incredible threats": examples

A Nash equilibrium represents a strategically stable situation because no player anticipates beneficial payoff consequences from unilateral deviations. Of course, for an appropriate assessment of these consequences, the player in question must

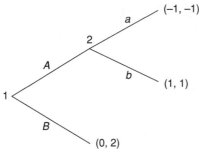

Figure 4.1: An extensive-form game with a "noncredible" equilibrium.

take into account the strategies to be played by the remaining players. In particular, she must be in a position to anticipate what reactions would follow from the opponents' strategies in response to any possible deviation on her part. Sometimes, such reactions (even though optimal in the Nash equilibrium sense) may embody suboptimal behavior at unreached (and therefore payoff-irrelevant) information sets. The equilibrium may then be interpreted as supported by "incredible threats," a feature that calls into question its presumed strategic stability. A simple first illustration of these ideas is provided by the game in extensive form represented in Figure 4.1.

This game has two Nash equilibria: (B, a) and (A, b). The first one, however, is not reasonable (or strategically robust) because it is supported by the incredible threat on the part of 2 that she would adopt action a if player 1 were to give her an opportunity by *not* playing the equilibrium action B. Since, at this equilibrium, player 1 in fact chooses B, such a threat does not materialize and, therefore, its *potential* payoff suboptimality is of no consequence to player 2. However, player 1 chooses action B only *because* she believes in that threat. But, if she knows that player 2 is rational,[47] player 1 should be able to anticipate that 2 would not carry out her threat if she (player 1) were to play A. That is, the hypothetical response of a is no longer credible, thus rendering the equilibrium (B, a) a very fragile prediction.

Instead, the alternative Nash equilibrium (A, b) is fully credible (or reasonable, robust, etc.), and it is so because this strategy profile follows from a procedure of *backward induction* (i.e., a sequence of nested optimization problems solved from the future to the present) akin to that used in standard dynamic programming. This inductive procedure ensures that, when a decision is to be adopted at some particular point in the game (e.g., when player 1 starts the present game), the assessment of the different options then available internalizes the decisions that would prove optimal in the future (i.e., action b in the second stage of the game). Following Selten (1965, 1975), any Nash equilibrium that enjoys this feature is called a *subgame-perfect equilibrium*. The name given to this new concept already points to its distinctive property: it must induce a Nash equilibrium in *every* subgame, whether *or not* the subgame is reached along the equilibrium path induced. Hence, in particular, the "threats" that (out of the equilibrium path) support the equilibrium choices should

---

[47] Except when explicitly mentioned, it is always assumed that rationality (in the stronger sense of players being payoff maximizers for some suitable beliefs) is common knowledge – cf. Section 2.7.

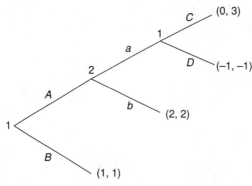

Figure 4.2: An extensive-form game with several "noncredible" equilibria.

be credible in the following sense. If need be, rational agents will be ready to carry out those threats under the belief that others will also do so, i.e., will behave thereafter as the equilibrium prescribes.

Returning to the game represented in Figure 4.1, note that players display opposite preferences concerning its two Nash equilibria: player 1 prefers the equilibrium (A, b), whereas 2 prefers (B, a). Thus, subgame perfection is a refinement criterion that one of the players (player 1) will not be ready to ignore in analyzing the situation. In contrast, consider now the game represented in Figure 4.2, borrowed from van Damme (1987).

In this game, we can also discard some of the Nash equilibria as not being subgame perfect. Thus, the strategy profile $((A, D), b)$ defines a Nash equilibrium in which the second choice of player 1 (i.e., D) is not credible. Paradoxically, player 2 would like to believe this action is an optimal choice for player 1 at her last decision node. For, otherwise, if subgame perfection is required, $((B, C), a)$ is the only admissible equilibrium.[48] In it, each player obtains a payoff of 1, which is lower than the payoff of 2 that each obtains with $((A, D), b)$. However, if the players are rational and this is common knowledge, they are forced into an equilibrium outcome that both would like to avoid. If they could just commit to being naively rational (i.e., not concerned about whether the opponent is indeed behaving rationally), they would both be better off!

As explained, the notion of subgame-perfect equilibrium can be understood as embodying the requirement that players' strategies define a Nash equilibrium at *all* possible subgames (i.e., visited and unvisited). However, not all subgames that conceivably could be reached along the game allow one to apply the notion of Nash equilibrium. This occurs only when the subgame in question qualifies as "proper." In essence, what characterizes a *proper subgame* is that it inherits from the full game the following crucial feature: it displays a *unique root*. A proper subgame is like a "game proper" in that it starts with a singleton information set and includes all its possible successors. Any such subgame admits a clear-cut analysis on the part of

---

[48] Additionally, there is also the pure-strategy Nash equilibrium $((B, D), a)$, which is *not* subgame perfect but that induces the same outcome as the subgame-perfect equilibrium $((B, C), a)$. The profile $((B, D), a)$ is not perfect because, again, it involves the suboptimal action D by player 1 in her last decision node.

the players because, once it is reached, they are fully informed of previous history (i.e., they know exactly their position in the game). Thus, as it happens before the start of any (ordinary) game, players can identify *unambiguously* at the beginning of proper subgames the outcome induced by each possible strategy profile. Therefore, it is only for those subgames – including of course the whole game – that the notion of subgame-perfect equilibrium requires verification of the Nash conditions.

In view of these considerations, it should be clear that the notion of subgame-perfect equilibrium bears its full strength in those multistage games in which each intermediate node defines by itself an information set (see, for example, the games described in Figures 4.1 and 4.2). These games are called of *perfect information*. In them, each of the actions available at any point in the game induces a proper subgame from there onward. Therefore, the criterion of subgame perfection affords in those games the largest number of "test situations" and thus obtains a maximum refinement power.

In comparison, when players' actions are not perfectly observed by others (as when they are simultaneous) or some decision by Nature is only partially revealed to some players (e.g., in the so-called incomplete-information games studied in Chapter 6), subgame perfection typically has very little discriminating force. Indeed, if there is never full revelation of some prior choice of at least one player (this occurs in many applications), the only singleton information set is the initial one and, therefore, this criterion is fully devoid of any additional implications, i.e., all Nash equilibria are subgame perfect. To illustrate this point and explore possible ways of tackling it, consider the extensive-form game represented in Figure 4.3.

This game has two Nash equilibria in pure strategies: (A, b) and (B, a). Since there are no proper subgames (other than the full game, of course), the requirement of subgame perfection is equivalent to that embodied by Nash equilibrium. Therefore, both of those Nash equilibria are subgame perfect as well. However, the first one does not seem at all reasonable. Specifically, the prediction that, if player 2 is

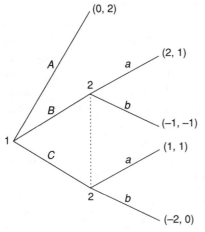

Figure 4.3: An extensive-form game with a "noncredible" equilibrium and no proper subgames.

called upon to move, she will choose *b* is blatantly inconsistent with the maintained assumption that she is rational. For, even though this player is incapable of distinguishing between the two nodes of her information set, choosing *b* is a uniformly worse action for her in either of them. That is, no matter what her subjective beliefs are on each of those two nodes, action *b* provides a lower expected payoff than *a*. Thus, if player 2 is rational and player 1 knows it, the equilibrium supported by player 2's strategy (or threat) of playing *b* if given a chance should be ruled out. Such a threat is incredible, in a sense very similar to that indicated above for the complete-information games of Figures 4.1 and 4.2.

This idea is captured in a simple fashion by the concept we call *weak perfect Bayesian equilibrium*.[49] In addition to a strategy profile, a weak perfect Bayesian equilibrium requires the specification of a set of "compatible" beliefs (or perceptions) for every player at each of her information sets. These beliefs are taken to reflect the subjective probability attributed by the player in question to each of the possible nodes she cannot discriminate among. Heuristically (see Section 4.4 for a formal definition), a strategy profile defines a weak perfect Bayesian equilibrium if there exists a collection of associated beliefs such that the following two conditions hold:

(a) For every player and each of her information sets, the actions prescribed by her strategy are optimal responses to the opponents' strategies in terms of the specified beliefs.

(b) The beliefs held by each player at any of her respective information sets embody probability updates that are consistent with Bayes rule (when this rule may be applied), given the opponents' strategies.

Condition (a) is merely an extension (to any information set) of the optimality condition required by the notion of subgame-perfect equilibrium at *singleton* information sets. To see this, note that, for information sets consisting of a single node, beliefs must be trivially concentrated in that node. In those cases, therefore, condition (a) simply boils down to what is a direct implication of subgame perfection, namely, that the player who initiates a proper subgame must choose (because she is playing an equilibrium for that subgame) a best response to the opponents' strategies.

Condition (b), on the other hand, can also be seen as extending the implicit (degenerate) beliefs postulated by subgame-perfect equilibrium at the beginning of a proper subgame to any other decision point in the game. When information sets include more than one node, condition (b) requires that players' beliefs be consistent (i.e., not contradictory) with the opponents' strategies *and* Bayes rule (the only coherent procedure of statistical updating). For those cases in which Bayes rule is well defined (i.e., when the equilibrium strategies induce positive *prior* probability for the information set in question), application of that rule defines uniquely the corresponding *posterior* beliefs. This happens along the so-called "equilibrium path," which is simply identified with the *set* of possible paths of play that can

---

[49] As explained in Section 4.4, this concept is a significant weakening (suitable for our present purposes) of the more involved notion of *perfect Bayesian equilibrium*, which was proposed by Fudenberg and Tirole (1991).

occur with positive probability for *some* materialization of the players' equilibrium strategies. Outside of it, since the prior probability is zero, Bayes rule cannot be applied to obtain a suitable posterior probability. Therefore, condition (b) allows for any arbitrary beliefs to be held at those information sets – note that if Bayes rule cannot be applied, it cannot be contradicted either!

Even accepting as admissible any players' perceptions outside of the equilibrium path, it is clear that the notion of weak perfect Bayesian equilibrium may have important implications not induced by the criterion of subgame perfection. For example, consider again the game represented in Figure 4.3. As we have explained, action b is never an optimal response to any beliefs that could be assigned off the equilibrium path induced by (A, b).[50] The strategy profile (A, b) is *not*, therefore, a weak perfect Bayesian equilibrium; only (B, a) is so. For the latter case, since player 2's information set is reached at equilibrium, her beliefs in it are no longer arbitrary. Specifically, player 2 must have all her subjective probability concentrated on the node induced by player 1's action B.

4.3 Subgame-perfect equilibrium

Let $\Gamma = \{N, \{K_i\}_{i=1}^n, R, \{H_i\}_{i=1}^n, \{A(x)\}_{x \in K \setminus Z}, \{[\pi_i(z)]_{i=1}^n\}_{z \in Z}\}$ be a game in extensive form (without Nature)[51] and consider a subset of nodes $\hat{K} \subset K \equiv (\bigcup_{i=1}^n K_i) \bigcup Z$ that satisfies the following twofold condition:

(S.1) There exists an information set $\hat{h}$ such that $\hat{K} = \hat{h} \cup \{x' : x \in \hat{h}, \ x R x'\}$, i.e., $\hat{K}$ includes the nodes in $\hat{h}$ and *every* other node following those;

(S.2) $\forall h \in H \equiv \bigcup_{i \in N} H_i$,

$$(h \subset \hat{K}) \vee (h \subset K \setminus \hat{K}),$$

that is, *any* information set h is *wholly* included in $\hat{K}$ or its complement.

Given any $\hat{K}$ satisfying (S.1) and (S.2), one can define an associated *subgame*

$$\hat{\Gamma} = \left\{ N, \{\hat{K}_i\}_{i=1}^n, \hat{R}, \{\hat{H}_i\}_{i=1}^n, \{\hat{A}(x)\}_{x \in \hat{K} \setminus \hat{Z}}, \left\{[\hat{\pi}_i(z)]_{i=1}^n\right\}_{z \in \hat{Z}} \right\}$$

as follows:

- $\hat{K}_i \equiv K_i \cap \hat{K}$ $(i = 1, 2, \ldots, n)$, $\hat{Z} \equiv Z \cap \hat{K}$;
- $\forall x, x' \in \hat{K}, x \hat{R} x' \Leftrightarrow x R x'$;
- $\hat{H}_i \equiv \{h \in H_i : h \subset \hat{K}\}$ $(i = 1, 2, \ldots, n)$;
- $\forall x \in \hat{K} \setminus \hat{Z}, \hat{A}(x) = A(x)$;
- $\forall z \in \hat{Z}, \hat{\pi}_i(z) = \pi_i(z)$.

---

[50] Since in this game strategy a (weakly) dominates b for any strategy of player 1, *any* beliefs by 2 can support her former action as optimal response. Sometimes, however, the scope of arbitrariness that in principle is allowed off the equilibrium path must be carefully narrowed down to support the equilibrium choice. In fact, we may often want to "refine" these off-equilibrium beliefs, as indeed is the motivation that underlies the collection of Nash refinements discussed in Sections 4.5–4.7.

[51] As usual, an explicit reference to Nature is avoided when it plays no significant role in the discussion.

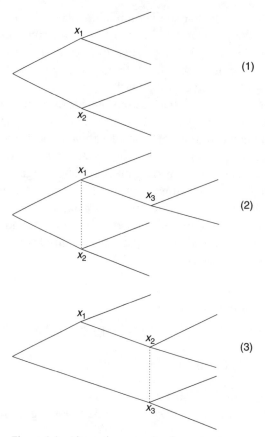

Figure 4.4: Alternative extensive-form structures.

Heuristically, the subgame $\hat{\Gamma}$ is simply a "projection" of the original game on the nodes in $\hat{K}$ that, in view of (S.1) and (S.2), preserves the same relative structure and information conditions they had in Γ. If the information set $\hat{h}$ initiating the subgame $\hat{\Gamma}$ consists of a single node, the subgame is said to be *proper*. As explained, the crucial feature of a proper subgame is that it displays the same structure as (i.e., is isomorphic to) an ordinary extensive-form game and can therefore be analyzed as such (see below for the details).

To illustrate these new theoretical constructs, refer to the three different extensive-form structures displayed in Figure 4.4.

In the first example, either node x_1 or node x_2 induces a corresponding subgame, both of them proper. In the second example, both the information set $\{x_1, x_2\}$ and the singleton $\{x_3\}$ induce respective subgames, only the latter one proper. Finally, in the third example, only the set $\{x_2, x_3\}$ defines a (nonproper) subgame. In this case, the singleton information set $\{x_1\}$ does *not* define a subgame because it violates condition (S.2) above. Specifically, the information set $\{x_2, x_3\}$ is not included in the set of successors of x_1 or in its complement.

Now, we define formally the notion of subgame-perfect equilibrium (SPE). Under the maintained assumption that the game displays perfect recall (cf. Subsection

1.5.2),[52] it is useful to focus on behavioral-strategy profiles in the set $\Psi \equiv \Psi_1 \times \Psi_2 \times \cdots \times \Psi_n$ rather than on mixed-strategy profiles in the set Σ. Since every behavioral-strategy profile γ is payoff equivalent to any mixed-strategy profile σ that induces it, we may abuse notation and define the payoff function $\pi_i : \Psi \to \mathbb{R}$ for each player $i = 1, 2, \ldots, n$ in the natural fashion. That is, for each $\gamma \in \Psi, \pi_i(\gamma)$ is made equal to $\pi_i(\sigma)$, where σ is any mixed strategy inducing γ.

Consider any given strategy profile $\gamma = (\gamma_1, \gamma_2, \ldots, \gamma_n) \in \Psi$ and let $\hat{\Gamma}$ be a subgame of Γ. Clearly, every γ_i induces a corresponding behavioral strategy $\gamma_i \mid_{\hat{\Gamma}}$ for every such subgame $\hat{\Gamma}$ by simply making

$$\forall h \in \hat{H}_i, \quad \gamma_i \mid_{\hat{\Gamma}}(h) = \gamma_i(h).$$

Restrict attention to proper subgames. Because those subgames have the same structure as an ordinary game, one may suitably formulate the requirement that, for every such proper subgame $\hat{\Gamma}$, the induced profile $\gamma \mid_{\hat{\Gamma}} \equiv (\gamma_1 \mid_{\hat{\Gamma}}, \gamma_2 \mid_{\hat{\Gamma}}, \ldots, \gamma_n \mid_{\hat{\Gamma}})$ defines a Nash equilibrium for the subgame. This is precisely the requirement demanded by SPE concept, as formally expressed in the following definition.

Definition 4.1 (Selten, 1965): *A profile $\gamma^* \in \Psi$ is a* subgame-perfect equilibrium *of Γ if, for every proper subgame $\hat{\Gamma} \subseteq \Gamma$, $\gamma^* \mid_{\hat{\Gamma}}$ is a Nash equilibrium of $\hat{\Gamma}$.*

Let us now return to the examples presented in Figures 4.1 and 4.2 and recast the previous discussion formally. In the first game, only the Nash equilibrium $\gamma^* = [(\gamma_{1A}^*, \gamma_{1B}^*), (\gamma_{2a}^*, \gamma_{2b}^*)] = [(1, 0), (0, 1)]$ is subgame perfect. To see this, note that the restriction of this profile to the last proper subgame – which gives rise to the induced "profile" $(\gamma_{2a}^*, \gamma_{2b}^*) = (0, 1)$ – is the only Nash equilibrium of that subgame (trivially so, because only player 2 moves in it).

Concerning the second game (i.e., the one represented in Figure 4.2), the unique subgame-perfect equilibrium is $\gamma^* = [((\gamma_{1A}^*, \gamma_{1B}^*), (\gamma_{1C}^*, \gamma_{1D}^*)), (\gamma_{2a}^*, \gamma_{2b}^*)] = [((0, 1), (1, 0)), (1, 0)]$. On the one hand, its restriction to the last (proper) subgame yields $(\gamma_{1C}^*, \gamma_{1D}^*) = (1, 0)$, which is obviously the only Nash equilibrium of that subgame. On the other hand, the restriction to the subgame where player 2 moves first, $[(\gamma_{1C}^*, \gamma_{1D}^*), (\gamma_{2a}^*, \gamma_{2b}^*)] = [(1, 0), (1, 0)]$, is obviously a Nash equilibrium of that subgame, and the only one that embodies the unique Nash equilibrium already identified for the last subgame, $(\gamma_{1C}^*, \gamma_{1D}^*) = (1, 0)$.

4.4 Weak perfect Bayesian equilibrium

As illustrated in Section 4.2, when the game is *not* of perfect information (i.e., some information set is not a singleton) the SPE notion may fail to weed out every unreasonable Nash equilibrium. To address this problem, we outlined the concept called weak perfect Bayesian equilibrium (WPBE). As will be recalled, its most notable variation over SPE is that it involves an *explicit* description of players' beliefs and demands that agents respond optimally to them.

---

[52] If the game exhibits imperfect recall, a Nash equilibrium in behavioral strategies can fail to have a counterpart Nash equilibrium in mixed strategies – see Exercise 4.13.

Formally, a WPBE involves a pair (μ, γ) that, following Kreps and Wilson (1982a), we call an *assessment*. Its second component γ is just a behavioral-strategy profile, as formulated above. On the other hand, its first component μ is interpreted as a pattern of players' beliefs (or perceptions) specifying, for each information set $h \in H$, the subjective probability $\mu(x)$ attributed to each node $x \in h$ by the player who moves at h. Naturally, for every such h, one must insist that

$$\sum_{x \in h} \mu(x) = 1 \tag{4.1}$$

if the suggested belief (i.e., probability) interpretation is to make sense. In principle, the pattern μ is arbitrary. In equilibrium, however, it should be required that the pair (μ, γ) display the kind of "reciprocal consistency," as explained below.

On the one hand, it must be demanded that the pattern of beliefs μ be *statistically consistent* with the strategy profile γ. This is taken to mean that, whenever the information set in question allows (i.e., when γ induces some positive *ex ante* probability of reaching the information set), μ is obtained from γ via Bayes rule. To be more precise, let $P^\gamma : 2^K \to [0, 1]$ stand for the mapping that specifies, for any subset of nodes $V \subset K$, the *ex ante* probability $P^\gamma(V)$ attributed to it by the strategy profile γ.[53] Then, the statistical consistency of μ requires that, for all $h \in H$ and $x \in h$,

$$P^\gamma(h) > 0 \Rightarrow \mu(x) = \frac{P^\gamma(x)}{P^\gamma(h)}. \tag{4.2}$$

That is, for every information set h that (given the strategy profile γ) may be reached with positive *ex ante* probability, the beliefs $\mu(x)$ associated with any node $x \in h$ must coincide with its conditional probability, as computed through Bayes rule.

When $P^\gamma(h) = 0$, Bayes rule is not well defined and (4.2) does not apply. If information set h is indeed reached, the player who has to move there is facing an event of *ex ante* probability zero, given the strategy profile γ. In any case, the belief pattern μ cannot dispense with the need of attributing some beliefs within h, since that player must still make a "rational" (i.e., belief-based) decision at that point. As advanced, the WPBE admits at this juncture that any arbitrary beliefs with support on the nodes in h might be used. That is, one may then rely on any probability vector $(\mu(x))_{x \in h}$ satisfying (4.1) to support rational behavior at h.

A compact way of accounting for the two possibilities (i.e., a positive or a null *ex ante* probability) is to require that, for any given information set $h \in H, x \in H$, we should have

$$\mu(x)\, P^\gamma(h) = P^\gamma(x). \tag{4.3}$$

This condition implies (4.2) when $P^\gamma(h) > 0$ but admits any arbitrary probability imputation (satisfying (4.1)) otherwise.

The second "consistency" condition required by the WPBE concept is of a somewhat reciprocal nature; i.e., it does not have strategies impose conditions

---

[53] As usual, the notation 2^K stands for the *power set* of K, i.e., the family of all subsets of K.

on beliefs but rather *vice versa*. It demands that, given the pattern of beliefs $\mu \equiv \{(\mu(x))_{x \in h}\}_{h \in H}$ to be applied at every information set h, the strategy γ_i played by each player i should be optimal, given the opponents' strategies, at every one of her information sets $h \in H_i$ (i.e., once she knows she is at any one of her information sets). To write matters formally, denote by $\pi_i (\gamma \mid \mu, h)$ the payoff expected by any given player i at information set $h \in H_i$ when the prevailing strategy profile is γ and the belief pattern is μ. Then, what is required is that, for all $i \in N$ and every $h \in H_i$,

$$\pi_i (\gamma \mid \mu, h) \geq \pi_i \left((\gamma_i', \gamma_{-i}) \mid \mu, h\right) \tag{4.4}$$

for any possible $\gamma_i' \in \Psi_i$.

The former discussion may be summarized through the following definition.

Definition 4.2: *A behavioral-strategy profile $\gamma^* = (\gamma_1^*, \gamma_2^*, \ldots, \gamma_n^*) \in \Psi$ is a* weak perfect Bayesian equilibrium *for Γ if there exists a pattern of beliefs $\mu^* = \{(\mu^*(x))_{x \in h}\}_{h \in H}$ such that the assessment (μ^*, γ^*) satisfies the following conditions:*

(a) $\forall i \in N, \forall h \in H_i, \forall \gamma_i \in \Psi_i,$
$$\pi_i (\gamma^* \mid \mu^*, h) \geq \pi_i \left((\gamma_i, \gamma_{-i}^*) \mid \mu^*, h\right).$$

(b) $\forall h \in H, \ \forall x \in h,$
$$\mu (x) \, P^\gamma (h) = P^\gamma (x).$$

Items (a) and (b) in the above definition are the formal counterparts of the heuristic requirements (labeled (a) and (b) as well) introduced in our informal discussion of WPBE in Section 4.2. Note that, in games of perfect information (i.e., when all information sets are singletons), these requirements are equivalent to the demands embodied by subgame perfection. In those cases, therefore, the sets of SPE and WPBE coincide.

For arbitrary games, however, SPE and WPBE need not be identical. In fact, we already saw in Section 4.2 that the notion of WPBE may significantly refine SPE in cases in which information sets are not singletons and the latter notion can have no bite. (Recall, for example, the game represented in Figure 4.3, where both (A, b) and (B, a) are SPEs but only the latter is a WPBE.) In general, therefore, one might expect that, in any extensive-form game, every WPBE should also be an SPE. Unfortunately, this is not true, as shown by the game represented in Figure 4.5.

In this game, the pure-strategy profile (B, X, D) induces a WPBE that is *not* an SPE. First, to see that it is not subgame perfect, note that the unique Nash equilibrium of the proper subgame where 2 starts playing is (X, C). This simply follows from the fact that X is a strictly dominant strategy for player 2 in this subgame and player 3's best response to it is C. On the other hand, to verify that (B, X, D) is indeed a WPBE, let $\hat{h}$ be player 3's information set and denote by $\hat{\mu}$ the beliefs on it that are concentrated on player 2 having chosen Y. These beliefs (defined on the only nonsingleton information set of the game) are part of an admissible assessment. For, being $\hat{h}$ off the equilibrium path, they can be set arbitrarily by part (b) of

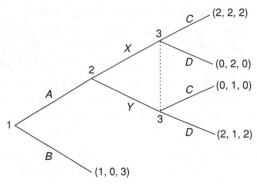

Figure 4.5: An extensive-form game with a weak perfect Bayesian equilibrium that is not subgame perfect.

Definition 4.2. Furthermore, given these beliefs, we have

$$\pi_3\big(D; B, X \mid \hat{\mu}, \hat{h}\big) = 2 > \pi_3\big(C; B, X \mid \hat{\mu}, \hat{h}\big) = 0,$$

where D and C are the two possible choices in $\hat{h}$. Thus, the strategy profile considered satisfies the optimality required at the information set $\hat{h}$ (part (a) of Definition 4.2). It is straightforward to check that it is satisfied as well at all other information sets, thus confirming that (B, X, D) is indeed a WPBE.

The above example illustrates a substantial drawback of the WPBE concept. Its attempt to introduce explicit beliefs into the analysis of multistage games appears to backfire. Even though WPBE achieves some sort of belief-based rationality at every information set, it fails to guarantee the equilibrium features ensured by SPE at proper subgames. It is easy to see that this problem cannot arise in very simple games (e.g., those involving just two stages). But for games of even moderate complexity (recall the game represented in Figure 4.5), WPBE may be too weak and more stringent refinements need to be considered. One possibility in this respect is afforded by a notion proposed by Fudenberg and Tirole (1991), *Perfect Bayesian Equilibrium*, which strengthens WPBE by imposing some natural constraints on how beliefs can be formed off the equilibrium path. Another earlier concept that addresses the issue in a quite different fashion, sequential equilibrium, was proposed by Kreps and Wilson (1982*a*). Since both of these approaches end up arriving at similar solutions of the problem, our attention focuses on just one of them, namely, sequential equilibrium, which is discussed at some length in Section 4.6.

Supplementary Material

4.5   Refinements excluding "untenable beliefs": examples

In previous sections, our objective has been to propose robustness criteria that might refine (i.e., selectively discard) Nash equilibria that include threats (contingent behavior out of equilibrium) that would never be carried out by rational players. Those threats were conceived as "incredible," and thus unsuitable to support the equilibrium in question.

It should be clear by now that the credibility of a particular threat (that is, whether it would be rational to carry it out) must depend crucially on the beliefs held by the player in question at the point (i.e., information set) where it would have to be carried out. When trying to distinguish between credible and incredible threats in Section 4.4, we admitted the possibility of "rationalizing" threats on the basis of *any* arbitrary pattern of beliefs *not* contradicting Bayes rule or the equilibrium strategies. In a sense, we allowed players to "choose" their out-of-equilibrium beliefs to support their particular threats. Undertaking a step forward that is conceptually analogous, our aim in this section is to explore the "credibility" of beliefs. A discrimination between those that are sustainable (or credible) and those that are not provides additional criteria of refinement within the general set of Nash equilibria.

However, the task is now more subtle and also less conclusive than before. The credibility or not of some specific beliefs hinges on the kind of counterfactual rationalizations (i.e., justifications or "stories") that are admitted as plausible after observing an (unexpected) deviation from equilibrium. To facilitate the discussion, it is useful to associate the corresponding Nash refinements to alternative ways of explaining or justifying a player's deviation. Specifically, we consider the following three possibilities[54]:

1. The deviant player has made a mistake.
2. The deviant player holds a different "theory" of play (i.e., is aiming at another equilibrium).
3. The deviant player is, in fact, sending a signal to her opponents.

4.5.1 *Deviations interpreted as mistakes*

Accepting that agents are playing (or, at least, are intending to play) a particular Nash equilibrium, it seems natural that one should try to understand any observed deviation from it as a possible mistake. One possible formalization of this idea gives rise to the concept of *Perfect Equilibrium* (Selten, 1975), sometimes also known as "trembling-hand perfect" for reasons that will become apparent below. Let us now describe it informally, postponing a precise formulation to Definition 4.6.

Assume that, given a particular game and some corresponding equilibrium strategies that agents aim to play, none of them can be sure to do as desired. Specifically, suppose that every time each player has to make a decision during the game, she cannot avoid choosing an action different from the intended one with some small (but positive and independent) probability no larger than some $\varepsilon > 0$. With this motivation in mind, let us define an ε-perfect equilibrium as a Nash equilibrium of the "perturbed" game in which the referred probabilities of deviation cannot be avoided. The perturbed game essentially plays an instrumental role in the analysis: since all strategies are played in it with some positive probability, such a game has *no* information sets "off the equilibrium path." Therefore, in contrast with what generally happens when mistakes are not allowed, the beliefs applicable at each

---

[54] The discussion here follows closely the approach of Kreps (1987).

information set are a *direct* consequence of Bayes rule. Naturally, we want to think of the mistake probability as small. Accordingly, we make ε converge to zero, any limit of ε-perfect equilibria for the corresponding sequence of perturbed games being called a perfect equilibrium of the original game.

Consider now the implications of the perfect equilibrium concept for the game represented in Figure 4.3. Suppose that both players adopt each of their respective actions with positive probability (due to mistakes) and, for simplicity, make the mistake probability equal to $\varepsilon > 0$. Then, for a particular strategy of player 2 to be optimal, it must prescribe that when this player is called upon to play (something that occurs with probability no lower than 2ε), the probability of adopting action b is the minimum possible; i.e., it is equal to ε. But then, neither can the equilibrium strategy of player 1 attribute to action A a probability higher than the minimum ε. This implies that, as ε approaches zero, the corresponding equilibrium strategy profile must converge to (B, a), which turns out to be the (unique) perfect equilibrium of the game. Recall from our discussion of Section 4.2 that (B, a) is also the unique Nash equilibrium of the game supported by credible threats on the part of player 2. As shown below (cf. Theorem 4.1), such "off-equilibrium credibility" is, in fact, a general property displayed by any perfect equilibrium. It derives from the feature that, at any of the ε-perfect equilibria that approximate it, all subgames are reached with some positive (albeit arbitrarily small) probability. Thus, because all subgames are on the equilibrium path, strategies cannot prescribe suboptimal behavior in any of them.

A further elaboration on the interpretation of deviations as unlikely mistakes is provided by a refinement of the perfect equilibrium concept proposed by Myerson (1978) known as *proper equilibrium* – itself then, of course, an even more stringent refinement of Nash equilibrium. According to this concept, if unexpected deviations are to be conceived of as the outcome of players' mistakes, it is natural to attribute a substantially lower probability to those more detrimental ones that are themselves payoff dominated by other possible deviations. The motivation here is that the care a player devotes to avoiding mistakes should depend on what relative (always negative) consequences are associated with each of them. More precisely, consider, for each information set, a ranking of the different possible action choices according to their payoff consequences. If we postulate that, as the overall error probability tends to zero, the *order of magnitude* of the probabilities associated with each possible mistake should reflect their payoff ranking, the resulting limit equilibrium is called a proper equilibrium (see Definition 4.7 for a precise formulation).

Let us now illustrate heuristically the differences between the perfect and proper equilibrium concepts through the game represented in Figure 4.6.

This game has two Nash equilibria: (F, b) and (A, a), and both are perfect. The second one qualifies as such because, simply, it does not allow for any off-equilibrium behavior. The first one, on the other hand, is also perfect because, in case player 2 was called upon to play (something that should *not* occur in the contemplated equilibrium), this player can rationalize her action b as a best response to the belief that (by mistake) it is more likely that player 1 has deviated to B than to A. This belief, however, is incompatible with the proper equilibrium concept.

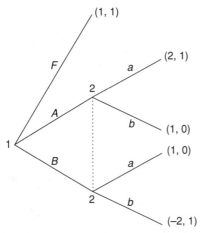

Figure 4.6: An extensive-form game with two pure-strategy Nash equilibria that are both perfect.

Since strategy A payoff dominates B for player 1 – given that the equilibrium being played is (F, b) – a mistake toward A must be attributed a higher subjective probability by player 2 than a deviation toward B. We must conclude, therefore, that the Nash equilibrium (F, b) is not proper. In contrast, the strategy profile (A, a) does define a proper equilibrium because, as indicated above, it involves no off-equilibrium behavior.

4.5.2   *Deviations interpreted as alternative theories*

Each equilibrium represents a particular "theory" on how the game will (or should) be played. If a certain equilibrium is predicted, it is implicit in such a prediction that all players share that same theory of play. If this equilibrium represents the only coherent theory on how the game can be played (e.g., it is the unique Nash equilibrium – recall Subsection 2.2.1), no ambiguities might arise. Often, however, no such uniqueness prevails. Then, the deviation from a particular equilibrium by a certain player may be interpreted by the other players as a confusion on her part about what equilibrium "really" is being played. In fact, the existence of some such alternative equilibrium may sometimes determine univocally the beliefs to be held off the intended equilibrium path.

   To illustrate matters, consider the game represented in Figure 4.7. This game has two pure-strategy WPBEs: (F, b) and (A, a), that are perfect as well.[55] Suppose that the first of these equilibria is the one that player 2 assumes (or insists, given her payoffs) should be played. What might player 2 think if, nevertheless, player 1 deviates from it? It is natural that she allow for the possibility that this deviation has occurred because player 1 assumes (or again, insists, given her payoffs) that it is the equilibrium (A, a) that represents the "appropriate" theory of the game. If player

---

[55] The equilibrium (F, b) may be supported by the belief on the part of player 2 that a deviation toward B (say, by mistake) is more likely than one toward A.

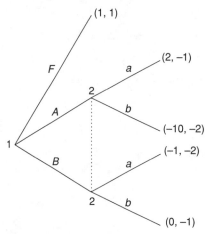

Figure 4.7: An extensive-form game with two pure-strategy WPBEs that are both perfect.

2 indeed accepts that possible explanation, her beliefs should be concentrated on player 1 having chosen action A. Hence, her optimal response to player 1's deviation should be a. But then, if player 1 reasons in this fashion and becomes convinced that player 2 will argue as indicated, she will indeed deviate from the equilibrium (F, b). That is, the alternative equilibrium (A, a) is the only one robust to the possibility of interpreting observed deviations as a manifestation of disagreement (or confusion) among the players about which equilibrium is being played.

In fact, the former considerations used to discard the equilibrium (F, b) may be reinforced by the following observation. Only by deviating toward A can player 1 hope to achieve a payoff higher than what she may *ensure* for herself by playing F. (Note that, after B, any choice by player 2 provides a payoff to player 1 lower than 1.) Thus, whatever might have been her original beliefs, the only way player 2 can reconcile the assumption that player 1 is rational and the observation that she has deviated from F is to believe that player 1 has chosen action A.

This complementary route to discard the equilibrium (F, b) exploits an argument of *forward induction*, which is to be contrasted with the *backward* induction logic reflected, for example, by the SPE concept (cf. Section 4.2).[56] Forward induction interprets the actions adopted by the players along the game in terms of what they could have previously done but did not do. In the context of the previous game, any action by player 1 that leads player 2 to move (that is, A or B) is interpreted by the latter player in terms of the action F that the former could have chosen but did not choose. Specifically, player 2 may be conceived as reasoning along the following lines:

> "If player 1 allows me to participate in the game, it must be because she must be aiming to earn a payoff higher than what she could guarantee with action F. The only way she can obtain that payoff is by playing A. Therefore, she

[56] As will be recalled, backward induction evaluates *current* choice possibilities in terms of the predicted *future* courses of action. Its logic, therefore, is performed "backward" in time.

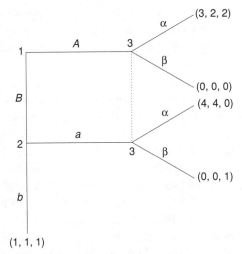

Figure 4.8: A three-player extensive-form game with two pure-strategy Nash equilibria, only one of which is a WPBE.

must have chosen A and my optimal response to it is to 'yield' and, rather than choosing b as I had (possibly) planned, adopt a instead."

Arguments of forward induction such as that outlined above are an important part of the more interesting (and advanced) developments of the recent literature on Nash refinements. Consequently, they will be revisited several times in a variety of different contexts in this and subsequent chapters. In particular, a good further illustration of their potential is discussed in the ensuing Subsection 4.5.3, where deviations are studied in terms of their signaling content.

To close our present discussion, we now turn to another example where the existence of "conflicting theories" gives rise to difficult conceptual problems. Consider the three-player game represented in Figure 4.8.

This game has two pure-strategy Nash equilibria: (A, b, α) and (B, b, β) – the second is a WPBE (even perfect), but not the first one. The strategy profile (A, b, α) is not a WPBE because if player 2 were given the opportunity to make a choice, it would never be rational for her to choose b – she should select a instead. (Note that player 3 is supposed to choose α at this equilibrium and she cannot make her action depend on whether 2 moves or not.) However, let us now sketch a heuristic argument that suggests that, despite the fact that (A, b, α) is not a WPBE, it might still be a "reasonable" way to play.

In the only WPBE of the game, (B, b, β), player 3 does not move. Supposing that this is indeed the equilibrium expected by player 3, consider now what she might think if player 1 chooses A and gives her (i.e., player 3) the opportunity to move. If, once recovered from the initial surprise, she replaces her primitive "theory" (B, b, β) by the alternative Nash equilibrium (A, b, α), her optimal choice is α. But then, if player 1 is able to anticipate this mental process on the part of player 3, she will choose A in the first place and induce the strategy profile (A, b, α), which is more profitable for player 1 than the WPBE (B, b, β).

The "mental processes" of players, however, need not stop here. Suppose player 1 is also capable of anticipating that player 2 may think in a way similar to herself (in particular, that player 2 can understand the hypothetical reasoning by 3 explained above). In this case, if player 2 were given the opportunity to move, she would choose a instead of b, because she should predict that player 3 would subsequently move α. But then, taking this into account, player 1 should choose B and the strategy profile (B, a, α) would prevail. This logic, of course, may be taken one further step to ask: what prevents player 3 from performing, mimetically, the former mental reasoning? If she does, her choice must be β, and the whole argument collapses completely.

What can we make of this seemingly "self-destructive" chain of contradictory arguments? Taken to an extreme, even the prediction that *some* Nash equilibrium will be played seems questionable. (Recall in this respect the motivation underlying the much weaker notion of rationalizability discussed in Section 2.7.) As we shall argue repeatedly throughout, the "message" that transpires from this state of affairs is a rather eclectic one: the value and relevance of any equilibrium notion (for prediction or otherwise) is necessarily context dependent; i.e., it cannot abstract from the specific circumstances in which it is applied.

4.5.3 *Deviations interpreted as signals*

In a general sense, any intermediate action played in a game with sequential structure may be regarded as a signal sent by the player who adopts it. In certain asymmetric-information contexts (e.g., in the so-called signaling games studied in Section 6.4, where a certain piece of relevant knowledge on the environment is private information to the player that moves first in the game), this phenomenon arises explicitly and sharply. However, it is not only in such games that the idea of "deviation as signal" may play an important role. By way of illustration, we discuss now a simple variation on a game proposed by Ben-Porath and Dekel (1992). As a starting point for it, we consider the (simultaneous) battle of the sexes described by Table 1.2. Then, before this game (which becomes a subgame of the whole game), we introduce an initial stage where the boy can, *publicly*, "burn money." That is, he may choose to decrease his utility in, say, one unit in an irreversible way (observed by the girl). Adding this prior stage, the full game displays the extensive form represented in Figure 4.9.

Suppose the boy decides to burn money publicly (i.e., chooses X) in the first stage of the game. How should the girl interpret this action on his part? A reasonable possibility would be to view this as a signal that, in the ensuing battle of the sexes, the boy intends to play S. For otherwise (i.e., if he planned to play B instead), the maximum payoff the boy can hope to get is 1 (but perhaps even less if the girl chooses S rather than B). In contrast, playing Y first (i.e., not burning money) and then S, the boy *guarantees* for himself the same payoff of 1.

Once the girl analyzes the situation in this way (i.e., understands that playing X and then B is weakly dominated for the boy), she should predict that, after observing X, the boy will play S. Therefore, she should react by playing S on her part as well after this observation. But then, if despite these considerations, the boy decides

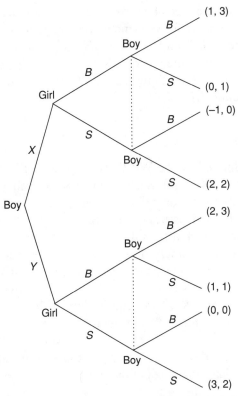

Figure 4.9: Battle of the sexes with the prior choice of "money burning" (X) or not (Y) on the part of the boy. (Payoff vectors specify first the boy's payoff, followed by the girl's.)

to start the game with Y (*not* burning money) rather than X, it must be because he has the intention or hope of earning a payoff higher than 2 – the payoff that he can be sure to attain in view of the previous argument. This higher payoff is possible only if, after Y, the boy plays S. Thus, it seems reasonable that the girl should predict a choice of S on the part of the boy in *every* case (i.e., both after X and Y). Consequently, she should *always* play S as well. In view of this fact, the best (undominated) strategy for the boy is to eschew burning money altogether and then play S, because this will be responded by the girl (even though she observes only Y but not S) with a choice of S. Finally, the option of burning money that triggered the whole argument is not used by the boy, even though its *possibility* is indeed the crucial feature allowing the boy to achieve his most preferred outcome.

The previous argument of forward induction (recall Subsection 4.5.2, where this logic was originally discussed) is, to a certain extent, shocking and controversial. Why should one suppose that only one of the players can burn money publicly? How is it possible that an *ex post* irrelevant possibility may have such an overpowering effect on the analysis of the game? All this illustrates the subtle and interesting considerations raised by forward induction in the study of many multistage games. It also hints at some potential fragility of the underlying arguments, an issue that has been the source of a lively (and still open) debate among game theorists.

The iterative reasoning illustrated here can be formalized in a rigorous manner. As we shall see in Section 4.8, its chain of forward-induction arguments essentially amounts to a corresponding process of elimination of *weakly* dominated strategies. Quite interestingly, we shall see that the outcome of this iterative process contrasts sharply with the seemingly similar process of elimination of (strongly) dominated strategies that was studied in Section 2.1.

4.6   Sequential equilibrium

The important shortcomings exhibited by the WPBE concept were illustrated in Section 4.4. There, we showed that this equilibrium notion does not even guarantee subgame perfection; i.e., it may allow for nonequilibrium behavior in some proper subgames. To tackle the problem, the main issue concerns finding natural conditions that suitably narrow down the unrestricted off-equilibrium beliefs permitted by the WPBE concept. Of course, one of the primary objectives in this respect must be to guarantee that the induced equilibria satisfy the basic requirement of subgame perfection. But more generally, the objective should be to rule out all awkward (thus, arguably "untenable") belief imputations off the equilibrium path. To illustrate some of the considerations involved in this task, consider the game represented in Figure 4.10.

In this game, the strategy profile (A, b, U) defines a Nash equilibrium. This equilibrium is weak perfect Bayesian for any belief pattern $\hat{\mu}$ that satisfies

$$\hat{\mu}(x_{31}) \geq 2(1 - \hat{\mu}(x_{31})) \tag{4.5}$$

or $\hat{\mu}(x_{31}) \geq 2/3$. Clearly, any assessment (recall Section 4.4) that involves a belief pattern consistent with (4.5) and the strategy profile (A, b, U) satisfies both (a) and

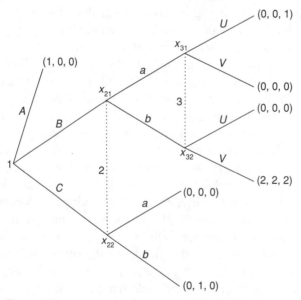

Figure 4.10: An extensive-form game with a WPBE that is not a sequential equilibrium.

(b) in Definition 4.2. On the other hand, this strategy profile is an SPE because the game has no proper subgames (thus, trivially, every Nash equilibrium is subgame perfect).

However, it is reasonable to claim that any off-equilibrium beliefs that satisfy (4.5) are contradictory with the strategy profile (A, b, U), which prescribes that player 2 would choose b if given the opportunity to move. In view of the structure of the game, the only beliefs by player 3 that are compatible with such a strategy of player 2 are those that have all probability concentrated on the node x_{32} (or, equivalently, attribute zero weight to the node x_{31}). Thus, recalling (4.5), we may argue that the beliefs required to support (A, b, U) as a WPBE are incompatible (although statistically consistent, given the inapplicability of Bayes rule at player 3's information set) with the structure of the game *and* the equilibrium strategies.

Essentially, the root of the problem here is the same as that discussed for the game represented by Figure 4.5 (Section 4.4). It derives from the fact that, if any given information set displays zero *ex ante* probability, the same applies to every other information set that follows it in the game. Therefore, from the viewpoint of statistical consistency alone (i.e., Bayes rule), the beliefs to be had at both information sets admit an arbitrary – and, in principle, *independent* – specification. However, once the beliefs have been determined in the first of the information sets, it seems natural to require that any *subsequent* beliefs should exhibit full statistical coherence with those former beliefs, the structure of the game, *and* the contemplated (equilibrium) strategies. In other words, given the beliefs specified at the first information set, a new resort to "discretion" in determining beliefs should be allowed again only when it is absolutely necessary. To be more precise, the suggested condition may be formulated as follows. Let γ be the prevailing strategy profile and consider any information set $h \in H$ (possibly, with $P^\gamma(h) = 0$) where $(\mu(x))_{x \in h}$ are the corresponding beliefs. Then, the requirement is that the beliefs $(\mu(x))_{x \in h'}$ associated with any other h' following h in the game should be statistically consistent with $(\mu(x))_{x \in h}$, the strategies in γ, and Bayes rule.

The justification of this condition on how beliefs are to be formed off the equilibrium path not only derives from its intuitive appeal. As shown below (cf. Theorem 4.1), it also remedies the problems of subgame imperfection found for the (unrestricted) WPBE concept. An effective way of imposing that condition on any given assessment (μ, γ) is through a natural requirement of continuity in the process of belief formation. Specifically, note that, on the one hand, any strategy profile γ may always be conceived as the *limit* of some sequence $\{\gamma_k\}_{k=1,2,...}$ where every profile γ_k in the sequence is *completely mixed*; i.e., each player i's strategy $\gamma_{i,k}$ attributes positive probability to *all* her actions available in every one of her information sets. Of course, any such completely mixed strategy profile γ_k guarantees that every information set in the game has positive *ex ante* probability. Therefore, we can univocally associate with it a belief pattern μ_k through Bayes rule alone and refer unambiguously to the pair (γ_k, μ_k) as a *consistent assessment*. Then, the continuity requirement used to evaluate the consistency of *any* assessment (possibly associated with a strategy profile not completely mixed) may be simply formulated as follows: a general assessment (μ, γ) is declared consistent if it is "approachable" by a sequence of consistent assessments $\{(\mu_k, \gamma_k)\}_{k=1,2,...}$, where each strategy profile γ_k in the sequence is completely mixed. Formally, we define the following.[57]

Definition 4.3: *Let $\gamma \in \Psi$ be a strategy profile that is* completely mixed *in Γ (that is, $\forall i = 1, 2, \ldots, n$, $\forall h \in H_i$, $\forall a \in A(h)$, $\gamma_i(h)(a) > 0$). A corresponding assessment (μ, γ) is said to be* consistent *if $\forall h \in H$, $\forall x \in h$, $\mu(x)$ coincide with the posterior updating of $P^\gamma(x)$ that results from the application in h of Bayes rule.*

Definition 4.4: *Let $\gamma \in \Psi$ be a general strategy profile, not necessarily completely mixed. A corresponding assessment (μ, γ) is* consistent *if it is the limit of a sequence of consistent assessments $\{(\mu_k, \gamma_k)\}_{k=1,2,...}$ where each γ_k is completely mixed (cf. Definition 4.3).*

Consider again the game represented in Figure 4.10 and denote $\gamma_1 \equiv (\gamma_1(A), \gamma_1(B), \gamma_1(C))$, $\gamma_2 \equiv (\gamma_2(a), \gamma_2(b))$, $\gamma_3 \equiv (\gamma_3(U), \gamma_3(V))$. In such a behavioral-strategy format, the equilibrium (A, b, U) is defined by the following strategies:

$$\hat{\gamma}_1 = (1, 0, 0); \quad \hat{\gamma}_2 = (0, 1); \quad \hat{\gamma}_3 = (1, 0).$$

Fix any arbitrary $\rho > 0$ and focus on the sequence of completely mixed strategies $\{\gamma_{1,k}, \gamma_{2,k}, \gamma_{3,k}\}_{k=1}^\infty$ given by

$$\gamma_{1,k} = (1 - (1 + \rho)\varepsilon_{1k}, \varepsilon_{1k}, \rho\varepsilon_{1k}); \quad \gamma_{2,k} = (\varepsilon_{2k}, 1 - \varepsilon_{2k});$$

$$\gamma_{3,k} = (1 - \varepsilon_{3k}, \varepsilon_{3k}); \tag{4.6}$$

where $\varepsilon_{rk} \downarrow 0$ for each $r = 1, 2, 3$. Associated with this sequence of strategy profiles, Bayes rule induces a corresponding sequence of beliefs as follows:

$$\mu_{2k} \equiv (\mu_k(x_{21}), \mu_k(x_{22})) = \left(\frac{1}{1 + \rho}, \frac{\rho}{1 + \rho} \right)$$

$$\mu_{3k} \equiv (\mu_k(x_{31}), \mu_k(x_{32})) = (\varepsilon_{2k}, 1 - \varepsilon_{2k}).$$

Obviously, $\gamma_{r,k} \to \hat{\gamma}_r$ for each $r = 1, 2, 3$, and

$$\hat{\mu}_2 \equiv \lim_{k \to \infty} \mu_{2k} = \left(\frac{1}{1 + \rho}, \frac{\rho}{1 + \rho} \right) \tag{4.7}$$

$$\hat{\mu}_3 \equiv \lim_{k \to \infty} \mu_{3k} = (0, 1). \tag{4.8}$$

This provides a rigorous formalization of the former discussion heuristically excluding unsuitable beliefs for the game represented in Figure 4.10. Specifically, it shows that, given the WPBE $\hat{\gamma}$ (or (A, b, U)), the only belief pattern $\hat{\mu}$ giving rise to a *consistent* assessment $(\hat{\mu}, \hat{\gamma})$ must attribute full probability to the node x_{32} in

---

[57] Note that, whereas Definition 4.3 restricts to assessments associated with *completely mixed* strategy profiles, Definition 4.4 builds on the former one to extend the notion of consistent assessment to the general case.

player 3's information set, even though it may allow for any beliefs (associated with different values of ρ above)[58] in the information set of player 2.

As explained, the notion of consistency embodied by Definition 4.4 requires from any assessment (μ, γ) that it should *not* be contradictory with (i) statistical updating (i.e., Bayes rule); (ii) the structure of the game; (iii) the equilibrium strategies. But, of course, for any such consistent assessment to support an equilibrium, it is also required (as in (a) of Definition 4.2 for WPBE) that it should induce *sequentially optimal* behavior. That is, each strategy γ_i must prescribe optimal action for player i at every one of her information sets $h \in H_i$, given the beliefs $(\mu(x))_{x \in h}$ that prevail there. The twin requirements of consistency and sequential optimality character-ize the notion of sequential equilibrium proposed by Kreps and Wilson (1982a). Relying on former notational conventions, it can be formally defined as follows.

Definition 4.5 (Kreps and Wilson, 1982a): *A strategy profile* $\gamma^* = (\gamma_1^*, \gamma_2^*, \ldots, \gamma_n^*) \in \Psi$ *is a sequential equilibrium of* Γ *if there exists a pat-tern of beliefs* μ^* *such that* (μ^*, γ^*) *is a consistent assessment and* $\forall i \in N, \forall h \in H_i, \forall \gamma_i \in \Psi_i,$

$$\pi_i(\gamma^* \mid \mu^*, h) \geq \pi_i\left((\gamma_i, \gamma_{-i}^*) \mid \mu^*, h\right). \tag{4.9}$$

Returning to the game represented in Figure 4.10, it is clear that the WPBE (and SPE) $\hat{\gamma}$ is *not* sequentially optimal (i.e., it does not satisfy (4.9)) for *any* of the belief patterns $\hat{\mu}$ for which $(\hat{\gamma}, \hat{\mu})$ is a consistent assessment (cf. (4.7) and (4.8)). In contrast, the pure strategy profile (B, b, V) – or, equivalently, the behavioral strategy profile $\tilde{\gamma}$ given by

$$\tilde{\gamma}_1 = (0, 1, 0), \quad \tilde{\gamma}_2 = (0, 1), \quad \tilde{\gamma}_3 = (0, 1), \tag{4.10}$$

does define a sequential equilibrium (which is in fact unique – see Exercise 4.5). To verify it, note that these strategies lead to positive (in fact, full) probability of visiting every information set. Therefore, the corresponding beliefs are uniquely induced by Bayes Rule as follows:

$$\tilde{\mu}_2 = (1, 0), \quad \tilde{\mu}_3 = (0, 1),$$

rendering the pair $(\tilde{\gamma}, \tilde{\mu})$ a consistent assessment. On the other hand, it is clear that, given the belief pattern $\tilde{\mu}$, the strategies $\tilde{\gamma}_i$ defined in (4.10) are optimal for each respective player i in her respective (single) information set. Thus, the strategy profile defines a sequential equilibrium for the game, as claimed.

4.7 Perfect and proper equilibria

As might be recalled, the informal discussion conducted in Subsection 4.5.1 out-lined an approach to refining Nash equilibria that, unlike what had been done so far, involved formulating a *comprehensive* theoretical framework where a coherent

---

[58] Strictly speaking, the procedure described produces only limit beliefs $\hat{\mu}_2$ that are interior, i.e., attribute positive weight to both nodes in player 2's information set. However, it is straightforward to check that if (4.6) is modified so that $\gamma_{1,k} = (1 - (1 + \rho_k)\varepsilon_{1k}, \varepsilon_{1k}, \rho_k\varepsilon_{1k})$, any of the two extreme beliefs, $(0, 1)$ or $(1, 0)$, are, respectively, obtained by making $\rho_k \to \infty$ (with $\rho_k\varepsilon_{1k} \to 0$) or $\rho_k \downarrow 0$.

explanation for *both* on- and off-equilibrium behavior is explicitly provided. In particular, the natural proposal we made in this respect was to allow for the possibility of (unlikely) mistakes. These mistakes were then invoked to justify that even suboptimal behavior might be occasionally observed as the outcome of players' unintended decisions. In fact, depending on how the relative probabilities of these mistakes were specifically conceived, two different equilibrium notions were outlined: perfect equilibrium and proper equilibrium. Each of them is now formally presented in turn.

First, we introduce the concept of (trembling-hand) perfect equilibrium. Heuristically, it may be interpreted as a "limit equilibrium situation" (or, more precisely, as the limit of a sequence of equilibrium situations) where players display progressively lower probabilities of mistakes. To formalize this notion precisely, it is useful to rely on the following notation. Given some behavioral strategy γ_i of player i, let a be one of the actions she has available in the information set $h \in H_i$. Denote by $\gamma_i \backslash a$ the strategy that results from playing always action a at h, maintaining unchanged all other prescriptions of γ_i at any other information set $h' \in H_i$. The concept of perfect equilibrium is then defined as follows.

Definition 4.6 (Selten, 1975): *A strategy profile $\gamma^* \in \Psi$ is a* perfect equilibrium *of Γ if there exists a sequence $\{(\mu_k, \gamma_k)\}_{k=1,2,...}$ of consistent assessments (cf. Definition 4.3) satisfying*

> *(i) $\forall k = 1, 2, \ldots, \gamma_k$ is completely mixed;*
> *(ii) $\exists \{\varepsilon_k\}_{k=1}^{\infty}, \quad \varepsilon_k \downarrow 0, \quad$ such that $\forall k = 1, 2, \ldots, \quad \forall i \in N, \quad \forall h \in H_i,$*
> *$\forall a, a' \in A(h),$*
> $$\pi_i((\gamma_{i,k}\backslash a, \gamma_{-i,k}) \mid \mu_k, h) > \pi_i((\gamma_{i,k}\backslash a', \gamma_{-i,k}) \mid \mu_k, h)$$
> $$\Rightarrow \gamma_{i,k}(h)(a') \leq \varepsilon_k;$$
> *(iii) $\{\gamma_k\} \to \gamma^*$.*

Part (i) of the previous definition ensures that, since all information sets are visited with positive probability for each strategy profile along the sequence, the consistency demanded from the assessments $\{(\mu_k, \gamma_k)\}_{k=1,2,...}$ follows from a direct application of Bayes rule. From a technical viewpoint, this is the essential motivation for this condition. At a more conceptual level, however, the idea embodied by (i) is that agents cannot behave in a tremble- (or mistake-) free manner. Part (ii) is an "almost" optimality condition. It requires that suboptimal decisions (i.e., "wrong" actions at any information set) can occur only by mistake, i.e., with probabilities no higher than the corresponding $\{\varepsilon_k\}_{k=1}^{\infty}$, that are independent across information sets and converge to zero along the sequence considered. Finally, part (iii) simply states that the equilibrium profile γ^* may be conceived as the limit of (or an approximation to) a situation in which, as reflected by (i) and (ii), strategy profiles always allow for some, but vanishingly small, probabilities of mistake.

It is easy to verify (Exercise 4.9) that the perfect equilibrium concept may be reformulated in the following more compact and manageable fashion, along the lines of our previous formulation of sequential equilibrium (Definition 4.5).

Definition 4.6′: *A strategy profile $\gamma^* \in \Psi$ is a* perfect equilibrium *for Γ if there exists a sequence $\{(\mu_k, \gamma_k)\}_{k=1,2,...}$ of consistent assessments such that* *(i)* $\forall\, k = 1, 2, \ldots,\, \gamma_k$ *is completely mixed*;

(ii) $\forall k = 1, 2, \ldots, \forall i \in N, \forall h \in H_i, \forall \gamma_i \in \Psi_i,$

$$\pi_i(\gamma^* \mid \mu_k, h) \geq \pi_i((\gamma_i, \gamma^*_{-i,k}) \mid \mu_k, h);$$

(iii) $\{\gamma_k\} \to \gamma^*$.

The perfect equilibrium concept contemplates no particular restriction on the structure of the different mistake probabilities experienced by the players. As explained in Subsection 4.5.1, it is of quite some interest to study a variation on (in fact, a refinement of) perfect equilibrium that introduces a hierarchy of players' mistakes according to their relative payoff consequences. Responding to this hierarchy, if a certain mistake is more costly than another in a given information set (i.e., it induces a lower expected payoff in that information set, given prevailing beliefs and opponents' strategies), the former must display a significantly lower mistake probability than the latter. More precisely, it is required that, as the "benchmark" mistake probability ε_k becomes progressively lower ($\varepsilon_k \downarrow 0$), the different suboptimal actions should be played with infinitesimal probabilities whose order in ε_k reflects the referred hierarchy. Formally, this gives rise to the concept of proper equilibrium, which is defined as follows.

Definition 4.7 (Myerson, 1978): *A strategy profile* $\gamma^* \in \Psi$ *is a* proper equilibrium *of* Γ *if there exists a sequence* $\{(\mu_k, \gamma_k)\}_{k=1,2,\ldots}$ *of consistent assessments satisfying*

(i) $\forall\, k = 1, 2, \ldots,\, \gamma_k$ *is completely mixed;*

(ii) $\exists \{\varepsilon_k\}_{k=1}^{\infty},\quad \varepsilon_k \downarrow 0,\quad such\quad that\quad \forall k = 1, 2, \ldots, \forall i \in N,\quad \forall h \in H_i,$ $\forall a, a' \in A(h),$

$$\pi_i((\gamma_{i,k} \backslash a, \gamma_{-i,k}) \mid \mu_k, h) > \pi_i((\gamma_{i,k} \backslash a', \gamma_{-i,k}) \mid \mu_k, h)$$
$$\Rightarrow \gamma_{i,k}(h)(a') \leq \varepsilon_k \cdot \gamma_{i,k}(h)(a);$$

(iii) $\{\gamma_k\} \to \gamma^*$.

Given any extensive-form game Γ, consider the following short-hand notation:

- $SP(\Gamma)$: Set of subgame-perfect equilibria in Γ;
- $Sq(\Gamma)$: Set of sequential equilibria in Γ;
- $Pf(\Gamma)$: Set of (trembling-hand) perfect equilibria in Γ;
- $Pr(\Gamma)$: Set of proper equilibria in Γ.

With this notation in place, we end the present section with the following basic result.

Theorem 4.1: *Every finite game in extensive form* Γ *satisfies*

$$SP(\Gamma) \supseteq Sq(\Gamma) \supseteq Pf(\Gamma) \supseteq Pr(\Gamma) \neq \emptyset.$$

Proof: The stated inclusion relations are a straightforward consequence of the respective definitions for each equilibrium concept. We focus, therefore, on proving that $Pr(\Gamma) \neq \emptyset$, which obviously guarantees existence for all of them.

Let $\varepsilon \in (0, 1)$ be chosen arbitrarily. For each $h \in H$, denote

$$\delta_h = \frac{\varepsilon^{|A(h)|}}{|A(h)|},$$

where $|A(h)|$ stands for the cardinality of the set $A(h)$. Define

$$\tilde{\Psi}_i \equiv \{\gamma_i \in \Psi_i : \forall h \in H_i, \ \forall a \in A(h), \ \gamma_i(h)(a) \geq \delta_h\},$$

$$\tilde{\Delta}(A(h)) \equiv \{\gamma_i(h) \in \Delta(A(h)) : \forall a \in A(h), \ \gamma_i(h)(a) \geq \delta_h\}.$$

For each $h \in H_i$, consider the mapping (a correspondence)

$$\varphi_h : \tilde{\Psi} \equiv \tilde{\Psi}_1 \times \tilde{\Psi}_2 \times \cdots \times \tilde{\Psi}_n \rightrightarrows \tilde{\Delta}(A(h))$$

defined by

$$\varphi_h(\gamma) = \left\{ \begin{array}{c} \tilde{\gamma}_i(h) \in \tilde{\Delta}(A(h)) \mid \ \forall a, a' \in A(h), \\ \pi_i(\gamma_i \backslash a, \gamma_{-i} \mid \mu, h) > \pi_i(\gamma_i \backslash a', \gamma_{-i} \mid \mu, h) \\ \Rightarrow \tilde{\gamma}_i(h)(a') \leq \varepsilon \tilde{\gamma}_i(h)(a) \end{array} \right\}.$$

It may be checked (see Exercise 4.10) that, $\forall h \in H$, $\forall \gamma \in \tilde{\Psi}$, the set $\varphi_h(\gamma)$ is nonempty, closed, and convex. Since, moreover, each φ_h is upper hemicontinuous, the product correspondence

$$\varphi \equiv (\varphi_h)_{h \in H} : \tilde{\Psi} \rightrightarrows \tilde{\Psi} \tag{4.11}$$

satisfies the hypotheses of Kakutani's fixed-point theorem (recall Section 2.4). Therefore, one can guarantee the existence of some $\gamma^* \in \tilde{\Psi}$ such that $\gamma^* \in \varphi(\gamma^*)$. Choose some such fixed point and, to reflect its dependence on the given ε, denote it by $\gamma^*(\varepsilon)$.

Consider now any sequence $\{\varepsilon_k\}_{k=1}^{\infty}$ with $\varepsilon_k \downarrow 0$ and, for each ε_k, choose a strategy profile $\gamma^*(\varepsilon_k)$, i.e., a fixed point of φ for $\varepsilon = \varepsilon_k$. By construction, the sequence $\{\gamma^*(\varepsilon_k)\}$ satisfies (i) and (ii) in Definition 4.7. Therefore, its limit (of a subsequence, if necessary) is a proper equilibrium, the desired conclusion. ∎

As indicated, Theorem 4.1 establishes, in particular, that all the Nash refinement concepts contemplated in the present chapter have their existence guaranteed. It also contains a nested chain of inclusions among these concepts, whose main implications may be summarized as follows.

(a) In contrast with, say, the WPBE concept, sequential equilibrium is not only effective in guaranteeing (by construction) consistent beliefs, but it also ensures subgame perfection (i.e., a Nash equilibrium is played in every proper subgame, both on as well as off the equilibrium path).

(b) Those two essential features of consistency and subgame perfection can also be achieved through an *explicit* modeling of out-of-equilibrium behavior, as reflected (with different levels of detail) by the perfect equilibrium and proper equilibrium concepts.

4.8   Strategic-form refinements

So far, the different Nash refinements considered in this chapter have been geared toward either discarding incredible threats (Sections 4.2–4.4) or ruling out untenable off-equilibrium beliefs (Sections 4.5–4.7). Implicitly, therefore, the analysis has been restricted to multistage games, which is the only context where these notions (threats and off-equilibrium beliefs) can be of any significance.

Many strategic situations of interest, however, are best modeled as simultaneous games (i.e., games displaying no strategically relevant order of moves). Furthermore, any game (even if it involves a multiplicity of different stages) can always be described through its "simultaneous" strategic-form representation (cf. Section 1.3), which is sometimes more amenable to analysis. This suggests that, in some cases, it may be worthwhile to shift from the previous extensive-form approach to Nash refinements to a similar endeavour based on a strategic-form approach.

These considerations notwithstanding, one may be inclined to think that the strategic-form representation is too compact a description of a game to allow for the study of interesting Nash refinements. In particular, it could be argued that this representation "hides" some of the essential features of the game (order of moves, information, etc.) that are essential to any refining criterion. The aim of this section, however, is to highlight the contrary viewpoint. In particular, we show that interesting conclusions may arise through strategic-form refinements that are close analogues of extensive-form concepts. Moreover, we find that, quite surprisingly, some of the former refining ideas that would seem to hinge crucially on the extensive-form representation of a game (e.g., discarding incredible threats or responding to forward-induction considerations) are in fact embodied by suitably formulated strategic-form counterparts.

Thus, in this section, our discussion pertains to any game in strategic form $G = \{N, \{S_i\}_{i=1}^{n}, \{\pi_i\}_{i=1}^{n}\}$ (recall Section 1.4), with strategy spaces S_i being finite, and the mixed extension defined in terms of the strategy spaces $\Sigma_i = \Delta^{r_i-1}$ $(r_i \equiv |S_i|)$.[59] To open the discussion, it is useful to start with the simple-minded refinement of Nash equilibrium that results from insisting that *every* player should have a *strict* incentive to play as prescribed by the equilibrium. This is the idea reflected by the concept of *strict Nash equilibrium*, which is defined as follows.

Definition 4.8: *A strategy profile* σ^* *is a* strict Nash equilibrium *of* G *if* $\forall i = 1, 2, \ldots, n$, $\forall \sigma_i \neq \sigma_i^*$, $\pi_i(\sigma^*) > \pi_i(\sigma_i, \sigma_{-i}^*)$.

Often, the strictness condition demanded by the above equilibrium concept is too strong to allow for existence. For example, when all Nash equilibria of the game involve some player adopting a genuinely mixed strategy, no strict Nash equilibrium can exist (Exercise 4.12).

Even though it is often too demanding to insist that players have *strict* incentives to play a particular Nash equilibrium, it will be generally desirable to rule out

---

[59] By returning to the primitive (i.e., nonbehavioral) formulation of mixed strategies, we underscore the fact that extensive-form notions and constructs (e.g., information sets, beliefs, off-equilibrium reactions, etc.) play no explicit role in the present strategic-form approach.

Table 4.1: *A strategic-form game with two Nash equilibria, one of them involving a weakly dominated strategy*

1 \ 2	A	B
X	0, 0	0, 0
Y	0, 0	1, 1

certain cases of payoff indifference. By way of illustration, consider the game whose strategic form is given by Table 4.1.

This game has two Nash equilibria: (X, A) and (Y, B). Intuitively, it is clear that the first equilibrium is not very reasonable. If, say, player 1 were to deviate from X to Y, she would be sure not to lose with the change. The same happens with player 2 if she were to choose B instead of A. In both cases, those deviations can just bring in payoff gains for the deviating player, something that will indeed occur if the opponent deviates as well. In fact, if players reason in this way, it seems very likely that, even if they were planning to play (X, A), they would both end up deviating, which just reconfirms the advantages of a deviation in the first place. Summing up, the Nash equilibrium (X, A) appears to be very fragile, and there seem to be good reasons to reject it as a robust equilibrium configuration.

Essentially, what underlies the previous discussion is simply the idea that strategies X and A are *weakly dominated* by Y and B, respectively, in the following precise sense.

Definition 4.9: *The (pure)[60] strategy $s_i \in S_i$ is weakly dominated for player i in G if $\exists \sigma_i \in \Sigma_i$ such that*

(a) $\forall s_{-i} \in S_{-i} \equiv S_0 \times \cdots S_{i-1} \times S_{i+1} \times \cdots \times S_n$,
$$\pi(\sigma_i, s_{-i}) \geq \pi(s_i, s_{-i});$$
(b) $\exists \tilde{s}_{-i} \in S_{-i}$ for which $\pi(\sigma_i, \tilde{s}_{-i}) > \pi(s_i, \tilde{s}_{-i})$.

In contrast with the concept of (strongly) dominated strategy introduced in Definition 2.1, the present weaker notion of dominance requires only that the dominating strategy produce a strictly higher payoff for *some* strategy profile of the opponents (and no lower, of course, for all of them). On the basis of it, we propose our next strategic-form refinement of Nash equilibrium.

Definition 4.10: *The strategy profile $\sigma^* \in \Sigma$ is a Nash equilibrium in (weakly) un-dominated strategies if it is a Nash equilibrium such that $\forall i = 1, 2, \ldots, n,$ $\sigma_i^*(s_i) = 0$ for every strategy $s_i \in S_i$ that is weakly dominated.*

It is important to understand the very different implications of the two notions of payoff dominance considered thus far: weak (Definition 4.9) and strong

---

[60] The present notion of weak domination has analogous implications for mixed strategies as its strong counterpart (recall Section 2.1). For example, any mixed strategy that gives positive weight to a weakly dominated strategy is itself weakly dominated, even though the converse statement is not generally true.

Table 4.2: *A strategic-form game sensitive to the order of elimination of weakly dominated strategies*

1 \\ 2	a	b
A	1, 0	0, 1
B	0, 0	0, 2

(Definition 2.1). At a very basic level, an obvious difference has already been illustrated through the game represented by Table 4.1. Whereas no strongly dominated strategy can form part of a Nash equilibrium, weakly dominated strategies may do so. Playing weakly dominated strategies, therefore, is consistent with the hypothesis of common knowledge of rationality, even though in an admittedly weak sense. As explained next, other less straightforward differences between these two concepts arise when they are applied iteratively.

First, we illustrate the fact that, in contrast with the concept of strong dominance (recall Exercise 2.2), the final outcome resulting from an iterative application of the weaker notion does depend on the order in which it is carried out. Consider the game whose strategic form is given in Table 4.2.

In this game, if one first eliminates the strongly (and therefore weakly) dominated strategy of player 2 (strategy a), player 1 is indifferent about her two strategies (A and B). Thus, the two strategy profiles (A, b) and (B, b) arise as admissible outcomes. Instead, if one first eliminates player 1's strategy B (which originally appears as weakly dominated) and then player 2's strategy a (which is strongly dominated), the unique resulting outcome is the profile (A, b). Therefore, in contrast to the first order of strategy elimination, the profile (B, b) does not survive the process in the second case.

Another very interesting feature displayed by the iterative elimination process based on weak dominance may be illustrated through the game whose extensive-form representation is described in Figure 4.9. Recall that this game contemplated the possibility that one of the players (the boy) might decide to "burn money" before playing a standard battle of the sexes. In Subsection 4.5.3, we proposed an iterative argument that, relying on the signaling content implicit in the different initial actions (specifically, on whether the boy "burns money" or not), excluded any outcome other than the one the boy prefers the most, i.e., no money burning and subsequent coordination in S.

The logic underlying this argument was interpreted heuristically as one of forward induction – i.e., previous decisions that are brought forward to bear on current decisions. As we now explain, such forward-induction considerations can also be formally identified (at least within the present game)[61] with an iterative process of elimination of *weakly* dominated strategies in the strategic-form representation of the game. This representation is given by Table 4.3, where strategies are

---

[61] The issue of what is the correct and general formalization of forward-induction arguments is still under debate by game theorists. Early instances of this way of reasoning can be found in Kohlberg and Mertens (1986).

Table 4.3: *Strategic-form representation of the game in extensive form displayed in Figure 4.9 (battle of the sexes with prior money burning)*

Boy \ Girl	SS	SB	BS	BB
XS	2, 2	2, 2	0, 1	0, 1
XB	−1, 0	−1, 0	1, 3	1, 3
YS	3, 2	1, 1	3, 2	1, 1
YB	0, 0	2, 3	0, 0	2, 3

distinguished by the two action labels corresponding to the respective (relevant) choices made in each of the two information sets corresponding to each player.[62]

As a first round of elimination, observe that, for the boy, strategy XB is weakly dominated by YS (that is, by playing B after X the boy can *never* obtain a larger payoff – sometimes it could be lower – than what he can guarantee for himself by playing Y – i.e., not burning money – and then S). Once XB has been eliminated on these grounds in the first round, the girl finds that playing B after the boy has chosen X is weakly dominated for her. Thus, in the second round, the girl's strategies BS and BB can be eliminated, because they are weakly dominated, respectively, by SS and SB. Entering then the third round, note that the boy now has the strategy YB weakly dominated by XS, i.e., to "risk" playing B after Y is weakly dominated by the strategy ("safer" at this round) of playing X and then S. Having ruled out that the boy may play the strategy YB, the girl, already in the fourth round of the iterative process, should discard playing B after observing that the boy has chosen Y, i.e., SS weakly dominates SB. Finally (fifth round), given that after the former considerations only the strategy SS remains on the girl's part, it is clear that the boy must play YS, because this strategy dominates (now strongly) XS. So doing against the strategy SS on the part of the girl, the boy obtains his maximum payoff of 3, without the need to "burn any money." As will be recalled, this was precisely the conclusion obtained in Subsection 4.5.3.[63]

To close our discussion on the iterative elimination of strategies based on weak payoff dominance, it is worth mentioning that this process may also yield sharp implications reflecting a backward (rather than forward) logic – recall Section 4.2. This occurs, for example, in games of perfect information (i.e., all subgames are proper) that display no payoff ties. In these games, it may be shown (Exercise 4.14) that if the iterative process is performed in a suitable order it leads to the (unique)

---

[62] For example, XS denotes the *boy*'s strategy: "burn money (i.e., choose X) first, S later"; or SB stands for the *girl*'s strategy: "after X, choose S; after Y choose B". Note that, for simplicity, we identify (i.e., do not distinguish between) the boy's alternative strategies that prescribe different actions in information sets that cannot be reached, given his first action chosen (X or Y). If this identification were not performed, the boy would have eight strategies, half of them redundant.

[63] Ben-Porath and Dekel (1992) have established a general result for games such as the present battle of the sexes, where there are several pure-strategy equilibria that Pareto-dominate any other equilibrium in mixed strategies. These authors prove that, if the original situation is embedded into a larger game where any one (but only one) player can "burn sufficient money," the unique equilibrium that survives an iterative elimination of weakly dominated strategies is the one preferred by the player who has the money-burning option, despite the fact that this possibility does not materialize.

subgame-perfect equilibrium.[64] In light of this fact, it is interesting to observe that the same iterative process eliminating weakly dominated strategies may reflect "inductions" of such a contrasting nature (forward or backward) in different contexts.

Proceeding now with the discussion of strategic-form Nash refinements, we turn to exploring the implications of allowing for players' mistakes in the adoption of their desired strategies. In the present strategic-form scenario, since the strategies are to be conceived as chosen once and for all at the beginning of the game, the formulation becomes significantly simpler than in the extensive-form approach. First, we consider the counterpart of the perfect equilibrium concept.

Definition 4.11 (Selten, 1975): *A strategy profile $\sigma^* \in \Sigma$ is a* perfect equilibrium *of G if there exists a sequence $\{\sigma_k\}_{k=1,2,\ldots}$ such that*

> *(i) $\forall k = 1, 2, \ldots, \sigma_k$ is completely mixed; that is, $\forall i \in N$, $\forall s_i \in S_i$, $\sigma_{i,k}(s_i) > 0$;*

> *(ii) $\exists \{\varepsilon_k\}_{k=1}^{\infty}$, $\varepsilon_k \downarrow 0$, such that $\forall k = 1, 2, \ldots, \forall i \in N$, $\forall s_i, s_i' \in S_i$ $\pi_i(s_i, \sigma_{-i,k}) < \pi_i(s_i', \sigma_{-i,k}) \Rightarrow \sigma_{i,k}(s_i) \leq \varepsilon_k$;*

> *(iii) $\{\sigma_k\} \to \sigma^*$.*

The definitions for perfect equilibrium in the strategic and extensive forms are of a parallel nature. However, the mistake probabilities that are contemplated in each case pertain to a different space of decisions. In the extensive-form concept (Definition 4.6), mistakes are conceived as independent events associated with each separate information set; i.e., they may occur at each point in the game where an action is to be adopted. In contrast, for the version of this concept that is defined on the strategic form (Definition 4.11), the mistakes are viewed as taking place when a player has to choose (irreversibly) one of the contingency plans of action (i.e., strategic-form strategies) that she will then faithfully apply throughout the game.

Next, we present two different results concerning the concept of strategic-form perfect equilibrium. The first one, which concerns existence, states that every finite game in strategic form has some perfect equilibrium. The second one establishes that this equilibrium notion is itself a refinement of the one described in Definition 4.10. That is, *no* (strategic-form) perfect equilibrium involves weakly dominated strategies.

Theorem 4.2: *Every finite game in strategic form G has a perfect equilibrium.*

Proof: Given any strategic-form game $G = \{N, \{S_i\}_{i=1}^n, \{\pi_i\}_{i=1}^n\}$, the proof may be carried out along the lines of that of Theorem 4.1, as applied to the (simultaneous) extensive-form game where each player $i \in N$ chooses independently her strategy $s_i \in S_i$ in her *unique* information set and the induced payoffs are as given by $\pi_i(\cdot)$.[65] ∎

---

[64] As a further line of contrast between the strong and weak dominance criteria, it is worth stressing that this conclusion does *not* hold for the stronger notion contemplated in Definition 2.1.

[65] In fact, the direct analogue of the proof of Theorem 4.1 applies to the strategic-form counterpart of proper equilibrium, as formulated in Definition 4.12 below.

Theorem 4.3: *Let $\sigma^* \in \Sigma$ be a perfect equilibrium of the finite game in strategic form G. For each $i = 1, 2, \ldots n$, if $s_i \in S_i$ is a weakly dominated strategy, then $\sigma_i^*(s_i) = 0$.*

Proof: Let σ^* be a perfect equilibrium of G and suppose, for the sake of contradiction, that there is some player $i \in N$ such that $\sigma_i^*(s_i) > 0$ for strategy s_i that is weakly dominated. By Definition 4.9, there exists some strategy, $\hat{\sigma}_i \in \Sigma_i$, such that, if $\sigma_{-i} \in \Sigma_{-i}$ is *completely* mixed,

$$\pi_i(\hat{\sigma}_i, \sigma_{-i}) > \pi_i(s_i, \sigma_{-i}).$$

This implies that, for any such completely mixed σ_{-i}, there exists a pure strategy, $\hat{s}_i(\sigma_{-i}) \in S_i$, satisfying

$$\pi_i(\hat{s}_i(\sigma_{-i}), \sigma_{-i}) > \pi_i(s_i, \sigma_{-i}). \tag{4.12}$$

Consider now a sequence of strategy profiles $\{\sigma_k\}_{k=1}^{\infty}$ that satisfy (i), (ii), and (iii) in Definition 4.11. Given the corresponding sequence $\{\varepsilon_k\}_{k=1}^{\infty}$, (4.12) implies that, $\forall k = 1, 2, \ldots$, the following inequality must hold:

$$\sigma_{i,k}(s_i) \leq \varepsilon_k.$$

Since $\varepsilon_k \downarrow 0$, (iii) implies that $\sigma_i^*(s_i) = 0$, which leads to the desired contradiction and thus completes the proof. ∎

Remark 4.1: *Equivalence in finite bilateral games*

It can be shown (see van Damme, 1987, Theorem 3.2.2) that in finite bilateral games (i.e., games involving only two players), every Nash equilibrium in weakly undominated strategies is also (strategic-form) perfect. Thus, in this restricted context, both equilibrium notions are equivalent, in view of Theorem 4.3. This conclusion does not generalize to games with more than two players. ♦

Remark 4.2: *Perfection in the strategic and extensive forms*

As explained, the alternative notions presented in Definitions 4.6 and 4.11 reflect a similar requirement of perfection on players' behavior but applied to a different representation of the game (strategic or extensive form). From this viewpoint, it is natural to wonder what the relationship is between the outcomes induced by each of them. Interestingly, neither of these concepts is more restrictive than the other. In other words, it is possible to find extensive-form games where an (extensive-form) perfect equilibrium does not correspond to a perfect equilibrium in the induced strategic form (cf. Exercise 4.15) and vice versa, i.e., extensive-form games where a perfect equilibrium in the induced strategic form does not lead to a perfect equilibrium in the original extensive form (cf. Exercise 4.16). ♦

The Nash refinement literature has proposed a very wide variety of alternative concepts, whose often very fine differences may be quite hard to disentangle. Given this state of affairs, it is natural to pose the following question: How sharp and effectively different are these concepts in discriminating among (i.e., "refining") Nash equilibria? If, to fix ideas, this question is particularized to the concept of strategic-form perfect equilibrium, a clear-cut, but seemingly disappointing, answer is provided by the next result.

Theorem 4.4: *Generically,*[66] *every Nash equilibrium of a strategic-form game G is perfect.*

The proof of this theorem requires using tools in differential topology that go well beyond the mathematical level set for this book. At first glance, its statement is rather surprising. In fact, it turns out that the same generic equivalence can be extended to almost all the strategic-form refinement concepts proposed in the literature (the counterpart of proper, for example, but also to those known as *essential, persistent, regular,* etc.). In a sense, this appears to indicate that, other than for "exceptional" nongeneric cases, there is little to be gained in strategic-form games by insisting on any equilibrium notion different from Nash equilibrium.

The key to making sense of this "puzzle" derives from the following somewhat subtle point. In extensive-form games with a genuinely sequential structure (i.e., those involving several strategically relevant stages), the induced strategic forms are nongeneric. More specifically, the induced payoff tables display exact equalities (payoff ties) among those strategy profiles that lead to the same path of play – see, for example, the game represented in Figure 4.9 and its induced strategic form given by Table 4.3. Thus, even if an extensive-form multistage game displays no precise relationships among the payoffs attributed to its final nodes, its corresponding strategic form will necessarily do so; i.e., it will exhibit "nongeneric features." In fact, it is because of such inherent nongenericity (in the mathematical sense of the word – cf. footnote 66) that the strategic-form refinements may play a fruitful role in discriminating among Nash equilibria of an underlying (generic) extensive form.

The previous considerations notwithstanding, game theorists long shared the view that the strategic-form representation of a game was largely inadequate for an appraisal of the credibility (or sequential rationality) of agents' behavior – recall the discussion of these matters undertaken at the start of this section. This received position, however, started to change in the early 1980s, when a different methodological standpoint started gaining a foothold. The fresh methodological perspective then proposed may be succinctly described as follows[67]:

> Every decision problem (whether it involves a single agent or several of them) may be suitably represented and analyzed through its strategic form,

---

[66] The qualifier "generically" applied to a certain property of strategic-form games is to be understood as follows. Fix the game form – i.e., the set of players N and their respective strategy spaces S_i. Then, the property is said to hold generically if it is true for "almost all" payoff tables consistent with the given game form. Or, more precisely, if it holds for the whole payoff space $\mathbb{R}^{(r_1 \times r_2 \times \cdots \times r_n) \times n}$ (where payoff entries lie), except for a closed subset of Lebesgue measure zero.

[67] One of the earliest instances of this novel approach can be found in the work of Kohlberg and Mertens (1986). These authors pose the problem in an axiomatic fashion and formulate a set of requirements to be demanded from a suitable equilibrium concept. Finally, their analysis settles on the concept they call *stable equilibrium*, which displays partial consistency with their proposed axioms.

that is, by means of a *complete ex ante* description of all possible (contingent) decisions that will (or may) be confronted by individuals. The resulting strategic form has to be sufficient to formulate and apply any of the "refinements" that might be judged appropriate. In particular, it must be sufficient to evaluate the sequential rationality of whatever behavioral plan is considered.

The question of whether the viewpoint just outlined represents a sound methodological position has led to a heated controversy among game theorists that is still ongoing. It cannot be our objective here to summarize this multifaceted and still open debate, let alone venture into it. We shall only provide a brief glimpse of matters by dwelling on one of the early "discoveries" of this literature, a result that has been used to support the above approach. It establishes that a certain strategic-form refinement, i.e., the counterpart of (extensive-form) proper equilibrium, succeeds in capturing a suitable notion of sequential rationality.

Before stating and proving the advanced result, we present, in parallel to Definition 4.7, a formal description of concept of proper equilibrium for a strategic-form game.

Definition 4.12 (Myerson, 1978): *A strategy profile $\sigma^* \in \Sigma$ is a* proper equilibrium *of G if there exists a sequence $\{\sigma_k\}_{k=1}^{\infty}$ such that*

(i) $\forall k = 1, 2, \ldots, \sigma_k$ *is completely mixed*;

(ii) $\exists \{\varepsilon_k\}_{k=1}^{\infty}, \varepsilon_k \downarrow 0,$ *such that* $\forall k = 1, 2, \ldots, \forall i \in N, \forall s_i, s_i' \in S_i,$
$\pi_i(s_i, \sigma_{-i,k}) < \pi_i(s_i', \sigma_{-i,k}) \Rightarrow \sigma_{i,k}(s_i) \leq \varepsilon_k \cdot \sigma_{i,k}(s_i')$;

(iii) $\{\sigma_k\}_{k=1}^{\infty} \to \sigma^*$.

Originally, the concept of proper equilibrium was proposed only for strategic-form games,[68] with the aim of remedying what appeared to be an unappealing feature of the perfect equilibrium concept, namely, the possibility that the set of equilibria might be affected by the addition of (strongly) dominated strategies (see Exercise 4.18). Ironically, however, it turns out that proper equilibrium is subject to an identical problem (cf. Exercise 4.19). We shall not discuss this issue in any detail here because, as indicated, our sole objective here is to rely on this concept to illustrate the general idea announced before: strategic-form Nash refinements may be effective in sieving out sequentially irrational behavior. This is the content of our last result.

Theorem 4.5: *Every proper equilibrium of a finite strategic-form game G induces a sequential equilibrium in any extensive-form game Γ such that $G = G(\Gamma)$.*

Proof: Let $\{\sigma_k\}_{k=1}^{\infty}$ be a sequence satisfying (i)–(iii) of Definition 4.12 so that $\sigma^* = \lim_{k \to \infty} \sigma_k$ is a proper equilibrium of $G(\Gamma)$. Denote by γ^* and γ_k the behavioral-strategy profiles induced, respectively, by σ^* and each σ_k. Correspondingly, let μ^* and μ_k be such that (μ^*, γ^*) and every (μ_k, γ_k) are consistent assessments (in the sense of Definitions 4.3 and 4.4) with $\mu_k \to \mu^*$ (note that each γ_k is completely mixed, for all $k = 1, 2, \ldots$). It

---

[68] Concerning the existence of strategic-form proper equilibrium, see Footnote 65.

must be proven that $\forall i \in N$, $\forall h \in H_i$, $\gamma_i^*(h)$ is an optimal response for player i, given γ_{-i}^* and μ^*.

For the sake of contradiction, suppose not, and let i_0 be a player whose strategy $\gamma_{i_0}^*$ prescribes a suboptimal response at some of her information sets. Denote by $\hat{h}$ the last of her information sets with this feature, according to the order displayed by the game. In that $\hat{h}$, therefore, there must exist one of the available actions, say a, such that $\gamma_{i_0}^*(a) > 0$ and the payoff that player i_0 earns by playing it is lower, given $(\gamma_{-i_0}^*, \mu^*)$, than that obtained by playing some other available action, say b. Thus, if $\{\varepsilon_k\}_{k=1}^{\infty}$ is the sequence underlying $\{\sigma_k\}_{k=1}^{\infty}$ (cf. (ii) of Definition 4.12) there must be some sufficiently small ε_k such that b also dominates a, given the corresponding opponents' profile $\sigma_{-i_0,k}$. By part (ii) of Definition 4.12, the probability $\sigma_{i_0,k}(s_{i_0})$ assigned to any strategy s_{i_0} that prescribes action a at $\hat{h}$ must be no larger than $\varepsilon_k \, \sigma_{i_0,k}(s_{i_0}')$ for any other strategy s_{i_0}' that differs from the former only in playing b at $\hat{h}$. Adding up over all strategies such as s_{i_0} that prescribe a in $\hat{h}$, the weight that $\gamma_{i_0,k}$ associates with this action cannot exceed $q \cdot \varepsilon$, where q is the number of pure strategies of i_0 in $G(\Gamma)$. In the limit, as $\varepsilon_k \downarrow 0$, this probability converges to zero, which leads to the desired contradiction. ∎

Summary

This chapter has been concerned with the so-called refinements of Nash equilibrium. We have considered a wide variety of them, differing both in the stringency of their requirements (i.e., how much they "refine" Nash equilibrium) and their framework of application (extensive- or strategic-form games).

One of the weakest notions is subgame-perfect equilibrium (SPE), which requires that a Nash equilibrium should materialize in every proper subgame, i.e., in each subgame starting with a singleton information set. This concept is most useful in games of perfect information, where every information set consists of a single node. In other kinds of games, where not all players are fully informed of past history at their decision nodes, this concept may have little or no cutting power over Nash equilibrium.

Many games of interest are not of perfect information. This motivates introducing other equilibrium notions such as weak perfect Bayesian equilibrium (WPBE), in which players' beliefs are made explicit at every information set and are required to be statistically consistent with players' equilibrium strategies. The fact that WPBE imposes no restrictions whatsoever on off-equilibrium beliefs (i.e., full discretion is allowed at nonvisited information sets) has been shown to be a significant drawback of this concept. In particular, it renders it too weak in some games, where it may even fall short of meeting the basic requirement of subgame perfection.

In a sense, we may conceive SPE and WPBE as being Nash refinements geared toward excluding *only* incredible threats. Some of their conceptual problems follow from the fact that they abstract from the need to "refine" beliefs and therefore may admit some that, in fact, should be judged as untenable. To exclude untenable beliefs is the motivation underlying the concepts of sequential equilibrium, perfect equilibrium, and proper equilibrium. The first one attains this objective by demanding a certain continuity requirement on the formation of out-of-equilibrium beliefs. The latter two do it by introducing an explicit theory of deviations (i.e., out-of-equilibrium behavior) that allows for the possibility that players may make choice mistakes with small probability.

Most of our discussion has been concerned with Nash refinements that build on a dichotomy between choices (or beliefs) arising on- and off-equilibrium, thus requiring them to be defined on the extensive-form representation of a game. However, we have seen that refinements defined on the strategic form (e.g., the exclusion of weakly dominated strategies, or the counterparts of perfect and proper) are of special interest as well and may go well beyond a narrow strategic-form interpretation. They may reflect, for example, considerations that would have seemed to belong exclusively to the realm of extensive-form Nash refinements, such as those based on backward induction, forward induction, or even sequential rationality.

Exercises

Exercise 4.1: Within the game represented in Figure 4.11, find all pure-strategy profiles that define (a) a Nash equilibrium, (b) a subgame-perfect equilibrium, (c) a weak perfect Bayesian equilibrium.

Exercise 4.2: Consider the extensive-form game represented in Figure 4.12.

(a) Specify the strategy spaces of each player.
(b) Find every pure-strategy profile that defines (i) a Nash equilibrium, (ii) a subgame-perfect equilibrium, (iii) a weak perfect Bayesian equilibrium.
(c) Construct an extensive-form "simultaneous" game whose strategic-form game coincides with the game originally considered.

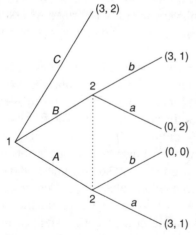

Figure 4.11: An extensive-form game.

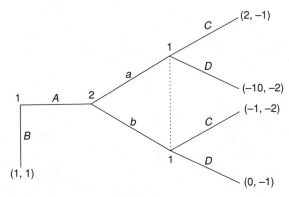

Figure 4.12: An extensive-form game.

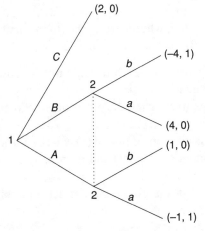

Figure 4.13: An extensive-form game.

(d) In the game specified in (c), determine the pure-strategy profiles that define (i) Nash equilibria, (ii) subgame-perfect equilibria, (iii) weak perfect Bayesian equilibria. Compare each of these with the respective equilibria obtained in (b).

Exercise 4.3: For the game represented in Figure 4.13, determine all the following equilibria, both in pure and mixed strategies: (i) Nash equilibria, (ii) subgame-perfect equilibria, (iii) weak perfect Bayesian equilibria.

Exercise 4.4: A government and an agent are involved in the following strategic context. The agent must choose action a from the set $A = \{0, 1\}$. The government would like to influence the agent's choice. To try to do so, the government publicly announces, *before* the agent selects her action, a monetary transfer rule $t : A \to \mathbb{R}$ that is to be automatically implemented after the agent has made her decision. For simplicity, assume that the monetary transfers induced by t (i.e., the values of $t(a)$, for each $a \in A$) can take only two values: zero and a certain fixed positive value, which is normalized to one.

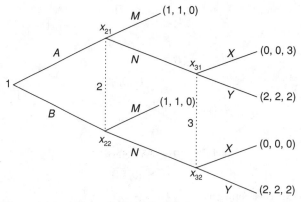

Figure 4.14: A three-player extensive-form game.

Let the objective of the government be to maximize $U_g(a, t) \equiv 2a - t$ and that of the agent to maximize $U_a(a, t) \equiv t - c(a)$, where $c(a)$ is the (monetary) cost of her action. Furthermore, postulate that $c(0) = 0$ and $c(1) = 1/2$.

(a) Represent the game in extensive form under the assumption that the transfer rule cannot depend on the agent's choice.

(b) Represent the game in extensive form when the government can choose a transfer rule that depends on the agent's choice.

(c) Define, for each of the two scenarios considered in (a) and (b), the strategy spaces of each player (government and agent) and represent the game in strategic form.

(d) Find, for both scenarios, the Nash and subgame-perfect equilibria and discuss their salient features.

Exercise 4.5: Show that, in the extensive-form game represented in Figure 4.10, the pure strategy profile (B, b, V) is the *unique* sequential equilibrium.

Exercise 4.6: Consider the extensive-form game represented in Figure 4.14.

(a) Find a weak perfect Bayesian equilibrium of this game that is *not* sequential.

(b) Determine all its (several) sequential equilibria.

Exercise 4.7: Rosenthal (1981) proposed the following strategic context, often known as the "centipede game." Two partners, 1 and 2, become involved in a certain joint venture and agree on building up their investment in it in a gradual and alternating fashion. They start with 1,000 dollars each. Then, in odd (even) periods, agent 1 (respectively, 2) faces the decision of whether to invest further (I) or stop altogether (S). If the agent in question chooses I, she must contribute a *net* amount of 1,000 dollars to the partnership (i.e., her wealth decreases by this amount), but her partner obtains a net additional benefit of 2,000 dollars (i.e., the partner experiences a wealth increase of this magnitude). If she chooses S instead, no further investment is made and the whole process stops irreversibly, each player obtaining a payoff equal to the wealth accumulated thus far. Assume that this process can continue for

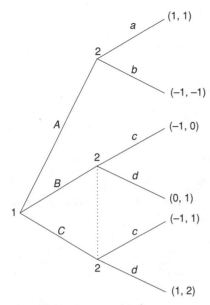

Figure 4.15: An extensive-form game.

at most 100 periods.

1. Represent the game in extensive and strategic forms (not exhaustively, given the large size of the game).
2. Determine its Nash, subgame-perfect, and sequential equilibria.

Exercise 4.8: Consider the extensive-form game represented in Figure 4.15 and find *all pure-strategy* profiles that define (i) a Nash equilibrium, (ii) a subgame-perfect equilibrium, (iii) a sequential equilibrium, (iv) a (trembling-hand) perfect equilibrium.

Exercise 4.9*: Prove, formally, that Definitions 4.6 and 4.6′ are equivalent.

Exercise 4.10: Show that the correspondence $\varphi \equiv (\varphi_h)_{h \in H}$ defined in (4.11) – as part of the proof of Theorem 4.1 – satisfies the hypotheses of Kakutani's fixed-point theorem. That is, it is upper hemicontinuous and $\forall h \in H$, $\forall \gamma \in \tilde{\Psi}$, the sets $\varphi_h(\gamma)$ are nonempty, closed, and convex.

Exercise 4.11: Compute the perfect equilibria of the game described in part (iii) of Exercise 2.4 (Chapter 2). Are there any other Nash equilibria? Do you need to reconsider your previous answer to Exercise 2.4?

Exercise 4.12: Show that any Nash equilibrium where a player chooses more than one pure strategy with positive probability cannot define a strict Nash equilibrium.

Exercise 4.13*: Construct a game Γ with imperfect recall where a Nash equilibrium in behavioral strategies has no counterpart equilibrium in mixed strategies for the associated strategic-form game $G(\Gamma)$.

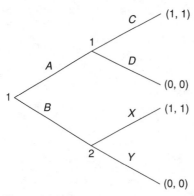

Figure 4.16: An extensive-form game with an equilibrium that is perfect in the extensive form but not in the induced strategic form.

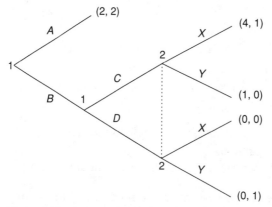

Figure 4.17: An extensive-form game with an equilibrium that is perfect in the induced strategic form but not in the extensive form.

Exercise 4.14*: Let Γ be an extensive-form game with perfect information that displays no payoff ties (i.e., no agent obtains the same payoff at two different final nodes). Prove that when the iterative process of elimination of weakly dominated strategies is carried out in a suitable order on $G(\Gamma)$ it leads to a strategy profile s that corresponds to the subgame-perfect equilibrium of Γ.

Exercise 4.15*: Consider the game in extensive form represented by Figure 4.16, which is borrowed from van Damme (1987).

Show that the behavioral strategy profiles $((A, C), X))$ and $((B, C), X))$ are perfect in the extensive form, but only the strategic-form profile (AC, X) defines a perfect equilibrium in the induced strategic form.

Exercise 4.16*: Consider the game in extensive form represented by Figure 4.17, again taken from van Damme (1987).

Show that the behavioral strategy profile $((B, C), X))$ is the unique perfect equilibrium in the extensive form but the two strategic-form profiles (AC, Y) and (AD, Y) define perfect equilibria in the induced strategic form.

Table 4.4: *A strategic-form game*

1 \ 2	a	b
A	2, 2	1, 0
B	2, 2	2, 2

Table 4.5: *A strategic-form game*

1 \ 2	a	b	c
A	2, 2	1, 0	0, −1
B	0, 1	1, 1	1, −1
C	−1, 0	−1, 1	−1, −1

Table 4.6: *A strategic-form game*

1 \ 2	a	b
A	1, 1	10, 0
B	0, 10	10, 10

Exercise 4.17: Find the Nash and perfect equilibria of the two different strategic-form games described by Tables 4.4 and 4.5.

Exercise 4.18: Determine the perfect and proper equilibria of the two different strategic-form games described by Tables 4.6 and 4.7. Compare the conclusions obtained in each case.

Exercise 4.19*: Consider the two different trilateral games given by Tables 4.8 and 4.9, where player 1 chooses rows, player 2 columns, and player 3 boxes (in the first game, just trivially). Find the perfect and proper equilibria in each case, contrasting the results with those of Exercise 4.18.

Exercise 4.20: Two players, 1 and 2, have to share the contents of a basket containing 4 units of two different goods, a and b. Given that these goods are assumed perfectly divisible, an allocation in this context is simply a pair of two-dimensional real vectors, $x = (x^1, x^2) \in \mathbb{R}_+^2 \times \mathbb{R}_+^2$, each vector $x^i = (x_a^i, x_b^i)$ specifying the amounts allocated to player i. Naturally, the feasibility of any such allocation requires

$$x_h^1 + x_h^2 \leq 4$$

for each good $h = a, b$. Player 1 has preferences represented by the Cobb-Douglas utility function

$$U^1\left(x_a^1, x_b^1\right) = x_a^1 \cdot x_b^1,$$

whereas player 2's preferences display fixed-proportion requirements and are

Table 4.7: *A strategic-form game*

1\2	a	b	c
A	1, 1	10, 0	−1, −2
B	0, 10	10, 10	0, −2
C	−2, −1	−2, 0	−2, −2

Table 4.8: *A strategic-form game*

1\2	a	b
A	1, 1, 1	0, 0, 1
B	0, 0, 1	0, 0, 1

Table 4.9: *A strategic-form game*

1\2	a	b
A	1, 1, 1	0, 0, 1
B	0, 0, 1	0, 0, 1
3	M	

1\2	a	b
A	0, 0, 0	0, 0, 0
B	0, 0, 0	1, 0, 0
	N	

represented by

$$U^2\left(x_a^2, x_b^2\right) = \min\left\{x_a^2, x_b^2\right\}.$$

The allocation mechanism considered is as follows:

- In the first stage, player 1 proposes two vectors in $\mathbb{R}_+^2$, $y \equiv (y_a, y_b)$ and $z \equiv (z_a, z_b)$, such that

$$y_h + z_h = 4 \qquad (h = a, b).$$

  The two vectors proposed, y and z, are interpreted as alternative "subbaskets" dividing the total amounts available for both goods.
- In the second stage, player 2 chooses one of these subbaskets, y or z, this choice then becoming her own allocation. The subbasket *not* chosen by player 2 determines the allocation of player 1.

1. Formulate the allocation mechanism proposed as a two-stage game and define precisely the strategy spaces for each player.
2. Find a subgame-perfect equilibrium of this game.
3. Is there any other Nash equilibrium whose payoffs are different from those obtained in the previous point? Discuss your answer.
4. Reconsider the three previous points for a *modified* mechanism in which player 2 is given the *additional* option of destroying the whole basket. (If player 2 decides to destroy the basket, its contents are fully wasted.)
5. Reconsider the four previous points for the case in which the basket to be divided still contains 4 units of good a but has instead 5 units of good b.

CHAPTER 5

Refinements of Nash equilibrium: applications

5.1 Oligopoly (II): sequential moves

5.1.1 *Stackelberg model*

Nearly a century had elapsed since Cournot (1838) published his seminal work, when von Stackelberg (1934) proposed an alternative model of oligopolistic competition. This model, in contrast with Cournot's and Bertrand's (cf. Sections 3.1.1 and 3.1.2), embodies an important asymmetry between the competing firms. Specifically, one of the firms, called the "leader," is assumed to adopt its output decision first. More generally, the leader may be simply conceived as having the capacity of committing itself to whatever output it wishes before the other firms make their corresponding decision. Formally, the strategic situation thus induced is modeled as a two-stage game where

(a) in the first stage, the leader determines its output;
(b) in the second stage, the remaining firms (the "followers") choose simultaneously their respective outputs.

Consider, for simplicity, the case of just two firms (a duopoly) that display constant and identical marginal costs and face a linear demand function (recall (3.8) and (3.9)). That is, the cost and inverse-demand functions are as follows:

$$C_i(q_i) = c\, q_i, \quad c > 0, \ i = 1, 2, \tag{5.1}$$

$$P(Q) = \max\left[M - d\, Q, 0\right], \quad M, d > 0, \tag{5.2}$$

where each q_i stands for the output produced by firm i and $Q \equiv q_1 + q_2$ is the aggregate output.

Suppose firm 1 is the leader and firm 2 is the follower. Then, the strategy space of firm 1 in the Stackelberg game is simply given by

$$S_1 = \mathbb{R}_+,$$

with a typical element s_1 sometimes also denoted by q_1, the usual notation for output choices. On the other hand, the strategy space of firm 2 is

$$S_2 = \{s_2 : \mathbb{R}_+ \to \mathbb{R}_+, \ q_2 = s_2(q_1)\}.$$

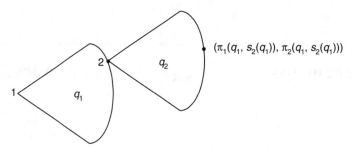

Figure 5.1: Stackelberg duopoly.

Given these strategy spaces, the payoff functions $\pi_i : S_1 \times S_2 \to \mathbb{R}$ determine the profits earned by each firm as follows:

$$\pi_1(s_1, s_2) = \{\max[M - d(s_1 + s_2(s_1)), 0] - c\}\, s_1$$

$$\pi_2(s_1, s_2) = \{\max[M - d(s_1 + s_2(s_1)), 0] - c\}\, s_2(s_1).$$

The extensive-form representation of the game is informally illustrated in Figure 5.1.

As explained in Chapter 4, the natural approach to analyze such a multistage game is to focus on its subgame-perfect equilibria. To compute them, one must proceed backward in the game and first determine the equilibrium reactions by firm 2 to every initial decision of firm 1. More precisely, one has to find the optimal actions of firm 2 in each of the subgames induced by *every* possible strategy by firm 1. Such contingent pattern of optimal *actions* defines the only "credible" strategy of firm 2, $\tilde{s}_2(\cdot)$, that may form part of any subgame-perfect equilibrium.

To compute $\tilde{s}_2$, we solve the optimization problem:

$$\max_{q_2 \in \mathbb{R}_+} \{\max[M - d(q_1 + q_2), 0]\, q_2 - c\, q_2\},$$

for every possible *given* value of q_1. The first-order necessary conditions for an *interior* solution $\tilde{q}_2 > 0$ are

$$M - dq_1 - 2d\tilde{q}_2 - c = 0,$$

which, allowing for boundary solutions, induce a strategy $\tilde{s}_2(\cdot)$ defined as follows:

$$\tilde{s}_2(q_1) = \max\left\{\frac{M - c - dq_1}{2d}, 0\right\}. \tag{5.3}$$

Note that this optimal strategy $\tilde{s}_2(\cdot)$ coincides with the reaction function of firm 2, $\eta_2(\cdot)$, as defined by (3.12) for the traditional Cournot model with simultaneous decisions. Anticipating such behavior by firm 2 in the second stage of the game, the optimal decision by firm 1 in the first stage is obtained by solving the following optimization problem:

$$\max_{q_1 \in \mathbb{R}_+} \{\max[M - d(q_1 + \tilde{s}_2(q_1)), 0]\, q_1 - c\, q_1\}$$

which, abstracting for notational simplicity from non-negativity constraints, can be rewritten as follows:

$$\max_{q_1 \in \mathbb{R}_+} \left\{ \left[M - d \left(q_1 + \frac{M - c - dq_1}{2d} \right) \right] q_1 - c q_1 \right\}.$$

As formulated, the above decision problem embodies the idea that firm 1 correctly predicts what would be the (optimal) subsequent reactions by firm 2 to any of its own possible choices. The corresponding first-order condition for an interior maximum yields the solution:

$$\tilde{q}_1 = \frac{M - c}{2d}. \tag{5.4}$$

If the "market size" is large enough relative to production costs (specifically, if $M > c$) their respective optimization problems indeed yield interior solutions for both firms. In that case, the unique subgame-perfect equilibrium of the game $(\tilde{s}_1, \tilde{s}_2(\cdot))$ has $\tilde{s}_1 = \tilde{q}_1$, as given in (5.4), and $\tilde{s}_2(\cdot)$ as defined by (5.3). Introducing $\tilde{q}_1$ in (5.3), the output produced by firm 2 in equilibrium becomes

$$\tilde{q}_2 = \frac{M - c}{4d}. \tag{5.5}$$

Comparing (5.4) and (5.5) to the (symmetric) equilibrium output profile (q_1^*, q_2^*) obtained in the Cournot model for the same scenario (cf. 3.11), we observe that, in line with intuition, the Stackelberg model induces a larger production for the leader ($\tilde{q}_1 > q_1^*$) but smaller for the follower ($\tilde{q}_2 < q_2^*$). In fact, it is easy to check that the equilibrium profits of each firm in the two contexts maintain an analogous relationship. This is illustrated diagrammatically in Figure 5.2, which should be compared with Figure 3.1 for the Cournotian model.

5.1.2 *Price competition under capacity constraints* *

As explained in Subsections 3.1.1 and 3.1.2, oligopoly models in which either prices or quantities are the strategic variables may lead to sharply different conclusions. In view of this state of affairs, one may naturally wonder which of these two scenarios provides a better model of oligopolistic competition. From a descriptive viewpoint, it might be claimed that Bertrand's approach seems a better approximation to reality. For, as casual observation suggests, firms tend to set their own prices (i.e., their decision variables are prices), the associated demand then following from those prices as a result of consumers' aggregate reaction to them.

Furthermore, it may be argued that Bertrand's approach has a certain modeling advantage over the Cournot setup. Since in the Bertrand model prices are not an endogenous *consequence* of the firms' decisions but the decisions themselves, one does not need to resort to any additional mechanism (often artificial, such as the theoretical construct of an auctioneer) to determine market-clearing prices. In this sense, therefore, the Bertrand setup may be said to include an *explicit* description of *all* components required to understand how the market actually operates. Instead, this same viewpoint would argue that, in contrast, the Cournot framework is either

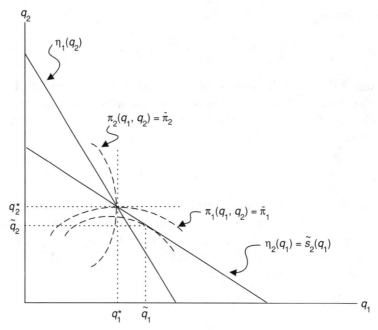

Figure 5.2: Cournot and Stackelberg equilibria.

an incomplete model of market-based competition or an approach based on weak (ad hoc) theoretical foundations.

The previous considerations notwithstanding, a well-known contribution by Kreps and Scheinkman (1983) shows that a certain natural variant of Bertrand competition is not, after all, so different from Cournot competition. Here, we present a simplified description of their approach that nevertheless is sufficient to bring across the main insights.

Kreps and Scheinkman follow the lead of Edgeworth (1897) and embed Bertrand competition in a context in which firms experience capacity constraints. The capacity constraint faced by each firm defines an upper bound on the amount that firms may produce and sell in the market once their prices are set. The key difference with Edgeworth's approach is that Kreps and Scheinkman postulate that the capacity enjoyed by a firm is not an exogenous parameter of the model but an *endogenous* choice adopted by firms in a stage preceding that of price competition. Of course, to make the problem interesting, capacity building is assumed costly, its level being decided by a (correct) anticipation of its implications in the ensuing phase of price competition. Overall, the problem is formulated as a two-stage game, the first stage having firms fix their capacity and the second one making them determine their prices. As we shall see, the main conclusion obtained from the model is that, at a subgame-perfect equilibrium, the market outcome coincides with that induced by the Cournot model when costs (incurred both by capacity and actual production) are added across the two stages.

Next, the model is presented formally. There are two firms, 1 and 2, involved in a game displaying two stages. In the first stage, both firms choose independently (i.e., "simultaneously") their respective capacities K_i, $i = 1, 2$. Then, in the second stage, having accurately observed each other's capacity choice, they choose, again independently, their respective prices p_i, $i = 1, 2$. Given the capacity K_i decided by each firm i in the first stage, its output q_i produced (and sold) in the second stage must satisfy $q_i \leq K_i$. That is, capacity variables are measured in terms of the output they allow firms to produce.

To fix ideas, we shall find it useful to focus our discussion on a symmetric and linear model of duopoly, where the demand function is linear,

$$P(Q) = \max [M - d Q, 0], \quad M, d > 0,$$

and capacity and production costs are linear as well:

$$C_i(K_i) = cK_i, \quad c \geq 0$$
$$\tilde{C}_i(q_i) = \tilde{c}q_i, \quad \tilde{c} \geq 0$$

with $c + \tilde{c} < M$. We also find it convenient to rely on two further simplifications. First, it will be postulated that only capacity building is costly; i.e., $c > 0$ but $\tilde{c} = 0$. Second, the ranges of admissible capacity choices (in the first stage) and prices (in the second stage) are bounded above, for each $i = 1, 2$, as follows:

$$K_i \leq \frac{M}{3d} \equiv \bar{K} \tag{5.6}$$

$$p_i \leq M. \tag{5.7}$$

Note that the upper bound $\bar{K}$ on capacity choice coincides with what would be the ordinary Cournot equilibrium outputs at *zero* total costs. (Bear in mind, however, that Cournot equilibrium outputs in the present context are $(M - c)/(3d) < (M)/(3d)$, since total costs c are positive.) On the other hand, the upper bound M on prices simply reflects the idea that firms should not set prices above the point where they are already sure to fetch no demand.

Most of the above simplifications (linearity, zero production costs, or upper bound on prices) can be relaxed easily – cf. Exercise 5.5. The only difficult assumption to dispense with concerns the upper bound on capacities contemplated in (5.6). Its main role is to allow the analysis to focus on pure-strategy equilibria. Whereas the main conclusion still goes through without such a restriction (i.e., Cournot outcomes still obtain at equilibrium), the argument becomes substantially more involved since mixed strategies must then be used to allow for randomized behavior off the equilibrium path.

Given the previous simplifications, the strategy spaces of the game S_i can be identified with the Cartesian product $[0, \bar{K}] \times G_i$, where

$$G_i \equiv \{g_i : [0, \bar{K}] \times [0, \bar{K}] \to [0, M], \ p_i = g_i(K_1, K_2)\}$$

is interpreted as the set of pricing rules, which are functions of observed capacities. To complete the specification of the game, we need to define the payoff functions $\pi_i : S_1 \times S_2 \to \mathbb{R}, i = 1, 2$. To do so, we divide the strategy profiles into two different classes:

(a) If $s = (s_1, s_2) = ((K_1, g_1(\cdot)), (K_2, g_2(\cdot)))$ is such that $p_i = g_i(K_1, K_2) < p_j = g_j(K_1, K_2), j \neq i$, then

$$\pi_i(s) = \min\left[\frac{M - p_i}{d}, K_i\right] p_i - cK_i \tag{5.8}$$

$$\pi_j(s) = \min\left\{\max\left[\frac{M - p_j}{d} - K_i, 0\right], K_j\right\} p_j - cK_j. \tag{5.9}$$

(b) If $s = (s_1, s_2) = ((K_1, g_1(\cdot)), (K_2, g_2(\cdot)))$ is such that $p_i = g_i(K_1, K_2) = p_j = g_j(K_1, K_2), j \neq i$, then

$$\pi_i(s) = \min\left\{\frac{1}{2}\frac{M - p_i}{d} + \max\left[\frac{1}{2}\frac{M - p_j}{d} - K_j, 0\right], K_i\right\} p_i - cK_i \tag{5.10}$$

$$\pi_j(s) = \min\left\{\frac{1}{2}\frac{M - p_j}{d} + \max\left[\frac{1}{2}\frac{M - p_i}{d} - K_i, 0\right], K_j\right\} p_j - cK_j. \tag{5.11}$$

The interpretation of the above expressions is as follows. On the one hand, (a) deals with the case in which some firm i "posts" alone the lowest price. This leads firm i to absorb the whole demand up to capacity, i.e., $\min[(M - p_i)/d, K_i]$, obtaining the profits specified in (5.8). Therefore, if $K_i > (M - p_i)/d$, firm i's capacity is not a binding restriction and this firm serves the whole of prevailing demand (correspondingly, firm $j(\neq i)$ obtains *no* residual demand). However, if the opposite inequality applies, firm i is forced to exhaust its own capacity, leaving still some residual demand unsatisfied. In this case, firm j gains access to that fraction of the residual demand that is consistent with its own price, i.e., $(M - p_j)/d - K_i$. Once the capacity constraint of firm j is taken into account, this results into the profits indicated in (5.9).

Note that the latter considerations embody an important implicit assumption concerning the rationing scheme operating in the market. Specifically, rationing is assumed to be efficient, in that every consumer who purchases the good has a willingness to pay for it that is above p_j, the highest posted price, which is also the marginal cost to consumers of buying the good. This feature of the rationing mechanism would necessarily result *ex post* if "fortunate" (nonrationed) consumers could frictionlessly resell the good to other rationed consumers with a higher valuation for it. But, of course, there are conceivable rationing mechanisms that would not have this property (e.g., proportional schemes – cf. Exercise 5.4). For those cases, our analysis does not necessarily apply, as explained below.

Let us now turn to explaining (b) above. This addresses the situation where both firms offer the same price $p_i = p_j$. In this case, (5.10) and (5.11) simply reflect the idea that both firms are *entitled* to share the induced market demand equally. Thus, if half of the total demand (i.e., $1/2(M - p_i)/d$) can be served by firm i given its capacity constraint K_i, this firm is sure to sell at least this amount. But, if the other firm j cannot satisfy its "notional" demand $1/2(M - p_i)/d$, then firm i can also serve that part of the induced residual, $1/2(M - p_i)/d - K_j$, to the extent that it is feasible given its own capacity constraint K_i.

We shall be interested in the pure-strategy subgame-perfect equilibria of the two-stage game just described. Let $s^* = (s_1^*, s_2^*) = ((K_1^*, g_1^*(\cdot)), (K_2^*, g_2^*(\cdot)))$ be some such equilibrium. The characterization of these equilibria follows from the following two claims.

Claim 1: *Given any* $(K_1, K_2) \in (0, \bar{K}]^2$, $g_1^*(K_1, K_2) = g_2^*(K_1, K_2) = M - d(K_1 + K_2)$ *and, therefore, the firms produce to full capacity.*

To prove this first claim, we start by ruling out that, given any (K_1, K_2) as described, any of the different alternative possibilities may be consistent with equilibrium behavior.

(i) First, suppose that $p \equiv g_1^*(K_1, K_2) = g_2^*(K_1, K_2) < M - d(K_1 + K_2)$. Then, both firms ration their consumers and either of them, say i, could benefit from deviating to a price slightly above p. Then, it would still be able to sell the same amount K_i at that higher price.

(ii) Suppose now that $p \equiv g_1^*(K_1, K_2) = g_2^*(K_1, K_2) > M - d(K_1 + K_2)$. Then, some firm i is not selling to its full capacity K_i. Therefore, if it were to deviate and offer a price slightly lower than p, it would increase its sales by some amount bounded above zero, which would increase its profits.

(iii) Finally, consider the possibility where firms charge different prices, say $p_i \equiv g_i^*(K_1, K_2) < p_j \equiv g_j^*(K_1, K_2)$. In this case, if firm i is rationing some consumers (and thus selling at full capacity), raising its price slightly would increase its profits. Thus, suppose that firm i is not rationing consumers. Then, since p_i has to be optimal for this firm, it must be obtaining the monopoly profit. But this implies that firm j is facing zero demand and could therefore benefit by deviating and offering a price $p_j' \leq p_i$.

The previous considerations establish that every equilibrium must be as described for each feasible (K_1, K_2). That is, the above conditions are *necessary* for equilibrium behavior. To show that they are also *sufficient*, we need to verify that no unilateral deviation is profitable. In what follows, we discard downward and upward deviations in turn.

– Concerning a deviation downward (i.e., some firm i choosing a price $p_i' < p_i = p_j = M - d(K_1 + K_2)$), the fact that each firm i is already selling at full capacity with price p_i means that a lower price is obviously detrimental to its profits. This rules out such a deviation.

– Concerning a deviation upward (i.e., to some price $p_i'' > p_i = p_j = M - d(K_1 + K_2)$), the induced profits are (in view of (5.9)) given by

$$\tilde{\pi}_i(p_i'', p_j) \equiv \left(\frac{M - p_i''}{d} - K_j \right) p_i'' - cK_i$$

or, if we denote by q_i'' the output which satisfies

$$p_i'' = M - d(q_i'' + K_j)$$

we can rewrite firm i's profits as follows:

$$\tilde{\pi}_i(p_i'', p_j) = q_i''(M - d(q_i'' + K_j)) - cK_i.$$

In the game being considered, once capacities K_i and K_j are chosen in the first stage, they are irreversibly fixed. Therefore, maximizing $\tilde{\pi}_i(p_i'', p_j)$ in the second stage is equivalent to maximizing $q_i''(M - d(q_i'' + K_j))$. On the other hand, the fact that $K_j \leq \bar{K} \equiv M/3d$ implies that firm i's profit is increasing in q_i'' and, therefore, decreasing in p_i''. Thus, within the range $p_i'' \in [p_i, M]$ (or, equivalently, for $q_i'' \in [0, K_i]$), $\tilde{\pi}_i(p_i'', p_j)$ is maximized at $p_i'' = p_i$ (or $q_i'' = K_i$). This shows that an upward deviation on prices is not profitable either and completes the proof of claim 1.

Claim 2: *Given the second-stage pricing rules specified in Claim 1 (i.e., $g_i^*(K_1, K_2) = M - d(K_1 + K_2)$ for each $i = 1, 2$), the capacity profile $(K_1^*, K_2^*) = ((M - c)/3d, (M - c)/3d)$ defines a Nash equilibrium in the first stage of the game; i.e., capacities (and therefore ensuing outputs) induce a Cournot equilibrium for underlying total costs given by c (recall (3.11)).*

To prove this second claim, we build on claim 1 as follows. First, note that, given $K_j^*, g_1^*(\cdot)$ and $g_2^*(\cdot)$, the payoff to be earned by each firm i from any particular choice of K_i in the first stage is equal to $K_i(M - d(K_i + K_j^*)) - cK_i$. Then, it follows from the analysis undertaken in Subsection 3.1.1 (cf. (3.11)) that

$$K_i\left(M - d\left(K_i + \frac{M - c}{3d} \right) \right) - cK_i$$

$$\leq \frac{M - c}{3d}\left(M - d\left(2\frac{M - c}{3d} \right) \right) - c\frac{M - c}{3d}$$

for all $K_i \geq 0$. Hence, the claim is readily confirmed.

We conclude, therefore, that if firms must commit to costly production capacities before price competition determines actual production needs, there is a (unique)[69] subgame-perfect equilibrium that reproduces the traditional Cournot outcome. Specifically, firms set capacities (and also, subsequently, corresponding

[69] See Exercise 5.6.

productions) that coincide with the Cournot-Nash equilibrium values for the total costs involved (i.e., capacity and production costs). Thus, quite surprisingly, we find out that the *endogenous* quantity rigidity imposed on the second stage by the prior, and therefore irreversible, capacity choices deprives price (or Bertrand) competition of much of its otherwise aggressively competitive features – recall Subsection 3.1.2.

5.2 Markets (II): decentralized price formation

So far in this book, the crucial issue of how prices are formed in a market context has either been abstracted from (e.g., the Cournot model) or has been approached in a quite asymmetric fashion (e.g., the Bertrand model, where prices are the object of choice of only *one* side of the market). In this section, we model the phenomenon of price determination *explicitly*, conceiving it as the strategic outcome of a *bilateral* bargaining setup. First, in Subsection 5.2.1, only two fixed parties are involved throughout the intertemporal process of bargaining. Then, in Subsection 5.2.2, this stylized setup is extended to a large-population environment, where every bilateral encounter unfolds under the threat that, in the case of disagreement, bargaining may proceed afresh with different partners.

5.2.1 *Bilateral strategic bargaining*

Consider a process of bargaining between two individuals, 1 and 2, who have to decide how to divide a certain surplus. Possible examples for this surplus are, say, a monetary prize to which both agents are jointly entitled or the relative contribution of each of them to the production of a bilateral public good. Here, however, our preferred motivation is to view the surplus in question as the *monetary* gains from trade to be divided between a buyer and a seller of a certain indivisible object (see Subsection 5.2.2 for details). In this case, the surplus can be conceived as the difference between the monetary value of the good for the buyer (say, player 2) and that of the seller (player 1). Without loss of generality, we normalize the first magnitude to be equal to unity and the second to zero. Thus, any bargaining proposal can be identified with a "price" $x \in [0, 1]$ to be paid for the good in question. If the transaction materializes at that price, player 1 (the seller) receives a net benefit equal to x and player 2 (the buyer) a net benefit of $1 - x$.

In this setup, the intertemporal bargaining process is modeled as a sequence of alternating offers, corresponding responses, and possible counteroffers. Time is taken to be discrete, with periods indexed by $t \in \{1, 2, \ldots, T\}$. Initially, T is assumed finite (i.e., the bargaining process lasts for at most a finite number of periods). Later on, we make $T \to \infty$, thus considering a process with unbounded time horizon.

The rules of the bargaining process are as follows.

- In odd periods, $t = 1, 3, 5, \ldots$, player 1 is the proposer and suggests a certain division of the surplus of the form $(x(t), 1 - x(t))$, where the first and second components of this vector are interpreted as the shares associated to players 1 and 2, respectively. In even periods, $t = 2, 4, 6, \ldots$, it is player 2's turn to be the proposer, suggesting some surplus division with the same format.[70]

- In any period t, after the corresponding player i (1 or 2, depending on whether t is odd or even) has made her proposal $(x(t), 1 - x(t))$, the other player $j \neq i$ (the "responder") may accept or reject it.

  – If player j accepts the proposal, the corresponding division of the surplus is carried out and players 1 and 2 receive the respective payoffs

  $$(\delta^{t-1}x(t), \ \delta^{t-1}(1 - x(t))),$$

  where $\delta < 1$ is a common discount rate. Thus, when an agreement occurs, the induced payoffs are taken to be linear in the share of the surplus received but discounted over time at a constant rate.

  – If player j rejects i's proposal, two possibilities may arise:
  ∗ when $t < T$, the process enters period $t + 1$, and then it is player j's turn to make her proposal;
  ∗ when $t = T$, the process ends and each player receives a zero payoff.

The above described multistage game models the bargaining process as a stylized concatenation of proposals and counterproposals. If an agreement is not reached early on, as the game is pushed toward further stages, the consequent passage of time is costly to the players because the payoffs resulting from late agreements are correspondingly discounted. Such payoff discounting can be provided with different interpretations. For example, one may suppose that the surplus actually shrinks (deteriorates) over time or, perhaps more naturally, that players are impatient and value positively an early resolution of matters. In any case, it will become clear that payoff discounting with time plays a crucial role in the model. It is only because time is costly that players may display any inclination to compromise.

The extensive-form representation of the game is schematically illustrated in Figure 5.3. Its analysis will be carried out inductively on T, the bargaining horizon.

Consider first the case with $T = 1$. The *unique* subgame-perfect equilibrium of this game is trivial: player 1 proposes $(1, 0)$ and player 2 accepts *any* proposal. To see this, first note that any strategy by player 2 that should qualify as optimal in every subgame must involve accepting all $(x, 1 - x)$ with $1 - x > 0$ (i.e., as long as $x < 1$). This uniquely determines player 2's equilibrium strategy except for the subgame associated to the proposal $(1, 0)$ by player 1. In this subgame, either "accept" or "reject" is an optimal reaction by player 2, because both provide her with the same payoff of zero. Consider first the possibility that player 2 might choose to "reject" in this subgame. Then, player 1 would have no *best* proposal (i.e., no optimal strategy) in response to it. For, in this case, player 1 would like to propose an "infinitesimally positive" share for her opponent, a magnitude which is not well

---

[70] Alternatively, which player (1 or 2) starts the bargaining process as the proposer could be chosen randomly. In fact, this is the formulation adopted in Subsection 5.2.2 to render the buyer and seller positions fully symmetric.

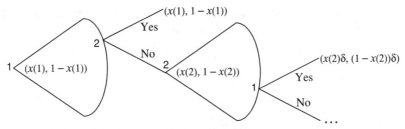

Figure 5.3: Bargaining process with alternating offers.

defined.[71] Therefore, no equilibrium would exist. Instead, if player 2's strategy prescribes accepting the proposal $(1, 0)$ – as well as all the others, of course – the optimal proposal by player 1 is exactly this proposal, thus leading to the unique subgame-perfect equilibrium indicated.

Now, let $T = 2$. In this case, we know from the above considerations that if the process were to reach the last period ($t = 2$), the whole surplus would be taken by player 2 (the one who proposes then). Therefore, taking into account the time discount of δ this possibility would entail, it is clear that player 2 will accept proposals by player 1 only at $t = 1$, $(x(1), 1 - x(1))$, that satisfy

$$1 - x(1) \geq \delta \cdot 1. \tag{5.12}$$

In other words, since any subgame-perfect equilibrium of the whole game must involve playing the (unique) subgame-perfect equilibrium from $t = 2$ onward, every optimal strategy by player 2 must prescribe rejecting at $t = 1$ any proposal that violates (5.12). In fact, by an argument analogous to the one explained above for $T = 1$, the equilibrium strategy of player 2 should accept all proposals that satisfy such (weak) inequality. In view of this, the equilibrium strategy by player 1 must involve a first-period proposal that maximizes her own share of the surplus subject to (5.12). That is, she must propose $(1 - \delta, \delta)$, which, as indicated, player 2 accepts. This is the outcome induced by the (again unique) subgame-perfect equilibrium of the game.

Next, let $T = 3$. Proceeding in an analogous manner, it follows that, in a subgame-perfect equilibrium, player 2 accepts any first-period proposal that satisfies

$$1 - x(1) \geq \delta(1 - \delta). \tag{5.13}$$

For, if she were to reject the initial proposal by player 1, player 2 would find herself as the initial proposer of a two-period bargaining game. She would then be in the same position as player 1 in the above considered game (with $T = 2$) where, in the unique subgame-perfect equilibrium, she would obtain a share of the surplus equal to $(1 - \delta)$. Appropriately discounted, this yields a payoff of $\delta(1 - \delta)$, the lower bound contemplated in (5.13). Thus, if player 2 accepts in equilibrium any proposal that satisfies such a lower bound, the first-period equilibrium proposal by player 1 must coincide with the largest $x(1)$ consistent with it. That is, she proposes $(1 - \delta(1 - \delta), \delta(1 - \delta))$ at $t = 1$ and player 2 accepts it.

---

[71] More precisely, the problem here is that player 1's relevant choice set (i.e., the set of proposals acceptable to player 2) is not compact.

Iterating the argument for any finite T, we conclude that the unique subgame-perfect equilibrium induces the following surplus division:

$$\left(1 - \delta + \delta^2 - \delta^3 + \cdots + (-1)^{T-1}\delta^{T-1}, \delta - \delta^2 + \delta^3 - \cdots + (-1)^T \delta^{T-1}\right),$$

or, more compactly,

$$\left(\frac{1 - (-1)^T \delta^T}{1 + \delta}, \frac{\delta + (-1)^T \delta^T}{1 + \delta}\right). \tag{5.14}$$

This outcome is supported by strategies that, as required by the notion of subgame-perfect Equilibrium, define a Nash equilibrium in *every* possible subgame. For each player $i = 1, 2$, these strategies may be described as follows:

(a) For any $t = 1, 2, \ldots$, if player i is the proposer at t, she demands for her the following share of the surplus

$$\frac{1 - (-1)^{T-t+1}\delta^{T-t+1}}{1 + \delta},$$

and offers the complementary amount to $j \neq i$.

(b) For any $t = 1, 2, \ldots$, if player i is the responder, she accepts any proposal by $j \neq i$ where i's share is at least as large as

$$\frac{\delta + (-1)^{T-t+1}\delta^{T-t+1}}{1 + \delta}$$

and rejects all the rest.

The above strategies lead to immediate agreement on (5.14) and therefore provide an *actual* response for only *one* of the shortest possible "histories" of play. Of course, this does not mean that those strategies can either remain silent or behave abitrarily (albeit only hypothetically) for all other histories. As explained, they must define a Nash equilibrium for every "continuation subgame," even for those arising after very long (and counterfactual) histories. At this point, it is worthwhile stressing that such a requirement of subgame perfection is crucial for our former clear-cut analysis. For, if we allowed for arbitrary Nash (nonperfect) equilibria, essentially *any* agreement (no matter how asymmetric or delayed it might be) could be supported as an equilibrium outcome of the bargaining game – see Exercise 5.8. By way of illustration, consider (assuming that T is even) the following strategies:

(i) For player 1,
   – in each $t = 1, 3, 5, \ldots, T - 1$, she proposes (1,0);
   – in each $t = 2, 4, 6, \ldots, T$, she accepts any player 2's proposal $(x, 1 - x)$.
(ii) For player 2,
   – in each $t = 2, 4, 6, \ldots, T$, she proposes (0,1);
   – in each $t = 1, 3, 5, \ldots, T - 1$, she rejects any player 1's proposal $(x, 1 - x)$.

The former pair of strategies define a Nash equilibrium. On the one hand, player 1 cannot gain from any unilateral deviation because, given the strategy of player 2, the most player 1 can ever attain is a zero payoff (either a null share of the surplus or eventual disagreement). On the other hand, given that player 1 never offers 2 any positive share of the surplus but accepts any of the latter's proposals, the best player 2 can do is to propose $(0, 1)$ in the first period when she acts as a proposer (i.e., $t = 2$). This is precisely what her strategy prescribes.

The strategies (i) and (ii) give rise to an outcome very different from immediate agreement on (5.14). Specifically, they lead to a situation in which player 2 obtains the full surplus at stake with one-period delay. As explained, this is possible only because the behavior prescribed is not "credible"; i.e., those strategies do not define a Nash equilibrium in every subgame. For example, in contrast with what player 2's strategy postulates, it can never be optimal for this player to reject any proposal $(x, 1 - x)$ by player 1 with $1 - x > \delta$. The *maximum* discounted payoff player 2 can conceivably achieve by rejecting any such proposal is δ, i.e., the discounted payoff (as viewed from the current period) derived from obtaining the whole surplus with one-period delay. Thus, if she rejected a proposal $(x, 1 - x)$ with $1 - x > \delta$, she would be playing a strictly dominated strategy (therefore, never part of an equilibrium) in the subgame following that proposal.

The finite-horizon bargaining model just considered was proposed by Stahl (1972). Later, Rubinstein (1982) studied an infinite-horizon version of it where players' bargaining is not constrained to a maximum preestablished duration and, in case an agreement is *never* reached, both players earn a null payoff. Heuristically, one can think of such an infinite-horizon context as one where $T = \infty$. To find one subgame-perfect equilibrium for this infinite-horizon context, it turns out to be enough to take $T \to \infty$ on the finite-horizon equilibrium strategies described by (a) and (b). Doing so, we obtain the following strategies for each player $i = 1, 2$.

(†) For any $t = 1, 2, \ldots$, if player i is the proposer at t, she demands (for her) the following share of the surplus:

$$\frac{1}{1 + \delta},$$

and offers the complementary amount to $j \neq i$.

(‡) For any $t = 1, 2, \ldots$, if player i is the responder, she accepts any proposal by $j \neq i$ where $i's$ share is at least as large as

$$\frac{\delta}{1 + \delta}$$

and rejects all the rest.

To verify that these strategies indeed define a subgame-perfect equilibrium of the infinite-horizon game, it is useful to observe that the underlying bargaining context is essentially stationary. Specifically, note that every two subgames starting at the beginning of an even period are isomorphic and, on the other hand, the same happens with all those starting at the beginning of every odd period. Because of this stationarity, to verify that (†) and (‡) define a subgame-perfect equilibrium, it is enough to check that these strategies induce a Nash equilibrium of the continuation game at any arbitrary even or odd period.

Consider, for concreteness, the case of player 1 and assume that player 2's strategy is given by (†) and (‡). If the period in question is odd and player 1 is the proposer, the division $(1/(1 + \delta), \delta/(1 + \delta))$ prescribed by (†) is the best proposal she can offer among those that would be accepted by player 2. And if she were to propose instead something more ambitious (i.e., a proposal $(x, 1 - x)$ with $x > 1/(1 + \delta)$), this would lead to its rejection by player 2 and thus to a discounted payoff which could be no higher than $\delta^2/(1 + \delta)$, i.e., the "present value" of obtaining a share of the surplus equal to $\delta/(1 + \delta)$ next period, which is obviously lower than $1/(1 + \delta)$.

Now suppose that the period in question is even and 1 plays the responder role. Then, as prescribed by (†), it is optimal for her to reject any surplus share strictly lower than $\delta/(1 + \delta)$. For, by so doing, the continuation equilibrium provides her with the share $1/(1 + \delta)$ next period and a present value equal to $\delta/(1 + \delta)$. On the other hand, the acceptance of a share no smaller than the lower bound $\delta/(1 + \delta)$ is also optimal because, again, that lower bound is the present value of what she may expect to get from rejecting the offer and starting as a proposer next period. Combining these considerations, we conclude that, given the strategy played by her opponent, the strategy specified by (†) and (‡) is indeed optimal for player 1 in every subgame. The confirmation of a similar conclusion for player 2 can be done analogously.

Once confirmed that the strategies given by (†) and (‡) define a subgame-perfect equilibrium of the infinite-horizon bargaining game, a full parallelism with the analysis conducted for the finite-horizon context still requires establishing its uniqueness. To do so, we shall rely on an argument proposed by Shaked and Sutton (1984) that again exploits in an elegant manner the stationarity of the dynamic game. Even though their original argument applies generally to any subgame-perfect equilibrium, we shall restrict our consideration here to those that will be labeled as *pseudo-stationary,* namely, equilibria whose strategies may possibly depend on time but *not* on any of the events of past history that occurred before the current period of play.[72] This will simplify matters substantially by allowing us to speak unambiguously of the *continuation payoffs* that any given equilibrium induces for either player from any period t onward. For convenience, these payoffs are evaluated (i.e., discounted) from that same t onward – thus, for example, any agreement $(x, 1 - x)$ achieved at $t' \geq t$ yields, when evaluated at t, a continuation payoff vector equal to $(x\delta^{t'-t}, (1 - x)\delta^{t'-t})$.

Consider any given pseudo-stationary subgame-perfect equilibrium of the infinite-horizon bargaining game, and denote by ω_1 the payoff obtained in it by player 1. On the other hand, let ω_1' stand for the continuation payoff which player 1 would earn in that equilibrium if (after some unpredicted deviations) the process were to reach $t = 3$. We now want to verify that ω_1 and ω_1' are related through the

---

[72] In a heuristic sense, these equilibria reflect the idea that "bygones are bygones"; i.e., the past can have no bearing on the future if it does not affect the available possibilities (strategic or otherwise).

following expression:

$$\omega_1 = 1 - \delta + \delta^2 \omega_1'. \tag{5.15}$$

This follows from a slight variation of the backward-induction logic explained above for a game whose horizon is $T = 3$. First, note that, since player 1 obtains the payoff ω_1' if the process reaches $t = 3$, the unique equilibrium proposal on 2's part at $t = 2$ must be $(\delta\omega_1', 1 - \delta\omega_1')$. Taking this into account, the unique equilibrium proposal by 1 at $t = 1$ becomes $(1 - \delta + \delta^2\omega_1', \delta - \delta^2\omega_1')$, which must be accepted by player 2. This induces an equilibrium payoff ω_1 for player 1 that fulfills (5.15).

Let $\hat{\omega}_1$ be the *supremum* computed over the payoffs that player 1 may obtain in *some* pseudo-stationary subgame-perfect equilibrium. (This supremum is well-defined, because the set of such equilibria includes the one given by (†) and (‡) and therefore is nonempty.) To compute $\hat{\omega}_1$, define the function $h(\cdot)$ from (5.15) as follows:

$$\omega_1 = h(\omega_1') \equiv 1 - \delta + \delta^2 \omega_1'.$$

Since the function $h(\cdot)$ is increasing and continuous, it follows that the highest payoff player 1 can earn in the game through a pseudo-stationary subgame-perfect equilibrium is obtained when precisely this same highest payoff is also the continuation payoff at $t = 3$. Formally, this allows us to write

$$\hat{\omega}_1 = 1 - \delta + \delta^2 \hat{\omega}_1.$$

That is, the maximum equilibrium payoff (at $t = 1$) coincides with that obtained when the continuation payoff at $t = 3$ is also maximum. Hence we obtain

$$\hat{\omega}_1 = \frac{1}{1 + \delta}.$$

On the other hand, let $\tilde{\omega}_1$ be the *infimum* computed over the payoffs that player 1 can obtain in *some* pseudo-stationary subgame-perfect equilibrium. Again, this infimum is well defined. The above argument can be trivially adapted to conclude that the infimum equilibrium payoff must exactly coincide with that induced by the infimum continuation payoff at $t = 3$. Therefore, we have

$$\tilde{\omega}_1 = \frac{1}{1 + \delta}.$$

Since, as it turns out, $\hat{\omega}_1 = \tilde{\omega}_1$, this common value must be the unique payoff obtained by player 1 in *any* pseudo-stationary subgame-perfect equilibrium. Thus, payoff-wise, every such equilibrium is equivalent to the one given by (†) and (‡). In fact, since the above argument is history independent, it is easy to see that, strategy-wise as well, the only pseudo-stationary subgame-perfect equilibrium is the one given by (†) and (‡) – cf. Exercise 5.10.

5.2.2   *Strategic bargaining in a population context**

We now turn to a model due to Rubinstein and Wolinsky (1985) where bargaining is still formulated as a two-party affair. It is not conceived, however, as an isolated phenomenon but as part of an unfolding population process that *endogenously* determines the relevant outside option. This option, therefore, is simply the outcome predicted for an analogous process of bargaining that could be started in the future with some other partner, if an agreement fails to be reached with the current one. Thus, in the present case, the payoff to be expected by any pair of agents if their bilateral process of bargaining is discontinued is not a parameter of the model (i.e., a zero payoff, as in Subsection 5.2.1) but an endogenous variable of the model. To fix ideas, we shall think of this context as a *market* consisting of many agents, buyers and sellers, involved in "parallel bargaining." Therefore, when an agreement materializes, it can be viewed as the bilateral "price" at which the transaction takes place, and a reflection of the prevailing "market conditions."

More precisely, the theoretical framework is as follows. The market consists of B buyers and S sellers, both to be conceived present in large numbers. Each seller has only one unit of an indivisible good, for which it has a zero valuation. Every buyer has one unit of a fully divisible commodity (it can be thought of as money) and displays a valuation of the indivisible good that, in monetary terms, equals one. Time is discrete and unbounded. Every period $t = 1, 2, \ldots$, a certain (same) number of buyers and sellers meet. Some of them meet for the first time while others may have already been matched in the preceding period (i.e., they are involved in *ongoing* bargaining).

At each t, bargaining between any matched pair of buyer and seller proceeds in the following manner. First, one of them is chosen at random (with equal probability) to be the proposer. The one so chosen proposes a "price" $x \in [0, 1]$. If accepted by the other party, the transaction takes place at that price, the buyer receiving a payoff equal to $(1 - x)\delta^{t-1}$ and the seller a payoff equal to $x\delta^{t-1}$, where $\delta < 1$ represents the common discount factor. Those agents then exit the market and are replaced by a new pair of (yet unmatched) buyer and seller.

Instead, if the price being proposed is not accepted, the buyer–seller pair in question faces a number of different possibilities next period. On the one hand, with probability β, the buyer is rematched in $t + 1$ with some other seller and the previous relationship is irreversibly discontinued. Analogously, the seller may be rematched afresh in $t + 1$, a possibility that occurs with probability α. Since those two rematching events are assumed stochastically independent, it turns out that with probability $(1 - \beta)\alpha$ only the buyer is left unmatched (her former partner having been rematched with some other buyer) and with probability $\beta(1 - \alpha)$ only the seller is left unmatched. Finally, with probability $(1 - \beta)(1 - \alpha)$ neither of them is rematched afresh, an event that is taken to mean both of them continue to face each other at $t + 1$ in a new bargaining round.

To complete the specification of the matching dynamics, we still need to describe what happens at any t with those agents who were unmatched at $t - 1$. For simplicity, they are assumed to face the same possibilities as those who were formerly matched.

That is, any formerly unmatched buyer meets a seller with probability β, and any previously unmatched seller meets a buyer with probability α. Therefore, with the respective complementary probabilities, $1 - \beta$ and $1 - \alpha$, the corresponding agent (i.e., a formerly unmatched buyer or seller) continues to be unmatched in the current period.

The matching probabilities, β and α, are assumed proportional to $1/B$ and $1/S$, respectively. Thus, it is posited that

$$\frac{\beta}{\alpha} = \frac{S}{B}, \tag{5.16}$$

which simply embodies the idea that matching selection is conducted in an unbiased fashion over the relevant population. Therefore, the relative odds faced by a typical buyer or seller reflect the underlying "market conditions," i.e., the relative scarcity of either of them.

What should be the format of a player's strategy in the context described? In principle, it could be any mapping from past history to current choices, as contemplated in any general game-theoretic framework (cf. Subsection 1.3.1). Here, however, we restrict to the much simpler notion that Rubinstein and Wolinsky (1985) label a *semistationary strategy,* which postulates that players make their behavior depend only on observations that belong to the current match.[73] That is, whatever happened earlier with other players is taken to have no bearing on the proposals and responses to be issued in the prevailing bargaining phase conducted with the most recent partner. With this restriction in place, a strategy for a buyer or a seller is simply a proposed price $x \in [0, 1]$ and a contingent pattern of responses to be applied at each t (each to be used in either the proposer or responder role), whose specification depends only on the history of the present ongoing matching.

Focusing on symmetric situations, let us make the "working assumption" that the bargaining process may be characterized by two given (semistationary) strategies, σ_b for buyers and σ_s for sellers. Then, our first task is to compute the expected payoffs induced by some such pair of strategies for a matched buyer and a matched seller. To this end, we find it useful to introduce some notation. First, let V_b and V_s stand for the expected (discounted) payoffs respectively obtained by a buyer and seller when they are currently *unmatched*. On the other hand, denote by W_b and W_s the expected payoffs respectively obtained by a *matched* buyer and seller before bargaining roles have been assigned. Note that these magnitudes can be defined independently of t and the agent's identity due to the assumption that the same *semistationarity* strategy is used by all buyers and, correspondingly, by all sellers. This allows one to describe compactly the game played by each pair of matched buyer and seller as illustrated in Figure 5.4.

---

[73] Despite the fact that the ensuing argument restricts consideration to semistationary strategies, it is not difficult to see that an equilibrium in those strategies still qualifies as an equilibrium when players are not thus restricted and may use any arbitrary strategies. The reason justifying this conclusion is simple: if other players use semistationary strategies, there must always be a best response that is also semistationary.

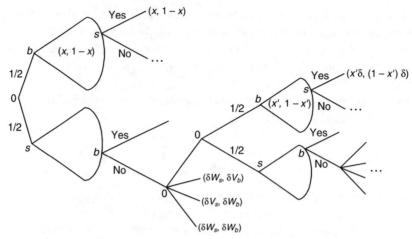

Figure 5.4: Bargaining process in a population environment.

The payoff continuation values given by V_h and W_h, $h = b, s$, are related as follows:

$$V_b = \delta[\beta W_b + (1 - \beta)V_b] \tag{5.17}$$

$$V_s = \delta[\alpha W_s + (1 - \alpha)V_s], \tag{5.18}$$

that is, the payoff of being currently unmatched is a discounted convex combination of the payoffs associated with either being matched or staying unmatched next period, with respective weights given by the prior probabilities of each of those two events. Expressions (5.17) and (5.18) can be rewritten as follows:

$$V_b = \frac{\delta\beta}{1 - \delta(1 - \beta)} W_b$$

$$V_s = \frac{\delta\alpha}{1 - \delta(1 - \alpha)} W_s,$$

which indicate that the continuation payoffs for an unmatched agent are a simple linear function of the payoffs predicted when being matched. To compute the latter payoffs, we obviously need to know the proposals and responses chosen by each type of matched agent (buyer and seller) in each of the two roles, proposer and responder. In this respect, let us conjecture (for the moment, again, just a working hypothesis) that there are two prices, x_b and x_s, which are always put forward by a buyer or a seller when playing the proposer role. Further conjecture that, in the responder role, their strategies are of the following simple form:

- For a buyer, accept any price x if, and only if, it satisfies $x \leq x_b$;
- For a seller, accept any price x if, and only if, it satisfies $x \geq x_s$.

Then, we could close the computation of the induced payoffs and write:

$$W_b = 1 - \frac{x_b + x_s}{2} \tag{5.19}$$

$$W_s = \frac{x_b + x_s}{2}; \tag{5.20}$$

i.e., the expected payoff of a matched agent would be simply given by the average payoff induced by the two possible proposals (buyer- or seller-originated).

Our objective now is to identify suitable proposals, x_b^* and x_s^*, whose induced strategies (with the above format)[74] define a subgame-perfect equilibrium for every *bilateral* encounter when the ensuing payoffs that players anticipate if their relationship is discontinued are as determined by those proposals as well. Let V_h^* and W_h^* ($h = b, s$) denote the values obtained from (5.17)-(5.18) and (5.19)-(5.20) when these expressions are particularized to $x_b = x_b^*$ and $x_s = x_s^*$. Then, a straightforward adaptation of the arguments used in Subsection 5.2.1 for the isolated bilateral case indicates that any pair of proposals (x_b^*, x_s^*) – together with the associated values V_h^* and W_h^* ($h = b, s$) – defines a subgame-perfect equilibrium of every bilateral encounter if they satisfy the following payoff-indifference conditions:

$$x_b^* = (1 - (1 - \alpha)(1 - \beta))V_s^* + (1 - \alpha)(1 - \beta)\delta W_s^* \tag{5.21}$$

$$1 - x_s^* = (1 - (1 - \alpha)(1 - \beta))V_b^* + (1 - \alpha)(1 - \beta)\delta W_b^*. \tag{5.22}$$

The interpretation of the above conditions is the familiar one. For example, (5.21) embodies the requirement that the equilibrium proposal offered by the buyer when she is the proposer is the minimum price that makes the seller *not* prefer to reject the proposal and enter the following period. An analogous interpretation can be attributed to (5.22), now concerning the seller's proposal and the buyer's incentives.

Overall, the above conditions give rise to a system of six equations with six unknowns: V_b^*, V_s^*, W_b^*, W_s^*, x_b^*, x_s^*. Straightforward algebraic derivations (cf. Exercise 5.12) show that the unique solution of this system involves the following buyer and seller proposals:

$$x_b^* = \frac{\delta\alpha + \delta(1 - \delta)(1 - \alpha)(1 - \beta)}{2(1 - \delta) + \delta\alpha + \delta\beta} \tag{5.23}$$

$$x_s^* = \frac{2(1 - \delta) + \delta\alpha - \delta(1 - \delta)(1 - \alpha)(1 - \beta)}{2(1 - \delta) + \delta\alpha + \delta\beta}. \tag{5.24}$$

This model was originally proposed by Rubinstein and Wolinsky (1985) as a stylized way of shedding light on the following important issue: Can interagent bargaining be conceived as a decentralized (and auctioneer-free) mechanism to generate Walrasian outcomes? Of course, a positive answer to this question can be hoped for only as a limit result, obtained under the assumption that the bargaining

---

[74] Thus, in particular, the values x_b^* and x_s^* also mark the threshold of acceptance for buyers and sellers, respectively.

process is almost frictionless.[75] For otherwise, if bargaining were sluggish or wasteful, this would necessarily introduce a significant wedge between realized and Walrasian outcomes for reasons akin to other well-understood sources of market imperfections. (Recall, for example, the problem of market coordination failure arising in Section 3.4 as a consequence of time irreversibilities, another particular instance of trade frictions.)

To be precise, the desired question is posed as follows. How does the equilibrium outcome of the bargaining population game compare with the Walrasian allocation when $\delta \to 1$? The focus, therefore, is on a context with an arbitrarily small cost of delay, which is the key source of (potential) inefficiency in the present context.[76] Taking limits on δ in (5.23) and (5.24), we obtain

$$\lim_{\delta \to 1} x_b^* = \lim_{\delta \to 1} x_s^* = \frac{\alpha}{\alpha + \beta}. \tag{5.25}$$

That is, as delay becomes insignificantly costly, the equilibrium outcome induces a limit price that divides the surplus between each side of the market in exact proportion to their respective probabilities of being (re)matched. Therefore, the equilibrium biases the surplus share in favor of that side of the market whose probability of being (re)matched is higher. This accords with intuition since, when delay is almost costless, matching probabilities fully reflect the bargaining power of each party in the bilateral bargaining conducted between any buyer and seller.

How does this bargaining outcome compare with the Walrasian price? Here, the crucial first step is to identify the "right" benchmark economy one should use to define the Walrasian equilibrium. One possibility in this respect is to focus on the underlying economy with B buyers and S sellers, out of which individuals are randomly matched to face a bilateral bargaining situation. Then, unless we are in the exceptional case where there are precisely as many buyers as sellers ($B = S$), the Walrasian price is either one (if $B > S$) or zero (if $B < S$). This contrasts with (5.25), which, in view of (5.16), can be rewritten as

$$\lim_{\delta \to 1} x_b^* = \lim_{\delta \to 1} x_s^* = \frac{B}{B + S}.$$

Thus, with this approach, one finds that the asymmetries between each side of the market (supply and demand) induce much less drastic consequences in the bargaining context than in the Walrasian model.

This approach, however, has been criticized by Gale (1987), who argues that the discrepancy between both outcomes (the Walrasian and the bargaining-induced prices) derives from the fact that the wrong benchmark economy is being

---

[75] Note that the process could not be utterly void of time friction (i.e., agents could not display an absence of time preference) because, in that case, there would be no pressure toward reaching any agreement in finite time – cf. Subsection 5.2.1.

[76] One possible way of understanding the procedure of making the discount rate approach one is as follows. Suppose the discount rate over *calendar* time is fixed but the time period shrinks (i.e., bargaining, with its offers and counteroffers, becomes faster – or less subject to friction). Then, if the time period becomes very short (formally, converges to zero), the effective payoff discounting is very low as well (i.e., the discount rate converges to one).

considered. In essence, the main issue at stake is connected to our assumption that, as transactions take place and agents exit the market (buyers and sellers, in equal numbers), they are correspondingly replaced to keep the total number of agents in each side of the market unchanged. This means, in particular, that the relative scarcity of buyers or sellers reflected by B and S never shows up in the market flows: by construction, they are always composed by the same number of buyers and sellers. It is as if, in terms of flows, the economy were placed in the exceptional case mentioned above where there is an equal number of buyers and sellers. But then, if we view this flow specification as the appropriate benchmark economy, the Walrasian price is undetermined: any price between zero and one is a possible Walrasian price, including that in (5.25). This suggests that, at least under some formalizations of the "Walrasian test," the bargaining framework is not really incompatible with the Walrasian model but rather provides a selection device for it.[77]

5.3   Oligopoly (III): differentiated products

As explained in Chapter 3 (recall, in particular, Exercises 3.5 and 3.6), when firms produce a homogenous good in an oligopolistic market and set prices (i.e., interact à la Bertrand) there is often little room for noncompetitive profits at equilibrium. However, the state of affairs substantially changes if firms' strategic interaction does not strictly abide by the simple Bertrand paradigm. For example, in Subsection 5.1.2, we discussed an enrichment of the original Bertrand setup where firms have to commit beforehand to a given production capacity and the situation becomes outcome-equivalent to Cournot competition. In this context, therefore, firms are generally able to sustain above-competitive profits at equilibrium, despite the fact that they compete in prices in the second stage of the game.

In a different vein, another consideration that should generally improve firms' performance under price competition is the existence of some degree of product differentiation among the goods they supply. This was illustrated through a simple, but rather primitive, model in Section 3.1.2, where each firm was postulated to face a specific demand function that reflected an *exogenously given* form of product differentiation. Now, our objective is to study a model in which the degree of differentiation displayed by the goods produced is endogenously determined by the firms themselves within a multistage game. Specifically, we postulate a game with only two stages. In the first stage, firms select the type of product they want to produce; in the second stage, they compete à la Bertrand, determining their prices simultaneously.

This approach, which originated in the work of Hotelling (1929), admits several alternative interpretations. One of them associates the product type of each firm with

---

[77] This literature (cf. Gale, 1987; or Rubinstein and Wolinsky, 1990) has also considered alternative variations of the present bargaining context where the competitive outcome obtains at equilibrium. For example, the latter paper studies a model in which the number of agents is given at the beginning of time and none enter thereafter. In it, the competitive price results at any subgame-perfect equilibrium in which the strategies condition behavior only on the set of agents currently present and time (e.g., *not* on the identity or past history of the current partner).

the physical location where its output is being delivered. (This is why the models studied in this literature are often called *location models.*) The good is assumed homogeneous across all firms but consumers are spread throughout the relevant territory. Consequently, each consumer has to incur a twofold cost in acquiring the good from a particular firm. On the one hand, she has to pay the price charged for it. On the other hand, the consumer also has to incur the transportation cost involved in visiting the firm's location.

An alternative interpretation of the model identifies the "location" chosen by a particular firm as the point in characteristic space occupied by its produced good. Then, consumers' distribution over the space is viewed as reflecting taste hetero-geneity, each consumer placed at the point that reflects her ideal (most preferred) product characteristics. As the consumer is forced to buy a good whose characteris-tics differ more (i.e., are further away) from her ideal point, she incurs an increasing "preference cost," which is formally identical to the aforementioned transportation cost.

The model is now formally introduced. (In presenting it, we adhere, for the sake of concreteness, to the first of the interpretations proposed above: a geographic one.) Let there be two firms, $i = 1, 2$, that produce a homogeneous good with an identical constant-returns technology and marginal cost $c > 0$. The region served by these firms has a continuous spatial structure, its locations represented by points in the interval $[0, 1]$. Consumers are distributed in this space according to a uniform distribution (i.e., there is an identical *density* of consumers of "infinitesimal size" in every location). Each one of them wants to consume at most one (indivisible) unit of the good, from which she derives a gross utility of $\hat{u} > 0$, expressed in monetary terms.

The net utility obtained by each consumer is obtained by substracting from $\hat{u}$ both the price paid for the good and the transportation cost incurred by visiting the point in space where the good is delivered. It is assumed that each firm can deliver its good only in a single point of the interval $[0, 1]$. For each firm $i = 1, 2$, this point is called its *delivery point* and is denoted by s_i.

Transportation costs are supposed identical for every consumer and quadratic in the distance traveled, which is denoted by d. That is, they are of the form

$$C(d) = vd^2, \quad v > 0.$$

Thus, for a consumer located at point $h \in [0, 1]$ – who is simply called "consumer h" – the cost of traveling to any given s_i is

$$C(|h - s_i|) = v(h - s_i)^2.$$

Given any pair of delivery points (s_1, s_2) and a corresponding vector of prices (p_1, p_2) charged by both firms, any particular consumer $h \in [0, 1]$ is naturally taken to buy the good from any firm $i \in \{1, 2\}$ that maximizes the expression

$$\hat{u} - p_i - v(h - s_i)^2,$$

provided, of course, that this expression is not negative for the price-location configuration of at least one of the firms. If it is negative in both cases, consumer h does not buy the good at all. And if the *net* utility derived from both firms is identical (and nonnegative), we simply assume that the consumer in question buys the good from any *one* of them with equal *ex ante* probability.

Without loss of generality, assume that $s_2 \geq s_1$, i.e., firm 2 is located to the right of, or at the same point as, firm 1. As a first step in the analysis, it is useful to identify, for each price-location profile $[(p_1, s_1), (p_2, s_2)]$, the consumer who is indifferent between buying from either of the two firms. If such a consumer $\tilde{h}$ exists, the following expression is to hold:

$$p_1 + v\left(\tilde{h} - s_1\right)^2 = p_2 + v\left(\tilde{h} - s_2\right)^2,$$

which in turn implies:

$$\tilde{h} = \frac{p_2 - p_1}{2v\left(s_2 - s_1\right)} + \frac{s_1 + s_2}{2}, \tag{5.26}$$

under the implicit assumption that $s_1 \neq s_2$.[78] If the value of $\tilde{h}$ that follows from the above expression is negative, this reflects a situation in which firm 1 has a zero aggregate demand; if, on the contrary, that value exceeds unity, it is the aggregate demand for the good of firm 2 that vanishes.

The above description of consumers' behavior allows one to define demand functions for each firm that express their respective total sales for every possible price-location profile. Suppose, for simplicity, that *every* consumer buys the good from one of the firms at equilibrium. This can be ensured (see Exercise 5.14) if, for example

$$\hat{u} > 3v + c. \tag{5.27}$$

In this case, the demands of firms 1 and 2 (i.e., the total mass of consumers served by each of them) are, respectively, given by

$$D_1(s_1, s_2, p_1, p_2) = \min\left\{\max\left[\tilde{h}, 0\right], 1\right\} \tag{5.28}$$

$$D_2(s_1, s_2, p_1, p_2) = \min\left\{\max\left[1 - \tilde{h}, 0\right], 1\right\}. \tag{5.29}$$

Rewriting (5.26) as follows:

$$\tilde{h} = s_1 + \frac{s_2 - s_1}{2} + \frac{p_2 - p_1}{2v(s_2 - s_1)} \tag{5.30}$$

or, equivalently,

$$1 - \tilde{h} = 1 - s_2 + \frac{s_2 - s_1}{2} + \frac{p_1 - p_2}{2v(s_2 - s_1)},$$

we are led to an insightful interpretation of the demand captured by each firm in an interior case. Focus, for example, on (5.30), which reflects the demand enjoyed

---

[78] Of course, if $s_1 = s_2$, either *all* consumers are indifferent between the two firms (when $p_1 = p_2$) or *none* is (when $p_1 \neq p_2$).

by firm 1. This expression includes, as a *benchmark*, the size of firm 1's captive market of consumers, which is the set $\{h : h \leq s_1\}$ whose consumer mass is equal to s_1. On the other hand, out of the "no man's land" $\{h : s_1 \leq h \leq s_2\}$, firm 1 is postulated to obtain in addition half of it, i.e., $(s_2 - s_1)/2$, plus (or minus) a bonus (or penalty) determined by the price difference $p_2 - p_1$. In accord with intuition, the bonus (or penalty) experienced by firm 1 is higher (or smaller) the larger the price difference. In fact, the bonus (or penalty) could be so high as to make firm 1 gain (or lose) some of the competitor's (or its own) *a priori* captive market.

As advanced, the strategic interaction between firms is modeled as a two-stage game:

- In the first stage, they select simultaneously their respective locations in $[0, 1]$, i.e., their s_i, $i = 1, 2$.
- In the second stage, fully aware of the locations determined in the previous stage, they choose (also simultaneously) their respective prices p_i, $i = 1, 2$.

As usual, the game is solved backward. First, we compute the Nash equilibria of the second stage for every possible location profile. Then, we build on the pattern of second-stage Nash equilibria thus generated to find the firms' equilibrium decisions in the first stage, when they select their respective locations.

Given any location profile (s_1, s_2), a Nash equilibrium of the second-stage game is formally akin to that analyzed in Section 3.1.2. It is easy to compute (see Exercise 5.15) that the associated equilibrium prices are given by

$$p_1^*(s_1, s_2) = c + v(s_2 - s_1)\left(1 + \frac{s_1 + s_2 - 1}{3}\right) \tag{5.31}$$

$$p_2^*(s_1, s_2) = c + v(s_2 - s_1)\left(1 + \frac{1 - s_1 - s_2}{3}\right). \tag{5.32}$$

The above expressions uniquely determine the second-stage equilibrium induced by *any* possible pair of prior location decisions. From the viewpoint of the first stage of the game, (5.31) and (5.32) may be used to represent the original two-stage framework as a one-shot game with payoff functions that depend only on location choices (s_1, s_2) as follows:

$$\pi_i(s_1, s_2) = \tilde{\pi}_i(s_1, s_2, p_1^*(s_1, s_2), p_2^*(s_1, s_2)) \tag{5.33}$$

where the following notation is used:

$$\tilde{\pi}_i(s_1, s_2, p_1^*(s_1, s_2), p_2^*(s_1, s_2))$$
$$\equiv (p_i^*(s_1, s_2) - c)D_i(s_1, s_2, p_1^*(s_1, s_2), p_2^*(s_1, s_2)).$$

To characterize the Nash equilibria associated to the above first-stage payoff functions, we may rely on the corresponding first-order necessary conditions to be satisfied at equilibrium by both firms. To this end, we need to compute the first derivatives of each function $\pi_i(\cdot)$ with respect to its own s_i for each $i = 1, 2$.

From (5.33), we readily obtain

$$
\frac{\partial \pi_i}{\partial s_i}(s_1, s_2) = \frac{\partial \tilde{\pi}_i}{\partial s_i}(s_1, s_2, p_1^*(s_i, s_2), p_2^*(s_1, s_2))
$$

$$
+ \frac{\partial \tilde{\pi}_i}{\partial p_i}(s_1, s_2, p_1^*(s_1, s_2), p_2^*(s_1, s_2))\frac{\partial p_i^*}{\partial s_i} \qquad (5.34)
$$

$$
+ \frac{\partial \tilde{\pi}_i}{\partial p_j}(s_1, s_2, p_1^*(s_1, s_2), p_2^*(s_1, s_2))\frac{\partial p_j^*}{\partial s_i}.
$$

The above expression is greatly simplified by the observation that, by the optimality embodied by the functions $p_i^*(\cdot)$, one must have

$$
\frac{\partial \tilde{\pi}_i}{\partial p_i}(s_1, s_2, p_1^*(s_1, s_2), p_2^*(s_1, s_2)) = 0,
$$

because the equilibrium outcome prevailing in the second stage of the game must always be interior (cf. (5.31) and (5.32)). This implies that the second term in (5.34) vanishes. With respect to the other two, it may be checked (see Exercise 5.16) that (5.28)-(5.29) and (5.31)-(5.32) imply, say for firm 1, that

$$
\frac{\partial \tilde{\pi}_1}{\partial s_1}(s_1, s_2, p_1^*(s_1, s_2), p_2^*(s_1, s_2)) = (p_1^*(s_1, s_2) - c)\frac{2 + s_2 - 5s_1}{6(s_2 - s_1)}
$$

$$ (5.35) $$

$$
\frac{\partial \tilde{\pi}_1}{\partial p_2}(s_1, s_2, p_1^*(s_1, s_2), p_2^*(s_1, s_2))\frac{\partial p_2^*}{\partial s_1} = (p_1^*(s_1, s_2) - c)\frac{s_1 - 2}{3(s_2 - s_1)}.
$$

$$ (5.36) $$

Consequently, adding (5.35) and (5.36), it follows that, for every (s_1, s_2),

$$
\frac{\partial \pi_1}{\partial s_1}(s_1, s_2) < 0. \qquad (5.37)
$$

Thus, at the first stage of the game (and in correct anticipation of the subsequent equilibrium price behavior), firm 1 would always want to move toward the lower extreme of the interval $[0, 1]$. Symmetrically, one can easily compute as well that, for every (s_1, s_2),

$$
\frac{\partial \pi_2}{\partial s_2}(s_1, s_2) > 0. \qquad (5.38)
$$

Hence it follows that firm 2 would always want to move toward the upper extreme of the location interval $[0, 1]$ in the first stage of the game. Combining (5.37) and (5.38), we conclude that the unique Nash equilibrium (s_1^*, s_2^*) of the first-stage game with payoff functions defined by (5.33) has

$$
s_1^* = 0, \quad s_2^* = 1. \qquad (5.39)
$$

Hence, in combination with the functions $p_1^*(\cdot)$ and $p_2^*(\cdot)$ defined by (5.31) and

(5.32), the above location decisions define the unique subgame-perfect equilibrium of the whole (two-stage) game. Introducing (5.39) into (5.31) and (5.32), we obtain the prices actually set at this equilibrium:

$$p_1^* \left(s_1^*, s_2^*\right) = p_2^* \left(s_1^*, s_2^*\right) = c + v. \tag{5.40}$$

Thus, in contrast with the basic Bertrand model, we find that firms end up imposing a markup over production cost that depends positively on the magnitude of the transportation costs (as parametrized by v). Since this transportation cost is the basis for potential product differentiation in the present context, this conclusion underscores the insights obtained from our former analysis in Section 3.1.2.

Even though the *pricing* decisions in (5.40) are of an expected form, it is somewhat surprising that the equilibrium *location* choices given in (5.39) should have both firms maximize their distance (or product differentiation). For, at first glance, one would think either firm has an incentive to come as close as possible to its competitor in order to "grab from it" the maximum number of consumers. In fact, this effect is (for firm 1) sharply captured by (5.35), which, for sufficiently small values of s_1, implies that $\partial \tilde{\pi}_1 / \partial s_1 (\cdot) > 0$. Thus, *given* a low enough value of s_1 (in particular, for the equilibrium value of zero), firm 1 would indeed like to approach 2's location *provided that prices were to remain fixed*. Nevertheless, prices are not fixed, independently of location decisions, in the present model. When this price flexibility is taken into account, (5.37) shows that the distance-cutting incentives just explained are always offset by an opposite and stronger effect on prices; i.e., a greater proximity to firm 2 induces too strong a downward pressure on prices to make it worthwhile. It is this second effect (which is embodied by (5.36) and always overcomes the first effect) that leads firms to maximize their distance at equilibrium. By so doing, they limit effectively the detrimental (and perfectly anticipated) payoff consequences of having a too aggressive round of price competition in the subsequent stage of the game.

5.4   Mechanism design (III): efficient allocation of an indivisible object*

When confronting the problem of reconciling incentives and efficiency in the allocation of public goods, the perspective adopted in Subsection 3.2.2 was the "creative" one of a mechanism designer. We were not content, therefore, with taking the interaction context as given – in contrast, for example, with what had been formerly done with the inefficient subscription procedure (cf. Subsection 3.2.1) – but searched instead for a suitable mechanism tailored to the problem at hand. The issue, in other words, was to design a mechanism that, albeit possibly not so transparent or intuitive, tackled satisfactorily the free rider problem and guaranteed the desired efficiency in allocation of resources.

This approach was extended in Section 3.3, where the implementation problem was formulated in a general, and consequently abstract, manner. In this fashion, we aimed at addressing a wide variety of different design problems in a common theoretical setup. Given any desired *social choice rule* (SCR), the challenge was to define a mechanism whose induced game produced the required performance at its

Nash equilibria; i.e., we were concerned with so-called Nash implementation. The key (necessary) condition underlying the Nash implementability of a social choice rule was called monotonicity (recall Theorem 3.1). Even though this condition was found to be satisfied in many problems of interest, it was also seen to be violated in some others of relevance. A simple illustration of the latter was provided by King Solomon's dilemma, a particularly clear-cut instance of an interesting general problem, namely, the efficient allocation of an indivisible object.

One possible proposal to address the problem confronted by King Solomon, which seems quite natural (at least to an economist, if not necessarily to the "wise King"), is to enrich the allocation framework by allowing for monetary payments. In a sense, the perfect divisibility of these payments might be hoped to bypass the strict indivisibility of the good in question that is at the very heart of the problem. Is such a broadening of the allocation space sufficient to tackle King Solomon's implementation challenge satisfactorily? In what follows, we show that it is not, because the corresponding SCR continues to be nonmonotonic even in this case.

Recall the original King Solomon's dilemma, as it was precisely described in Subsection 3.3.2. Now, however, we allow for the possibility that the agents (the mothers) might be asked to make (never receive) monetary payments, which are either received directly by the planner (King Solomon) or simply "wasted." Then, the previous outcome space must be extended as follows:

$$\Omega = \{a, b, c\} \times X_A \times X_B,$$

a typical element denoted by $\omega = (\theta, x_a, x_b)$. Each of the elements in $\{a, b, c\}$ is understood as before:

   a : "the baby is given to woman A";

   b : "the baby is given to woman B";

   c : "the baby is killed";

while each $x_i \in \mathbb{R}_+$ is interpreted as the monetary payment made by woman $i \in \{A, B\}$.

As before, there are two environments, α and β. In environment α the true mother is A, whereas in environment β it is B. On the other hand, the SCR ϕ that embodies King Solomon's objectives is postulated as follows:

$$\phi(\alpha) = (a, 0, 0); \quad \phi(\beta) = (b, 0, 0). \tag{5.41}$$

That is, the King is interested in allocating the child to the true mother and, being altruistic, he would rather have no payments made by either woman A or B.

Individual utilities over outcomes are given by respective functions $V_i^e : \Omega \to \mathbb{R}$ for each woman $i \in \{A, B\}$ and every environment $e \in \{\alpha, \beta\}$. For any given outcome $\omega = (\theta, x_A, x_B) \in \Omega$, they are assumed to be of the following form:

$$V_i^e(\omega) = U_i^e(\theta) - x_i,$$

where $U_i^e(\theta)$ represents the *monetary* evaluation of the baby's state $\theta \in \{a, b, c\}$.

As in Subsection 3.3.2, these valuations are assumed to satisfy the following conditions:

(i) In environment α, woman A has $U_A^\alpha(a) > U_A^\alpha(b) > U_A^\alpha(c)$, whereas woman B has $U_B^\alpha(b) > U_B^\alpha(c) > U_B^\alpha(a)$.

(ii) In environment β, woman A has $U_A^\beta(a) > U_A^\beta(c) > U_A^\beta(b)$, and woman B has $U_B^\beta(b) > U_B^\beta(a) > U_B^\beta(c)$.

For our present purposes, we find it convenient to postulate as well that

(iii) $U_A^\alpha(a) - U_A^\alpha(b) < U_A^\beta(a) - U_A^\beta(b);\quad U_B^\beta(b) - U_B^\beta(a) < U_B^\alpha(b) - U_B^\alpha(a)$,

that is, for any of the two women, A or B, the payoff loss induced by having the child given away to the other woman is lower when she is the true mother. This may be motivated as a reflection of the fact that the true mother has a much stronger desire to see her child stay alive, even if it is at the cost of remaining with the other woman. In any case, bear in mind that, since our present objective is to establish a negative (i.e., impossibility) result, it is enough to identify reasonable circumstances (such as those in (iii) above) where this result holds.

Under the former three conditions, we now state two claims:

Claim 1: For woman A and any $\theta \in \{b, c\}$, $x_A \in \mathbb{R}_+$,

$$U_A^\alpha(a) \geq U_A^\alpha(\theta) - x_A \Rightarrow U_A^\beta(a) \geq U_A^\beta(\theta) - x_A.$$

Claim 2: For woman B and any $\theta \in \{b, c\}$, $x_B \in \mathbb{R}_+$,

$$U_B^\alpha(a) \geq U_B^\alpha(\theta) - x_B \Rightarrow U_B^\beta(a) \geq U_B^\beta(\theta) - x_B.$$

Concerning Claim 1 and the particularization of Claim 2 for $\theta = c$, simply note that both are a trivial consequence of the fact that, by (ii) above, we have

$$\forall \theta \in \{b, c\}, \quad U_A^\beta(a) - U_A^\beta(\theta) \geq 0 \geq -x_A$$

and

$$U_B^\beta(a) - U_B^\beta(c) \geq 0 \geq -x_B.$$

Now, to prove Claim 2 for $\theta = b$, suppose, for the sake of contradiction, that there exists some $x_B \in \mathbb{R}_+$ such that

$$x_B \geq U_B^\alpha(b) - U_B^\alpha(a)$$

but

$$x_B < U_B^\beta(b) - U_B^\beta(a).$$

Then, we have

$$U_B^\beta(b) - U_B^\beta(a) > U_B^\alpha(b) - U_B^\alpha(a),$$

which contradicts (iii) above.

Recall that the SCR ϕ is taken to satisfy $\phi(\alpha) = (a, 0, 0) \equiv \omega_a$; i.e., the desired outcome in environment α is that the child be given to mother A and no payments are made. Consider now environment β and its associated preferences U_i^β. Claims 1 and 2 imply that, for any outcome $\omega = (\theta, x_A, x_B)$ such that $V_i^\alpha(\omega_a) \geq V_i^\alpha(\omega)$, the inequality $V_i^\beta(\omega_a) \geq V_i^\beta(\omega)$ must also hold. Therefore, if the SCR ϕ were monotonic (recall condition (M) in Subsection 3.3.2), we should have $\omega_a \in \phi(\beta)$, a contradiction with the fact that $\phi(\beta) = (b, 0, 0)$. In view of Theorem 3.1, this implies that King Solomon's objective (as specified in (5.41)) *cannot* be implemented in Nash equilibrium by any conceivable mechanism with the general format introduced in Subsection 3.3.1.[79]

To be sure, the previous considerations indicate that the possibility of monetary payments *alone* cannot solve the problem of allocating efficiently an indivisible object. Given this state of affairs, one may still wonder whether there is a richer approach to the problem (i.e., a still wider universe of mechanisms and/or more sophisticated tools to analyze them) that may prove successful. In this respect, it is worthwhile stressing that the mechanisms considered so far have been implicitly restricted in the following two important dimensions:

- the induced games have been either given in strategic form or have been analyzed in this manner;
- the equilibrium concept used has been that of "unrefined" Nash equilibrium.

Thus, along these lines, it could be conjectured that by resorting, for example, to

- dynamic (i.e., multistage) mechanisms,
- some suitable refinement of Nash equilibrium, e.g., subgame-perfect equilibrium,

the implementation possibilities might be substantially improved. Indeed, we now illustrate the validity of this conjecture in a context that generalizes King Solomon's dilemma and considers the problem of allocating (efficiently) an indivisible object to one of two individuals. The specific mechanism proposed is from Glazer and Ma (1989).

Consider the following situation. A planner faces the problem of deciding to which of two agents, 1 or 2, he should allocate a certain indivisible good (e.g., the child in dispute, in King Solomon's problem). His desire is to give the good to the individual who has the highest valuation for it, without penalizing either of them. However, the planner does not know the individual valuations. He is only certain that they belong to some finite set V, where each $z \in V$ represents a valuation expressed in monetary terms (thus, it is a real number). Each individual $i = 1, 2$ knows her own valuation $v_i \in V$ and also knows the valuation v_j of her opponent $j \neq i$. More precisely, the valuation profile (v_1, v_2) is assumed common knowledge

---

[79] Recall that for an SCR to be Nash implementable (cf. Definition 3.1), the desired performance must be achieved at any of the environments under consideration. Thus, since conditions (i)–(iii) define a relevant subset of such environments, having shown the impossibility of Nash implementation within this subset is enough for our purposes.

for the two of them. As in King Solomon's dilemma, it is convenient to postulate that $v_1 \neq v_2$ (i.e., there is only *one* true mother).

To address the problem, and in view of the fact that the SCR reflecting his objectives cannot be guaranteed to be monotonic (recall above), the planner designs a multistage mechanism, as described next. In this mechanism, a suitable Nash refinement (specifically, subgame-perfect equilibrium) will be shown to allow for positive results.

Let

$$\eta \equiv \min\{|z - z'| : z \neq z', \ z, z' \in V\}.$$

Since V is a finite set, $\eta > 0$, and the planner knows it (because he knows V). Therefore, he can use it in the mechanism designed to allocate the good. This mechanism consists of the following stages:

1. First, individual 1 states whether her valuation is highest (action H) or not (action L). If she chooses L, the process terminates and the good is assigned to individual 2. If she chooses H, the following stage is reached.
2. Individual 2 accepts (action L') or not (action H') that individual 1 has the highest valuation. If she accepts it, the process ends and the good is assigned to individual 1. Otherwise, the mechanism proceeds to the following stage and *each* player has to make a (monetary) payment equal to $\eta/4$, fixed by the planner as part of the mechanism specification.
3. If the process enters the third stage, individual 1 announces some $\rho_1 \in V$, to be interpreted as a monetary offer (or "bid") to obtain the good.
4. Next, knowing the announcement ρ_1 made by player 1 in the preceding stage, individual 2 makes her own announcement $\rho_2 \in V$.
5. Finally, once the mechanism has completed stages 3 and 4 and the bids ρ_1 and ρ_2 have been issued, the good is assigned to the individual with the highest bid. If it happens that $\rho_1 = \rho_2$, the tie is resolved by assigning the good to individual 1. In any case, the individual who obtains the good pays for it the amount $[\max\{\rho_1, \rho_2\} - \eta/2]$, whereas the other one does not make any payment at this stage. (Note, however, that the payment made by both individuals at the end of stage 2 is irreversible or "sunk.")

The extensive form of the game proposed is schematically illustrated in Figure 5.5.

As advanced, the analysis of the game induced by the above mechanism will focus on its subgame-perfect equilibria. First, we need to specify the strategy spaces of the two players. For player 1, we have

$$S_1 = \{H, L\} \times V,$$

and for player 2,

$$S_2 = \{H', L'\} \times \{r : V \to V\}$$

with the following interpretations. For player 1, her strategy determines whether she

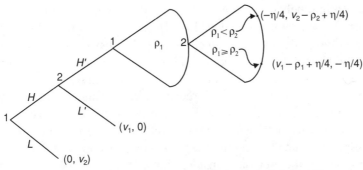

Figure 5.5: A successful mechanism for allocating an indivisible object.

claims that her valuation is highest (the first component of the strategy), together with the bid she *would* announce if the third stage is reached (the second component). On the other hand, a strategy of player 2 reflects similar considerations, with the only (but important) difference that this player acts as a "follower." Therefore, she can make her decisions contingent on the actions previously adopted by the other player – in particular, the bid announced by player 2 in the last stage of the game may depend on that announced by player 1 in the preceding stage.

To find the subgame-perfect equilibria, we perform, as usual, a backward sequential determination of the optimal behavior to be displayed at the different decision points (here, singleton information sets). Consider first the last subgames to be reached along the mechanism when both individuals have chosen to claim that each has the highest valuation (H and H', respectively) and player 1 has announced a certain bid equal to ρ_1. At this point, any optimal strategy by player 2, $s_2^* = (x_2^*, r^*) \in S_2$, must satisfy

$$v_2 \leq \rho_1 \Rightarrow r^*(\rho_1) \leq \rho_1 \tag{5.42}$$

$$v_2 > \rho_1 \Rightarrow r^*(\rho_1) = \min\{\rho_2 \in V : \rho_2 > \rho_1\}. \tag{5.43}$$

Proceeding backward one further stage in the game, let $r^*(\cdot)$ be any given function satisfying (5.42) and (5.43) and consider what would be an optimal bid by player 1 in the third stage. Naturally, the decision must depend on her valuation v_1, as well as on the valuation v_2 of player 2 (both known by each player).[80] For concreteness (see Exercise 5.18 for the reciprocal situation), consider the case in which $v_1 > v_2$. Then, it is straightforward to check that the unique optimal decision for player 1 (who anticipates an *equilibrium* reaction $r^*(\cdot)$ on the part of 2) is to announce a bid $\rho_1^* = v_2$. Doing so, she is able to guarantee for herself the obtention of the good at the minimum possible cost.

Knowing what would be the equilibrium behavior of each individual if the third and fourth stages of the mechanism were reached, we can now consider what must

---

[80] Recall that only the planner (e.g., King Solomon) is taken to ignore both v_1 and v_2. This lack of information on the planner's part is precisely what prevents him from imposing a suitable allocation (because he cannot identify it), despite the fact that he is implicitly supposed to have the authority to "impose" a particular mechanism.

be their equilibrium behavior in the first two stages. Again, we proceed backward and consider first the subgame induced by a prior decision of H by player 1. In this subgame (and under the maintained assumption that $v_1 > v_2$), it is clear that player 2 should *not* challenge the "claim" H of player 1 by choosing H'. For, given the subsequent (equilibrium) behavior to be played on both sides, such a challenge would not finally give her the good. Moreover, it would entail for her a cost of $\eta/4$ (i.e., the cost imposed on *each* player by the rules of the mechanism if the later bidding stages are reached) that she might as well save by simply choosing L'. Now, we may complete the analysis by focusing on player 1's choice at the beginning of the game. In view of the previous considerations, the optimal decision for player 1 at this point is clear: she should choose H under the (correct) anticipation that player 2 will subsequently choose L'.

In sum, we conclude that, if $v_1 > v_2$, any subgame-perfect equilibrium of the game $\big((x_1^*, \rho_1^*), (x_2^*, r^*(\cdot))\big)$ has $x_1^* = H$ and $x_2^* = L'$. Therefore, the good is assigned to individual 1 after the second stage of the mechanism, without any cost or monetary transaction. This occurs under the equilibrium prediction that, if the third stage were reached, player 1 would choose $\rho_1^* = v_2$, which in turn is an optimal response to the ensuing reaction by player 2 given by function $r^*(\cdot)$ satisfying (5.42) and (5.43).

The analysis conducted here illustrates in a particularly transparent fashion the power enjoyed by the perfectness criterion in multistage games. From the point of view of the planner/designer, it is an extremely useful principle that allows him to circumvent the nonmonotonicity of the efficient SCR in the present context. In fact, this idea is extremely general and goes well beyond the specific context considered here, as established Moore and Repullo (1988). They prove that *any* SCR that is *single-valued* (i.e., a function) can be implemented through *some* multistage mechanism in (unique) subgame-perfect equilibrium.[81] In view of this striking general result, the main contribution of the above "Solomonic" mechanism is simply to show that, in some particular cases, the general implementation *possibility* established by Moore and Repullo can be realized through especially simple and intuitive procedures.

Summary

This chapter has discussed a number of different economic models in which players' rationality is assumed to be more stringent than that embodied by the basic notion of Nash equilibrium. In fact, as a reflection of what is the bulk of applications in this vein, all our models involved some multistage game and the concept used was subgame-perfect equilibrium, i.e., the least demanding of those considered in Chapter 4 for extensive-form games.

---

[81] Analogous broadenings of the range of implementability can be achieved through other Nash refinements. A good case in point can be found in the work of Palfrey and Srivastava (1991), who show that monotonicity is no longer required for implementation through "simultaneous" mechanisms if one restricts to undominated Nash equilibria (cf. Definition 4.10).

We started with two oligopoly models that have important bearing on related contexts studied in Subsections 3.1.1 and 3.1.2. First, we considered a model in which quantity-setting firms play asymmetric roles in the timing (or commitment credibility) of their decisions. Second, we studied a model in which firms are simultaneous price setters but must commit beforehand to some costly production capacity. Both variations on the traditional Cournot and Bertrand models have been shown to display significant differences with their respective original counterparts. In the first case, the postulated interfirm asymmetry benefits the first mover, which can exploit profitably its commitment ability to increase its profits. In the second case, the initial stage in which capacities are determined impinges decisively on the second-stage Bertrand competition so as to produce Cournot outcomes.

Next, we presented a stylized model of bargaining between two individuals (say, a buyer and a seller) who must agree on how to share some prespecified surplus. The theoretical framework considered has individuals propose their offers in alternation, the partner then responding with either acceptance or rejection. Even though the game could proceed indefinitely and the wealth of possible intertemporal strategies is staggering, the game has a unique subgame-perfect equilibrium in which players agree immediately on a certain division of the surplus. Building on this bilateral model of bargaining, we have then studied a population-based process in which pairs of individuals bargain in "parallel" and may switch partners in case of disagreement. The resulting game again displays a unique subgame-perfect equilibrium, which in turn determines a uniform price. This price, however, turns out to be different from the Walrasian price, at least under a certain interpretation of what is the right "benchmark economy."

Then, we studied a model of oligopolistic competition with differentiated products and price competition. In contrast with other simpler (but unsatisfactory) models studied before, the approach proposed has the advantage of endogenizing product differentiation in the first stage of the game, before prices are determined in the second stage. We solved for the unique subgame-perfect equilibrium and found that the extent of product differentiation prevailing in it is maximal. Abstracting from price considerations, firms have strong incentives to lower product differentiation. However, anticipating the detrimental (price undercutting) effects of such a move reverses those incentives at equilibrium.

Finally, we turned to a problem, the so-called King Solomon's dilemma, that was first introduced in Chapter 3 when discussing the topic of Nash implementation. The key condition of monotonicity required for an SCR to be Nash implementable is violated in this case, thus ruling out that the desired SCR (i.e., the assignment of the child in dispute to the true mother) might be implemented in Nash equilibrium. We have shown, however, that the problem (in fact, a generalization of it, which concerns the allocation of an indivisible object) can be solved if a multistage mechanism is used and the individuals play according to a subgame-perfect equilibrium of the induced game. This suggests a rich interplay between mechanism design and equilibrium theory (in particular Nash refinements), which has in fact been explored quite exhaustively in recent literature.

Exercises

Exercise 5.1: Provide a rigorous verbal argument for the following general assertion:

"The leading firm in the model of Stackelberg always obtains at least as much profits as it would obtain in a Cournot framework with the same underlying data (demand, costs, etc.)."

Exercise 5.2: Consider the following statement:

"Every Nash equilibrium of a Cournot oligopoly model is also a Nash equilibrium of the corresponding Stackelberg game in which one of the firms acts as a leader."

Indicate whether this statement is true or false, supporting your answer with a rigorous argument.

Exercise 5.3: Consider a linear oligopoly context with three firms, the cost functions given by (5.1) and the demand function by (5.2).

(a) Compute the Nash equilibrium of the corresponding (simultaneous) Cournot game.
(b) Compute the subgame-perfect equilibrium of a sequential game in which firms' decisions are taken in two stages:
  (i) in a first stage, firm 1 decides its output level;
  (ii) in a second stage, having observed the outcome of the first stage, firms 2 and 3 simultaneously decide their output levels.

Exercise 5.4*: Recall the efficient rationing mechanism proposed in Subsection 5.1.2 within a duopoly context. Suppose that instead there operates a proportional rationing mechanism formulated as follows. Let firms i and j ($i, j = 1, 2$, $i \neq j$) offer prices p_i and p_j with, say, $p_i < p_j$. Let $D(\cdot)$ be the aggregate demand function for the single homogeneous good produced by both firms and denote by K_i and K_j their respective capacity constraints. Suppose that $D(p_i) > K_i$, so that firm i cannot serve the full market demand at price p_i. Then, the residual market demand $\tilde{D}(p_j)$ confronted by firm j is given by

$$\tilde{D}(p_j) = D(p_j) \frac{D(p_i) - K_i}{D(p_i)}.$$

The rationing mechanism implied may be interpreted as one in which every unit "notionally" demanded at price p_i (i.e., a total of $D(p_i)$) has the same prior probability of being subject to rationing (in which case it becomes available only at the higher price p_j). Prove that this rationing scheme is inefficient in the sense that there could be mutually beneficial trades (i.e., arbitrage opportunities) between rationed and nonrationed consumers.

Exercise 5.5: Show that the conclusions obtained in Subsection 5.1.2 for the Kreps-Scheinkman model with capacity constraints can be adapted to a context with (a) an arbitrary decreasing and concave demand function $P(\cdot)$; (b) constant

marginal costs associated with capacity and production, c and $\tilde{c}$, both positive;
(c) no upper bound on the prices that firms may set.

Exercise 5.6*: Prove that the subgame-perfect equilibrium constructed in Subsection 5.1.2 for the Kreps-Scheinkman model is unique. Is it also the unique Nash equilibrium? That is, are there other Nash (possibly non-subgame-perfect) equilibrium *outcomes*?

Exercise 5.7: Consider a context as in Exercise 3.10 where the "community" in question involves only *two* individuals. Suppose they operate the following (sequential) subscription mechanism. First, individual 1 proposes her contribution. If this contribution covers K, the cost of the public good, this good is immediately provided. Otherwise, it is individual 2's turn to propose her respective contribution. If having reached the second stage of the mechanism, the sum of the two contributions covers K, the public good is provided but the net utility of each individual is discounted by a certain factor, $\delta < 1$. That is, the utility each individual i receives in this second stage is

$$\delta U_i(x, c_i) = \delta(V_i(x) - c_i).$$

Suppose, for simplicity, that for each $i = 1, 2$, $V_i(1) = 1$, $V_i(0) = 0$, $\delta = 1/2$.

(a) Compute the subgame-perfect equilibria as a function of the value of $K \in [0, 2]$. (That is, partition the interval $[0, 2]$ into subintervals in which the set of equilibria displays different characteristics.)
(b) Compare the subgame-perfect equilibria computed in (a) with those obtained in Exercise 3.10. Is it true that every Nash equilibrium outcome in that exercise is also attained at a Nash equilibrium in the present context? Discuss your answer.
(c) Finally, study how the features of the subgame-perfect equilibria are affected if the individuals' utility function (for first-stage consumption) is changed as follows:

$$U_i(x, c_i) = V_i(x) - (c_i)^2.$$

Exercise 5.8: Show that in the Rubinstein bargaining game with infinite time horizon *any* outcome of the process (that is, any agreement materialized at any time) is induced by some Nash equilibrium.

Exercise 5.9: Consider a variation of the Rubinstein (infinite-horizon) bargaining model in which each of the two individuals displays possibly different discount factors δ_1 and δ_2. Find the (unique) subgame-perfect equilibrium.

Exercise 5.10: Recall the definition of pseudo-stationary subgame-perfect equilibrium introduced in Subsection 5.2.1. Prove that any such equilibrium of the Rubinstein bargaining game in which the payoff of player 1 equals $1/(1 + \delta)$ must involve the strategies given by (†) and (‡) in that subsection.

Exercise 5.11*: Consider the following extension of the Rubinstein bargaining model involving n players. As time proceeds, players submit, in fixed order, proposals of the kind $x \equiv (x_1, x_2, \ldots, x_n)$, with $\sum_{i=1}^{n} x_i = 1$ and each component x_j is interpreted as the share of the surplus proposed for player j. (That is, every player i submits some such vector of proposals in every $t \in \{i, i+n, i+2n, \ldots\}$.) Right after any player i has issued her proposals, and before the process enters the following period, the rest of the individuals $j \neq i$ decide simultaneously whether to accept them. If all accept, the process comes to an end and the proposals are implemented. If not, player $i + 1$ (modulo n) is the one who submits the next proposals. Assuming that all players have a common discount factor, δ, prove that there exists a subgame-perfect equilibrium where player 1 proposes

$$\left(\frac{1}{1 + \delta + \cdots + \delta^{n-1}}, \frac{\delta}{1 + \delta + \cdots + \delta^{n-1}}, \ldots, \frac{\delta^{n-1}}{1 + \delta + \cdots + \delta^{n-1}} \right),$$

which is accepted at $t = 1$ by every $j = 2, 3, \ldots, n$.

Exercise 5.12: Show that (5.23) and (5.24) form part of the unique solution to the system of equations given by (5.17)–(5.22). Discuss its dependence on δ, the discount rate.

Exercise 5.13: Consider a model, as the one studied in Subsection 5.2.2, but with the following variation on the bargaining process: at the start of any bilateral stretch of bargaining between two persistently matched players, the seller always has the option to propose first. Compare its solution with that induced by (5.21) and (5.22).

Exercise 5.14*: Recall the Hotelling model studied in Section 5.3. Show that, within the price range relevant for equilibrium, (5.27) guarantees that every consumer will buy the good from one of the firms.

Exercise 5.15: Prove expressions (5.31) and (5.32).

Exercise 5.16: Prove expressions (5.35) and (5.36).

Exercise 5.17: Consider a planner whose objective is to maximize the aggregate welfare of an economy consisting of a single market of the type described in Section 5.3. More specifically, assume that the planner maximizes the sum of firms' profits and the aggregate (or, equivalently, average) utility of consumers. Suppose that the planner can force each firm to locate at a certain point in the interval $[0, 1]$, subsequently letting them compete freely in prices. What locations should be chosen by the planner? Contrast your answer with that derived in the text.

Exercise 5.18: Suppose that, in the context of the mechanism presented in Section 5.4, we have $v_2 > v_1$.

    (a) Determine the subgame-perfect equilibria in this case.
    (b) Suppose now that, in addition to $v_2 > v_1$, the order of movement of the players is reversed but the tie-breaking rule continues to favor individual 1. Determine the subgame-perfect equilibria in this case.

Exercise 5.19*: Consider a variation of the mechanism discussed in Section 5.4 where, if individuals' bids coincide, the assignment of the good is carried out stochastically with equal *ex ante* probabilities for each of the two individuals. Determine the subgame-perfect equilibria in this case.

Exercise 5.20*: Recall the original King Solomon's dilemma, in which the two women can have only two possible valuations (associated with being either the true or the false mother of the child). Allowing each woman to be treated asymmetrically (in particular, concerning possible monetary penalties), design a mechanism with *only two* stages guaranteeing that, at the subgame-perfect equilibria of the induced game, the true mother receives the child.

CHAPTER 6

Incomplete information: theory

6.1 Introduction and examples

Many strategic problems of interest take place in contexts where, unlike what has been implicitly assumed so far, players do *not* have complete information on the underlying features of the situation. Often, this happens because, even though players accurately know their individual payoffs, they have only imprecise information on the payoffs earned by others for some possible paths of play. And then, of course, any uncertainty about their opponents' payoffs typically must have an important bearing on how players analyze the strategic situation and make their respective choices. To obtain a preliminary glimpse of the important considerations involved, let us first consider some illustrative (yet informal) examples.

Recall the game we labeled battle of the sexes, first introduced in Section 1.1 (Table 1.2). As in that game, suppose the boy and the girl confront (simultaneously) the decision of whether to go shopping or attend the basketball game. The payoffs for the boy are as postulated before. Concerning the girl, however, now suppose that her payoffs may *a priori* be of two different sorts: she may either be a "shopping fan," or a "basketball fan." If she is the first, she always prefers to go shopping, no matter what the boy does; if she is the second (a basketball fan), her best option is always to go to the basketball game, again independently of what the boy decides. Nevertheless, for any of the two possibilities (shopping or basketball), she prefers to be joined by the boy rather than going alone.[82] For concreteness, let the payoffs for both players be as given in Table 6.1 if the girl is a basketball fan, whereas they are as in Table 6.2 if she is a shopping fan.

Assume the girl knows her preferences (as well as the boy's, which can be of just one sort), but the boy knows only his own. *A priori*, the only information the boy has is that the girl's preferences are one of those described in the above payoff tables. In particular, suppose the boy attributes subjective probability p to the girl being a basketball fan, and probability $1-p$ to her being a shopping fan. Thus, succinctly, the information conditions can be described as follows: the girl knows what payoff table applies (Table 6.1 or 6.2), whereas the boy attributes probability p to the first one and $1 - p$ to the second.

---

[82] Note that the game considered is quite different from the ordinary battle of the sexes in that, from the girl's viewpoint, there is no incentive to coordinate with the boy's choice. This important contrast notwithstanding, we label it a "modified battle of the sexes" because we find it useful to motivate this game (as well as other future variations of it) in terms of the story proposed for the original battle of the sexes.

Table 6.1: *Modified battle of the sexes if the girl is a "basketball fan"*

Boy Girl	B	S
B	3, 2	2, 1
S	0, 0	1, 3

Table 6.2: *Modified battle of the sexes if the girl is a "shopping fan"*

Boy Girl	B	S
B	1, 2	0, 1
S	2, 0	3, 3

In this context, the decision problem of the girl is straightforward: she should simply play B or S if, respectively, Table 6.1 or 6.2 applies because those strategies are dominant in each case. On the other hand, for the boy (who should anticipate this contingent behavior on the girl's part), what is optimal depends on the value of p. If $p > 3/4$, then

$$2p + 0(1 - p) > 1p + 3(1 - p)$$

and he must play B, which yields a higher expected payoff than S. Otherwise, if $p < 3/4$, the highest expected payoff is obtained by playing S, which is then the optimal action. Of course, in the exact case where $p = 3/4$, any behavior on the boy's part (pure or mixed) is equivalently optimal. As we formally describe below, this is indeed the behavior resulting from the appropriate generalization of the Nash equilibrium concept to be applied in games of incomplete information – what we later call Bayes-Nash equilibrium.

As a second example, consider a variation of the model of Cournot duopoly studied in Subsection 3.1.1, with each firm $i = 1, 2$, displaying *identical* linear costs of the form given by

$$C_i(q_i) = c \, q_i, \tag{6.1}$$

for some common $c > 0$ and some linear (inverse) demand function:

$$P(Q) = \max\{M - d \, Q, \, 0\}, \quad M, d > 0. \tag{6.2}$$

The demand parameters M and d are given and commonly known. Costs, however, can be high (for concreteness, we make $c = 2$) or low ($c = 1$). Both firms know they share identical costs $c \in \{1, 2\}$ (i.e., they face the same production conditions) but the exact value of c is known only by firm 1. Firm 2, on the other hand, has subjective probabilities of p and $1 - p$ that, respectively, costs are low or high.

In this context, if firm 1 were to know the output to be chosen by firm 2, say $\hat{q}_2$, it could readily find its best response to it. Of course, this best response must depend on cost parameter c, a piece of information firm 1 is taken to know precisely. If we now take the viewpoint of firm 2 (which is uninformed of the marginal cost), its prediction of 1's behavior may be formalized through a pair $(\hat{q}_1(1), \hat{q}_1(2))$, where $\hat{q}_1(c)$ stands for the output of firm 1 anticipated for each possible $c \in \{1, 2\}$. Given any such *contingent* pair of predicted actions *and* its subjective probability p, a best response by firm 2 can be easily computed as that which maximizes its expected profit. Combining all the above considerations, a (Bayes-Nash) equilibrium may be defined as reflecting the usual considerations. That is, it must embody a best response by each firm, when the predicted behavior on the competitor's part (now only contingently specified for firm 1) is a fully accurate description of its behavior. A formal description of matters and an explicit computation of the equilibrium is postponed to Subsections 6.2.2.2 and 6.3.2.2 below.

To complete this introductory section, let us consider two simple variations on the following public-good problem. Two individuals, 1 and 2, live in neighboring houses at a remote and isolated location. Since there is no paved road accessing the place (only a small dirt path), they consider whether to build a paved road that would connect their houses to a nearby highway. Building this road is known to cost 20 thousand dollars. The only reason why any of the two individuals might be interested in having the road built is if she plans to buy a car. In that case, let us suppose the monetary value of the road (abstracting from the cost) equals 30 thousand dollars for the individual in question.

Suppose that, to tackle the problem of whether to build the road, the individuals contemplate two alternative mechanisms. The first mechanism – called mechanism A in what follows – requires that both of them send independent letters to a neutral third party (a "mediator"), expressing whether they have any interest for the undertaking. If any agent $i \in \{1, 2\}$ expresses an interest for the road, this may be interpreted as the "message" that she plans to buy a car, i.e., her gross valuation v_i for the project is 30 (thousand dollars). Otherwise, the reported valuation v_i may be identified with zero.

Given such a dichotomic interpretation of messages (i.e., the reported valuation is identified with either zero or 30), it is natural to postulate that mechanism A should operate as follows. If both individuals happen to express interest in the paved road, the project goes ahead and they share equally its cost (i.e., they pay 10 thousand dollars each). If only one does so, this individual covers by herself the full cost of the road. Finally, if neither of them conveys any interest, the road is not built and the situation is left at the original status quo (i.e., the houses are connected to the highway only through a small dirt path).

The second mechanism to be considered (called mechanism B) displays a sequential structure. First, individual 1 indicates how much she is willing to contribute to the financing of the road, i.e., any $\xi_1 \in [0, 20]$, expressed in thousands of dollars. Then, unless $\xi_1 = 20$ (in which case the road is exclusively financed by 1), individual 2 must state whether she is willing to pay for the difference $20 - \xi_1$. If so, the project goes ahead and each of the individuals pays the implied contributions, ξ_1 and $\xi_2 \equiv 20 - \xi_1$. Otherwise, if individual 2 rejects covering the difference $20 - \xi_1$, the situation remains at the status quo and the paved road is not built.

Since the two mechanisms proposed are of a very different Nature, each of them poses specific issues of its own (e.g., considerations of "credibility" pertaining to the sequential mechanism B). In either case, however, the problem becomes most interesting when it is posited that each individual agent is privately informed of her own valuation of the road. Under these conditions, while each individual knows whether she herself plans to buy a car, she is uncertain (say, has some nondegenerate subjective probabilities, p and $1 - p$, common to both) about whether the other individual is planning to buy one. Then, the strategic conflict between incentives and efficiency arises in full strength. On the one hand, every high-valuation individual would like to conceal her interest in the road, with the hope that the other individual also has a high valuation and may then be prepared to bear the full burden of the cost. On the other hand, any such attempt at strategic manipulation is subject to risks. For if both were to proceed analogously, the road might never be built, even though each of them (or perhaps only one) could benefit amply from it. Indeed, this is the tension markedly displayed by the Bayes-Nash equilibria that is computed below. For both mechanisms, these equilibria yield some *ex ante* positive probability that an inefficient outcome regrettably obtains *ex post*, a consequence of agents' attempts at manipulating the outcome.

6.2   Bayesian games

The above simple examples illustrate the point that many situations of economic interest arise under incomplete-information conditions. That is, they often take place when relevant pieces of information are *not* commonly shared by all players. The most paradigmatic instance of this state of affairs occurs when, as in all those previous examples, some (or all) of the agents are exclusively informed of their respective payoffs. This turns out to be an important consideration in the analysis because, to evaluate the different choices available, each player is forced to rely on some assessment (possibly probabilistic) of the opponents' private payoff information and thus associated behavior.

How can one model those contexts where information is incompletely (or, as is often said, asymmetrically) distributed among the players? The seminal work of Harsanyi (1967–68) provides a simple and elegant form of doing it. It introduces into the model the fictitious agent we have called Nature (recall Section 1.2) and postulates that such an agent chooses stochastically, at the beginning of the game, every detail that is not common knowledge. Then, before actual play begins (i.e., before genuine players start choosing their respective actions), information about Nature's choice is asymmetrically disseminated among the agents. That is, each one of them becomes exclusively informed of the specific object of her *private information*, which in Harsanyi's terminology is simply identified with the player's *type*.

Thus, to sum up Harsanyi's proposal, his approach may be described heuristically as follows. From an *ex ante* viewpoint, players know only the probabilities with which Nature selects the different features of the game that are not common knowledge (i.e., the full profile of player types). In the *interim* (before actual play starts), each player becomes aware of her own private information (her type) but is left completely ignorant about information that belongs to others (i.e., the opponents' types). On the basis of this information (which is accurate concerning one's own type but probabilistic concerning those of others) each player adopts a plan of action. This, *ex post*, leads to a payoff profile that depends on the full array of players' choices, including that of Nature. A formal presentation of this model is presented next.

6.2.1 *Harsanyi formalization*

Harsanyi's (1967–68) formulation of a *Bayesian game* consists of the following items:

1. A finite set of players $N = \{1, 2, \ldots, n\}$.
2. For each player $i \in N$:
   (a) *a space of types* T_i,
   (b) *a set of (pure) actions* A_i,
   (c) *a payoff function*

   $$\pi_i : T \times A_1 \times \cdots \times A_n \to \mathbb{R}, \tag{6.3}$$

   where $T \equiv T_1 \times T_2 \times \cdots \times T_n$ is the space of type profiles. For the sake of formal convenience, each T_i and every A_i are posited here to be finite.[83]
3. A (discrete) *probability* function

   $$P : T \to [0, 1]$$

   that specifies the probabilities with which Nature selects each type profile $t \equiv (t_1, t_2, \ldots, t_n) \in T$.

A Bayesian game may be interpreted as the reduced (i.e., compact) model of an ordinary extensive-form game involving $n + 1$ players where

- in the first stage, Nature (player 0) moves alone and selects the type $t_i \in T_i$ of each player $i \in N$;
- subsequently, each player $i \in N$ is informed (only) of her own type t_i and must then choose a *continuation* strategy (or action) in A_i.

The implicit assumption underlying the construct of a Bayesian game is that the analysis of the *interim* situations (i.e., once players are informed of their respective types) can be suitably conducted in "strategic form."[84] Note, however, that in contrast with what happens in strategic-form games, players in a Bayesian game must choose their actions (continuation strategies) without precise information on the payoff function $\pi_i(t, \cdot)$. At the time of choice, each player i knows only t_i (not

---

[83] In some of our future examples and applications (cf. Subsection 6.2.2.2 or Section 6.5), the type and/or action spaces display the cardinality of the continuum and thus are not finite. In those cases, the present framework has to be adapted in a natural way.

[84] Of course, this does not rule out that, once individuals are informed of their own type, the ensuing play may involve a multiplicity of different stages. But then, if one wants to apply perfection-like criteria of equilibrium refinement, an explicit description of the sequential (extensive-form) structure of the game may be required – see, for example, the so-called signaling games studied in Section 6.4.

the full vector t) and this is generally insufficient to have (accurate) *point* beliefs about $\pi_i(t, \cdot)$.

In a Bayesian game, the particular type of some player i embodies all information she has available at the time of making her (single) decision. Thus, in our customary terminology, we may identify each type $t_i \in T_i$ with a separate information set of player i and conceive any (pure) strategy on her part as a mapping

$$\gamma_i : T_i \to A_i. \tag{6.4}$$

Note that, by imposing no constraints on this mapping, we are implicitly assuming that the set of available actions is independent of the player's type. This is just a convenient simplification, which could be generalized at some notational cost.

In general, we shall be interested in allowing for the possibility that players may choose to rely on stochastic decision procedures. (As for ordinary games, this is partly motivated by the desire to guarantee equilibrium existence.) To do so, we simply enlarge the action space of each player i to the set $\mathcal{A}_i \equiv \Delta(A_i)$ of probability vectors on A_i. This set is interpreted as the space of "mixed actions" and the payoff functions (6.3) are extended in the usual fashion to reflect expected magnitudes (recall the analogous procedure described in Section 1.4). This then requires that the concept of pure strategy given by (6.4) be reformulated to display, for each $i \in N$, the more general form

$$\gamma_i : T_i \to \mathcal{A}_i.$$

The set of all such strategies will be denoted by Υ_i. Conceptually, one may simply think of them as the player's "behavioral" strategies in the Bayesian game (cf. (1.6)).

6.2.2 *Examples*

Having introduced the theoretical construct of a Bayesian game, let us now recast in this format the incomplete-information examples presented just informally in Section 6.1.

6.2.2.1 *Modified battle of the sexes.* Recall the variation on the battle of the sexes described in Section 6.1, where the girl's preferences (or payoffs) were linked to whether she is a basketball or a shopping fan. First, concerning the type spaces of the players, they can be defined as follows:

$$T_1 = \{t_{11}, t_{12}\}, \quad T_2 = \{t_2\},$$

reflecting the fact that player 1 (the girl) has two possible pieces of information (i.e., whether Table 6.1 or Table 6.2 applies), whereas player 2 (the boy) is fully *uninformed* and therefore his type space is a singleton. Let t_{11} be the type associated with the first possibility (the girl is a basketball fan) and t_{12} to the second (she is a shopping fan). Then, to model the situation as a Bayesian game, Nature is postulated to select type profiles $t \in T \equiv T_1 \times T_2$ with respective probabilities

$$P(t_{11}, t_2) = p; \quad P(t_{12}, t_2) = 1 - p.$$

The pure action spaces are given by $A_i = \{B, S\}$, where for simplicity we do not distinguish notationally between the two homonymous actions of different players. Finally, Tables 6.1 and 6.2 readily define the payoff functions $\pi_i : T \times A_1 \times A_2 \to \mathbb{R}$. In the latter respect, it is worthwhile noticing that, for every action profile $(a_1, a_2) \in A_1 \times A_2$, player i's payoffs $\pi_i(t_1, t_2, a_1, a_2)$ are independent of t_j, $j \neq i$. That is, one's own payoffs are unaffected by the information a player does not hold. Of course, this does not mean that the players – here, specifically, the boy – would be indifferent about learning the opponent's type. For, in this game, if the boy had such information he would be able to anticipate the girl's action and thus ensure his desired coordination.

6.2.2.2 *Cournot duopoly with uncertain costs.* Let us now formulate the model of Cournot competition induced by (6.1) and (6.2) as a Bayesian game. Recall that, in this context, firms can display *ex ante* one of two possible marginal costs, $c \in \{1, 2\}$, but the realized cost is common to both of them. The fact that firm 1 is informed of c (and thus may receive two distinct pieces of information) whereas firm 2 is not so informed leads to the following type spaces:

$$T_1 = \{1, 2\}, \quad T_2 = \{t_2\},$$

where firm 1's type is identified with the prevailing marginal cost. Thus, concerning the choice of Nature, each of the two possible type profiles is selected with the following probabilities:

$$P(1, t_2) = p; \quad P(2, t_2) = 1 - p.$$

The action space of each $i = 1, 2$ is $A_i = \mathbb{R}_+$. Thus, denoting a typical element of each A_i by q_i, the payoff functions are defined as follows:

$$\pi_i(t_1, t_2, q_1, q_2) = \{\max [M - d (q_1 + q_2), \, 0] - t_1\} \, q_i,$$

where t_1 enters the above expression as the marginal cost c. Note that, unlike what happened in the previous example, the type of one of the players (firm 1) now affects the payoffs of both of them, not just of itself. In contrast, the (single) type of firm 2 has no payoff or informational implications whatsoever. The latter observation helps to underscore an important feature of the notion of type in Bayesian games: it may reflect solely individual information and nothing else. Thus, in particular, it is perfectly possible that, as in the present example, players display an asymmetric type structure (because they enjoy different information) but share nevertheless symmetric payoff conditions.

6.2.2.3 *A public-good problem: mechanisms A and B.* Recall the alternative procedures labeled mechanisms A and B, which were proposed in Section 6.1 to have players 1 and 2 decide whether to build a paved road. Formulating the induced strategic contexts as a Bayesian game, players' types may be simply associated with their respective valuations for the road. Depending on whether each individual i plans to buy a car or not, these were taken to be $v_i = 30$ or $v_i = 0$ for both. Thus, the type spaces for either of the two mechanisms are as follows:

$$T_i = \{0, 30\}, \quad i = 1, 2.$$

In this case, and unlike the previous two examples, the asymmetry of information is fully "symmetric": each individual exclusively knows the key piece of information (her valuation) that defines her payoffs. Nature's choice of these players' types is governed by the following probabilities:

$$P(t_1, t_2) = \begin{cases} p^2 & \text{if } t_1 = t_2 = 30 \\ (1 - p)^2 & \text{if } t_1 = t_2 = 0 \\ p(1 - p) & \text{if } t_1 \neq t_2. \end{cases}$$

Clearly, this implies that both agents must share the same subjective probability p that the neighbor is planning to buy a car (i.e., has a high valuation).

The differences between the Bayesian games induced by the two mechanisms arise only in connection with their action spaces (and, therefore, with their payoff functions as well). For mechanism A, the available actions for each player i can be identified with whether she conveys a positive valuation ($a_i \equiv 30$) or not ($a_i \equiv 0$). Thus we have

$$A_i^A = \{0, 30\}, \quad i = 1, 2.$$

Given these action spaces, the payoff functions for mechanism A are, for each $i = 1, 2$, as follows:

$$\pi_i^A(t_1, t_2, a_1, a_2) = \begin{cases} t_i - 20 & \text{if } a_i > a_j \ (j = 1, 2, \ j \neq i) \\ t_i & \text{if } a_i < a_j \ (j = 1, 2, \ j \neq i) \\ t_i - 10 & \text{if } a_1 = a_2 = 30 \\ 0 & \text{if } a_1 = a_2 = 0. \end{cases}$$

Turning now to mechanism B, the asymmetric role played in it by the two individuals induces different action sets for each of them. As explained in Subsection 6.2.1, their actions must represent complete continuation strategies for each of the contingencies that follow Nature's revelation of their respective private information. For player 1, this simply amounts to the specification of a proposed contribution $a_1 \equiv \xi_1 \in [0, 20]$. On the other hand, for player 2, her actions may be formalized as contingent rules specifying whether, for *any* given proposal a_1 put forward by 1, player 2 is willing to cover the difference $20 - a_1$ required to finance the road. Thus, formally, we have

$$A_1^B = [0, 20] \tag{6.5}$$

$$A_2^B = \{a_2 : [0, 20) \rightarrow \{Y, N\}\}, \tag{6.6}$$

where Y is interpreted as player 2's acceptance to cover the difference ("Yes") and N is interpreted as a refusal to do so ("No").

Given these action spaces, the payoff functions are specified as follows:

$$\pi_1^B(t_1, t_2, a_1, a_2) = \begin{cases} t_1 - a_1 & \text{if either } a_1 = 20 \text{ or } a_2(a_1) = Y \\ 0 & \text{if } a_2(a_1) = N \end{cases}$$

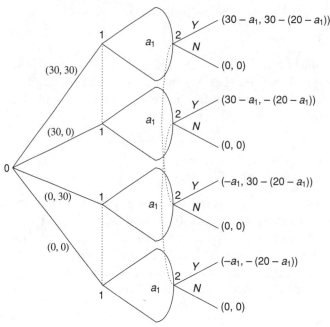

Figure 6.1: Mechanism B.

$$\pi_2^B(t_1, t_2, a_1, a_2) = \begin{cases} t_2 - (20 - a_1) & \text{if either } a_1 = 20 \text{ or } a_2(a_1) = Y \\ 0 & \text{if } a_2(a_1) = N. \end{cases}$$

Figure 6.1 provides an illustration of the Bayesian game induced by mechanism B, conceived as an extensive-form game where Nature is the first mover.[85]

6.3   Bayes-Nash equilibrium

6.3.1   Formalization

Consider any given Bayesian game $BG \equiv \{N, \{T_i\}_{i=1}^n, \{A_i\}_{i=1}^n, (\pi_i(\cdot))_{i=1}^n, P(\cdot)\}$, where its different items were described in Subsection 6.2.1. As explained, such an n-player Bayesian game can be conceived essentially equivalent to an ordinary $(n + 1)$-player game in extensive form where Nature moves first (cf. Figure 6.1 and recall Subsection 1.2.1). Given such a formal equivalence, or isomorphism, between both setups, it is natural to require that the equilibrium concepts to be applied in each case (a Bayesian game and an extensive-form game with Nature) should be isomorphic as well. Indeed, this is the idea reflected by the concept of *Bayes-Nash equilibrium* that is defined below. It may be viewed as embodying the following requirement: the strategy profile played by the n players of the Bayesian game should be part of a Nash equilibrium for the extended $(n + 1)$-player game where

---

[85] Each of the arcs in the figure represents the range of possible actions for player 1. Concerning player 2, only a "typical" representative node is included for each possible pair of types.

Nature "plays" (indifferently)[86] according to the exogenously specified probability function $P(\cdot)$. Formally, the concept proposed may be defined as follows.

Definition 6.1: *Let* $BG = \{N, \{T_i\}_{i=1}^n, \{A_i\}_{i=1}^n, (\pi_i(\cdot))_{i=1}^n, P(\cdot)\}$ *be some given Bayesian game. The strategy profile* $\gamma^* = (\gamma_i^*)_{i=1}^n$, $\gamma_i^* : T_i \to A_i$, *is a Bayes-Nash equilibrium for* BG *if* $\forall i = 1, 2, \ldots n$, $\forall \gamma_i \in \Upsilon_i$,

$$\sum_{t \in T} P(t)\, \pi_i(t, \gamma_1^*(t_1), \ldots, \gamma_i^*(t_i), \ldots, \gamma_n^*(t_n))$$

$$\geq \sum_{t \in T} P(t)\, \pi_i(t, \gamma_1^*(t_1), \ldots, \gamma_i(t_i), \ldots, \gamma_n^*(t_n)). \tag{6.7}$$

The optimality conditions (6.7) demanded by the Bayes-Nash equilibrium concept view the players' decision problems from an *ex ante* viewpoint, i.e., before any of them is informed of her own type. However, under the natural assumption that $P(t) > 0$ for all $t \in T$ (since those types that are never chosen may be simply eliminated from the description of the game), it should be clear that such an *ex ante* optimality is equivalent to what is often called *interim optimality*. That is, any given strategy γ_i^* satisfies the equilibrium optimality condition (6.7) if, and only if, it prescribes an optimal action $\gamma_i^*(t_i)$ once the particular type t_i is known by player i. Or, to express it in somewhat different but by now familiar terms: for a strategy γ_i^* to be part of a Bayes-Nash equilibrium, it must be optimal at each of the "subgames" reached with positive probability – in effect, all of them because, as explained, one may suppose that any type profile has positive prior probability.

To render the former discussion more precise, let $P_i(\cdot \mid t_i)$ stand for the conditional probability induced by $P(\cdot)$ on $T_{-i} = \prod_{j \neq i} T_j$ when the type of player i is known to be t_i. Then, the concept of Bayes-Nash equilibrium can be equivalently reformulated as follows.

Definition 6.1': *Let* $BG = \{N, \{T_i\}_{i=1}^n, \{A_i\}_{i=1}^n, (\pi_i(\cdot))_{i=1}^n, P(\cdot)\}$ *be some given Bayesian game. The strategy profile* $\gamma^* = (\gamma_i^*)_{i=1}^n$, $\gamma_i^* : T_i \to A_i$, *is a Bayes-Nash equilibrium for* BG *if* $\forall i = 1, 2, \ldots, n$, $\forall t_i \in T_i$, $\forall \alpha_i \in A_i$,

$$\sum_{t_{-i} \in T_{-i}} P_i(t_{-i} \mid t_i) \pi_i(t_i, t_{-i}, \gamma_1^*(t_1), \gamma_2^*(t_2), \ldots, \gamma_i^*(t_i), \ldots, \gamma_n^*(t_n))$$

$$\geq \sum_{t_{-i} \in T_{-i}} P_i(t_{-i} \mid t_i) \pi_i(t_i, t_{-i}, \gamma_1^*(t_1), \gamma_2^*(t_2), \ldots, \alpha_i, \ldots, \gamma_n^*(t_n)).$$

Having defined a new equilibrium concept, our first immediate concern should be that of its existence. Specifically, we are led to the following question: Does a Bayes-Nash equilibrium exist in any Bayesian game? By building on the parallelism between an n-player Bayesian game and the corresponding $(n + 1)$-person ordinary game with Nature, a straightforward adaptation of former arguments (recall, specifically, the proof of Theorem 2.2) leads to the following existence result.

---

[86] Recall from Subsection 1.2.1 that if, fictitiously, Nature is assigned payoffs over the different end nodes of the game, these payoffs are posited to be constant across all of these nodes.

Theorem 6.1: *Let* $BG = \{N, \{T_i\}_{i=1}^n, \{A_i\}_{i=1}^n, (\pi_i(\cdot))_{i=1}^n, P(\cdot)\}$ *be some finite Bayesian game.*[87] *A Bayes-Nash equilibrium* $\gamma^* \equiv (\gamma_i^*)_{i=1}^n$ *always exists.*

Proof: Exercise 6.10. ∎

6.3.2　Examples

To illustrate the implications of the Bayes-Nash equilibrium (BNE) concept, let us review in turn the different examples discussed in Subsection 6.2.2 and compute for each of them the corresponding Bayes-Nash equilibria.

6.3.2.1 *Modified battle of the sexes (continued).* Recall the modified battle of the sexes that was formally modeled as a Bayesian game in Subsection 6.2.2.1. The computation of its BNE follows immediately from the fact that the girl (the only informed party) has a dominant action in either case (i.e., action B if her type is t_{11} and action S if her type is t_{12}). This allows us to fix her equilibrium strategy accordingly:

$$\gamma_1^*(t_{11}) = B; \quad \gamma_1^*(t_{12}) = S. \tag{6.8}$$

Then, as explained in Section 6.1, the optimal response on the part of the boy comes to depend on p as follows[88]:

$$\gamma_2^*(t_2) = \begin{cases} B & \text{if } p > 3/4 \\ (x, 1-x), \ x \in [0, 1] & \text{if } p = 3/4 \\ S & \text{if } p < 3/4. \end{cases} \tag{6.9}$$

The expressions (6.8) and (6.9) jointly characterize the strategy profile γ^*, which defines a BNE of the game, as a function of $p \equiv P(t_{11}, t_2)$. Generically (i.e., if $p \neq 3/4$), the BNE is unique.

6.3.2.2 *Cournot duopoly with uncertain costs (continued).* Consider now the Bayesian game described in Subsection 6.2.2.2. A pure-strategy BNE γ^* for it can be identified with three output choices. On the one hand, one must specify the two outputs chosen by firm 1, depending on its type:

$$q_{11}^* \equiv \gamma_1^*(1), \quad q_{12}^* \equiv \gamma_1^*(2).$$

On the other hand, one has to indicate as well the output to be chosen by firm 2,

$$q_2^* \equiv \gamma_2^*(t_2),$$

which is associated with its unique (uninformed) type.

Suppose, for simplicity, that M and d are such that there is an interior BNE given by the outputs $(q_{11}^*, q_{12}^*, q_2^*)$. Then, these outputs must satisfy the following

---

[87] Finiteness, in this case, concerns the set of players N and each of their respective T_i and A_i.

[88] As usual, when a strategy is deterministic, we find it convenient to identify it with the action being adopted with probability one rather than writing such a strategy in the (degenerate) probability-vector format.

conditions for firm 1:

$$\left[M - d(q_{11}^* + q_2^*) - 1\right] q_{11}^* \geq \left[M - d(q_1 + q_2^*) - 1\right] q_1 \quad \forall q_1 \in \mathbb{R}_+;$$
(6.10)

$$\left[M - d(q_{12}^* + q_2^*) - 2\right] q_{12}^* \geq \left[M - d(q_1 + q_2^*) - 2\right] q_1 \quad \forall q_1 \in \mathbb{R}_+;$$
(6.11)

and, for firm 2:

$$\left\{p\left[M - d(q_{11}^* + q_2^*) - 1\right] + (1 - p)\left[M - d(q_{12}^* + q_2^*) - 2\right]\right\} q_2^*$$
$$\geq \left\{p\left[M - d(q_{11}^* + q_2) - 1\right] + (1 - p)\left[M - d(q_{12}^* + q_2) - 2\right]\right\} q_2$$
$$\forall q_2 \in \mathbb{R}_+.$$
(6.12)

These conditions simply reflect the optimality requirements formulated in Definition 6.1′: each firm must choose an optimal action, conditional on the information it receives (i.e., its type).

Associated with (6.10), (6.11), and (6.12), we have the following system of first-order necessary conditions:

$$M - d\,q_2^* - 1 - 2d\,q_{11}^* = 0$$
$$M - d\,q_2^* - 2 - 2d\,q_{12}^* = 0$$
$$p\left[M - dq_{11}^* - 1\right] + (1 - p)\left[M - dq_{12}^* - 2\right] - 2dq_2^* = 0,$$

which is solved to yield

$$q_{11}^* = \frac{2M - 1 - p}{6d}$$

$$q_{12}^* = \frac{2M - 4 - p}{6d}$$

$$q_2^* = \frac{M - 2 + p}{3d}.$$

The above expressions define the unique BNE of the game. Its dependence on p is clear-cut: while the uninformed firm 2 increases its equilibrium quantity as p rises (i.e., as its subjective probability of a low cost grows), the opposite applies to the informed firm 1.

Such an opposite effect of p on the equilibrium behavior of each firm has an intuitive interpretation worth explaining. On the one hand, for firm 2, an increase in p unambiguously improves its (expected) cost conditions and, consequently, it is natural that it should also increase its equilibrium output. For firm 1, however, the value of p has no direct consequence on its *interim* profit possibilities. At the time of choice, this firm is informed about the value of c and, therefore, the probability p has no consequence *per se* on its payoffs (i.e., on the profits obtained for any *given* output profile). It follows, therefore, that the effect of p on the equilibrium choices of firm 1 is purely strategic. In other words, it is only because firm 1 anticipates how the value of p will affect the (equilibrium) behavior of the competitor that it has an effect on its own equilibrium decision. Its output falls (rises) with a rise (fall) in p because firm 2's output is correctly predicted to increase (decrease) accordingly.

6.3.2.3 *A public-good problem: mechanisms A and B (continued).* We consider first the Bayesian game induced by mechanism A (cf. Subsection 6.2.2.3). Since this game is fully symmetric between players, we focus on symmetric BNE. These are equilibria given by a *common* strategy $\gamma_i^* = (\gamma_i^*(0), \gamma_i^*(30))$ which, allowing for mixed actions, displays the following general form:

$$\gamma_i^*(0) = [\gamma_i^*(0)(0), \gamma_i^*(0)(30)] \equiv (u, 1 - u) \tag{6.13}$$

$$\gamma_i^*(30) = [\gamma_i^*(30)(0), \gamma_i^*(30)(30)] \equiv (w, 1 - w) \tag{6.14}$$

with the same $u \in [0, 1]$ and $w \in [0, 1]$ for both $i = 1, 2$.

The first immediate observation to make is that, at equilibrium, it can be guaranteed that $u = 1$. That is, no player with the low valuation of zero will ever want to send the message that she has a high valuation. For, if she were to do it with positive probability, the probability that she might be called to finance part (or even the whole) of the cost of building the road would also be positive, thus yielding a negative expected payoff. Instead, by never expressing a high valuation, her payoff is certain to be zero.

On the other hand, it also follows that any *symmetric* BNE must have $w < 1$. For, if we had $w = 1$, neither type would ever communicate a high valuation (because $u = 1$), which would imply that the payoff would be uniformly zero for both types. However, in that case, it would be clearly in the interest of a high type (i.e., one with a valuation $v_i = 30$) to behave truthfully, because the entailed payoff would be $30 - 20 > 0$.

Thus, since any BNE γ^* must have type $t_i = 30$ play $a_i = 30$ with positive probability, this action must be an optimal response for this type when the opponent plays the equilibrium strategy. This implies that, say, for player 1, the expected payoff[89] of playing $a_1 = 30$,

$$p\{w\pi_1^A(30, 30; 30, 0) + (1 - w)\pi_1^A(30, 30; 30, 30)\}$$
$$+ (1 - p)\pi_1^A(30, 0; 30, 0), \tag{6.15}$$

must be at least as large as that corresponding to $a_1 = 0$,

$$p\{w\pi_1^A(30, 30; 0, 0) + (1 - w)\pi_1^A(30, 30; 0, 30)\}$$
$$+ (1 - p)\pi_1^A(30, 0; 0, 0). \tag{6.16}$$

Such a requirement can be simply rewritten as follows:

$$p\{w(30 - 20) + (1 - w)(30 - 10)\} + (1 - p)(30 - 20)$$
$$\geq p(1 - w)(30 - 0),$$

---

[89] Note that these payoff expressions already incorporate the fact that, at equilibrium, $u = 1$.

On the other hand, concerning the optimality of the other component of her strategy, $\hat{\gamma}_1(30)$, the precise value of the probability p must naturally have a crucial effect on it. To assess this effect, denote by $\psi(a_1, p)$ the expected payoff earned by a high type of player 1 when she chooses action a_1 and the high-valuation probability is p, of course assuming that player 2 relies on the strategy $\hat{\gamma}_2$ given by (6.20). This function is of the following form:

$$\psi(a_1, p) = \begin{cases} p \times (30 - a_1) + (1 - p) \times 0 & \text{if } a_1 < 20 \\ 10 & \text{if } a_1 = 20. \end{cases}$$

It is easy to see that, independently of the value of p, the only possible values for a_1 that may qualify as optimal are 20 and 0. Thus, a direct comparison of the payoffs induced by each of these two possibilities yields

$$\hat{\gamma}_1(30) = \begin{cases} 0 & \text{if } p > 1/3 \\ 20 & \text{if } p < 1/3 \end{cases} \tag{6.22}$$

and for the exact (nongeneric) case in which $p = 1/3$, any mixture between both options ($a_1 = 0, 20$) is optimal.

The expressions (6.20), (6.21), and (6.22) define the BNE for mechanism B that is consistent with the contemplated requirement of perfection. However, as advanced, there are many other BNE that do not satisfy this requirement. To illustrate this possibility most simply, let us focus on an alternative collection of BNE that yield the same equilibrium *outcome* as $\hat{\gamma}$, i.e., they lead to an identical allocation of resources. These alternative equilibria differ from the previous one only in how player 2 reacts to interior proposals a_1 such that $0 < a_1 < 20$. Specifically, instead of (6.19), let us consider the following much weaker condition

$$a_2(0) = Y \tag{6.23}$$

that just fixes player 2's response to the proposal $a_1 = 0$. Denote by $\tilde{A}_2^B$ the set of player 2's actions that are compatible with (6.23). Then, it is easy to verify (cf. Exercise 6.2) that any strategy profile $\tilde{\gamma} = (\tilde{\gamma}_1, \tilde{\gamma}_2)$, where $\tilde{\gamma}_1$ satisfies (6.21) and (6.22), and $\tilde{\gamma}_2$ is of the form

$$\tilde{\gamma}_2 = [\tilde{\gamma}_2(0), \tilde{\gamma}_2(30)] \in \{a_{2N}\} \times \tilde{A}_2^B, \tag{6.24}$$

is a BNE for the Bayesian game induced by mechanism B. Clearly, all these equilibria (which include, of course, the one formerly determined) yield the *same* pattern of *actual* play.

When contrasting the equilibrium performance induced by the two alternative mechanisms considered, A and B, it is worth highlighting the following differences:

- Unlike what happens for mechanism A, mechanism B always guarantees an efficient outcome when the second mover (i.e., player 2) has a high valuation.
- Instead, when player 2 has a low valuation, mechanism B leads to an inefficient outcome with *certainty* if (somewhat paradoxically) there is a high prior probability p that each agent might display a high

valuation – specifically, when $p > 1/3$. Even though large values for p also increase the likelihood of inefficiency in the case of mechanism A, this is never a sure outcome, even for $p = 1$.

- In terms of the probability p, the range of *possible* inefficiency is larger for mechanism B (i.e., $p \in (1/3, 1]$) than for mechanism A (where, for possible inefficiency, one must have $p \in (1/2, 1]$). However, this seeming drawback displayed by mechanism B is mitigated by the following observation: for large p, the *ex ante* probability that such inefficiency occurs is very low (as explained, it requires that player 2 have a low valuation). In contrast, the analogous probability remains significant (in fact increases) as p becomes large in the context of mechanism A. (See Exercises 6.1, 6.3, and 6.4 for elaboration on these matters.)

6.4   Signaling games

6.4.1   *Introduction and examples*

As explained in Section 6.2, the formulation proposed by Harsanyi to study player interaction under incomplete (or asymmetric) information implicitly assumes that the situation at hand can be suitably modeled in strategic form. However, as our former discussion of mechanism B illustrates, many problems of interest lead to a sequential modeling of the decision process. They require, therefore, careful treatment of issues pertaining to off-equilibrium behavior and off-equilibrium beliefs. In the context of mechanism B, these issues could be dealt with quite trivially because, in effect, one could abstract from any explicit consideration of players' beliefs. However, this is not typically the case in many applications, which then demand a more sophisticated approach. Here, our discussion of these important matters is not undertaken in the most general framework but instead is restricted to a particular class of games: the so-called *signaling games*. Albeit very stylized, this class of games provides a framework that is rich enough to understand some of the key theoretical questions involved.

Signaling games have been widely used to understand some of the core strategic issues arising in the economics of information. Its theoretical framework can be informally described as follows. There are two agents moving in sequence. The first one (e.g., a salesman who supplies a good of a given quality – Akerlof (1970) – or a worker of a certain ability – Spence (1973)) has private information (the specific quality of the product she sells or her work ability) that is relevant for the second mover (an interested buyer or a potential employer). The action first chosen by the informed party (e.g., a price offer, or a certain level of education) is assumed perfectly observed by the uninformed agent, who moves subsequently. This second agent, on the basis of her observation, may *indirectly* infer some knowledge (full or only partial) about the underlying information she did not originally hold. Then, with this possibly improved knowledge in hand, the second player makes her choice and concludes the game. Naturally, the payoff each player obtains in the game is taken to depend on the actions chosen by both players as well as the underlying piece of private information held by the first player.

Some of the games discussed in Section 6.2.2 to illustrate the construct of a Bayesian game can be readily transformed into signaling games by introducing a sequential order of moves. Consider, for example, the modified battle of the sexes presented in Subsection 6.2.2.1 or the Cournot duopoly with uncertain costs introduced in Subsection 6.2.2.2. If, instead of the simultaneous (type-contingent) choice of actions postulated there, it is posited that player 1 (the only one with relevant private information in either example) moves first, those games accurately fit the format of a signaling game. Both of them will be precisely cast as such below (see Subsection 6.4.4), once we have completed the formal description of the signaling model. For the moment, we close this introductory section with a yet informal description of another signaling game, which is a minor variation on a famous example proposed by Cho and Kreps (1987). This game has been used repeatedly in the literature to illustrate many of the subtleties and problems raised by equilibrium refinements in games under incomplete information.

Two individuals, 1 and 2, belonging to rival clans (also denoted, respectively, by 1 and 2) meet some early morning at the saloon bar of a town in the American West. Although everyone in clan 1 is peaceful and dislikes violence, all members in clan 2 are aggressive and would like to enter into a duel with anyone of the other clan, provided they can win it. Suppose this duel is won or not depending on whether individual 1 is *strong* or *weak*, something individual 2 does not observe. *A priori*, the only information the latter has available is that 90% of the individuals of clan 1 are strong (the complementary fraction being of course weak) and that every one of them has the same probability of being at the saloon that day.

Even though the type of individual 1 is not known by individual 2, the latter observes the sort of "breakfast" the former one chooses that morning. There are two options: beer and quiche. Further assume that while the strong individuals of clan 1 prefer beer, the weak ones prefer quiche. The issue that arises may be succinctly described as follows: Under what conditions will individual 2 be able to infer the type of player 1 from the observation of his breakfast? Can such a type revelation be part of an equilibrium of the incomplete-information game?

When the situation is modeled as a signaling game, the breakfast ordered by 1 that morning plays the role of a signal (possibly revealing, but perhaps not) of the underlying private information (his strength or weakness) held by player 1. Then, of course, the answer to the previous questions must depend on the concrete payoffs posited for each of the possible outcomes of the game. To fix ideas, let these payoffs be given as follows. On the one hand, for player 2, associate a payoff of 1 to a duel that ends in victory, a payoff of -1 to one that ends in defeat, and simply a payoff of zero if no duel takes place. On the other hand, for player 1, his payoffs must depend not only on whether there is a duel but also on what he has for breakfast. Specifically, suppose that, whatever his type, player 1 obtains a payoff of 3 if he does not face a duel *and* has his most preferred breakfast (beer if strong, quiche if weak). If, even having avoided the duel, his breakfast is not his preferred one, his payoff is only 2. If he is confronted in duel, but his breakfast is the preferred one, his payoff is equal to 1. Finally, in the remaining case (he faces the duel and his breakfast is not the one he likes best), his payoff is taken to be equal to zero.

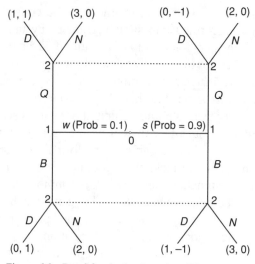

Figure 6.2: Breakfast in the American West.

How can we model the strategic dilemma faced by the two individuals meeting in the saloon bar? Following Harsanyi again (see Subsection 6.4.2 for the formal details), we may do it by introducing Nature – player 0 – into the game, leading to the extensive-form representation displayed in Figure 6.2. In this game, Nature is the first mover and selects the type of player 1 (whether he is weak (w) or strong (s)) with probabilities equal to the respective frequencies in clan 1. Then, this choice by Nature is revealed to player 1 alone who, on the basis of this information, chooses his breakfast. Finally, after observing player 1's breakfast, player 2 adopts his own action (i.e., whether to duel) and ends the game.

6.4.2 *Formalization*

Now, we describe precisely the theoretical framework that defines a bilateral signaling game between players 1 and 2 (the first fully informed, the second wholly uninformed).[90] Along the lines proposed by Harsanyi for Bayesian games (recall Subsection 6.2.1), a signaling game may be decomposed into the following different stages:

1. First, Nature selects a certain $t \in T$ with respective probabilities $P(t) > 0$ that are common knowledge. Player 1 is accurately informed of Nature's choice, which is therefore identified with player 1's type. Formally, that is, we identify the type space of player 1 with T, while we dispense with the specification of what would be a trivial (singleton) type space of player 2.

---

[90] For notational simplicity, we restrict the theoretical framework to only two players. The extension to more than two players is conceptually simple to do, provided that (a) one maintains the dichotomy between the players who are *completely* informed and those who are not at all, and (b) players within each of these two groups are treated symmetrically. In fact, some of the applications discussed in Chapter 7 (e.g., see Section 7.1) display an interaction among more than two players.

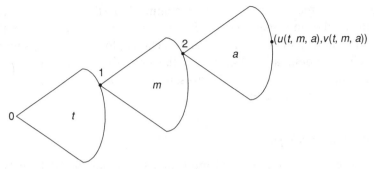

Figure 6.3: A signaling game.

2. Having been informed of her type, player 1 sends a message m belonging to some prespecified message space M (here, for convenience, assumed finite). That message is accurately observed by player 2.
3. Having observed player 1's message, player 2 then reacts by choosing action a in her action (finite) set A. This ends the signaling game.

Given any chosen type t, message m, and action a, the induced payoffs to player 1 and 2, $u(t, m, a)$ and $v(t, m, a)$, respectively, are given by corresponding payoff functions

$$u, v : T \times M \times A \to \mathbb{R}.$$

A schematic extensive-form illustration of a signaling game is presented in Figure 6.3.

In the context of a signaling game, a typical (behavioral) strategy of player 1 is formally identical to that of a Bayesian game.[91] It is a mapping of the form

$$\gamma_1 : T \to \mathcal{M} \equiv \Delta(M),$$

which associates with every possible information received t (i.e., her particular type) a probability vector $\gamma_1(t) = [\gamma_1(t)(m)]_{m \in M}$ over the space of messages. As usual, this vector is taken to reflect choice probabilities, thus allowing for the possibility that the agent's decision may display some *ex ante* randomness.

On the part of player 2, a strategy in the signaling game is a function

$$\gamma_2 : M \to \mathcal{A} \equiv \Delta(A)$$

associating with each of the possible messages m she may receive from player 1, a mixed action $\gamma_2(m) = [\gamma_2(m)(a)]_{a \in A}$. Since player 2 does not receive any information from Nature (i.e., has no private information), her strategy depends only on the information she does receive by virtue of the position she occupies in the game as second mover. Thus, as usual, both players' strategies display the same

---

[91] Note that, in fact, the present signaling scenario could also be modeled as a Bayesian game. Then, the "actions" of player 1 would coincide with her messages and those of player 2 would be identified with the (message-contingent) strategies of the signaling game. Despite this formal parallelism, the reason why we find it useful here to formulate an alternative extensive-form framework is essentially instrumental, as explained at the beginning of Subsection 6.4.3.

general format, i.e., they prescribe behavior contingent on the information received. However, the kind of information they rely on in each case is different: in the case of player 1, this information concerns Nature's choice; for player 2, it is merely the opponent's choice. For notational simplicity, the respective set of all those strategies will be denoted, as in the context of Bayesian games, by $\Upsilon_i(i = 1, 2)$. Given the context, no confusion should arise.

6.4.3   *Signaling equilibrium*

In Subsection 6.3.1, we viewed and motivated the notion of BNE in Bayesian games as the counterpart of Nash equilibrium for a suitably extended game with Nature. An analogous approach is pursued here for any given signaling game $SG \equiv \{\{1, 2\}, T, P(\cdot), M, A, u(\cdot), v(\cdot)\}$, now pertaining to the notion we call signaling equilibrium. More precisely, a signaling equilibrium (SE) is conceived as a weak perfect Bayesian equilibrium (WPBE) for a corresponding three-player game with Nature.

The motivation for introducing yet another equilibrium concept tailored to the specific context of signaling games derives from the subtle strategic issues raised by the phenomenon of signaling in games. Signaling is an inherently dynamic (multistage) phenomenon and thus leads to a rich scope of already familiar issues. In particular, it raises the need to have perfection (or credibility) considerations off equilibrium impinge on the behavior that may be sustained as optimal on the equilibrium path. These considerations are not easily tackled within the context of Bayesian games, because they are cast in a strategic-form framework (recall Footnote 91).

As indicated, the route undertaken here represents a direct counterpart of what was done in Section 4.4 for the WPBE concept. Credibility pertaining to behavior prescribed at *all* possible contingencies is assessed by imputing *explicit* beliefs at all relevant decision points in the game. But since, in a signaling game, player 1 is fully informed, only the beliefs of player 2 need to concern us here. As usual, these beliefs are to be defined at each of player 2's "information sets," i.e., after each possible message received from player 1. For each of these messages, a probability vector must be specified that formalizes player 2's beliefs about player 1's type after receiving that message. And, as in the WPBE concept, the crucial requirement concerning these beliefs is that they should be consistent with player 1's strategy *and* Bayes rule when the latter is applicable (i.e., when the *ex ante* probability is positive); otherwise, beliefs are simply unrestricted. Then, by adding to this condition on beliefs the requirement that players' strategies be optimal responses (either to admissible beliefs in the case of player 2 or to the opponent's strategy in the case of player 1), one arrives at the notion of SE.

To present the SE notion formally, we introduce some notation that represents just a slight adaptation of that used in Section 4.4. For each message $m \in M$, let $\mu(m) \in \Delta(T)$ stand for the *beliefs* held by player 2 abouts 1's type after receiving message m. Correspondingly, let a *pattern of beliefs* be a collection $\mu \equiv \{\mu(m)\}_{m \in M}$ representing the specification of some beliefs for every possible message in M. With this notation in place, the SE concept may be defined as follows.

Definition 6.2: *Let $SG \equiv \{\{1, 2\}, T, P(\cdot), M, A, u(\cdot), v(\cdot)\}$ be a signaling game. A strategy profile (γ_1^*, γ_2^*) is a* signaling equilibrium *if there exists a belief pattern $\mu^* = \{\mu^*(m)\}_{m \in M}$ such that the following conditions are satisfied:*

(i) $\forall t \in T, \forall v \in \mathcal{M},$

$$\sum_{m \in M} \gamma_1^*(t)(m) \left[\sum_{a \in A} u(t, m, a)\, \gamma_2^*(m)(a) \right]$$

$$\geq \sum_{m \in M} v(m) \left[\sum_{a \in A} u(t, m, a)\, \gamma_2^*(m)(a) \right],$$

i.e., player 1's strategy prescribes an optimal message for each type, given player 2's strategy.

(ii) $\forall m \in M, \forall \alpha \in \mathcal{A},$

$$\sum_{a \in A} \gamma_2^*(m)(a) \left[\sum_{t \in T} v(t, m, a)\, \mu^*(m)(t) \right]$$

$$\geq \sum_{a \in A} \alpha(a) \left[\sum_{t \in T} v(t, m, a)\, \mu^*(m)(t) \right],$$

i.e., player 2's strategy responds optimally to every message, given the belief pattern μ^*.

(iii) $\forall m \in M,$

(a) $T^*(m) \equiv \{t \in T : \gamma_1^*(t)(m) > 0\} \neq \emptyset \Rightarrow$

$$\forall t' \in T, \quad \mu^*(m)(t') = \frac{P(t')\, \gamma_1^*(t')(m)}{\sum_{t \in T} P(t)\, \gamma_1^*(t)(m)};$$

(b) $T^*(m) = \emptyset \Rightarrow \mu^*(m)(\cdot)$ *may be specified arbitrarily.*

That is, the beliefs associated with every possible message are consistent with player 1's strategy and Bayes rule whenever the message in question has positive prior probability.

Definition 6.2 formalizes the equilibrium requirements verbally explained above concerning both individual optimality and belief consistency. As indicated, these requirements are the same as those reflected by WPBE, the concept introduced in Chapter 4 for ordinary multistage games. In particular, SE shares with WPBE the convenient but "simple-minded" feature of allowing for any arbitrary beliefs at those junctures in the game that lie off the contemplated equilibrium path (i.e., when Bayes rule is not well defined). It should be stressed, however, that this wide range of discretion does not allow for some of the paradoxical features illustrated in Section 4.4 for the WPBE concept. (Recall, in particular, the game represented in Figure 4.5, where a WPBE was shown not to be necessarily subgame perfect.) For, as it might be recalled, we argued that those problems cannot arise when, as happens in signaling games, there are only *two* players (genuine ones, excluding Nature) who move *once* each throughout the game.

There are, however, other grounds on which certain imputations of beliefs off equilibrium may be questioned as yielding unreasonable outcomes. This is discussed at some length in Section 6.6, where we observe that, even though SE does display "backward-induction perfection," it may fail to satisfy other reasonable criteria of forward induction. With the aim of tackling this problem, specific refinements on off-equilibrium *beliefs* will be proposed that, at least for some specific games, will display the desired features.

We close this section by addressing the basic issue of existence of SE. In analogy with Theorem 6.1, the isomorphism between signaling games and corresponding (ordinary) games with Nature provides an easy route to establishing existence.

Theorem 6.2: *Let $SG \equiv \{\{1, 2\}, T, P(\cdot), M, A, u(\cdot), v(\cdot)\}$ be a (finite) signaling game. A signaling equilibrium $\gamma^* \equiv (\gamma_i^*)_{i=1}^n$ always exists.*

Proof: Exercise 6.10.   ∎

6.4.4   *Examples*

6.4.4.1 *Modified battle of the sexes (continued).* Reconsider the modified battle of the sexes, whose payoffs were given by Tables 6.1 and 6.2 for each of the two girl types (basketball or shopping fan). In Subsection 6.2.2.1, we assumed that both players adopted their decisions simultaneously and modeled the situation as a Bayesian game. Now, suppose the girl (i.e., the informed player) moves first and the boy second. This transforms the context into a signaling game.

Formally, the type space of the signaling game is equal to $T = \{t_{11}, t_{12}\}$ where, as before, t_{11} is identified with the girl being a basketball fan and t_{12} a shopping fan. Their respective prior probabilities are $P(t_{11}) = p$ and $P(t_{12}) = 1 - p$, with p being a parameter of the model. Both the "message" space of the girl as well as the "action" space of the boy can be identified (for notational simplicity) with the same set, i.e., $\{B, S\} = M = A$. Finally, the payoff functions $u(\cdot)$ and $v(\cdot)$ readily obtain from Tables 6.1 and 6.2.

In the signaling game thus specified, a pure strategy of player 1 (the girl) is a mapping of the form $\gamma_1 : T \to \{B, S\}$, and that of player 2 (the boy) a mapping $\gamma_2 : \{B, S\} \to \{B, S\}$. It is easy to find an SE (γ_1^*, γ_2^*) for this game. On the one hand, since the boy's payoffs are not affected by the girl's type and always favor matching the girl's (previous) choice of action, we must have

$$\gamma_2^*(B) = B; \quad \gamma_2^*(S) = S. \tag{6.25}$$

And then, the optimal type-contingent response by the girl is simply

$$\gamma_1^*(t_{11}) = B; \quad \gamma_1^*(t_{12}) = S. \tag{6.26}$$

In sum, we conclude that (6.25) and (6.26) define the unique SE of the game,

Table 6.3: *Modified battle of the sexes if the girl is a "basketball fan": second version*

Boy Girl	B	S
B	1, 2	3, 1
S	0, 0	2, 3

Table 6.4: *Modified battle of the sexes if the girl is a "shopping fan": second version*

Boy Girl	B	S
B	2, 2	0, 1
S	3, 0	1, 3

supported by the belief pattern μ^* given by

$$\mu^*(B)(t_{11}) = 1; \quad \mu^*(S)(t_{12}) = 1. \tag{6.27}$$

If we contrast this SE with the BNE obtained in the counterpart Bayesian game where decisions are simultaneous (cf. Subsection 6.3.2.1), we observe that the girl's strategies are formally identical in both cases – compare (6.8) and (6.26). One might be tempted to argue (wrongly, however) that this coincidence follows from the fact that, in both situations, the girl has a dominant action for each type. Indeed, when players make their decisions *simultaneously*, the fact that, at equilibrium, the girl must play as given by (6.8) does follow from a mere dominance argument. For, if the boy cannot make his action contingent on hers (as is assumed in the Bayesian game), to play the "dominant action" for each type must be a dominant *strategy* for the corresponding Bayesian game. However, no similar logic can be used, in general, for the signaling-game version of the interaction. In this case, the fact that the boy may react to (i.e., make his choice contingent on) the girl's choice could well make playing B (or S) a suboptimal decision even when her type is t_{11} (or t_{12}).

To illustrate the former point, suppose the original payoff tables are replaced by Tables 6.3 and 6.4. Along the heuristic lines we have used to motivate the battle of the sexes, one may interpret these payoffs as follows: even though the girl still prefers B or S (depending on whether her type is t_{11} or t_{12}) for *any* fixed action of the boy, she enjoys going alone to her most preferred alternative (not for the other one, where the opposite applies).

Consider first the case in which the decisions are adopted simultaneously and thus the appropriate model of the situation is a Bayesian game. Then, the fact that B and S are still dominant actions in, respectively, the first and second payoff tables continue to imply that the strategy played by the girl in any BNE must be as before, i.e., given by either (6.8) or (6.26).

However, if we now consider the sequential version of the model where the girl moves first, the unique SE $\hat{\gamma} = (\hat{\gamma}_1, \hat{\gamma}_2)$ in the corresponding signaling game is no longer as before. On the one hand, the boy's equilibrium strategy remains unchanged, because his decision problem is essentially the same:

$$\hat{\gamma}_2(B) = B; \quad \hat{\gamma}_2(S) = S.$$

But now, in response to $\hat{\gamma}_2$, the optimal strategy by the girl is

$$\hat{\gamma}_1(t_{11}) = S, \quad \hat{\gamma}_1(t_{12}) = B.$$

Thus, in view of the fact that her action affects the ensuing choice of the boy, the girl's optimal strategy involves playing the "dominated" action for each payoff table. In turn, the belief pattern $\hat{\mu}$ that supports this SE is as follows:

$$\hat{\mu}(B)(t_{12}) = 1; \quad \hat{\mu}(S)(t_{11}) = 1. \tag{6.28}$$

The previous two versions of the modified battle of the sexes have involved SE that are of the so-called *separating* kind. That is, they have each type of informed player choose a different action and therefore fully reveal her respective information. In the above examples, this is reflected by the fact that the corresponding belief patterns μ^* and $\hat{\mu}$ yield the boy's perceptions that are concentrated, for each of the girl's actions, in a *single* type of hers (cf. (6.27) and (6.28)).

The polar case is given by the so-called *pooling* SE. To provide a simple illustration of this alternative kind of SE, let us remain within the context motivated by the original battle of the sexes and consider a third variant of it. Continue to suppose that the girl may be of two types, t_{11} and t_{12}, each of them interpreted again as a basketball or shopping fan, respectively. Now, however, if the girl is a basketball fan (i.e., her type is t_{11}), her payoffs are as given by Table 6.1. Instead, if she is a shopping fan (her type is t_{12}), her payoffs are given by Table 6.4. Then, we may easily see that the unique SE $\tilde{\gamma} = (\tilde{\gamma}_1, \tilde{\gamma}_2)$ is of the pooling kind. On the one hand, the boy's equilibrium strategy is as before because, again, his decision problem remains unchanged:

$$\tilde{\gamma}_2(B) = B; \quad \tilde{\gamma}_2(S) = S.$$

In view of this strategy, the optimal response by the girl is

$$\tilde{\gamma}_1(t_{11}) = \tilde{\gamma}_1(t_{12}) = B;$$

that is, her choice of action is independent of her type.

Concerning the belief pattern $\tilde{\mu}$ that supports this equilibrium, first note that the girl's strategy renders B as the unique "message" that is delivered at equilibrium. Therefore, associated with this message, Bayes' rule implies

$$\tilde{\mu}(B)(t_{11}) = p; \quad \tilde{\mu}(B)(t_{12}) = 1 - p.$$

That is, nothing new is learned (compared with the original *a priori* beliefs) by observing B. In contrast, action S should never be observed at equilibrium. Consequently, Bayes rule is unapplicable in that case, and the corresponding beliefs are unrestricted. That is, we may choose any beliefs of the form

$$\tilde{\mu}(S)(t_{11}) = q, \quad \tilde{\mu}(S)(t_{12}) = 1 - q,$$

for some $q \in [0, 1]$. Whatever such beliefs are specifically posited, the optimality of the boy's strategy $\tilde{\gamma}_2$ is preserved.

6.4.4.2 *Cournot duopoly with uncertain costs (continued).* Recall the duopoly scenario with uncertain costs presented in Subsection 6.2.2.2. Now, instead of postulating simultaneous decisions, suppose that firm 1 (the informed player) moves first and its output decision is observed by firm 2 before making its own choice. This strategic situation can be readily modeled as a signaling game with the following components:

- type space $T = \{1, 2\}$ with $P(1) = p$, $P(2) = 1 - p$ and $p \in [0, 1]$;
- firm 1's message space $M = \mathbb{R}_+$, a typical element of it denoted by q_1;
- firm 2's action space $A = \mathbb{R}_+$, its typical element denoted by q_2;
- firm 1's payoff function $u(\cdot)$ defined by $u(t, q_1, q_2) = \{\max[M - d(q_1 + q_2), 0] - t\}q_1$ for each $t \in T$, $q_1 \in M$, $q_2 \in A$;
- firm 2's payoff function $v(\cdot)$ defined by $v(t, q_1, q_2) = \{\max[M - d(q_1 + q_2), 0] - t\}q_2$ for each $t \in T$, $q_1 \in M$, $q_2 \in A$.

To focus ideas, let us look for a separating equilibrium $\hat{\gamma} = (\hat{\gamma}_1, \hat{\gamma}_2)$, where each type of firm 1 decides on a different output and so reveals its private information. In this case, firm 1's strategy is of the following form:

$$\hat{\gamma}_1(1) = \hat{q}_{11}, \quad \hat{\gamma}_1(2) = \hat{q}_{12}, \tag{6.29}$$

for some specific outputs $\hat{q}_{11} \neq \hat{q}_{12}$. Since, after observing either of these outputs, firm 2 becomes informed of the respective underlying cost, its strategy $\hat{\gamma}_2$ must satisfy the following two-fold condition, for all $q_2 \in \mathbb{R}_+$:

$$[M - d(\hat{q}_{11} + \hat{\gamma}_2(\hat{q}_{11})) - 1]\,\hat{\gamma}_2(\hat{q}_{11})$$
$$\geq \{\max[M - d(\hat{q}_{11} + q_2), 0] - 1\}\, q_2; \tag{6.30}$$

$$[M - d(\hat{q}_{12} + \hat{\gamma}_2(\hat{q}_{12})) - 2]\,\hat{\gamma}_2(\hat{q}_{12})$$
$$\geq \{\max[M - d(\hat{q}_{12} + q_2), 0] - 2\}\, q_2. \tag{6.31}$$

In other words, $\hat{\gamma}_2(\hat{q}_{11})$ must be a best response to output $\hat{q}_{11}$ under the assumption that the marginal cost $c = 1$, and $\hat{\gamma}_2(\hat{q}_{12})$ must be a best response to output $\hat{q}_{12}$ under the assumption that $c = 2$. For future purposes, we find it useful to reformulate these conditions by relying on the format of reaction functions, as these were defined in Subsection 3.1.1. Let $\eta_{21}(\cdot)$ and $\eta_{22}(\cdot)$ be the reaction functions of firm 2 when the marginal cost c is, respectively, assumed to be equal to 1 or 2. Then, (6.30) and (6.31) can be compactly rewritten as follows:

$$\hat{\gamma}_2(\hat{q}_{11}) = \eta_{21}(\hat{q}_{11}), \quad \hat{\gamma}_2(\hat{q}_{12}) = \eta_{22}(\hat{q}_{12}). \tag{6.32}$$

The beliefs by firm 2 inducing this behavior are as follows:

$$\mu(\hat{q}_{11})(1) = 1; \quad \mu(\hat{q}_{12})(2) = 1. \tag{6.33}$$

To complete the description of our (yet tentative) separating equilibrium, one still has to determine the values $\hat{q}_{11}$ and $\hat{q}_{12}$ that define firm 1's strategy as well as the behavior (and underlying beliefs) by firm 2 for all other possible outputs of firm 1. Concerning the first task, a natural candidate arises from the following observation. Because, at the desired separating equilibrium, firm 1 is to fully reveal its private information, its (type-contingent) optimal behavior should anticipate a perfectly informed response by firm 2. Heuristically, this suggests choosing $\hat{q}_{11}$ and $\hat{q}_{12}$ as in the Stackelberg model for each of the two possible cost conditions, $c = 1$ or $c = 2$, respectively. That is (cf. (5.4)),

$$\hat{q}_{11} = \frac{M - 1}{2d} \tag{6.34}$$

$$\hat{q}_{12} = \frac{M - 2}{2d}. \tag{6.35}$$

Next, we turn to completing the strategy $\hat{\gamma}_2(\cdot)$ by specifying $\hat{\gamma}_2(q_1)$ for $q_1 \notin \{\hat{q}_{11}, \hat{q}_{12}\}$. To do so, it must be kept in mind that our objective here is to support (6.29) as firm 1's optimal response to $\hat{\gamma}_2$. Of course, the easiest way to do it is to have any possible deviation by firm 1 trigger the most "harmful" reaction by firm 2, consistent with the restriction that the latter be a best response to some suitably chosen off-equilibrium beliefs. Since, in choosing those beliefs, the SE concept allows full discretion, an extreme (i.e., most "aggressive") reaction by firm 2 is given by

$$\hat{\gamma}_2(q_1) = \eta_{21}(q_1), \quad \forall q_1 \notin \{\hat{q}_{11}, \hat{q}_{12}\}, \tag{6.36}$$

which is supported by the beliefs

$$\hat{\mu}(q_1)(1) = 1, \quad \forall q_1 \notin \{\hat{q}_{11}, \hat{q}_{12}\}. \tag{6.37}$$

Those reactions by firm 2 induce the highest possible outputs on its part that are consistent with playing a best response to *some* beliefs. A less artificial (but analogously effective) possibility would be to postulate

$$\hat{\gamma}_2(q_1) = \begin{cases} \eta_{21}(q_1) & \text{if } q_1 > \hat{q}_{12} \\ \eta_{22}(q_1) & \text{if } q_1 \leq \hat{q}_{12}, \end{cases} \tag{6.38}$$

supported by the beliefs

$$\hat{\mu}(q_1)(1) = \begin{cases} 1 & \text{if } q_1 > \hat{q}_{12} \\ 0 & \text{if } q_1 \leq \hat{q}_{12}. \end{cases} \tag{6.39}$$

The *candidate* SE $\hat{\gamma} = (\hat{\gamma}_1, \hat{\gamma}_2)$ is now fully specified by (6.32), (6.34), (6.35), and (6.36), supported by the belief pattern given by (6.33) and (6.37) – alternatively to (6.36), we can contemplate (6.38), supported by (6.39). By construction, all items in it have been computed to satisfy the equilibrium conditions, except for the outputs $\hat{q}_{11}$ and $\hat{q}_{12}$ that define firm 1's strategy $\hat{\gamma}_1$. What needs to be finally verified is that neither of the two types of firm 1 would gain by deviating from those outputs, in view of the anticipated reaction by firm 2 reflected by $\hat{\gamma}_2$.

For type $t = 1$, this requires that

$$[M - d(\hat{q}_{11} + \eta_{21}(\hat{q}_{11})) - 1]\,\hat{q}_{11} \geq [M - d(\hat{q}_{12} + \eta_{22}(\hat{q}_{12})) - 1]\,\hat{q}_{12},$$

$$(6.40)$$

because no deviation to $q_1 \neq \hat{q}_{12}$ needs to be considered (i.e., it cannot be profitable), in view of the reaction by firm 2 implied by (6.36). Using (6.34) and (6.35) and the fact that the functions $\eta_{21}(\cdot)$ and $\eta_{22}(\cdot)$ are given by (cf. (3.12))

$$\eta_{21}(q_1) = \max\left\{0, \frac{M-1}{2d} - \frac{1}{2}q_1\right\} \qquad (6.41)$$

$$\eta_{22}(q_1) = \max\left\{0, \frac{M-2}{2d} - \frac{1}{2}q_1\right\}, \qquad (6.42)$$

we can rewrite (6.40) as follows:

$$\left[M - d\left(\frac{M-1}{2d} + \frac{M-1}{4d}\right) - 1\right]\frac{M-1}{2d}$$

$$\geq \left[M - d\left(\frac{M-2}{2d} + \frac{M-2}{4d}\right) - 1\right]\frac{M-2}{2d}.$$

On the other hand, for type $t = 2$, the required condition is that, for all $q_1 \in \mathbb{R}_+$,

$$[M - d(\hat{q}_{12} + \eta_{22}(\hat{q}_{12})) - 2]\,\hat{q}_{12}$$

$$\geq [M - d(q_1 + \eta_{21}(q_1)) - 2]\,q_1, \qquad (6.43)$$

which may be rewritten as follows:

$$\left[M - d\left(\frac{M-2}{2d} + \frac{M-2}{4d}\right) - 2\right]\frac{M-2}{2d}$$

$$\geq \left[M - d\left(\frac{1}{2}q_1 + \frac{M-1}{2d}\right) - 2\right]q_1,$$

where we rely on (6.36).

It may be checked (Exercise 6.6) that the verification of (6.40) and (6.43) imposes quite stringent conditions on the parameters of the model. In particular, one must have that $M \leq 5/2$, which amounts to saying that the "market size" is to be quite small relative to the cost parameters. If this condition is not satisfied, SE may require some pooling for the two types of firm 1 (see Exercise 6.7).

6.4.4.3 *Breakfast in the American West.* To end our collection of examples involving signaling games, we now tackle formally the American West conflict between rival clans represented in Figure 6.2. To cast it as a signaling game, the type space of player 1 is chosen equal to $T = \{w, s\}$ with the above indicated interpretations (weak and strong type, respectively). The probabilities associated with each type are equated to their respective population frequencies, so that $P(w) = 0.1$ and $P(s) = 0.9$. For player 1, his message space is identified with his breakfast menu,

$M = \{Q, B\}$. For player 2, his action space is $A = \{D, N\}$, which includes his two possible reactions (dueling or not) after observing player 1's breakfast. Finally, the payoffs corresponding to each possible type, message, and action combination are simply as described in Figure 6.2.

A first observation to be made is that this signaling game can have no separating SE (cf. Exercise 6.9). The reason is simple: in any separating equilibrium, the strong type of player 1 would reveal himself as such through his breakfast, which in turn should be different from that of the weak type. Thus, after the former kind of breakfast, player 2 should never duel at equilibrium (because he is sure to be defeated) while he would do so after the latter kind. But then, given that player 1 (independently of his type) always values more avoiding duel than having his most preferred breakfast, both types of this player would have an incentive to share the same breakfast (i.e., the one originally associated with the strong type). This, of course, would break the supposed intertype separation.

In view of the former observation, we direct our attention toward finding pooling SE where both types choose the same breakfast. There are two different *classes* of strategy profiles that are possible candidates for such SE. In one of them, whose SE are generically denoted by $\hat{\gamma} = (\hat{\gamma}_1, \hat{\gamma}_2)$, both types have beer for breakfast, i.e.,

$$\hat{\gamma}_1(w) = \hat{\gamma}_1(s) = B. \tag{6.44}$$

In the alternative class, whose SE are denoted by $\tilde{\gamma} = (\tilde{\gamma}_1, \tilde{\gamma}_2)$, the pooling "message" is quiche and

$$\tilde{\gamma}_1(w) = \tilde{\gamma}_2(s) = Q. \tag{6.45}$$

Consider each of these two possibilities in turn. For the first one, it is clear that the equilibrium reaction to B must be

$$\hat{\gamma}_2(B) = N, \tag{6.46}$$

supported by the belief

$$\hat{\mu}(B)(s) = 0.9. \tag{6.47}$$

As in previous examples, we now ask ourselves how to complete player 2's strategy with a suitable reaction to Q (the off-equilibrium message) so that the pooling strategy (6.44) indeed becomes optimal for 1. Looking again for the "most harmful" such reaction, we propose

$$\hat{\gamma}_2(Q) = D, \tag{6.48}$$

which may be supported by the belief

$$\hat{\mu}(Q)(w) = 1. \tag{6.49}$$

Of course, we could also consider less extreme beliefs by 2 after observing Q, as well as less extreme reactions to this off-equilibrium breakfast. In particular, a high enough probability of playing D after Q (not necessarily one) would suffice – see Exercise 6.8. However, the above specification is the simplest and most clear-cut one for our purposes. As desired, it renders player 1's pooling strategy optimal, thus confirming that (6.44), (6.46), and (6.48) define an SE, supported by the belief pattern given by (6.47) and (6.49).

By relying on an analogous line of reasoning, it should be clear that the alternative pooling strategy (6.45) also leads to an SE when completed as follows:

$$\tilde{\gamma}_2(Q) = N \tag{6.50}$$

$$\tilde{\gamma}_2(B) = D. \tag{6.51}$$

Clearly, such a strategy of player 2 is supported by the following beliefs after observing the equilibrium message

$$\tilde{\mu}(Q)(s) = 0.9$$

and, say, the following off-equilibrium beliefs:

$$\tilde{\mu}(B)(w) = 1.$$

Even though the two kinds of pooling SE specified above are formally symmetric, they seem intuitively very different. In the first one, both types pool by having the sort of breakfast that the strong one prefers. In a heuristic sense, this seems to be the most natural pooling outcome, because it is the weak type (i.e., the one who could not deter the duel by revealing himself) who pays the cost of a less preferred breakfast. Instead, the second pooling equilibrium displays the seemingly paradoxical feature that it is the strong type (i.e., the one who could reveal himself as such and avoid the duel) who has to incur the pooling cost.

In fact, there are natural and precise arguments that, by exploiting forward-induction considerations, allow us to discriminate between these two kinds of pooling equilibria. A classic example in this respect is afforded by the notion called the *intuitive criterion*, proposed by Cho and Kreps (1987). This and related concepts are discussed in some detail in Section 6.6. There, in particular, we attempt to understand more precisely the features that render the quiche-pooling SE in the American West signaling game quite counterintuitive.

Supplementary material

6.5   Mixed strategies, revisited: a purification approach

As indicated in Subsection 2.2.3, the notion of mixed strategy has led to an intense controversy among game theorists. It has been argued, for example, that individuals definitely do *not* randomize when confronting important decision problems. Moreover, these misgivings are reinforced by the observation that, at mixed-strategy Nash equilibria, there seems to be an acute tension between the following two facts:

- players are typically required to mix (i.e., randomize) among several pure strategies in a very *precise* fashion;
- they must also be *indifferent* between any particular way of mixing among those pure strategies – otherwise (cf. Exercise 4.12), it could not be optimal to play each of them with positive probability.

In Subsection 2.2.1, we suggested that one of the possible reasons that can be invoked to justify the use of mixed strategies is that, in some games, it is not inconceivable that players may indeed resort to mechanisms (perhaps only "internal," not necessarily explicit or visible) to hide their action from the opponents. This was illustrated with the familiar game of matching pennies (cf. Table 1.4). In this game, if either player were to choose heads or tails with probabilities different from $1/2$, she had better make sure her opponent is not able to anticipate it. Otherwise, the opponent would gain a significant strategic advantage, which in a zero-sum game should have detrimental payoff consequences for the player in question.

To elaborate on this idea, suppose the matching-pennies game is repeatedly played by the same two players over time, with each of them trying to learn from experience what precise rule is used by her opponent to choose between heads and tails. Even if one of the players did not, in fact, use the stochastic equal-probability rule prescribed by Nash equilibrium, her induced behavior should at least be indistinguishable from that induced by such a rule. In other words, it should not allow the opponent to detect any "vulnerability" (e.g., some intertemporal correlation or different long-run frequencies for each strategy) that could be profitably exploited.

The former discussion points to what is, in essence, the role played by mixed strategies in achieving the interagent consistency of behavior demanded by Nash equilibrium. The incentives of players to use mixed strategies at equilibrium are *not* direct payoff advantages – as explained, any mixture with the same support as the equilibrium strategy yields comparable expected payoffs. Rather, what will generally motivate players to rely on mixed strategies is their desire to protect themselves from being exploited (i.e., their behavior anticipated) by the opponents. Thus, as suggested above, even if a player does not in fact use the precise mixture of pure strategies prescribed by equilibrium, typically, she should try not to let other players suspect it.

Heuristically, the previous discussion may be summarized as follows. What counts in a mixed-strategy Nash equilibrium is not what players actually do (as long as it is optimal, given their beliefs) but what others perceive them to do. Strictly speaking, this statement would seem to contradict the tenet of rational expectations that is supposed to underlie Nash equilibrium (recall Subsection 2.2.1). Harsanyi (1973), however, proposed a very elegant way of formulating the gist of this intuitive idea, rendering it fully precise and coherent with equilibrium behavior.

Customarily, Harsanyi's proposal is described as an approach that involves the *purification* of mixed-strategy Nash equilibria. More specifically, it transforms mixed-strategy equilibria into equilibria in *pure* strategies of a perturbed (Bayesian) game that is arbitrarily close to the original game. In that perturbed game, players have *strict* incentives to follow a pure Bayesian-game strategy, whose pattern of choice probabilities (induced by the corresponding pattern of realized types) approximately matches the corresponding probabilities displayed by the original mixed-strategy equilibrium. In this sense, therefore, we may conceive players' uncertainty about the opponent's choices as a mere reflection of the uncertainty they hold on their underlying private information (i.e., their realized types). A full discussion of Harsanyi's purification approach is beyond the scope of this book. Instead, we merely describe

Table 6.5: *Perturbed matching-pennies game under incomplete information*

1 \ 2	H	T
H	$1 + \varepsilon_1, -1 + \varepsilon_2$	$-1 + \varepsilon_1, 1 - \varepsilon_2$
T	$-1 - \varepsilon_1, 1 + \varepsilon_2$	$1 - \varepsilon_1, -1 - \varepsilon_2$

its general approach in what follows, first introducing the essential ideas in the specific context of the matching-pennies game.

Recall the matching-pennies game and assume that its "base payoffs" (as specified in Table 1.4) are perturbed stochastically by a pair of *independent* random variables, $\tilde{\varepsilon}_1$ and $\tilde{\varepsilon}_2$, distributed uniformly on some interval $[-\delta, \delta]$ with $0 < \delta \leq 1$. Each $\tilde{\varepsilon}_i$ is taken to affect only the payoffs of the respective player i. Specifically, given any particular realization $\varepsilon_i \in [-\delta, \delta]$, the payoffs of player i experience an additive shift by ε_i if she chooses H and a shift equal to $-\varepsilon_i$ if she chooses T. Thus, for any pair of realizations, $(\varepsilon_1, \varepsilon_2) \in [-\delta, \delta] \times [-\delta, \delta]$, the induced payoffs may be summarized by Table 6.5.

The key informational assumption we make is that each player $i \in \{1, 2\}$ is *privately* informed of the realization of her respective $\tilde{\varepsilon}_i$. This allows one to model the strategic setup as a two-player Bayesian game where the realization of each random variable $\tilde{\varepsilon}_i$ is viewed as player i's type, her type space being $T_i = [-\delta, \delta]$ for each $i = 1, 2$. Since these type spaces have the cardinality of the continuum, the stochastic choice by Nature cannot be formalized through some discrete density, as postulated simply in Section 6.2.1. Instead, it will be assumed given by the continuous *uniform density* $f(\cdot)$ with

$$f(\varepsilon_1, \varepsilon_2) = \left(\frac{1}{2\delta}\right)^2, \quad \forall (\varepsilon_1, \varepsilon_2) \in [-\delta, \delta]^2.$$

In this Bayesian game, a pure strategy of player i is a mapping

$$\gamma_i^* : [-\delta, \delta] \to \{H, T\} \tag{6.52}$$

prescribing whether to play heads or tails, depending on her realized type $t_i = \varepsilon_i$. We next show that the strategy profile $\gamma^* = (\gamma_1^*, \gamma_2^*)$ given by

$$\begin{aligned} \gamma_i^*(\varepsilon_i) &= H, \quad \text{if } \varepsilon_i > 0, \\ \gamma_i^*(\varepsilon_i) &= T, \quad \text{if } \varepsilon_i \leq 0, \end{aligned} \tag{6.53}$$

defines a BNE and reproduces (for *any* arbitrarily small δ) the performance induced by the unique Nash equilibrium of matching pennies. As explained above, this is then interpreted to represent a "purification" of that (mixed-strategy) equilibrium.

Take one of the two players, say player 1, and consider any particular realization of her type, $\varepsilon_1 \in [-\delta, \delta]$. Given the strategy γ_2^* played by the opponent, her expected payoff of playing H, denoted by $\psi_1(H, \gamma_2^*)$, is given by

$$\psi_1(H, \gamma_2^*) = (1 + \varepsilon_1) \Pr[\gamma_2^*(\varepsilon_2) = H] + (-1 + \varepsilon_1) \Pr[\gamma_2^*(\varepsilon_2) = T].$$

And the expected payoff of playing T is given by

$$\psi_1(T, \gamma_2^*) = (-1 - \varepsilon_1) \Pr[\gamma_2^*(\varepsilon_2) = H] + (1 - \varepsilon_1) \Pr[\gamma_2^*(\varepsilon_2) = T].$$

Since, in view of (6.53),

$$\Pr[\gamma_2^*(\varepsilon_2) = H] = \Pr[\varepsilon_2 > 0] = \frac{1}{2}$$

$$\Pr[\gamma_2^*(\varepsilon_2) = T] = \Pr[\varepsilon_2 \le 0] = \frac{1}{2},$$

it is immediate to check that

$$\psi_1(H, \gamma_2^*) \lesseqgtr \psi_1(T, \gamma_2^*) \Leftrightarrow \varepsilon_1 \lesseqgtr 0, \tag{6.54}$$

while the two actions, H and T, provide the same payoff in the exceptional (thus irrelevant) case where $\varepsilon_1 = 0$. Analogously, we would obtain

$$\psi_2(H, \gamma_1^*) \lesseqgtr \psi_2(T, \gamma_1^*) \Leftrightarrow \varepsilon_2 \lesseqgtr 0. \tag{6.55}$$

Combining (6.54) and (6.55), one readily concludes that, indeed, the strategy profile $\gamma^* = (\gamma_1^*, \gamma_2^*)$ given by (6.53) defines a BNE of the game of incomplete information that results from perturbing the original matching-pennies game in the manner described.

In this BNE, players choose each of their two actions, H and T, with an identical *ex ante* probability of $1/2$. Furthermore, their beliefs about what the opponent actually plays also assign an equal weight of $1/2$ to her two actions. We find, therefore, that the BNE induces the same pattern of choice and the same beliefs as those of the unique mixed-strategy Nash equilibrium in the ordinary (unperturbed) game of matching pennies. An important observation to make in this respect is that the above considerations are fully independent of δ (of course, as long as $\delta > 0$, so that there is some genuine amount of incomplete information). Thus, in this sense, we find that the mixed-strategy equilibrium profile of the original game coincides with the pure-strategy BNE of the perturbed game, *independently* of how small the payoff perturbation might be.

This example illustrates much of what is the essential bearing of Harsanyi's (1973) purification approach. To describe it formally, let $G = \{N, \{S_i\}_{i=1}^n, \{\pi_i\}_{i=1}^n\}$ be any finite game in strategic form and consider, for each $s \in S \equiv \prod_{i \in N} S_i$ and every $i \in N$, a corresponding random variable $\tilde{\varepsilon}_i(s)$, interpreted as the payoff perturbation experienced by player i if the strategy profile s is played. These random variables are assumed distributed according to smooth density functions, that are absolutely continuous, and with support on the interval $[-1, 1]$. Furthermore, the vector of random variables $\tilde{\varepsilon}_i \equiv (\tilde{\varepsilon}_i(s))_{s \in S}$ is assumed stochastically independent of any other $\tilde{\varepsilon}_j \equiv (\tilde{\varepsilon}_j(s))_{s \in S}$ with $j \ne i$. Given any such family of player-based perturbations and any given $\delta > 0$ (a parameter of the construction), denote by $G(\delta)$ the Bayesian game where

(a) each player i's type space T_i coincides with the support of the vector random variable $\tilde{\varepsilon}_i \equiv (\tilde{\varepsilon}_i(s))_{s \in S}$;

(b) player i's payoff function is defined by

$$\hat{\pi}_i(\varepsilon_1, \ldots, \varepsilon_n, s) = \pi_i(s_1, \ldots, s_n) + \delta\varepsilon_i(s),$$

each $\varepsilon_i(s)$ representing a typical realization of the corresponding random variable $\tilde{\varepsilon}_i(s)$. (Here, we denote the payoff function of the Bayesian perturbed game by $\hat{\pi}_i(\cdot)$ to differentiate it from that of the original game, denoted by $\pi_i(\cdot)$.)

In this general setup, Harsanyi established the following purification result.

Theorem 6.3 (Harsanyi, 1973): *Let G be a game in strategic form, as described. Then, generically,[92] the following statement holds. Given any Nash equilibrium σ^* for G, there exists a collection of strategy profiles $\{\gamma(\delta)\}_{\delta>0}$ for the family of Bayesian perturbed games $\{G(\delta)\}_{\delta>0}$ such that*

(i) for any δ, $\gamma(\delta)$ is a pure-strategy BNE of the game $G(\delta)$;
(ii) there exist $\{\delta_k\}_{k=1}^{\infty}$ with $\delta_k \to 0$ and $\gamma(\delta_k) \to \gamma^*$ such that for each $i \in N$, $s_i \in S_i$,

$$\Pr\{\gamma_i^*(\varepsilon_i) = s_i\} = \sigma_i^*(s_i).$$

In contrast with the discussion undertaken for the matching-pennies game, Theorem 6.3 underscores the fact that the purification of a mixed-strategy Nash equilibrium does not (generically) presume a specific form for the payoff perturbations, the only requirement being that they should be stochastically independent across players and satisfy some natural regularity conditions. However, again in contrast with our simple example, the desired purification is attained only as a limit result, i.e., for an "infinitesimal" magnitude of the perturbation as $\delta_k \to 0$.

6.6 Forward induction

6.6.1 *Intuitive criterion: motivation*

As explained in Subsection 6.4.3, the concept of signaling equilibrium may be viewed as representing a refinement of BNE that fulfills a twin requirement of perfection and belief consistency. In the latter respect (belief consistency), no restrictions are imposed off the equilibrium path, where any arbitrary assignment of beliefs is viewed as consistent with Bayes rule (inapplicable there). Now, we go beyond such a full discretionary flexibility and ask the following question: What off-equilibrium beliefs are indeed reasonable? In addressing this question, we propose the so-called *intuitive criterion*, which demands that off-equilibrium beliefs should "interpret" any particular deviation in terms of the full signaling content it potentially embodies.

The belief-based refinement reflected by the intuitive criterion is a particular application of the general forward-induction logic described in Chapter 4 – specifically, recall Subsection 4.5.3 and Section 4.8. Before formalizing this

---

[92] Recall Footnote 66 of Chapter 4

criterion precisely in the next subsection, we first provide a motivation of it here within the game represented in Figure 6.2.

Recall that this game has two different pooling SE. In one of them (given by (6.44), (6.46), and (6.48)), both types of player 1 pool by having beer for breakfast. Instead, in the second one (given by (6.45), (6.50), and (6.51)), both types of player 1 pool by having quiche. At the end of Subsection 6.4.4.3, it was informally suggested that the latter SE seems hardly intuitive. We now elaborate on that heuristic discussion and clarify that the quiche-pooling SE is to be regarded as counterintuitive because, if a beer breakfast were to be observed, the corresponding off-equilibrium beliefs ignore reasonable rationalizations of such a deviation.

Suppose that players indeed have "agreed" to play the second pooling SE $\tilde{\gamma}$ but, contrary to its prescription, player 2 observes that player 1 has beer for breakfast. Then, player 2 could undergo the following reasoning:

> "If player 1 were weak, he could not benefit from this deviation (i.e., having beer), *independently* of what my reaction to it might be. Thus, if I discard the possibility that he might have made a mistake, I cannot admit that this deviation is carried out by a player 1 of type w. In this case, therefore, he must be strong and, contrary to what my equilibrium strategy prescribes, I had better not enter into a duel."

In essence, what the above line of reasoning reflects is that the off-equilibrium beliefs supporting the equilibrium strategy of player 2 are not plausible. Thus, if a deviation indeed occurs, player 2 should not be expected to react as induced by those beliefs.

To understand matters from a somewhat different viewpoint, suppose players had the opportunity to (re-)discuss the pattern of equilibrium play *before* any actual choices are made but *after* player 1 is informed of his type. Then, of course, player 2 could argue, along the lines outlined above, that the beliefs underlying strategy $\tilde{\gamma}_2$ are not reasonable. On the other hand, it is also conceivable that player 1 could take the initiative to point to those considerations. For, if player 1 is the strong type (and he is assumed to know it at this communication stage), it will be profitable for him to deviate from equilibrium *if* he is able to convince player 2 of the above argument. In a sense, one may view such a *forward-induction* argument as underlying a kind of implicit "meta-signal," which helps interpret the tangible signal (i.e., the kind of breakfast) sent by the informed party.

Thus, based on the above considerations of forward induction, it appears that the pooling SE $\tilde{\gamma}$ should be ruled out as a robust prediction for the American West game. In contrast, the alternative pooling SE $\hat{\gamma}$ is not affected by analogous problems. It would seem, therefore, that beer is the only breakfast on which both types of player 1 can solidly pool. However, as explained in Chapter 4, forward-induction arguments must always be treated with caution. In particular, they may hide subtle conceptual problems that affect their seemingly solid internal coherence. (Recall, specifically, some of the examples discussed in Subsections 4.5.2 and 4.5.3.) Indeed, we now show that those problems unfortunately arise in the present example.

Suppose that, contrary to what has been suggested, players are set on playing the SE $\tilde{\gamma}$. Further suppose that, at the time of play, both players jointly understand the above forward-induction arguments (and this is commonly known). Then, player 2 should expect that the strong type of player 1 deviates to beer, in which case he must respond by avoiding duel. But, if this is so, how should player 2 interpret the observation that player 1 chooses quiche for breakfast? Naturally, he should be quite confident that his opponent is of the weak type, thus wanting to enter into a duel in this case. Clearly, matters should not stop here. For, if player 1 understands the former argument, he should have beer for breakfast, *independently* of his type. But, in this case, the forward-induction considerations that initiated the reasoning process fall completely apart. That is, the working hypothesis that underlies those considerations leads to a self-contradictory conclusion. What could player 2 conclude therefore, from the observation of a beer breakfast? Anything would seem possible.

The previous discussion should not be interpreted as an unqualified dismissal of forward induction as a useful basis for the analysis of games. Rather, it should be read as a forceful word of caution about the use of these arguments in multistage games with incomplete information. With this pragmatic caveat in mind, we now turn to a more precise formalization of matters in the next subsection. For the sake of focus, the discussion is still restricted to the context of signaling games.

6.6.2 *A formal definition for signaling games*

Consider a signaling game, as introduced in Subsection 6.4.2. Given a belief pattern, μ, we define the *pure best-response correspondence* $\rho(\cdot; \mu) : M \rightrightarrows A$ as follows:

$$\rho(m; \mu) \equiv \arg \max_{a \in A} \sum_{t \in T} v(t, m, a) \mu(m)(t), \quad m \in M.$$

And, for any subset of types $\tilde{T} \subseteq T$, define

$$\zeta\left(m, \tilde{T}\right) \equiv \bigcup_{\{\mu: \sum_{t \in \tilde{T}} \mu(m)(t) = 1\}} \rho(m, \mu), \tag{6.56}$$

that is, the set of player 2's actions that are a best response to *some* belief pattern whose support is included in $\tilde{T}$.

Let $\gamma^* = (\gamma_1^*, \gamma_2^*)$ be an SE and denote by $u^*(t)$ the expected payoff obtained in this equilibrium by player 1 if her type is t.

Definition 6.3: *A signaling equilibrium (γ_1^*, γ_2^*) satisfies the* intuitive criterion *if whenever some $m \in M$ satisfies that $\gamma_1^*(t)(m) = 0$ for every $t \in T$, there is* not *any proper and nonempty subset of the type space $T_0 \subset T$ (i.e., $\emptyset \neq T_0 \neq T$) satisfying the following two conditions:*

> *(i) $\forall t \in T_0, \forall a \in \zeta(m, T), u^*(t) > u(t, m, a)$;*
> *(ii) $\exists t' \in T \backslash T_0 : \forall a \in \zeta(m, T \backslash T_0), u^*(t') < u(t', m, a)$.*

Verbally, the intuitive criterion requires that, given any possible deviation m from the maintained SE γ^*, there must *not* exist a proper subset of types $T_0 \subset T$ ($T_0 \neq T$) that verifies, jointly, the two following conditions:

(i)′ If the type of player 1 belongs to T_0, this player can never benefit from the deviation toward m, *independently* of the induced beliefs and corresponding best response of player 2.

(ii)″ If, in view of (i)′, the beliefs of player 2 after observing m are required to have their support in $T \setminus T_0$, there exists some type $t' \notin T_0$ such that, whatever such beliefs and the corresponding best response, the payoff of t' is *always* improved relative to that induced by equilibrium γ^*.

In line with our former discussion, the motivation for the intuitive criterion should be quite apparent. If a certain SE violates it relative to some message m and a type subset T_0, there exists some type of player 1 who, after deviating to m, may be conceived as implicitly arguing in the following fashion:

"It is clear – says player 1 – that my type is not in T_0. For if it were (and I know it), I have no chance (given that you, player 2, are rational) of improving my payoff over what I can obtain at the contemplated equilibrium. We can therefore agree (since I am rational and you know it) that my type is *not* in T_0, i.e., it is in the complement subset $T \setminus T_0$. Form your beliefs restricted to this latter subset as you wish. Any best response to these beliefs improves my payoff over what I would have obtained with my equilibrium strategy."

If player 2 becomes convinced that a deviation toward m reflects credibly such an implicit signal, her beliefs and induced best response will indeed improve the equilibrium payoff obtained by player 1 under one of her types. Thus, it will lead this type to deviate, destroying the incentives underlying the equilibrium in question.

In a heuristic sense, the intuitive criterion allows player 2 to reevaluate any original off-equilibrium beliefs she might initially have entertained, in response to an "unexpected" deviation by player 1. The logic, therefore, that underlies this criterion is one of a forward-induction nature: the implications of any "past" deviation are projected forward to the determination of "future" beliefs. This logic has been formulated in a general and precise fashion for any finite multistage game by Cho (1987). He has also established the existence of equilibria consistent with forward induction (what he simply calls forward-induction equilibria) for this general context. Since, naturally, every forward-induction equilibrium turns out to satisfy the intuitive criterion, the following existence result then obtains as an immediate corollary.[93]

Theorem 6.4 (Cho, 1987): *Let* $SG \equiv \{\{1,2\}, T, P(\cdot), M, A, u(\cdot), v(\cdot)\}$ *be any (finite) signaling game. The game SG has a SE* $\gamma^* = (\gamma_1^*, \gamma_2^*)$ *satisfying the intuitive criterion.*

---

[93] Recall from Subsection 6.4.3 that a signaling game can be reformulated as a three-player game with Nature.

Summary

In this chapter, we have elaborated on the framework and concepts developed in previous chapters to model the important class of situations in which players do not share complete information about the details of the interaction. Such incomplete-information games arise, for example, when there is an asymmetric distribution of information among the players concerning the underlying payoffs. Key parts of modern economic theory, such as the study of market imperfections or mechanism design, focus on scenarios displaying these features.

The starting point of our discussion has been Harsanyi's model of a Bayesian game. In this context, Nature is attributed the role of specifying all the relevant details of the environment, which are *a priori undetermined*, and then distributing the information to the different agents (possibly in an asymmetric fashion) before they enter into actual play. In essence, a so-called Bayes-Nash equilibrium (BNE) in this setup can be identified with an ordinary Nash equilibrium for the extended game where Nature participates as an additional player. This identification settles a number of important issues. For example, it guarantees that a BNE always exists in a finite Bayesian game, as an immediate corollary of previous results.

By construction, a Bayesian game defines a strategic-form framework and a BNE is a strategic-form notion. They do not lend themselves naturally, therefore, to the study of considerations of credibility, perfectness, or (most importantly) signaling, all of which are at the core of some of the most interesting applications in this context. To model matters more effectively, we have defined the framework of a signaling game that introduces the aforementioned considerations in the simplest possible setting. It merely involves two parties moving in sequence, the first fully informed about the decision of Nature, the second one ignorant of it but perfectly aware of the action chosen by the first agent. The main merit of this stylized framework is that it allows for the explicit introduction of the notion of beliefs and, consequently, provides a natural criterion of perfectness as well as the possibility of useful signaling. A natural adaptation (in fact, a refinement) of the former BNE concept to a signaling context gives rise to the concept of SE. Elaborating on the parallelisms on which we built for BNE, an SE can be simply viewed as a perfect Bayesian equilibrium for an enlarged multistage game with Nature. Again, this settles a number of issues such as that of existence of SE.

The incomplete-information framework presented in this chapter is very rich and versatile as well as often quite subtle. All this will receive ample confirmation in Chapter 7, where we discuss a wide variety of applications. Here, it has been exemplified in two different ways. First, we have seen that it may be used to provide a rather solid basis for the often controversial notion of mixed strategies. Specifically, it can be shown that, generically, any Nash equilibrium in mixed strategies can be "purified," i.e., approximated by a pure-strategy BNE if the game in question is slightly perturbed by some asymmetric incomplete information. Second, we have also briefly illustrated the intricacies displayed by incomplete-information (signaling) games when their analysis is tested against forward-induction arguments. In some cases, this has been shown to yield a series of contradictory implications that are reminiscent of considerations already encountered in Chapter 4.

Exercises

Exercise 6.1: Consider the Bayesian game induced by mechanism A, as formalized in Subsection 6.2.2.3. Compute the expected efficiency losses of its symmetric BNE for each possible value of p (the independent probability that each individual displays a high valuation) and determine how these losses depend on this parameter.

Exercise 6.2: Consider now mechanism B, also described in Subsection 6.2.2.3. Show that every strategy profile satisfying (6.21), (6.22), and (6.24) defines a BNE for the induced game. Is there any other BNE that yields a *different* allocation of resources? Discuss you answer.

Exercise 6.3: Pertaining to mechanism B, address the same questions that were posed in Exercise 6.1 for mechanism A but now concerning its (nonsymmetric) BNE – note that, in this case, equilibria cannot be symmetric because players do not play symmetric roles in the induced game.

Exercise 6.4*: Within the public-good context described in Subsection 6.2.2.3, suppose individual 1 already knows her type (i.e., valuation) and may decide which of the two mechanisms, A or B, to rely on. What will be her decision? And if she does not know yet her valuation but only anticipates that it will be equal to either 30 or zero with respective probabilities p and $1 - p$?

Exercise 6.5: Show that definitions 6.1 and 6.1' are equivalent forms of defining the concept of BNE.

Exercise 6.6: Consider the duopoly signaling game studied in Subsection 6.4.4.2. Show that for (6.32), (6.34), (6.35), and (6.36) to define an SE, the vertical intercept of the (linear) demand function must satisfy $M \leq 5/2$.

Exercise 6.7*: Again consider the duopoly signaling game discussed in Subsection 6.4.4.2. Find an SE when $M > 5/2$.

Exercise 6.8: Recall the American West signaling game described in Subsection 6.4.4.3. Find a pooling SE that embodies (nondegenerate) probabilistic behavior off the equilibrium path.

Exercise 6.9: Consider a variation of the American West signaling game of Subsection 6.4.4.3 where either type of player 1 would rather have her preferred breakfast and enter into a duel than avoid the duel and have her least desired breakfast. Specifically, associate a payoff of 2 to the former possibility and a payoff of 1 to the latter. Find the SE of the new game and compare them with those obtained in the text.

Exercise 6.10: Show that every finite Bayesian game BG, as defined in Section 6.2.1, has a BNE. Also show that every finite signaling game SG, as introduced in Section 6.4.2, has an SE.

Exercise 6.11: Consider a context of duopolistic competition between two firms, $i = 1, 2$, which choose simultaneously the quantities they produce of a certain homogenous product (recall Subsection 3.1.1). The firms confront a linear (inverse) demand function,

$$P(Q) = \max\{10 - Q, 0\},$$

and aim at maximizing their individual profit. The marginal cost of firm 1 is constant and equal to 2, this being common knowledge. The marginal cost of firm 2 is also constant, but its precise magnitude is known only by this same firm. *A priori*, the belief held by firm 1 on the marginal cost of firm 2 is that it attains the value of either 1 or 2 with equal probability. Model the situation as a Bayesian game and compute its BNE.

Exercise 6.12: Consider a duopolistic context as in Exercise 6.11, now with an inverse demand function of the following general linear form:

$$P(Q) = \max\{M - d\, Q, 0\}, \quad M, d > 0. \tag{6.57}$$

The cost functions of each firm are also linear and given by

$$C_i(q_i) = c_i\, q_i \tag{6.58}$$

for some $c_i \in \{c^h, c^l\}$ where $c^h > c^l$ and $c^h < M$. Each firm i is informed of its own cost c_i but ignores that of its competitor. *A priori*, the independent probability with which each firm has a high cost c^h is p, where $0 < p < 1$. Model the situation as a Bayesian game, compute its BNE, and discuss its dependence on p.

Exercise 6.13: Two players, $i = 1, 2$, are involved in the following strategic situation under incomplete information. Player 1 must choose between two actions, A and B; player 2 must choose between two other actions, C and D. The resulting payoffs are as given by either of the two subtables displayed in Table 6.6. Player 1 is informed of which subtable applies. In contrast, player 2 is uninformed, but her beliefs are that both possibilities are equiprobable. Model the situation as a Bayesian game and compute *all* its BNE in pure strategies.

Exercise 6.14: Two firms, $i = 1, 2$, compete à la Bertrand (i.e., simultaneously choose their respective prices) in a market with product differentiation. Both firms display *identical* costs, as determined by a function

$$C(q_i) = c\, q_i,$$

for some given $c > 0$. On the other hand, the demand function confronted by each firm is of the form

$$F_i(p_1, p_2) = \max\{K - p_i + v\, p_j, 0\}, \quad i, j = 1, 2, \quad j = 3 - i,$$

Table 6.6: *Type-dependent payoff tables for a two-player BG*

1 \ 2	C	D	1 \ 2	C	D
A	1, 1	0, 0	A	1, 2	0, 4
B	0, 0	0, 0	B	0, 1	1, 3

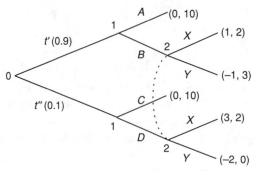

Figure 6.4: An extensive-form game with Nature.

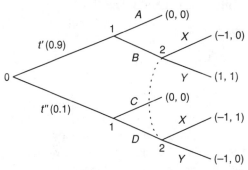

Figure 6.5: An extensive-form game with Nature.

where $v > 0$ is taken to be fixed and common knowledge, while K may display two different values: K^a, K^b $(K^a > K^b)$, with probabilities q and $(1 - q)$, respectively. Suppose firm 1 becomes fully informed of the value of K, whereas firm 2 has no such information at the time it must take its pricing decision. Model the situation as a Bayesian game, compute its BNE, and discuss its dependence on q.

Exercise 6.15: Consider the game represented in Figure 6.4, where Nature (player 0) moves first by selecting t' and t'' with respective probabilities of 0.9 and 0.1. Model it as a signaling game and determine its SE in pure strategies.

Exercise 6.16: Focus on the game represented in Figure 6.5, with the same conventions as in Exercise 6.15. Model it as a signaling game and determine its SE in pure strategies.

Exercise 6.17*: Consider the game represented in Figure 6.6. Model it as a signaling game and verify that there exists an SE inducing an expected payoff vector of $(2, 2)$. Confirm as well that this particular SE satisfies the intuitive criterion (cf. Definition 6.3). Would you nevertheless criticize the "intuitive" basis for it?

Exercise 6.18: Particularize the linear version of a quantity-setting duopoly given in Exercise 6.12 and make $d = c_1 = c_2 = 1$ in (6.57) and (6.58). That is, postulate demand and cost functions given by

$$P(Q) = \max\{M - Q, 0\}, \quad M > 0$$

$$C_i(q_i) = q_i, \qquad i = 1, 2.$$

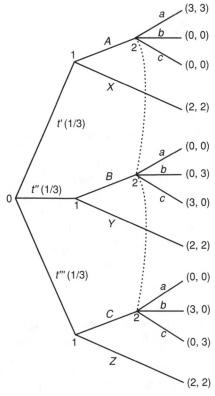

Figure 6.6: An extensive-form game with Nature.

These features of the environment are taken to be common knowledge but not so the precise value of M. *A priori*, M may attain one of two values, $M = 9$ or $M = 25$, both possibilities with identical *ex ante* probability. Only firm 1 is assumed to be informed of the particular realization of M. The decision process is sequential. First, firm 1 chooses its output q_1. Subsequently, after observing firm 1's decision (but yet uninformed of the value of M), firm 2 chooses its own q_2.

1. Model the situation as a signaling game.
2. Find a separating SE (i.e., an equilibrium in which firm 1 selects a different output depending on the information it obtains).
3. Is there any pooling SE? If so, specify it formally.

Exercise 6.19*: Two players are involved in a strategic-form game with payoffs as given in Table 6.7. Introduce explicitly in it a (small) payoff perturbation which purifies, à la Harsanyi, its unique (mixed-strategy) equilibrium.

Exercise 6.20: Two individuals must jointly produce a certain public good. To this end, each of them must contribute some amount of labor input $\ell_i \in [0, 1]$. The productivity of individual 2 is common knowledge, whereas that of individual 1 is private information (i.e., it is known only to herself). *A priori*, this productivity can be either *high* with probability p or *low* with the complementary probability. Both individuals decide simultaneously how much to contribute to the production of the

Table 6.7: *A strategic-form game with a*
unique Nash equilibrium in mixed strategies

1 \ 2	A	B
X	3, 0	2, 4
Y	1, 2	3, 0

public good. Once their decisions have been made, the output produced is as given by the following production function:

$$y(\ell_1, \ell_2) = \begin{cases} \sqrt{2\ell_1 + \ell_2} & \text{if individual 1 is highly productive} \\ \sqrt{\ell_1 + \ell_2} & \text{otherwise.} \end{cases}$$

Given the individuals' labor contributions and the induced production of the public good, each individual $i \in \{1, 2, \}$ obtains a utility (i.e., payoff) given by the function $U_i(\ell_i, y) = (1 - \ell_i) y^2$.

1. Formalize the situation as a Bayesian game.
2. Define and compute its BNE.
3. Determine the effect of an increase of p (the probability that individual 1 be highly productive) on the labor contributions decided at equilibrium.

Exercise 6.21: Consider now a context as described in Exercise 6.20, but with the following variation: individual 1 takes her decision first, then followed by individual 2 who has previously observed 1's decision.

1. Formulate the situation as a signaling game.
2. Is there any separating SE? If so, specify it precisely.
3. Is there any pooling SE? Again, if there is any, specify at least one precisely.

CHAPTER 7

Incomplete information: applications

7.1 Markets (III): signaling in the labor market

In this section, we study a stylized model of signaling in the labor market that is based on the influential work of Spence (1973, 1974). Informally described, the setup is as follows. Two identical firms sell a certain homogeneous good whose price is fixed. The sole dimension in which firms compete concerns the wage they offer to the only worker available. The ability (or competence) of this worker in undertaking the required tasks is known only to herself. However, despite the fact that firms do not observe the worker's ability, they do observe her education level. The key assumption in this respect is that the cost incurred by the worker in attaining her particular level of education depends on her ability. Specifically, it is supposed that this cost is lower the higher is her ability. In this context, the following natural question is posed: Is it possible to have (as an equilibrium) a situation in which the worker, depending on her ability, chooses different education levels? If so, the ability and education level of the worker must be positively correlated, workers with different education levels also obtaining different equilibrium wages. The education level may then be seen as playing the role of a (credible) signal of the underlying ability, even if the education *per se* has no influence on productivity.

To study these issues formally, we formulate a game involving a single worker, two firms, and Nature that displays the following four stages:

1. Nature selects the worker's type, which is identified with her ability θ. This ability can be high ($\theta = H$) or low ($\theta = L$) with respective probabilities p and $(1 - p)$.
2. Having received precise information about the choice of Nature (i.e., knowing her type), the worker selects her education level $\eta \in \mathbb{R}_+$.
3. After observing the level of education chosen by the worker (although *not* her ability), each firm $i = 1, 2$ proposes *simultaneously* a corresponding wage $\omega_i \in \mathbb{R}_+$.
4. In view of the wages offered by each firm, the worker chooses the firm for which to work.

As explained, the problem is interesting only if the education is an activity less costly for the worker with higher ability. Denote by $c(\theta, \eta)$ the cost (or disutility) experienced by a worker of type θ when obtaining education level η. Such a cost is measured in the same monetary terms as the wage, so the net payoff of a worker of type θ when she receives wage ω and chooses education level η is given by

$$u(\theta, \eta, \omega) = \omega - c(\theta, \eta).$$

For our analysis, it is *not* enough to posit that $c(H, \eta) < c(L, \eta)$ for all $\eta > 0$, i.e., the high type experiences a lower cost in attaining any given (positive) level of education. It must also be required that an analogous wedge holds for marginal costs. That is,

$$\forall \eta \geq 0, \quad \frac{\partial c(H, \eta)}{\partial \eta} < \frac{\partial c(L, \eta)}{\partial \eta}, \tag{7.1}$$

where the function $c(\theta, \cdot)$ is taken to be twice continuously differentiable for each θ. For technical convenience, it is also assumed that the function $c(\theta, \cdot)$ is strictly convex, i.e.,

$$\forall \eta \geq 0, \quad \frac{\partial^2 c(\theta, \eta)}{\partial \eta^2} > 0.$$

The ability and education level of the worker jointly determine her productivity in the firm. This productivity is given (also in monetary terms) by a certain function, $f(\theta, \eta)$, that is supposed concave in η. Naturally, we also posit that

$$\forall \eta \geq 0, \quad f(H, \eta) > f(L, \eta),$$

which simply embodies the idea that, given the same education for both types, the one with higher ability displays a larger productivity. However, it is worth stressing at this point that it is *not* necessary to require that the education should strictly improve the worker's productivity. Thus, in line with our motivation for the model, one may have education act as a *pure* signaling device. That is, even allowing for the (admittedly extreme) possibility that the education might be irrelevant for production (that is, even if $f(\theta, \eta)$ were constant in η), there could well be equilibria where, by virtue of the signaling role of education, each type of worker chooses a different level of it. In those extreme cases, therefore, one can be certain that the economy invests too much in education (which would be costly but unproductive), just because of the desire of high-ability workers to signal their type.

As a *first step* in the analysis and a useful benchmark for the ensuing discussion, we start by studying the context where the ability of the worker is precisely known by both firms. Next, we compare such a complete-information setup with that obtained in the original one with incomplete information where firms are taken to be uninformed of the worker's ability.

Thus, let us start by modifying stage (3) above, assuming instead that firms become at that point *perfectly informed* of whether the worker they face has a high or low ability. In other words, the original game is transformed into one in which all participants are perfectly (i.e., symmetrically) informed of prior choices by all players (in particular, that of Nature). Under those circumstances, once the worker has chosen her education level η in the second stage of the game, *both* firms know her productivity $f(\theta, \eta)$ in the third stage. Consequently, a situation of acute wage competition arises, where firms must offer (at equilibrium) identical wages

$\omega_1 = \omega_2 = \omega = f(\theta, \eta)$. The reason for this should be clear. Once the wages are set, the worker of course decides (in the fourth stage) to work for the firm that offers the highest wage. Firm interaction in the third stage then becomes analogous to that undergone by a Bertrand duopoly producing a homogenous good (recall Section 3.1.2). Their competition exerts an extreme upward pressure on the wage (polar to the downward pressure on prices displayed by Bertrand competition), which shrinks to zero the share of the available surplus enjoyed by the firms. That is, all that surplus (at that point, the value of production) is appropriated by the worker as a consequence of the aggressive interfirm competition on wages.

Anticipating that the outcome in the third stage will be as described, the worker must select in the second stage the education level that solves the following problem:

$$\textbf{Max} \quad f(\theta, \eta) - c(\theta, \eta) \tag{7.2}$$
$$\eta$$

whose solution (assumed unique) is denoted by $\eta^*(\theta)$, a function of θ. This function defines the optimal strategy for the worker prescribed by the unique subgame-perfect equilibrium of the complete-information version of the game. The corresponding wage received, which coincides with its productivity $f(\theta, \eta^*(\theta))$, is denoted by $\omega^*(\theta)$. Overall, the resource allocation thus induced is obviously efficient, as illustrated in Figure 7.1.

Let us now consider the original game with incomplete information described in (1)–(4). Our objective is to find its signaling equilibria, with the concept introduced in Definition 6.2 being adapted in the natural fashion to the present scenario. The main modification concerns the fact that, unlike what was considered in Chapter 6, the game now involves *two* uninformed agents (the firms) that act simultaneously

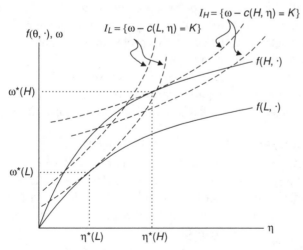

Figure 7.1: Separation of types under complete information. The optimal decision by a worker of type $\theta \in \{H, L\}$ is depicted as a tangency point between her respective "production function" $f(\theta, \cdot)$ and a corresponding "indifference curve" I_θ. The latter is obtained as an education–wage locus yielding a constant payoff K (specific for each indifference curve).

once they have observed the message (the education level) of the informed party.[94] However, by treating both firms symmetrically (in wage offers as well as beliefs), the analysis can be conducted as if there were only one uninformed firm whose action must always be to set a wage equal to the worker's expected productivity. (Here, we rely on the argument already used under complete information: since firms are involved in "Bertrand-like competition" in wages, their offer to the worker must grant her the whole expected surplus.) With these considerations in mind, a *signaling equilibrium* (SE) for the present scenario is identified with a tuple $[(\eta(\theta))_{\theta=H,L}, (\omega(\eta))_{\eta\geq0}]$ so that the following two requirements are satisfied:

(a) The worker's strategy $(\eta(\theta))_{\theta=H,L}$ is optimal, given the anticipated wage schedule $(\omega(\eta))_{\eta\geq0}$ to be used by the firms, as a function of the worker's education level.

(b) There exists some pattern of firms' beliefs $(\mu(\eta))_{\eta\geq0}$ about the worker's type that is statistically consistent (in the sense explained for Definition 6.2) with the worker's strategy, and such that for all education levels $\eta \geq 0$,

$$\omega(\eta) = \mu(\eta)(L) f(L, \eta) + \mu(\eta)(H) f(H, \eta);$$

i.e., the wage offered by firms coincides with the expected productivity of the worker.

In general, the incomplete-information model will be seen to generate a wide range of SE. It will also be shown, however, that the refinement afforded by the so-called intuitive criterion (recall Definition 6.3) is very effective in tackling this equilibrium multiplicity. For the sake of focus, we start our discussion by centering on just three kinds of equilibria: pooling, separating, and hybrid.

- In the *pooling equilibria*, the firms are fully unable to discriminate whether the worker is of a high or low type because both types "pool" at the same education level. Therefore, after observing that common education level, the firms maintain their initial subjective probabilities, p and $(1 - p)$, on the worker being of a high or low type.
- In the *separating equilibria*, each type of worker selects a different education level. Therefore, once her particular educational choice is observed, the firms may infer exactly the worker's ability, i.e., these equilibria "separate" types.
- Finally, in the *hybrid equilibria*, one of the types chooses a certain education level deterministically, whereas the other type plays randomly and associates to that education level only a positive (less than full) probability. Thus, *ex post*, firms may either be able to learn the worker type or simply be in a position to revise (nondrastically) the prior type probabilities, i.e., both separation and pooling may obtain.

---

[94] Another difference pertains to the fact that the action space in the present case displays the cardinality of the continuum. This raises some technical issues concerning the formulation of mixed strategies, akin to those discussed in Section 2.4. Here, we abstract from these issues by restricting our attention to either pure strategies or simple mixed strategies with a finite support.

We start our discussion of SE with those of the pooling variety. By definition, these equilibria have both types choose a common education level, say

$$\eta_0 = \eta(H) = \eta(L). \tag{7.3}$$

Then, concerning the associated beliefs, we must have

$$\mu(\eta_0)(H) = p \tag{7.4}$$

because, after observing η_0, the posterior probabilities are to coincide with the prior ones (i.e., nothing new is learned by that observation). Therefore, the wage ω_0 offered by both firms at equilibrium has to satisfy

$$\omega_0 = pf(H, \eta_0) + (1 - p) f(L, \eta_0)$$

by virtue of the "Bertrand-like competition" thus induced – recall the analogous situation arising in the benchmark setup with complete information.

To close the specification of the equilibrium, one still must indicate the wages that would be offered out of equilibrium, i.e., for education levels $\eta \neq \eta_0$. These wage offers must satisfy two requirements.

1. They must deter worker's deviations from equilibrium, thus rendering it optimal to abide by the contemplated pooling decision, $\eta(\theta) = \eta_0$ for each $\theta = H, L$.
2. They must be supported by some suitable firms' beliefs about the worker's type.

An extreme and direct way of trying to fulfill the previous two requirements is to posit that firms display the following off-equilibrium beliefs:

$$\mu(\eta)(H) = 0 \quad \text{if } \eta \neq \eta_0. \tag{7.5}$$

Thus, any education level different from η_0 (even if it is larger) is conceived to be chosen by the worker of type L. Admittedly, this is a somewhat artificial choice of beliefs, but there is nothing in the concept of SE that rules them out (see Exercise 7.4). With these beliefs, the contingent pattern of wage offers meeting the second requirement is

$$\omega(\eta_0) = \omega_0; \tag{7.6}$$

$$\omega(\eta) = f(L, \eta), \quad \eta \neq \eta_0. \tag{7.7}$$

And then, given such a strategy by the firms, the equilibrium conditions for each worker type $\theta \in \{H, L\}$ that embody the first of the above requirements are as follows:

$$\forall \eta \geq 0, \quad \omega_0 - c(H, \eta_0) \geq f(L, \eta) - c(H, \eta)$$

$$\forall \eta \geq 0, \quad \omega_0 - c(L, \eta_0) \geq f(L, \eta) - c(L, \eta).$$

The first inequality expresses the idea that the worker of type H should not find it profitable to deviate from η_0. The second one embodies a similar condition for the worker of type L. If both are verified, (7.3), (7.6)–(7.7) define a pooling SE

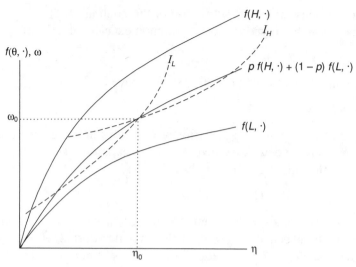

Figure 7.2: Pooling equilibrium.

supported by beliefs given by (7.4) and (7.5). By way of illustration, Figure 7.2 depicts a particular (graphical) specification of the underlying data of the problem (i.e., production functions, worker's indifference curves and prior probabilities) where the above listed conditions for a pooling SE are satisfied.

Figure 7.2 illustrates that, in general, the game should be expected to allow for an ample scope of different pooling equilibria (with correspondingly different pooling education levels). For example, it is clear that, given the concrete scenario represented in this figure, one may construct different pooling equilibria for education levels above or below η_0. However, it is worth noting as well that, if the underlying scenario were different (see Exercise 7.1), one could find instead that *no* equilibrium of the pooling kind exists.

Next, we turn to separating equilibria. First, let us focus on the case in which the underlying data of the environment are such that the following condition holds:

$$f(L, \eta^*(L)) - c(L, \eta^*(L)) \geq f(H, \eta^*(H)) - c(L, \eta^*(H)), \qquad (7.8)$$

with $\eta^*(L)$ and $\eta^*(H)$ denoting the (unique) solutions of the optimization problem (7.2). The above condition implies that if a low-type worker were presented with the two alternative education-wage pairs that *would* materialize under complete information for each type, i.e., $[\eta^*(H), f(H, \eta^*(H))]$ and $[\eta^*(L), f(L, \eta^*(L))]$, she would (weakly) prefer the latter. This case is often described as one where (if complete information prevailed) the worker of a low ability would not "envy" the outcome attained by the high type. Thus, even though the low type would certainly obtain a higher salary in the latter case, the higher education level also required would be too high to be judged worthwhile by the low type. Under these circumstances, there is an obvious separating equilibrium $[\eta(L), \eta(H), \omega(\cdot)]$

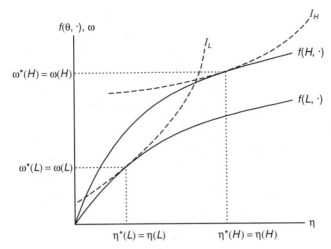

Figure 7.3: Separating equilibrium under "no envy."

in which

$$\eta(\theta) = \eta^*(\theta) \quad (\theta = H, L),$$
$$\omega(\eta) = f(L, \eta) \quad \text{if } \eta < \eta^*(H), \qquad\qquad (7.9)$$
$$\omega(\eta) = f(H, \eta) \quad \text{if } \eta \geq \eta^*(H),$$

that may be supported by the following beliefs:

$$\mu(\eta)(H) = 0 \quad \text{if } \eta < \eta^*(H);$$
$$\mu(\eta)(H) = 1 \quad \text{if } \eta \geq \eta^*(H).$$

In this equilibrium, a worker of type θ receives the wage $\omega(\theta) \equiv f(\theta, \eta(\theta)) = \omega^*(\theta)$, the efficient allocation of resources thus induced being the same as that obtained under complete information. Figure 7.3 illustrates the situation (to be compared with Figure 7.1).

Concerning intertype separation at equilibrium, the most interesting situation arises when condition (7.8) does *not* apply. Then, a pattern of behavior such as the one described by (7.9) cannot define an equilibrium: the worker of type L would prefer to choose the education level assigned to type H (thus experiencing a cost increase $c(L, \eta^*(H)) - c(L, \eta^*(L))$ so as to obtain a higher wage equal to $\omega(H) = f(H, \eta^*(H))$. Of course, the anticipation of this low-type behavior on the part of firms would make them no longer offer the wage $\omega(H)$ after observing $\eta^*(H)$ – they would offer instead $\omega' = [(1 - p)f(L, \eta^*(H)) + pf(H, \eta^*(H))]$ – thus leading to the collapse of the tentative equilibrium configuration.

It follows, therefore, that if under *complete* information the low-ability worker would "envy" that of high ability, the latter type has to incur some "separating cost" to be credibly singled out under *incomplete* information. In particular, the high type must increase her education level above $\eta^*(H)$ if she wants to make sure the low

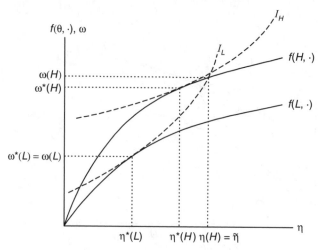

Figure 7.4: Separating equilibrium under "envy."

type does not want to imitate him. The *minimum* education $\tilde{\eta}$ that achieves this state of affairs is the one that satisfies the following equality:

$$f(L, \eta^*(L)) - c(L, \eta^*(L)) = f(H, \tilde{\eta}) - c(L, \tilde{\eta}). \tag{7.10}$$

That is, intertype separation requires that a worker of type H selects at least that education level, $\tilde{\eta}$, such that even if firms then pay the best wage consistent with it (i.e., $f(H, \tilde{\eta})$), the low-ability worker should judge this high wage insufficient to more than strictly offset the large cost entailed (larger for her, of course, than for the high type).

Based on the value $\tilde{\eta}$ determined by (7.10), one can construct the following separating equilibrium for the present "envy-laden" case:

$$\begin{aligned}
\eta(L) &= \eta^*(L) \\
\eta(H) &= \tilde{\eta} \\
\omega(\eta) &= f(L, \eta) \quad \text{if } \eta < \tilde{\eta} \\
\omega(\eta) &= f(H, \eta) \quad \text{if } \eta \geq \tilde{\eta}
\end{aligned} \tag{7.11}$$

that can be supported by the following beliefs:

$$\begin{aligned}
\mu(\eta)(H) &= 0 \quad \text{if } \eta < \tilde{\eta} \\
\mu(\eta)(H) &= 1 \quad \text{if } \eta \geq \tilde{\eta}.
\end{aligned} \tag{7.12}$$

In this separating equilibrium, the worker of type L chooses her efficient education $\eta^*(L)$, but the one of type H distorts upward her decision ($\tilde{\eta} > \eta^*(H)$) to deter being mimicked by type L. The wages $\omega(L)$ and $\omega(H)$ received by each type at equilibrium fully reflect their respective productivities, but the induced allocation is clearly inefficient.[95] Specifically, the high type overeducates herself as the only way to separate herself from the low type. Figure 7.4 illustrates graphically the situation. Clearly, similar considerations will generally allow other education

---

[95] However, if we were to take into account the informational constraints (i.e., the asymmetry of information) displayed by the problem at hand, this separating equilibrium need not be "constrained inefficient."

levels $\eta(H) > \tilde{\eta}$ to be supported as well through analogous separating equilibria (cf. Exercise 7.6).

We now proceed with a case that is a hybrid of the previous two. In particular, we are interested in equilibria in which one of the worker types does not play in a deterministic fashion but rather randomizes (i.e., plays a mixed action) between an education level that separates her from the other type and another level that does not. Out of the many kinds of such hybrid equilibria that could be considered, let us simply illustrate matters and restrict to a very particular class of them. In this class, whereas the worker of type H always selects a fixed education level, the low type randomizes between the education level chosen by the high type and some alternative one.

Thus, on the one hand, with some probability, say $\alpha > 0$, the type L is taken to choose a differentiated (type-specific) education level $\check{\eta}$, which separates itself from type H. Since, after observing such $\check{\eta}$, the firms become certain the worker has a low ability, they must then offer a low-productivity wage $\omega(\check{\eta}) = f(L, \check{\eta})$. Consequently, at equilibrium, it is clear that we must have $\check{\eta} = \eta^*(L)$. That is, if the low type separates itself, it must do so through its *optimal* education level under *complete information*.

On the other hand, with a complementary probability $(1 - \alpha) > 0$, the worker of type L pools with the high type. Denote by $\hat{\eta}$ the education level chosen in this case. It follows that $\omega(\hat{\eta}) < f(H, \hat{\eta})$, because after the firms observe $\hat{\eta}$ their subjective probability $\mu(\hat{\eta})(H)$ of facing a worker of type H must be lower than 1. More specifically, Bayes rule indicates that

$$\mu(\hat{\eta})(H) = \frac{p}{p + (1 - p)(1 - \alpha)} \equiv q. \tag{7.13}$$

Correspondingly, the equilibrium wage that will be offered by the firms when the worker displays an education level $\hat{\eta}$ is given by

$$\omega(\hat{\eta}) = q\, f(H, \hat{\eta}) + (1 - q)\, f(L, \hat{\eta}), \tag{7.14}$$

which is indeed lower than $f(H, \hat{\eta})$.

As we know from the usual payoff-indifference condition that must be fulfilled by equilibrium mixed strategies, the payoffs expected by a low-type worker from either $\eta^*(L)$ and $\hat{\eta}$ have to coincide; that is,

$$\omega(\hat{\eta}) - c(L, \hat{\eta}) = f(L, \eta^*(L)) - c(L, \eta^*(L)). \tag{7.15}$$

Then, by simply introducing (7.14) in (7.15), we can readily find the precise value of $\hat{\eta}$ (associated with q, that is itself determined by p and α through (7.13)) that is consistent with a hybrid equilibrium of the contemplated kind. Of course, such an education level $\hat{\eta}$ must also satisfy the following further conditions

$$\forall \eta \geq 0, \quad \omega(\hat{\eta}) - c(L, \hat{\eta}) \geq \omega(\eta) - c(L, \eta) \tag{7.16}$$

$$\forall \eta \geq 0, \quad \omega(\hat{\eta}) - c(H, \hat{\eta}) \geq \omega(\eta) - c(H, \eta), \tag{7.17}$$

where $\omega(\eta)$ is the contingent wage pattern induced by firms' strategies.

As in former cases, the most direct way of trying to meet the incentive conditions (7.16) and (7.17) is to postulate that, off-equilibrium (i.e., whenever $\eta \notin \{\eta^*(L), \hat{\eta}\}$), the associated wage coincides with the productivity of the low-type worker. This leads to a hybrid equilibrium of the following form:

$$\eta(H) = \hat{\eta};$$

$$\eta(L) = \begin{cases} \eta^*(L) & \text{with probability } \alpha \\ \hat{\eta} & \text{with probability } (1 - \alpha) \end{cases}$$

$$\omega(\eta) = q f(H, \eta) + (1 - q) f(L, \eta) \quad \text{if } \eta = \hat{\eta}$$

$$\omega(\eta) = f(L, \eta) \quad \text{if } \eta \neq \hat{\eta}$$

that can be supported, for example, by the following beliefs:

$$\mu(\eta)(H) = q, \quad \text{if } \eta = \hat{\eta}$$

$$\mu(\eta)(H) = 0, \quad \text{if } \eta \neq \hat{\eta}.$$

Thus, we simply posit the extreme belief pattern by which *any* education level different from $\hat{\eta}$ is interpreted by the firms as chosen by a low-ability worker. Figure 7.5 illustrates conditions under which such a hybrid equilibrium exists.

We end our discussion of the model by showing that, when the intuitive criterion (cf. Section 6.6) is applied to select among the rich variety of SE found above for the context with envy, only one of them meets this criterion. The one selected is the separating equilibrium given by (7.11), which involves the minimum signaling distortion. We show, therefore, that an "intuitive" belief refinement is sharply effective in tackling the problem of equilibrium multiplicity otherwise arising in the model.

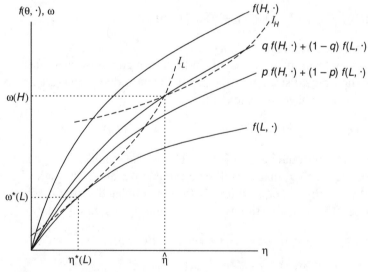

Figure 7.5: Hybrid equilibrium.

To arrive at this conclusion, we dismiss in turn each of the alternative equilibria that are different from the one mentioned. First, let us focus on any separating equilibrium whose associated education level for the high type, $\eta(H)$, satisfies $\eta(H) > \tilde{\eta}$, where $\tilde{\eta}$ is given by (7.10). This equilibrium must embody a contingent (off-equilibrium) pattern of wage offers satisfying

$$\tilde{\eta} < \eta < \eta(H) \Rightarrow \omega(\eta) < f(H, \eta). \tag{7.18}$$

For, if it were the case that

$$\exists \check{\eta} \in (\tilde{\eta}, \eta(H)) : \omega(\check{\eta}) = f(H, \check{\eta}),$$

then, the high-ability worker would find it profitable to deviate from the equilibrium by choosing education level $\check{\eta}$.

However, the wage offers described in (7.18) are inconsistent with the intuitive criterion. Any education level $\eta > \tilde{\eta}$ is dominated for type L by $\eta^*(L)$, regardless of the ensuing wage that conceivably could be offered by the firms. In other words, not even the maximum wage the firms would offer under the assumption that the worker is of type H could compensate a low type for an education level higher than $\tilde{\eta}$. Thus, off-equilibrium beliefs for $\eta \in (\tilde{\eta}, \eta(H))$ should satisfy

$$\mu(\eta)(H) = 1$$

and, therefore, the corresponding wage offer should be

$$\omega(\eta) = f(H, \eta).$$

This contradicts (7.18) and thus refutes that an equilibrium of the kind suggested can be consistent with the intuitive criterion.

Somewhat more generally, we now show that an argument analogous to the one just explained implies that, if $\pi(H)$ stands for the payoff earned by a high-ability worker at equilibrium, consistence with the intuitive criterion requires

$$\pi(H) \geq f(H, \tilde{\eta}) - c(H, \tilde{\eta}). \tag{7.19}$$

For, if the above inequality did not hold, type H could deviate toward some $\eta' > \tilde{\eta}$ satisfying

$$f(H, \eta') - c(H, \eta') > \pi(H) \tag{7.20}$$

$$f(H, \eta') - c(L, \eta') < f(L, \eta^*(L)) - c(L, \eta^*(L)). \tag{7.21}$$

But then, if $\pi(L)$ denotes the equilibrium payoff earned by the low type, we should have

$$\pi(L) \geq f(L, \eta^*(L)) - c(L, \eta^*(L))$$

that, in view of (7.21), implies

$$\pi(L) > f(H, \eta') - c(L, \eta'). \tag{7.22}$$

Thus, if the intuitive criterion is to be met, the wage offered by firms after observing η' must be

$$\omega(\eta') = f(H, \eta')$$

because, by (7.22), the corresponding beliefs have to satisfy

$$\mu(\eta')(L) = 0$$

or, equivalently,

$$\mu(\eta')(H) = 1.$$

However, such a wage offer for η' is incompatible with equilibrium since, from (7.20), we have

$$\omega(\eta') - c(H, \eta') > \pi(H),$$

and therefore the high-type worker would gain by deviating toward η'.

Building on the former considerations, we next argue that *any* SE of the pooling or hybrid kind can also be discarded by invoking the intuitive criterion. First, suppose p is relatively low so that the indifference curve of type H that goes through the point $(\tilde{\eta}, f(H, \tilde{\eta}))$ is above the locus of points

$$\{(\eta, \omega) : \omega = p f(H, \eta) + (1 - p) f(L, \eta)\}$$

where the wage associated with each education level equals the expected productivity based on the prior type probabilities – refer to Figure 7.6 for an illustration of this situation.

In this case, there can be *no* intuitive pooling equilibrium because the education–wage pair (η_0, ω_0) where pooling could take place has to fulfill

$$pf(H, \eta_0) + (1 - p) f(L, \eta_0) = \omega_0.$$

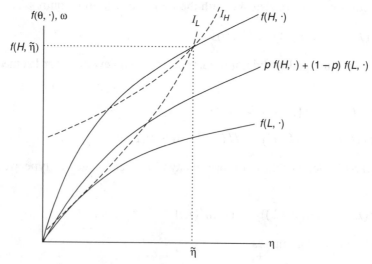

Figure 7.6: Impossibility of an *intuitive* pooling equilibrium, low p.

Therefore, condition (7.19) must be violated since the indifference curve I_H (cf. Figure 7.6) does not intersect the expected-productivity locus given by the function $pf(H, \cdot) + (1 - p)f(L, \cdot)$. Clearly, the same applies to those hybrid equilibria where the high-ability worker mixes over her education choice. For, in this case, the equilibrium wage associated with the common education level chosen by both types with positive probability must be given by the function $qf(H, \eta) + (1 - q)f(L, \eta)$, for some $q < p$. And, of course, since

$$qf(H, \eta) + (1 - q)f(L, \eta) < pf(H, \eta) + (1 - p)f(L, \eta)$$

for all η, condition (7.19) is violated *a fortiori*.

Consider now the alternative hybrid equilibria where the worker of type L randomizes between $\eta^*(L)$ and some alternative $\hat{\eta}$ (which is the education level chosen deterministically by the high-type H). Then, by the condition of payoff indifference displayed by equilibrium mixed strategies, we must have

$$f(L, \eta^*(L)) - c(L, \eta^*(L)) = \hat{\omega} - c(L, \hat{\eta}),$$

where

$$\hat{\omega} = rf(H, \hat{\eta}) + (1 - r)f(L, \hat{\eta})$$

for some suitable posterior probability $r < 1$. Since, from the definition of $\tilde{\eta}$, it follows that

$$f(L, \eta^*(L)) - c(L, \eta^*(L)) = f(H, \tilde{\eta}) - c(L, \tilde{\eta}),$$

the single-crossing assumption[96] embodied by (7.1) implies

$$\hat{\omega} - c(H, \hat{\eta}) = \pi(H) < f(H, \tilde{\eta}) - c(H, \tilde{\eta})$$

that again amounts to a violation of (7.19).

Finally, let us rule out that either a pooling or a hybrid equilibrium can satisfy the intuitive criterion when p is relatively high. Consider, for example, a situation as illustrated in Figure 7.7, where the curve given by $pf(H, \cdot) + (1 - p)f(L, \cdot)$ intersects the indifference curve of type H that passes through the point $(\tilde{\eta}, f(H, \tilde{\eta}))$.

In this context, the intuitive criterion is inconsistent with pooling equilibria. To see this, consider any such equilibrium and let η_0 be the education level chosen by both types at equilibrium. Then, there always exist a range of education levels (i.e., those between η' and η'' in Figure 7.7) such that, if the worker of type H were to choose some $\hat{\eta}$ in this range (i.e., $\eta' < \hat{\eta} < \eta''$), she can "credibly separate" herself from type L through the implicit argument underlying the intuitive criterion. Specifically, this argument builds on the following threefold considerations:

1. The worker of type L would always obtain a payoff lower than in equilibrium if she chose an education level $\hat{\eta} \in (\eta', \eta'')$, even if the firms were to

---

[96] The requirement that the *marginal* cost of the high type is uniformly below that of the low type is often conceived as a "single-crossing condition" because it implies that any two indifference curves corresponding to different types can never cross more than once.

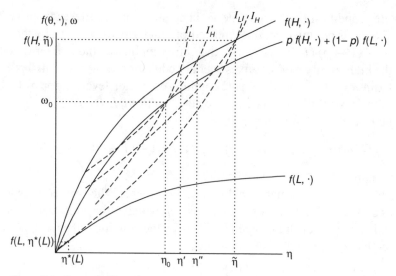

Figure 7.7: Impossibility of an *intuitive* pooling equilibrium, high p.

consider her as being of the high type with probability one (i.e., in the best possible circumstances).

2. In view of the previous point, the firms' beliefs after observing $\hat{\eta}$ should be $\mu(\hat{\eta})(H) = 1$ and the corresponding wage offer $\hat{\omega} = f(H, \hat{\eta})$.

3. If the firms issue the wage offer $\hat{\omega} = f(H, \hat{\eta})$ in response to $\hat{\eta}$, the high-ability worker may obtain a payoff equal to $\hat{\omega} - c(H, \hat{\eta})$ by choosing $\hat{\eta}$, which is higher than the equilibrium payoff $\omega_0 - c(H, \eta_0)$.

The above considerations show that the intuitive criterion rules out any pooling equilibrium in the present context (p high). On the other hand, concerning hybrid equilibria in either of its two forms (i.e., either when the high or the low type mixes) to prove an analogous conclusion is the object of Exercise 7.10. Thus, summing up our discussion for the different scenarios considered, we conclude that, by relying on the intuitive criterion to refine out-of-equilibrium beliefs, only the separating SE given by (7.11) remains. In a sense, this equilibrium is the one that, both heuristically as well as theoretically, would seem to be the most appealing. In it, the worker takes full advantage of the signaling (i.e., separating) potential that the setup avails, exploiting this potential in the most cost-effective manner.[97]

7.2   Markets (IV): insurance markets and adverse selection*

In this section, we present a model that bears some similarities to the signaling context studied in Section 7.1, although it also displays important differences. The theoretical setup was originally proposed by Rotschild and Stiglitz (1976) to study

[97] Nevertheless, note that it may well be possible (as it happens, for example, in the context depicted in Figure 7.7) that the *two* types of worker would prefer to play a (nonintuitive) equilibrium where no separation occurs. Such an equilibrium, however, would not be robust in the sense of permitting some deviations from it which would benefit – if beliefs are refined in the "intuitive" manner – to one of the two types.

interfirm competition in the insurance market when the insurance-providing firms only have incomplete (asymmetric) information over the underlying risk conditions faced by the different individuals. The fact that agents who are subject to heterogenous risk contingencies may nevertheless buy the (same) insurance policy "intended" for only one of them (thus affecting the profit of the insurance companies offering that policy) raises important issues of so-called *adverse selection*. As we shall see, the market implications of this phenomenon may be quite negative, affecting in particular the possibility of sustaining a suitable range of insurance contracts at equilibrium.

Let there be just two insurance firms and one individual, the latter facing the possibility of an accident. This accident occurs with a certain exogenous probability that is determined by the specific risk circumstances of the individual in question. In contrast with the setup considered in Section 7.1, here we suppose the firms are those that start the game. They do so by deciding (simultaneously) on a respective menu of contracts offered to the individual. Each of these contracts is a different insurance policy (α, β) specifying the premium $\alpha \in \mathbb{R}_+$ to be paid by the individual in case the accident does *not* take place (a state that is labeled ξ_1) in exchange for the *net* compensation $\beta \in \mathbb{R}_+$ that would be paid by the insurance company in case the accident does occur (a state labeled ξ_2). After observing the range of contracts offered by the firms, the individual is taken to choose that particular one that best suits her personal circumstances (e.g., her accident probability). Naturally, the individual may decide as well to remain uninsured if none of the contracts being offered proves advantageous, given her specific risk characteristics. As mentioned, these characteristics are assumed to be known only by the individual, although the *prior* probabilities that determine them *ex ante* are supposed to be commonly known by everyone (in particular, by the insurance companies).

More formally, the structure of the game between the firms and the individual (with the usual addition of Nature) may be decomposed into the following stages:

(i) Nature selects the type θ of the individual, i.e., her risk level, that can be high ($\theta = H$) or low ($\theta = L$). The *prior* probabilities of each case are p and $(1 - p)$, respectively.

(ii) Without knowing the individual's type, each firm $i = 1, 2$ offers simultaneously a finite menu of insurance contracts $J_i \equiv \{(\alpha_{ik}, \beta_{ik})\}_{k=1}^{r_i} \subset \mathbb{R}^2$, each of them with the interpretation described above.

(iii) The individual becomes informed of her type (i.e., Nature's choice) and then selects at most one (possibly none) of the contracts offered by the firms.

As customary, it will be assumed that the individual's preferences are representable by a von Neumann-Morgenstern utility $U(\cdot)$. This function is defined over a space of lotteries of the form $L = (\rho, W_1, W_2)$, where

- $\rho \in [0, 1]$ is the accident probability;
- W_1 is the wealth in state ξ_1 (when the accident does not happen);
- W_2 is the wealth in state ξ_2 (when the accident occurs).

For any lottery L with the indicated format, the individual's expected utility is computed as follows:

$$U(L) = (1 - \rho)\, V(W_1) + \rho\, V(W_2), \tag{7.23}$$

where $V : \mathbb{R}_+ \to \mathbb{R}$ is the underlying elementary utility function that is defined over (deterministic) levels of wealth. It will be postulated that $V(\cdot)$ is differentiable and strictly concave, i.e., the individual is assumed to be risk averse.[98]

Let $\hat{W}_1$ and $\hat{W}_2$ ($\hat{W}_1 > \hat{W}_2$) stand for the wealth levels respectively obtained in the states ξ_1 and ξ_2 when the individual chooses *no* insurance. On the other hand, denote by ρ^H and ρ^L ($\rho^H > \rho^L$) the accident probabilities of each of the two types, H and L. Once these parameters of the model are specified, the setup described in (i)–(iii) defines a multistage Bayesian game in which the two insurance firms and the sole individual are the genuine players and Nature is the first fictitious mover. The payoffs for the firms are identified with their respective expected profits whereas the payoff for the individual is given by her expected utility, as specified in (7.23).

In this game, a strategy for each firm $i = 1, 2$ consists of the specification of a contract menu $J_i = \{(\alpha_{ik}, \beta_{ik})\}_{k=1}^{r_i}$ that is offered to the individual. The set of all such possible menus is denoted by $\mathcal{J}$. On the other hand, a strategy for the individual is a type-contingent prescription of what contract to choose among those offered by the firms. To be precise, let Φ represent the set of decision rules of the form

$$\phi : \mathcal{J} \times \mathcal{J} \to \mathbb{R}^2 \cup \{\otimes\},$$

where $\otimes$ simply stands for the choice of remaining uninsured and, for each pair of contract menus offered by the firms, $(J_1, J_2) \in \mathcal{J} \times \mathcal{J}$, we have $\phi(J_1, J_2) \in J_1 \cup J_2 \cup \{\otimes\}$ – that is, the choice $\phi(J_1, J_2)$ is either one of the contracts offered or the no-insurance possibility. With this notation in hand, a strategy for the individual may be formalized as a mapping

$$\gamma : T \to \Phi$$

with the interpretation that, for each $\theta \in T \equiv \{H, L\}$, $\gamma(\theta)$ is the decision rule followed by the individual of type θ.

Our analysis focuses on the weak perfect Bayesian equilibria (WPBE) of the proposed game with Nature (recall Definition 4.2). Thus, considering only the behavior of the genuine players (the firms and the individual), a WPBE may be identified with Bayes-Nash equilibrium strategies (J_1^*, J_2^*, γ^*) satisfying the following additional requirement: for each $\theta \in T$, $\gamma^*(\theta)$ is a decision rule ϕ that leads to the selection of an optimal contract for *any* pair of menus (J_1, J_2), i.e., *not only* for the equilibrium menus (J_1^*, J_2^*). Note that, in contrast with the signaling setup studied in Section 7.1, a WPBE for the present context does not depend on a suitable specification of out-of-equilibrium beliefs. This is because the uninformed players (the insurance companies) move first in the game and thus have no prior observations on the basis of which to refine their initial information. At the time of their decision, therefore,

---

[98] Thus, heuristically, the individual always prefers to exchange some expected payoff for more certainty (cf. Varian, 1992, Section 11.5).

the firms' beliefs over the individual's type must coincide with those given by the exogenous prior probabilities $(p, 1 - p)$.

We find it useful to restrict our attention to *pure-strategy* WPBE, referred to henceforth by the acronym PWPBE. Such a restriction will not only simplify matters substantially, it will also play a crucial role in our subsequent analysis – for example, it is at the basis of the nonexistence problems that are discussed at some length below.

We start with a preliminary conclusion that will later prove very useful in our discussion of the model: at *any* PWPBE, both firms must obtain zero profits. To confirm this general claim suppose, to the contrary, that there were some PWPBE where firms obtained *aggregate* profits $\hat{\pi} > 0$. (Since each firm can always guarantee for itself nonnegative profits, if some firm earns nonzero equilibrium profits, aggregate profits at equilibrium must be positive.) Let $\chi^H \equiv (\alpha^H, \beta^H)$ and $\chi^L \equiv (\alpha^L, \beta^L)$ be the two contracts, not necessarily distinct, respectively chosen by type H and L at that equilibrium.[99] Consider the firm that obtains equilibrium profits no larger than $\hat{\pi}/2$ (or any of the two firms, if profits are equal for both). This firm may deviate and offer alternative contracts $\tilde{\chi}^H \equiv (\tilde{\alpha}^H, \tilde{\beta}^H)$ and $\tilde{\chi}^L \equiv (\tilde{\alpha}^L, \tilde{\beta}^L)$ with

$$\tilde{\alpha}^H = \alpha^H, \tilde{\alpha}^L = \alpha^L$$

but

$$\tilde{\beta}^H = \beta^H + \varepsilon, \tilde{\beta}^L = \beta^L + \varepsilon$$

for some $\varepsilon > 0$, arbitrarily small. Obviously, these alternative contracts would be chosen by the two types instead of those originally offered. Thus, after such a deviation, the firm in question would obtain profits arbitrarily close to $\hat{\pi}$, provided that ε is chosen small enough. In particular, those profits could be made larger than $\hat{\pi}/2$, contradicting the hypothesis that the original configuration defined an equilibrium.

As a benchmark for future comparison, it is again helpful to proceed as in Section 7.1 and study first the simple context where there is *no* asymmetric information between the firms and the individual. For concreteness, let us focus on the case where the individual happens to be of the high-risk type and both firms know it at the time of their decision. (The case in which the individual is of the low-risk type is fully analogous.) Then, an immediate particularization of former reasoning implies that, in this complete-information case as well, firms' profits must vanish at equilibrium. Therefore, the insurance contract chosen by the individual must belong to the set

$$C^H \equiv \{\chi = (\alpha, \beta) : \alpha (1 - \rho^H) = \beta \rho^H\}. \tag{7.24}$$

This set consists of all those contracts that "transform" the payments made in state ξ_1 into compensations obtained in state ξ_2 at the rate $(1 - \rho^H)/\rho^H$. Or, equivalently, they can be viewed as the contracts that expand the original no-insurance

---

[99] Note that, at any PWPBE, at least the high-risk type must be offered acceptable insurance by one of the firms. If, on the other hand, the equilibrium were such that the low-risk type accepts none of the contracts offered by the firms, the argument below would have to be adapted to focus alone on the contract accepted by the high-risk type.

configuration $(\hat{W}_1, \hat{W}_2)$ by allowing for *any* extent of insurance (i.e., net compensation) at the *unitary* premium $\rho^H/(1 - \rho^H)$. This set of contracts spans the range of wealth configurations $(W_1(\chi), W_2(\chi))$ given by

$$W_1(\chi) = \hat{W}_1 - \alpha$$

$$W_2(\chi) = \hat{W}_2 + \beta = \hat{W}_2 + \frac{1 - \rho^H}{\rho^H}\,\alpha,$$

which can be parametrized along a single dimension by the premium α.

Next, we argue that, of all contracts in C^H, only the one that provides *complete* insurance can be actually chosen at an *equilibrium*. That is, the contract $\chi^* = (\alpha^*, \beta^*)$ implemented at any PWPBE must have the individual's wealth be independent of the prevailing state, i.e.,

$$W_1(\chi^*) = W_2(\chi^*),$$

so that

$$\alpha^* = (\hat{W}_1 - \hat{W}_2)\rho^H \tag{7.25}$$

$$\beta^* = (1 - \rho^H)(\hat{W}_1 - \hat{W}_2). \tag{7.26}$$

This follows directly from the observation that the individual's indifference curves, i.e., loci of points defined in the space of state-contingent wealths (W_1, W_2) by the condition

$$(1 - \rho^H)\,V(W_1) + \rho^H\,V(W_2) = K \quad (K \in \mathbb{R}),$$

display a slope *different* from $-(1 - \rho^H)/\rho^H$ at any (W_1, W_2) such that $W_1 \neq W_2$. Consequently, if $\chi = (\alpha, \beta) \in C^H$ but $\alpha \neq \alpha^*$, there exists an alternative contract $\chi' = (\alpha', \beta')$ that satisfies the following two conditions (see Figure 7.8 for an illustration):

$$(1 - \rho^H)\,V(\hat{W}_1 - \alpha') + \rho^H\,V(\hat{W}_2 + \beta')$$
$$> (1 - \rho^H)\,V(W_1(\chi)) + \rho^H\,V(W_2(\chi)) \tag{7.27}$$

$$(1 - \rho^H)\alpha' - \rho^H\,\beta' > 0. \tag{7.28}$$

By (7.27), the individual prefers the insurance contract χ' to χ. On the other hand, from (7.28), any firm that were to offer χ' would obtain positive profits if the individual (who is currently taken to be of type H) were to choose it. Combining both considerations, it follows that there cannot exist an equilibrium where the individual chooses a contract $\chi = (\alpha, \beta)$ that belongs to C^H (a necessary condition for equilibrium) but $\alpha \neq \alpha^*$. If that were the case, either firm would profit by deviating to a contract such as χ' above, satisfying (7.27) and (7.28). In sum, we conclude that only the contract χ^* may be actually chosen at equilibrium, the high-risk individual who subscribes it thus obtaining full insurance.

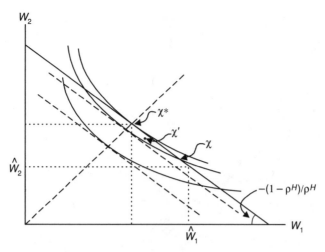

Figure 7.8: Equilibrium in the insurance market under complete information for the high-risk type. (Alternative insurance contracts are identified in terms of their induced pair of state-contingent wealths.)

The previous considerations have been carried out under the assumption that firms know they face a high-risk individual, i.e., in a context of complete information. Now, we turn to the richer and more interesting scenario in which the information is genuinely asymmetric between the firms and the individual, the former holding nondegenerate subjective probabilities p and $(1 - p)$ that the latter is a high- or low-risk individual, respectively. We organize the discussion in three parts.

- First, in part (a), we show that there is no PWPBE where the two types of individual pool and choose the same insurance contract.
- Second, in part (b), we identify the unique configuration of contracts that is capable of sustaining a (separating) equilibrium.
- Finally, in part (c), we describe conditions for which the equilibrium cannot involve intertype separation and, therefore (by part (b)), no PWPBE exists.

(a) *There exists no pooling PWPBE.*

Suppose, for the sake of contradiction, that there exists a pooling PWPBE (J_1, J_2, γ), where the two types of individual choose, at equilibrium, the same contract $\chi = (\alpha, \beta)$, i.e.,

$$\gamma(H)(J_1, J_2) = \gamma(L)(J_1, J_2) = \chi.$$

Since the expected equilibrium profits induced by this contract must be zero, χ must satisfy

$$\alpha (1 - \bar{\rho}(p)) = \beta \, \bar{\rho}(p)$$

where $\bar{\rho}(p) \equiv p \, \rho^H + (1 - p)\rho^L$ is the expected accident probability when the individual's type is unknown and each of the two possibilities, H and L, is attributed respective probabilities p and $(1 - p)$. Consider the state-contingent wealth pair

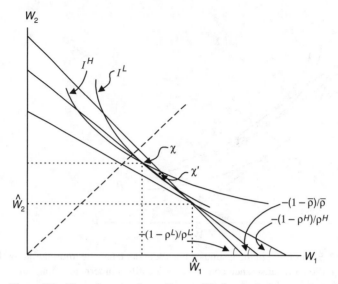

Figure 7.9: Nonexistence of a pooling equilibrium in the insurance market under incomplete information. Indifference curves for the high and low type are, respectively, denoted by I^H and I^L.

$(W_1(\chi), W_2(\chi))$ resulting from this contract:

$$W_1(\chi) \equiv \hat{W}_1 - \alpha \tag{7.29}$$

$$W_2(\chi) \equiv \hat{W}_2 + \beta = \hat{W}_2 + \frac{1 - \bar{\rho}(p)}{\bar{\rho}(p)}\alpha. \tag{7.30}$$

At $(W_1(\chi), W_2(\chi))$, the marginal rate of substitution of each type $\theta = H, L$ is given by

$$-\frac{1 - \rho^\theta}{\rho^\theta} \frac{V'(W_1(\chi))}{V'(W_2(\chi))}$$

and, therefore, the marginal rate of substitution of type H is lower (in absolute value) than that of type L. Since

$$\frac{1 - \rho^L}{\rho^L} > \frac{1 - \bar{\rho}}{\bar{\rho}}$$

it follows that there must exist a contract $\chi' = (\alpha', \beta')$ such that (see Figure 7.9)

$$(1 - \rho^H) V(\hat{W}_1 - \alpha') + \rho^H V(\hat{W}_2 + \beta')$$
$$< (1 - \rho^H) V(\hat{W}_1 - \alpha) + \rho^H V(\hat{W}_2 + \beta) \tag{7.31}$$
$$(1 - \rho^L) V(\hat{W}_1 - \alpha') + \rho^L V(\hat{W}_2 + \beta')$$
$$> (1 - \rho^L) V(\hat{W}_1 - \alpha) + \rho^L V(\hat{W}_2 + \beta) \tag{7.32}$$
$$(1 - \rho^L)\alpha' - \rho^L \beta' > 0. \tag{7.33}$$

By virtue of (7.31), an individual of type H will not subscribe to the contract χ' if the original one, χ, is indeed available. However, from (7.32), an individual of type L would prefer χ' to χ if both were offered. This implies that one of the firms may profit by deviating and including only the contract χ' in its menu, thus attracting solely the individual of type L. In view of (7.33), this would render positive expected profits to that firm, a contradiction to the hypothesis that the original strategy profile defines a PWPBE.

(b) *There exists a unique contract pair that may prevail at a separating PWPBE.*

By the former discussion, we know that any PWPBE must be separating, i.e., each individual type must choose a different insurance contract at equilibrium. Denote by χ^H and χ^L the distinct contracts underlying some such hypothetical equilibrium. First, we argue that $\chi^H = (\alpha^H, \beta^H)$ is to coincide with $\chi^* = (\alpha^*, \beta^*)$, where α^* and β^* are given by (7.25) and (7.26) – that is, the individual of type H insures herself completely at equilibrium.

Suppose the contrary, i.e., $\chi^H \neq \chi^*$. Then, since $\chi^H \in C^H$ (due to the zero-profit condition to hold at equilibrium),[100] one must have $W_1(\chi^H) \neq W_2(\chi^H)$ – recall the notation introduced in (7.29) and (7.30). This in turn implies that the indifference curve of type H at the point $(W_1(\chi^H), W_2(\chi^H))$ displays a slope *different* from $-(1 - \rho^H)/\rho^H$ and, therefore, there has to be an insurance contract $\chi' = (\alpha', \beta')$ such that

$$(1 - \rho^H) V(\hat{W}_1 - \alpha') + \rho^H V(\hat{W}_2 + \beta')$$
$$> (1 - \rho^H) V(\hat{W}_1 - \alpha^H) + \rho^H V(\hat{W}_2 + \beta^H)$$

$$\forall \rho \leq \rho^H, \quad (1 - \rho)\alpha' - \rho \beta' > 0. \tag{7.34}$$

Consequently, any firm would profit by deviating from the hypothetical equilibrium and offering χ', because at least the high types would subscribe χ' and the profits induced by it are certain to be positive, i.e., higher than the zero profits obtained with χ^H. (Note that, by (7.34), this conclusion applies even if both type H *and* L were to subscribe the alternative contract χ'.)

Once confirmed that $\chi^H = \chi^*$, we turn to determining what must be the features of the contract $\chi^L = (\alpha^L, \beta^L)$ chosen by the low-risk type in a separating PWPBE. Again, for the zero-profit condition to be met at equilibrium it must be required that

$$\chi^L \in C^L \equiv \{\chi = (\alpha, \beta) : \alpha (1 - \rho^L) = \beta \rho^L\}.$$

Next we argue that, among all possible insurance contracts belonging to C^L, we can rule out all of them except the particular one $\hat{\chi} = (\hat{\alpha}, \hat{\beta})$ that satisfies

$$(1 - \rho^H) V(\hat{W}_1 - \alpha^*) + \rho^H V(\hat{W}_2 + \beta^*)$$
$$= (1 - \rho^H) V(\hat{W}_1 - \hat{\alpha}) + \rho^H V(\hat{W}_2 + \hat{\beta}).$$

---

[100] Clearly, the zero-profit condition must *separately* hold for χ^H and χ^L.

We proceed in two steps. First, to exclude that $\chi^L = (\alpha^L, \beta^L)$ might have $\alpha^L > \hat{\alpha}$, note that, in that case,

$$(1 - \rho^H) V(\hat{W}_1 - \alpha^L) + \rho^H V(\hat{W}_2 + \beta^L)$$
$$> (1 - \rho^H) V(\hat{W}_1 - \alpha^*) + \rho^H V(\hat{W}_2 + \beta^*), \tag{7.35}$$

which would imply that the contracts χ^H and χ^L do not "separate" types, a contradiction with part (a) above.

On the other hand, concerning the alternative possibility that $\alpha^L < \hat{\alpha}$, this of course leads to a reversal of the inequality (7.35), which in principle is consistent with a separating equilibrium. However, an argument akin to one used above (recall (7.31)–(7.33)) indicates that, in this case, there must be a contract $\chi' = (\alpha', \beta')$ such that

$$(1 - \rho^H) V(\hat{W}_1 - \alpha') + \rho^H V(\hat{W}_2 + \beta')$$
$$< (1 - \rho^H) V(\hat{W}_1 - \alpha^*) + \rho^H V(\hat{W}_2 + \beta^*)$$
$$(1 - \rho^L) V(\hat{W}_1 - \alpha') + \rho^L V(\hat{W}_2 + \beta')$$
$$> (1 - \rho^L) V(\hat{W}_1 - \alpha^L) + \rho^L V(\hat{W}_2 + \beta^L)$$
$$(1 - \rho^L) \alpha' - \rho^L \beta' > 0.$$

The above expressions imply that if any of the two firms were to unilaterally add the contract χ' to its menu, the individual of type L (and only this type) would subscribe it. This would lead the firm in question to obtaining positive expected profits, thus contradicting the hypothesis that χ^L is the contract chosen by the low-risk individual at equilibrium.

From the above considerations we may conclude that there is just *one* pair of insurance contracts that may separate types H and L at a PWPBE. These two contracts, $\chi^H = \chi^*$ and $\chi^L = \hat{\chi}$, are illustrated graphically in Figure 7.10.

(c) *Possible nonexistence of a (separating) PWPBE.*

The argument developed in the preceding part (b) implies that only if the contracts χ^* and $\hat{\chi}$ are among the offered contracts, and the high type chooses the former while the low type chooses the latter, can one possibly be at a PWPBE. This, however, is just a necessary condition for equilibrium, not by itself a confirmation that such an equilibrium exists. In general, whether a PWPBE exists depends on p, the prior probability that the individual be of high risk. If p is sufficiently high, we have the situation illustrated in Figure 7.10 and the contract pair $(\chi^*, \hat{\chi})$ can indeed be used to support the equilibrium. In contrast, if the data of the problem are as depicted in Figure 7.11 (that is, p is relatively low), the only *candidate contracts* to support an equilibrium (again χ^* and $\hat{\chi}$) cannot meet the required incentive conditions and, therefore, no PWPBE exists.

Consider, for example, what would happen in the context of Figure 7.11 if one of the firms were to deviate from the target separating equilibrium and offer a contract such as $\chi' = (\alpha', \beta')$. After such a deviation, any individual (either of type H or L) would choose χ' rather than their respective (tentatively separating) contracts

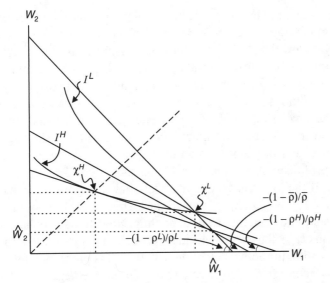

Figure 7.10: Separating equilibrium in the insurance market under incomplete information.

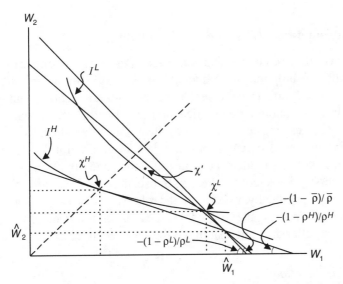

Figure 7.11: Nonexistence of a (separating) equilibrium in the insurance market under incomplete information.

χ^H or χ^L. Besides, the deviating firm would obtain positive expected profits because

$$(1 - \bar{\rho}(p))\alpha' - \bar{\rho}(p)\beta' > 0.$$

Therefore, the contemplated deviation would be profitable for the firm under consideration, thus rendering it impossible that the pair $(\chi^*, \hat{\chi})$ may be the type-contingent contracts underlying separation at a PWPBE.

We may interpret these nonexistence problems as a consequence of the negative externality that high-risk agents exert on the market – more specifically, on those individuals displaying low risk. If the probability that an individual be of high risk is quite large (as in Figure 7.10), the market adapts to such a high-risk environment and offers separating conditions for each type, which cannot be destroyed by pooling contracts – these conditions involve, in particular, only *partial* insurance for the *relatively infrequent* low-risk individuals. In essence, the robustness displayed by the separating menu in this case is a direct consequence of the following simple fact: the average accident probability is so high that any pooling would impose (through the zero-profit condition) unacceptable terms on type L.

On the contrary, if the low-risk type is relatively likely (as in Figure 7.11), the required separation of types can be destroyed through a single contract that both types prefer to the status quo and thus leads to pooling. Now this is possible because, unlike in the previous case, the average accident probability is so low that there is a contract that is appealing for both a deviating firm (i.e., it is profit making) and for each type (i.e., it is pooling). Under these circumstances, the negative externality exerted by the infrequent high types on the more frequent low types is so large that separation becomes inviable at equilibrium.[101]

7.3   Mechanism design (IV): one-sided auctions

Auctions are one of the primary mechanisms used in modern economies to allocate a wide variety of consumption or production goods (works of art, mining rights, or even, quite recently, wave frequencies to operate communication technologies). This has given rise to a booming theoretical and empirical literature, out of which we select just two topics here concerning the allocation of a single indivisible good among a certain number of potential buyers. First, in Subsection 7.3.1, we study the most basic (or simple-minded) auction procedure one could imagine to this end: a so-called first-price auction. Then, in Subsection 7.3.2 we turn to issues of mechanism design. Specifically, we explore the relative performance of alternative allocation procedures in this context and tackle the issue of how to design an optimal mechanism for the seller, i.e., one that maximizes the resulting expected revenue.

7.3.1   *First-price auctions*

Consider the owner of an indivisible good who decides to sell it through a public auction. For simplicity, let us suppose there are only two individuals interested in this good, identified by the index $i = 1, 2$. The auction used is of the kind labeled *first-price*.[102] Specifically, the potential buyers are asked to issue their offers (bids)

---

[101] These nonexistence problems can be tackled by resorting to equilibria in mixed strategies (see Dasgupta and Maskin, 1986*b*). An alternative route involves the consideration of certain variations on the game that might be able to restore equilibrium. For example, Wilson (1977) allows each firm to react to the deviations of the competitor (in particular, it may withdraw contracts already offered if they incur losses), which obviously limits substantially the ability of firms to find profitable *unilateral* deviations. In a related vein, the reader may find alternative approaches by Riley (1979*a*) and Hellwig (1986).

[102] See Exercise 7.17, where a "second-price" auction is discussed.

by, say, introducing them in a closed envelope. Then, these envelopes are given to the seller, who opens them and delivers the good to the highest bidder in exchange for the *exact* price put forward by the latter. In case the bids of both buyers are identical, the good is allotted randomly to one of the two, each being chosen with the same probability.

Denote by v_i the (monetary) valuation of the good for buyer $i = 1, 2$. Both of these agents are taken to know their own respective valuation but are uninformed of the valuation v_j ($j \neq i$) of the other one. Each buyer knows only that the other's valuation belongs to some finite interval, say $[0, 1]$, from where she assumes that it has been selected in a random and independent fashion according to a *uniform* probability distribution.

The context described may be modeled as a Bayesian game as follows. On the one hand, the type of each player i is identified with her valuation v_i. That is, $T_i = [0, 1]$ for each $i = 1, 2$. On the other hand, the action spaces A_i consist of all possible bids that agents may conceivably issue in an independent fashion. Without any essential loss of generality, we can make $A_i = [0, 1]$, i.e., agents never bid above the maximum possible valuation. Finally, we posit that Nature selects the players' types (v_1, v_2) with a density $f(v_1, v_2)$ that is constant over the whole square $[0, 1]^2$. For any given vector of players' and Nature's decisions, the payoff functions $\pi_i(\cdot)$ are defined as follows:

$$
\pi_i(v_1, v_2, a_1, a_2) = \begin{cases} v_i - a_i, & \text{if } a_i > a_j \\ \dfrac{v_i - a_i}{2}, & \text{if } a_i = a_j \\ 0, & \text{if } a_i < a_j \end{cases} \quad i, j = 1, 2; \; j \neq i.
$$

In the Bayesian game thus defined, the players' (mixed) strategies are functions

$$
\gamma_i : [0, 1] \to \Delta([0, 1])
$$

that, for any possible type (valuation) $v_i \in [0, 1]$ of each player i, associate a probability distribution over the interval $[0, 1]$, which is the action (bid) space for each agent. As a particular case, the *pure* strategies of the form

$$
g_i : [0, 1] \to [0, 1] \tag{7.36}
$$

have each player i choose deterministically a bid $g_i(v_i)$ for any given valuation v_i.

We focus on the computation of a Bayes-Nash equilibrium (BNE) displaying the following set of characteristics:

(i) players follow *pure* strategies of the sort contemplated in (7.36);
(ii) players' (pure) strategies are *affine* functions of their type given by

$$
g_i(v_i) = \min\{1, \max\{\alpha_i + \beta_i v_i, 0\}\} \tag{7.37}
$$

for some given real numbers, α_i and β_i;
(iii) players' (pure and affine) strategies are identical, i.e., the equilibrium is *symmetric*; therefore, $\forall i = 1, 2$, $\alpha_i = \alpha$, $\beta_i = \beta$.

It is important to emphasize that our objective is *not* to compute a BNE subject to the constraint that players can only choose strategies that satisfy (i)–(iii). Rather, what we shall do is to limit our search for (unrestricted) equilibria to those strategy profiles that meet those conditions. That is, we hope to find that there is an affine and symmetric pure-strategy profile that defines an equilibrium even if players may deviate to any unrestricted (i.e., possibly mixed or nonaffine) strategy.

Thus, suppose players use strategies of the kind contemplated in (ii), with identical coefficients α and β as indicated in (iii). As a first step, it is immediate to observe (see Exercise 7.14) that, if any such profile is to define a BNE, it should have $\alpha \geq 0$. But, on the other hand, it is also true that $\alpha \leq 0$. For, if $\alpha > 0$, there would be some types (i.e., those with $v_i < \alpha + \beta v_i$) who would be issuing a bid above their valuation. This is obviously a suboptimal strategy at equilibrium because agents would then be making an expected payment above their valuation. We may conclude, therefore, that any affine strategy in a symmetric equilibrium must have $\alpha = 0$. But then, this strategy may also be restricted to have $\beta > 0$. To see this, note that, if $\beta \leq 0$, (7.37) would prescribe a *zero* bid uniformly across all types. This is obviously inconsistent with equilibrium because, in that case, any individual of type $v_i > 0$ would profit by issuing a positive bid lower than v_i.

In view of the former considerations, we direct our search toward strategies of the following form:

$$g_i(v_i) = \beta v_i, \quad 0 < \beta \leq 1. \tag{7.38}$$

That is, we focus on strategies that are increasing and linear functions (i.e., affine with a zero intercept) of each player's type. In equilibrium, of course, given any strategy of this form on the other buyer's part, the strategy adopted by each $i = 1, 2$ must be a suitable best response. This implies that, for any valuation $v_i \in [0, 1]$, the prescribed bid $a_i^* = \beta v_i$ must be a solution to the following optimization problem:

$$\max_{a_i \in [0, 1]} \left\{ \left((v_i - a_i) \Pr\{a_i > \beta v_j\} \right) \right.$$

$$\left. + \left(\frac{1}{2} (v_i - a_i) \Pr\{a_i = \beta v_j\} \right) \right\} \quad j \neq i. \tag{7.39}$$

The second term in the above expression can be ignored because, given that types are continuously distributed, the probability *mass* (not the density) associated with the event that βv_j might coincide with any particular a_i is zero. That is,

$$\Pr\{a_i = \beta v_j\} = 0 \tag{7.40}$$

for any given $a_i \in [0, 1]$. On the other hand, the uniform distribution postulated for v_j implies

$$\Pr\{a_i > \beta v_j\} = \Pr\left\{v_j < \frac{a_i}{\beta}\right\} = \min\left[\frac{a_i}{\beta}, 1\right]. \tag{7.41}$$

Thus, using (7.40) and (7.41), the optimization problem confronted by individual i

may be simply rewritten as follows:

$$\max_{a_i \in [0, 1]} \left\{ (v_i - a_i) \min \left[\frac{a_i}{\beta}, 1 \right] \right\}.$$

For the solution to the above optimization problem to be always responsive to the agent's valuation, it must be required that $\beta \geq 1/2$.[103] Thus, in the quest of an equilibrium in linear strategies, this lower bound on β can be assumed without loss of generality. Then, for each $v_i \in [0, 1]$, the solution to the above optimization is easily seen to be of the form

$$a_i^* = g_i(v_i) = \frac{v_i}{2}. \tag{7.42}$$

Note that, curiously enough, this expression does *not* depend on the precise value of β (the coefficient attributed to player j's strategy). Thus, the unique equilibrium in symmetric linear strategies must have $\beta = 1/2$, each agent always issuing a bid equal to half her valuation. In fact, it turns out that the following much stronger conclusion is also true (see Gibbons, 1992): under certain regularity conditions (in particular, differentiability and monotonicity of players' bidding behavior), the *unique* symmetric equilibrium must involve the linear strategies given in (7.42).

To sum up, we conclude that the very simple strategies that specify the bid of each individual to be half of her valuation define a BNE for the game induced by the first-price (two-buyer) auction. The outcome thus obtained is efficient since the individual with the highest valuation ends up obtaining the good. The price she pays for it, however, is lower than her true valuation. This is simply a reflection of the fact that, because of the asymmetric information conditions in which the auction takes place, buyers strategically manipulate their bids at equilibrium.

7.3.2 *Optimal auction design: the revelation principle**

Consider now the previous allocation problem as seen from the seller's viewpoint. From her perspective, the key "decision variable" to consider is of an institutional kind. Specifically, she may well ask herself the following question: What is the best *mechanism* to be used in allocating the good and determining payments? In this respect, the first-price auction considered above might be considered a "natural" candidate, but only that: one of the possible options. In principle, if the seller has no *a priori* restrictions in choosing the allocation rules, a wide range of other mechanisms (auction-like or not) could be considered instead. Is there any hope of finding out which of those mechanisms are optimal for the seller? If, in this case, "optimality" is defined from the standpoint of the seller and thus identified with expected revenue maximization, the question would seem far too ambitious even to allow for a meaningful formalization. What is the universe of mechanisms under

---

[103] Note that, if $\beta < 1/2$, there is a sufficiently high valuation $\hat{v}_i < 1$ such that, for all $v_i \geq \hat{v}_i$, the optimal bid is constant. This happens because the corresponding subjective probability of obtaining the good is already one and, therefore, the bid does not rise as the valuation does.

consideration? Isn't it too vast? And, if attention is restricted to a particular class (e.g., auctions), how can one be sure that there is not some other approach (possibly, quite "imaginative" or involved) that might prove more fruitful?

A sharp and effective route to tackle the problem is afforded by the so-called revelation principle, which was first applied to a Bayesian setting by Myerson (1979). As we shall explain, the key implication to be derived from this principle is far-reaching. It amounts to the guarantee that, in exploring the implementation possibilities available through *any* mechanism, it is enough to restrict attention to a much smaller class. Specifically, it turns out to be sufficient to focus on *direct mechanisms* where agents are simply asked to reveal their information (i.e., their respective types) and, in addition, they have incentives (at a BNE of the induced game) to *behave truthfully*. This relatively small subset of the full space of conceivable mechanisms (i.e., direct and truthful mechanisms) spans the whole performance possibilities achievable by *any other* mechanism, however complex it might be. Since the revelation principle is not only a fundamental contribution to the theory of mechanisms but is also used later in other contexts (cf. Subsection 7.4.2), we next provide a formal and separate treatment of it.

7.3.2.1 *The revelation principle for Bayesian mechanisms**. Recall the mechanism-design viewpoint to the Nash implementation problem, formulated in Section 3.3. The implicit assumption there was that the players enjoy complete (symmetric) information about the underlying characteristics of the environment. The mechanism $M = \{\{S_i\}_{i=1}^n, g\}$ was the *variable* of the problem, the aim being to find some such mechanism that, given any environment (or utility profile) $U = (U_1, U_2, \ldots, U_n)$, guarantees the desired performance $\phi(U)$ at the Nash equilibria of the induced game $G\langle M, U \rangle$. The standard of *satisfactory performance* was embodied by some social choice rule (SCR) $\phi : \mathcal{E} \rightrightarrows \Omega$, an exogenous datum of the implementation problem, where $\mathcal{E}$ represents the space of possible environments and Ω is the outcome space (cf. Subsection 3.3.1). This problem was diagrammatically illustrated in terms of Figure 3.4, its solution identified with the equivalence (or commutation) of the following two mappings: on the one hand, the desired SCR $\phi(\cdot)$; on the other hand, the composition of the Nash equilibrium correspondence $\mathcal{N}(G\langle M, \cdot \rangle)$ and the outcome function $g(\cdot)$.

A similar approach can be pursued to formulate the implementation problem in the present Bayesian setup. The key difference here is that each player is assumed informed only of her own characteristics (i.e., "utility function"). But again, the variable of the problem is identified as the *mechanism M* that, to recall, specifies

- the messages to be sent by the agents, as given by their respective action spaces S_i, $i = 1, 2, \ldots, n$;
- the rules of the mechanism that define the implementation procedure, as given by the outcome function $g : S_1 \times \cdots \times S_n \to \Omega$.

Let us follow Harsanyi's approach and postulate that there is some exogenous probability function $P(\cdot)$ governing the selection by Nature of the prevailing environment $U = (U_1, U_2, \ldots, U_n) \in \mathcal{E}$. Then, each agent i becomes informed of her

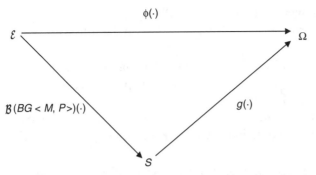

Figure 7.12: The Bayesian implementation problem through some general mechanism.

own U_i but remains uninformed about the others' realized U_j. This readily defines a Bayesian game, $BG \langle M, P \rangle$, where the type space coincides with the set of environments $\mathcal{E}$ (for simplicity, supposed finite), and the payoff function $\pi_i : \mathcal{E} \times S \to \mathbb{R}$ of each player $i = 1, 2, \ldots, n$ is defined as follows:

$$\pi_i[(U_1, U_2, \ldots, U_n), (s_1, s_2, \ldots, s_n)] = U_i[g(s_1, s_2, \ldots, s_n)].$$

Consider any given SCR ϕ, and let $\mathcal{B}(BG \langle M, P \rangle)$ denote the set of pure-strategy[104] BNE of the Bayesian game $BG \langle M, P \rangle$. For the mechanism M to be conceived as a suitable "solution" to the implementation problem posed by ϕ, the following two conditions are required in the present Bayesian setup.

(i) Let $f : \mathcal{E} \to \Omega$ be any particular selection of ϕ. Then, there must exist a corresponding BNE $\gamma \in \mathcal{B}(BG \langle M, P \rangle)$ such that

$$\forall U \equiv (U_1, U_2, \ldots, U_n) \in \mathcal{E}, \quad g(\gamma_1(U_1), \gamma_2(U_2), \ldots, \gamma_n(U_n)) = f(U).$$
$$(7.43)$$

(ii) Let γ be any BNE of the Bayesian game $BG \langle M, P \rangle$. Then, it is required that

$$\forall U \equiv (U_1, U_2, \ldots, U_n) \in \mathcal{E}, \quad g(\gamma_1(U_1), \gamma_2(U_2), \ldots, \gamma_n(U_n)) \in \phi(U).$$

Conditions (i) and (ii) are reciprocal inclusions between the set of equilibrium and the set of desired "performances," as functions of the underlying environment. Therefore, if jointly satisfied, they imply an equality of both sets. Any mechanism M that fulfills these conditions is said to *Bayes-implement* the SCR ϕ. The notion of Bayesian implementation is informally illustrated in Figure 7.12, which can be regarded as the present counterpart of Figure 3.4 for Nash implementation.

We are now in a position to state precisely the revelation principle, as applied to the present context. Consider any SCR ϕ that is *Bayes-implementable*. This implies, in particular, that there exists some mechanism M such that, for any selection f of

---

[104] As in Section 3.3 concerning Nash implementation, we restrict our attention here to pure-strategy equilibria, for the sake of simplicity. However, the essence of the approach is unaffected if one extends it to allow for mixed-strategy equilibria.

ϕ, (7.43) is satisfied for some corresponding BNE γ. Now associate with M another mechanism derived from it, $M' = \{\{S_i'\}_{i=1}^n, g'\}$, with the following features.

- It is a *direct mechanism* in the sense that players are asked in it to reveal their respective types. That is, the action space of each player is $S_i' = \mathcal{U}_i$ and, therefore, $S' = S_1' \times \cdots \times S_n' = \mathcal{E}$.
- The outcome function $g' : \mathcal{E} \to \Omega$ is designed as the composition of the original outcome function g and the BNE strategy profile γ. That is,

$$\forall U \in \mathcal{E} = S', \quad g'(U) = g(\gamma_1(U_1), \gamma_2(U_2), \ldots, \gamma_n(U_n)).$$

Heuristically, one can think of the direct mechanism M' as formalizing the following two-stage procedure. First, each player reports what she claims (truthfully or not) to be her type to an impartial mediator. Second, this mediator implements the outcome in Ω that would have materialized if each player had played according to her strategy γ_i in the original game $BG \langle M, P \rangle$ and the type of each one had been the reported one. Thus, in a sense, we can view the mediator as mimicking the behavior of agents in the BNE γ on the basis of the reported types.

In this context, the revelation principle simply states that the *truthful* strategy profile $\gamma^* = (\gamma_1^*, \gamma_2^*, \ldots, \gamma_n^*)$ where each player i reveals her type honestly, i.e.,

$$\forall U_i \in \mathcal{U}_i \quad \gamma_i^*(U_i) = U_i,$$

defines a BNE of the Bayesian game $BG \langle M', P \rangle$. This equilibrium, of course, also reproduces the selection of the admissible (or desired) performance embodied by f. The intuitive reason why this principle applies is easy to understand in terms of the mediator-based heuristics used above to motivate the direct mechanism M'. If the revelation principle were violated, the impartial character of the mediator would imply that, whenever in the direct mechanism there is some player who would benefit from lying, this player would also benefit by lying to herself in the original mechanism – an obvious absurdity! Diagrammatically, the implications of the revelation principle are illustrated in Figure 7.13.

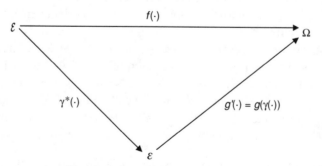

Figure 7.13: The Bayesian implementation problem through some direct mechanism and truthful revelation.

To fix ideas, it may be useful to provide a formal argument for the revelation principle. Thus, reasoning by contradiction, suppose that it were false. Then, there would be some Bayes-implementable SCR ϕ and a selection of it, f, such that, while γ would be a BNE for the game induced by some mechanism M that satisfies (7.43), the corresponding truthful strategy profile γ^* would not be a BNE of the game $BG\langle M', P\rangle$ induced by the associated direct mechanism M'. Consider any player i for which γ_i^* is not an equilibrium strategy. Then, for some $\hat{U}_i, \tilde{U}_i \in \mathcal{U}_i$, we must have

$$\sum_{U_{-i}\in\mathcal{U}_{-i}} P_i(U_{-i} \mid \hat{U}_i)\,\pi_i'\big((\hat{U}_i, U_{-i}), \gamma_1^*(U_1), \dots, \tilde{U}_i, \dots, \gamma_n^*(U_n)\big)$$

$$> \sum_{U_{-i}\in\mathcal{U}_{-i}} P_i(U_{-i}\mid\hat{U}_i)\pi_i'\big((\hat{U}_i, U_{-i}), \gamma_1^*(U_1), \dots, \gamma_i^*(\hat{U}_i), \dots, \gamma_n^*(U_n)\big)$$

where $\pi_i'(\cdot)$ stands for the payoff function of player i in the game $BG\langle M', P\rangle$ and $P_i(\cdot \mid \cdot)$ represents conditional probabilities induced by player i's information (cf. Subsection 6.3.1). But this clearly implies that, in the game $BG\langle M, P\rangle$,

$$\sum_{U_{-i}\in\mathcal{U}_{-i}} P_i(U_{-i} \mid \hat{U}_i)\,\pi_i\big((\hat{U}_i, U_{-i}), \gamma_1(U_1), \dots, \tilde{s}_i, \dots, \gamma_n(U_n)\big)$$

$$> \sum_{U_{-i}\in\mathcal{U}_{-i}} P_i(U_{-i}\mid\hat{U}_i)\pi_i\big((\hat{U}_i, U_{-i}), \gamma_1(U_1), \dots, \gamma_i(\hat{U}_i), \dots, \gamma_n(U_n)\big),$$

for $\tilde{s}_i = \gamma_i(\tilde{U}_i)$, which contradicts the hypothesis that γ is a BNE of this game.

The main contribution of the revelation principle is to provide a powerful *instrument* in the analysis of implementation issues rather than a solution *per se*. This principle, for example, does *not* ensure that direct mechanisms are effective ways of tackling general implementation problems. The fact that there always exists a truthful equilibrium for an associated direct mechanism that yields the desired performance (i.e., condition (i) above holds for the direct mechanism) does not imply that the equilibrium is unique. Or, somewhat less stringently, it does not guarantee either that, if other equilibria exist, they all yield equivalent (or even admissible) performance (i.e., condition (ii) need not apply for the direct mechanism). In fact, this second requirement is generally violated, as illustrated in Exercise 7.18 through a simple example.

However, what the revelation principle does permit is an *exhaustive* exploration of all performance *possibilities* available in any given implementation problem.[105] Thus, for example, it allows one to identify the full range of outcomes that are attainable (respecting agents' incentives and private information) when allocating an indivisible object among a number of buyers – cf. Subsection 7.3.1. Or, as explained in Subsection 7.4.1, it permits as well a complete characterization of the possible terms of trades on which a buyer and seller may settle on in any

---

[105] In fact, the revelation principle is not only useful in problems of Bayesian implementation as the ones considered here but is also relevant for the study of implementation problems posed in other informational setups (e.g., it can be applied to Nash implementation, as explained in Exercise 7.19).

bilateral trade mechanism. By virtue of the revelation principle, the restriction to direct mechanisms and the corresponding focus on their truthful equilibria alone can be done without loss of generality if our sole concern is to "map" the range of implementation possibilities for the problem at hand. In a sense, this principle can be seen as the theoretical basis of a convenient "algorithm" that renders tractable what otherwise would be a practically unfeasible task.

7.3.2.2 *Revenue-maximizing auctions**. We are now in a position to revisit the seller's revenue-maximizing problem outlined at the beginning of this subsection. In particular, we want to study whether the seller is at all limited by relying on a mechanism such as the first-price auction studied in Subsection 7.3.1. To underscore the generality of our approach,[106] we extend the context formerly discussed to the case in which

    (i) there is any *arbitrary* finite number n of potential buyers;

    (ii) the valuation (or type) of each buyer is independently selected for each of them according to a *general* distribution function $F(\cdot)$ with corresponding well-defined density $f(\cdot)$ on the interval [0, 1].

By the revelation principle, for *any* arbitrary mechanism that allocates the good and corresponding payments among the different buyers, its performance can be replicated by the BNE of a direct mechanism where players communicate their types (i.e., valuations) in an honest fashion. The behavior of direct mechanisms in the present context is easy to formulate. It is simply given, for each individual i, by a respective pair of functions[107]

$$P_i : [0, 1]^n \to \mathbb{R}_+, \quad X_i : [0, 1]^n \to [0, 1], \tag{7.44}$$

with the interpretation that, for every type profile $v = (v_1, v_2, \ldots, v_n) \in [0, 1]^n$ specifying the reports (truthful or not) of the n agents,

    • $P_i(v)$ specifies the payment made by individual i, and

    • $X_i(v)$ stands for the probability with which this individual receives the good in question.

Naturally, for $X_i(\cdot)$ to admit a coherent interpretation as assignment probabilities, we must have $\sum_{i=1}^n X_i(v) \leq 1$. (Thus, in principle, it is possible that the assignment probabilities fall short of one and therefore the good remains in the seller's hands with positive probability.)

Given the functions introduced in (7.44), one can define, for each individual i, corresponding functions

$$p_i : [0, 1] \to \mathbb{R}_+, \quad x_i : [0, 1] \to [0, 1],$$

---

[106] The ensuing discussion heavily borrows from Burguet (2000).

[107] Note that, without loss of generality, the payments and allocation probabilities can be specified through separate functions because players' preferences depend on those payments and the (monetary) valuation for the good in an additively separable fashion.

where $p_i(v_i)$ is interpreted as the (conditional) *expected payment* buyer i has to make if her reported valuation is v_i, and $x_i(v_i)$ stands for the (conditional) *probability* with which she obtains the good. These functions are derived from the respective $P_i(\cdot)$ and $X_i(\cdot)$ as follows:

$$p_i(\hat{v}_i) = \int_{v_{-i} \in [0,1]^{n-1}} P_i(\hat{v}_i, v_{-i}) \prod_{j \neq i} f(v_j) \, dv_{-i} \qquad (7.45)$$

$$x_i(\hat{v}_i) = \int_{v_{-i} \in [0,1]^{n-1}} X_i(\hat{v}_i, v_{-i}) \prod_{j \neq i} f(v_j) \, dv_{-i}. \qquad (7.46)$$

Now, we may invoke the revelation principle to restrict the analysis to those direct mechanisms where honest revelation of types is an equilibrium. In terms of the functions specified in (7.45) and (7.46), truthful revelation requires that, for each $i = 1, 2, \ldots, n$ and every valuation $v_i \in [0, 1]$ that might *actually* prevail on player i's part, the following condition is satisfied[108]:

$$v_i \in \arg \max_{z \in [0,1]} \; x_i(z) \, v_i - p_i(z). \qquad (7.47)$$

But this implies that the functions $p_i(\cdot)$ and $x_i(\cdot)$ must satisfy *identically* (i.e., for all v_i) the following first-order necessary condition (FONC) characterizing (7.47):

$$x_i'(v_i) \, v_i - p_i'(v_i) \equiv 0 \,, \qquad (7.48)$$

where the notation $h'(\cdot)$ stands for derivative of any given (single-variable) function $h(\cdot)$. Expression (7.48) defines a differential equation in v_i whose solution is of the following form:

$$p_i(v_i) = \int_0^{v_i} z \, x_i'(z) \, dz + p_i(0) \,, \qquad (7.49)$$

for some boundary conditions $p_i(0) \geq 0$. It is natural to postulate that no buyer, whatever is her valuation, should have *interim* incentives (cf. Section 6.2) to block the operation of the mechanism. This implies that we must choose $p_i(0) = 0$, because otherwise (i.e., if $p_i(0) > 0$) there would be individuals with a sufficiently low valuation who would prefer not to participate in the mechanism. Such a restriction on the mechanism that ensures buyers' "voluntary participation" is customarily known as the *individual rationality (IR)* condition.

Expression (7.49) reflects the following important idea: if a mechanism is consistent with incentive compatibility constraints (i.e., satisfies (7.48)), its performance is uniquely determined (up to the specification of $p_i(0)$) by the respective probabilities with which each individual obtains the good. To see this, simply note that, given the assignment probabilities $x_i(\cdot)$, expected prices $p_i(\cdot)$ are univocally obtained through (7.49). Thus, in particular, the range of outcomes induced by the different incentive-compatible mechanisms is essentially one-dimensional. In fact, integrating (7.49) by parts, we obtain that the following interesting property has to

---

[108] Note that, in the present case, v_i stands for the *actual* valuation of player i, whereas z denotes her report.

be satisfied by *any* incentive-compatible (direct) mechanism:

$$x_i(v_i)\, v_i - p_i(v_i) = \int_0^{v_i} x_i(z)\, dz. \tag{7.50}$$

That is, the "expected rents" accruing to any individual i must be increasing in her valuation v_i. More specifically, at any such v_i, these rents are to grow at a (marginal) rate that depends only on

$$x_i(v_i) = \frac{\partial}{\partial \hat{v}_i} \left[\int_0^{\hat{v}_i} x_i(z)\, dz. \right]\Bigg|_{\hat{v}_i = v_i},$$

i.e., the probability with which the good is allocated to an individual with valuation v_i.

Having characterized the behavior of direct mechanisms that are compatible with individual incentives (i.e., are both individually rational and consistent with truthful behavior), we can now address the central question posed above: Which of these mechanisms maximize expected revenues? Formally, the issue concerns finding the mechanisms $M \equiv \{P_i, X_i\}_{i=1}^n$ in the contemplated class that solve the problem

$$\max_M \sum_{i=1,\dots,n} \mathbf{E}\,[p_i(v_i)]. \tag{7.51}$$

Using (7.50) for each $i = 1, 2, \dots, n$, we have

$$\mathbf{E}\,[p_i(v_i)] = \int_0^1 p_i(v_i)\, f(v_i)\, dv_i$$

$$= \int_0^1 \left[x_i(v_i)\, v_i - \int_0^{v_i} x_i(z)\, dz \right] f(v_i)\, dv_i$$

$$= \int_0^1 x_i(v_i)\, v_i\, f(v_i)\, dv_i - \int_0^1 \int_0^{v_i} x_i(z) f(v_i)\, dz\, dv_i. \tag{7.52}$$

Focusing on the second term of (7.52), note that, by changing the order of integration on the triangle $\{(v_i, z) \in [0, 1]^2 : 0 \le z \le v_i \le 1\}$, we can write[109]:

$$\int_0^1 \int_0^{v_i} x_i(z) f(v_i)\, dz\, dv_i = \int_0^1 \int_z^1 x_i(z) f(v_i)\, dv_i\, dz$$

$$= \int_0^1 \int_{v_i}^1 x_i(v_i) f(z)\, dz\, dv_i,$$

where the last equality simply reflects a change of notation (i.e., permuting z and v_i) in the variables of integration. Introducing the above expression in (7.52), we

---

[109] Note that the set $\{(v_i, z) : v_i \in [0, 1] \wedge z \in [0, v_i]\}$ is exactly the same as the set $\{(v_i, z) : z \in [0, 1] \wedge v_i \in [z, 1]\}$.

obtain

$$\mathbf{E}\left[p_i(v_i)\right] = \int_0^1 \left[x_i(v_i)\, v_i\, f(v_i) - \int_{v_i}^1 x_i(v_i) f(z)\, dz\right] dv_i$$

$$= \int_0^1 \left[v_i - \frac{1}{f(v_i)} \int_{v_i}^1 f(z)\, dz\right] x_i(v_i)\, f(v_i)\, dv_i$$

$$= \int_0^1 \left[v_i - \frac{1 - F(v_i)}{f(v_i)}\right] x_i(v_i)\, f(v_i)\, dv_i. \tag{7.53}$$

Denote

$$\eta(v_i) \equiv v_i - \frac{1 - F(v_i)}{f(v_i)},$$

which is usually known as the *virtual valuation* of individual i when her (actual) valuation is v_i. With this notation in hand, and relying on expressions (7.46) and (7.53), the optimization problem (7.51) can be reformulated as follows:

$$\max_M \sum_{i=1}^n \mathbf{E}\left[p_i(v_i)\right] = \max_M \sum_{i=1}^n \int \eta(v_i)\, x_i(v)\, f(v_i)\, dv_i$$

$$= \max_M \sum_{i=1}^n \int \eta(v_i)\, X_i(v) \prod_{j=1}^n f(v_j)\, dv$$

$$= \max_M \int \left(\sum_{i=1}^n \eta(v_i)\, X_i(v)\right) \prod_{j=1}^n f(v_j)\, dv. \tag{7.54}$$

Given a valuation profile $v = (v_1, v_2, \ldots, v_n)$, denote by

$$\Lambda(v) \equiv \{i \in \{1, 2, \ldots, n\} : \eta(v_i) \geq 0\}$$

the set of individuals with nonnegative *virtual* valuations. Furthermore, let

$$\Lambda^*(v) \equiv \{i \in \Lambda(v) : \eta(v_i) \geq \eta(v_j), \; j \in \Lambda(v)\}$$

stand for the *subset* of those individuals in $\Lambda(v)$ whose virtual valuation is maximal. Then, consider any mechanism $M = \{P_i, X_i\}_{i=1}^n$ with the property

$$\sum_{j \in \Lambda^*(v)} X_j(v) = 1 \quad \text{if } \Lambda(v) \neq \emptyset; \tag{7.55}$$

$$\sum_{i=1}^n X_i(v) = 0 \quad \text{otherwise.} \tag{7.56}$$

In such a mechanism, the good is assigned to any of the buyers whose *virtual* valuation is both maximal *and* nonnegative, provided one such individual exists (if there are several of them, the selection can be done in an arbitrary – possibly random – fashion). On the other hand, if *every* buyer has a negative virtual valuation, *none* of the buyers receives the good. Clearly, in view of (7.54), *any* mechanism that satisfies (7.55) and (7.56) is a possible solution to the seller's optimization problem posed in (7.51).

Suppose that $\eta(v_i)$ is increasing in v_i, which is a "regularity condition" satisfied by many interesting probability distributions (e.g., the uniform distribution). Under this condition, we now argue that a particularly simple *optimal* mechanism is provided by the first-price auction (cf. Subsection 7.3.1), but with the important complement of a *reservation price* $\hat{p}$, which is computed as follows:

$$\hat{p} = \min \{v_i \in [0, 1] : \eta(v_i) \equiv v_i - \frac{1 - F(v_i)}{f(v_i)} \geq 0\}. \tag{7.57}$$

Thus, $\hat{p}$ is made equal to the minimum v_i that induces a nonnegative virtual valuation.[110] The interpretation of this reservation price is the usual one: the seller does not accept any bid below $\hat{p}$. It is easy to check that any equilibrium strategies for the Bayesian game induced by such a *modified first-price auction* (MFPA) must satisfy the following:

(a) Individuals with valuation larger than $\hat{p}$ (and essentially only those)[111] participate in the auction;

(b) For those individuals i who do participate in the auction, their strategies $g_i(v_i)$ are increasing in v_i.

The fact that the MFPA displays the above features implies that, provided there is at least one individual with $v_i \geq \hat{p}$ who actually participates in the auction, the winner is one of those whose valuation (both actual and virtual) is maximal. Therefore, (7.55) and (7.56) are satisfied, in turn ensuring that the MFPA (or, equivalently, the associated direct mechanism under the truthful equilibrium) is an optimal procedure for the seller.

But, under the maintained assumption that $\eta(\cdot)$ is increasing, it should be clear that the seller would obtain an *identical* expected payoff from *any* other mechanism that guarantees as well that, in equilibrium, the good is assigned to the buyer with the maximum virtual valuation $\eta(v_i) \geq 0$. By way of illustration, another interesting mechanism displaying this performance is the so-called second-price auction, provided it is subject to the same reservation price $\hat{p}$ specified in (7.57). In a (modified) second-price auction, the winning individual (the one who submits the highest bid, which has to be at least equal to $\hat{p}$) does not pay her bid but the second-highest one (or $\hat{p}$, if she is the only one willing to participate). It may be verified (see Exercise 7.17) that conditions (7.55) and (7.56) continue to hold for this alternative mechanism and hence the same *expected* gains for the seller are obtained as in an MFPA if the same reservation price $\hat{p}$ is applied.

What has been just learned for both the first- and second-price auctions represents particular instances of a quite general result: the so-called *income equivalence theorem* (Myerson, 1981). This result, which is an immediate consequence of

---

[110] For example, if the underlying distribution is uniform on $[0, 1]$ – i.e., $F(v_i) = v_i$ for each v_i – the reservation price $\hat{p}$ is equal to $1/2$.

[111] The decision adopted by indifferent individuals whose valuation $v_i = \hat{p}_i$ is irrelevant, because this possibility has null *ex ante* probability.

the form of expression (7.54), establishes the following conclusion: *any* two mechanisms that induce the same allocation pattern for the good (that is, assign the good with the same probabilities $X_i(v), i = 1, 2, \ldots, n$, for each valuation profile v) lead to the same expected payoff for the seller. Thus, despite the fact that, for example, first- and second-price auctions induce a very different pattern of actual *payments*, both produce (even irrespectively of the reservation price) the *same* expected payoff for the seller.

As (7.57) indicates, either when using a first- or a second-price auction, the seller will always want to impose some *positive* reservation price. Of course, this is just a reflection of the privileged position she holds in the "market," which allows an exploitation of her entailed "monopoly power." As in other analogous cases well understood in the industrial organization literature, the aim of such a reservation price is to extract some rents (here, of an informational kind) from the buyers. And, as usual, this maneuver does not come without an efficiency cost. For example, if $\hat{p}$ is determined as in (7.57) in a first- or second-price auction, the good will not be traded when the valuation profile v is such that $0 < v_i < \hat{p}$ for each $i = 1, 2, \ldots, n$. In those cases, whose *a priori* probability is $(F(\hat{p}))^n > 0$, the resulting allocation is obviously inefficient.

7.4 Mechanism design (V): buyer–seller trade

In this section, we focus on the study of trade mechanisms between buyers and sellers of an indivisible good, all of them playing an active role in the process – thus, unlike in Section 7.3, the allocation problem is now genuinely two-sided. For simplicity, we restrict attention to a stylized setup involving only one buyer and one seller. First, in Subsection 7.4.1, we study the natural ("simple-minded") mechanism in which both parties offer their respective terms of trade (i.e., a price) and an actual transaction takes place if, and only if, both offers are compatible. This mechanism is seen to be *ex post* inefficient, in the sense that *not* all gains from trade are sure to be exhausted in every case. In view of this state of affairs, we adopt in Subsection 7.4.2 a mechanism-design viewpoint (akin to that pursued in Subsection 7.3.2.2) and pose the following natural question: Is it possible to construct a more "sophisticated" mechanism that (at least in the simple bilateral context considered) guarantees allocation efficiency? As we explain, the answer to this question leads, essentially, to an impossibility result.

7.4.1 *Double auctions*

Consider a simple "market" where just one seller and one buyer face each other, the former in the possession of a certain indivisible good that the latter may purchase. They are assumed to participate in a *double auction*, both submitting simultaneously a certain proposal indicating the *worst* terms of trade (i.e., "price") each finds admissible.[112] More specifically, identify the buyer and seller by b and s, respectively, and denote by p_b and p_s their corresponding proposals. Then, the rules of the

---

[112] This auction was first studied by Chatterjee and Samuelson (1983).

procedure are as follows:

- If $p_b \geq p_s$, trade ensues at the average proposal $p_s + p_b/2$.
- If $p_b < p_s$, no trade takes place.

Let v_b and v_s represent the respective valuations of buyer and seller, customarily called their "reservation values." For the buyer, v_b may be conceived as the cost of acquiring a substitute for the good in question, whereas for the seller v_s may be identified with the payoff (or profit) she could obtain if the good were devoted to some other purpose. That is, v_b and v_s are to be thought of as, respectively, the buyer's and seller's opportunity costs. Their precise magnitude is taken to be private information for the agent in question, buyer or seller. And, as usual, it is assumed that each agent believes the valuation of the other agent is selected, *independently* of her own, according to some specific distribution function. For simplicity, this probability distribution is assumed uniform on the interval [0, 1] in either case.

The context described may be modeled as a Bayesian game where, for each player $i = b, s$, the type space is $T_i = [0, 1]$, the action space is $A_i = \mathbb{R}_+$, and the payoff functions are defined as follows:

$$\pi_b(v_b, v_s, p_b, p_s) = \begin{cases} v_b - \dfrac{p_s + p_b}{2} & \text{if } p_b \geq p_s \\ 0 & \text{otherwise;} \end{cases}$$

$$\pi_s(v_b, v_s, p_b, p_s) = \begin{cases} \dfrac{p_s + p_b}{2} - v_s & \text{if } p_b \geq p_s \\ 0 & \text{otherwise.} \end{cases}$$

In this game, the pure strategies of each player are functions of the form

$$p_i : [0, 1] \to [0, 1], \quad i = b, s,$$

that specify, for each player (buyer and seller), the way in which her proposal depends (deterministically) on her respective valuation.

The game displays a large number of pure-strategy equilibria. To illustrate this point, fix any arbitrary $\zeta \in (0, 1)$ and consider the following associated strategies:

- For the buyer,

$$\tilde{p}_b(v_b) = \begin{cases} \zeta & \text{if } v_b \geq \zeta \\ 0 & \text{if } v_b < \zeta. \end{cases} \tag{7.58}$$

- For the seller,

$$\tilde{p}_s(v_s) = \begin{cases} \zeta & \text{if } v_s \leq \zeta \\ 1 & \text{if } v_s > \zeta. \end{cases} \tag{7.59}$$

It is easy to check that this pair of strategies defines a BNE for any given ζ – cf. Exercise 7.20. Trade always takes place in it at the fixed price ζ, but only with probability

$$\Pr\{v_b \geq \zeta\} \Pr\{v_s \leq \zeta\} = \zeta (1 - \zeta).$$

On the other hand, with the complementary probability $(1 - \zeta (1 - \zeta))$ no trade occurs. As the parameter ζ is made to vary over the interval $[0, 1]$, one traces a continuum of different equilibria, all with the same format but quite different terms of trade.[113] Clearly, the particular equilibrium in this class that induces highest *ex ante* probability of trade is obtained for $\zeta = 1/2$.

The equilibria of the form (7.58) and (7.59) display an important drawback: they depend very discontinuously on the players' types. More precisely, each of these equilibria allows for the possibility that just a slight change in the players' valuations may lead to the abrupt collapse of otherwise substantial gains from trade and thus a large inefficiency.[114] This suggests that, in contrast, it would be interesting to have a BNE that exhibits a more gradual (say, continuous) dependence on the underlying agents' types. In this respect, of course, a natural candidate is one that involves affine strategies, formally akin to those contemplated in Section 7.3.1 for one-sided auctions. To find an equilibrium of this sort is the task undertaken in what follows.

Consider, therefore, strategies for the induced Bayesian game of the form

$$p_i (v_i) = \alpha_i + \beta_i v_i, \quad \alpha_i, \beta_i \geq 0, \ i = b, s.$$

In equilibrium, the strategies adopted by each agent must be a mutual best response. For the buyer, this implies that, given any valuation v_b, the induced proposal $p_b^* = p_b(v_b)$ is to be a solution of the following optimization problem:

$$\max_{p_b \in [0, 1]} \left\{ v_b - \frac{p_b + \mathbf{E}\left[\alpha_s + \beta_s v_s \mid p_b \geq \alpha_s + \beta_s v_s \right]}{2} \right\}$$
$$\times \Pr \{ p_b \geq \alpha_s + \beta_s v_s \}. \tag{7.60}$$

And for the seller, given any v_s, the induced $p_s(v_s)$ must be a solution of the problem

$$\max_{p_s \in [0, 1]} \left\{ \frac{p_s + \mathbf{E}\left[\alpha_b + \beta_b v_b \mid p_s \leq \alpha_b + \beta_b v_b \right]}{2} - v_s \right\}$$
$$\times \Pr \{ p_s \leq \alpha_b + \beta_b v_b \}. \tag{7.61}$$

Given that the seller's strategy is taken to be affine, her proposal p_s is (from the viewpoint of the buyer) uniformly distributed on the closed interval $[\alpha_s + (\beta_s \times 0), \alpha_s + (\beta_s \times 1)] = [\alpha_s, \alpha_s + \beta_s]$. Therefore, it follows that the buyer's problem (7.60) may be rewritten as follows:

$$\max_{p_b \in [0, 1]} \left\{ v_b - \frac{1}{2} \left(p_b + \frac{\alpha_s + p_b}{2} \right) \right\} \frac{p_b - \alpha_s}{\beta_s}.$$

---

[113] Note the marked parallelism between the present equilibria and those Nash (nonperfect) equilibria considered in Section 5.2.1 within a bargaining context (cf. Exercise 5.8). There, as well, one could span the full range of possible surplus shares through strategies that are rigidly linked to a certain minimum proposal/demand.

[114] By way of example, suppose v_s is close to zero and v_b falls from, say, $\zeta + \varepsilon$ to $\zeta - \varepsilon$ for any small $\varepsilon > 0$. This small change in the buyer's valuation leads to the breakdown of trade despite the fact that, if ζ is high, the potential gains to be obtained from it are large.

Since, on the other hand, the buyer's proposal p_b is *ex ante* distributed on the interval $[\alpha_b, \alpha_b + \beta_b]$ in a uniform fashion, we may proceed analogously for the seller and write her optimization problem (7.61) as follows:

$$\max_{p_s \in [0, 1]} \left\{ \frac{1}{2} \left(p_s + \frac{p_s + \alpha_b + \beta_b}{2} \right) - v_s \right\} \frac{\alpha_b + \beta_b - p_s}{\beta_b}.$$

The FONC for those two optimization problems (the buyer's and the seller's) yield, for interior solutions p_b^* and p_s^*, the following expressions:

$$p_b^* = \frac{\alpha_s}{3} + \frac{2}{3} v_b$$

$$p_s^* = \frac{\alpha_b + \beta_b}{3} + \frac{2}{3} v_s.$$

Hence, we conclude that the equilibrium strategies must have $\beta_b = \beta_s = 2/3$, which in turn leads to the following linear system of equations for α_b and α_s:

$$\alpha_b = \frac{\alpha_s}{3}$$

$$\alpha_s = \frac{\alpha_b + 2/3}{3}.$$

By solving this system, we find that $\alpha_b = 1/12$ and $\alpha_s = 1/4$, thus obtaining the following equilibrium strategies:

$$p_b(v_b) = \frac{2}{3} v_b + \frac{1}{12} \tag{7.62}$$

$$p_s(v_s) = \frac{2}{3} v_s + \frac{1}{4}. \tag{7.63}$$

Trade occurs only when the buyer's and seller's proposals satisfy $p_b \geq p_s$. Rewriting this inequality in terms of the equilibrium strategies (7.62) and (7.63), we obtain that, for trade to materialize one must have

$$\frac{2}{3} v_b + \frac{1}{12} \geq \frac{2}{3} v_s + \frac{1}{4}$$

or, equivalently,

$$v_b \geq v_s + 1/4.$$

The above condition characterizes the type (valuation) profiles where, given the double-auction mechanism used, the good in question is transferred to the buyer. This condition clearly indicates that, *a priori*, there is positive probability that, even though it would be efficient that the buyer obtains the good (i.e., $v_b > v_s$), trade does not occur because the submitted proposals do not warrant it (i.e., $p_b < p_s$). Of course, this is just a reflection of the strategic considerations (or, in a sense, manipulation attempts) arising, under incomplete information, in the Bayesian game

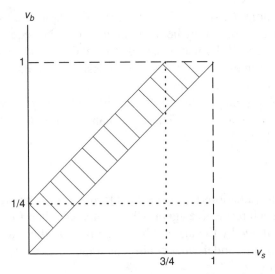

Figure 7.14: Inefficiency range in the double auction between buyer and seller.

induced by a double auction. The extent of the potential inefficiency entailed is graphically illustrated in Figure 7.14 .

The unit square depicted in Figure 7.14 encompasses the full set $[0, 1] \times [0, 1]$ of possible realizations in the space of buyer–seller valuations (or types). The points above the diagonal, where $v_b > v_s$, reflect all those situations where it is *ex post* efficient that trade should take place. However, trade does not materialize (at equilibrium) for the type realizations lying in the shaded area. Therefore, the relative size of this area quantifies, in expected terms, the magnitude of the inefficiency resulting from the interplay of individual incentives, incomplete information, and the allocation mechanism considered.

7.4.2 *The impossibility of efficient trade**

The former subsection has shown that the operation of a buyer–seller double auction cannot guarantee efficiency because, at least for some of the BNE of the induced game, some trades that are mutually beneficial *ex post* are not realized. In view of this state of affairs, one may naturally wonder whether this unsatisfactory situation may be overcome either by relying on other equilibria of the same game or the use of an alternative, perhaps more sophisticated, mechanism. Again, since the issue thus raised concerns the full performance achievable over the *whole universe* of relevant mechanisms, an effective theoretical tool for addressing it is provided by the revelation principle (cf. Subsection 7.3.2.1).

Thus, the approach to be pursued here is analogous to that of Subsection 7.3.2.2, where similar issues were tackled concerning one-sided allocation mechanisms. As in that case, we underscore the generality of our conclusions by generalizing significantly the framework proposed in Subsection 7.4.1. Specifically, it is assumed that the buyer and seller valuations are independently selected according to *general* respective distribution functions $F_b(\cdot)$ and $F_s(\cdot)$. These distributions are assumed to display a common support on $[0, 1]$ (any bounded interval could be equivalently used) and have corresponding well-defined densities $f_b(\cdot)$ and $f_s(\cdot)$. In this broad context, we ask the following question: Is it possible to design some buyer–seller mechanism that guarantees *ex post* efficiency?

By invoking the revelation principle, one may focus without loss of generality on truthful equilibria of direct mechanisms.[115] These mechanisms are characterized, on the one hand, by a pair of transfer functions

$$Y_b, \ Y_s : [0, 1]^2 \to \mathbb{R}$$

that, for each pair of reported valuations $(v_b, v_s) \in [0, 1]^2$, determine the monetary transfers to be *received* by each respective agent – these transfers, therefore, are to be interpreted as payments *made* by the agent when negative. On the other hand, the mechanism must also specify under what conditions trade takes place. This is formalized through a function

$$X : [0, 1]^2 \to [0, 1]$$

that, for each pair of reported valuations $(v_b, v_s) \in [0, 1]^2$, determines the probability with which trade occurs.

Consider any particular direct mechanism $M = [Y_b(\cdot), \ Y_s(\cdot), \ X(\cdot)]$ and suppose that, at a truthful BNE of the induced game, the resulting outcome is always efficient. This mechanism must then satisfy

$$v_b > v_s \Rightarrow X(v_b, v_s) = 1 \tag{7.64}$$

$$v_b < v_s \Rightarrow X(v_b, v_s) = 0. \tag{7.65}$$

As in Subsection 7.3.2.2, we require the further condition that the mechanism be *individually rational*. That is, in the *interim* stage (when agents already know their respective types), neither the buyer nor the seller should ever want to block the operation of the mechanism. At this point, therefore, they should never prefer to stay with the status quo rather than committing to follow whatever happen to be the *ex post* prescriptions of the mechanism. To formalize this condition, consider any given $(\hat{v}_b, \hat{v}_s) \in [0, 1]^2$, and let

$$y_b(\hat{v}_b) \equiv \int_0^1 Y_b(\hat{v}_b, v_s) \ f_s(v_s) \, dv_s$$

$$y_s(\hat{v}_s) \equiv \int_0^1 Y_s(v_b, \hat{v}_s) \ f_b(v_b) \, dv_b$$

represent the expected payments respectively anticipated by the buyer and seller, contingent on their respective information. On the other hand, define the corresponding expected trade probabilities perceived by the buyer and seller as

---

[115] The formal approach pursued here parallels that of Úbeda (1997).

follows:

$$x_b(\hat{v}_b) \equiv \int_0^1 X(\hat{v}_b, v_s)\, f_s(v_s)\, dv_s$$

$$x_s(\hat{v}_s) \equiv \int_0^1 X(v_b, \hat{v}_s)\, f_b(v_b)\, dv_b.$$

Then, the *IR* conditions can be expressed as follows:

$$y_b(\hat{v}_b) + x_b(\hat{v}_b)\, \hat{v}_b \geq 0 \tag{7.66}$$

$$y_s(\hat{v}_s) + (1 - x_s(\hat{v}_s))\, \hat{v}_s \geq \hat{v}_s. \tag{7.67}$$

By (7.64) and (7.65), we must have

$$x_b(\hat{v}_b) = F_s(\hat{v}_b)$$

$$x_s(\hat{v}_s) = 1 - F_b(\hat{v}_s)$$

so that the IR conditions (7.66)–(7.67) can be simply rewritten as follows:

$$y_b(\hat{v}_b) \geq -F_s(\hat{v}_b)\, \hat{v}_b \tag{7.68}$$

$$y_s(\hat{v}_s) \geq (1 - F_b(\hat{v}_s))\, \hat{v}_s. \tag{7.69}$$

Now, we introduce the key requirement (which is justified by the revelation principle) that the direct mechanism under consideration must support truthful behavior at BNE in the induced Bayesian game. Formally, this implies that, for each $i, j \in \{b, s\}$, $j \neq i$, one must have

$$\forall \hat{v}_i, \tilde{v}_i \in [0, 1], \quad F_j(\hat{v}_i)\, \hat{v}_i + y_i(\hat{v}_i) \geq F_j(\tilde{v}_i)\, \hat{v}_i + y_i(\tilde{v}_i), \tag{7.70}$$

where we implicitly rely again on (7.64) and (7.65). But, of course, by permuting the role of $\hat{v}_i$ and $\tilde{v}_i$ in (7.70), the following condition must also hold:

$$\forall \hat{v}_i, \tilde{v}_i \in [0, 1], \quad F_j(\tilde{v}_i)\, \tilde{v}_i + y_i(\tilde{v}_i) \geq F_j(\hat{v}_i)\, \tilde{v}_i + y_i(\hat{v}_i). \tag{7.71}$$

Therefore, given any pair of valuations $\hat{v}_i, \tilde{v}_i \in [0, 1]$, (7.70) and (7.71) can be integrated into the following single expression:

$$-[F_j(\hat{v}_i) - F_j(\tilde{v}_i)]\, \tilde{v}_i \geq y_i(\hat{v}_i) - y_i(\tilde{v}_i) \geq -[F_j(\hat{v}_i) - F_j(\tilde{v}_i)]\, \hat{v}_i. \tag{7.72}$$

Without loss of generality, let $\hat{v}_i > \tilde{v}_i$. Then, divide through (7.72) by $(\hat{v}_i - \tilde{v}_i)$ and make $\tilde{v}_i \to \hat{v}_i$ to obtain

$$\left. \frac{\partial y_i(v_i)}{\partial v_i} \right|_{v_i = \hat{v}_i} = -\hat{v}_i \left. \frac{\partial F_j(v_j)}{\partial v_j} \right|_{v_j = \hat{v}_i}$$

or

$$y_i'(\hat{v}_i) = -\hat{v}_i\, f_j(\hat{v}_i), \tag{7.73}$$

which is a condition that must be satisfied for all $\hat{v}_i \in [0, 1]$ if truthful revelation is to be a BNE.

Through integration, the above differential equation can be used to construct the expected transfer functions as follows:

$$y_b(\hat{v}_b) = y_b(0) + \int_0^{\hat{v}_b} y_b'(v_b)\, dv_b = y_b(0) + \int_0^{\hat{v}_b} -v_b\, f_s(v_b)\, dv_b \quad (7.74)$$

$$y_s(\hat{v}_s) = y_s(1) - \int_{\hat{v}_s}^1 y_s'(v_s)\, dv_s = y_s(1) - \int_{\hat{v}_s}^1 -v_s\, f_b(v_s)\, dv_s, \quad (7.75)$$

for some suitably chosen boundary conditions, $y_b(0)$ and $y_s(1)$.

The issue at hand may then be posed precisely as follows. Is there a *feasible* direct mechanism that is compatible with the IR conditions (7.68) and (7.69) and the incentive-compatibility constraints (7.74) and (7.75)? (Note that all of these conditions already embody implicitly the efficiency requirements (7.64) and (7.65).) Of course, the key point here concerns the question of what is to be understood as a "feasible mechanism." Minimally, an uncontroversial demand in this respect would seem to be that the mechanism in question be self-reliant, in the sense of *never* requiring outside funds to implement it. Unfortunately, it turns out that no such feasible, efficient, and individually rational mechanism exists. To see this, use (7.74) and (7.75) to compute the total net payment jointly expected by the buyer and seller as follows:

$$\mathbf{E}_{(v_b, v_s)} \left[y_b(v_b) + y_s(v_s)\right] = y_b(0) + y_s(1)$$

$$+ \mathbf{E}_{(v_b, v_s)} \left[\int_{v_s}^1 z\, f_b(z)\, dz - \int_0^{v_b} z\, f_s(z)\, dz\right]. \quad (7.76)$$

Now note that, particularizing the IR constraints (7.68) and (7.69) to $v_b = 0$ and $v_s = 1$, we have

$$y_b(0) \geq 0; \quad y_s(1) \geq 0.$$

Therefore, in view of (7.76), we can conclude

$$\mathbf{E}_{(v_b, v_s)} \left[y_b(v_b) + y_s(v_s)\right] \geq \mathbf{E}_{(v_b, v_s)} \left\{ \begin{array}{l} \mathbf{E}_{v_b}\left[v_b \mid v_b \geq v_s\right] \Pr(v_b \geq v_s) + \\ \mathbf{E}_{v_s}\left[v_s \mid v_s \leq v_b\right] \Pr(v_s \leq v_b) \end{array} \right\}$$

$$= \mathbf{E}_{(v_b, v_s)} \left\{v_b - v_s \mid v_s \leq v_b\right\} \Pr(v_s \leq v_b)$$

$$> 0.$$

That is, any *efficient* mechanism that were to satisfy the incentive constraints given by (7.68)–(7.70) would require that some outside funds be used, on average, to render it viable. This means, in essence, that efficiency and incentives are incompatible requirements and that, in the absence of outside ("costly") support, one should be prepared to admit that gains from trade are not always materialized.

In view of this negative conclusion, one might still wonder (much along the lines pursued in Subsection 7.3.2.2 for one-sided mechanisms) what are the "second-best" mechanisms that, given the prevailing incentive constraints, maximize expected gains from trade. Again relying on the revelation principle, Myerson and Satterthwaite (1983) established the following conclusion:

> Assume that the buyer's and seller's valuations are uniformly distributed on a compact interval , say [0, 1]. Then, among *all* exchange mechanisms and corresponding equilibria that one could possibly construct, agents' (aggregate) expected gains are maximized by the first-price auction and its Bayesian equilibrium in affine strategies (cf. Subsection 7.4.1).

Thus, much as in the case of one-sided mechanisms, it is interesting to learn that rather simple and natural mechanisms can perform as well as any other, at least in some paradigmatic contexts (e.g., under uniform prior distributions).

Summary

This chapter has discussed a number of economic applications where agent interaction takes place under incomplete (or asymmetric) information on relevant details of the strategic situation. We have started with the classical model due to Spence that focuses on the potential role played by education as a *signal* of unobserved worker productivity in labor markets. Specifically, the setup involves two firms that may discern the education level of the worker they face but not her underlying productivity. Under these circumstances, the fact that education is assumed to be more costly an activity for low-productivity types introduces the possibility that, at SE, different education levels "separate" types and thus allow firms to infer the worker's productivity. We have discussed conditions under which other kind of equilibria also exists, such as pooling (or even hybrid) equilibria where intertype separation does not (at least completely) take place. Finally, we have relied on a forward-induction refinement of SE (the intuitive criterion) to select, among the typical multiplicity of equilibria, the one that permits intertype separation at the lowest possible "cost" for the high-productivity type.

Next, we have discussed a model proposed by Rotschild and Stiglitz whose focus is on the implications of incomplete information (and the resulting adverse selection) on the functioning of insurance markets. As in Spence's model, their theoretical context also involves two uninformed firms and one informed agent, although the order of move is now reversed. First, the firms decide simultaneously on the set of insurance contracts offered to the individual, in ignorance of the latter's particular risk conditions (i.e., her type, high or low). Then, the individual (aware of her own type) chooses the contract that, among those offered, yields her the highest expected payoff. We have shown that, in general, there *can* exist only (weak perfect Bayesian) equilibria that are separating, i.e., strategy configurations in which each type chooses a different contract. However, we have also seen that there are reasonable parameter configurations (specifically, a relatively low *ex ante* probability for the high-risk type) where *no* equilibrium whatsoever exists in pure strategies. This has been understood as the effect of a negative (information-based) externality imposed by the high-risk type on the low-risk one, whose effect naturally becomes important when the latter is relatively frequent.

Then, we have addressed two different problems of mechanism design concerning the allocation of a given indivisible object. The first of them involves a *one-sided* context, since only the buyers' side of the market is genuinely involved in the strategic interaction. Specifically, we have studied a simple first-price auction, conducted in the presence of two potential buyers who are privately informed of their own valuations for the good. Modeled as a Bayesian game, we have solved for its unique BNE in affine strategies. In this equilibrium, individuals try to exploit strategically their private information by bidding only half of their true valuation of the good. Of course, this implies that, in equilibrium, the individual with the highest valuation ends up obtaining the good but at a price that is below his reservation value. This has led to the following mechanism-design questions. Is there any procedure for allocating the good that the seller might prefer to a first-price auction? If so, can one identify the mechanism that maximizes expected revenues?

To tackle such "ambitious" questions, we have relied on the powerful revelation principle. In a nutshell, this principle establishes that the performance achievable through any arbitrary mechanism can be reproduced through truthful equilibria of a direct mechanism where players' messages concern their respective characteristics. From a practical viewpoint, it permits narrowing down "mechanism search" substantially and thus answering the questions posed above in a clear-cut fashion. Quite surprisingly, we have found that not only the first-price auction but also any other mechanism where the highest-valuation individual obtains the good at equilibrium is (equivalently) optimal for the seller, provided the seller can impose some suitable minimum (i.e., reservation) price. In essence, this is the content of the so-called income-equivalence theorem.

Finally, we have turned to a two-sided context in which both buyers and sellers actively participate in the mechanism for allocating an indivisible object. Focusing on the simplest case where there is only a single buyer and a single seller, we have studied a double auction in which agents are asked to submit simultaneously their worst acceptable terms of trade. Under the assumption that agents' valuations are private information, we have modeled it as a Bayesian game and solved for the (unique) BNE in affine strategies. In this equilibrium, players' underbidding incentives induce, with positive probability, *ex post* inefficiency, i.e., trade is not carried out in some cases where, nevertheless, there would be aggregate gains to do so. Motivated by this negative conclusion, we again have been led to a mechanism-design question. Is there any mechanism that, at equilibrium, guarantees *ex post* efficiency? By resorting once more to the revelation principle, this question has been provided with an essentially negative answer. That is, no such mechanism exists, if players must always be furnished with incentives to participate in it (i.e., if the requirement of individual rationality is to be satisfied).

Exercises

Exercise 7.1: Within the Spence signaling model presented in Section 7.1, construct a graphical example where there is *no* pooling SE.

Exercise 7.2: Recall the multistage labor-market context given by (1)–(4) in Section 7.1.

(a) Model it as a Bayesian game (that is, *not* as a signaling game). Show that, for any education level $\eta_o < \eta^*(H)$, there exists a BNE in which both types of worker choose η_o. (Recall that $\eta^*(\theta)$ stands for the optimal education level chosen by each type $\theta = H, L$ under complete information.)

(b) Recast the strategic context as a signaling game and show that there exists a certain $\check{\eta} > 0$ such that there can be no pooling SE where both types choose an education level $\eta < \check{\eta}$.

(c) Explain the contrast between (a) and (b).

Exercise 7.3*: In the Spence signaling model, posit linear production functions of the form

$$f(\theta, \eta) = a(\theta) + b(\theta)\, \eta$$

with $a(H) \geq a(L) \geq 0$ and $b(H) > b(L)$. Propose conditions on the cost functions $c(\theta, \cdot)$ that guarantee the existence of a pooling SE for any given value of $p > 0$ (the prior probability of type H).

Exercise 7.4: In the context of Exercise 7.3, consider any of the pooling equilibria existing under the conditions specified there. Let ω_0 and η_0 be the wage and education level materialized at this equilibrium and define the education level $\check{\eta} \neq \eta_0$ that solves the following equation:

$$\omega_0 - c(H, \eta_0) = [pf(H, \check{\eta}) + (1 - p)\, f(L, \check{\eta})] - c(H, \check{\eta});$$

that is, at the education level $\check{\eta}$, the worker of type H is indifferent between being paid the expected productivity or, alternatively, choosing the level η_0 and being paid ω_0.

(a) Prove that $\check{\eta}$ is well defined and unique if

$$\frac{\partial c(H, \eta_0)}{\partial \eta} < p\, b(H) + (1 - p)\, b(L)$$

and $\partial^2 c(H, \eta) / \partial \eta^2$ is bounded below, above zero.

(b) Show that the common education level η_0 may be supported as a pooling SE by the following off-equilibrium beliefs (much less extreme than those contemplated in the text):

$$\mu(\eta)(H) = p \quad \text{if } \eta \geq \check{\eta},$$

$$\mu(\eta)(H) = 0 \quad \text{if } \eta < \check{\eta},\ \eta \neq \eta_0.$$

Exercise 7.5: Prove or refute the following assertion:

If the no-envy condition (7.8) applies, the Spence signaling model displays a separating SE but has *no* pooling SE.

Exercise 7.6: Under the assumption that

$$f(L, \eta^*(L)) - c(L, \eta^*(L)) < f(H, \eta^*(H)) - c(L, \eta^*(H)),$$

find a separating SE for the Spence signaling model that (both on- and off-equilibrium) is different from the one specified in the text under these circumstances. Determine the maximum education level for the high type that may be supported at some such equilibrium.

Exercise 7.7: Suppose that, in the context of the Spence signaling model, a hybrid SE is being played in which the worker of type L chooses a mixed action with a two-point support $\{\hat{\eta}, \check{\eta}\}$, $\hat{\eta} > \check{\eta}$, whereas the worker of type H selects a deterministic education level. Prove or refute the validity of the following statements.

   (a) The education level $\hat{\eta}$ is always lower than $\eta^*(H)$.
   (b) The education level $\hat{\eta}$ is always lower than $\tilde{\eta}$, where $\tilde{\eta}$ is given by (7.10).

   If any of these two statements is not generally true, propose additional conditions on the data of the environment that render them valid.

Exercise 7.8*: In the context of Exercise 7.3 make

$$a(\theta) = 0, \quad \theta = H, L$$
$$b(H) = 2, \quad b(L) = 1,$$

and posit cost functions given by

$$c(\theta, \eta) = \frac{\eta^2}{b(\theta)}.$$

Under the assumption that $p > 1/2$, characterize *all* SE.

Exercise 7.9: Define a hybrid SE for the Spence signaling model that is polar to the class of those equilibria considered in Section 7.1 – that is, an SE where type L plays a deterministic action but type H randomizes between two education levels (one of these being the same as that chosen by type L). Illustrate the equilibrium diagrammatically.

Exercise 7.10*: In the scenario graphically depicted in Figure 7.7, use the intuitive criterion to rule out the possibility of a hybrid SE where only one of the two types, H or L, separates itself from the alternative one with positive probability.

Exercise 7.11: In the insurance-market context described in Section 7.2, postulate the following specific data for the environment. The elementary utility function $V(\cdot)$ is given by

$$V(W) = \ln W,$$

whereas $\hat{W}_1 = 2$, $\hat{W}_2 = 1$, $\rho^H = 2/3$, and $\rho^L = 1/3$. Identify, as exhaustively as you can, the set of prior probabilities p for a high-risk type that are consistent with the existence of a PWPBE.

Exercise 7.12*: Consider the following variation on the context described in Exercise 7.11. Before the firms propose their respective menus of insurance contracts, the individual can choose whether to reveal her own risk characteristics (i.e., her accident probability), as decided by Nature in the first stage of the game. If she does provide this information (which then becomes common knowledge) she must incur a verification cost $c > 0$ (which could be interpreted as the fee charged by an expert who is in a position to certify the information revealed). Subsequently, the game unfolds as described in the text, except that now firms can make their contract offers contingent on the (verified) information possibly disclosed by the individual in the first stage of the game.

(a) Show that if c is sufficiently low, both types of individual (high- and low-risk) obtain full insurance in the unique PWPBE of the present enlarged game.

(b) Explain the features of a PWPBE when the individual chooses not to reveal her information.

Exercise 7.13: Consider a context with a worker and two firms akin to the labor-market scenario described in Section 7.1. (In particular, the underlying data of the environment, such as preferences and productivities, satisfy the assumptions made there.) However, in contrast with the order of moves (1)–(4) postulated in the text, consider the following alternative sequence of decisions:

(1') Nature selects the type (ability) of worker, which is chosen as high ($\theta = H$) or low ($\theta = L$) with respective probabilities p and $(1 - p)$.

(2') In ignorance of the worker's type, each firm $i = 1, 2$ *simultaneously* proposes a *wage pattern* $\omega_i(\cdot)$ that specifies the wage that would be payed to the worker for each possible education level η (to be observed accurately at the time of employment).

(3') Given the proposals of both firms, the worker (who is aware of her ability) chooses a certain education level and either to work for a particular firm or to remain idle. (If she remains idle, she obtains a zero payoff.)

Show that all PWPBE of the game induced by (1')–(3') are separating, i.e., each worker type chooses in it a different education level.

Exercise 7.14: Prove *formally* that any equilibrium strategy of the kind considered in (7.37) for the two-buyer first-price auction must have $\alpha \geq 0$.

Exercise 7.15: Extend the first-price auction studied in Subsection 7.3.1 to a context with three potential buyers and compute the symmetric BNE in affine strategies. Can you extrapolate matters to the general case with n buyers?

Exercise 7.16: Consider a two-buyer setup where buyers' valuations for the single indivisible good are private information and *a priori* chosen from the set $V = \{v^0, v^1\}$ according to probabilities $P(v, v') = 1/4$, $\forall (v, v') \in V^2$. Define the Bayesian game induced by a first-price auction where bids are restricted to the set $B = \{v^0, v^1, (v^0 + v^1)/2\}$ and find two different BNE for this game.

Exercise 7.17*: Consider an allocation setup in which n individuals participate in a so-called *second-price auction* for a given indivisible object. In this auction, bids are submitted simultaneously and, given any bid profile $(a_1, a_2, \ldots, a_n) \in \mathbb{R}_+^n$, the object is assigned to the individual (or one of the individuals, randomly chosen, if there are several) who has issued the highest bid. In this respect, therefore, it is just like the first-price auction. The difference resides in that the individual i who obtains the good does *not* pay for it her own bid a_i but pays the second-highest bid given by $\max\{a_j : a_j \le a_i, \ j \ne i\}$.

(a) Assuming that each individual is privately informed of her own valuation, model the situation as a Bayesian game and find all its BNE.
(b) Now suppose there is a minimum bid, $\hat{p} > 0$, that buyers must be prepared to submit if they wish to participate in the mechanism. (If only one buyer chooses to participate, the second-highest bid is identified with $\hat{p}$.) Determine the BNE in this case.

Exercise 7.18*: Consider a Bayesian implementation context, as described in Subsection 7.3.2.1, where the underlying uncertainty is degenerate in the following sense. First, the type spaces are identical across agents, i.e., $\mathcal{U}_1 = \mathcal{U}_2 = \cdots = \mathcal{U}_n$. Second, the types across agents are fully correlated so that only profiles in the "diagonal" of $\mathcal{E}$ (i.e., with all agents being of the same type) display positive *ex ante* probability. Show that *any* single-valued SCR ϕ can be "Bayes implemented" if one restricts to *truthful* BNE of a suitably chosen direct mechanism. Is it generally true, however, that such a direct mechanism implements ϕ in the usual sense (i.e., satisfies both conditions (i) and (ii) in Subsection 7.3.2.1, when *any* BNE are allowed)?

Exercise 7.19*: Recall the notion of Nash implementation, as formulated in Section 3.3 under the implicit assumption that agents enjoy complete information about the underlying details of the environment. State and prove an analogue of the revelation principle for this implementation scenario.

Exercise 7.20: Verify that the strategies given by (7.58) and (7.59) define a BNE for the Bayesian game induced by the bilateral double auction described in Subsection 7.4.1.

Exercise 7.21*: Consider a first-price auction (as described in Subsection 7.3.1) with three potential buyers and the following additional feature: before the auction starts, the seller can demand from each buyer a deposit $x \ge 0$ to participate in it. However, if a buyer who has committed this deposit does not eventually obtain the good, she is entitled to recover it fully.

In this context, consider two different variations. In the first one, each buyer knows how many others *may* participate in the mechanism (i.e., two more) but not how many are finally involved (that is, who pays the deposit). In the second one, information about who is actually involved in the auction is common knowledge before it actually starts.

Which of these two possibilities would the seller choose? Which would be her preferred value of x?

CHAPTER 8

Repeated interaction: theory

8.1   Introduction and examples

In many situations of interest, the strategic context involves a *given* number of players who interact in a *repeated* fashion over time – e.g., the firms serving a common market, the provider of a certain service and her regular customers, or the members of a sports club. Often, it may also happen that the conditions underlying the interaction remain more or less constant throughout the process. (Thus, referring to the former examples, the aggregate demand and production technology faced by the firms are largely stable, the service provided remains essentially the same, or the activities of the club do not experience any significant change.) Then, we see in this chapter that the players' repeated interaction introduces rich intertemporal considerations that often have an important bearing on the outcome. More precisely, interesting behavior may arise in the *repeated* game that would be unattainable (say, it would not be consistent with equilibrium) in a one-shot play of the constituent *stage* game.

As a first illustration of matters, let us consider the prisoner's dilemma, whose payoffs are recalled in Table 8.1.

If this game is played only once, we know that (D, D) is the unique Nash equilibrium because D is a dominant strategy for each player. Now suppose this game is repeated a certain number of times, say T, between the same two players. Further assume that, at each $t = 1, 2, \ldots, T$, both players are fully informed of what happened at all prior $t' < t$. Then, in the induced multistage game, it is clear that a repetition of (D, D) every round (independently of what has happened beforehand) defines a subgame-perfect (and therefore, Nash) equilibrium – see Exercise 8.5. In contrast, of course, the more interesting question concerns whether it is possible to sustain some different (e.g., more "cooperative") kind of behavior at equilibrium. Intuitively, it would seem that an *initial* string of action pairs (C, C) could form part of a "consistent agreement" (i.e., an equilibrium), grounded on the players' strong incentives to extract, however partially, the gains potentially available for both from cooperation. As we presently see, however, the validity of this intuition depends crucially on the cardinality of the horizon of interaction T – specifically, on whether it is finite or infinite.

Consider first the case where T is finite (although arbitrarily large) and let $\gamma^* \equiv (\gamma_1^*, \gamma_2^*)$ be a subgame-perfect equilibrium of the corresponding repeated game. Since D is a strictly dominant strategy in the prisoner's dilemma (the stage game),

Table 8.1: *Prisoner's dilemma*

1 \ 2	D	C
D	−10, −10	0, −12
C	−12, 0	−1, −1

neither of the strategies γ_i^* ($i = 1, 2$) may prescribe C with positive probability in the last period $t = T$. Thus, γ^* must necessarily induce the action pair (D, D) in the last period, *independently* of what may have happened before. In view of this fact, the period before last comes to reflect the same considerations as the last one. From a strategic viewpoint, the period $t = T - 1$ is now essentially the "last one" because whatever actions are chosen then by either player, the ensuing behavior at $t = T$ is independent of those. Therefore, γ^* must also prescribe the action pair (D, D) at $t = T - 1$, this again independently of what may have occurred before, i.e., at *any* of the subgames starting at $t = T - 1$. Clearly, we can now proceed inductively to ever earlier periods in the repeated game to conclude that γ^* must have each player choose D at every period and for any corresponding subgame.

Consider now how matters are affected if rather than focusing on the notion of subgame-perfect equilibrium, we are concerned instead with the more general one of Nash equilibrium. As before, in the last period, the equilibrium strategies must induce (D, D), at least on the *equilibrium path*, i.e., at contingencies actually materializing at equilibrium. But then, in period $t = T - 1$, there is no reason why either player should play (again, on the equilibrium path) an action different from D. Thus, in analogy with our former inductive procedure, an iterative process unfolds that implies that, at equilibrium, both players must *actually* choose D at every t. Even though off the equilibrium path a wider range of "counterfactual" possibilities exist (cf. Exercise 8.2), these have no implications on realized behavior as long as players adhere to the equilibrium. We conclude, therefore, that the finite repetition of the prisoner's dilemma does not enlarge (compared with its one-shot version) the extent of players' cooperation actually materialized at equilibrium (either subgame perfect or the less restrictive of Nash).

Now suppose that the prisoner's dilemma is repeated an unbounded number of times where, naturally, the infinite repetition of a game is to be conceived only as a theoretical abstraction – i.e., a model of those situations in which the "last period" does not play any significant role in the analysis. If T is not finite, there is no longer a *last period* from where players can start the inductive process formerly described for the finite-horizon case. One may then conjecture that, in the infinitely repeated case, players should be able to reap (at least partially) the potential gains available from cooperation.

To address this issue precisely, let us postulate (as in Subsection 5.2.1) that each player has intertemporal preferences that discount future stage payoffs at a rate $\delta \in (0, 1)$. That is, the intertemporal payoff to player $i \in \{1, 2\}$ associated to a flow of stage payoffs $\{\pi_i^t\}_{t=1,2,\dots}$ is given by

$$\pi_i \equiv \sum_{t=1,2,\dots} \delta^{t-1} \pi_i^t.$$

On the one hand, of course, one still has (because this is independent of T) that a strategy profile inducing the stage-game Nash equilibrium (D, D) for *every* t and *every* possible past history is a Nash equilibrium of the repeated game. Now, however, it is not the only one if δ is large enough. Suppose, for concreteness, that $\delta = 2/3$ and consider the strategies for each player i that may be verbally described as follows:

For each $t = 1, 2, \ldots,$

(i) play C, if neither of the players has played D in one of the $t - 1$ preceding periods;

(ii) play D otherwise (that is, if at least one of the players has chosen D in some $t' < t$).

Let us now confirm that the above strategies define a Nash equilibrium of the infinitely repeated prisoner's dilemma. On the one hand, if both players follow their respective strategy, each of them obtains an overall payoff

$$\pi_i = \sum_{t=1,2,\ldots} (2/3)^{t-1} (-1) = -3.$$

On the other hand, if any particular player i deviates unilaterally at some particular time t_0, this player obtains at most

$$\pi_i' = \sum_{t=1}^{t_0-1} (2/3)^{t-1} (-1) + 0 + \sum_{t=t_0+1}^{\infty} (2/3)^{t-1} (-10),$$

which induces a maximum payoff difference

$$\Delta \pi_i \equiv \pi_i' - \pi_i = (2/3)^{t_0-1} \left(1 + (2/3) \sum_{\tau=1,2,\ldots} (2/3)^{\tau-1} (-9) \right),$$

which is obviously negative. Thus, it follows that, by resorting to the strategies described in (i) and (ii), the players are able to sustain cooperative behavior from the very first period as a Nash equilibrium of the repeated game.

At this point, it is worth stressing that the equilibrium described by (i) and (ii) is *not* the unique one in this case – e.g., a constant play of (D, D) throughout is, as noted, a Nash equilibrium as well for the (finitely or infinitely) repeated game. In fact, such an equilibrium multiplicity is not just an idiosyncratic feature of the present example. As we shall see, it arises quite generally as one of the distinctive implications of repeated interaction in most interesting contexts. This is one of the main insights provided by the wide variety of results in this chapter that fall under the label of "folk theorems." To introduce them precisely, we first turn in the following section to a formal description of the theoretical framework used to model repeated interaction.

8.2 Repeated games: basic theoretical framework

Consider a given set of n players who are involved in a strategic-form game $G = \{N, \{A_i\}_{i\in N}, \{W_i\}_{i\in N}\}$ that repeats itself unchanged along a series of stages or periods $t = 1, 2, \ldots, T$, where T may be finite or infinite. The game embodied by the (vectorial) payoff function

$$W \equiv (W_i)_{i=1}^{n} : A_1 \times A_2 \times \cdots A_n \to \mathbb{R}^n \tag{8.1}$$

is known as the *stage game* and the full intertemporal game is labeled the *repeated game*. Each A_i is called the *action set* of player i, for simplicity taken to be finite.

We assume that, at each stage t, players have observed and perfectly recall the actions chosen by all of them in the past (i.e., at any $t' < t$). Therefore, a strategy for the repeated game by each player $i = 1, 2, \ldots, n$ is a function

$$\gamma_i : \bigcup_{t \in \mathbb{N}} H^{t-1} \to \Delta(A_i) \equiv \mathcal{A}_i$$

where, for each t, H^{t-1} stands for the set of all possible histories h^{t-1} that may take place up to (including) the *preceding* stage $t - 1$. That is, H^{t-1} consists of strings of play of the form

$$h^{t-1} \equiv \left(\left(a_1^1, a_2^1, \ldots, a_n^1 \right), \left(a_1^2, a_2^2, \ldots, a_n^2 \right), \ldots, \left(a_1^{t-1}, a_2^{t-1}, \ldots, a_n^{t-1} \right) \right)$$

that describe a path of play prior to stage t. Naturally, at $t = 1$, the corresponding H^0 is just a singleton including only the "empty history." As usual, for all those histories, a strategy must prescribe a certain action, possibly mixed.

As indicated, the time horizon of the interaction T may be finite or infinite. In the first case (T finite), the repeated-game payoffs of each player i, $\pi_i^T(h^T)$, are identified with any affine function of her stage payoffs. For simplicity, we posit their time-average[116]:

$$\pi_i^T \left(h^T \right) \equiv (1/T) \sum_{t=1,\ldots,T} W_i \left(a^t \right) \tag{8.2}$$

where, as usual, we rely on the notational shorthand $a^t \equiv (a_1^t, a_2^t, \ldots, a_n^t)$. The finitely repeated game whose payoffs are given by (8.2) will be denoted by $\mathcal{R}^T(W)$, the stage game G being thus identified for the sake of notational convenience with the function (8.1) that determines stage payoffs.

On the other hand, when the horizon of interaction is not bounded (i.e., $T = \infty$), we focus on two alternative ways of defining intertemporal payoffs: discounted sum of stage payoffs and their (equal-weighted) limit average.

(i) *Discounted payoffs*: Given some discount rate δ with $0 \leq \delta < 1$ (for simplicity, assumed common to all players), the discounted payoff of player i associated with a certain path of play, h^∞, is defined as follows:

$$\pi_i^\delta \left(h^\infty \right) \equiv (1 - \delta) \sum_{t=1}^{\infty} \delta^{t-1} W_i \left(a^t \right). \tag{8.3}$$

---

[116] Alternatively, one could have future stage payoffs discounted at a certain rate δ, as is posited below for infinitely repeated games. This would have no relevant implications for the analysis, provided δ were chosen high enough.

The coefficient $(1 - \delta)$ that precedes the above summatory is merely a normalization factor. Its purpose is to have the repeated-game payoffs lie in the convex hull of the stage-game payoffs.[117] In this way, the payoffs obtained throughout the repeated game can be meaningfully compared with those that would result from a one-shot play of the stage game. The infinitely repeated game whose payoffs are given by (8.3) for a certain discount rate, δ, is denoted by $\mathcal{R}^{\delta}(W)$.

(ii) *Limit average payoffs*: A different approach to evaluating alternative paths of play in the infinitely repeated game identifies intertemporal payoffs with the *limit* of the average payoffs obtained for finite, but arbitrarily, long time horizons. Formally, given a certain (infinite) path of play h^{∞}, the limit average payoff for player i is defined as follows:

$$\pi_i^{\infty}(h^{\infty}) = \lim_{T \to \infty} \inf \frac{1}{T} \sum_{t=1}^{T} W_i(a^t), \tag{8.4}$$

which is always well defined.[118] The infinitely repeated game whose payoffs are defined in (8.4) is denoted by $\mathcal{R}^{\infty}(W)$.

If one relies on the payoff criterion given by (i) – i.e., discounted sum of stage payoffs – players' "patience" can be parametrized by the discount rate δ. As δ approaches unity, their patience rises in the sense that the relative weight attributed to future (as compared with more recent) stage payoffs increases. Equivalently, higher values of δ can also be understood as the reflection of a situation in which the interaction takes place at a faster pace – that is, the length of *real* time separating consecutive stages shrinks (cf. Subsection 5.2.2).

In contrast, the payoff criterion specified in (ii) – limit average payoffs – may be conceived as a direct formalization of the extreme context where players are infinitely patient. Heuristically, this case may be interpreted as one where players have a discount rate that is "arbitrarily close to unity" (or a context where the interaction takes place at an "arbitrarily fast rate"). Indeed, a particularly stark manifestation of the extreme patience embodied by criterion (ii) is that, according to it, players should view any *finite* (arbitrarily long) segment of an infinite path of play as payoff *irrelevant*.[119]

---

[117] Note that $(1 - \delta) \sum_{t=1}^{\infty} \delta^{t-1} \equiv 1$ for all $\delta < 1$.

[118] Note that the real sequence $\{1/T \sum_{t=1}^{T} W_i(a_1^t, a_2^t, \ldots, a_n^t)\}_{T=1}^{\infty}$ is uniformly bounded, above and below. Therefore, its lim inf (i.e., the infimum across the set of points which are the limit of some convergent subsequence) is finite.

[119] Another evaluation criterion proposed in the literature that also reflects "infinite patience" is the so-called *overtaking criterion*. For any two given paths of play, $h^{\infty} = (a^1, a^2, \ldots)$ and $\hat{h}^{\infty} = (\hat{a}^1, \hat{a}^2, \ldots)$, any particular player $i \in N$ is taken to prefer the first one to the second according to this criterion if, and only if

$$\exists \tau_0 \in \mathbb{N} : \forall \tau > \tau_0, \ \sum_{t=1}^{\tau} W_i(a^t) > \sum_{t=1}^{\tau} W_i(\hat{a}^t).$$

Thus, as for the limit average payoffs, later payoffs are weighted as much as earlier ones. The overtaking criterion, however, is technically more delicate to use because it cannot be represented through a real function nor does it always guarantees that two alternative sequences are comparable.

8.3   Folk theorems: Nash equilibrium

Briefly stated, our aim in much of this chapter is to understand what expanded range
of behavior may be attained when a certain strategic-form game is repeated over
time with the same set of players involved.[120] Of course, when all equilibria of the
stage game are somehow unsatisfactory (e.g., they are inefficient, as in the prisoner's
dilemma) an obvious concern pertains to whether repeated interaction may help
players sustain, at equilibrium, some better "cooperative" outcome. However, as
we shall see, repeated interaction may also render it possible (i.e., achievable at an
equilibrium) that players attain payoffs that are uniformly worse for all of them than
those obtained at any equilibrium of the stage game.

The results that provide a rigorous formalization of the heuristic ("folk") idea that
repeated interaction should typically allow for a wide scope of equilibrium behavior are traditionally labeled *folk theorems*. In fact, the literature includes an ample
variety of them, differing in their time horizon (finite or infinite), equilibrium concept (Nash, subgame perfect), or information conditions (complete or incomplete
information, perfect or imperfect observability). The large equilibrium multiplicity typically established by these folk theorems may be judged either positively or
negatively. Positively, one may stress the fact that these results often allow game-
theoretic models to regain the consistency with empirical observations that is lost
when the situation is analyzed as a one-shot game. On the negative side, however,
it can also be pointed out that this very "success" sometimes does away with the
usefulness of the approach – i.e., not much explanatory power can be claimed if the
model is compatible with very diverse outcomes!

In the next two subsections we present the simplest versions of the folk theorems.
They concern those that involve the (unrefined) Nash equilibria of a repeated game,
either with an infinite horizon (Subsection 8.3.1) or a finite one (Subsection 8.3.2).
Later on, we turn toward folk theorems that restrict to equilibria meeting suitable
perfection criteria (Section 8.5) or allow for repeated contexts where informational
conditions are either asymmetric or imperfect (Sections 8.4 and 8.6).

8.3.1   *Infinite horizon*

Let $G = \{N, \{A_i\}_{i \in N}, \{W_i\}_{i \in N}\}$ be a strategic-form game that is infinitely repeated
over time, as described in Section 8.2. Define

$$V \equiv \mathbf{conv} \left\{ v \in \mathbb{R}^n : v = W(a), \ a \in A_1 \times \cdots \times A_n \right\},$$

where "**conv** $\{\cdot\}$" stands for the convex hull of the set in question. The set V
includes all those payoff vectors that are attainable in the stage game through
random, possibly correlated, mechanisms of coordination among the players (recall
Section 2.6).[121]

---

[120] An exception is the analysis undertaken in Subsection 8.6.2, where players with different time horizons are
taken to interact under asymmetric information.
[121] Formally, $V \equiv \{v \in \mathbb{R}^n : v = \sum_{k=1}^{r} \lambda^k W(a^k)$, where $a^k \in A_1 \times \cdots \times A_n$, $\lambda^k \geq 0$, and $\sum_{k=1}^{r} \lambda^k = 1$ for
some $r \in \mathbb{N}\}$.

For each $i = 1, 2, \ldots, n$, let V_i denote the projection of the set V on the coordinate associated with player i. There are two payoff magnitudes in V_i that will play an important role in the analysis.

- The first one is the *lowest payoff* that player i may obtain in some *Nash equilibrium* of the stage game. It is denoted by $\tilde{v}_i$ for each player $i = 1, 2, \ldots, n$.
- The second payoff magnitude of interest is player i's *minimax* in the stage game, which is denoted by $\hat{v}_i$. As defined in Section 2.3 within the context of zero-sum games, it is given by

$$\hat{v}_i = \min_{\alpha_{-i} \in \mathcal{A}_{-i}} \max_{\alpha_i \in \mathcal{A}_i} W_i(\alpha_i, \alpha_{-i}), \tag{8.5}$$

where $\mathcal{A}_i$ and $\mathcal{A}_{-i} \equiv \prod_{j \neq i} \mathcal{A}_j$ stand for the spaces of "mixed actions" by player i and the remaining players, respectively.

Intuitively, $\hat{v}_i$ is the lowest payoff to which player i can be forced by a coordinated action by the other players. Thus, in particular, one must have that $\hat{v}_i \leq \tilde{v}_i$ for each $i = 1, 2, \ldots, n$; i.e., the minimax payoff can be no higher than the payoff attained at any Nash equilibrium of the stage game. To see this, simply note that, by reacting optimally to whatever action profile the opponents might be playing (an information implicitly held at an equilibrium of the stage game), player i can block any payoff lower than $\hat{v}_i$. Carrying over these considerations to the repeated game, the condition that player i's intertemporal payoff should *not* fall below her respective $\hat{v}_i$ may be conceived as a mere constraint of *individual rationality*.[122] That is, no equilibrium of the repeated game can provide a payoff to any player i below her corresponding $\hat{v}_i$ (cf. Exercise 8.4).

Our first two results are surprisingly drastic. They establish that *any* payoff *vector* that is individually rational (strictly so) for *each* player i can be supported as a Nash equilibrium of the repeated game if individuals are sufficiently patient. Theorem 8.1, which focuses on discounted repeated games (cf. (i) in Section 8.2), introduces the patience proviso by positing a discount rate that is close enough to 1. On the other hand, Theorem 8.2 accounts for this directly by assuming that players are concerned with average payoffs (cf. (ii) in Section 8.2) and therefore are infinitely patient – i.e., all stage payoffs, independently of when they accrue, carry the same relative weight.

Theorem 8.1: *Let $v = (v_1, \ldots, v_n) \in V$ with $v_i > \hat{v}_i$, $\forall i = 1, 2, \ldots, n$, $\exists \bar{\delta} < 1$ such that, if $1 > \delta > \bar{\delta}$, there exists a Nash equilibrium of $\mathcal{R}^\delta(W)$ whose payoffs for each player $i = 1, 2, \ldots, n$ coincide with v_i.*

Theorem 8.2: *Let $v = (v_1, \ldots, v_n) \in V$ with $v_i > \hat{v}_i$, $\forall i = 1, 2, \ldots, n$. There exists a Nash equilibrium of $\mathcal{R}^\infty(W)$ whose payoffs for each player $i = 1, 2, \ldots, n$ coincide with v_i.*

---

[122] Recall the analogous notion introduced in Subsections 7.3.2.2 and 7.4.2 within the framework of mechanism design.

Proof of Theorem 8.1: Consider any $v \in V$ with $v_i > \hat{v}_i$ for each $i = 1, 2, \ldots, n$, and suppose for simplicity (see Remark 8.1 below) that there exists some $a = (a_1, a_2, \ldots a_n) \in A$ with $W(a) = v$. Denote by $(\hat{\alpha}_1^j, \hat{\alpha}_2^j, \ldots, \hat{\alpha}_n^j)$, $j = 1, 2, \ldots, n$, one of the (possibly mixed) action profiles that underlie the minimax payoff $\hat{v}_j$, i.e.,

$$\hat{\alpha}_{-j}^j \in \arg \min_{\alpha_{-j} \in A_{-j}} \left\{ \max_{\alpha_j \in A_j} W_j \left(\alpha_j, \alpha_{-j} \right) \right\}$$

$$\hat{\alpha}_j^j \in \arg \max_{\alpha_j \in A_j} W_i \left(\alpha_j, \hat{\alpha}_{-j}^j \right).$$

We now argue that the following strategies define a Nash equilibrium of the repeated game for a discount rate δ sufficiently close to unity.

For each $i = 1, 2, \ldots, n, t = 1, 2, \ldots,$[123]

$$\gamma_i \left(h^{t-1} \right) = a_i \quad \text{if } \forall \tau \leq t - 1, \text{ there exists } no \text{ player } j \text{ who}$$
$$\text{has deviated } unilaterally \text{ (i.e., only herself)}$$
$$\text{from action } a_j \text{ in } \tau;$$

$$\gamma_i \left(h^{t-1} \right) = \hat{\alpha}_i^j \quad \text{otherwise, where } j \text{ is the index of the player}$$
$$\text{who has } first \text{ deviated unilaterally from } a_j.$$

$$(8.6)$$

The above strategies are particularly simple in that they divide the set of histories into just two classes, i.e., those histories where no unilateral deviation has yet occurred and those where a single individual, i, first deviated from her respective a_i. (Note, in particular, that they react to a deviation of more than one player as if no deviation had occurred at all.) To check that those strategies indeed define a Nash equilibrium, consider the situation of a particular player, i, who, at a certain t where still no single player $j = 1, 2, \ldots, n$ has deviated from her respective a_j, considers the possibility of choosing some $a_i' \neq a_i$. If she does not deviate (i.e., keeps playing a_i) and assumes that no other player will deviate either (at t or later), her ensuing discounted payoff is simply v_i. If, instead, player i deviates unilaterally and other players follow the strategies specified in (8.6), player i's payoff is bounded above by the following expression:

$$\left(1 - \delta^{t-1} \right) v_i + (1 - \delta) \delta^{t-1} v_i^* + \delta^t \hat{v}_i,$$

where

$$v_i^* \equiv \max_{a \in A} W_i \left(a \right) \qquad (8.7)$$

---

[123] For notational convenience, we rely on the slight abuse of identifying $\gamma_i(h^{t-1})$ with the action that is being deterministically selected at t after history h^{t-1}.

is the maximum payoff that player i can earn in the stage game. Let $\bar{\delta}_i > 0$ be such that

$$\left(1 - \bar{\delta}_i^{t-1}\right) v_i + \left(1 - \bar{\delta}_i\right) \bar{\delta}_i^{t-1} v_i^* + \bar{\delta}_i^t \hat{v}_i = v_i$$

or, equivalently,

$$\left(1 - \bar{\delta}_i\right) \bar{\delta}_i^{t-1} v_i^* + \bar{\delta}_i^t \hat{v}_i = \bar{\delta}_i^{t-1} v_i,$$

which can be simplified to

$$\left(1 - \bar{\delta}_i\right) v_i^* + \bar{\delta}_i \hat{v}_i = v_i. \tag{8.8}$$

Since $v_i > \hat{v}_i$, we have $\bar{\delta}_i < 1$. On the other hand, if the discount rate $\delta > \bar{\delta}_i$, it is clear from (8.8) that no unilateral deviation from (8.6) can be profitable to player i. Therefore, if we make

$$\bar{\delta} \equiv \max_i \bar{\delta}_i,$$

whenever $\delta > \bar{\delta}$, none of the players can profit by deviating unilaterally from the strategies given in (8.6). Thus, in this case, the profile given by these strategies defines a Nash equilibrium with corresponding payoff vector v, as desired. The proof is complete. ∎

Proof of Theorem 8.2: It is straightforward to check that the strategies described in (8.6) also define a Nash equilibrium for the repeated game $\mathcal{R}^\infty(W)$. ∎

Remark 8.1: *Supporting convex payoff combinations*

The argument presented in the proof of Theorem 8.1 pertains to the case where the payoff vector v to be supported at equilibrium has some $a \in A$ with $W(a) = v$. If v were not achievable through some deterministic action profile in the stage game, an easy way of tackling the problem is to suppose that any randomization required to produce v (even if it embodies correlation of actions) is observed by all players, i.e., it is a public randomization. In this case, any unilateral deviation (even in the presence of randomization of actions) can be detected and reacted upon by the remaining players, just as before.

Suppose now that one wants to avoid resorting to public randomization. Then, there is an alternative way of addressing the problem, although at the cost of relying on a significantly more involved procedure. In essence, what is required is that players generate (at equilibrium) a sequence of action profiles whose realized frequencies over time reproduce the weights associated to the contemplated randomization. This, of course, requires that players' monitoring of the opponents' behavior (to check that no deviation has taken place) should involve a "careful accounting" stretching over past history. But, under these conditions, the logic of the argument can be

Table 8.2: *Stage game with the lowest equilibrium payoff equal to the minimax payoff for both players*

1 \ 2	A	B
X	5, 1	0, 0
Y	4, 4	1, 5

Table 8.3: *Stage game with the unique equilibrium payoff higher than the minimax payoff for both players*

1 \ 2	A	B	C
X	2, 2	3, 3	1, 0
Y	3, 3	4, 4	0, 0
Z	0, 1	0, 0	0, 0

adapted to show that *any* $v \in V$ is attainable at equilibrium provided that players' patience is high enough. ◆

To illustrate some of the implications of the previous results, let us turn to the strategic-form game introduced in Section 2.6, whose payoffs are recalled in Table 8.2.

Suppose this stage game is infinitely repeated over time between the same two players. By virtue of the above results, the payoff vector $v = (4, 4)$ can be supported at an equilibrium of the repeated game (in the discounted-payoff version, if players are sufficiently patient). This simply follows from the observation that the *minimax* payoff for both players is $\hat{v}_1 = \hat{v}_2 = 1 < 4$. Thus, in contrast with the correlation devices discussed in Section 2.6 for this game, repeated interaction is here a more effective way of attaining symmetric and efficient configurations.

To provide some further illustration on the implications of the above results, suppose now that the (symmetric) stage game is as described in Table 8.3.

Again, the *minimax* payoff for each player is $\hat{v}_1 = \hat{v}_2 = 1$. On the other hand, the unique Nash equilibrium of the stage game is (Y, B), which implies that $\tilde{v}_1 = \tilde{v}_2 = 4$. Of course, there is always a Nash equilibrium of the repeated game in which the action profile (Y, B) is reiterated indefinitely. But, provided players are sufficiently patient, the above results imply that there is also a Nash equilibrium where, on the equilibrium path, players always play the action profile *(X, A)* – this simply follows from the fact that, for each player i, $\hat{v}_i = 1 < 2$. Thus, in this alternative equilibrium of the repeated game, one finds a rather perverse state of affairs: players "cooperate" to implement a bad outcome at *equilibrium*. That is, they obtain a payoff vector that is Pareto dominated by the unique Nash equilibrium of the stage game and therefore could only be improved (at equilibrium) in the absence of repeated interaction. This represents a particularly forceful illustration of the wide range of possibilities (both good and bad) that repeated interaction may avail.

Remark 8.2: *Cooperation and imperfect information in repeated games*

The repeated-interaction framework posited so far displays a crucial feature that is worth stressing at this point. Throughout, we have assumed that all players are able to single out and remember with accuracy the whole sequence of past actions of their opponents. It is precisely this fact that allows each of them to establish a precise link between her own current action and the opponents' past behavior.

However, in some contexts of interest, the assumption that past history is accurately perceived by all players is hardly appropriate. As a natural example, think of a market where a given set of firms repeatedly compete à la Cournot but can only observe overall market conditions – say, the prevailing market price every period (or, equivalently, total market sales). Section 9.1.2 considers an oligopoly scenario with these features, introducing a certain amount of exogenous uncertainty that impinges on the ("noisy") mechanism of price determination. Obviously, such an uncertainty generally impairs the potential of the observed price to reveal the actions (outputs) actually chosen by competitors. It should come as no surprise, therefore, that the potential for implementing collusive outcomes is then significantly curtailed. ◆

To summarize, Theorems 8.1 and 8.2 establish that repeated interaction opens up a broad set of new Nash equilibrium possibilities, well beyond those attainable in the context of the stage game alone. These results, however, raise a legitimate concern pertaining to the equilibrium perfection of the supporting equilibria. Indeed, this worry is warranted by the "highly imperfect" nature of the equilibria that are used in the constructive proofs to support the desired outcomes. Specifically, these equilibria embody the threat that, should any player ever deviate, she would be subject to an indefinite punishment by others that forces on her the minimax payoff. However, if some such deviation does occur, carrying out this threat could sometimes be far from optimal on the part of the punishers. We are then led to the following question: Would the requirement of (subgame) perfection significantly curtail the equilibrium-supporting possibilities displayed by the above folk theorems? As we see in Section 8.5.1, the answer is reassuring, at least if the time horizon under consideration is unbounded. Specifically, it turns out (albeit the arguments required to prove it become substantially more involved) that the payoff range attainable at equilibria of infinitely repeated games is essentially unaffected by the restriction to subgame perfection. Matters, however, will happen to be somewhat more mixed in finite-horizon repeated games. A discussion of this scenario is started in the following Subsection by focusing on its Nash equilibria and then continued in Subsection 8.5.2 by studying its subgame-perfect equilibria.

8.3.2 *Finite horizon*

As illustrated in Section 8.1, the nature of repeated interaction (and therefore its equilibrium-supporting possibilities) may crucially depend on whether the time horizon under consideration is finite or infinite. This suggests the need of exploring in detail the conditions under which the main insights underlying the infinite-horizon folk theorems are maintained in finite (but sufficiently long) time horizons. In a heuristic sense, the issue here is essentially one of "modeling continuity" between infinite and finite-but-long horizons of interaction.

Suppose a given set of players is involved in a *finitely* repeated game where a certain stage game W (i.e., our shorthand for the strategic-form game $G = \{N, \{A_i\}_{i \in N}, \{W_i\}_{i \in N}\}$) is repeated some finite number of times T. Thus, using the terminology introduced in Section 8.2, players are engaged in the game $\mathcal{R}^T(W)$, where $T < \infty$. In this context, Theorem 8.3 below may be regarded as a natural counterpart of the folk theorems established in Subsection 8.3.1. It asserts that any individually rational payoff vector can be *approximated* in an arbitrarily close fashion at some Nash equilibrium of the repeated game, provided the following two conditions hold:

(a) the stage game admits some punishment leeway (specifically, some discrepancy between Nash and *minimax* outcomes), which can be used to deter deviations;

(b) the time horizon is long enough, i.e., the conditions are sufficiently akin to those of the infinite horizon case so that, at least as seen from the beginning of the game, players have enough periods to enjoy any benefits from "cooperation."

Intuitively, one can think of (a) and (b) as the two complementary factors ("stick" and "carrot," respectively) that must underlie any equilibrium of the repeated game where players behave differently from how they would do in the stage game. More precisely, the result may be stated as follows

Theorem 8.3 (Benoit and Krishna, 1987): *Suppose that, for every player $i = 1, 2, \ldots, n$, there exists a Nash equilibrium of the stage game W, $\bar{\alpha}^i$, where $W_i(\bar{\alpha}^i) > \hat{v}_i$. If $v \in V$ satisfies $v_i > \hat{v}_i$ for each i, then, $\forall \varepsilon > 0$, $\exists T^*$ such that if $T > T^*$, the repeated game $\mathcal{R}^T(W)$ has a Nash equilibrium whose payoffs v_i' for each player i verify $|v_i' - v_i| \leq \varepsilon$.*

Proof: Given the Nash equilibria $\bar{\alpha}^i$ $(i = 1, 2, \ldots, n)$ specified in the statement of the theorem, let $\alpha = (\bar{\alpha}^1, \bar{\alpha}^2, \ldots, \bar{\alpha}^n)$ be an n-period *path* of action *profiles* where these equilibria are played in consecutive order. Since the payoff attained by any player in *every* Nash equilibrium of the stage game can be no lower than her *minimax* payoff, we have

$$W_i(\bar{\alpha}^j) \geq \hat{v}_i, \quad \forall i, j = 1, 2, \ldots, n. \tag{8.9}$$

Thus, since it has been assumed that (8.9) holds strictly when $i = j$ (i.e., we have $W_i(\bar{\alpha}^i) > \hat{v}_i$), the *average* payoff of each player i along the path α must exceed her *minimax* $\hat{v}_i$ in some positive magnitude, say μ_i. Let $\mu \equiv \min_{i=1}^n \mu_i > 0$. If we now produce a concatenation of q paths such as α above to form a path of length $q \cdot n$, it follows that the average payoff of any player i along this extended path must exceed $\hat{v}_i$ in at least $q \cdot \mu$. Of course, the latter magnitude can be made arbitrarily large by simply choosing q (the number of replicas of α) sufficiently high. Building on this fact, we now demonstrate how to construct equilibrium strategies that support any payoff vector v with $v_i > \hat{v}_i$ for every $i \in N$.

Let v be any such payoff vector and suppose, for simplicity, that $v = W(a)$ for some $a \in A$. Consider the following strategies: for each player $i = 1, 2, \ldots, n$, and any $t = 1, 2, \ldots,$

(i) $\gamma_i \left(h^{t-1} \right) = a_i$ if $t \leq T - q \cdot n$ and $\forall \tau \leq t - 1$ there exists *no* player j who has deviated unilaterally (only she) from a_j in τ;

(ii) $\gamma_i \left(h^{t-1} \right) = \bar{\alpha}_i^j$ if $t > T - q \cdot n$ and *no* single player deviated from (i) for all $\tau \leq T - q \cdot n$, where the mixed-action profile $\bar{\alpha}^j$ is chosen so that $j = n - [T - t]_n$[124];

(iii) $\gamma_i \left(h^{t-1} \right) = \hat{\alpha}_i^j$ otherwise, where j is the player who first deviated from a_j for some prior $\tau \leq T - q \cdot n$.

The above strategies can be verbally described as follows. The whole length of play, T, is divided into two parts. The early part, $t = 1, 2, \ldots, T - qn$, has agents play the intended action profile a, as long as no one unilaterally deviates. However, if someone does so, she is punished thereafter by the remaining players, who impose on her the minimax payoff until the end of the game. On the other hand, if the game reaches $t = T - qn + 1$ without witnessing any unilateral deviation, the strategies prescribe that players should enter a q-long chain of n-fold sequences of Nash equilibria such that, in each of these sequences, every player has at least one Nash equilibrium where her payoff is strictly higher than her respective minimax payoff.

Let us verify that the above strategies define a Nash equilibrium of the finitely repeated game $\mathcal{R}^T(W)$ for a sufficiently high value of q. To see this, note that, if q is chosen high enough, no optimal deviation may exist prior to entering the terminal phase of the game that consists of the last $q \cdot n$ periods. Then, within the terminal phase itself, the fact that the strategies merely induce (at equilibrium) a sequence of Nash equilibria of the stage game also implies, by an already familiar argument, that no optimal deviation can exist there either.

Now, to conclude the argument, fix any particular q as required by the former considerations. Then, if T^* is chosen large enough, it is clear that, for $T \geq T^*$, the payoffs for each player i induced by the above strategies approximate v_i in an arbitrarily close fashion. This completes the proof. ∎

---

[124] The notation $[\cdot]_n$ indicates that the number in question is interpreted as "modulo n" (that is, it is the resulting remainder when the number is divided by n).

In contrast with the folk theorems established in Subsection 8.3.1, finite-horizon repeated games require an additional "punishment-margin condition" (cf. (a) above) to have their Nash equilibria span (approximately) the whole set of individually rational payoffs. For example, if the stage game is that represented in Table 8.3, we may still conclude that the payoff vector $v = (2, 2)$ can be arbitrarily approximated at a Nash equilibrium of the repeated game if the horizon T is sufficiently long (cf. (b)).

Let us now return to the example where the stage game is the prisoner's dilemma (cf. Table 8.1). As explained in Section 8.1, for any T, the unique payoff vector supportable at a Nash equilibrium of the repeated game is $v = (-10, -10)$, i.e., the Nash equilibrium payoff of the stage game. Theorem 8.3 helps us understand, in a somewhat different light than before, the reason for this clear-cut conclusion. In the prisoner's dilemma, the Nash and *minimax* payoffs coincide for both players. This leaves no effective punishment margin to be used and thus prevents the implementation of any outcome other than indefinite joint defection, i.e., forces a constant play of the unique Nash equilibrium of the stage game.

Finally, and in analogy with infinitely repeated games, one may wonder what would be the implications of introducing (subgame) perfection considerations into the analysis. Again, this is to be regarded as a very legitimate concern but one whose somewhat more intricate study is best relegated to the supplementary material (cf. Subsection 8.5.1). There, we find that subgame perfection is a more restrictive consideration in finite-horizon games than it is in repeated games with an unbounded horizon. Specifically, the existence of some (stage) equilibrium *multiplicity* will turn out to be crucial if players are to enjoy not only the punishment *credibility* but also the punishment *flexibility* that, as explained in (a) above, must underlie all nontrivial equilibria in repeated games.

8.4   Reputation and "irrationality": informal discussion

In a loose sense, every equilibrium of a multistage game embodies a certain idea of *reputation*. At every point of the game, each player anticipates what the opponents will do on the basis of their current reputation, as this has been shaped by previously observed behavior. Intuitively, this view seems particularly well suited to the case in which the game involves *repeated* interaction according to a *fixed* stage game. Then, the range of available actions and entailed payoffs remain unchanged, a scenario that lends itself quite naturally to having players rely on past (observed) behavior when shaping their ensuing predictions.

In everyday life, we typically think of a (good) reputation as a certain asset, i.e., something valuable that, once acquired, is worth preserving. Of course, the value of any such reputation must depend on the time horizon during which one envisages to benefit from it. Thus, if gaining a good reputation is costly[125] (otherwise, it would be essentially meaningless), any decision concerning its possible preservation must

---

[125] Often, the kind of costs involved in building a reputation are *opportunity costs*, i.e., costs associated with letting some gains (say, short-run or opportunistic ones) slip away.

crucially depend on the remaining length of time during which it can still be used. In this section, we informally illustrate the multifaceted considerations involved in this respect through a variety of examples, all of them in the context of repeated games. The intuitive features just outlined already arise quite starkly in these examples. However, for a precise analysis of matters the reader is referred to Section 8.6 (in the Supplementary Material of this chapter), where these issues are studied in formal detail.

Let us start by considering again the *infinitely* repeated prisoner's dilemma. In this context, the simplest cooperative equilibrium is that which sustains (C, C) by the threat of responding drastically to any deviation with a constant adoption of action D throughout (that is, with the threat of turning irreversibly to playing the unique Nash equilibrium of the stage game). In a sense, we may conceive the support of cooperation in such an equilibrium as the outcome of a joint "reputation for good will" that is maintained over time through cooperative behavior. This reputation, however, is extremely fragile: a single failure to abide by it is enough for its irreversible collapse.

Let us now reconsider the *finite* repetition of the prisoner's dilemma. As explained, every Nash equilibrium of this game leads to the action profile (D, D) being played throughout, independently of how protracted the (finitely lived) interaction might be. This may be viewed as the reflection of an unsatisfactory "modeling discontinuity at infinity," i.e., what appears to hold for $T = \infty$ (the possibility of supporting cooperation) is nevertheless completely unfeasible at equilibrium for *every* given $T \in \mathbb{N}$. In general, such an acute discontinuity should be interpreted as a "warning" that the model might be imperfectly or incompletely specified. But, in the present context, that theoretical uneasiness is even reinforced by an empirical concern. In laboratory experiments, where real subjects (often students) have been made to play a repeated prisoner's dilemma under significant monetary rewards, long stretches of cooperation are typically observed when the number of periods involved is large. More specifically, a significant fraction of cooperative behavior is found in the early stages, although the backward-induction logic seems to take over in the final stages and lead to a steep rise of defection.[126]

The literature has pursued a variety of different approaches to tackle the theoretical and empirical issues raised by the above observations. Here, we focus on the incomplete-information route proposed by Kreps, Milgrom, Roberts, and Wilson (1982).[127] These authors slightly perturb the game with a small amount of asymmetric information, allowing for some small probability that either of the two players involved in the finitely repeated prisoner's dilemma be of an "irrational" type. More specifically, they model the situation as a Bayesian game with Nature

---

[126] There has been a long experimental literature concerned with the finitely repeated prisoner's dilemma. For the earlier part of it, Lave (1962) is a good representative, whereas interesting examples of more recent experimental research in this context can be found in Selten and Stocker (1986) or Andreoni and Miller (1993). These experiments are summarized in Subsection 12.7.3, where we also contrast at some length both their different focus and their alternative theoretical underpinnings.

[127] An alternative approach based on the notion of ε-rationality (or ε-equilibrium) is described in Subsection 8.5.2.

(recall Section 6.2), where there is a low *a priori* probability that the (Harsanyi) type of each player holds preferences that render the following *tit-for-tat (TFT)* strategy dominant:

"At each t, choose C if the other player chose C in the preceding period; otherwise, choose D."

Under those circumstances, Kreps *et al.* show that, in every sequential equilibrium of the perturbed game with Nature (cf. Section 4.6), each rational-type player (i.e., one with the original preferences of the prisoner's dilemma) mimics the irrational-type player during most of the game, provided the time horizon is long enough. That is, precisely *because* of her rationality, each player behaves most of the time as prescribed by TFT, under the prediction that the other player will also behave in this fashion. Indeed, such a prediction is *always* confirmed at equilibrium, even though the opponent is very likely to be rational and thus not hold TFT preferences.

A *general* result in this vein is stated and proven in Subsection 8.6.1 (cf. Theorem 8.11). Along the lines of our former discussion, one can interpret this result as reflecting an *equilibrium* process of "investment in reputation." Given that both players share a common belief that the opponent could possibly be a rare but "useful" type (e.g., a TFT type in the repeated prisoner's dilemma), both players prefer to behave as this type would, at least in the early phase of the game. In this way, the equilibrium reputation that they will continue to play in a "constructive" manner is preserved. Of course, keeping such a reputation will generally entail short-run opportunity costs. Thus, for a rational type to find it a worthwhile pursuit at equilibrium, the game must be long enough to allow for a sufficiently protracted enjoyment of the future payoff benefits.

Heuristically, the result just outlined displays an interesting, somewhat paradoxical, feature: players are interested in concealing their rationality. Or, in other words, they prefer *not* to carry its logical implications through, consciously clinging to any small doubt in this respect that the (incomplete-information) game may avail. This, in sum, allows even small subjective probabilities for a certain type of irrationality to entail important payoff consequences.

However, a potentially controversial issue then arises as to what "manifestations of irrationality" players could, or should, admit in their analysis of the game. In contrast with the fact that there are only limited ways of modeling rationality (i.e., they must all involve some suitable embodiment of payoff maximization and, perhaps, rational expectations – recall Sections 2.2 and 2.7), the scope for possible "irrationalities" seems vastly unrestricted. For example, in the model proposed by Kreps *et al.* (1982) for the repeated prisoner's dilemma, it was convenient to consider a particular kind of reciprocity-inducing irrationality (i.e., that reflected by the TFT strategy). But, of course, many other different such possibilities could have been contemplated instead. In general, one may suspect that, as different types of irrationality are being considered for a particular stage game, a wide range of equilibrium (and therefore payoff) possibilities could arise under repeated interaction. Indeed, this conjecture will be proven essentially true in Subsection 8.6.1, where it will lead to an incomplete-information counterpart of our previous folk theorems. Informally, that is, it will be shown that every individually rational payoff may be approximated at a sequential equilibrium of a suitably perturbed finitely repeated game.

As will be recalled (cf. Section 8.3), one of the issues that can be raised against folk-type results concerns the large equilibrium multiplicity they typically span. Such a multiplicity, however, cannot be tackled by perturbing the game with some incomplete information because, as suggested above, there is seldom an obvious way to choose the "suitable perturbation." This problem would seem exacerbated even further if, instead of *just one* irrationality, several of them are allowed *simultaneously* with positive probability. But, in this case, one would also expect that a conflict might arise among the players, who could become involved in a *tour de force* to settle what reputation should steer equilibrium play. Which player might be expected to end up succeeding in this struggle? Intuitively, it seems that the one who has more at stake should prevail. In particular, if players differ in their discount rates, it may be conjectured that the one who is more patient (i.e., places more weight on future payoffs) is bound to gain the upper hand in imposing her own preferred reputation.

To facilitate a precise discussion of these subtle issues, the literature has mostly focused on a very stylized theoretical framework. In it, a long-term player (i.e., one with an infinite time horizon) interacts with a sequence of short-run agents whose concerns span just one period (i.e., the only period where they interact with the long-run player). A paradigmatic example of this setup is provided by the so-called *chain-store game*, originally proposed by Selten (1978). We rely on this game to illustrate some of the main issues involved.

Consider a large chain store that operates in a given set of different (say, spatially separated) markets. In each of them, the chain faces the potential entry of a specific and independent competitor, which is circumscribed to that particular market. Every one of these potential entrants must take, in sequence, the decision of whether to actually enter in competition with the chain. More precisely, let $t = 1, 2, \ldots, T$ stand for the different dates at which these decisions must be adopted. Then, at each such t, the corresponding market-specific firm (which is supposed to be informed of all previous history) adopts one of two possible decisions: entry (E) or not entry (N). Having observed this choice, the chain store then responds in one of two different ways: it can either fight entry (F) or acquiesce (A).

To fix ideas, let the "profit potential" of each market be equal to 2, which can be either peacefully shared by the chain store and the corresponding firm (thus inducing a payoff of 1 for each) or simply enjoyed by the former. Suppose, on the other hand, that the "cost of fighting" is equal to -2 for both firms, which induces a net payoff of -1 if they enter a fight. With these conventions, the extensive-form (two-stage) game that is played by the chain store and each of the potential entrants may be represented as in Figure 8.1.

Clearly, the only subgame-perfect equilibrium of the game represented in Figure 8.1 is given by the strategy profile (E, A). Now suppose that, as suggested above, this game is embedded into the larger context where the same chain store plays repeatedly and in sequence with a *finite* number T of potential entrants. Then, by resorting to a by now familiar backward-induction argument, it is straightforward

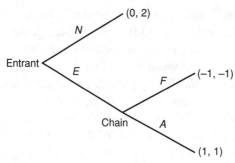

Figure 8.1: Chain-store stage game.

to check that the only subgame-perfect equilibrium of such a repeated game also involves playing (E, A) in every $t = 1, 2, \ldots, T$.

Let us now focus on an extension of the previous context to the case in which the chain store faces in sequence an *unbounded* number of potential entrants, its overall (intertemporal) payoffs being identified with, say, the flow of stage payoffs discounted at a certain given rate $\delta \in (0, 1)$.[128] Of course, in such an infinite-horizon game, there still is a subgame-perfect equilibrium where (E, A) is played every period. However, if δ is large enough, there is now also an alternative subgame-perfect equilibrium where, on the equilibrium path, no potential entrant ever enters under the fear that, if it were to do so, the chain store would respond by fighting. In a sense, this fear is to be conceived as a reflection of the "fighting reputation" the chain store enjoys, at equilibrium, in the eyes of the potential entrants. And again, the long-term value of this reputation derives from its own fragility. It is only because this reputation would immediately collapse if the chain store ever tolerated entry that every potential entrant understands that entry would always be fought and is thus best avoided altogether.

Formally, the aforementioned considerations are embodied by the following equilibrium strategies: for each $t = 1, 2, \ldots$, and every possible history h^{t-1} prevailing at t, the chain store (denoted by c) and the potential entrant (identified by e) respectively react as follows[129]:

$$\gamma_c\left(h^{t-1}\right) = F \tag{8.10}$$

$$\gamma_e\left(h^{t-1}\right) = \begin{cases} N & \text{if } \forall \tau \leq t-1, \ a_c^\tau \neq A \\ E & \text{otherwise.} \end{cases} \tag{8.11}$$

An interesting feature of this equilibrium (only Nash? subgame-perfect as well? – cf. Exercise 8.13) is that, in contrast with the infinitely repeated prisoner's dilemma

---

[128] Alternatively, one could consider the possibility (also contemplated in Section 8.2 for ordinary repeated games) that the intertemporal preferences of the chain store are given by the limit average payoffs earned throughout the whole game.

[129] The present example deviates from the theoretical framework introduced in Section 8.2 because not all players display the same time horizon. A reformulation of the original setup that accommodates for this feature is introduced in Subsection 8.6.2. Of course, an additional difference resides in the fact that, because the game played at every t involves two distinct stages, the chain store has to take no action when the potential entrant decides to keep out of the market (i.e., chooses N). To tackle this problem formally, one can simply resort to the notational convention that, in that case, $a_1^t = \emptyset$.

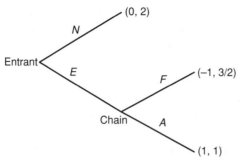

Figure 8.2: Chain-store stage game, alternative version.

discussed earlier, the chain-store reputation can be maintained at equilibrium without ever being put to any tangible test. That is, its fighting reputation would only have to be "honored" if a short-run firm enters, an event never observed at equilibrium. Despite this contrast, the repeated prisoner's dilemma and the chain-store game do display an analogous discontinuity in the length of the time horizon; i.e., both lead to drastically different (equilibrium) analysis when the horizon of the interaction passes from being finite to infinite.[130] In the present case, this discontinuity (again to be judged counterintuitive and theoretically problematical) has been labeled the *chain-store paradox*.

Kreps and Wilson (1982*b*) and Milgrom and Roberts (1982) addressed independently the "resolution" of this paradox along lines quite similar to those described above for the repeated prisoner's dilemma. Specifically, they postulated that, in the finite-horizon version of the game, there is a small *a priori* probability that the chain store could display payoffs different from those contemplated in Figure 8.1; for example, one may suppose that in this alternative case they are as indicated in Figure 8.2.

If payoffs were as described in Figure 8.2, the chain store would always fight the entry of any short-run firm and, therefore, it would be unambiguously optimal for *every* potential entrant to remain on the sidelines. Thus, suppose that, with some small subjective prior probability, short-run firms allow for the possibility that the chain-store's payoffs might be as in this second alternative version. Then, it can be shown that, if the time horizon (i.e., number of potential entrants) is large enough, the so-perturbed repeated game with Nature leads to no entry by the short-run firms in an arbitrarily high fraction of the initial periods. Or, to be more precise, this behavior occurs at every sequential equilibrium of the game, no matter how small their subjective probability on the second type. For the short-run firms, staying out is an optimal response to the credible threat on the part of the chain store that it will maintain its reputation (i.e., fight entry), at least in the early part of game. Through this reputation, the long-run firm obtains average payoffs that are arbitrarily close to those of monopoly (that is, close to 2) provided the game is long enough.

Even though this conclusion has obvious parallelisms with our above discussion of the finitely repeated prisoner's dilemma, it is worth stressing that there are

---

[130] Recall that a *finite* repetition of the chain-store game induces entry by every potential entrant in its *unique* subgame-perfect equilibrium.

important differences as well. In the chain-store game, sustaining the equilibrium reputation is *not* jointly advantageous for all players. That is, this reputation benefits only the chain-store firm, which is prepared to uphold it if necessary by fighting any entry decision. In contrast, of course, any of the short-run firms would like that, at its time of play, such a reputation had collapsed somehow and therefore the chain store would be ready to share the market. However, those firms have no way (nor incentives) to struggle to that effect because their individual time horizon is too short.[131] Thus, exploiting the entailed asymmetry, the chain store is able to maintain, at equilibrium, its most profitable reputation. As we formally show in Subsection 8.6.2 (cf. Theorem 8.12), this is a phenomenon that arises with some generality in contexts of repeated interaction where a long-run player coexists with a finite (but sufficiently long) series of short-run players.

Supplementary material

8.5   Folk theorems: subgame-perfect equilibrium

8.5.1   *Infinite horizon*

As explained (cf. Subsection 8.3.2), the folk theorems established so far raise serious concerns as to whether their conclusions are robust to the demand of subgame perfection. Motivated by these concerns, we are specifically led to the following question. Is repeated interaction still an effective way of achieving payoffs that could not possibly be attained at Nash equilibria of the stage game? Addressing first this question for the case of *infinitely* repeated games, a preliminary (and yet partial) answer to this question is provided by the following two results. These results address in turn the discounted- and the average-payoffs scenario, as given, respectively, for a certain stage game W, by the repeated games $\mathcal{R}^{\delta}(W)$ and $\mathcal{R}^{\infty}(W)$ – cf. Section 8.2. In either setup, they establish that, for some payoff vector v to be achievable at an equilibrium of the repeated game, it is enough that every player prefers it to *some* Nash equilibrium of the stage game. That is, one must have $v_i > \tilde{v}_i$ for each player i; recall from Section 8.3 that $\tilde{v}_i$ is the worst payoff attained by this player across all possible Nash equilibria of the stage game W.

Theorem 8.4 (Friedman, 1971): *Let* $v \in V$ *with* $v_i > \tilde{v}_i, \forall i = 1, 2, \ldots, n.$ $\exists \bar{\delta} < 1$ *such that if* $1 > \delta > \bar{\delta}$*, there exists a subgame-perfect equilibrium of* $\mathcal{R}^{\delta}(W)$ *whose payoffs for each player* $i = 1, 2, \ldots, n$ *coincide with* v_i.[132]

Theorem 8.5: *Let* $v \in V$ *with* $v_i > \tilde{v}_i, \forall i = 1, 2, \ldots, n.$ *There exists a subgame-perfect equilibrium of* $\mathcal{R}^{\infty}(W)$ *whose payoffs for each player* $i = 1, 2, \ldots, n$ *coincide with* v_i.

---

[131] As explained in Remark 8.6, the key considerations here concerning both the players' time horizons and discount rates are their relative (i.e., not absolute) magnitudes.

[132] Friedman (1971) proved only the slightly weaker result in which the payoff vector v to be supported at a subgame-perfect equilibrium of the repeated game is required to dominate component-wise (i.e., in the strong Pareto sense) the payoff vector obtained at a Nash equilibrium of the stage game.

Proof for Theorem 8.4 and 8.5: Since the arguments are parallel for both results, we combine them in a single proof. The logic is quite similar to that used for Theorems 8.1 and 8.2. In the present case, however, the supporting equilibria embody the threat that, if a unilateral deviation should occur, subsequent play will settle on a Nash equilibrium of the stage game. In general, of course, the particular such equilibrium then played is tailored to the identity of the player having deviated first.

More precisely, let $v \in V$ with $v_i > \tilde{v}_i$, $\forall i = 1, 2, \ldots, n$, and suppose, for simplicity (recall Remark 8.1), that $\exists a \in A$ such that $W(a) = v$. Denote by $\tilde{\alpha}^j \equiv (\tilde{\alpha}_i^j)_{i=1,2,\ldots,n}$ a Nash equilibrium of the stage game W with a payoff of $\tilde{v}_j$ for player j (that is, an equilibrium whose payoff for j is minimum among all Nash equilibria of W). Consider the following strategies.

For each player $i = 1, 2, \ldots, n$, $t = 1, 2, \ldots$,

$$\gamma_i \left(h^{t-1} \right) = a_i \text{ if } \forall \tau \leq t-1, \text{ there exists } no \text{ player } j$$
$$\text{who has deviated unilaterally from action } a_j \text{ in } \tau;$$
$$\gamma_i \left(h^{t-1} \right) = \tilde{\alpha}_i^j \text{ otherwise, where } j \text{ is the index of the player}$$
$$\text{who has } first \text{ deviated unilaterally from } a_j.$$

First, by relying on the line of argument used for Theorem 8.1, it should be clear that the above strategies define a Nash equilibrium of the repeated game $\mathcal{R}^\delta(W)$ for any δ close enough to unity. Thus, they prescribe optimal behavior for each separate player at any point in the game, provided that no player has ever deviated nor is predicted to do so in the future. Clearly, this applies to the repeated game $\mathcal{R}^\infty(W)$, where players evaluate intertemporal strings of stage payoffs according to their limit average.

Next, consider a situation such that, at a certain prior point in the game, some deviation (unilateral or multilateral) has occurred. If all prior deviations have involved more than one player, then the contemplated strategies prescribe ignoring those deviations and have players still playing the action profile a. Since the considerations then involved are equivalent to those prevailing at the beginning of the game, this behavior defines a Nash equilibrium of the continuation subgame. On the other hand, if some unilateral deviation did occur in some previous period, the strategies induce playing forever that particular Nash equilibrium of the stage game which is more detrimental to the first (unilaterally) deviating player. Again (cf. Exercise 8.5), this defines a Nash equilibrium of the ensuing repeated subgame, both in the scenario given by $\mathcal{R}^\delta(W)$ as well as in $\mathcal{R}^\infty(W)$. This completes the proof of the results. ∎

Recall from Section 8.3 that we always have $\tilde{v}_i \geq \hat{v}_i$ for every player i, and therefore

$$\{v \in V : v_i > \tilde{v}_i\} \subseteq \{v \in V : v_i > \hat{v}_i\}.$$

Thus, if Theorems 8.4 and 8.5 are compared with their Nash equilibrium counterparts (Theorems 8.1 and 8.2, respectively), it follows that, in general, the former establish narrower equilibrium possibilities than the latter. By way of illustration, suppose the stage game were as represented in Table 8.3. Then, since $\tilde{v}_1 = \tilde{v}_2 = 4$ is the highest payoff in the stage game, we have

$$\{v \in V : v_i > \tilde{v}_i, \quad i = 1, 2\} = \emptyset$$

while it can be readily seen that

$$\{v \in V : v_i > \hat{v}_i \quad i = 1, 2\} = \{(v_1, v_2) \in \mathbb{R}^2 : 1 < v_i \leq 1 + \frac{3}{4}v_j,$$

$$\forall i, j = 1, 2 \ (i \neq j)\}.$$

We find, therefore, a significant contrast between the payoff-supporting possibilities stated in Theorem 8.4 (or 8.5) when restricting to subgame-perfect equilibria and those established by Theorem 8.1 (or 8.2) when extending consideration to the Nash equilibria of the corresponding repeated game. Thus, whereas the former yield nothing beyond the vector $(\tilde{v}_1, \tilde{v}_2) = (4, 4)$ obtained by continuously playing the stage-game equilibrium (which is always a subgame-perfect equilibrium of the repeated game), the latter encompass a significantly wider range of payoff vectors otherwise unattainable through Nash equilibria of the stage game.

Is this significant curtailment of possibilities an unavoidable implication of subgame perfection? The next two results indicate that this is not the case. Specifically, they show that, by increasing the sophistication of the underlying construction, subgame perfection can be made compatible, in essence,[133] with the same range of equilibrium payoffs obtained in Theorems 8.1 and 8.2. That is, they establish that any vector of (strictly) individually rational payoffs is attainable at some subgame-perfect equilibrium of either $\mathcal{R}^\delta (W)$ or $\mathcal{R}^\infty (W)$ – in the former case, under the customary proviso that δ is large enough.

Theorem 8.6 (Fudenberg and Maskin, 1986): *Consider any $v \in V$ with $v_i > \hat{v}_i$, $\forall i = 1, 2, \ldots, n$. Then, if the set of feasible payoffs V displays full dimension (i.e., equal to n), $\exists \bar{\delta} < 1$ such that for all $\delta \in (\bar{\delta}, 1)$ there exists a subgame-perfect equilibrium of $\mathcal{R}^\delta (W)$ whose payoffs for each player $i = 1, 2, \ldots, n$ coincide with v_i.*

Theorem 8.7 (Aumann and Shapley, 1976): *Consider any $v \in V$ with $v_i > \hat{v}_i$, $\forall i = 1, 2, \ldots, n$. Then, there exists a subgame-perfect equilibrium of $\mathcal{R}^\infty (W)$ whose payoffs for each player $i = 1, 2, \ldots, n$ coincide with v_i.*

The proofs of these two theorems rely on different variations of the same basic idea: to deter deviations, it is enough to punish them for a sufficiently *long but finite* stretch of time. Despite this similarity, the actual construction of the supporting equilibrium strategies is significantly more involved in the case of Theorem 8.6. Thus, for example, this result requires that the dimension of the set V coincide with the total number of players. The intuitive basis for this requirement is quite

---

[133] As explained below, the discounted-payoff scenario now requires an additional dimensionality condition on the set of stage payoffs.

clear. Sometimes, to deter certain deviations credibly, some players may have to be threatened with *selective* punishments (or rewards) that do not punish (or reward) the remaining players. In general, this is possible only if the set of possible stage payoffs is dimensionally rich.

These complications, however, do not arise in the infinitely repeated game if players are concerned with the limit average payoffs. In this case, because the players display an "infinite" patience, no finitely lived punishment has any payoff implications and, therefore, the particular details of any such punishment leave every player fully indifferent. Since this feature facilitates the proof of Theorem 8.7 quite substantially, we choose to exemplify the basic ideas by presenting a formal proof of this latter result alone.

Proof of Theorem 8.7: As in previous cases, let us make the convenient simplification that the payoff vector v to be supported satisfies $v = W(a)$ for some $a \in A$. Partition the set of possible histories

$$\mathcal{H} = \bigcup_{t \in \mathbb{N}} H^{t-1}$$

into $n + 1$ equivalence classes: $\mathcal{H}_0, \mathcal{H}_1, \ldots, \mathcal{H}_n$ with the following interpretation

- $\mathcal{H}_0$ consists of all those histories after which players are supposed to behave in a "cooperative fashion," i.e., each player is to choose her respective action a_i in the target profile a.
- $\mathcal{H}_i$, $i = 1, 2, \ldots, n$, is composed of those histories after which player i must be "punished" by all other players $j \neq i$.

Let us posit that h^0, the "empty history" prevailing at $t = 1$, belongs to $\mathcal{H}_0$. Starting at it, the *law of motion* for histories that governs their assignment to the different equivalence classes is specified as follows.

On the one hand, postulate that if at any given period t the prevailing history h^{t-1} has the game be in a cooperative phase, the game stays in a cooperative phase at $t + 1$ if

(a) each player $i = 1, 2, \ldots, n$ adopts her respective target action a_i at t, or

(b) there is a multilateral deviation from $a = (a_1, a_2, \ldots, a_n)$ involving two or more players.

Formally, this amounts to specifying the following conditions:

(i) $\left(h^{t-1} \in \mathcal{H}_0, \ a^t = a \right) \Rightarrow h^t \in \mathcal{H}_0$;
(ii) $\left(h^{t-1} \in \mathcal{H}_0, \ a_i^t \neq a_i, \ a_j^t \neq a_j, \ i \neq j \right) \Rightarrow h^t \in \mathcal{H}_0$.

On the other hand, let us also postulate that, at any t where the game is in a cooperative phase, any *unilateral* deviation by some given player i triggers a punishment phase where this player is kept at her minimax payoff for r periods, where $r \in \mathbb{N}$ is a parameter (to be determined below), which specifies the duration of punishment phases. Naturally, after those r periods are over, the game is assumed to return to a cooperative phase. Formally, this is embodied by the following additional conditions:

(iii) $\left(h^{t-1} \in \mathcal{H}_0, \; a_i^t \neq a_i, \; \left(\forall j \neq i, \; a_j^t = a_j\right)\right) \Rightarrow h^t \in \mathcal{H}_i;$

(iv) $\left(h^{t-1} \in \mathcal{H}_0, \; h^t, \ldots, h^{t+s-1} \in \mathcal{H}_i, \; s \leq r\right) \Rightarrow h^{t+s} \in \mathcal{H}_i;$

(v) $\left(h^t, h^{t+1}, \ldots, h^{t+r} \in \mathcal{H}_i\right) \Rightarrow h^{t+r+1} \in \mathcal{H}_0.$

Given (i)–(v), now consider the following strategies: for each player $i = 1, 2, \ldots, n$, and every t,

$$
\begin{aligned}
\gamma_i \left(h^{t-1}\right) &= a_i \quad \text{if} \quad h^{t-1} \in \mathcal{H}_0, \\
\gamma_i \left(h^{t-1}\right) &= \hat{\alpha}_i^j \quad \text{if} \quad h^{t-1} \in \mathcal{H}_j,
\end{aligned}
\tag{8.12}
$$

where $\hat{\alpha}_i^j$ is a (possibly mixed) action of player i underlying the minimax payoff $\hat{v}_j$ for player j (recall the analogous procedure used in the proof of Theorem 8.1). Of course, those strategies are not yet fully defined because one still needs to specify the parameter r determining the length of the punishment phases. Thus choose r so that, for all $i = 1, 2, \ldots, n$, the following inequality is satisfied:

$$
v_i^* + r \hat{v}_i < \underline{v}_i + r v_i
\tag{8.13}
$$

where we define

$$
\underline{v}_i = \min_{a \in A} W_i \left(a\right),
\tag{8.14}
$$

i.e., the minimum payoff attainable by player i in the stage game, and recall that

$$
v_i^* = \max_{a \in A} W_i \left(a\right).
$$

Since, by assumption, $\hat{v}_i < v_i$ for every $i = 1, 2, \ldots, n$, some such (finite) r exists.

Finally, let us verify that the strategies described in (8.12) define a subgame-perfect equilibrium of $\mathcal{R}^\infty \left(W\right)$ for any r that satisfies (8.13). Clearly, given any such r, no player i can enjoy any payoff gain by deviating from her respective target action a_i. This certainly implies that those strategies define a Nash equilibrium of the repeated game. However, if this equilibrium is to be subgame perfect as well, the punishment phases to be suffered by any given player i must involve optimal (i.e., credible) responses by the remaining players $j \neq i$. But this is a trivial consequence of the fact that, because players are concerned only with their limit average payoffs, any payoff stretch involving just a *finite* number of periods (note that punishment phases are so designed) is payoff irrelevant. The proof of the theorem is thus complete.   ∎

Remark 8.3: *Renegotiation-proof equilibria in repeated games.*

To tackle the equilibrium multiplicity typically displayed by repeated games, a natural course to take would seem to be that explored in Chapter 4.

There, it might be recalled, we introduced a variety of further strategic-stability requirements that, by strengthening those embodied by Nash equilibrium, were in some cases effective in ruling out some of the original Nash equilibria.

However, Theorems 8.6 and 8.7 make it apparent that, by limiting to refinement criteria that reflect considerations of perfection *alone*, nothing essential is gained in tackling the problem. Instead, an alternative route that has proven partially effective in this respect has revolved around the general notion labeled renegotiation-proof equilibrium, which has been formalized in different specific ways. Early proponents were Farrell and Maskin (1989) for infinitely repeated games and Benoit and Krishna (1988) for finitely repeated ones.

Succinctly, the main idea put forward by this literature may be explained as follows. Consider a given multistage game and suppose that players may "pause" at any intermediate stage of it to reevaluate the situation. At every such point, they should have the opportunity of "renegotiating" whatever equilibrium they might have originally settled on, if all of them so desire. But this must also imply that, when contemplating a *future* hypothetical deviation, players should be able to anticipate this possibility. That is, they should consider whether, if such a deviation were indeed to occur, players would afterward be interested in jointly revising the ensuing (equilibrium) reactions that should follow. In particular, it could well happen that, even though the ensuing equilibrium behavior does define an equilibrium of the continuation game (i.e., the equilibrium considered is perfect, in some appropriate sense), there is another continuation equilibrium that all players prefer to the original one. Then, players could argue at that juncture (i.e., after the deviation) as follows:

> *If we must 'agree' on a particular equilibrium to apply henceforth, it is silly for us to focus on one for which an alternative equilibrium exists that we uniformly prefer (i.e., whose outcome Pareto-dominates that of the former). Bygones are bygones: if one of us has deviated from a putative equilibrium, there is nothing we can now do about it – it would be unreasonable to punish ourselves (i.e., all of us) for that irreversible state of affairs.*

As suggested in Subsection 2.2.1, to admit the implicit "conversation" outlined above as a legitimate basis for the analysis of a game is somewhat at odds with the tenet of independent decision making that underlies non-cooperative game theory. In general, that is, one should insist that if the description of the strategic situation allows for the possibility of interplayer communication, this communication should be formally modeled as part of the game itself.

In fact, it is partly because this underlying communication is not modeled explicitly that this literature has produced quite a diverse range of renegotiation-proof concepts. All of them embody the same rough idea: no equilibrium should qualify as renegotiation proof if its off-equilibrium ("punishment") strategies admit the possibility of a jointly beneficial revision toward an equilibrium of the continuation game. Their implications, however, are sometimes quite diverse and depend as well on the particular context of application. They range from cases where equilibria of this kind do not exist, to others where they are successful in ensuring uniqueness, to still others where the original equilibrium multiplicity of subgame-perfect equilibria persists even when renegotiation proofness is imposed. Overall, it seems fair to say that the difficult issues raised by renegotiation proofness must be understood far better before this idea can be widely and consistently used in the analysis of general repeated games.   ◆

8.5.2   *Finite horizon*

Here, we carry out for *finitely* repeated games the analogue of the task performed in the previous subsection for games that are infinitely repeated. That is, we explore how the folk theorem proven in Section 8.3.2 for those games (Theorem 8.3) fares under the requirement of subgame perfection.[134]

First, we establish that, unlike what we concluded in Subsection 8.5.1 for infinitely repeated games, there are circumstances where the requirement of subgame perfection may have drastic ("nonfolk") implications if the horizon of interaction is finite. Consider, for example, the case where the stage game has a unique Nash equilibrium. Then, the next result shows that by demanding subgame perfection the repeated game is forced to inherit rigidly the same equilibrium uniqueness of the stage game. Thus, repeated interaction adds in this case no further payoff possibilities, beyond what is already available in the stage game alone.

Theorem 8.8: *Suppose that the stage game W has a unique Nash equilibrium, $\bar{\alpha}$. Then, given any $T < \infty$, the unique subgame-perfect of $\mathcal{R}^T (W)$ has every player $i = 1, 2, \ldots, n$ choose $\bar{\alpha}_i$ in every $t = 1, 2, \ldots, T$, independently of history.*

Proof: The proof is a straightforward generalization of the argument described in Section 8.1 for the finitely repeated prisoner's dilemma (see Exercise 8.7).   ∎

The above result stands in stark contrast with Theorem 8.3, whose statement did not depend at all on the lack of equilibrium uniqueness of the stage game. Here, it is the combination of such uniqueness and the demand of subgame perfection that jointly imply the uniqueness of equilibrium in the finitely repeated game. Thus, for example, if we again let the stage game W be as given by Table 8.3, the unique payoff vector sustainable at a subgame-perfect equilibrium of the repeated game $\mathcal{R}^T (W)$ is $\tilde{v} = (4, 4)$. This contrasts with the fact, already discussed, that a payoff vector such as $v = (2, 2)$ may be supported through a Nash equilibrium of $\mathcal{R}^T (W)$, provided T is high enough.

---

[134] Recall that the constructive proof of Theorem 8.3 involved "nonperfect" strategies, much as it was also the case in the counterpart results for *infinitely* repeated games (Theorems 8.1 and 8.2).

It follows, therefore, that to have finitely repeated interaction expand "credibly" (i.e., through subgame-perfect equilibria) the payoff possibilities attainable in the stage game, this game must display at least two distinct Nash equilibria. In fact, as we show next, one must require a somewhat stronger condition: every individual must have two alternative Nash equilibria of the stage game that she does *not* find payoff indifferent. Intuitively, what this avails is a sufficient degree of freedom to threaten each player in a credible fashion.

Theorem 8.9 (Benoit and Krishna, 1985): *Suppose that,* $\forall i = 1, 2, \ldots, n$, *there exists a Nash equilibrium of* W, $\breve{\alpha}^i$, *such that* $W_i(\breve{\alpha}^i) > W_i(\tilde{\alpha}^i)$.[135] *If* $v \in V$ *satisfies* $v_i > \hat{v}_i$ *for each* i *and* $\dim V = n$,[136] *then* $\forall \varepsilon > 0$, $\exists T^*$ *such that if* $T > T^*$, *the repeated game* $\mathcal{R}^T(W)$ *has a subgame-perfect equilibrium whose induced payoff vector* v' *satisfies* $|v_i' - v_i| \leq \varepsilon$ *for each player* i.

Proof (partial): Let $v \in V$. Here, to avoid some intricate details, we shall posit, in addition to the usual simplification that $v = W(a)$ for some $a \in A$, the further assumption that $v_i > \tilde{v}_i$ for each $i = 1, 2, \ldots, n$. That is, we posit that the target payoff vector can be attained by a pure-strategy profile, each player receiving with it a payoff larger than what she would obtain in her worst Nash equilibria of the stage game.[137]

As in Theorem 8.3, consider a terminal path of actions, $(\alpha^{T-n+1}, \alpha^{T-n+2}, \ldots, \alpha^T)$, with $\alpha^{T-n+i} = \breve{\alpha}^i$, $i = 1, 2, \ldots, n$. By hypothesis, the average payoff for each player i along this path exceeds that of the constant path given by $\alpha^{T-n+j} = \tilde{\alpha}^i$ for every $j = 1, 2, \ldots, n$. Let $\mu_i > 0$ represent the magnitude of this excess average payoff and make $\mu \equiv \min_i \mu_i$. Consider now a concatenation of q paths as the one formerly described, which produces a terminal path q times longer involving the last $q \cdot n$ periods (here, of course, it is implicitly supposed that $T > q \cdot n$). Then, if one compares the path so constructed with another constant one (also of length $q \cdot n$) in which every element coincides with $\tilde{\alpha}^i$, it follows that the average payoff of each player i along the constant path must fall below that of the alternative one by at least $q \cdot \mu$. On the other hand, it should be clear that both of these paths can be supported as a subgame-perfect equilibrium in any subgame involving the last $q \cdot n$ stages of the repeated game $\mathcal{R}^T(W)$.

---

[135] Recall that $\tilde{\alpha}^i$ stands for the Nash equilibrium of the stage game W where player i obtains the lowest equilibrium payoff, which was denoted by $\tilde{v}^i$.

[136] As explained in connection with Theorem 8.6, the condition $\dim V = n$ guarantees that the stage game admits a sufficiently *discriminating* leeway to construct a rich (player-specific) set of punishment strategies. In the *partial* proof outlined below this consideration plays no role because the argument focuses on the case where the payoff vector to be supported Pareto-dominates that obtained at some Nash equilibrium of the stage game.

[137] Note that this case is the analogue, for finitely repeated games, of that considered in Theorems 8.4 and 8.5 for repeated games with an unbounded time horizon.

Motivated by the aforementioned considerations, we define the following strategies for each player $i = 1, 2, \ldots, n$[138]:

(i) $\gamma_i \left(h^{t-1} \right) = a_i$ if $t \leq T - q \cdot n$ and $\forall \tau \leq t - 1$, there exists *no* player j who has deviated unilaterally from a_j in τ;

(ii) $\gamma_i \left(h^{t-1} \right) = \breve{\alpha}_i^j$ if $t > T - q \cdot n$ and *no* single player deviated from (i) for all $\tau \leq T - q \cdot n$, where the mixed-action profile $\breve{\alpha}^j$ is chosen so that $j = n - [T - t]_n$;

(iii) $\gamma_i \left(h^{t-1} \right) = \tilde{\alpha}_i^j$ otherwise, where j is the player who first deviated from a_j for some prior $\tau \leq T - q \cdot n$.

As in the proof of Theorem 8.3, it is easy to check that, for sufficiently high q, the above strategies define a subgame-perfect equilibrium of $\mathcal{R}^T (W)$ if $T > n \cdot q$. Therefore, given q (independently of T), there exists some T^*, large enough, such that if $T > T^*$ the overall average payoffs induced by those strategies approach her respective v_i in an arbitrarily close fashion. This completes the proof. ∎

The former result shows that, in finitely repeated games, a crucial factor is whether the stage game W admits some punishment margin that could be selectively implemented for *each* player in a credible fashion (i.e., through corresponding Nash equilibria of W). If this happens, any individually rational payoff can be sustained by some subgame-perfect equilibrium when the time horizon under consideration is long enough. This then implies that, under those conditions, the requirement of subgame perfection does not shrink (as compared with Nash equilibrium alone – cf. Theorem 8.3) the scope of payoff possibilities that can be attained at equilibrium in a long enough repeated game.

These payoff possibilities, on the other hand, are also essentially the same as those attainable with an unbounded time horizon (recall Theorems 8.6 and 8.7). At first sight, it is intriguing that the anticipation by the players that their interaction will definitely end at some prespecified date should not alter matters in this respect. Wouldn't players then face progressively weaker incentives to avoid deviations as the finitely repeated game approaches its end? This, in turn, should bring over analogous implications to the earlier stages of the game through the familiar procedure of backward induction. Indeed, it is true that, as the end of the game is reached, the incentives of the players to abide by (nonequilibrium stage) behavior deteriorates – simply, the future consequences of any deviation become less important. This problem, however, has been tackled in the above equilibrium construction by exploiting the wedge experienced by every player between her worst equilibrium outcome in the stage game and an alternative equilibrium possibility. If this wedge is applied to a long enough final stretch, it maintains the required incentives till the very end of the game. In particular, it precludes the backward-induction unraveling, which might otherwise be possible in view of the prespecified end of the interaction.

---

[138] Recall the notational conventions explained in Footnote 124.

By way of illustration, recall the strategic-form game represented in Table 8.2. This game has two pure-strategy Nash equilibria: (X, A) and (Y, B), with different payoffs for each player. Its only symmetric Nash equilibrium (which involves each player choosing both of her pure strategies with the same probability) is clearly inefficient. However, it follows from Theorem 8.9 that the payoff vector $v = (4, 4)$ can be arbitrarily approximated in a subgame-perfect equilibrium if the stage game is repeated a sufficiently large (but finite) number of times. The reason is that the two aforementioned pure-strategy Nash equilibria, precisely because of their asymmetry, provide the punishment leeway required to support the symmetric efficient profile along (most of) the equilibrium path.

Theorem 8.9 leaves aside those contexts where the stage game has a unique Nash equilibrium, in which case we know (cf. Theorem 8.8) that there is a unique subgame-perfect equilibrium where the stage Nash equilibrium is repeated over time. A case in point is the finitely repeated prisoner's dilemma, where defection prevails throughout in its unique subgame-perfect equilibrium. The theoretical and empirical problems raised by this fact were already discussed in Section 8.4. There, we suggested a way out of these problems that involved perturbing the game slightly with a small degree of incomplete information. Here, we pursue a somewhat reminiscent methodological approach, in that play will also be slightly perturbed. In the present case, however, the perturbation will impinge on the equilibrium concept itself, that will be relaxed slightly to accommodate for an approximate notion of optimality (or rationality) on the part of the agents.[139]

Let us parametrize by $\varepsilon \geq 0$ the payoff magnitude by which players are allowed to divert from optimality – or, more precisely, the extent to which they may ignore profitable deviations. Associated with any such ε, we introduce two generalized equilibrium notions labeled ε-*Nash equilibrium* and ε-*subgame-perfect equilibrium*. As should be apparent, the ordinary notions of Nash and subgame-perfect equilibria (cf. Definitions 2.2 and 4.1) are obtained as particular cases when the tolerance level $\varepsilon = 0$.

Definition 8.1: *Let* $G = \{N, \{S_i\}_{i=1}^n, \{\pi_i\}_{i=1}^n\}$ *be a game in strategic form. Given* $\varepsilon \geq 0$, *a strategy profile* $\sigma^* = (\sigma_1^*, \sigma_2^*, \ldots, \sigma_n^*)$ *is said to be an* ε-Nash *equilibrium if* $\forall i = 1, 2, \ldots, n, \forall \sigma_i \in \Sigma_i, \pi_i(\sigma^*) \geq \pi_i(\sigma_i, \sigma_{-i}^*) - \varepsilon$.

Definition 8.2: *Let* Γ *be a game in extensive form. Given* $\varepsilon \geq 0$, *a strategy profile* γ^* *is said to be an* ε-subgame-perfect equilibrium *if, for all proper subgames* $\hat{\Gamma}$ *of* Γ, $\gamma^* \mid_{\hat{\Gamma}}$ *is an* ε-Nash equilibrium of $\hat{\Gamma}$.

Thus, if $\varepsilon > 0$, the standpoint adopted by the ε-equilibrium concepts is that deviations that entail only a small payoff gain may be ignored. This contrasts with the standard notion of (exact) rationality considered so far, where no profitable deviations are allowed, no matter how small. The approach based on ε-(ir)rationality may be conceived as an indirect formalization of bounded rationality, as it pertains to

---

[139] Thus, in contrast with the Nash refinement approach, our present aim is to relax the Nash criterion itself, consequently tending to *enlarge* the set of strategy profiles that qualify as equilibria.

players' perception – i.e., only if payoff potential gains are substantial enough, they are necessarily reacted to. As we shall see (cf. Theorem 8.10), such ε-rationality can open up ample cooperation opportunities that would otherwise be unreachable. In this sense, therefore, a strict bounded-rationality interpretation of matters might be questionable. In a sense, one could heuristically say (for example, concerning play in the finitely repeated prisoner's dilemma) that letting oneself slide into "too much" rationality (more specifically, its being common knowledge) might be somewhat irrational. For, if players insist on responding even to the most minute payoff gains (and this is commonly known), they might in effect be foregoing large payoff gains.

A formalization of these ideas in a general repeated-interaction framework is the object of the following result.

Theorem 8.10 (Radner, 1980): *Let $v \in V$ with $v_i > \tilde{v}_i$, $\forall i = 1, 2, \ldots, n$. Given any $\varepsilon > 0, \eta > 0$, $\exists T^*$ such that if $T > T^*$ the repeated game $\mathcal{R}^T(W)$ has an ε-subgame-perfect equilibrium whose payoffs v'_i for each player i satisfy $|v'_i - v_i| \leq \eta$.*

Proof: Consider any $v \in V$ such that $v_i > \tilde{v}_i$ $(i = 1, 2, \ldots, n)$ and suppose, as usual, that $v = W(a)$ for some $a \in A$. Let $\tilde{\alpha}^i$ stand for a Nash equilibrium of the stage game W where the payoff of player i is equal to $\tilde{v}_i$; i.e., it is minimum across all Nash equilibria of W. Then, given some $s \in \mathbb{N}, s < T$, and any particular Nash equilibrium $\bar{\alpha}$ of the stage game W, consider the following strategies for each player $i = 1, 2, \ldots, n$:

(i) $\gamma_i\left(h^{t-1}\right) = a_i$ if $t \leq T - s$ and $\forall \tau \leq t - 1$, there exists *no* player j who has deviated unilaterally (only she) from a_j in τ;

(ii) $\gamma_i\left(h^{t-1}\right) = \tilde{\alpha}_i^j$ if $t \leq T - s$ and (i) does not apply, where j is the player who first deviated unilaterally from a_j for some $\tau \leq t - 1$;

(iii) $\gamma_i\left(h^{t-1}\right) = \bar{\alpha}_i$ if $t > T - s$.   (8.15)

Choose $q \in \mathbb{N}$ such that

$$q(v_i - \tilde{v}_i) > v_i^* - v_i$$

for every $i = 1, 2, \ldots, n$, where v_i^* is defined in (8.7). Then, if players are taken to follow the strategies described in (8.15), no player has an incentive to deviate for all $t \leq T - s - q$. Naturally, no deviation is profitable either for $t > T - s$ because, in each of these periods, play coincides with a Nash equilibrium of the stage game.

Let us finally turn to the possibility that deviations might occur for t such that $T - s - q < t \leq T - s$. Fix $\varepsilon > 0$, arbitrarily low. Then, if s (and therefore T) is chosen large enough, no deviation by any player in those periods may produce an increase in average payoffs larger than ε. Specifically, it is enough to select

$$s + 1 > \frac{\max_i v_i^* - \min_i v_i}{\varepsilon}.$$

In that case, the strategies given in (8.15) define an ε-Nash equilibrium of $\mathcal{R}^T(W)$ that, as is it is easy to confirm, is ε-subgame-perfect as well.

Finally, note that the previous argument (in particular, the fact that the strategies in (8.15) define an ε-equilibrium) is independent of T, provided that $T \geq s + q$. Therefore, if T is chosen high enough (keeping s and q fixed), the equilibrium described induces average payoffs that approximate v_i for each player $i = 1, 2, \ldots, n$ in an arbitrarily close manner. The proof is thus complete. ∎

By way of example, let us apply Theorem 8.10 to the finitely repeated prisoner's dilemma with stage payoffs as described in Table 8.1. Given any $\varepsilon > 0$ and $\eta > 0$, we may guarantee that there exists a sufficiently protracted (but finite) horizon such that if the repeated game extends beyond this point, the two players can sustain, through an ε-subgame-perfect equilibrium, average payoffs (v_1, v_2) such that $v_i \geq -1 - \eta$ for each $i = 1, 2$ – that is, average payoffs arbitrarily close to the cooperative levels. If we follow the same construction used in the proof above, such an equilibrium would have players choose action D in the last s periods, where s must be chosen so that $s > (1 - \varepsilon)/\varepsilon$. And then, it can be easily checked that, for the stated conclusion to hold, it is enough that the time horizon T satisfies $T > 9s/\eta$.

8.6   Reputation and "irrationality": formal analysis

To complement the informal illustrations discussed in Section 8.4, our present objective is to gain some rigorous understanding of the role that reputation-building phenomena can have in repeated games. More specifically, we focus on how different behavioral reputations unfold in scenarios that are perturbed, just slightly, by some prior probability for "irrational" behavior. In line with our former examples, we divide the analysis in two parts. First, in Subsection 8.6.1, we are concerned with setups where all players involved display the same (long) time horizon. Then, in Section 8.6.2, our attention turns to contexts where agents with different time horizons coexist – specifically, the focus is on a case where a single long-run player faces an infinite sequence of short-run ones.

8.6.1   *A common time horizon*

First, we want to render precise the idea that, under "slight" incomplete information, the incentives of forward-looking players to buttress a certain behavioral reputation (even if this reputation is, in a sense, of irrationality) may sustain, at equilibrium, payoffs that would not be attainable otherwise, i.e., under complete information. In essence, the folk-type result of this kind that is proven below may be summarized as follows:

In a long process of repeated interaction that is subject to small uncertainty as to the underlying types of the opponents, there is a suitable choice for the possible alternative types that allows one to obtain any payoff vector that dominates Nash stage payoffs at an associated sequential equilibrium.

To establish this result formally, let us consider a theoretical framework that, for simplicity, is restricted to just two players, 1 and 2. Suppose that, *a priori*, each of these players can be either of a "normal" or of a "rare" type, the latter possibility happening with a prior independent probability $\eta > 0$, conceived as small. Modeling matters in the Harsanyian fashion, let Nature select first the type of each player i, who is then informed privately. (This, of course, has player j ($\neq i$) hold subjective beliefs on player i's type that are given by Nature's choice probabilities, η and $1 - \eta$.) If both players are of the normal type, their payoffs are as given by some $\mathcal{R}^T(W)$. That is, they are in fact involved in the T-fold repetition of the (finite) stage game given by

$$W : A_1 \times A_2 \to \mathbb{R}^2,$$

even though neither of them can be completely sure of that (because they are uncertain of the opponent's payoffs). Instead, if either player $i \in \{1, 2\}$ happens to be of the rare type, she is assumed confronted with a situation (or game form) just as in $\mathcal{R}^T(W)$, but her corresponding payoffs are then different. Specifically, her intertemporal payoffs (defined over the set of complete histories) are as given by some payoff function of the form

$$\psi_i : H^T \to \mathbb{R}.$$

For the moment, these payoff functions (or alternative "reputations") are left unspecified, because they will be used to parametrize the ensuing analysis. For any given pair of such payoff functions, $(\psi_i)_{i=1,2}$, the induced incomplete-information game will be denoted $\mathcal{R}^T(W, (\psi_i)_{i=1,2}, \eta)$.

In this context, the aforementioned folk-type result can be formally stated as follows.[140]

Theorem 8.11 (Fudenberg and Maskin, 1986): *Let $v \in V$ with $v_i \geq \tilde{v}_i$, $\forall i = 1, 2$. $\forall \eta > 0$, $\forall \varepsilon > 0$, there exists some T^* and suitable payoff functions for the rare types, $(\psi_i)_{i=1,2}$, such that if $T > T^*$, the game $\mathcal{R}^T(W, (\psi_i)_{i=1,2}, \eta)$ has a sequential equilibrium[141] whose payoffs v_i' for the normal type of each player i satisfy $|v_i - v_i'| \leq \varepsilon$.*

Proof: Suppose, for simplicity, that $v = W(a)$ for some $a \in A$. First, we need to define the *rare types* used to support the payoff vector v at equilibrium. This amounts to specifying what are the intertemporal payoffs $\psi_i(\cdot)$ displayed by these types. In this respect, it will be convenient to postulate simply that, for each player i, her corresponding payoff function $\psi_i(\cdot)$ when

---

[140] Fudenberg and Maskin (1986) show a stronger theorem where any individually rational payoff vector (i.e., any $v \in V$ such that $v_i > \hat{v}_i$ for each player i) can be supported at a sequential equilibrium of the incomplete-information game. Here, to simplify the argument, we focus on the weaker version where $v_i \geq \tilde{v}_i$ ($\geq \hat{v}_i$) – cf. Subsection 8.3.1.

[141] As explained, the game is modeled to have Nature as the first mover. Thus, the sequential equilibrium referred pertains to the induced trilateral game involving Nature and players 1 and 2.

being of the rare type renders it *dominant* for her to follow the following strategy[142]:

$$\check{\gamma}_i \left(h^{t-1} \right) = a_i \quad \text{if } \forall \tau \leq t - 1, \text{ there exists } \textit{no} \text{ player } j \text{ who}$$
$$\text{has } \textit{unilaterally} \text{ deviated from } a_j \text{ in } \tau; \quad (8.16)$$

$$\check{\gamma}_i \left(h^{t-1} \right) = \tilde{\alpha}_i^j \quad \text{otherwise, where } j \text{ is the index referring to}$$
$$\text{the player who has } \textit{first} \text{ deviated unilaterally}$$
$$\text{from } a_j. \quad (8.17)$$

Fix a certain $\hat{T}$, and consider any particular sequential equilibrium of the game $\mathcal{R}^{\hat{T}} \left(W, (\psi_i)_{i=1,2}, \eta \right)$. Let the behavior for the normal types in this equilibrium be given by (interim) strategies that are denoted by $(\hat{\gamma}_i)_{i=1,2}$. Next, consider time horizons T with $T > \hat{T}$, and suppose that the strategy for a normal type of player i in this game is as follows:

$$\gamma_i \left(h^{t-1} \right) = \check{\gamma}_i \left(h^{t-1} \right) \quad \text{if } t < T - \hat{T}; \quad (8.18)$$

$$= \hat{\gamma}_i \left(h^{t-1} \right) \quad \text{if } t \geq T - \hat{T} \quad \text{and} \quad \forall \tau < T - \hat{T},$$
$$\text{no player deviated unilaterally;} \quad (8.19)$$

$$= \check{\gamma}_i \left(h^{t-1} \right) \quad \text{otherwise.}[143] \quad (8.20)$$

We claim that, for any given $\eta > 0$, the strategies defined by (8.16) and (8.17) for the rare types and (8.18)–(8.20) for the normal ones define a sequential equilibrium of $\mathcal{R}^T (W, (\psi_i)_{i=1,2}, \eta)$, provided T is large enough. For the rare types, the strategies defined in (8.16) and (8.17) are sequentially optimal by hypothesis. On the other hand, for the normal types, in order to show that the strategies given by (8.18)–(8.20) are optimal as well at every possible period t, it is useful to decompose the argument in three steps.

1. Let $t \geq T - \hat{T}$, and suppose that *no* unilateral deviation has occurred in $\tau \in \{1, 2, \ldots, T - \hat{T} - 1\}$. Then, (8.19) prescribes behavior according to $(\hat{\gamma}_i)_{i=1,2}$ that, by construction, is supposed to define a sequential equilibrium for the final part of the game of duration $\hat{T}$. (Note that, if no deviation from a has occurred up to $T - \hat{T} - 1$, the subjective probabilities on the opponent's type coincide with those prevailing at the beginning of the game.)

2. Suppose now that, at a certain $t' < t$, there has been a unilateral deviation by some player j. Then, the prescription of (8.17) and (8.20) is that in t (and all later periods) the Nash equilibrium $\tilde{\alpha}^j$ of the stage

---

[142] In the present incomplete-information context, a well-defined strategy must involve a mapping from observed history (i.e., past actions) *and* the player's type to the set of possible actions. For simplicity, however, we choose to abuse this notion and speak of a strategy as a mapping that, for any *given* type, depends on observed history alone. No confusion should arise.

[143] Note that, if $t \geq T - \hat{T}$ and some player j deviated at some $\tau < T - \hat{T}$ (i.e., neither of the two first cases apply), then $\check{\gamma}_i \left(h^t \right) = \tilde{\alpha}_i^j$. Despite the fact that players' behavior is then constant, the general formulation $\check{\gamma}_i \left(h^t \right)$ is maintained for expositional reasons.

game will be played. This obviously induces a sequential equilibrium of the ensuing game.

3. Finally, we consider the third possibility. Let $t < T - \hat{T}$ and suppose that no unilateral deviation has taken place before then. It has to be shown that no player $i = 1, 2$ will find it optimal to deviate from the contemplated strategies – i.e., it is optimal for each of them to play her respective a_i in t. On the one hand, if she were to deviate, her maximum *total sum* of stage payoffs would be

$$v_i^* + (T - t)\,\tilde{v}_i, \tag{8.21}$$

where recall that v_i^* was defined as the maximum payoff of player i in the stage game W (cf. (8.7)). On the other hand, under the maintained assumption that her opponent (if of a normal type) will keep playing the strategy defined by (8.18)–(8.20), each player i can *guarantee* (by, say, mimicking the strategy $\check{\gamma}_i$ of the rare type) an ensuing flow of stage payoffs that, in expected terms, provide a total sum that is at least

$$\eta\,(T - t + 1)\,v_i + (1 - \eta)\left(\underline{v}_i + (T - t)\,\tilde{v}_i\right), \tag{8.22}$$

where recall that $\underline{v}_i$ stands for the minimum payoff of i in the stage game W (cf. (8.14)). Thus, it is enough to show that if T is high enough, the expression in (8.22) must exceed that in (8.21). Subtracting (8.21) from (8.22), we obtain

$$\eta\,(T - t)\,(v_i - \tilde{v}_i) + (1 - \eta)\,\underline{v}_i + \eta v_i - v_i^*.$$

Since $t < T - \hat{T}$ (i.e., $T - t > \hat{T}$), the above expression is positive if $\hat{T}$ is high enough. Specifically, it is sufficient that

$$\hat{T} > \frac{v_i^* - (1 - \eta)\underline{v}_i - \eta v_i}{\eta\,(v_i - \tilde{v}_i)}.$$

To conclude, note that, because $\hat{T}$ (the length of the "terminal phase") can be determined independently of T (the length of the whole game), the *average* payoffs of each player i over the full game can be drawn arbitrarily close to v_i (i.e., within any prespecified $\varepsilon > 0$). This simply follows from the fact that the contemplated equilibrium yields v_i to player i in the first $T - \hat{T}$ stages of the game, and these stages represent an arbitrarily high fraction of the whole game if (given $\hat{T}$) the time horizon T is long enough. This completes the proof. ∎

Remark 8.4: *Equilibrium robustness in finitely repeated games*

Theorem 8.11 underscores the fact (also illustrated in Section 8.4) that some of the results proven in Section 8.5.2 for repeated games with a finite time horizon (e.g., Theorem 8.8) are not robust to small perturbations in either the description or the analysis of the game. Here, the perturbation has concerned the *information conditions* under which the interaction takes place. In contrast, Theorem 8.10 focused on "perturbations" of the traditional, perfect rationality, *behavioral paradigm.*   ◆

8.6.2   *Different time horizons*

As discussed in Section 8.4, the scope of possible reputations (and corresponding equilibrium payoffs) that should be expected to arise and consolidate in a repeated process of interaction must crucially depend on the particular time horizons of the different players. This point was illustrated through the (finitely repeated) chain-store game. In this example, the fact that the chain store has a time horizon much longer than the market-specific potential entrants allows the former to impose its preferred reputation to each of the latter. That is, at equilibrium, the potential entrants come to believe (rightly so) that the chain store would always fight entry, at least for the early part of the game. This, in the end, deters the entry of most of the potential entrants and allows the chain store to earn profits that are close to those it would obtain if, rather than being the second mover in every stage game, it were the "Stackelberg" leader.

Here, we explore whether the insights obtained in this example can be extended to general repeated games involving players with different time horizons. To render the analysis specially simple (see Remark 8.6 below), we focus on a clear-cut context akin to that of the chain-store game. In it, just one long-run player interacts bilaterally (according to a fixed stage game) with a collection of short-run players entering the process in sequence. However, in contrast to the chain-store game, we maintain the theoretical approach adopted throughout and postulate that the stage game may be suitably described in strategic form.[144]

Thus, consider a context in which the interaction in every period always takes place according to the same bilateral stage game in strategic form, specified through a function

$$W : A_1 \times A_2 \to \mathbb{R}^2.$$

In what follows, we adhere to the notational convention that player 1 is the long-run player while player 2 stands for the *changing* short-run player. The interaction spans for T periods, where T is assumed to be finite. The long-run player is involved in each and every one of the different periods. However, at every $t = 1, 2, \ldots, T$, there is a new short-run player (indexed by t) who plays in that (and only that) period. At each t, players are assumed fully informed of past history, i.e., they know all those action pairs (a_1^τ, a_2^τ) chosen in every $\tau < t$. Their intertemporal payoffs are identified with the average payoffs earned over the whole game (or, equivalently in the case of short-run players, with the single-stage payoffs). Modifying the notation proposed in Section 8.2, such a game is denoted by $\widehat{\mathcal{R}}^T(W)$.

The game $\widehat{\mathcal{R}}^T(W)$ defines the benchmark framework and describes the strategic interaction when the long-run player is of the "normal" type. Again, we perturb

---

[144] Thus, the analysis is not directly applicable to the chain-store setup where the stage game is sequential. However, the ideas can be readily extended to this case, as indicated in Exercise 8.16.

matters by allowing that, with a small probability, player 1 might be of some different "rare" type. Specifically, it is convenient to posit that her space of rare types consists of those who simply repeat a particular action from the stage game W throughout (say, because each of these types finds repeating that action a dominant strategy). Then, the overall situation is formulated as an incomplete-information game where player 1 is taken to be informed of her type, whereas each of the short-run players starts the game with some common and nondegenerate beliefs about the type of player 1.

More formally, let $\mathcal{J}_1$ be the space of possible rare types of player 1 that are alternative to the normal one. As explained, we associate $\mathcal{J}_1$ with the action space of player 1 in the stage game W. Thus, restricting to pure actions alone, we make $\mathcal{J}_1 = \{\theta(a_1) : a_1 \in A_1\}$, where $\theta(a_1)$ is interpreted as the type who finds it dominant to play a_1 throughout. Consequently, the full type space of player 1 is

$$\widetilde{\mathcal{J}}_1 = \mathcal{J}_1 \cup \{\theta_n\},$$

where θ_n stands for the normal type whose payoffs are as given by $\widehat{\mathcal{R}}^T(W)$. The *ex ante* probabilities used (by Nature) to select the fixed type of player 1 are given by a certain probability function $P_1(\cdot)$. Naturally, to make the problem interesting, we suppose that $0 < P_1(\theta_n) < 1$, i.e., there is some *ex ante* uncertainty about the type of player 1. In contrast, each of the T short-run players is *for sure* of a "normal" type. That is, their payoffs are always as given by $W_2(\cdot)$, the second of the components of the vectorial function $W(\cdot)$. The incomplete-information game thus defined is denoted by $\widehat{\mathcal{R}}^T(W, \widetilde{\mathcal{J}}_1, P_1)$.

If player 1 could commit to a fixed *pure* action (say, if the stage game were sequential and she could move first in it), the maximum payoff she can guarantee for herself in each period (assuming that the opponent in question reacts optimally) is given by

$$\bar{v}_1 = \max_{a_1 \in A_1} \min_{\alpha_2 \in \rho_2(a_1)} W_1(a_1, \alpha_2),$$

where

$$\rho_2 : A_1 \rightrightarrows \mathcal{A}_2$$

represents the *best-response correspondence* of the short-run players. That is, for each $a_1 \in A_1$, $\rho(a_1)$ embodies the set of (mixed) actions in $\mathcal{A}_2$, which are a best response to a_1. The payoff magnitude $\bar{v}_1$ is called the Stackelberg payoff of player 1, with $\bar{a}_1 \in A_1$ standing for any one of the actions of player 1 that guarantees this payoff when the short-run player responds optimally.

Clearly, the long-run player can hope to establish no better reputation than that of being a rare type fixed on playing action $\bar{a}_1$. Suppose the corresponding type $\theta(\bar{a}_1)$ has positive *a priori* probability, i.e., $P_1(\theta(\bar{a}_1)) > 0$. Then, in line with the insights developed in Section 8.4 for the chain-store game, the next result establishes that, at *any* sequential equilibrium of the induced game with Nature, the long-run player is able to approximate the Stackelberg payoff $\bar{v}_1$ if the time horizon is long enough. Thus, in this case, she is able to approximate the payoff associated with her best possible "reputation."

Theorem 8.12 (Fudenberg and Levine, 1992): *Suppose $P_1(\theta(\bar{a}_1)) > 0$. $\forall \varepsilon > 0$, $\exists T^*$ such that if $T > T^*$, the payoffs v_1' obtained by the normal type of player 1 in the game $\widehat{\mathcal{R}}^T(W, \widetilde{\mathcal{J}}_1, P_1)$ satisfy $v_1' \geq \bar{v}_1 - \varepsilon$ in any of the sequential equilibria.*

Proof: Let $(\tilde{\gamma}_1, \tilde{\gamma}_2)$ be the players' strategy profile in a sequential equilibrium of $\widehat{\mathcal{R}}^T(W, \widetilde{\mathcal{J}}_1, P_1)$, where $\tilde{\gamma}_2(\cdot) = [\tilde{\gamma}_{21}(\cdot), \tilde{\gamma}_{22}(\cdot), \ldots, \tilde{\gamma}_{2T}(\cdot)]$ stands for the collection of strategies played by each of the T short-run players. As induced by this equilibrium, one can determine, for each history h^{t-1}, the probability $\chi(a_1^t = \bar{a}_1 \mid h^{t-1})$ that player 1 adopts action $\bar{a}_1$ right after that history. First we argue, by relying on a simple continuity argument, that there must exist some $\tilde{\chi} < 1$ such that if

$$\chi\left(a_1^t = \bar{a}_1 \mid h^{t-1}\right) \geq \tilde{\chi}$$

then

$$\tilde{\gamma}_2\left(h^{t-1}\right) \in \rho_2\left(\bar{a}_1\right). \tag{8.23}$$

To verify it, suppose otherwise, which implies that there exists some $\tilde{a}_2 \notin \rho_2(\bar{a}_1)$ and a sequence, $\{\alpha_1^n\}_{n=1}^\infty$, of mixed actions of player 1 (or, equivalently, beliefs about her pure actions) such that

$$\forall n = 1, 2, \ldots, \ \forall a_1 \in A_1, \quad \alpha_1^n(a_1) > 0$$

$$\lim_{n \to \infty} \alpha_1^n(\bar{a}_1) = 1$$

$$\forall n = 1, 2, \ldots, \ \forall a_2 \in A_2, \ W_2(\alpha_1^n, \tilde{a}_2) \geq W_2(\alpha_1^n, a_2).$$

But, by the continuity of (the mixed extension of) $W_2(\cdot)$, it follows that

$$\lim_{n \to \infty} W_2(\alpha_1^n, \tilde{a}_2) = W_2(\bar{a}_1, \tilde{a}_2) \geq \lim_{n \to \infty} W_2(\alpha_1^n, a_2) = W_2(\bar{a}_1, a_2)$$

for all $a_2 \in A_2$, which contradicts the hypothesis that $\tilde{a}_2 \notin \rho_2(\bar{a}_1)$.

Now suppose the normal type of player 1, θ_n, were to mimic the constant strategy played by type $\theta(\bar{a}_1)$. It is next shown that, in this case, at least one of the following two statements is true for each $t = 1, 2, \ldots, T$:

(i) $\chi\left(a_1^t = \bar{a}_1 \mid h^{t-1}\right) \geq \tilde{\chi}$,

or

(ii) $P_1\left(\theta(\bar{a}_1) \mid h^{t-1}\right) \geq \frac{1}{\tilde{\chi}} P_1\left(\theta(\bar{a}_1) \mid h^{t-1}\right)$,

where $P_1(\cdot \mid h^{t-1})$ denotes the posterior probability over player 1's type after some given history h^{t-1}.

To establish this disjunction, consider any particular t where (i) does *not* hold. Then, applying Bayes rule, one has

$$P_1\left(\theta\left(\bar{a}_1\right) \mid h^{t-1}\right) = \frac{\chi\left(a_1^t = \bar{a}_1 \mid h^{t-1}, \theta\left(\bar{a}_1\right)\right) \; P_1\left(\theta\left(\bar{a}_1\right) \mid h^{t-1}\right)}{\chi\left(a_1^t = \bar{a}_1 \mid h^{t-1}\right)},$$

where, adapting previous notation, $\chi(a_1^t = \bar{a}_1 \mid h^{t-1}, \theta(\bar{a}_1))$ stands for the probability that player 1 adopts action $\bar{a}_1$ after history h^{t-1} if she is of type $\theta\left(\bar{a}_1\right)$. Naturally, $\chi(a_1^t = \bar{a}_1 \mid h^{t-1}, \theta(\bar{a}_1)) = 1$, which readily implies (ii).

Maintaining for the moment the hypothesis that the type θ_n of player 1 follows the same strategy as $\theta\left(\bar{a}_1\right)$, consider any arbitrary period t. If (i) holds at t, then (8.23) readily follows at that same t, as explained above. But if, alternatively, (i) does *not* hold at t (and therefore (ii) applies), the posterior probability prevailing on type $\theta\left(\bar{a}_1\right)$ grows at the rate $1/\tilde{\chi}$. Therefore, since its prior probability $P_1(\theta\left(\bar{a}_1\right)) > 0$, there is some maximum number of periods, s, such that

$$t' > t + s \Rightarrow P_1\left(\theta(\bar{a}_1) \mid h^{t'-1}\right) \geq \tilde{\chi}. \tag{8.24}$$

The previous considerations imply that, by mimicking the strategy followed by the type $\theta\left(\bar{a}_1\right)$, the normal type of player 1 (i.e., θ_n) may attain a stage payoff of $\bar{v}_1$ in at least $T - s$ periods. Thus, because one can choose s in (8.24) independently of T (i.e., it depends only on $P_1\left(\theta\left(\bar{a}_1\right)\right)$ and $\tilde{\chi}$), type θ_n may guarantee for herself an average payoff no lower than $\bar{v}_1 - \varepsilon$, for any $\varepsilon > 0$, if T is high enough. Obviously, no sequential equilibrium can provide her with a payoff lower than that, which is the desired conclusion. This completes the proof. ∎

Recall the game whose payoffs were given in Table 8.2. This game has two (asymmetric) pure-strategy Nash equilibria, (X, A) and (Y, B). Let this be the stage game played between a long-run player (of the normal type) and multiple short-run opponents, and suppose their interaction is perturbed by allowing for a small *ex ante* probability that the long-run player might be fixed on action X. Then, Theorem 8.12 indicates that, if the (finite) time horizon is long enough, player 1 can obtain an intertemporal payoff arbitrarily close to that obtained at the best of the two-stage Nash equilibria, i.e., the payoff of 5 obtained through (X, A).

This simple example shows that the long-run player may exploit any small doubts harbored by the short run player as to her own (player 1's) type to "select" her best Nash payoff available. But, in fact, in other cases she could proceed analogously and attain an advantageous payoff that does *not* correspond to any Nash equilibrium of the stage game. To illustrate this possibility, assume the stage game is as described by Table 8.4.

This game has a unique Nash equilibrium, (Y, B), which induces a payoff of 2 to both players. However, by the former considerations, it should be clear that the long-run player can approximate her larger Stackelberg payoff of 5, if the reputation

Table 8.4: *Stage game with the unique equilibrium payoff for player 1 lower than her Stackelberg payoff*

1 \ 2	A	B
X	5, 1	0, 0
Y	6, 0	2, 2

associated with her playing X forever has positive probability and the time horizon is long enough.

Remark 8.5: *Maintaining a reputation in an infinite-horizon setup*

It is easy to see that the conclusion of Theorem 8.12 may be strengthened (specifically, the payoff $\bar{v}_1$ becomes exactly attainable) if the time horizon is unbounded and the intertemporal payoffs of the long-run player are made equal to her limit average flow of stage payoffs. If one focuses instead on the infinitely repeated context with discounted payoffs, the corresponding conclusion would have to be formulated again in terms of an approximate lower bound (i.e., as in Theorem 8.12), the magnitude of this bound growing toward $\bar{v}_1$ as the discount rate is drawn closer to one. ◆

Remark 8.6: *Different time horizons*

To facilitate the discussion, the theoretical framework considered in this subsection has been quite extreme; i.e., it has involved a single player who displays a long time horizon and a collection of short-run players who have no future concerns whatsoever. In general, it would be desirable to study richer models that allow for less marked asymmetries among the interacting agents. Thus, for example, in the context of the chain-store game, it would seem interesting to admit the possibility that not only the chain store but also the potential entrants might have nontrivial time horizons. Then, all of them could attempt to consolidate profitable (and therefore conflicting) reputations along their interaction.

In those more general scenarios, it is intuitive that the success of each of the alternative players in "imposing" a certain reputation to her individual advantage should depend (among a variety of other factors) on (i) the relative length of their respective time horizons; and (ii) their relative impatience, e.g., their corresponding discount rates. For a detailed analysis of these issues, the reader is referred to the work of Schmidt (1993). ◆

Summary

In this chapter, we have proposed a general framework to analyze strategic situations in which the same set of players repeatedly interact under stable circumstances (i.e., a fixed-stage game). The discussion has been organized into two alternative, and qualitatively quite distinct, scenarios. In one of them, players do not envisage any prespecified end to their interaction – that is, *their* understanding (and, therefore, *our* model) of the situation is an *infinitely* repeated game. Instead, in the second scenario, their interaction is known by the players to last a certain finite (predetermined) number of rounds and, therefore, the appropriate model turns out to be that of a *finitely* repeated game.

Much of our concern in this chapter has revolved around the so-called folk theorems. These results – which are cast in a variety of different forms, reflect different time horizons, and rely on different equilibrium concepts – all share a similar objective. Namely, they aim at identifying conditions under which repeated interaction is capable of sustaining, at equilibrium, a large variety of different outcomes and intertemporal payoffs. More specifically, their main focus is on whether payoffs distinct from those attainable at Nash equilibria of the stage game (e.g., those that are Pareto-superior to them, but even those that are Pareto-inferior) can be supported at an equilibrium of the repeated game.

As it turns out, the answers one obtains are surprisingly wide in scope, at least if the repeated game is infinitely repeated and players are sufficiently patient (e.g., if they are concerned with limit average payoffs or their discount rate is high enough). Under those conditions, essentially all payoff vectors that are individually rational (i.e., dominate the minimax payoff for each player) can be supported by some Nash (or even subgame-perfect) equilibrium of the repeated game. However, matters are somewhat less sharp if the horizon of interaction is finite. In this case, to obtain similar "folk results," the *stage* game must display sufficient punishment leeway through alternative Nash equilibria. This rules out, for example, cases such as the finitely repeated prisoner's dilemma where, because the stage game has a unique Nash equilibrium, the unique subgame-perfect equilibrium involves repeated defection throughout.

This and other examples – such as the chain-store game – that display a sharp contrast between the conclusions prevailing under finite and infinite time horizons have led us to wonder about the possible lack of robustness of the referred conclusions. Indeed, we have found that the analysis undertaken in the *finite*-horizon framework may be rather fragile to small perturbations in at least two respects. First, they do not survive a slight relaxation of the notion of rationality that allows players to ignore deviations that are only marginally (ε-)profitable. Second, they are not robust to the introduction of a small degree of incomplete information that perturbs the players' originally degenerate beliefs about the types of others. In either case, one recovers the folk-type conclusions for long (but finite) repeated games.

Having allowed for the possibility that players may entertain some doubt about the opponents' types, it is natural to ask whether some players might try to exploit this uncertainty to shape for themselves a profitable reputation as the game unfolds. To analyze this issue, we have focused on a simple and stylized context where just one long-run player faces a long sequence of short-run players in turn. In this setup, the asymmetric position enjoyed by the former player (she is the only one who can enjoy the future returns of any "investment in reputation") yields a stark conclusion: along any sequential equilibrium, the long-run player can ensure for herself almost the Stackelberg payoff.

Exercises

Exercise 8.1: Consider a prisoner's dilemma (Table 8.1) repeated *twice*. Represent it in extensive form, describing as well *all* the strategies of each player. Which of those define a Nash equilibrium? Which are rationalizable (cf. Section 2.7)?

Exercise 8.2: Consider a *finitely* repeated prisoner's dilemma with a time horizon, T, arbitrarily large. Prove or refute the following assertion: the unique Nash equilibrium of the game coincides with its (unique) subgame-perfect equilibrium.

Exercise 8.3: Now consider the *infinitely* repeated prisoner's dilemma where future stage payoffs are discounted at some common rate δ. Particularize to this case the strategies used in the proof of Theorem 8.1 so as to sustain the constant play of (C, C) as a Nash equilibrium of the repeated game. Answer then the following questions:

  (a) What is the minimum discount rate $\bar{\delta}$ that is consistent with those strategies defining a Nash equilibrium?
  (b) Let $\delta \geq \bar{\delta}$, where $\bar{\delta}$ is the value found in (a). Do the strategies considered define as well a subgame-perfect equilibrium? Explain your answer.

Exercise 8.4: Let $\hat{v}_i$ denote the minimax payoff of player i in a certain stage game W (cf. (8.5)). Show that, given any δ, every Nash equilibrium of the infinitely repeated game $\mathcal{R}^\delta (W)$ must provide player i with a payoff no smaller than $\hat{v}_i$.

Exercise 8.5: Given any particular stage game W, show that every strategy profile of the repeated games $\mathcal{R}^\delta (W)$, $\mathcal{R}^\infty (W)$, and $\mathcal{R}^T (W)$ that induce for each t a particular Nash equilibrium of W (not necessarily the same one, but independently of history) defines a subgame-perfect equilibrium of the corresponding repeated game.

Exercise 8.6: Consider a context with n (≥ 3) firms involved in an oligopolistic market for a homogeneous product, the production cost being constantly equal to zero for all of them. The (inverse) demand function is linear, as given by

$$P(\Sigma_{i=1}^n x_i) = \max[0, a - b\Sigma_{i=1}^n x_i], \quad a > 0, \ b > 0,$$

where x_i is the production (and sales) of firm $i = 1, 2, \ldots, n$. Further suppose that

  (i) firms compete à la Cournot over time, i.e., choose their outputs simultaneously every period $t = 1, 2, \ldots$;
  (ii) each firm, when making its choice at any particular t, knows only (besides its own past choices) the prices materialized in past periods $\tau < t$;
  (iii) the firms are "infinitely patient," i.e., their intertemporal payoffs coincide with their limit average profits along the whole process.

Answer the following questions:

(a) What is the range of average profits sustainable at a subgame-perfect equilibrium?
(b) Compare your answer in (a) with the conclusion of Theorem 8.7.
(c) How are matters affected if the time horizon is finite?

Exercise 8.7: Provide a rigorous proof of Theorem 8.8.

Exercise 8.8: Let the stage game W be the battle of the sexes, whose payoffs are described in Table 1.2.

(a) Determine the set of intertemporal payoffs that can be supported in a Nash equilibrium of $\mathcal{R}^{\infty}(W)$. Are these payoffs affected if one restricts to subgame-perfect equilibria?
(b) Compute the maximum *symmetric* payoff that can be obtained at a subgame-perfect equilibrium of $\mathcal{R}^{0.95}(W)$ (i.e., the discount rate $\delta = 0.95$), when play off-equilibrium path consists exclusively of Nash equilibria of the stage game. Is the equilibrium efficient? Describe explicitly the equilibrium strategies.
(c) Reconsider (b) above for the repeated game $\mathcal{R}^{0.1}(W)$.

Exercise 8.9*: Let the stage game be again the battle of the sexes, as in Exercise 8.8.

(a) Compute the maximum symmetric payoff that may be sustained in a subgame-perfect equilibrium of $\mathcal{R}^{T}(W)$ for $T = 2$. Can one support an even larger payoff if $T = 100$? Describe the equilibrium strategies in each case.
(b) Answer the questions posed in (a), but now with respect to the *minimum symmetric* payoff.

Exercise 8.10: Let the stage game be the one described in Table 8.2. Referred to this game, answer the same questions as in (a), (b), and (c) of Exercise 8.8.

Exercise 8.11*: Let the stage game be again the one described in Table 8.2. Referred to this game, answer the same questions as in (a) and (b) of Exercise 8.9.

Exercise 8.12: Prove that, given any stage game W, $\exists \hat{\delta}$ such that if $\delta \leq \hat{\delta}$ and γ is a Nash equilibrium of $\mathcal{R}^{\delta}(W)$, then for every history h^{t-1} that has positive *ex ante* probability (according to γ), $\gamma(h^{t-1}) = \alpha^*$ for some Nash equilibrium α^* of W (possibly dependent on h^{t-1}). Is this conclusion also true if h^{t-1} has zero *ex ante* probability?

Exercise 8.13: Consider the chain-store game with an infinite horizon, as described in Section 8.4. Compute the minimum discount rate $\bar{\delta}$ that is consistent with the fact that the (constant) strategies described in (8.10) and (8.11) define a Nash equilibrium of the repeated game. Is the lower bound $\bar{\delta}$ affected if those strategies are required to define a subgame-perfect equilibrium?

Exercise 8.14*: Recall the so-called chain-store paradox discussed in Section 8.4. Explain whether the ε-rationality approach (as embodied by Definitions 8.1 and 8.2) may bring a "solution" to this paradox.

Exercise 8.15*: Consider the stage game W given by the following payoff table:

2＼1	D	C
D	1, 1	$b, 0$
C	0, b	a, a

Suppose $b > a > 1$, so that the game is of the same kind as the prisoner's dilemma given in Table 8.1. Now consider the game of incomplete information $\mathcal{R}^T(W, (\psi_i)_{i=1,2}, \eta)$ where, for some given T and ε, the "alternative reputation" for each $i = 1, 2$ is associated with payoffs ψ_i that display the following features:

- If, at any given period, the opponent has *not* played D before, it is a dominant strategy to play C then.
- If, at any given period, the opponent has played D sometime in the past, the stage payoffs are given by the above payoff table.

(a) Let $\eta = 0.1$ and $T = 2$. Determine some parameter configuration for a and b such that there exists a sequential equilibrium where the normal type of either player is indifferent between playing C or D in the first period of the game.

(b) Fix the values of a and b determined in (a) and suppose $\eta = 0.01$. Determine *some* value of T for which the normal type of either player decides to play C in the *first* period at some sequential equilibrium.

Exercise 8.16*: Consider the chain-store game with a finite number of potential entrants and the stage game (in extensive form) represented in Figure 8.1. This game reflects the strategic situation prevailing in each stage with prior probability $1 - \eta$, where $\eta \in (0, 1/2)$. On the other hand, with the complementary probability η, the payoffs in the stage game are not as described by Figure 8.1 but instead are as described by Figure 8.2. The chain store is informed by Nature which of these two stage games applies throughout but not so the potential entrants. In this context, discuss the validity of the following statement:

> Given η, arbitrarily low, if the number of potential entrants is large enough, the chain store will find it optimal to fight any possible entry for most of the game.

Hint: Refer to the proof of Theorem 8.12, with special focus on the behavior that will take place in the later periods of the game. (Note, however, that a direct application of that result is not possible here, because the "intended actions" of the chain store need not be observed in the stage game.)

CHAPTER 9

Repeated interaction: applications

9.1 Oligopoly (IV): intertemporal collusion in a Cournot scenario

9.1.1 *Perfect observation*

Consider a context as described in Section 3.1.1, with a finite set of n oligopolists competing in a market where the good is homogenous. Let the demand side of the market be modeled by an aggregate demand function

$$F : \mathbb{R}_+ \to \mathbb{R}_+ \tag{9.1}$$

that specifies, for each price $p \in \mathbb{R}_+$, the induced total demand $F(p)$. The inverse of this function (assumed well-defined) is denoted by $P(\cdot)$.

Each firm $i \in \{1, 2, \ldots, n\}$ is taken to display a cost function

$$C_i : \mathbb{R}_+ \to \mathbb{R}_+$$

where $C_i(q_i)$ stands for the cost of producing output q_i. Correspondingly, profit functions are defined as follows:

$$\pi_i(q_1, \ldots, q_n) \equiv P \left(\sum_{i=1}^{n} q_i \right) q_i - C_i(q_i) \qquad (i = 1, 2, \ldots, n).$$

For simplicity, we restrict ourselves to symmetric contexts where $C_i(\cdot) = C(\cdot)$ for every $i = 1, 2, \ldots, n$. Consequently, the profit profiles $(\pi_i(q_1, \ldots, q_n))_{i=1}^{n}$ are invariant to any permutation of firm indices.

If each firm's choice variable is identified with its respective output q_i and market interaction can be suitably modeled as a one-shot event (say, because the firms are not forward looking in time), the analysis of the strategic situation may rely on the notion of Cournot-Nash equilibrium – recall Subsection 3.1.1. For future reference, denote by x^c the output that is produced by each firm in the (assumed unique) symmetric Nash equilibrium and let π^c be its corresponding profits.[145] The output x^c is to be regarded as the production undertaken by the firms if their one-shot decision is adopted strategically, i.e., in a strictly *independent* fashion.

---

[145] Let us clarify a notational convention used throughout this chapter. We use the letter x (e.g., x^c here, or x^m later) to denote specific outputs (say, the Cournot-Nash equilibrium output or the collusive one) that we are interested in singling out as possible firm choices, i.e., as possible values for any particular q_i. To denote the output *vector* where every firm chooses homogeneously some such output x, we use the notation $\mathbf{x}$ (e.g., $\mathbf{x}^c$ or $\mathbf{x}^m$).

Instead, if firms could *coordinate* themselves to some alternative (say symmetric) configuration, they would aim at producing the output x^m that, when produced uniformly by all of them, maximizes joint profits. Assuming again that this output is unique, it is defined as follows:

$$x^m \equiv \arg\max_{x \geq 0} \sum_{i=1}^{n} \pi_i(x, \ldots, x). \tag{9.2}$$

For example, in the simple case where the (inverse) demand is linear, i.e.,

$$P(Q) = \max\{M - dQ, 0\}, \quad Q \equiv \sum_{i=1}^{n} q_i, \quad M > 0, \ d > 0, \tag{9.3}$$

and the (identical) cost function is linear as well

$$C(q_i) = cq_i, \ c > 0, \tag{9.4}$$

we have

$$x^c = \frac{M - c}{(n+1)d} \tag{9.5}$$

$$x^m = \frac{M - c}{2nd}. \tag{9.6}$$

Obviously, if $n > 1$, $x^c \neq x^m$ and thus firms *cannot credibly* agree (or commit) to producing the individual outputs x^m that symmetrically maximize their joint profits. To suppose they could do so would violate either individual incentives (profit maximization) or rational expectations (i.e., the maintained assumption that each firm can correctly anticipate the behavior of competitors).

Now suppose that the *same n* firms anticipate being present in the market over a certain time horizon T and their decisions over time can be made contingent on past events. Then, as we know from an immediate application of the arguments spelled in Section 8.3.2, if T is finite, the *unique* subgame-perfect equilibrium of the induced repeated game involves a constant repetition of the output profile $(x^c, \ldots, x^c)$ in every period. In this case, therefore, repeated interaction does *not* enrich, over the stage game, the (credible) strategic possibilities enjoyed by firms.

In contrast, assume the horizon of interaction is unbounded (i.e., $T = \infty$) and, say, firms are concerned with the flow of stage payoffs discounted at a certain common rate δ. Then, it readily follows from an adaptation of Theorem 8.4 that the firms may sustain the collusive profile $(x^m, \ldots, x^m)$ at a subgame-perfect equilibrium of the induced repeated game, provided the rate δ is close enough to one.[146] In particular, this objective can be achieved by simple so-called "trigger strategies" where the outputs q_i^t to be produced by each firm $i = 1, 2, \ldots, n$ at every t are determined

---

[146] Even though the stage game was assumed finite in Chapter 8, it should be clear that the nature of the argument is applicable to any simultaneous game displaying some Nash equilibrium.

as follows:

(a) At $t = 1$, $q_i^1 = x^m$.
(b) For $t = 2, 3, \ldots,$
   (b.1) $q_i^t = x^m$ if $\forall t' < t, \forall j = 1, 2, \ldots, n,$ $q_j^{t'} = x^m$;
   (b.2) $q_i^t = x^c$, otherwise.

These strategies aim to sustain collusive behavior over time through the simple threat of playing the Cournot-Nash profile $(x^c, \ldots, x^c)$ indefinitely once any firm deviates – a threat that is *credible* because it defines a subgame-perfect equilibrium of the corresponding subgame. As indicated, for (a) and (b) to define an equilibrium, the (assumed common) discount rate δ must be high enough. More precisely (see Exercise 9.1), it is enough that

$$\delta \geq \frac{\hat{\pi}^m - \pi^m}{\hat{\pi}^m - \pi^c}, \tag{9.7}$$

where we set

$$\pi^m \equiv \pi_i(x^m, \ldots, x^m), \tag{9.8}$$

$$\pi^c \equiv \pi_i(x^c, \ldots, x^c), \tag{9.9}$$

$$\hat{\pi}^m \equiv \max_{q_i \geq 0} \pi_i(q_i, (\mathbf{x}^m)_{-i}), \tag{9.10}$$

with $\mathbf{x}^m$ standing for the vector $(x^m, \ldots, x^m)$, and $(\mathbf{x}^m)_{-i}$ denoting the $(n-1)$-dimensional vector obtained from $\mathbf{x}^m$ by removing the ith component. Naturally, we must have

$$\hat{\pi}^m \geq \pi^m > \pi^c.$$

The strategies specified in (a) and (b) display two conceptual drawbacks:

- On the one hand, these strategies have the (threats of) "punishment" restricted to an indefinite repetition of the Cournot-Nash equilibrium of the stage game. In general, this significantly limits the range of outcomes that can be attained at equilibrium, because the reversion to Cournot-Nash payoffs embodies only a relatively mild deterrence power. A good illustration of this point is found in Subsection 9.2.1, where the payoff-supporting potential of the trigger strategies (a) and (b) is compared with that of the analogous trigger strategies in the Bertrand (price-setting) scenario. The fact that the Cournot-Nash equilibrium is substantially less drastic a punishment than the counterpart threat in the Bertrand setup has significant consequences. In particular, it implies that the range of (symmetric) outcomes that are supportable at subgame-perfect equilibria of the induced repeated game is substantially wider in the Bertrand scenario.
- On the other hand, one might also question whether the *off-equilibrium* behavior prescribed by strategies (a) and (b) is intuitively robust, despite the fact that it certainly satisfies the formal criterion of subgame perfection. Heuristically, the fact that these strategies prescribe *irreversible* (i.e., indefinite) punishment after *any* deviation renders them particularly fragile to

the possibility of *ex post* renegotiation (cf. Remark 8.3). That is, wouldn't firms attempt to reconsider matters if they were drawn (say, by a "mistake") into an indefinite punishment spell that forever ignores the large collusive potential? If they might do so, one may legitimately cast some doubts on the *ex ante* credibility of the (irreversible) trigger punishments contemplated in (a) and (b).

Our analysis of Chapter 8 suggests that the former two drawbacks (i.e., limited deterrence potential and indefinite punishment phases) may be remedied quite effectively, but at the cost of a substantial increase in the complexity of the strategies involved (cf. Theorems 8.6 and 8.7). However, Abreu (1986) has shown that one can also do it by resorting to natural "carrot-and-stick" strategies (recall Subsection 8.3.2). As we now explain, such a simple kind of strategy may be constructed to display *both* powerful deterrence and short punishment phases.

Let x° be a particular output level chosen so that the uniform profile $\mathbf{x}^\circ \equiv (x^\circ, x^\circ, \ldots, x^\circ)$ is sufficiently costly for all firms (see below for details). Associated with such an $\mathbf{x}^\circ$, consider the following carrot-and-stick strategies for each firm $i = 1, 2, \ldots, n$:

(α) For $t = 1$, $\quad q_i^1 = x^m$;
(β) $\forall t = 2, 3, \ldots,$
    (β.1) $q_i^t = x^m$ if $\forall j = 1, 2, \ldots, n$, $q_j^{t-1} = x^m$;
    (β.2) $q_i^t = x^m$ if $\forall j = 1, 2, \ldots, n$, $q_j^{t-1} = x^\circ$;
    (β.3) $q_i^t = x^\circ$, otherwise.

These strategies aim at sustaining the collusive behavior embodied by x^m through the threat of just *one* period of "intense" punishment (as captured by the profile $\mathbf{x}^\circ$). Once this single punishment period has been completed, the strategies revert to the original collusive behavior. The reason why *all* firms should abide by such one-period punishment (that could be very costly for every one of them) is that, given the above strategies (see (β.2)), it is the only route to return to a collusive path.

Let us verify that, under suitable conditions, the strategies (α) and (β) define a subgame-perfect equilibrium. Denote by π° the *stage* profit obtained by each firm if all produce x° and let

$$W^\circ \equiv (1 - \delta)\pi^\circ + \delta\pi^m = (1 - \delta)\pi^\circ + (1 - \delta) \sum_{t=2}^{\infty} \delta^{t-1}\pi^m, \qquad (9.11)$$

which stands for the *discounted*[147] flow of profits obtained by each firm from any given t onward when all of them currently produce x° and the continuation strategies are given by (α) and (β). Also define

$$\hat{\pi}^\circ \equiv \max_{q_i \geq 0} \pi_i(q_i, (\mathbf{x}^\circ)_{-i}), \qquad (9.12)$$

---

[147] Note that, as it was posited in Chapter 8 (cf. Subsection 8.2), the discounted payoffs are multiplied by $(1 - \delta)$ to have them lie in the same space as the stage payoffs.

i.e., the maximum *stage* profits that a firm can obtain by *deviating* unilaterally from the homogenous profile $\mathbf{x}^\circ$ (recall the notation explained in Footnote 145).

For strategies (α) and (β) to define a subgame-perfect equilibrium, the following conditions must hold:

(E1) The discounted profits that any firm may earn by deviating from x^m (under the assumption that all of them will then follow those strategies) cannot exceed the collusive profits. That is,

$$\pi^m \geq (1 - \delta)\hat{\pi}^m + \delta W^\circ$$

or equivalently, using (9.11)

$$(1 + \delta)\pi^m \geq \hat{\pi}^m + \delta \pi^\circ. \tag{9.13}$$

(E2) If the game enters a punishment phase – i.e. $(\beta.3)$ applies and therefore x° is uniformly being produced – all firms must be willing to undertake the contemplated punishment rather than deviate and postpone it to the following period. That is,

$$W^\circ \geq (1 - \delta)\hat{\pi}^\circ + \delta W^\circ,$$

or simply

$$W^\circ \geq \hat{\pi}^\circ. \tag{9.14}$$

Under customary assumptions about the environment (and provided the discount rate is close enough to one), a suitable choice of x° allows firms to support full collusion by means of the carrot-and-stick strategies (α) and (β). The key requirement here is that the profile $\mathbf{x}^\circ$ should impose on firms a sufficiently sharp cost. In particular, the output level x° must be chosen sufficiently higher than x^c, the output prevailing in the Nash equilibrium of the stage game.

By way of illustration, consider the linear context given by (9.3) and (9.4). Denote $\hat{Q} \equiv M/d$, i.e., $\hat{Q}$ is the least aggregate output that fetches a zero price. Then, x° may be fixed as follows:

$$x^\circ = \max\left\{\frac{\hat{Q}}{n - 1}, \frac{2\hat{\pi}^m}{c}\right\}, \tag{9.15}$$

where c is the constant marginal (and average) production cost and $\hat{\pi}^m$ is the particularization of (9.10) to the present context. Given that $x^\circ \geq \hat{Q}/n - 1$, we have

$$\hat{\pi}^\circ = 0 \tag{9.16}$$
$$\pi^\circ = -cx^\circ. \tag{9.17}$$

Thus, provided $\delta \geq 1/2$,

$$\hat{\pi}^m + \delta \pi^\circ \leq 0$$

since $x^\circ \geq 2\hat{\pi}^m/c$. This ensures the fulfillment of (9.13), the first of the above equilibrium conditions. On the other hand, (9.16) implies that (9.14) – the second equilibrium condition – may be rewritten as follows:

$$(1 - \delta)\pi^\circ + \delta\pi^m \geq 0$$

which, in view of (9.17), is satisfied as long as

$$\delta \geq \frac{cx^\circ}{cx^\circ + \pi^m}.$$

Therefore, if the discount rate is such that

$$1 > \delta \geq \max\left\{\frac{cx^\circ}{cx^\circ + \pi^m}, \frac{1}{2}\right\},$$

the strategies given by (α) and (β) – where x° is as specified in (9.15) – define a subgame-perfect equilibrium for the linear environment under consideration. As intended, this equilibrium induces a path of indefinite collusion along which every oligopolist produces x^m (and earns π^m) at every stage t.

9.1.2 *Imperfect observation**

The strategies specified in (a)–(b) or (α)–(β) in Subsection 9.1.1 are based on the implicit assumption that every firm is able to observe perfectly the outputs formerly produced by its competitors. In contrast, it seems interesting (and arguably more realistic as well) to study an alternative scenario in which each firm is unable to observe the individualized outputs of others and, say, can ascertain only the overall market conditions.

Suppose, specifically, that firms can only observe prevailing market-clearing prices. Then, if the (fixed) demand function is decreasing, it is clear that *unilateral* deviations from any prespecified output profile can always be detected. That is, after any such a deviation, all firms become aware of its existence, even if they are not able to determine which of the firms caused it. It is easy to check that the mere availability of this anonymous evidence provides a sufficient basis for the onset of coordinated (and credible) punishment phases (cf. Exercise 8.6). Consequently, the gist of the analysis undertaken above (in particular, the equilibrium sustainability of collusion) applies essentially unchanged, just requiring some straightforward adaptations.

It follows, therefore, that for imperfect monitoring of individual firm choices to raise novel strategic considerations, one must have a less than rigid (e.g., noisy) link between price realizations and aggregate output. Indeed, the introduction of some such "noisy link" is the approach pursued by the important work of Green and Porter (1984). Their model is essentially as described in Subsection 9.1.1, with just one but crucial difference: the aggregate demand is stochastic. More precisely, they postulate that the prevailing price at any given t is a random variable $\tilde{p}^t$ determined as follows[148]:

$$\tilde{p}^t = \tilde{\theta}^t P(Q^t),$$

where Q^t is the aggregate production at t, $P(\cdot)$ is a decreasing real function, and $\{\tilde{\theta}^t\}_{t=1}^{\infty}$ is a sequence of random variables. Every particular $\tilde{\theta}^t$ is supposed to be distributed in an independent and identical fashion across periods, according to a distribution function $\Phi(\cdot)$ with corresponding well-defined density $\phi(\cdot)$ and expectation $\mathbf{E}(\tilde{\theta}^t) = 1$. Thus, given the output profile $q^t = (q_1^t, q_2^t, \ldots, q_n^t)$ prevailing at some given t, the *ex ante* (uncertain) profits earned by each firm $i = 1, 2, \ldots, n$ at t are given by

$$\tilde{\pi}_i^t(q_1^t, q_2^t, \ldots, q_n^t) \equiv \tilde{\theta}^t\, P\left(\sum_{i=1}^n q_i^t\right) q_i^t - C_i(q_i^t),$$

whereas the corresponding expected magnitudes are

$$\pi_i(q_1^t, q_2^t, \ldots, q_n^t) \equiv \mathbf{E}\left[\tilde{\theta}^t P\left(\sum_{i=1}^n q_i^t\right) q_i^t - C_i(q_i^t)\right]$$

$$= P\left(\sum_{i=1}^n q_i^t\right) q_i^t - C_i(q_i^t).$$

The firms are assumed risk neutral; i.e., they are concerned with expected payoffs. Their objective is to maximize the expected flow of discounted profits, with all firms assumed to display a common discount rate $\delta \in (0, 1)$. The core hypothesis of the model is that, at any t, each firm is informed *only* of the prices $\{p^\tau\}_{\tau=1}^{t-1}$ that materialized in previous periods. That is, *no* firm is assumed to have observed the (aggregate) output produced at any $\tau < t$ or, consequently, the corresponding realizations θ^τ.

Naturally, firms' strategies in this context must respect the aforementioned informational restrictions. Thus, abstracting from behavioral randomization, they are mappings of the form

$$s_i : \bigcup_{t \in \mathbb{N}} H^{t-1} \to \mathbb{R}_+,$$

which, at every t, determine for each firm i (simultaneously with all other firms $j \neq i$) its corresponding output

$$q_i^t = s_i(h^{t-1})$$

as a function of the preceding price history $h^{t-1} \equiv \{p^\tau\}_{\tau=1}^{t-1} \in H^{t-1}$. For simplicity, we restrict to *pure strategies* of this form, in what follows, the set of these strategies for each firm i denoted by S_i.

Adapting to the present context the customary requirements of subgame perfection, a strategy profile $s^* = (s_1^*, s_2^*, \ldots, s_n^*)$ is said to be an *equilibrium* if

---

[148] Throughout, we follow the general notational convention that tildes mark random variables and their absence indicates typical realizations of those random variables.

$\forall t = 1, 2, \ldots, \forall i = 1, 2, \ldots, n, \ \forall s_i \in S_i,$

$$\mathbf{E}\left[(1 - \delta) \sum_{\tau=t}^{\infty} \delta^{\tau-t} \, \tilde{\pi}_i^{\tau}(s^*(h^{\tau-1}))\right]$$

$$\geq \mathbf{E}\left[(1 - \delta) \sum_{\tau=t}^{\infty} \delta^{\tau-t} \, \tilde{\pi}_i^{\tau}(s_i(h^{\tau-1}), s_{-i}^*(h^{\tau-1}))\right],$$

where

$$s^*(h^{\tau-1}) \equiv (s_1^*(h^{\tau-1}), s_2^*(h^{\tau-1}), \ldots, s_n^*(h^{\tau-1})).$$

Thus, at every point in the game t and after every conceivable prior history h^{t-1}, the equilibrium strategies are required to define a Nash equilibrium of the induced subgame. The entailed equilibrium notion is akin to that of subgame-perfect equilibrium, even though the game has no proper subgames – note, in particular, that players are never fully informed whether the observation of a low price is due to a deviation or to a bad shock. This lack of information, however, has no direct[149] pay-off relevance on the continuation game and therefore still allows players to assess where any given strategy profile defines an ensuing equilibrium.

The issue to be addressed here is essentially the same as in Subsection 9.1.1: does repeated interaction allow firms to sustain collusive behavior? To address this question, the approach is constructive, i.e., it explicitly "constructs" a particular equilibrium with the desired performance. As it turns out, some especially simple and intuitive class of strategies prove suitable for the task. These strategies build on the contrasting notions of normal and regressive situations. In *normal situations*, the firms are taken to produce a certain (not necessarily symmetric) collusive profile $\hat{q} = (\hat{q}_1, \hat{q}_2, \ldots, \hat{q}_n)$ that satisfies

$$\pi_i(\hat{q}_1, \hat{q}_2, \ldots, \hat{q}_n) \geq \pi^c \equiv \pi_i(x^c, x^c, \ldots, x^c) \qquad (i = 1, 2, \ldots, n).$$

Instead, during *regressive situations*, firms are taken to revert to the (assumed unique) Nash equilibrium $\mathbf{x}^c = (x^c, x^c, \ldots, x^c)$.

With all firms moving in synchrony, the transition from normal to regressive situations is postulated to occur when they observe (all of them) that the prevailing price is below some predetermined $\bar{p}$. On the other hand, once firms enter a regressive phase, they *all* are taken to conceive it as lasting for some *fixed* and *finite* number of periods, T. That is, once a string of T regressive periods has been completed, *all* players turn (again, in a synchronized manner) to regard the ensuing situation as normal.

---

[149] Of course, it may typically have an *indirect* influence on payoffs through the responses to observed prices induced by the firms' *strategies*.

Formally, the behavior and transitions outlined are embodied by strategies that, for each firm $i = 1, 2, \ldots, n$, may be described as follows:

  (i) At $t = 1$, the situation is *normal* and $q_i^1 = \hat{q}_i$;
 (ii) $\forall t = 2, 3, \ldots,$
   (ii.a) $[(t - 1)$ is a *normal* period, $p^{t-1} \geq \bar{p}] \Rightarrow [t$ is *normal*, and $q_i^t = \hat{q}_i]$;
   (ii.b) $[(t - T - 1)$ is a *normal* period, $p^{t-T-1} < \bar{p}] \Rightarrow [t$ is *normal*, and $q_i^t = \hat{q}_i]$;
   (ii.c) otherwise, t is a regressive period and $q_i^t = x^c$.

Given the strategies specified in (i) and (ii), the decision setup faced by each firm may be formulated as a (stationary) Markovian decision problem with just two states: the *normal state* ω^a and the *regressive state* ω^b, each of them reflecting when the system is in a normal or regressive phase, respectively.[150] Note that, in a regressive phase (whose duration does *not* depend on what happens along it), an optimal strategy must involve producing x^c, where recall that $(x^c, x^c, \ldots, x^c)$ is the stage Nash equilibrium. This implies that, given a certain collusive profile $\hat{q} = (\hat{q}_1, \hat{q}_2, \ldots, \hat{q}_n)$, the crucial test required to confirm that the strategies given by (i) and (ii) indeed define an equilibrium concerns normal periods alone. For any one of these periods, it is enough to verify that producing $\hat{q}_i$ represents an optimal decision for every $i = 1, 2, \ldots, n$ when the other firms are playing accordingly.

Given the output vector $\hat{q}_{-i}$ embodying the choice of all firms $j \neq i$ in normal periods, define by $V_i^a(q_i, \hat{q}_{-i})$ the expected discounted payoff associated to any particular output q_i that could be chosen by firm i. Analogously, denote by $V_i^b(q_i, \hat{q}_{-i})$ the discounted payoff anticipated by firm i at the beginning of any recessive phase when in subsequent normal periods the output profile $(q_i, \hat{q}_{-i})$ is to be played. (As explained, in regressive periods, we may assume that firms always choose their Cournot-Nash outputs.) Both of these intertemporal payoff values can be obtained by solving the following system of simultaneous equations[151]:

$$V_i^a(q_i, \hat{q}_{-i}) = (1 - \delta)\, \pi_i(q_i, \hat{q}_{-i}) \tag{9.18}$$

$$+ \delta \left\{ \begin{array}{l} \Pr\left[\bar{p} \leq \tilde{\theta}\, P\big(q_i + \sum_{j \neq i} \hat{q}_j\big)\right] V_i^a(q_i, \hat{q}_{-i}) \\ + \Pr\left[\bar{p} > \tilde{\theta}\, P\big(q_i + \sum_{j \neq i} \hat{q}_j\big)\right] V_i^b(q_i, \hat{q}_{-i}) \end{array} \right\}$$

$$V_i^b(q_i, \hat{q}_{-i}) = (1 - \delta) \sum_{t=1}^{T} \delta^{t-1} \pi^c + \delta^T\, V_i^a(q_i, \hat{q}_{-i})$$

$$= (1 - \delta^T)\, \pi^c + \delta^T\, V_i^a(q_i, \hat{q}_{-i}), \tag{9.19}$$

---

[150] Rigorously speaking, one should define T separate regressive states in order to keep track of the number of periods left in a regressive phase, once the process enters in it. However, given that behavior in this phase is fixed at a Nash equilibrium, its overall performance can be associated with the single state that marks its commencement – see (9.19) for the formal details.

[151] To simplify notation, we dispense with the time superindex for the random variables since their distribution has been assumed identical (and independent) across periods.

where it is implicitly supposed that

- in regressive periods, *all* firms (including i) choose the Cournot output, and
- in normal periods, the firms $j \neq i$ choose their respective $\hat{q}_j$.

Using the fact that

$$\Pr\left[\bar{p} > \tilde{\theta}\, P\left(q_i + \sum_{j \neq i} \hat{q}_j\right)\right] = \Phi\left(\frac{\bar{p}}{P\left(q_i + \sum_{j \neq i} \hat{q}_j\right)}\right),$$

one solves for $V_i^a(q_i, \hat{q}_{-i})$ in the system (9.18) and (9.19) to obtain

$$V_i^a(q_i, \hat{q}_{-i})$$

$$= (1 - \delta)\frac{\pi_i(q_i, \hat{q}_{-i}) + \Phi\left(\bar{p}/P\left(q_i + \sum_{j \neq i} \hat{q}_j\right)\right)\left((\delta - \delta^{T+1})/(1 - \delta)\right)\pi^c}{1 - \delta + (\delta - \delta^{T+1})\,\Phi\left(\bar{p}/P\left(q_i + \sum_{j \neq i} \hat{q}_j\right)\right)}$$

$$= \frac{(1 - \delta)}{1 - \delta + (\delta - \delta^{T+1})\,\Phi\left(\bar{p}/P\left(q_i + \sum_{j \neq i} \hat{q}_j\right)\right)}\,[\pi_i(q_i, \hat{q}_{-i}) - \pi^c] + \pi^c.$$

The above expression is quite intuitive. It indicates that, at any given period, the ensuing discounted payoff expected by firm i if the output profile $(q_i, \hat{q}_{-i})$ is currently played does *not* improve over (a constant play of) the stage Cournot-Nash equilibrium in the *full* difference $\pi_i(q_i, \hat{q}_{-i}) - \pi^c$. Rather, this payoff magnitude is scaled down (given the discount rate δ) by the occasional but unavoidable interferences of regression phases of duration T.

With the previous constructs in hand, an intertemporal equilibrium of the sort considered may be characterized by an output profile $q^* = (q_1^*, \ldots, q_n^*)$ such that

$$V_i^a(q^*) \geq V_i^a(q_i, q_{-i}^*), \quad \forall q_i \geq 0 \qquad (i = 1, 2, \ldots, n). \tag{9.20}$$

Thus, assuming that the value functions involved are differentiable, we are led to the following necessary conditions for an interior equilibrium:

$$\frac{\partial V_i^a}{\partial q_i}(q^*) = 0 \qquad (i = 1, 2, \ldots, n),$$

or, equivalently,

$$\left[1 - \delta + (\delta - \delta^{T+1})\,\Phi\left(\frac{\bar{p}}{P\left(\sum_{j=1}^n q_j^*\right)}\right)\right]\frac{\partial \pi_i}{\partial q_i}(q^*) + (\delta - \delta^{T+1})$$

$$\times \phi\left(\frac{\bar{p}}{P\left(\sum_{j=1}^n q_j^*\right)}\right)\frac{\bar{p}\, P'\left(\sum_{j=1}^n q_j^*\right)}{\left(P\left(\sum_{j=1}^n q_j^*\right)\right)^2}\,(\pi_i(q^*) - \pi^c) = 0 \tag{9.21}$$

for each $i = 1, 2, \ldots, n$, where recall that ϕ denotes the density of Φ (and therefore $\phi = \Phi'$).

The expression (9.21) includes two terms, both evaluated at the collusive config-uration and capturing considerations of an opposing kind. On the one hand, the first term (whose sign is positive) simply reflects the fact that any oligopolist would like to increase its output unilaterally if only it could avoid a reaction of its opponents to-ward a regressive phase – such a "fortunate" event occurs only if the random variable displays a high realization that *masks the deviation*. On the other hand, the second term (whose sign is negative) captures the expected penalty attributed by any firm i to an output increase: it raises the probability of triggering a recessive phase, during which the expected payoff loss $(\pi_i(q^*) - \pi^c)$ is incurred relative to the collusive profile. In equilibrium, of course, both effects must exactly offset each other.

In general, the possibility of sustaining a collusive configuration must obviously depend on the underlying data of the environment (e.g., the discount rate, cost and demand conditions, form and magnitude of the noise, etc.). A detailed "comparative-statics" analysis concerning these matters has been conducted by Porter (1983) but only for the linear context given by (9.3) and (9.4). In this setup, he has computed the price threshold $\bar{p}$ and the time horizon T that characterize the best equilibrium for the oligopolists, i.e., the equilibrium (of the present dichotomous kind) that maximizes their expected discounted flow of profits. Interestingly, he finds that it is never optimal for the oligopolists to "squeeze" the collusive potential up to the point of aiming at the configuration $(x^m, \ldots, x^m)$ that maximizes aggregate profits – recall (9.6). For, if they did, the recessive phases required at equilibrium would be too costly (i.e., too long and/or frequent). At equilibrium, this leads to an optimal compromise where the profits earned at normal times are suitably restrained.[152]

Let us end our discussion of the model by contrasting its implications with the approach pursued in Subsection 9.1.1 under the assumption of perfect observability. The main point to stress here is somewhat paradoxical: even though the equilibrium paths in the present case do exhibit recurrent punishments (i.e., reversion to the stage Nash equilibrium), *none* of the firms ever deviates from its equilibrium strategy. Moreover, all firms must be completely sure (if rationality and the equilibrium being played are both common knowledge) that, whenever the price falls below the contemplated threshold, no firm has *in fact* deviated from equilibrium. However, a punishment spell must in that case ensue, as the involuntary but unavoidable cost to be paid by the firms if collusion is to be *credibly* supported under imperfect observability. This contrasts sharply with the role of the punishment phases under perfect observability, where (at equilibrium) those phases are never entered and thus remain in the limbo of never-exercised threats.

9.2   Oligopoly (V): intertemporal collusion in a Bertrand scenario

9.2.1   *Perfect observation*

Consider now the alternative oligopoly context in which the firms' strategic vari-ables are prices and individual firms $i \in \{1, 2, \ldots, n\}$ set their respective price p_i

---

[152] A formal exploration of these heuristic ideas is undertaken in Subsection 9.2.2 for the case of Bertrand competition.

simultaneously. Let us maintain the assumption that the good produced by every firm is homogenous, its *aggregate* market demand given by a certain function $F(\cdot)$ as in (9.1), strictly decreasing. For simplicity, postulate as well that all firms display an identical cost function of a linear form as given by (9.4), the constant average (and marginal) cost being equal to $c > 0$.

As explained in Section 3.1.2, when the strategic interaction is modeled as a one-shot phenomenon, the Bertrand-Nash equilibria of the price-setting game all have the prevailing (i.e., minimum) price equal to c. And if we restrict to *symmetric* equilibria, the unique one involves every firm setting the same price $p_i = c$ and thus obtaining an equal share of the aggregate induced demand $F(c)$.[153] In every one of these equilibria, symmetric or not, each firm obtains zero profits.

In contrast, it is easy to see that, just as for the Cournot (quantity-setting) oligopoly, price-setting firms can significantly enhance their profit possibilities by repeated interaction.[154] Thus, let p^m be the price that maximizes the aggregate profits of firms, i.e.,

$$p^m = \arg \max_{p \geq 0} (p - c) F(p). \tag{9.22}$$

Naturally, since there is a one-to-one correspondence between prices and the aggregate quantities induced by the (strictly decreasing) demand function $F(\cdot)$, it follows that

$$F(p^m) = n \cdot x^m, \tag{9.23}$$

where x^m is as defined in (9.2). If the firms wish to attain the maximally collusive configuration $(p^m, p^m, \ldots, p^m)$, again simple "trigger strategies" can sustain it at a subgame-perfect equilibrium of the infinitely repeated game if future profits are discounted at a rate close enough to one. Specifically, one may simply consider:

(a′) For $t = 1$, $p_i^1 = p^m$.
(b′) $\forall t = 2, 3, \ldots,$
    (b′.1) $p_i^t = p^m$ if $\forall t' < t, \forall j = 1, 2, \ldots, n,\ p_j^{t'} = p^m$;
    (b′.2) $p_i^t = c$, otherwise.

The above strategies reflect ideas analogous to those underlying (a) and (b) in Subsection 9.1.1 for the case of repeated Cournot interaction. They display, however, two interesting differences as well.

First, we observe that, by an obvious adaptation of the trigger strategies displayed in (a′) and (b′), firms may support not only collusive profits but any that lie between their perfectly collusive and perfectly competitive levels. To achieve any of these outcomes, it is enough to have a suitably chosen price $p \in [c, p^m]$ substitute p^m in (a′) and (b′), again assuming the discount rate δ is sufficiently high. In contrast, the range of *symmetric* subgame-perfect equilibrium payoffs sustainable in the

---

[153] Here, we implicitly assume that the market-sharing rule to be applied in case of equal prices is symmetric across firms.

[154] As we know, this is true only if the repeated interaction extends over an unbounded horizon. If not, Theorem 8.8 implies that the unique subgame-perfect equilibrium of the finitely repeated game involves playing the (unique) Nash equilibrium at every stage.

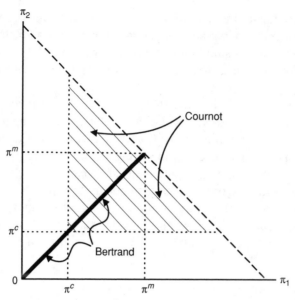

Figure 9.1: Range of discounted payoffs available through equilibrium trigger strategies in a duopoly with competition à la Cournot or Bertrand (linear costs and discount rate arbitrarily close to one). The payoffs π^m and π^c stand for the symmetric payoffs obtained by each firm under maximum collusion and the stage Cournot-Nash equilibrium, respectively.

Cournot setup by means of equilibrium *trigger* strategies is significantly narrower. Only the profits lying between the maximally collusive ones and those obtained at the Cournot-Nash equilibrium of the stage game are candidate payoffs for the repeated game under those strategies.[155]

Finally, another respect in which general trigger strategies display different implications under Cournot and Bertrand competition pertains to the possibility of sustaining *asymmetric* configurations. When firms are price setters, strategies of the form (a′) and (b′) must necessarily entail equilibrium outcomes that are fully symmetric. Instead, when firms are quantity setters, general trigger strategies of the type illustrated by (a) and (b) allow for substantially more flexibility. The fact that, in the latter case, output choices can be independently set across firms allows for quite heterogenous profiles (and therefore payoffs) to be achievable through different trigger-strategy equilibria of the repeated game. To fix ideas, a comparison of the payoff-supporting possibilities available within the Cournot and Bertrand setups are contrasted in Figure 9.1 for a simple duopoly case with linear costs.

9.2.2   *Imperfect observation**

Following up on our parallel treatment of the Cournot and Bertrand scenarios, we now explore the implications of the hypothesis of imperfect observability in

---

[155] Note, however, that such a limitation of the Cournot setup no longer applies if the set of admissible strategies is extended beyond those of the trigger kind (cf. Theorem 8.4).

the latter case. The theoretical approach will be, however, substantially simpler than the one studied in Subsection 9.1.2 for the Cournot setup. This allows us to provide a more detailed analysis of some of the issues (in particular, the optimal duration of punishment phases) that were only informally sketched for the Cournot setup.

To model imperfect observability, we continue to suppose that, at every $t = 1, 2, \ldots$, there is a corresponding random variable, $\tilde{\theta}^t$ that impinges multiplicatively on the demand prevailing in that period. Now, however, these random variables can adopt just one of two values, 0 or 1, and are distributed identically and independently with

$$\Pr\{\tilde{\theta}^t = 0\} = 1 - \Pr\{\tilde{\theta}^t = 1\} = \rho \in (0, 1).$$

At every t, the total demand for the homogenous good prevailing at t is a random variable, $\tilde{Q}^t$, given by

$$\tilde{Q}^t = \tilde{\theta}^t F \left(\min \left[p_1^t, p_2^t, \ldots, p_n^t \right] \right),$$

where each p_i^t is the price set by firm i, $F(\cdot)$ is a decreasing real function of the type introduced in (9.1), and $\{\tilde{\theta}^t\}_{t=1}^{\infty}$ is a sequence of independent random variables as defined above. Thus, with independent probability ρ, the demand confronted by firms at every t displays the usual characteristics and trade-offs. On the other hand, with the complementary probability $1 - \rho$, the market demand vanishes completely at *every* price, leaving no room for any positive revenue.

Firms are taken to set their prices simultaneously every period; i.e., they are involved in traditional Bertrand competition. Furthermore, in analogy with our former approach to Cournot competition under imperfect observability (Subsection 9.1.2), we posit that, at every t, every individual firm i observes only the demand q_i^t this firm has fetched for itself but *not* the prices p_j^t set by the other firms $j \neq i$. Thus, in particular, if a specific firm musters no demand at some t, this firm is unable to discern whether this has happened because other firms charged a lower price[156] or because $\theta^t = 0$ – i.e., it cannot discriminate "price undercutting" from simply "adverse market conditions."

For concreteness, let us focus on the symmetric outcome associated with the price vector $(p^m, p^m, \ldots, p^m)$ – recall (9.22) – and suppose the firms aim at sustaining it at equilibrium. Furthermore, let us assume that they again rely on the dichotomy of *normal* versus *regressive* situations to guide their behavior. Then, the strategies considered must specify

    (a) some criterion to switch from normal to regressive situations;
    (b) a predetermined duration T for the regressive phases;
    (c) the choices prescribed for normal and regressive situations.

---

[156] Recall that the good is homogenous, so the whole demand flows toward the firms setting the lowest price. This implicitly assumes that the market is transparent for consumers (recall Subsection 3.1.2), an assumption that is somewhat at odds with the opposite one currently made in this respect concerning the firms.

All three former items are addressed in the following description of the firms' strategies:

(i') At $t = 1$, the situation is labelled *normal* and $p_i^1 = p^m$;

(ii') $\forall t = 2, 3, \ldots,$

    (ii'.a) $[(t - 1)$ is a normal period, $q_i^{t-1} \geq x^m] \Rightarrow [t$ is normal, and $p_i^t = p^m]$, where x^m is the collusive output defined in (9.23) – recall Footnote 153;

    (ii'.b) $[(t - T - 1)$ is a normal period, $q_i^{t-T-1} < x^m] \Rightarrow [t$ is normal and $p_i^t = p^m]$;

    (ii'.c) otherwise, t is a regressive period and $p_i^t = c$, where c is the (constant) marginal cost.

Associated with the strategies described in (i') and (ii'), we may define the expected discounted payoffs, V^a and V^b, corresponding to each of the two states of the process that mark normal and (the start of)[157] regressive situations. These payoffs must satisfy the following relationships[158]:

$$V^a = (1 - \rho)((1 - \delta)\pi^m + \delta V^a) + \rho \delta V^b \tag{9.24}$$

$$V^b = \delta^T V^a, \tag{9.25}$$

where π^m is given by (9.8). Hence solving (9.24) and (9.25) for V^a and V^b, one readily obtains

$$V^a = \frac{(1 - \delta)(1 - \rho)\pi^m}{1 - \delta(1 - \rho) - \delta^{T+1}\rho} \tag{9.26}$$

$$V^b = \frac{(1 - \delta)\delta^T(1 - \rho)\pi^m}{1 - \delta(1 - \rho) - \delta^{T+1}\rho}. \tag{9.27}$$

To have the strategies (i') and (ii') define an equilibrium, we require (just as in Subsection 9.1.2) that every firm should find it optimal to behave as prescribed in both normal and regressive periods. Concerning regressive periods, the fact that firms are taken to play the (unique) symmetric Nash equilibrium of the stage game makes it trivially optimal for each of them to behave as specified by the strategies. Turning then to normal periods, the required optimality is simply captured by the following condition:

$$V^a \geq (1 - \rho)((1 - \delta)(n \cdot \pi^m) + \delta V^b) + \rho \delta V^b. \tag{9.28}$$

This inequality embodies the requirement that the payoff of behaving as prescribed at normal periods (i.e., setting p^m) must be no lower than the payoff obtained by deviating slightly to a lower price, say $p^m - \varepsilon$ for some small $\varepsilon > 0$. To understand it note that, if a firm implements a unilateral deviation toward $p^m - \varepsilon$ at a

---

[157] cf. Footnote 150.

[158] Note that, in contrast with (9.18) and (9.19), no arguments are specified for V^a or V^b. The reason is that, unlike in that case, we are currently restricting attention to the (tentative) *equilibrium* price choices for *all* firms prescribed by strategies (i') and (ii'). Therefore, we may simply fix those choices to being p^m in normal situations and c in regressive ones.

normal period, two possibilities arise. First, with probability $(1 - \rho)$, there is positive market demand, which this firm captures *wholly* (i.e., a total of $F(p^m - \varepsilon)$) and thus obtains immediate stage profits arbitrarily close to the highest monopoly level $n \cdot \pi^m$. But then, in the next period, (i′) and (ii′) imply that the process should enter a T-long regressive phase, thus leading to an ensuing discounted payoff equal to V^b. On the other hand, with the complementary probability ρ, the demand vanishes at the very time of deviation. In this case, the deviating firm obtains no immediate gain, although the process still enters into a regressive phase next period. Comparing the expected payoff derived from the above considerations (which take place in case of a unilateral deviation) with the payoff obtained by setting p^m at normal periods (which has been defined to be V^a), one obtains the equilibrium condition (9.28).

We now argue that for an equilibrium to exist in the present context, the probability ρ with which adverse market conditions materialize cannot be too close to 1. To verify this intuitive claim,[159] use (9.24) to rewrite the equilibrium condition (9.28) as follows:

$$(n - 1)(1 - \delta)\pi^m \leq \delta(V^a - V^b). \tag{9.29}$$

Then rely on (9.26) and (9.27) to restate (9.29) as follows:

$$(n - 1)(1 - \delta)\pi^m \leq \frac{\delta(1 - \delta)(1 - \rho)(1 - \delta^T)\pi^m}{1 - \delta(1 - \rho) - \delta^{T+1}\rho}$$

or, equivalently,

$$\delta(1 - \rho)(1 - \delta^T) \geq (n - 1)(1 - \delta(1 - \rho) - \delta^{T+1}\rho),$$

which may be simply formulated as

$$\zeta(\rho, T) \equiv (n\rho - 1)\delta^{T+1} + n\delta(1 - \rho) - n + 1 \geq 0. \tag{9.30}$$

Thus, if we were to make $\rho = 1$, we would have $\zeta(1, T) < 0$ for all T (since $\delta < 1$), which simply amounts to the formal confirmation of an obvious fact: no collusion can be supported at equilibrium if only "bad" (in effect vanishing) market conditions may arise with positive probability. But then, by continuity, it follows that, given T, no such equilibrium can be supported either (i.e., condition (9.29) is violated) if ρ is sufficiently close to 1.

Finally, we turn to studying the effect of T, the duration of the regressive phase, on the profit performance at equilibrium. An immediate preliminary observation is that

$$\zeta(\rho, 0) < 0 \tag{9.31}$$

for all ρ, which is reflection of the fact that, with the present dichotomic strategies, an equilibrium requires the threat of regressive phases displaying a *positive* time span. Next, to study the implications of varying this time span, it is useful to focus

---

[159] Heuristically, no collusion can be expected to persist if the future gains to be derived from it (which could offset short-run opportunistic incentives) are very low.

on the first differences of the function $\zeta(\cdot)$ in its argument T, as given by

$$\zeta(\rho, T + 1) - \zeta(\rho, T) = (n\rho - 1)(\delta^{T+2} - \delta^{T+1})$$
$$= \delta^{T+1}(1 - n\rho)(1 - \delta).$$

Mere inspection of the above expression reveals that $\zeta(\rho, \cdot)$ grows in T only if $1 - n\rho > 0$, or

$$n < \frac{1}{\rho}. \tag{9.32}$$

Thus, in view of (9.31), the above inequality becomes a *necessary* condition for equilibrium existence, i.e., for (9.30) to hold for *some* $T > 0$. Intuitively, it captures the following simple idea: the larger is n (the number of firms in the market), the more difficult it is to furnish the incentives required to deter unilateral deviations. In fact, it is easy to see (cf. Exercise 9.8) that, provided δ is high enough, some equilibrium of the format (i′) and (ii′) always exists for some suitable chosen T if (9.32) holds.[160] This condition, therefore, happens to be both necessary and sufficient for equilibrium existence when the firms are sufficiently patient.

The following question now arises: What is the value of T, the length of regressive phases, on which the firms would prefer to settle? Naturally, such a value of T must be the one that, within the admissible range consistent with equilibrium, leads to the highest expected discounted profits for firms. According to (i′) and (ii′), market interaction is supposed to start with firms placed at a normal situation (i.e., in a collusive state). This implies that the expected payoff obtained by playing an equilibrium built on those strategies is simply the value V^a specified in (9.26) – that is, the intertemporal payoff perceived at normal times. It follows, therefore, that the optimal length of regressive phases is to be identified with the value of T that maximizes (9.26), subject to the incentive (equilibrium) constraint (9.30).

The optimization problem so posed is extremely simple because, as one can directly check, V^a is decreasing in T. Consequently, we conclude that the desired value of T is merely the minimum one that satisfies (9.30). Formally, it is defined by

$$T^* = \min\{T \in \mathbb{N} : (n\rho - 1)\delta^{T+1} + n\delta(1 - \rho) - n + 1 \geq 0\}. \tag{9.33}$$

Of course, the set considered in (9.33) could be empty – even if (9.32) holds – thus rendering T^* ill-defined. However, as explained, this problem can be ruled out if firms are sufficiently patient. In that case, the time length defined in (9.33) characterizes the equilibrium preferred by firms among all those in the class considered (see Exercise 9.9).

Under *perfect* observability on the actions of the competitors (e.g., in the scenarios considered in Subsections 9.1.1 and 9.2.1), one can construct quite distinct but essentially equivalent equilibria that lead to the *same path of play* – in other words,

---

[160] To be sure, note that this assertion does not conflict with the former observation that, given any arbitrary length T for the regressive phases, no equilibrium exists if ρ is close enough to 1. Here, the value of ρ (<1) is taken as given, while the value of T is chosen accordingly.

they differ only in how *counterfactual* (i.e., merely hypothetical) deviations are deterred. Instead, when the interaction unfolds under imperfect action observability, the issue of finding the *optimal* way of precluding deviations becomes a key one. For, just as it occurred in Subsection 9.1.2 for Cournotian competition, imperfect observability forces the punishment spells to turn from hypothetical considerations to occasional (but certain) realities. Therefore, different alternative ways of inducing the same intended play need no longer be payoff equivalent, even when no deviation from equilibrium behavior occurs. This is precisely the idea underlying the determination of T^* in (9.33).

9.3   Markets (V): efficiency wages and unemployment

Unquestionably, one of the leading concerns marking the economic literature over much of the last century has been labor unemployment. In particular, the key issue has been to understand what economic mechanisms might underlie the persistence of significant unemployment levels in a market system. In Section 3.4, we presented a very stylized version of one of the early attempts on the problem, the Keynesian approach, which was reformulated there in a strategic vein. Here, we provide a game-theoretic formalization of the alternative approach proposed by Shapiro and Stiglitz (1984), whose essential considerations are of an informational kind. Specifically, labor unemployment is viewed as a consequence of the informational asymmetries prevailing between firms and workers that, in turn, cause detrimental "strategic" distortions on the equilibrium wages.

The theoretical framework is especially simple. Two workers and just one firm meet in an idealized "labor market." At that juncture, there are just three possibilities: the firm can hire no worker, only one, or the two of them for a full working period (i.e., no partial employment of a worker is possible). If any particular worker is hired, her corresponding productivity depends on two factors: whether the worker exerts effort or not and the firm's scale of production (i.e., the number of workers hired by the firm).

Denote by y_k the *per capita* productivity of each worker when she exerts the required effort and the number of employed workers is $k = 1, 2$. It is supposed that $y_2 \leq y_1$, i.e., the production technology exhibits nonincreasing returns. In contrast, if the worker in question does not exert effort, her corresponding productivity is assumed *ex ante* random; more precisely, we postulate that it continues to be equal to y_k with a certain probability, $p \in (0, 1)$, but it is equal to zero with the complementary probability $1 - p$.[161]

Suppose a firm and two workers participate in this market over a repeated chain of T periods (T finite or infinite). Assuming that the same firm and workers are involved throughout, their interaction is modeled as a repeated game. In each period

---

[161] Thus if two workers are employed by the firm, the productivity of each particular worker is *not* affected by whether her co-worker exerts effort or displays positive productivity. That is, the productivity of a worker is assumed to be affected only by her own effort and the level of firm's employment.

$t = 1, 2, \ldots, T$, the fixed *stage game* being played consists of the following three sequential moves.

1. The firm offers a pair of wages (ω_1, ω_2), each ω_i intended for the respective worker $i = 1, 2$.
2. Having received these wage offers, the workers then simultaneously (and independently) decide whether each of them accepts working for the firm (W) or not (NW).
3. Once the workers have irreversibly decided whether to work for the firm (and, say, this becomes common knowledge),[162] every employed worker decides (also simultaneously, if the two are employed) whether to exert effort (E) or not (NE).

To complete the description of the situation, the payoffs earned for each possible play of the stage game must be specified. First, let us focus on the case in which the two workers accept the firm offer (ω_1, ω_2). Then, if both make the effort, the firm obtains with certainty a payoff (profit) equal to $2y_2 - \omega_1 - \omega_2$. Correspondingly, if the (monetary) cost of effort incurred by workers (assumed common to both) is denoted by c, the payoff enjoyed in this case by each worker $i = 1, 2$ is respectively given by $\omega_i - c$.

Consider now the case in which both workers still accept the wage offer (ω_1, ω_2), but suppose that only one of the workers – say 1 – subsequently makes the effort. Then, with probability p, player 2 is nevertheless "effortlessly productive," which implies that the aggregate production is equal to $2y_2$ and thus the payoffs for the firm and the two workers are given by the triplet $(2y_2 - \omega_1 - \omega_2, \omega_1 - c, \omega_2)$ – note that worker 2 does not incur the effort cost c. On the other hand, with probability $(1 - p)$ player 2 is *not* productive and the payoff vector is $(y_2 - \omega_1 - \omega_2, \omega_1 - c, \omega_2)$. This simply reflects the fact that, in this case, the second worker does not contribute to the total production in this case.

Suppose now that neither worker exerts effort but both still accept the wage offer (ω_1, ω_2). Then, if the probabilities for high and low productivities are assumed independent between workers, it is clear that the different payoff configurations that may prevail in this case are as follows. With probability p^2 the payoff vector is $(2y_2 - \omega_1 - \omega_2, \omega_1, \omega_2)$, with probability $(1 - p)^2$ it is $(-\omega_1 - \omega_2, \omega_1, \omega_2)$, and with probability $2(1 - p)p$ it is $(y_2 - \omega_1 - \omega_2, \omega_1, \omega_2)$.

Similar considerations can be used to cover the case in which just one worker accepts the wage offered by the firm. In this case, of course, payoffs must involve the productivity y_1 displayed by a worker (again, deterministically or not, depending on her effort) when she is the only one employed by the firm.

Finally, one needs to specify the "outside option" to which the workers can resort in case of rejecting the firm's wage offer. In this respect, let us simply suppose that each worker can obtain in this case a payoff equal to a prespecified $\hat{\omega}$ that is to be interpreted as the payoff attainable in the best alternative she has outside of

---

[162] Whether the employment decision of a worker is observed by the other one prior to making the effort decisions is an unimportant feature of the model that bears no significance on the analysis.

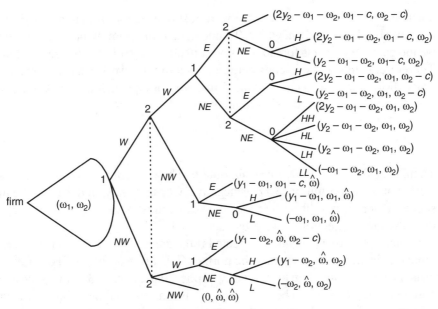

Figure 9.2: Stage game: a firm and two workers: 1 and 2; player 0 interpreted as Nature. W, NW: work, not work; E, NE: effort, no effort; H, L: high productivity, low productivity.

the firm (e.g., working by herself, or receiving unemployment benefits). Overall, an illustration of the extensive-form game played in *each* stage $t = 1, 2, \ldots, T$ is displayed in Figure 9.2.

To consider the most interesting scenario, assume that

$$(2y_2 - 2c) - (y_1 - c + \hat{\omega}) > 0. \tag{9.34}$$

This condition simply states that, from the point of view of the total payoffs earned by the three agents involved (the firm and the two workers), it is better to have the two workers employed rather than just one, provided they both exert effort. Condition (9.34) can be equivalently rewritten as follows:

$$y_2 - c - \hat{\omega} > y_1 - y_2, \tag{9.35}$$

which in turn implies, since $y_1 \geq y_2$, that

$$y_1 - c - \hat{\omega} > 0 \tag{9.36}$$

and

$$2y_2 - 2c - 2\hat{\omega} > 0. \tag{9.37}$$

In combination, (9.35)–(9.37) imply that, from the standpoint of aggregate payoffs, the very best outcome has the two workers employed and exerting effort. Of course, if monetary side payments among the agents are permitted *ex post* (and carried out in a way that does not have strategic consequences), this is also the only Pareto efficient outcome.

Can one guarantee such an efficiency desideratum (i.e., the employment of both workers) in the face of players' strategic incentives? If the stage game were considered in isolation – say, there were just one period of play and $T = 1$ – the answer would be clearly negative. To understand this, simply note that, in the one-period game, the firm is forced to commit itself *in advance* to a wage pair (ω_1, ω_2). Therefore, if this game is considered in isolation, no worker has any incentive to exert effort when she is hired by the firms. Now assume that the probability p with which workers are effortlessly productive is relatively low, i.e.,

$$p < \frac{\hat{\omega}}{y_1}. \tag{9.38}$$

Then, the expected payoff, $py_1 - \hat{\omega}$, obtained by the firm after hiring even just one worker at her opportunity cost $\hat{\omega}$ is negative. Consequently, in this case, the unique subgame-perfect equilibrium of the *stage game* must have wage offers $\omega_i \leq \hat{\omega}$ and the subsequent rejection to work by each $i = 1, 2$.[163]

Is such a negative conclusion affected if the game is repeated over time? Here, a crucial consideration is whether the horizon T is finite or infinite. For, if finite, the usual backward-induction logic readily implies that, under (9.38), the same negative outcome (i.e., no workers being employed) is materialized over time in the unique subgame-perfect equilibrium of the game. Incidentally, it is worth stressing that this state of affairs does *not* at all depend on whether the firm observes (and thus can make its actions contingent on) the effort exerted by the workers in preceding stages.

Let us see how matters are altered if the repeated interaction takes place over an *infinite* horizon and all players discount the resulting flow of stage payoffs at some common discount rate $\delta < 1$. In contrast with the finite-horizon case, observability conditions now play a crucial role in the analysis. In this respect, we may consider two polar cases. In the first one, the firm enjoys *perfect* observability on the effort undertaken by the workers at each point in the game. In the second one, no such observation is ever available to the firm. As it turns out, each of these cases displays very different implications concerning the possibility of sustaining efficient outcomes at equilibrium. We next address each of them separately.

9.3.1   *Perfect observation*

First, we consider the scenario with *perfect observability*. For concreteness, let us aim at constructing stationary equilibria that constantly display the following features *on the equilibrium path*:

(a) the firm always offers a suitably selected common wage $\tilde{\omega}$ to both workers throughout;

(b) the workers always choose to work and also exert the required effort.

Recalling previous discussion, it should be clear that any equilibrium with such a behavior on the equilibrium path must be supported by some effective *off-equilibrium* punishments by which the firm deters both workers from ever

---

[163] If p were not so low and $\hat{\omega}/y_1 < p < \hat{\omega}/y_2$, there are subgame-perfect equilibria that involve fixing different wages, $\omega_i \geq \hat{\omega} \geq \omega_j$ ($i \neq j$), with player i accepting the wage offer but *not* player j. A similar idea is applied later in the discussion of the infinitely repeated game under imperfect observability.

deviating and thus exerting no effort. For example, one may posit that, if any deviation is ever observed, the firm's strategy then induces a rather low wage offer $\omega^o < \hat{\omega}$ to both workers forever after.[164] In effect, because that wage offer is lower than the outside option, the implication is that the workers would never thereafter wish to work for the firm in that event.

To be precise, it is useful to introduce the following notation. Given any t, let $a_f^t \equiv (\omega_1^t, \omega_2^t)$ stand for the action chosen at that time by the firm, consisting of a pair of wages ω_i^t offered to each worker $i = 1, 2$. Concerning the workers, the "action" chosen by each of them at t is twofold. First, it must determine whether (in response to the firm's wage offer) the individual decides to work or not. Second, it must also indicate whether, in the case of working, she exerts effort or not. In essence, however, the options available can be reduced to just three: "not work" (NW), "work and exert effort" (E), "work and exert *no* effort" (NE). Thus, formally, the action a_i^t of worker i at t may be viewed as an element of the set $\{NW, E, NE\}$.

We are now in a position to formalize matters. First, we describe a strategy profile that leads to the outcome described in (a) and (b) above in terms of some prespecified wage $\tilde{\omega}$. Then, we verify that, for some suitable choice of $\tilde{\omega}$, the strategy profile satisfies the required equilibrium conditions.

Firm's strategy:

(F) $\forall t = 1, 2, \ldots$, the action (wage offer) a_f^t of the firm satisfies

* $a_f^t = (\tilde{\omega}, \tilde{\omega})$ if
$$\nexists \tau \leq t - 1 \quad \text{s.t.} \quad \begin{cases} a_f^\tau \neq (\tilde{\omega}, \tilde{\omega}) & \text{and/or} \\ a_j^\tau \neq E & \text{for some } j \in \{1, 2\}; \end{cases}$$
* $a_f^t = (\omega^o, \omega^o)$, otherwise.

Worker i's strategy, $i = 1, 2$:

(W) $\forall t = 1, 2, \ldots$, the action a_i^t of worker i satisfies:

* $a_i^t = E$ if $\omega_i^t \geq \tilde{\omega}$ and
$$\nexists \tau \leq t - 1 \quad \text{s.t.} \quad \begin{cases} a_f^\tau \neq (\tilde{\omega}, \tilde{\omega}) & \text{and/or} \\ a_j^\tau \neq E & \text{for some } j \in \{1, 2\}; \end{cases}$$
* $a_i^t = NE$ if $\omega_i^t \geq \tilde{\omega}$ and
$$\exists \tau \leq t - 1 \quad \text{s.t.} \quad \begin{cases} a_f^\tau \neq (\tilde{\omega}, \tilde{\omega}) & \text{and/or} \\ a_j^\tau \neq E & \text{for some } j \in \{1, 2\}; \end{cases}$$
* $a_i^t = NE$ if $\hat{\omega} \leq \omega_i^t < \tilde{\omega}$;
* $a_i^t = NW$ if $\omega_i^t < \hat{\omega}$.

---

[164] Admittedly, it would be more natural to postulate that the firm punishes only a worker who has deviated, leaving the future wage offers enjoyed by a nondeviant worker unaffected. This is not essential and would be easily accommodated in what follows, complicating the description of matters only in an irrelevant fashion.

Note, of course, that the above strategies implicitly assume that the underlying situation displays perfect observability. Let us now verify that, for sufficiently high discount rate δ, there exists some suitable choice for $\tilde{\omega}$ such that the above strategies define a subgame-perfect equilibrium of the corresponding infinitely repeated game. First note that if both workers indeed exert the required effort every period (i.e., they do not deviate from equilibrium), their induced discounted payoff $V^*(\tilde{\omega})$ must satisfy (recall footnote 147)

$$V^*(\tilde{\omega}) = (1 - \delta)(\tilde{\omega} - c) + \delta V^*(\tilde{\omega}),$$

which readily implies

$$V^*(\tilde{\omega}) = \tilde{\omega} - c. \tag{9.39}$$

Thus, for each worker to find it optimal to incur the effort cost at every period, the following condition must hold:

$$\tilde{\omega} - c \geq (1 - \delta)\,\tilde{\omega} + \delta\hat{\omega}, \tag{9.40}$$

that is, the discounted payoff $V^*(\tilde{\omega})$ obtained by not deviating can be no lower than the one derived from enjoying a full stage payoff of $\tilde{\omega}$ in a *single* period (i.e., saving on the cost c by deviating), followed by a constant stage payoff of $\hat{\omega}$ thereafter. The inequality (9.40) may be rewritten as follows:

$$\tilde{\omega} \geq \hat{\omega} + c\left(1 + \frac{1 - \delta}{\delta}\right), \tag{9.41}$$

which simply indicates that the firm must offer the workers a "sufficient premium" above their outside option $\hat{\omega}$ *and* the effort cost c if opportunistic deviations are to be deterred. This premium, which must be no lower than $c(1 - \delta)/\delta$, leads to what is often called an *efficiency wage*. It reflects the need to provide the worker being hired with supplementary incentives if, under the assumed strategic asymmetries (i.e., she moves after the firm in the stage game), efficient behavior on her part is to be induced.

Finally, we must check the incentive conditions on the part of the firm for some suitable $\hat{\omega}$. That is, we have to verify that, within the range of wages $\tilde{\omega}$ that satisfy (9.41), there exists a nonempty subrange where the firm earns nonnegative discounted profits. This requires only that y_2 be large enough. Specifically, in view of (9.41), one must have that

$$y_2 \geq \hat{\omega} + c\left(1 + \frac{1 - \delta}{\delta}\right), \tag{9.42}$$

which is always feasible, by (9.35), if δ is close enough to one. Thus, in this case, one can find some wage $\tilde{\omega}$ satisfying

$$y_2 \geq \tilde{\omega} \geq \hat{\omega} + c\left(1 + \frac{1 - \delta}{\delta}\right) \tag{9.43}$$

so that all the above requirements are satisfied and, therefore, the strategies given by (F) and (W) indeed define a subgame-perfect equilibrium of the underlying repeated game.

In view of the previous analysis, it may be argued that, under perfect observability, there are only *two* reasons why some unemployment might be unavoidable: either it is simply *not* efficient that the firm should hire the two workers (i.e., (9.35) is violated) or the workers are so impatient that it is impossible to offset short-run opportunistic benefits by the threat of long-run punishments (i.e., δ is so low that (9.42) cannot be met). Of course, another reason why unemployment may arise is that, unlike what has been assumed thus far, firms do not observe the workers' exerted effort. This introduces new and interesting considerations in itself, as explained in what follows.

9.3.2 *Imperfect observation*

Let us now postulate that the firm is incapable of observing the workers' efforts but is just able to gain indirect and noisy evidence of it through the (accurate) observation of the workers' respective productivity. Then, we wish to ask a question analogous to that posed before: Under what conditions is it possible to sustain an indefinite path of joint effort by both workers at equilibrium? We focus on the possibility of constructing an equilibrium akin to that given by (F) and (W), but adapted to the limitations imposed by unobservability. In such an equilibrium, workers are provided with incentives to exert effort by being paid a common (and relatively high) wage as long as there is no evidence that they have ever deviated in the past. That is, they are paid some $\tilde{\omega} > \hat{\omega}$ as long as each worker has always exerted effort so far or, even if she has not done so at some point, at least has been "lucky" to always display a high productivity. This, of course, must be complemented by a suitable threat as to how the firm would react if evidence of a deviation were to turn up (i.e., some worker were found to display a low productivity). As before, we focus on an equilibrium where, in that event, the firm threatens to punish both players by offering a low wage $\omega^o < \hat{\omega}$ at all subsequent periods, an offer that in fact would never be accepted.

Denote by $x_i^t \in \{y_1, y_2, 0\}$ the productivity of player i actually materialized at t.[165] Then, the above referred strategies may be formally described as follows.

Firm's strategy:
(F′) $\forall t = 1, 2, \ldots$, the action (wage offer) a_f^t of the firm satisfies

$\quad *\ a_f^t = (\tilde{\omega}, \tilde{\omega})$ if

$$\nexists \tau \le t - 1 \quad \text{s.t.} \quad \begin{cases} a_f^\tau \ne (\tilde{\omega}, \tilde{\omega}) & \text{and/or} \\ x_j^\tau = 0 & \text{for some } j \in \{1, 2\}; \end{cases}$$

$\quad *\ a_f^t = (\omega^o, \omega^o)$, otherwise.

---

[165] Recall that, from an *ex ante* viewpoint, the productivity displayed by any worker i who is employed at some t but exerts no effort is a random variable that displays a positive probability (less than one) of being equal to zero. On the other hand, if the worker is not employed, it will be convenient to view the situation as one in which her productivity is equal to zero with probability one.

Worker i's strategy, $i = 1, 2$:

(W') $\forall t = 1, 2, \ldots$, the action a_i^t of worker i satisfies

* $a_i^t = E$ if $\omega_i^t \geq \tilde{\omega}$ and

$$\nexists \tau \leq t - 1 \quad \text{s.t.} \quad \begin{cases} a_f^\tau \neq (\tilde{\omega}, \tilde{\omega}) & \text{and/or} \\ x_j^\tau = 0 & \text{for some } j \in \{1, 2\}; \end{cases}$$

* $a_i^t = NE$ if $\omega_i^t \geq \tilde{\omega}$ and

$$\exists \tau \leq t - 1 \quad \text{s.t.} \quad \begin{cases} a_f^\tau \neq (\tilde{\omega}, \tilde{\omega}) & \text{and/or} \\ x_j^\tau = 0 & \text{for some } j \in \{1, 2\}; \end{cases}$$

* $a_i^t = NE$ if $\hat{\omega} \leq \omega_i^t < \tilde{\omega}$;
* $a_i^t = NW$ if $\omega_i^t < \hat{\omega}$.

Note that, in comparison with the counterpart strategies (F) and (W) considered before for the perfect-observability scenario, (F') and (W') do reflect the imperfect-observability constraints presently assumed – specifically, the firm's strategy is made contingent only on the workers' productivities and not on their efforts. If the latter strategies are to define a subgame-perfect equilibrium of the repeated game, one must have, in particular, that the discounted payoff that a worker obtains by keeping at any given point in time with her respective strategy (W') is at least as high as that resulting from a unilateral deviation – in particular, if she were to eschew effort. To assess precisely the implications of this requirement, note that, on the one hand, the equilibrium payoff is

$$V^*(\tilde{\omega}) = \tilde{\omega} - c,$$

i.e., exactly as in (9.39) under perfect observability. Suppose now that, under the anticipation that the firm relies on strategy (W'), a deviation toward NE were optimal. Then, its payoff, denoted by $\check{V}(\tilde{\omega})$, would satisfy the following expression:

$$\check{V}(\tilde{\omega}) = (1 - \delta)\,\tilde{\omega} + \delta\{p\,\check{V}(\tilde{\omega}) + (1 - p)\,\hat{\omega}\}, \tag{9.44}$$

which leads to

$$\check{V}(\tilde{\omega}) = \frac{(1 - \delta)\,\tilde{\omega} + \delta\,(1 - p)\,\hat{\omega}}{1 - \delta p}.$$

Thus, to rule out that such a deviation might be optimal, one must have that

$$V^*(\tilde{\omega}) \geq \check{V}(\tilde{\omega}),$$

which may be simply written as follows:

$$\tilde{\omega} \geq \hat{\omega} + c \frac{1 - \delta p}{\delta\,(1 - p)}. \tag{9.45}$$

Naturally, if $p = 0$ (that is, workers's lack of effort always has *observable* consequences), condition (9.45) turns into (9.41), which is the inequality obtained under perfect observability. In this case, therefore, the minimum premium the firm needs to pay the workers to deter deviations coincides with that prevailing under perfect observability, i.e., $c(1 - \delta)/\delta$. Instead, when $p > 0$, the firm has to pay the *additional* premium

$$\Delta \equiv c\frac{1 - \delta p}{\delta(1 - p)} - c\left(1 + \frac{1 - \delta}{\delta}\right) = c\frac{(1 - \delta)p}{\delta(1 - p)} > 0,$$

which is a consequence of the more stringent incentive constraints imposed by the unobservability of effort. Of course, this extra premium leads to a higher *efficiency wage* than before, a reflection of the more acute informational asymmetries now afflicting the labor-market interaction. Naturally, the size of Δ grows with p, i.e., as effort becomes less important an input in ensuring the workers's productivity. For, as p grows, the worker can also try to conceal her lack of effort at a lower risk of being discovered.

What are the efficiency implications of effort unobservability? To gain a clear understanding of things, it is useful to assume that the underlying environment satisfies (9.35) and (9.42). Then, "full employment" (i.e., both workers being hired every period) is not only the efficient outcome but is also sustainable at equilibrium under *perfect observability*. In contrast, when effort is *unobservable* and p is low, the possibilities of sustaining full employment at equilibrium tend to be significantly curtailed. For example, it is possible that, despite (9.42), we also have

$$y_2 < \hat{\omega} + c\left(1 + \frac{1 - \delta}{\delta}\right) + \Delta. \tag{9.46}$$

Then, by playing the strategy given by (F') for any wage $\tilde{\omega}$ satisfying (9.45), the firm would incur losses. Thus, even though such a strategy would indeed induce the workers to exert a high effort at every stage of the game, the wage premium required is too high for the firm to find it worthwhile. This, in sum, prevents (F') and (W') from defining a subgame-perfect equilibrium of the repeated game in the present imperfect-observability scenario.

However, if production returns are *strictly* decreasing (i.e., $y_1 > y_2$), it is still possible to have that both (9.46) and the following inequality,

$$y_1 \geq \hat{\omega} + c\left(1 + \frac{1 - \delta}{\delta}\right) + \Delta, \tag{9.47}$$

simultaneously hold. Assume, in fact, that this is the case. Then, it seems natural to aim at an equilibrium where the two workers are treated asymmetrically; i.e., each worker receives a different wage offer from the firm, even on the equilibrium path. In this way, the firm may end up hiring only one of them, which in view of (9.46) and (9.47) is the only feasible way of earning positive profits at equilibrium. Indeed, as an immediate adaptation of (F') and (W') along these lines, it may be easily verified that the following strategies define a subgame-perfect equilibrium of the repeated game if (9.47) applies. In this equilibrium, only one worker, say worker 1, is employed throughout at a wage $\tilde{\omega}$ satisfying

$$y_1 \geq \tilde{\omega} \geq \hat{\omega} + c\frac{1 - \delta p}{\delta(1 - p)}.$$

Firm's strategy:

(F'') $\forall t = 1, 2, \ldots$, the action (wage offer) a_f^t of the firm satisfies

* $a_f^t = (\tilde{\omega}, \omega^o)$ if

$$\nexists \tau \le t - 1 \quad \text{s.t.} \quad \begin{cases} a_f^\tau \ne (\tilde{\omega}, \omega^o) & \text{and/or} \\ x_1^\tau = 0; \end{cases}$$

* $a_f^t = (\omega^o, \omega^o)$, otherwise.

Worker 1's strategy:

(W.1'') $\forall t = 1, 2, \ldots$, the action a_1^t of worker 1 satisfies:

* $a_1^t = E$ if $\omega_1^t \ge \tilde{\omega}$ and

$$\nexists \tau \le t - 1 \quad \text{s.t.} \quad \begin{cases} a_f^\tau \ne (\tilde{\omega}, \omega^o) & \text{and/or} \\ x_1^\tau = 0; \end{cases}$$

* $a_1^t = NE$ if $\omega_1^t \ge \tilde{\omega}$ and

$$\exists \tau \le t - 1 \quad \text{s.t.} \quad \begin{cases} a_f^\tau \ne (\tilde{\omega}, \omega^o) & \text{and/or} \\ x_1^\tau = 0; \end{cases}$$

* $a_1^t = NE$ if $\hat{\omega} \le \omega_1^t < \tilde{\omega}$;
* $a_1^t = NW$ if $\omega_1^t < \hat{\omega}$.

Worker 2's strategy:

(W.2'') $\forall t = 1, 2, \ldots$, the action a_2^t of worker 2 satisfies

* $a_2^t = NE$ if $\omega_2^t \ge \hat{\omega}$
* $a_2^t = NW$ if $\omega_2^t < \hat{\omega}$.

Obviously, we could have considered an analogous equilibrium where the roles of player 1 and 2 were interchanged. As explained, either of those two asymmetric strategy profiles reflects the need of the firm to limit employment to at most one player if losses are to be avoided and workers' effort incentives preserved. This, of course, does not mean it would be unfeasible for the firm to earn positive profits and also employ both workers voluntarily (i.e., at a wage they would be ready to accept). In fact, by (9.35), not only the firm but the workers too would gain if some such arrangement (which is feasible) were implemented somehow. Nevertheless, this turns out to be impossible by the demanding interplay of

(a) strategic incentives, which are associated to the "perverse" timing of decisions in the stage game, and

(b) observability conditions, which prevent the firm from using an effort-contingent strategy.

The consequent social cost is paid in the form of partial (un)employment, an inefficient state of affairs caused by the fact that the "efficiency wage" required to deter opportunistic behavior is too high. In turn, this can be attributed to the fact that the probability p with which effort-shirking workers can mask their action (i.e., still be productive) is itself too high.

Summary

This chapter has examined a number of different economic applications where forward-looking players are taken to interact along a repeated game. Much of our discussion has focused on models of oligopolistic competition where a given number of firms repeatedly compete in some fixed market for a homogeneous product. Along the lines pursued in Chapter 3, the discussion has been divided into two scenarios. In the first one, firms compete à la Cournot by setting their outputs independently every period. In the second one, firms set prices instead, their market interaction thus being modeled à la Bertrand in every period.

In each case (Cournot and Bertrand competition), matters have been approached in a parallel fashion, both concerning the theoretical framework proposed and the questions posed. The common leading motivation has been to shed light on the collusion possibilities afforded by repeated interaction, i.e., on the extent to which firms can improve over the static (Cournot- or Bertrand-) Nash equilibrium. By relying on the insights and techniques developed for the so-called folk theorems (recall Chapter 8), the following sharp and conclusive answer has been provided. If firms are relatively patient, the maximally collusive outcome can be supported at some subgame-perfect equilibrium of the corresponding infinitely repeated game, both in the Cournot and in the Bertrand scenarios. The main new insight gained in this respect is that even quite simple and intuitive strategies (e.g., those of a carrot-and-stick variety) are effective ways of achieving such a collusive outcome.

Naturally, the ability to collude in a repeated-oligopoly framework must crucially depend on the quality of the informational conditions enjoyed by firms when implementing their intertemporal strategies. To explore this issue, we have modified the benchmark setup where firms are supposed to be *fully informed* of past history, postulating instead that firms have access only to overall market information. Specifically, we have assumed that firms do not observe the individual decisions of their competitors but only *past prevailing prices*. Moreover, these prices are taken to be only noisy correlates of aggregate output, because independent shocks impinging on market demand every period break the usual deterministic link. Under these conditions, we have seen that collusive equilibria can still be constructed (both in the Cournot and the Bertrand setups), although now the target price cannot be constantly secured over time. Instead, the inability of firms to discriminate between *deviations* and *bad shocks* forces the process into finite but recurrent "punishment phases" where a Nash equilibrium of the stage game is played. At equilibrium, of course, these punishment spells are never the outcome of deviations but simply the consequence of bad shocks.

Finally, we have studied a very stylized model of a "repeated labor market" where a single firm and two workers meet every period. The constituent stage game involves sequential decisions, with the firm moving first (by issuing wage proposals) and the two workers subsequently (deciding whether to work for the firm at the offered wage and, in that case, whether to exert costly effort or not). In this stage game alone, no worker has any incentive to exert effort after accepting a wage offer, thus typically leading to an inefficient outcome in its unique subgame-perfect equilibrium. Such an inefficiency can be remedied in the (infinitely) repeated game if effort is observable and workers are sufficiently patient. That is, there is a subgame-perfect equilibrium of the repeated game where the firm offers a wage premium (i.e., proposes an *efficiency wage*) that offsets workers' opportunistic incentives. However, if the workers' effort is unobservable, the situation becomes substantially more problematic. For example, we have seen that, even if the underlying conditions would allow for "full employment" at equilibrium under effort observability, the absence of the latter may force some unemployment. That is, at any equilibrium of the game played under imperfect observability, at least one worker has to remain idle at every point in time.

Exercises

Exercise 9.1: Show that if the inequality (9.7) is satisfied, the trigger strategies described by (a) and (b) in Subsection 9.1.1 define a subgame-perfect equilibrium of the infinitely repeated game with discounted payoffs.

Exercise 9.2: Consider the linear environment given by (9.3) and (9.4) with $M = d = 1$, $c = 1/4$, and $n = 2$. Determine the highest lower bound on the discount rate δ such that the duopolists' strategies described in Subsection 9.1.1 define a subgame-perfect equilibrium of the infinitely repeated game. Allowing now c and n to vary (i.e., they become parameters of the model), study how the aforementioned lower bound on δ changes with them.

Exercise 9.3: In the same context as for Exercise 9.2, compute $\hat{\pi}^m$ and $\hat{\pi}^\circ$ in (9.10) and (9.12), the latter as a function of any arbitrary x°.

Exercise 9.4: Again in the setup of Exercise 9.2, make the discount rate $\delta = 1/2$ and determine the stick-and-carrot strategies (of the type indicated in (α) and (β) in Subsection 9.1.1) that support a constant output equal to $(x^c + x^m)/2$, where recall that x^c and x^m are, respectively, defined by (9.5) and (9.6).

Exercise 9.5*: Recall the general Cournot setup studied in Subsection 9.1.1. In this setup, define a particular scenario with two firms where, for some specific discount rate δ, the maximally collusive outcome cannot be sustained at a subgame-perfect equilibrium by trigger strategies of the kind (a) and (b) but it can be supported by strategies of the sort (α) and (β).

Exercise 9.6*: Consider a certain duopoly facing repeatedly over time (with no prespecified end) a fixed demand function for its homogenous good of the form

$$P(Q^t) = \tilde{\theta}^t (Q^t)^{-\alpha}, \ \alpha > 0,$$

where $\tilde{\theta}^t$ is an identically and independently distributed random variable in each time period t. Both firms display a fixed cost function given by

$$C(q_i) = \frac{1}{4}q_i \qquad (i = 1, 2).$$

Let $v \equiv p^m/p^c$ where $p^m > 0$ and $p^c > 0$ are the prices prevailing in the (static) Cournot-Nash equilibrium and the maximally collusive (symmetric) output profile, respectively. Assume the random variable $\tilde{\theta}^t$ takes only two values: $\tilde{\theta}^t = 1, v$, each arising with equal probability. In every period, firms choose their respective outputs simultaneously, but they observe only the prevailing prices (i.e., they do not observe the individual outputs chosen by other firms).

Model the situation as an infinitely repeated game with stage payoffs (profits) being discounted at a common rate $\delta \in (0, 1)$. Suppose firms wish to sustain the maximally collusive profile (q^m, q^m) through an equilibrium of the dichotomous sort presented in Subsection 9.1.2 (i.e., an equilibrium that responds to "normal" and "regressive" situations). Compute the optimal duration T^* of the regressive phases that achieve this objective. Furthermore, find how T^* depends on the discount rate δ.

Exercise 9.7: Consider a duopolistic scenario such as that of Exercise 9.6, although with perfect observability (i.e., each firm accurately observes the output chosen by its competitor) and no demand uncertainty (for simplicity, just make $\tilde{\theta} \equiv 1$). Suppose firms may decide to use prices or outputs as their strategic variables but, in either case, they consider relying only on trigger strategies of the kind introduced in Subsections 9.1.1 and 9.2.1. Find a value of $\delta > 0$ that will leave them exactly indifferent between the two possibilities (i.e., using prices or outputs).

Exercise 9.8: Within the context of Subsection 9.2.2 (i.e., repeated Bertrand competition under imperfect observability), show that if (9.32) holds and δ is high enough, some equilibrium of the format (i′) and (ii′) always exists for some suitable chosen T.

Exercise 9.9*: Reconsider the context described in Exercise 9.6, now assuming that firms adopt prices as their strategic variables.

1. What is the optimal duration T^* for the regressive phases in this case? Determine as well how T^* depends on δ, the discount rate.
2. Now suppose firms may choose prices or quantities as their strategic variables. Which of these two options will they choose? Discuss your answer.

Exercise 9.10: In the infinitely-repeated labor-market context of Section 9.3, assume that effort is unobservable and players' discount rate δ is not necessarily close to one. Further suppose that (9.38) does *not* hold, i.e., suppose that $py_1 \geq \hat{\omega}$.

(i) Is there a subgame-perfect equilibrium with full employment? Is it efficient (allowing for side payments)? Is every such subgame-perfect equilibrium efficient?

(ii) Discuss how your answers to (i) are affected if one may postulate effort observability and/or a high enough discount rate.

Exercise 9.11*: Consider a context with unobservability of the workers' effort such as that presented in Subsection 9.3.2 but with the following additional possibility. Now, if a particular worker exerts no effort, the situation is detected by the firm with some independent probability q, even if that worker turns out to be productive. (Note that the model described in the text follows from the particularization $q = 0$.)

Assume the probability q is a costly control variable of the firm. Specifically, suppose that, for any "chosen" q, the firm incurs a cost given by $C(q) = q^2$. Fix the values for the parameters of the model as follows: $p = 0.1$, $y_1 = 3$, $y_2 = 2$, $\hat{\omega} = 0$, $\delta = 0.5$. Then, compute the optimal value of q that maximizes the discounted profits of the firm at an equilibrium analogous to that considered in the text.

Exercise 9.12: In the context of Subsection 9.3.2 with effort unobservability, assume that (9.46) does *not* hold. Is there any subgame-perfect equilibrium where only *one* worker is hired every period? Discuss your answer.

Exercise 9.13: Consider a context as described in Section 9.3, but with worker 1 being uniformly more productive than worker 2 for each scale of production, and suppose this fact is common knowledge. (That is, if y_k^i denotes the productivity of worker i when k workers are employed by the firm, one has $y_k^1 > y_k^2$ for each $k = 1, 2$.) Specify conditions on the parameters of the model such that, with unobservability of workers' effort, there exists an equilibrium where worker 1 is always hired but worker 2 never is.

Exercise 9.14*: Consider a generalization of the setup described in Section 9.3 where there is an arbitrary number of $3n$ workers for some $n \in \mathbb{N}$ (i.e., the total number is some multiple of 3).

(a) Specify conditions on the parameters of the model such that, under perfect observability of workers' effort, no more than one-third of the workers can be hired at equilibrium. Define one such equilibrium.
(b) Address the same questions raised in (a) above but assuming that workers' effort is unobservable.

CHAPTER 10

Evolution and rationality

10.1   Introduction

So far in this book, we have implicitly assumed that players experience no cognitive limitations when confronting strategic situations. Consequently, any considerations pertaining to whether and how agents will be able to arrive at some optimal (or equilibrium) strategy have been fully abstracted from. It is clear, however, that a coherent and exhaustive analysis of some games can be exceedingly difficult. And this, of course, not only concerns many of our idealized *theoretical contexts* but is also much more applicable to the strategic interactions taking place in the *real world*. In many real contexts, players can seldom hope to understand the underlying game in a transparent manner, which in turn leads them to resorting to relatively simple rules to shape their behavior. But then, one expects that players should adjust over time their decision rules on the basis of their own and others' experience, those rules that are more effective tending to spread throughout the population in lieu of less successful ones.

From a theoretical viewpoint, the former considerations raise two related questions:

1. What reasonable features should be postulated on the dynamics of behavioral adjustment?
2. Under what conditions does the entailed adjustment dynamics converge to some optimal or equilibrium pattern of play?

The study of these important issues will attract much of our attention through the remainder of this book, not only here but also in the two subsequent chapters. In this chapter, the specific viewpoint adopted is of an evolutionary nature. This is an approach that has a long history in the economic literature, although, traditionally, it has been pursued only in a heuristic and informal fashion.[166] In essence, evolutionary theory builds upon the simple tenet that any suboptimal behavior eventually should be weeded out of the population (say, by the "pressure" of competing and better suited decision rules). Thus, rather than invoking players' reasoning ability to discipline behavior, some criterion of long-run performance and survival is used instead. Indeed, as it turns out, we shall see that there are a number of interesting

---

[166] A classical illustration of this approach can be found in the well-known essay by Friedman (1953).

scenarios where such an evolutionary approach is able to provide novel underpinnings for Nash equilibrium, or even some of its refinements.

10.2 Static analysis

Evolution, of course, is (and should be modeled as) a genuinely dynamic process. As a first approach, however, it is useful to study it from a static viewpoint and ask what kind of configurations can be suitably conceived as an "evolutionary equilibrium", i.e., a (robust) rest-point of some evolutionary dynamics. This is indeed our objective in the present section, undertaken in advance of the genuinely dynamic analysis that will be developed later on in Sections 10.3 and 10.4.

10.2.1 *Theoretical framework*

As in much of modern evolutionary theory, we focus here on a paradigmatic context where the individuals of a single *large* population are assumed to undergo a series of "parallel" and identical *pairwise contests* (i.e., games).[167] More precisely, we consider an infinite population (with the cardinality of the continuum) whose members are randomly matched in pairs to play a certain bilateral game in strategic form G. Let us suppose that this game is *symmetric* with $S = \{s_1, s_2, \ldots, s_n\}$ being the common strategy set and $A = (a_{qr})_{q,r=1,2,\ldots,n}$ the (square) payoff matrix. In this matrix, any given entry a_{qr} simply represents the payoff earned by an individual who adopts the pure strategy s_q when her opponent chooses s_r. By symmetry, of course, such an opponent then earns the payoff a_{rq}.

In general, we admit the possibility that individuals may choose mixed strategies. In that case, the expected payoff of an individual who plays the mixed strategy $\sigma = (\sigma_1, \sigma_2, \ldots, \sigma_n) \in \Delta^{n-1}$ against other that adopts σ' is given by[168]

$$\sigma A \sigma' = \sum_{q=1}^{n} \sigma_q \left[\sum_{r=1}^{n} a_{qr} \sigma'_r \right] = \sum_{q=1}^{n} \sum_{r=1}^{n} a_{qr} \sigma_q \sigma'_r.$$

The strategy simplex Δ^{n-1} may be used to represent not only mixed strategies but also *population profiles* $x = (x_1, x_2, \ldots, x_n)$ where each x_q now expresses the *ex post* frequency with which pure strategy s_q is played in the population. For example, if all players in the population happen to choose a common mixed strategy $\sigma \in \Delta^{n-1}$, it will be assumed that the induced population profile $x \in \Delta^{n-1}$ over pure strategies has $x_q = \sigma_q$ for all $q = 1, 2, \ldots, n$. That is, given that the population

---

[167] In Section 10.4, we extend this framework to allow for two populations interacting through a possibly asymmetric game, individuals from each population still randomly chosen to play. Alternatively, evolutionary theory has also focused on so-called *playing-the-field* models where, instead of random matching, there is joint simultaneous interaction among all the different individuals of the population. In economic contexts, a group of firms all competing in a single market is a classical example of this latter kind of interaction. Another classical one, but now of a biological nature, concerns the evolution of the sex ratio, a simplified version of which is discussed in Exercise 10.5.

[168] As in Chapter 2, we dispense for simplicity with the notation for matrix transposition, interpreting σ as a row vector and σ' as a column one.

is supposed to be very large, we shall heuristically invoke the law of large numbers and identify *ex ante* probabilities and *ex post* frequencies.[169]

Analogous considerations are used to identify *expected* and *average* payoffs in the following sense. Consider some positive measure of individuals who choose the mixed strategy σ and are randomly matched against a large pool of players whose profile over the different pure strategies is given by $x = (x_1, x_2, \ldots, x_n)$. Then, large-number considerations again lead us to identify the *expected* payoff $\sigma A x$ earned *ex ante* by each of the individuals playing σ with the *ex post* average payoff earned across all of those players.

10.2.2 *Evolutionarily stable strategy*

The first equilibrium concept introduced in the evolutionary literature was that of evolutionarily stable strategy (ESS), proposed by Maynard Smith and Price (1973). By virtue of its elegance and simplicity, this concept is still widely used in many evolutionary applications. Formally, it is defined as follows.[170]

Definition 10.1: *A (mixed) strategy* $\sigma \in \Delta^{n-1}$ *is an* evolutionarily stable strategy *if* $\forall \sigma' \neq \sigma$, $\exists \bar{\varepsilon} > 0$ *such that if* $0 < \varepsilon \leq \bar{\varepsilon}$,

$$\sigma A \left[(1 - \varepsilon)\sigma + \varepsilon\sigma'\right] > \sigma' A \left[(1 - \varepsilon)\sigma + \varepsilon\sigma'\right]. \tag{10.1}$$

The above definition has a quite transparent interpretation, at least in biological realms. Consider a certain (large) population that was initially playing strategy σ in a homogenous fashion – such a population is usually called *monomorphic*. The question implicitly posed by the ESS concept can be formulated as follows: Can the originally monomorphic population be *permanently* disturbed (i.e., "invaded") by a small number of alternative individuals ("mutants") who adopt a different strategy, $\sigma' \neq \sigma$? If one associates the ability to invade to obtaining at least as high payoffs (and therefore, it is assumed, as high an ability to survive and reproduce), the strategy σ qualifies as evolutionarily stable if the former question is answered in the negative for *any* alternative σ' and *some* maximum threshold $\bar{\varepsilon} > 0$ for the relative size of the invasion. That is, once any such σ'-mutants have entered at a frequency ε no higher than $\bar{\varepsilon}$, it is required that the latter's average payoff be lower than that of the original σ-incumbents, given that both of them face the same *post entry* population profile $(1 - \varepsilon)\sigma + \varepsilon\sigma'$.

At this stage, it is important to point to an important drawback of the ESS concept, which in turn is a key consideration in motivating future developments. By definition, the ESS concept restricts itself to the analysis of monomorphic

---

[169] In fact, such an identification is not devoid of technical problems because the law of large numbers applies only to a countable set (not a continuum) of random variables. We ignore these problems here, but the interested reader may refer to Judd (1985), Feldman and Gilles (1985), or Alós-Ferrer (1999) for a careful, but unavoidably technical, discussion of these matters.

[170] This concept can be readily adapted to contexts where individuals "play the field" (recall Footnote 167 and cf. Maynard Smith (1982) and Crawford (1991)) or the population is finite (cf. Riley, 1979b; Schaffer, 1988). All these different scenarios pose interesting questions of their own, which are nevertheless beyond the scope of our present concerns.

configurations, i.e., situations in which *all* individuals in the original population display the *same* strategy σ. Even though, *ex post*, individuals may differ in their actually displayed behavior (i.e., the pure strategy actually chosen), all of them are fully identical from an *ex ante* viewpoint. Naturally, the evolutionary performance of the strategy σ must be tailored to some global assessment of the payoff induced across all those individuals that adopt it. For simplicity, the ESS concept identifies such global performance with the corresponding average payoff. Thus, in view of the large-population scenario, the evolutionary stability of σ is linked to the *identical* expected payoff faced by all agents that *ex ante* determine their behavior according to the *same* σ.

In biology or economics alike, however, behavioral diversity (even *ex ante*) is an important feature of most interesting environments. That is, the checks and balances afforded by a suitable degree of heterogeneity are crucial to understand the (evolutionary) stability of the situation. For example, the fact that some individuals are risky and others prudent, or tall and short, or aggressive and compromising, provide the complementarities/substitutabilities that are often a key factor of stabilization and robustness of the population state. In some cases (see Subsection 10.2.4), such diversity can be suitably modeled in the way suggested above, i.e., as the *ex post* consequence of *ex ante* symmetry. However, in many others, the heterogeneity must be introduced explicitly into the framework if the problem is to be suitably modeled. (One can think, for example, of those archetypal economic scenarios where some agents are buyers and others sellers, or some are specialized in producing wool and others wine.) In those cases, the ESS concept is markedly unsatisfactory as an analytical tool and the situation must be approached in a richer way. This, indeed, is the task undertaken in Section 10.3, where evolution is modeled *explicitly* as a dynamic and polymorphic process.

10.2.3   *ESS and equilibrium*

In the introductory section of this chapter, we argued that evolution may provide an indirect but effective way of ensuring that agents end up displaying some extent of rationality. That is, evolution may act as a substitute for the players' deductive reasoning about the strategic situation implicitly presumed by classical game theory. To explore the possibilities in this respect, a natural first step is to contrast the behavioral implications of the ESS concept with those derived from the chief theoretical notion of classical game theory, Nash equilibrium. This is the objective of our next result, which readily implies that the former is a refinement – or a strengthening – of the latter (see the clarifying discussion below).

Proposition 10.1 (Maynard Smith, 1982): *Let σ be an ESS in a pairwise random-matching context with bilateral game G. Then*

> *(i) $\forall \sigma' \in \Sigma$, $\sigma A \sigma \geq \sigma' A \sigma$;*
> *(ii) $\forall \sigma' \in \Sigma$ $(\sigma' \neq \sigma)$, $\sigma A \sigma = \sigma' A \sigma \Rightarrow \sigma A \sigma' > \sigma' A \sigma'$.*

> *Reciprocally, if a certain strategy $\sigma \in \Sigma$ satisfies (i) and (ii), then it is an ESS.*

Proof: Let σ be an ESS. To prove (i) first, assume for the sake of contradiction that there is some $\sigma' \neq \sigma$ such that

$$\sigma A\sigma < \sigma' A\sigma.$$

Then, there is some $\hat{\varepsilon} > 0$ such that, for all $\varepsilon \leq \hat{\varepsilon}$, one has

$$(1 - \varepsilon)\sigma A\sigma + \varepsilon\sigma A\sigma' < (1 - \varepsilon)\sigma' A\sigma + \varepsilon\sigma' A\sigma'$$

or, equivalently,

$$\sigma A[(1 - \varepsilon)\sigma + \varepsilon\sigma'] < \sigma' A[(1 - \varepsilon)\sigma + \varepsilon\sigma'],$$

which contradicts Definition 10.1 and thus proves the claim. Concerning (ii), let σ' be any mixed strategy different from σ such that

$$\sigma A\sigma = \sigma' A\sigma. \tag{10.2}$$

Then, if, contrary to what is required, we had

$$\sigma A\sigma' \leq \sigma' A\sigma', \tag{10.3}$$

multiplying (10.2) by $(1 - \varepsilon)$, (10.3) by ε, and adding both of the resulting expressions, we would obtain, for any $\varepsilon \in (0, 1)$, that

$$(1 - \varepsilon)\sigma A\sigma + \varepsilon\sigma A\sigma' \leq (1 - \varepsilon)\sigma' A\sigma + \varepsilon\sigma' A\sigma'$$

or

$$\sigma A[(1 - \varepsilon)\sigma + \varepsilon\sigma'] \leq \sigma' A[(1 - \varepsilon)\sigma + \varepsilon\sigma'],$$

again a contradiction with Definition 10.1.

To prove the converse, assume that (i) and (ii) hold. Consider any given $\sigma' \neq \sigma$. If (i) applies with strict inequality, it is clear that (10.1) must hold for all ε that are small enough. Instead, if (i) is satisfied with equality, then (ii) implies that $\sigma A\sigma' > \sigma' A\sigma'$, which again implies that (10.1) follows for all $\varepsilon > 0$. ∎

In view of the above proposition, an ESS induces a symmetric Nash equilibrium of the underlying bilateral game G – this is simply what Condition (i) reflects. But, *in addition*, an ESS must also satisfy Condition (ii). Thus, as indicated, the ESS notion can be regarded as a refinement of (symmetric) Nash equilibrium.

Proceeding along these lines, one may still wonder how much of a refinement of Nash equilibrium is afforded by the ESS concept – that is, how does it fit in the large menu of other refinements considered in the literature (cf. Chapter 4). An exhaustive exploration of this question may be found in the monograph by van Damme (1987, Chapter 9). Here, we content ourselves with showing that ESS is a rather stringent refinement of Nash equilibrium, since it is no weaker than the concept of (strategic-form) perfect equilibrium. This is precisely the content of the following result.

Proposition 10.2 (Bomze, 1986): *Let σ be an ESS in a pairwise random-matching context with bilateral game G. Then, (σ, σ) is a perfect equilibrium of G.*

Proof: As explained in Remark 4.1, an equilibrium of a *bilateral* game in strategic form is perfect if, and only if, it is a Nash equilibrium that involves no weakly dominated strategies by either player (cf. Definition 4.10). Thus, to prove the desired conclusion it is enough to show that if any particular σ is an ESS, it cannot be weakly dominated.

Suppose the contrary is true. Then, there exists some $\sigma' \in \Delta^{n-1}$, $\sigma' \neq \sigma$, such that, for all $\sigma'' \in \Delta^{n-1}$,

$$\sigma' A \sigma'' \geq \sigma A \sigma''.$$

Particularizing σ'' above both to the ESS σ and the strategy σ' that weakly dominates it, we obtain

$$\sigma' A \sigma \geq \sigma A \sigma \qquad (10.4)$$

$$\sigma' A \sigma' \geq \sigma A \sigma'. \qquad (10.5)$$

By (i) of Proposition 10.1, the profile (σ, σ) defines a Nash equilibrium. Consequently, $\sigma' A \sigma \leq \sigma A \sigma$. This, together with (10.4), implies that

$$\sigma' A \sigma = \sigma A \sigma.$$

Thus, by (ii) in Proposition 10.1, we must have

$$\sigma' A \sigma' < \sigma A \sigma',$$

which is a contradiction with (10.5) and therefore completes the proof. ∎

The above results can be interpreted as a certain confirmation of the idea that evolutionary forces, at least as captured by the ESS concept, do impose some degree of rationality on behavior. Indeed, the kind of behavior that arises does not just embody *individual* rationality alone but a certain extent of consistency, or interagent rationality, as well. That is, if the situation is suitably described by an ESS, population behavior embodies Nash (even perfect) equilibrium play in every bilateral encounter.

At this point, however, it is worth stressing that the above considerations should not be overdone. Thus far, we have established only that *if* the population is settled at an ESS, then their overall behavior reproduces the pattern of a Nash (perfect) equilibrium. This, nevertheless, begs two important questions. First, there is the basic one of existence: does an ESS always exist? And second, one may legitimately wonder about the dynamic foundations of an ESS: is there any reasonable dynamics that would lead the population to playing an ESS (or an ESS-like state)? This dynamic issue is all the more important here since, unlike in classical game theory, we are not entitled to invoke players' reasoning as the procedure through which equilibrium might be attained.

Pertaining to both of these questions, matters are unfortunately not very positive. First, concerning existence, it turns out that no satisfactory result is available because there are simple and nonpathological finite games where no ESS exists (see Exercise 10.3 and Subsection 10.2.4.2). On the other hand, as for its dynamic foundations, note that the simple implicit dynamics underlying this concept reflect a purely *local* and *dichotomic* "test" of dynamic stability – i.e., it concerns the struggle between one mutant and an incumbent in the vicinity of an incumbent-monomorphic configuration. In essence, therefore, it is afflicted of the same rigid monomorphism that was criticized at the end of Subsection 10.2.2. Quite surprisingly, however, the ESS notion will come back again in Subsection 10.3.2, where the canonical model of (polymorphic) evolutionary dynamics – the so-called replicator dynamics – will be seen to provide some indirect but dynamic support for ESS configurations.

10.2.4 *Examples*

10.2.4.1 *Hawk–dove game.* Let us now consider a simple, and by now classic, example often used in the biological literature for purposes of illustration: the *hawk–dove game*. Its setup may be described as follows. There is a large population of a given species, its individuals competing for some scarce and indivisible resource (food, territory, etc.). They are matched in bilateral encounters involving randomly selected pairs. In every such encounter, the individuals in question can display one of two possible sorts of behavior (i.e., strategies):

- aggressive behavior (the "hawk" strategy H);
- peaceful behavior (the "dove" strategy D).

Identifying the first row (and column) with the strategy H and the second with strategy D, we posit the following payoff matrix:

$$A = \begin{pmatrix} \frac{V-C}{2} & V \\ 0 & \frac{V}{2} \end{pmatrix} \qquad (10.6)$$

where V is the "fitness" value of the resource,[171] and C is the cost of being defeated in a fight when both individuals display aggressive behavior. More specifically, the interpretation of the payoff entries is as follows.

- If both individuals adopt H (and thus enter into a fight), both enjoy the same probability (i.e., $1/2$) of overcoming the opponent (in which case they secure the resource at no cost and obtain a payoff of V) or being defeated (which leads to a negative payoff of $-C$ derived from losing both the fight and the resource).
- If both instead adopt D, again the probability of obtaining the resource is the same for each but, unlike before, the individual that is left without it does not incur any cost.
- Finally, if one of the individuals adopts H, whereas the other chooses D, the former is certain to obtain the resource at no cost, whereas the latter does not incur any cost either.

---

[171] As explained below, biological fitness is to be identified with the ability of producing viable offspring that inherit the same behavioral traits as the parent.

If $V > C$ the situation is trivial because, in this case, the strategy H is dominant. The unique ESS is then given by this *pure* strategy. The most interesting case arises when $V < C$.[172] In this case, no pure-strategy Nash equilibrium exists, and therefore no pure strategy can be an ESS. However, allowing for mixed strategies, we now show that

$$\sigma^* = \left(\sigma_H^*, \sigma_D^*\right) = (V/C, 1 - V/C) \tag{10.7}$$

is an ESS (in fact, the unique one). That is, a probabilistic mixing of aggressive and peaceful behavior (the latter being more likely the higher the cost C of being defeated) is evolutionarily stable in the sense of Definition 10.1.

To see this, first note that σ^* is the unique symmetric Nash equilibrium of the game G played by every matched pair of individuals. Thus, it is the only candidate for an ESS, by virtue of Proposition 10.1. Since this Nash equilibrium has full support on the full set of pure strategies, standard considerations indicate that, for all $\sigma = (\sigma_H, \sigma_D) \in \Delta$,

$$\sigma A \sigma^* = \sigma^* A \sigma^*,$$

i.e., all (mixed) strategies attain the same equilibrium payoff earned by σ^*. Therefore, by part (ii) of Proposition 10.1, we know that for σ^* to be an ESS, we must have

$$\sigma^* A \sigma > \sigma A \sigma$$

for all $\sigma \neq \sigma^*$. In view of (10.6), straightforward algebraic computations lead to

$$\sigma^* A \sigma - \sigma A \sigma = \frac{\sigma_H^* - \sigma_H}{2}(V - \sigma_H C),$$

where we use the fact that $\sigma_D = 1 - \sigma_H$. Thus, since $\sigma_H^* = V/C$, it follows that

$$\sigma^* A \sigma - \sigma A \sigma = \frac{1}{2C}(V - \sigma_H C)^2 > 0$$

for all $\sigma \neq \sigma^*$, as desired.

10.2.4.2 *Rock–scissors–paper game.* As a second example, suppose the strategic situation confronted by every pair of randomly matched individuals is the well-known rock–scissors–paper game (recall Exercise 1.7). Specifically, let the game display the following payoff matrix

$$A = \begin{pmatrix} 0 & 1 & -1 \\ -1 & 0 & 1 \\ 1 & -1 & 0 \end{pmatrix} \tag{10.8}$$

where the first row (and column) is associated with rock (R), the second with scissors (S), and the third with paper (P). This simply reflects the usual convention that R beats S, S beats P, and P beats R, with 1 being the payoff for victory and -1

---

[172] See Exercise 10.1 for the boundary configuration where $V = C$.

being that of defeat. If two same strategies play each other, the resulting tie is taken to entail a payoff of zero.

This game has a unique Nash equilibrium where every player chooses each pure strategy with equal probability, i.e., adopts the mixed strategy $\sigma^* = (1/3, 1/3, 1/3)$. Again, therefore, it follows that such σ^* is the only candidate for an ESS. Note, however, that if we choose, e.g., $\sigma' = (1, 0, 0)$ – i.e., the pure strategy R – we find

$$\sigma^* A \sigma' = \sigma' A \sigma' = 0 \tag{10.9}$$

and, on the other hand,

$$\sigma' A \sigma^* = \sigma^* A \sigma^* = 0. \tag{10.10}$$

Jointly, (10.9) and (10.10) imply that part (ii) of Proposition 10.1 is violated. This implies that σ^* is *not* an ESS. Thus, since it was the only candidate, we may conclude that *no* ESS whatsoever exists in this game. In view of the especially simple nature of the setup, this example provides an especially forceful illustration of the serious nonexistence problems afflicting the ESS.

10.3 Basic dynamic analysis

In this and subsequent sections, we undertake a genuinely dynamic approach to the study of evolutionary processes, i.e., one that is not limited by the straitjacket of static equilibrium analysis. In this way, we hope to overcome some of the conceptual and methodological objections raised above concerning the ESS approach (recall Subsections 10.2.2 and 10.2.3). As a first step in this direction, we start by focusing on the canonical model of evolutionary dynamics that embodies in the starkest manner the idea of Darwinian selection, i.e., the so-called replicator dynamics.

10.3.1 *Replicator dynamics*

Consider initially a context in which time is measured discretely, and in every time period $t = 1, 2, \ldots$, the agents' interaction is as described in Subsection 10.2.1. That is, suppose that, at any such t, the individuals of a large population are randomly matched in pairs to play a symmetric bilateral game, G, with payoff matrix A.

For simplicity, let us restrict attention to the case where agents adopt only pure strategies.[173] Denote by $x(t) = (x_1(t), x_2(t), \ldots, x_n(t)) \in \Delta^{n-1}$ the vector of population frequencies prevailing at some t (also called the *population state*), where $x_q(t)$ stands for the frequency of individuals playing strategy s_q. Then, if $v(t)$ represents the absolute size (or measure) of the population, the total number (or measure) of those adopting each pure strategy s_q $(q = 1, 2, \ldots, n)$ is simply given by $v_q(t) \equiv v(t) x_q(t)$.

---

[173] The replicator dynamics can be extended to the full set of mixed strategies at the cost of a substantial increase in complexity (in particular, the dynamical system becomes infinitely dimensional because the cardinality of Δ^{n-1}, the space of mixed strategies, is infinite). The interested reader is referred to Hines (1980) and Vega-Redondo (1996).

In biological contexts, payoffs have a very specific interpretation: they are a measure of *fitness* and thus quantify the "production" of viable offspring that inherit the same traits (i.e., behavior) as the parent. Such an interpretation of payoffs as fitness unambiguously determines the dynamics of $x(\cdot)$ and $v(\cdot)$. To see this, make the simplifying assumption that adult individuals live for only one period. Then, if the number of offspring left by each one of them is determined by (say, is proportional to) its respective payoffs, the total number of individuals that will adopt each pure strategy s_q at $t + 1$ can be readily computed as follows:

$$v_q(t + 1) = v_q(t) \left[\sum_{r=1}^{n} a_{qr} x_r(t) \right] \qquad (q = 1, 2, \ldots, n).$$

And, therefore, the respective frequencies at $t + 1$ are

$$x_q(t + 1) = \frac{v_q(t + 1)}{v(t + 1)} = \frac{x_q(t) v(t) \left[\sum_{r=1}^{n} a_{qr} x_r(t) \right]}{\sum_{u=1}^{n} x_u(t) v(t) \left[\sum_{r=1}^{n} a_{ur} x_r(t) \right]}$$

$$= \frac{x_q(t) \left[\sum_{r=1}^{n} a_{qr} x_r(t) \right]}{\sum_{u=1}^{n} x_u(t) \left[\sum_{r=1}^{n} a_{ur} x_r(t) \right]},$$

which can be equivalently rewritten as follows:

$$\frac{\Delta x_q(t)}{x_q(t)} \equiv \frac{x_q(t + 1) - x_q(t)}{x_q(t)} = \frac{\sum_{r=1}^{n} a_{qr} x_r(t) - x(t) A x(t)}{x(t) A x(t)}. \qquad (10.11)$$

The above expression captures the "bottom line" of Darwinian selection in a clear-cut fashion: the rate of change in the frequency displayed by any given strategy s_q is exactly *equal* to the *relative* difference between its average payoff $\sum_{r=1}^{n} a_{qr} x_r(t)$ and the average payoff earned across *all* strategies, $x(t) A x(t) = \sum_{u=1}^{n} x_u(t) [\sum_{r=1}^{n} a_{ur} x_r(t)]$. This expression gives rise to the dynamical system usually known as the *replicator dynamics* (RD) – here, "replication" is understood as *asexual* reproduction, given that each individual offspring is taken to be an exact copy of its *single* parent.

For analytical convenience, it is useful to treat time as a continuous variable by positing that the time period is of infinitesimal length. To make this precise, let $\theta \in (0, 1]$ parametrize the duration of each discrete time period and suppose that, within a time period of duration θ, only a θ-fraction of adult individuals die and bear offspring in it. (Therefore, if $\theta = 1$, the formulation is identical to that given in (10.11).) Adapting the former considerations to any such value of θ, it can be easily seen (cf. Exercise 10.6) that the corresponding generalization of (10.11) may be written as follows:

$$\frac{\Delta x_q(t)}{x_q(t)} \equiv \frac{x_q(t + \theta) - x_q(t)}{x_q(t)} = \frac{\sum_{r=1}^{n} \theta \, a_{qr} \, x_r(t) - x(t) \theta \, A x(t)}{x(t) \theta \, A x(t) + (1 - \theta)}.$$

$$(10.12)$$

Thus, dividing the above expression by θ and making $\theta \to 0$, we may rely on the customary definition of (time) derivative to write

$$\frac{\dot{x}_q(t)}{x_q(t)} = \frac{1}{x_q(t)} \lim_{\theta \to 0} \frac{x_q(t+\theta) - x_q(t)}{\theta}$$

$$= \sum_{r=1}^{n} a_{qr}\, x_r(t) - x(t)Ax(t), \quad t \geq 0, \quad (q = 1, 2, \ldots, n) \quad (10.13)$$

which is the *continuous-time* version of the RD to be used in most of our ensuing discussion. Reassuringly, observe that (10.13) displays the basic feature that, as argued above, characterizes Darwinian dynamics, namely, the rate of change in the frequency of any given strategy is proportional to its payoff differential over the average.[174]

The formulation of the RD given in (10.13) requires that $x_q(t) > 0$ for each $q = 1, 2, \ldots, n$. If we have $x_q(t) = 0$ for some q at any t (i.e., the set of individuals choosing strategy s_q display a zero measure), it is *inherent* in the strict Darwinian features embodied by the RD that no positive fraction of individuals choosing s_q may arise later on. Therefore, the growth rate of its frequency must be forced to be zero forever after. To accommodate for this possibility of zero frequencies, we may simply rewrite (10.13) as follows:

$$\dot{x}_q(t) = x_q(t) \left[\sum_{r=1}^{n} a_{qr}\, x_r(t) - x(t)Ax(t) \right], \quad t \geq 0, \quad (q = 1, 2, \ldots, n).$$

$$(10.14)$$

The above formulation of the RD highlights the fact that this dynamics *per se* allows for no mutation or innovation, a phenomenon that would have to be superimposed on the model as a separate component of the dynamics (see, for example, the explicit modeling of mutation carried out in the models studied in Chapter 12). Conversely, it is also easy to see that if $x_q(t) > 0$ at some t, the RD implies that $x_q(t') > 0$ for all future $t' > t$ (cf. Exercise 10.7). That is, no strategy that is ever present in the population at some positive frequency can fully disappear later on. In conjunction, the former two features of the RD may be combined into the following property:

---

[174] Note that, in contrast with (10.11), the law of motion in (10.13) displays a constant denominator of one in lieu of the average payoff. It is worth mentioning, however, that the inclusion or not of the latter (time-varying) denominator has no bearing on the qualitative behavior of the continuous-time system. That is, the following version of the continuous-time RD,

$$\frac{\dot{x}_q(t)}{x_q(t)} = \frac{\sum_{r=1}^{n} a_{qr}\, x_j(t) - x(t)Ax(t)}{x(t)Ax(t)},$$

displays the same long-run behavior and stability properties as (10.13). The key point to observe in this respect is that the term $1/x(t)Ax(t)$ is a *common* factor affecting the dynamics of *every* $x_q(\cdot)$.

Dynamic Invariance of Simplex Faces[175]: For any path $x(\cdot)$ of the RD and each $q = 1, 2, \ldots, n$,

$$x_q(0) > 0 \Leftrightarrow \forall t > 0, \; x_q(t) > 0. \tag{10.15}$$

Two further properties of the RD are worth mentioning at this point, because they represent an effective way of clarifying some of its theoretical implications.

Additive Invariance of Payoffs: Given the payoff matrix A, consider the alternative matrix A' where, for each $r = 1, 2, \ldots, n$, there is some $h_r \in \mathbb{R}$, such that

$$\forall q = 1, 2, \ldots, n, \quad a'_{qr} = a_{qr} + h_r.$$

Then, the trajectories induced by the RD with either payoff matrix A or A' coincide.

Quotient Dynamics: Let $q, r \in \{1, 2, \ldots, n\}$ be such that $x_q(t) > 0$ and $x_r(t) > 0$ for some t. Then, the RD implies

$$\frac{\dot{x}_q(t)}{x_q(t)} - \frac{\dot{x}_r(t)}{x_r(t)} = \sum_{u=1}^{n} a_{qu} x_u(t) - \sum_{u=1}^{n} a_{ru} x_u(t). \tag{10.16}$$

The above two properties are direct consequences of the RD formulation (cf. Exercises 10.8 and 10.9). They embody alternative but equally stark manifestations of what is the key feature of any Darwinian process: only *relative* payoffs matter. The first property, additive invariance of payoffs, underscores this fact by stating invariance to transformations of the underlying payoffs that leave differential magnitudes across strategies unchanged. In turn, the second property labeled quotient dynamics makes a related point: if one is interested only on how the differences between two given strategy frequencies evolve, it suffices to compare their payoff differences.

10.3.2 *Replicator dynamics and equilibrium*

Now, we ask a question on the RD much along the lines of the analogous question posed in Subsection 10.2.3 pertaining to the ESS concept. What is the relationship between the equilibria (i.e., rest points) of the RD and the equilibrium concepts posited by classical game theory?

First, we observe that every Nash equilibrium is a rest point of the RD. More precisely, let $D \equiv (D_1, \ldots, D_n) : \Delta^{n-1} \to \mathbb{R}^n$ be the *vector field* defining the RD

---

[175] To understand the terminology used to label this property, note that any particular simplex face is characterized by having some subset of components (or coordinates) vanish. Thus, as explained, any path of the RD that starts in any such face (or its interior) is bound to remain in it throughout. Customarily, this is formulated by saying that the RD leaves any such face "dynamically invariant."

in (10.14), i.e.,[176]

$$D_q(x) \equiv x_q \left[\sum_{r=1}^{n} a_{qr} x_r - x A x \right]$$

for each $x \in \Delta^{n-1}$ and every $q = 1, 2, \dots, n$. Then, we have the following.

Proposition 10.3: *Let σ^* be the strategy played at a symmetric Nash equilibrium of the game G. Then, the population state $x^* = \sigma^*$ is an equilibrium of the RD, i.e., $D(x^*) = 0$.*

This result follows immediately from the familiar fact that, at a Nash equilibrium, all strategies played with positive weight must yield an identical expected payoff. Thus, in contrast with the ESS approach (cf. Proposition 10.1), we find that the RD equilibria do not provide a refinement but rather an extension of the Nash equilibrium concept, with the population frequencies matching the corresponding probability weights. But, how large is such an extension? As it turns out, quite large (and also mostly uninteresting), as the following remark explains.

Remark 10.1: *Stationarity of simplex vertices*

Consider any simplex vertex of the form $e^q = (0, \dots, 1, \dots, 0) \in \Delta^{n-1}$, all its weight concentrated on some particular strategy s_q. Clearly, for every such e^q, we have that $D(e^q) = 0$. That is, *any* "degenerate" (or monomorphic) profile e^q is an equilibrium of the RD. In fact, depending on the underlying game G, it is easy to see that there can be *additional* (nonmonomorphic) rest points that do *not* correspond to Nash equilibria either – see Exercise 10.10. Overall, this indicates that stationarity (i.e., dynamic equilibrium) alone is too coarse a criterion to be of much interest by itself for the RD.   ◆

The above remark suggests that, to obtain sharper analytical conclusions from the RD, one needs to supplement the simplistic notion of stationarity with some additional requirement. A natural such requirement is that the rest point should pass some test of dynamic robustness in the face of suitable perturbations. If, minimally, those perturbations are taken to be only of a local character, one is led to the criterion called *asymptotic stability*. In general, this notion is defined as follows.

Definition 10.2: *Let $\dot{x} = F(x)$ be a dynamical system in a set $W \subset \mathbb{R}^m$, $m \in \mathbb{N}$. An equilibrium x^* (i.e., $F(x^*) = 0$) is said to be* asymptotically stable *if the following two conditions hold.*

(1) Given any neighborhood U_1 of x^*, there exists some other neighborhood of it, U_2, such that, for any path (or solution) $x(\cdot)$, if $x(0) \in U_2$ then $x(t) \in U_1$ for all $t > 0$.

---

[176] Informally, the vector field indicates the direction of (infinitesimal) movement at every point x in the state space of the system. Or, somewhat more formally, it specifies, for each x, a vector that is tangent to the trajectory passing through x, its modulus determining the corresponding "speed" of movement.

(2) There exists some neighborhood V of x^* such that, for any path $x(\cdot)$, if $x(0) \in V$ then $\lim_{t \to \infty} x(t) = x^*$.

Asymptotic stability involves two distinct requirements. First, Condition (1) demands that any path that starts sufficiently close to the equilibrium remains arbitrarily close to it. This condition is often labeled *Liapunov stability*. On the other hand, Condition (2) requires that any path that starts close enough to the equilibrium in question also converges to it.[177]

What can asymptotic stability provide for us in the task of shrinking the too-large set of RD equilibria? An encouraging answer is provided by the next result.

Proposition 10.4: *Let x^* be an asymptotically stable equilibrium of the RD. Then, if $\sigma^* = x^*$, the strategy pair (σ^*, σ^*) defines a (symmetric) Nash equilibrium of the game G.*

Proof: We argue by contradiction. Let x^* be an asymptotically stable equilibrium and suppose that the corresponding mixed strategy $\sigma^* = x^*$ does not define a symmetric Nash equilibrium. Then, there must exist some strategy s_u that obtains a higher payoff than σ^* against σ^*. Or, in terms of the corresponding population frequencies, we must have

$$\sum_{r=1}^{n} a_{ur} x_r^* > x^* A x^*, \tag{10.17}$$

which in turn obviously implies that

$$\sum_{r=1}^{n} a_{ur} x_r^* > \sum_{r=1}^{n} a_{vr} x_r^*$$

for some $v \neq u$ with $x_v^* > 0$. Since x^* is asymptotically stable, Condition (2) in Definition 10.2 requires that there should be a neighborhood V of x^* such that, for every path with $x(0) \in V$, $\lim_{t \to \infty} x(t) = x^*$. Thus, from (10.17), there must be some large enough T such that

$$\sum_{r=1}^{n} a_{ur} x_r(t) - \sum_{r=1}^{n} a_{vr} x_r(t) \geq \rho \tag{10.18}$$

for all $t \geq T$ and some given $\rho > 0$. Choose $x(0)$ to be an interior population state, i.e., $x_q(0) > 0$ for every $q = 1, 2, \ldots, n$. By the dynamic invariance of simplex faces implied by (10.15), we must also have that $x_u(t) > 0$ and $x_v(t) > 0$ for all t. Therefore, in view of (10.18) and the quotient RD (cf. (10.16)), it follows that

$$\frac{\dot{x}_u(t)}{x_u(t)} - \frac{\dot{x}_v(t)}{x_v(t)} \geq \rho$$

---

[177] At first sight, it might seem that Condition (2) implies Condition (1), i.e., is stronger and thus makes the latter redundant. However, this is not so and, in principle, one could have that a convergent trajectory is forced to move "far away" from x^* before returning to it. In fact, such examples are standard in the field of dynamical systems – see, for example, Hirsch and Smale (1974).

for all $t \geq T$. This is incompatible with the fact that $x(\cdot)$ converges to x^*, which obviously requires that $\lim \dot{x}_u(t) = \lim \dot{x}_v(t) = 0$. The proof is thus complete. ∎

By virtue of the above result, simply requiring that an equilibrium of the RD be dynamically robust to local perturbations (i.e., asymptotically stable)[178] is enough to guarantee that it induces a Nash equilibrium for the underlying game – or, more precisely, a population-based representation of it. Thus, in analogy with the ESS concept in Proposition 10.1, Proposition 10.4 indicates that asymptotic stability leads, in the context of the RD, to a refinement of Nash equilibrium – at least weakly so. A natural question then arises: Which of these two notions, ESS or asymptotic stability, is stronger, i.e., more "refined"? A clear-cut answer is provided by the following result, whose proof is merely sketched.

Theorem 10.1 (Hofbauer, Schuster and Sigmund, 1979): *Let $\sigma^* \in \Delta^{n-1}$ be an ESS. Then, the population state $x^* = \sigma^*$ is asymptotically stable in terms of the RD.*

Proof (*sketch*): Let $\sigma^* \in \Delta^{n-1}$ be an ESS and denote by x^* the corresponding population profile. The main step of the proof involves finding a suitable function $\psi : \Delta^{n-1} \rightarrow \mathbb{R}$ that displays the following two features:

(a) it achieves a unique maximum at x^* in some neighborhood V of this point;
(b) the value $\psi(x(t))$ increases along any trajectory with starting point $x(0) \in V$.

Locally, any such function $\psi(\cdot)$ defines a so-called Liapunov function, thus guaranteeing that every trajectory that starts close enough to x^* satisfies the twofold requirement contemplated in Definition 10.2. First, the trajectory never moves far away from x^* (since $\psi(x(t))$ always increases); second, it eventually converges to x^* (because $\psi(\cdot)$ attains the local maximum at x^*).

Prior to verifying that some such function exists, we need the following lemma, whose proof is relegated to Exercise 10.11.

Lemma 10.2: *Let σ^* be an ESS. Then, there exists some neighborhood of it, $N_{\sigma^*} \subset \Delta^{n-1}$, such that if $\sigma \in N_{\sigma^*} \backslash \{\sigma^*\}$, $\sigma^* A \sigma > \sigma A \sigma$.*

Assume, for simplicity, that $x^*(= \sigma^*)$ is an interior point of the simplex Δ^{n-1}, i.e., $x_q^* > 0$ for each $q = 1, 2, \ldots, n$. Then, consider the function $\psi : \Delta^{n-1} \rightarrow \mathbb{R}$ defined as follows:

$$\psi(x) = \sum_{q=1}^{n} x_q^* \log x_q$$

as the candidate for a local Liapunov function. As explained, the key point to show is that, for $x(t)$ in some sufficiently small neighborhood of x^* (we may choose it smaller than N_{σ^*} in Lemma 10.2) we have $\dot{\psi}(x(t)) > 0$.

---

[178] Note, however, that only Condition (2) in Definition 10.2 is actually used in the proof of the result.

To verify this, we compute

$$\dot{\psi}(x(t)) = \sum_{q=1}^{n} x_q^* \frac{\dot{x}_q(t)}{x_q(t)}$$

$$= \sum_{q=1}^{n} x_q^* \left[\sum_{r=1}^{n} a_{qr} x_r(t) - x(t) A x(t) \right]$$

$$= x^* A x(t) - x(t) A x(t),$$

which is indeed positive, by virtue of Lemma 10.2, as desired. ■

Theorem 10.1 provides an interesting link between our static and dynamic approaches to modeling evolution by establishing a new and surprising role to the ESS concept. As the reader will recall (cf. Subsection 10.2.2), the dynamic motivation of an ESS was conceived solely in terms of a simple and strictly *dichotomous* contest between incumbent and mutant subpopulations. The above result, however, shows that this concept also has interesting implications for the dynamic and inherently *polymorphic* scenario modeled by the RD. Specifically, it turns out to render a useful criterion of selection that refines (often strictly)[179] the set of its asymptotically stable states. Or, from an instrumental viewpoint, we could also regard the ESS notion as affording (when it exists) an indirect but effective way of selecting rest points of the RD that are dynamically robust, i.e., asymptotically stable.

10.3.3 *Examples*

10.3.3.1 *Hawk–dove game (continued).* Let us revisit the hawk–dove game described in Subsection 10.2.4.1, now approaching it from the dynamic perspective provided by the RD. A typical population profile $x = (x_H, x_D)$ specifies the frequencies of hawk and dove individuals in the population. In effect, however, because this vector is one-dimensional (i.e., $x_H + x_D = 1$), we may simply focus on the dynamics of one of these frequencies, say that of hawk strategists. Thus, denote $y \equiv x_H$ and particularize (10.14) to the present payoff matrix A given by (10.6) to obtain

$$\dot{y}(t) = y(t)(1 - y(t)) \left[\frac{V - C}{2} y(t) + V(1 - y(t)) - \frac{V}{2}(1 - y(t)) \right]$$

$$= \frac{1}{2} y(t)(1 - y(t))[V - Cy(t)].$$

The above dynamics implies that, for all interior $y(t) \in (0, 1)$,

$$y(t) < \frac{V}{C} \Rightarrow \dot{y}(t) > 0$$

$$y(t) = \frac{V}{C} \Rightarrow \dot{y}(t) = 0$$

$$y(t) > \frac{V}{C} \Rightarrow \dot{y}(t) < 0.$$

---

[179] One can construct simple examples where there is some asymptotically stable state for the (pure-strategy) RD that does *not* define an ESS (cf. Vega-Redondo, 1996, Chapter 3).

This indicates that the population state $x^* = (V/C, 1 - V/C)$ induced by the (unique) ESS is, in the present example, *globally* stable from any interior point of the space. It is worth stressing that such a conclusion is substantially stronger than that of Theorem 10.1, which, in general, establishes only *local* stability for ESS states, as embodied by the notion of asymptotic stability (cf. Definition 10.2).

10.3.3.2 *Rock–scissors–paper game (continued).* Consider now the rock–scissors–paper game described in Subsection 10.2.4.2. As explained there, this context allows for *no* ESS and, therefore, we can no longer rely on the associated ESS states to guide our dynamic analysis of the situation. This, of course, does not in general preclude the possibility that some other states might nevertheless display robust dynamic properties – the ESS conditions are only sufficient, *not* necessary, for asymptotic stability (recall Footnote 179).

In the absence of an ESS, the unique Nash-equilibrium strategy of the game, $\sigma^* = (1/3, 1/3, 1/3)$, appears as a natural benchmark to "anchor" (or at least start) the study of the situation. What are the stability/robustness properties displayed by the associated population profile $x^* = \sigma^*$? As we now show, even though they are not as stringent as required by the notion of asymptotic stability (cf. Definition 10.2), they are still partially satisfactory.

First, it is useful to note that, in the present example, the product of individual frequencies defines what is called a *constant of motion*, i.e., a magnitude that remains constant along *any* given trajectory of the system. That is, if one defines the function $\zeta : \Delta^2 \to \mathbb{R}$ by

$$\zeta(x) \equiv x_1 x_2 x_3,$$

the claim is that, along any path $x(\cdot)$ of the RD,

$$\dot{\zeta}(x(\cdot)) \equiv 0.$$

To verify it, simply observe that, given the payoff matrix A specified in (10.8), we have

$$x A x = x_1(x_2 - x_3) + x_2(x_3 - x_1) + x_3(x_1 - x_2) \equiv 0.$$

Therefore, the RD can be written simply as follows:

$$\dot{x}_q(t) = x_q(t)(x_{q+1}(t) - x_{q+2}(t)), \quad (q = 1, 2, 3),$$

where the indices 4 and 5 are interpreted as "modulo 3" (i.e., as 1 and 2, respectively). From the above set of differential equations, one may then readily compute

$$\dot{\zeta}(x(t)) = x_1(t)x_2(t)x_3(t)\left[(x_2(t) - x_3(t)) + (x_3(t) - x_1(t))\right.$$
$$\left. + (x_1(t) - x_2(t))\right] \equiv 0,$$

as claimed.

The previous derivations indicate that the interior trajectories of the RD coincide with the level sets of the function $\zeta(\cdot)$ – see Figure 10.1 for an illustration.

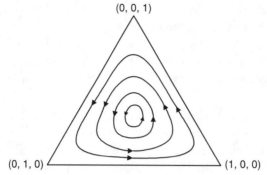

Figure 10.1: Rock–scissors–paper game, RD.

This implies, of course, that the unique interior rest point of the RD (which corresponds to the single Nash equilibrium of the underlying game) is *not* asymptotically stable – in particular, Condition (2) of Definition 10.2 is violated, because even when the system starts arbitrarily close to x^* the ensuing trajectories do not converge to it. However, its Condition (1) – what was labeled *Liapunov stability* – is clearly met. Heuristically, this means that although perturbations occurring at equilibrium will have *persistent* effects in moving the system away from it, those effects will be small if the perturbations are also small. In this sense, the equilibrium displays a sort of resilience – at least in the short or medium run – since only a repeated accumulation of (small) perturbations may lead to substantial changes in the population state.

10.4   Evolution in social environments

The static and dynamic models of evolution discussed in Sections 10.2 and 10.3 were originally conceived for, and have been mostly applied to, biological contexts. They have provided modern theoretical biology with a range of concepts and tools fruitfully used in the analysis of Darwinian processes of natural selection.[180] In social and economic environments, however, that biologically grounded approach can only be applied under quite restrictive behavioral assumptions. For, in socioeconomic contexts, the unfolding process of "selection" can no longer be closely tailored to the ability to generate viable offspring. Social evolution, that is, proceeds through a variety of rather flexible mechanisms (imitation, experimentation, introspection, etc.), which can hardly be modeled through the sharp (and thus rigid) formulation afforded by, say, the RD. For example, we see below that only under a set of behavioral assumptions that must be surely viewed as too special is it legitimate to regard the RD as a suitable model of social evolution. In general, therefore, one needs a more flexible model that, rather than spelling out the social dynamics in minute detail, allows for (i.e., is consistent with) a rich scope of evolutionary, payoff-responsive, adjustment.

---

[180] The monograph by Hofbauer and Sigmund (1988) provides an excellent discussion of the wide range of mathematical models that have been developed for the analysis of biological contexts. On the other hand, the reader may refer to Hammerstein and Selten (1992) for a good survey of concrete biological applications that rely on those theoretical developments.

10.4.1 *Social evolutionary systems*

In the present quest to extend the generality of our approach, it is worth the effort to allow for the possibility that several *distinct* populations interact – e.g., teachers with students and perhaps also parents, males with females, or consumers with firms and these with workers. Thus, let us suppose that there are several distinct populations, the members of which interact according to a certain multilateral game. In fact, to avoid unnecessary notational burden, let us simply posit that there are just *two* large (continuum) populations, indexed by $k = 1, 2$, both of equal size.

Concerning the modeling of time, we formulate it directly as a continuous variable. Thus, at every $t \geq 0$, we postulate that all individuals of population 1 are randomly paired with those of population 2. Each matched pair of agents plays a bilateral (not necessarily symmetric) game G. The finite strategy sets of this game are $S_1 = \{s_{11}, s_{12}, \ldots, s_{1n}\}$ for player 1 (i.e., the individual who belongs to population 1) and $S_2 = \{s_{21}, s_{22}, \ldots, s_{2m}\}$ for player 2 (the one who comes from population 2). On the other hand, the payoffs of the game are given by $(n \times m)$-matrices A and B whose entries

$$a_{qr} = \pi_1(s_{1q}, s_{2r})$$

$$b_{qr} = \pi_2(s_{1q}, s_{2r})$$

specify the respective payoffs of player 1 and 2 for every possible pair of strategies (s_{1q}, s_{2r}), $q \in \{1, 2 \ldots, n\}, r \in \{1, 2, \ldots, m\}$.

The state of the system at any given t is given by some $(n + m)$-dimensional vector $x(t) = (x_1(t), x_2(t)) \in \Delta^{n-1} \times \Delta^{m-1}$ specifying the frequencies with which *every* strategy s_{kq} is played in *each* population $k = 1, 2$. In general, the dynamics (or law of motion) for the system may be formalized through some system of $(n + m)$ differential equations:

$$\dot{x}_{1q}(t) = F_{1q}(x(t)) \qquad (q = 1, 2, \ldots, n) \tag{10.19}$$

$$\dot{x}_{2q}(t) = F_{2q}(x(t)) \qquad (q = 1, 2, \ldots, m) \tag{10.20}$$

where $F_1 \equiv (F_{1q})_{q=1}^n$ and $F_2 \equiv (F_{2q})_{q=1}^m$ define a vector field (i.e., a function mapping $\Delta^{n-1} \times \Delta^{m-1}$ into the possible directions of motion represented by vectors in $\mathbb{R}^n \times \mathbb{R}^m$). Naturally, for the system to be well defined, the induced paths cannot leave the state space $\Delta^{n-1} \times \Delta^{m-1}$ (i.e., the state space must be time invariant). This requires, in particular (see more on this below), that

$$\sum_{q=1}^n F_{1q}(x) \equiv \sum_{q=1}^m F_{2q}(x) \equiv 0 \tag{10.21}$$

for all $x \in \Delta^{n-1} \times \Delta^{m-1}$, which is enough to guarantee that

$$\sum_{q=1}^n x_{1q}(t) \equiv \sum_{q=1}^m x_{2q}(t) \equiv 1$$

for all $t > 0$, provided of course that, at the start of the process, we had $x(0) \in \Delta^{n-1} \times \Delta^{m-1}$.

To fix ideas, suppose that the previous vector fields can be written in the following form:

$$F_{1q}(x) = \sum_{r=1}^{n} x_{1r} \, w_{1r}(x) \, p_{1r}^{q}(x) - w_{1q}(x) \, x_{1q} \qquad (q = 1, 2, \ldots, n)$$

(10.22)

$$F_{2q}(x) = \sum_{r=1}^{m} x_{2r} \, w_{2r}(x) \, p_{2r}^{q}(x) - w_{2q}(x) \, x_{2q}, \qquad (q = 1, 2, \ldots, m)$$

(10.23)

where

- $w_{kr}(\cdot)$ is interpreted as the rate at which individuals in population k who were previously adopting pure strategy s_{kr} abandon it;
- $p_{kr}^{q}(\cdot)$ is viewed as the fraction of individuals in population k who, having abandoned strategy s_{kr}, switch to strategy s_{kq}.

The above formulation endows the evolutionary process with some structure by casting the underlying social adjustment as the composition of two opposite but complementary forces: the *inflow* of fresh strategy adoption and the *outflow* of strategy abandonment. Of course, the features displayed by the induced dynamics must depend on the properties postulated on the functions $p_{kr}^{q}(\cdot)$ and $w_{kr}(\cdot)$ that embody the aforementioned flows. Next, for the sake of illustration, we put forth some specific proposals in this respect.

First, consider the strategy inflows – i.e., the rate at which any particular player who abandons her prior strategy chooses a particular new strategy – and postulate that[181]

$$p_{kr}^{q}(x) = x_{kq}$$

(10.24)

for $k = 1$ and $q, r = 1, 2, \ldots, n$, or $k = 2$ and $q, r = 1, 2, \ldots, m$. This formulation can be conceived as the stylized description of an unsophisticated (i.e., payoff blind) *imitation* process. More specifically, we may assume that any player in a position to choose a new strategy (there is an "infinitesimal" measure of these at every t) mimics the particular choice displayed by some other randomly "met" individual from the same population (i.e., an individual who is selected in an unbiased manner). Thus, the probability with which this player adopts any particular strategy s_{kq} simply coincides with x_{kq}, the fraction of those individuals in population k who currently display that strategy.

On the other hand, concerning the strategy outflows, let us posit that players abandon their former strategies out of a certain sense of dissatisfaction or "frustration" with the payoffs they have been earning with them. Or, to be more specific, suppose individuals abandon any particular strategy at an overall rate that is decreasing in the average payoff currently received by those who play it. In terms of the induced

---

[181] Note that, in a continuous-time dynamical system, the rates of change (e.g., the rates of strategy abandonment or adoption considered here) are, in effect, defined only up to a proportionality constant, which is tailored to the overall speed of adjustment of the system (or, analogously, its time units).

abandonment rates, this amounts to the following formulation:

$$w_{1q}(x) = g_1 \left(\sum_{r=1}^{m} a_{qr} x_{2r} \right) \qquad (q = 1, 2, \dots, n)$$

$$w_{2r}(x) = g_2 \left(\sum_{q=1}^{n} b_{qr} x_{1q} \right) \qquad (r = 1, 2, \dots, m)$$

(10.25)

for some decreasing functions g_1, $g_2 : \mathbb{R} \to \mathbb{R}$, where note that

- the average payoff earned by a player of population 1 who chooses any given strategy s_{1q} $(q = 1, 2, \dots, n)$ is given by $\sum_{r=1}^{m} a_{qr} x_{2r}(t)$, and
- the average payoff obtained by a player of population 2 who chooses some strategy s_{2r} $(r = 1, 2, \dots, m)$ is $\sum_{q=1}^{n} b_{qr} x_{1q}(t)$.

Introducing (10.24)–(10.25) into (10.22)–(10.23), we arrive at an evolutionary system of the following form:

$$\dot{x}_{1q}(t) = \left\{ \left[\sum_{r=1}^{n} g_1 \left(\sum_{u=1}^{m} a_{ru} x_{2u}(t) \right) x_{1r}(t) \right] - g_1 \left(\sum_{u=1}^{m} a_{qu} x_{2u}(t) \right) \right\} x_{1q}(t)$$

(10.26)

$$\dot{x}_{2q}(t) = \left\{ \left[\sum_{r=1}^{m} g_2 \left(\sum_{u=1}^{n} b_{ur} x_{1u}(t) \right) x_{1r}(t) \right] - g_2 \left(\sum_{u=1}^{n} b_{uq} x_{1u}(t) \right) \right\} x_{2q}(t).$$

(10.27)

A simple particular case is obtained if one posits that both populations react to dissatisfaction in the same way, i.e., $g_1(\cdot) = g_2(\cdot) = g(\cdot)$, and this common function is *linear* of the form $g(z) = \alpha - \beta z$ for some parameters α, $\beta > 0$. Of course, for this specification to make sense, α and β must be chosen to satisfy

$$\alpha - \beta \sum_{r=1}^{m} a_{qr} x_{2r} \geq 0 \qquad (q = 1, 2, \dots, n)$$

$$\alpha - \beta \sum_{r=1}^{n} b_{rq} x_{1r} \geq 0 \qquad (q = 1, 2, \dots, m)$$

for all $x_1 \in \Delta^{n-1}$ and all $x_2 \in \Delta^{m-1}$. Then, (10.26) and (10.27) become

$$\dot{x}_{1q}(t) = \beta \left\{ \sum_{u=1}^{m} a_{qu} x_{2u}(t) - \left[\sum_{r=1}^{n} \left(\sum_{u=1}^{m} a_{ru} x_{2u}(t) \right) x_{1r}(t) \right] \right\} x_{1q}(t)$$

(10.28)

$$\dot{x}_{2q}(t) = \beta \left\{ \sum_{u=1}^{n} b_{uq} x_{1u}(t) - \left[\sum_{r=1}^{m} \left(\sum_{u=1}^{n} b_{ur} x_{1u}(t) \right) x_{2r}(t) \right] \right\} x_{2q}(t).$$

(10.29)

Note that, without any loss of generality, we can simply choose $\beta = 1$ in the above expressions – since β is a common factor to every equation, it has no effect on the dynamics other than scaling the measurement of time (cf. Footnote 181 and Exercise 10.16). Interestingly enough, we then find that (10.28) and (10.29) become a two-population counterpart of (10.14), the RD introduced in Subsection 10.3.1 for a *single*-population context. The above equations display, specifically, the following key feature: the proportional rate of change of any given strategy s_{kq} is equal to the difference between the average payoff of that strategy and the average payoffs earned within the corresponding population k. In view of this fact, it is straightforward to check (cf. Exercise 10.17) that the two-population dynamics (10.28)–(10.29) can be provided with a Darwinian interpretation fully analogous to that used to motivate our original version for a single population.

Even granting, however, that (10.24) and (10.25) might represent a useful representation of a certain class of social evolutionary processes, there is no solid reason to accept that players should revise their strategies as dictated by a common linear function $g(\cdot)$. What is the basis to postulate that payoffs should trigger a *linear* response on players' adjustment behavior? In general, it seems reasonable to *allow* for the possibility that players' "urge" for changing behavior might depend *non*-linearly on the payoffs they obtain. This suggests, in sum, that the conditions that have been shown to lead to the (two-population) RD should be conceived as too special, i.e., just an example that carries no special bearing for a suitably general model for social evolution.

In contrast, the purely *qualitative* tenet that "dissatisfaction should decrease with payoffs" seems a general and quite uncontroversial basis to model behavioral adjustment in the present stylized framework. Formally, this postulate merely translates into the condition that the functions $g_i(\cdot)$ should be decreasing mappings. Are there any interesting features to be expected from an evolutionary system if one just insists that such a general condition be met? Indeed there are. For in this case, any vector field $F = (F_1, F_2)$ of the form given by (10.22)–(10.23) and (10.24)–(10.25) can be easily seen to satisfy the following, quite appealing, property of *payoff monotonicity*:

$$\frac{F_{1q}(x)}{x_{1q}} > \frac{F_{1r}(x)}{x_{1r}} \Leftrightarrow \sum_{u=1}^{m} a_{qu} x_{2u} > \sum_{u=1}^{m} a_{ru} x_{2u}$$

$$(q, r = 1, 2, \ldots, n) \tag{10.30}$$

$$\frac{F_{2q}(x)}{x_{2q}} > \frac{F_{2r}(x)}{x_{2r}} \Leftrightarrow \sum_{u=1}^{n} b_{uq} x_{1u} > \sum_{u=1}^{n} b_{ur} x_{1u}$$

$$(q, r = 1, 2, \ldots, m), \tag{10.31}$$

for all $x \in \Delta^{n-1} \times \Delta^{m-1}$. These conditions lead to the following definition.

Definition 10.3: *An evolutionary system of the form (10.19)–(10.20) is said to be* payoff-monotonic *(or monotonic, for short) if (10.30)–(10.31) hold for all* $x \in \Delta^{n-1} \times \Delta^{m-1}$.[182]

In view of (10.19) and (10.20), the dynamic implications of payoff monotonicity are clear. This condition simply guarantees that, for any given pair of strategies in either population, their proportional rates of change are ordered in the same way as their respective average payoffs. Thus, in this sense, a process that satisfies (10.30) and (10.31) embodies, qualitatively, the key evolutionary feature that was repeatedly stressed when discussing the RD in Subsection 10.3.1. That is, whether any particular type of behavior grows (or survives) solely hinges on its relative payoffs, compared with those of other competing behavior. (Recall (10.16), the quotient representation of the RD, that displays this feature in the starkest – i.e., Darwinian – fashion.)

Payoff monotonicity is usually interpreted as reflecting the minimal criterion of evolutionary consistency (or payoff responsiveness) that any reasonable model of evolution, social or otherwise, should satisfy. Since it is an abstract requirement pertaining to the "reduced form" of the evolutionary process, it has the advantage of dissociating the analysis of the system from the particular details (often controversial, typically incomplete) of any "micro-model" of the underlying dynamics.[183] But, on the other hand, one may also legitimately fear that the very generality of such an abstract notion could, in effect, render it useless as an analytical tool. Will it have enough "bite" to shed light on some of our leading questions? Will it be sufficient, for example, to single out interesting conditions under which rational (even equilibrium) behavior should prevail in the long run? Indeed, as the next section explains, there are a number of interesting insights to be gained on such questions from the study of *general* evolutionary systems that are only required to satisfy the above *monotonicity* criterion.

10.4.2 *Payoff monotonicity and rationality*

As it will be recalled (cf. Subsection 10.3.2), the RD is quite effective in guaranteeing some measure of rationality in the long run. In a nutshell, our main task here will be to explore the extent to which this state of affairs is maintained when the underlying evolutionary process is required only to satisfy the weak criterion of payoff-monotonicity. In addressing this issue, our motivation is to investigate whether the flexibility afforded by such a general criterion still allows for a fruitful basis for the study of socioeconomic evolution.

First, we deal with some technical issues required for the mathematical analysis. Let $F = (F_1, F_2)$ be a vector field defining an evolutionary system of the type

---

[182] See Nachbar (1990), one of the seminal proposers of this notion, which he labeled *relative monotonicity*. Many other variants of the idea of monotonicty have been considered in the literature, as discussed for example by Friedman (1991), Weibull (1995), and Vega-Redondo (1996).

[183] In this respect, recall for example our former critical discussion concerning the assumption of linearity on the function $g(\cdot)$ that determines abandonment rates in (10.25).

given by (10.19) and (10.20). As a prerequisite to evaluate whether it satisfies the requirements of payoff monotonicity, it is clear that the proportional rates of change induced by F must be well-defined at any point x in the *state space* $\Delta^{n-1} \times \Delta^{m-1}$. This partly motivates the following definition.

Definition 10.4: *The evolutionary system with vector field F is said to be* regular *if, for all $x \in \Delta^{n-1} \times \Delta^{m-1}$, the function $G = (G_1, G_2) : \Delta^{n-1} \times \Delta^{m-1} \to \mathbb{R}^{n+m}$ defined by*

$$G_{kq}(x) \equiv \frac{F_{kq}(x)}{x_{kq}} \qquad (k = 1, \ q = 1, \ldots, n;$$

$$k = 2, \ q = 1, \ldots, m)$$

is a well-defined and continuously differentiable function.

Regularity of the evolutionary system obviously implies that the vector field F is continuously differentiable and, therefore, a unique solution (path or trajectory) of the induced dynamical system exists starting from any initial state.[184] It also ensures, as explained, that proportional rates of change are well defined at every point in the state space and thus payoff monotonicity can be assessed throughout. Finally, one can easily check that, in conjunction with (10.21), the above regularity condition guarantees that the evolutionary system leaves any simplex face invariant (either in Δ^{n-1} for population 1, or in Δ^{m-1} for population 2) in the following sense[185]:

$$x_{kq}(0) > 0 \Leftrightarrow \forall t > 0, \ x_{kq}(t) > 0 \qquad (k = 1, \ q = 1, \ldots, n;$$

$$k = 2, \ q = 1, \ldots, m).$$

In what follows, our analysis is mostly[186] restricted to regular and payoff-monotonic evolutionary systems (RPMES), i.e., those that satisfy the requirements expressed in Definitions 10.3 and 10.4.

As a preliminary step in the discussion, we start by simply stating the obvious fact that the counterpart of Proposition 10.3 extends immediately from the single-population RD to the whole class of RPMES. We have, that is, the following result.

Proposition 10.5: *Let $\sigma^* = (\sigma_1^*, \sigma_2^*)$ be a Nash equilibrium of the underlying game G. Then, the state $x^* = (x_1^*, x_2^*) = \sigma^*$ is an equilibrium of any RPMES, i.e., $F(x^*) = 0$, where F is its vector field.*

The above proposition underscores the fact that, as it was specifically the case for the RD, *no* "bite" is gained over that afforded by Nash equilibrium by focusing alone on the rest points of *any* RPMES. In fact, one can readily extend the considerations described in Remark 10.1 and show that, whatever might be the RPMES in place,

---

[184] See, e.g., Hirsch and Smale (1974, Chapter 8) for a statement and discussion of this fundamental result of the theory of ordinary differential equations.

[185] Recall the analogous condition (10.15) contemplated for the single-population RD.

[186] An exception can be found in Exercise 10.20, where the evolutionary system considered is *not* regular.

any degenerate population profile is always stationary. Stationarity alone, therefore, allows for too wide a range of possible outcomes and additional robustness requirements must be imposed if more interesting conclusions are to be obtained. This is precisely the route undertaken by the next result, which is a direct analogue of Proposition 10.4 (its proof is left to the reader as Exercise 10.19).

Proposition 10.6: *Let $x^* = (x_1^*, x_2^*)$ be an asymptotically stable equilibrium of an RPMES. Then, if $\sigma^* = x^*$, the strategy pair $\sigma^* = (\sigma_1^*, \sigma_2^*)$ defines a Nash equilibrium of the game G.*

Thus, if one restricts to rest points that satisfy a local robustness criterion (i.e., asymptotic stability), *any* RPMES is sure to deliver the extent of "interagent rationality" captured by the central notion of Nash equilibrium. Nothing is lost, therefore, if instead of the rigid formulation featured by the RD, the evolutionary process is modelled in the more open-ended fashion embodied by the twin conditions of regularity and payoff monotonicity.

But isn't the theoretical scope of asymptotic stability too narrow? What would happen if the evolutionary paths do not start close to some asymptotically stable equilibrium or, even worse, no such equilibrium exists? Indeed, the latter concern seems amply justified in the light of former discussion. For example, we have found that the basic static notion, ESS, is subject to serious existence problems (recall Subsection 10.2.3), or the canonical dynamic model embodied by the RD displays nonconvergent behavior even in very simple examples (cf. Subsection 10.3.3.2). And, obviously, those problems can just be expected to worsen now, in view of the substantially higher generality allowed by the notion of RPMES.

In view of the former considerations, we are led to the following question: Is some extent of rationality still attainable along an evolutionary process when the induced paths do not converge? As a preliminary negative conclusion in this respect, we may readily assert that, in the absence of convergence, no *equilibrium* behavior may ever materialize in the long run. (This simply follows from the fact that, as established by Proposition 10.5, every Nash equilibrium defines a rest point for *any* RPMES.) Thus, by way of "compromise," we may then ask: Is it nevertheless possible that some milder form of rationality may eventually arise? This, at last, has a reasonably positive answer. For, as we shall see, the quite *weak* form of rationality that eschews playing *strongly* dominated strategies is bound to prevail in the long run when the underlying evolutionary system is regular and payoff monotonic.

To make the former claim precise, we first need to discuss in some detail two of the different concepts of dominance that can be considered in a strategic-form game. On the one hand, there is the most common notion of dominance (sometimes, labeled "strict"), which was introduced in Definition 2.1. As it will be recalled, this notion declares a certain pure strategy s_{kq} of player k *dominated* if there is some mixed strategy σ_k that provides this player with a payoff higher than s_k against *any* profile of opponents' strategies. As it turns out, this concept is too weak for any RPMES to be effective (see more on this below). This suggests considering a stronger requirement of dominance that pronounces a certain strategy s_{kq} dominated only if there is some alternative *pure* strategy s_{kr}, which provides uniformly higher payoff than s_{kq}. If such stronger version of dominance is contemplated, clear-cut conclusions can be obtained. Specifically, any strategy that is dominated in the latter sense will be shown to have its frequency vanish along every interior path induced by *any* RPMES (Proposition 10.7 below).

For the sake of completeness, let us add to Definition 2.1 a precise formulation of the stronger dominance concept additionally considered here but particularized to the present bilateral case.

Definition 10.5: *Let G be a bilateral game as described above. The strategy $s_{kq} \in S_k$ of player k is dominated in pure strategies if there exists some $s_{kr} \in S_k$ such that*

$$\forall s_{\ell u} \in S_\ell \quad (\ell \neq k), \quad \pi_k(s_{kr}, s_{\ell u}) > \pi_k(s_{kq}, s_{\ell u}). \tag{10.32}$$

As advanced, we now establish the following result.

Proposition 10.7 (Samuelson and Zhang, 1992): *Let $x(\cdot)$ be a path induced by a RPMES that starts at interior initial conditions, i.e., $x(0) \in \text{int}(\Delta^{n-1} \times \Delta^{m-1})$. Then, if some s_{kq} is dominated in pure strategies ($k = 1$, $q = 1, \ldots, n$ or $k = 2$, $q = 1, \ldots, m$), $\lim_{t \to \infty} x_{kq}(t) = 0$.*

Proof: Let $x(\cdot)$ be a path as indicated, and suppose that some pure strategy s_{kq} is dominated for player (population) k. Then, from (10.32) and the compactness of the mixed-strategy spaces, there is some $s_{kr} \in S_k$ and some $\varepsilon > 0$ such that

$$\forall \sigma_\ell \in \Sigma_\ell \quad (\ell \neq k), \quad \pi_k(s_{kr}, \sigma_\ell) - \pi_k(s_{kq}, \sigma_\ell) \geq \varepsilon.$$

Thus, by the assumed regularity and payoff monotonicity of the evolutionary process, it follows that there exists some $\eta > 0$ such that, for all $x \in \text{int}(\Delta^{n-1} \times \Delta^{m-1})$,

$$\frac{F_{kr}(x)}{x_{kr}} - \frac{F_{kq}(x)}{x_{kq}} \geq \eta$$

and therefore, for all $t \geq 0$,

$$\frac{\dot{x}_{kr}(t)}{x_{kr}(t)} - \frac{\dot{x}_{kq}(t)}{x_{kq}(t)} \geq \eta, \tag{10.33}$$

where we rely on the fact that, since $x(0) \in \text{int}(\Delta^{n-1} \times \Delta^{m-1})$, we also have that $x(t) \in \text{int}(\Delta^{n-1} \times \Delta^{m-1})$ for all $t > 0$ (cf. Exercise 10.18). Define the variable $z(t) \equiv x_{kr}(t)/x_{kq}(t)$. Then, it is immediate to compute that

$$\frac{\dot{z}(t)}{z(t)} = \frac{\dot{x}_{kr}(t)}{x_{kr}(t)} - \frac{\dot{x}_{kq}(t)}{x_{kq}(t)}$$

and, therefore, in view of (10.33), we can write

$$z(t) \geq z(0) e^{\eta t}$$

which obviously implies that $z(t) \to \infty$ and therefore $x_{kq}(t) \to 0$, as desired.   ∎

Let us end our present discussion with three different remarks that elaborate and complement the previous analysis in some important respects.

Remark 10.2: *Iterative dominance*

As explained in Section 2.1, much of the effectiveness in the use of dominance arguments comes from the repeated use of it. That is, once a dominated strategy is removed (i.e., discarded as possible rational play), it may happen that other strategies that did not originally appear as dominated become so. This may then bring the elimination procedure much further than a single application of it would alone allow.

Since any RPMES eliminates over time (i.e. "eductively")[187] any dominated strategy, it should be clear that it must also reproduce the "deductive" arguments that underlie repeated elimination. For, once the frequency of a certain dominated strategy becomes insignificant, other strategies that appear as dominated in the former's absence will have their frequencies converge to zero in turn.

Naturally, the dynamic process of elimination thus induced proves particularly interesting when it leads to a *unique* pure-strategy profile. In that case, the underlying game may be called *dominance-solvable in pure strategies*, in analogy with the similar (but weaker) concept introduced in Section 2.1. In such games, it follows as an immediate corollary of the former considerations that any RPMES guarantees *global* convergence (from any point in the interior of the state space) to the monomorphic profile where each population plays its single iteratively undominated strategy. ◆

Remark 10.3: *Dominance in mixed strategies and the RD*

For the customary notion of dominance that allows for dominating mixed strategies (i.e., as formulated in Definition 2.1), even though not all RPMES are certain to carry out over time the iterative elimination of dominated strategies, some such processes do. In particular, the RD (which is of course a particular RPMES) eliminates all those strategies that are iteratively dominated in that sense, as the reader is asked to prove in Exercise 10.21. ◆

Remark 10.4: *Weak dominance*

Along the lines of Remark 10.3, one is led to wonder whether there are *some* evolutionary systems that might prove effective in removing behavior that is dominated in a sense even weaker than any of those two contemplated above. Consider, for example, the notion labeled *weak dominance*, which was introduced in Definition 4.9. Then, as we illustrate in what follows, it

---

[187] The term *eductive* was suggested by Binmore (1987, 1988) to refer to a gradual process of learning in "real time" that is to be contrasted with a timeless process of pure deductive reasoning.

turns out that *not* even the canonical RD is able to guarantee that a strategy that is weakly dominated in this sense is eliminated in the long run.

As the reader might recall, a certain (pure) strategy is said to be weakly dominated if there exists some mixed strategy that ensures no lower (but sometimes strictly higher) payoff against whatever strategy profile might be played by the opponents. To see that the RD might not be effective in discarding such weakly dominated strategies, let us rely on the simple bilateral game proposed by Samuelson and Zhang (1992) with the following payoff matrices:

$$A = \begin{pmatrix} 1 & 1 \\ 1 & 0 \end{pmatrix}; \qquad B = \begin{pmatrix} 1 & 0 \\ 1 & 0 \end{pmatrix}. \tag{10.34}$$

Note that, in this game, each player has her second strategy dominated (s_{12} and s_{22}, respectively). Nevertheless, while that of player 1 (i.e., s_{12}) is only weakly so, that of the second player (s_{22}) is dominated in the strongest sense – i.e., there exists a *pure* strategy that provides a strictly higher payoff for every strategy of the opponent.

Now, if one applies the RD to this example, Proposition 10.7 readily implies that s_{22} must have its frequency x_{22} vanish in the long run. In contrast, however, this does *not* happen for s_{12}, the weakly dominated strategy of population 1. The intuition here is that, as $x_{22} \rightarrow 0$, the payoff disadvantage of s_{12} versus s_{11} dwindles as well, slowing down very substantially the decrease of the former's frequency, x_{12}. Eventually, as it turns out, the latter consideration becomes preeminent, thus leading to a long-run frequency for s_{12} that remains bounded above zero. An indication on how to provide a formal proof of this conclusion may be found in Exercise 10.22.   ◆

10.4.3 *Examples*

10.4.3.1 *Trading complementarities.* Consider the following economic environment, which is inspired by the well-known work of Diamond (1982). There are two disjoint populations, 1 and 2. At any given point in time, every member of each population is in one of two states: employed or unemployed. In the former case, she produces $y > 0$ units of consumption and incurs a utility cost of $c > 0$; in the latter case, she simply produces no output and incurs no cost.

Suppose the good produced by either population can be consumed only by the individuals of the other population – i.e., the consumption of the good produced by oneself is impossible. If an individual consumes y units of the good produced by the other population she obtains a payoff equal to y. Thus, assuming that $c < y$, there is the potential for mutually *beneficial trade* if two employed individuals meet.

As is customary, let us assume that, at each point in (continuous) time t, individuals are randomly matched in pairs. If two employed individuals meet, they trade and each obtains a net payoff equal to $y - c$. On the other hand, if two agents who happen to be unemployed are matched, no trade of course can take place and their payoff is zero for both. Finally, if an employed individual meets an unemployed one, again no exchange is supposed to take place, which implies that the former obtains a negative payoff of $-c$, whereas the latter earns a payoff of zero.

The interaction between any two individuals of each population can be formalized by a bilateral game with the following payoff matrices:

$$A = \begin{pmatrix} 0 & 0 \\ -c & y-c \end{pmatrix} \qquad B = \begin{pmatrix} 0 & -c \\ 0 & y-c \end{pmatrix},$$

where the first strategy (s_{k1}, $k = 1, 2$) is interpreted as "unemployed," and the second one (s_{k2}, $k = 1, 2$) is interpreted as "employed." Note that the matrix B is simply the transpose of A. This reflects the fact that, even though the game has been formulated as a bimatrix (possibly asymmetric) game, it is nevertheless symmetric. Despite this symmetry, however, the interaction takes place between two distinct populations. It cannot be modeled, therefore, as in Section 10.3, with the members of a single population internally matched among themselves. It requires instead the two-population approach postulated here.

Assume that the population dynamics is governed by some RPMES. Then, we have five rest points. On the one hand, there are the four monomorphic states (i.e., states in which each population behaves homogeneously), from which we single out the following two:

$$\hat{x} = [(1, 0), (1, 0)]$$
$$\check{x} = [(0, 1), (0, 1)].$$

The first of these states, $\hat{x}$, has *all* the individuals of both populations unemployed, while the second one, $\check{x}$, has them employed. Furthermore, there is also the polymorphic rest point

$$\tilde{x} = \left[\left(1 - \frac{c}{y}, \frac{c}{y} \right), \left(1 - \frac{c}{y}, \frac{c}{y} \right) \right],$$

where there is a positive fraction of each type (employed and unemployed) in both populations.

Turning now to the dynamics, the following first observation should be clear. By virtue of the assumed payoff monotonicity, if the system starts in the interior of the state space with a sufficiently high fraction of employed (unemployed) agents in *both* populations, the ensuing path converges to the state in which everyone in each population is employed (unemployed). Or, more precisely, we have

$$\left[x_{k1}(0) > 1 - \frac{c}{y}, \; k = 1, 2 \right] \Rightarrow \lim_{t \to \infty} x(t) = [(1, 0), (1, 0)]$$

$$\left[x_{k2}(0) > \frac{c}{y}, \; k = 1, 2 \right] \Rightarrow \lim_{t \to \infty} x(t) = [(0, 1), (0, 1)].$$

In the remaining, less clear-cut case where the initial profile satisfies

$$\left[x_{k1}(0) - \left(1 - \frac{c}{y} \right) \right] \left[x_{\ell 1}(0) - \left(1 - \frac{c}{y} \right) \right] \equiv \left[x_{k2}(0) - \frac{c}{y} \right] \left[x_{\ell 2}(0) - \frac{c}{y} \right] < 0$$

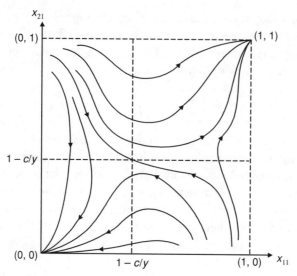

Figure 10.2: Trading complementarities under an RPMES.

for each $k, \ell = 1, 2$ ($k \neq \ell$), the induced path will also lead to one of the two monomorphic states, $\hat{x}$ or $\check{x}$, except for a "thin" (i.e., one-dimensional) subspace that by itself defines a path leading to the polymorphic (but very fragile) state $\tilde{x}$. In fact, this subspace precisely separates the basins of attraction of $\hat{x}$ and $\check{x}$ (i.e., the respective set of initial conditions from which convergence ensues toward each of them). This state of affairs is illustrated in Figure 10.2.

10.4.3.2 *Risky trading.* Consider again a trading context between two distinct and large populations, 1 and 2, whose members are matched in pairs (one individual from each population) at every point in time $t \in \mathbb{R}_+$. Every individual owns two *indivisible* units of a certain *population-specific* good. These goods provide a certain utility (say a constant payoff of 1 per each unit) if consumed alone. However, if either of them is consumed in combination with the other good in equal proportions, the utility of both goods is doubled (i.e., each unit attains a payoff of 2 if consumed in combination with another unit of the other good).

Clearly, this setup shares with the former example the feature that there are gains from trade – in particular, these gains fully materialize if one of the two units of the good originally held by each individual is "symmetrically" exchanged by one unit of the good in the hands of the other. There are, however, two key differences with the previous example. First, no costs are assumed for holding or producing the good owned by each individual. Second, the interaction is taken to be *non*symmetric, as described next.

Populations 1 and 2 display a different range of possible behavior. The essential difference between them is that the individuals of population 1 are *potentially* aggressive. Specifically, there is a certain fraction of them, $x_{11} \in [0, 1]$, who adopts the aggressive strategy s_{11}. This strategy results in the forceful deprivation of the amount held by the potential trading partner if the latter does not play protectively (see below). Aggressive behavior, however, is assumed to incur a *utility cost* of 1. In contrast, the complementary fraction $x_{12}(=1-x_{11})$ is peaceful and adopts the strategy s_{12}, which involves trading peacefully (and at no cost) one unit of the good originally owned for one of the units owned by the partner.

The individuals of population 2, on the other hand, can also adopt one of two possible strategies. The first one, s_{21}, involves playing protectively. This safeguards the two units owned by the individual, even in the presence of aggressive behavior on the partner's part. Thus, if the partner indeed plays aggressively, this strategy earns a payoff equal to 2 (resulting from the consumption of the two units owned). Instead, if the partner plays peacefully, there are gains from trade (with a gross total payoff of 4) but the individual of population 2 suffers a utility loss (say, due to "personal embarrassment") equal to 3. Thus, the resulting net payoff in this case is just equal to 1. The second strategy available to population 2, s_{22}, does not provide any protection. Thus, if aggressive behavior is met, it entails the loss of the full two units of the good originally owned and an additional utility loss of 1 – therefore, it leads to a net payoff equal to -1. If, on the contrary, the opponent is peaceful, the whole gains of trade are enjoyed and thus a net payoff of 4 is earned. As usual, the frequencies with which each of those two strategies is played in population 2 are denoted by x_{21} and x_{22}, respectively.

Combining all of the above considerations, the bilateral game faced by each pair of matched individuals may be described by the following two payoff tables[188]:

$$A = \begin{pmatrix} 1 \times 2 - 1 & 4 \times 2 - 1 \\ 2 \times 2 - 0 & 2 \times 2 - 0 \end{pmatrix} = \begin{pmatrix} 1 & 7 \\ 4 & 4 \end{pmatrix}$$

$$B = \begin{pmatrix} 1 \times 2 - 0 & 0 \times 2 - 1 \\ 2 \times 2 - 3 & 2 \times 2 - 0 \end{pmatrix} = \begin{pmatrix} 2 & -1 \\ 1 & 4 \end{pmatrix}.$$

$$(10.35)$$

Suppose, for concreteness, that the population dynamics in this context may be described by the RD. That is, the laws of motion for each population profile are given by the following two-dimensional system (note that $x_{k2}(t) = 1 - x_{k1}(t)$ for all t and each $k = 1, 2$):

$$\dot{x}_{11}(t) = x_{11}(t) \Big\{ x_{21}(t) + 7(1 - x_{21}(t))$$
$$- \Big[\begin{array}{l} x_{11}(t)(x_{21}(t) + 7(1 - x_{21}(t))) + \\ (1 - x_{11}(t))(4x_{21}(t) + 4(1 - x_{21}(t))) \end{array} \Big] \Big\}$$

$$\dot{x}_{21}(t) = x_{21}(t) \Big\{ 2x_{11}(t) + (1 - x_{11}(t))$$
$$- \Big[\begin{array}{l} x_{21}(t)(2x_{11}(t) + (1 - x_{11}(t))) + \\ (1 - x_{21}(t))(-x_{11}(t) + 4(1 - x_{11}(t))) \end{array} \Big] \Big\}.$$

---

[188] In these payoff matrices, all entries are of the form $a \times b - c$, where a is the number of units consumed, b is the utility per unit, and c is the possible cost entailed.

It can be shown (see Hofbauer and Sigmund, 1988, Chapter 27) that, for any generic 2×2 game displaying a *unique* completely mixed Nash equilibrium, the interior paths induced by the corresponding two-population RD lead to *closed* orbits around the equilibrium frequencies. Thus, in this sense, the dynamic behavior of this class of games is akin to that observed for the rock–scissors–paper game in Subsection 10.3.3.2. Since the bimatrix game given by (10.35) matches the required hypothesis (i.e., displays a unique mixed-strategy Nash equilibrium), let us attempt to provide a direct (constructive) confirmation of the aforementioned result in the context of the present example.

First, note that, as was argued for the single-population case (recall Subsection 10.3.1), the two-population RD also satisfies (a suitable version of) the property we called *additive invariance of payoffs*. That is, additive and independent transformations of the payoff matrix of each population that leave relative payoff differences unaffected have no bearing on the induced dynamics. This allows us to replace the previous payoff matrices, A and B in (10.35), by the following ones:

$$A' = \begin{pmatrix} -3 & 0 \\ 0 & -3 \end{pmatrix} \qquad B' = \begin{pmatrix} 3 & 0 \\ 0 & 3 \end{pmatrix},$$

where we simply add -4 to the first *column* of A (i.e., to its two entries) and -7 to the second, whereas we add 1 to the first *row* of B and -1 to the second. The game then becomes zero sum and the dynamics can be written in the following simplified form:

$$\dot{x}_{11}(t) = x_{11}(t)\{-3x_{21}(t) - [-3x_{11}(t)x_{21}(t) - 3(1 - x_{11}(t))(1 - x_{21}(t))]\}$$
$$= x_{11}(t)[1 - x_{11}(t)][3 - 6x_{21}(t)]$$
$$\dot{x}_{21}(t) = x_{21}(t)\{3x_{11}(t) - [3x_{11}(t)x_{21}(t) + 3(1 - x_{11}(t))(1 - x_{21}(t))]\}$$
$$= x_{21}(t)[1 - x_{21}(t)][-3 + 6x_{11}(t)].$$

Now introduce the function $\zeta : [0, 1] \times [0, 1] \to \mathbb{R}$ given by

$$\zeta(x_{11}, x_{21}) = \log x_{11} + \log(1 - x_{11}) + \log x_{21} + \log(1 - x_{21}).$$

This function defines a *constant of motion*, as the following computations show:

$$\dot{\zeta}(x_{11}(t), x_{21}(t)) = \frac{\dot{x}_{11}(t)}{x_{11}(t)} - \frac{\dot{x}_{11}(t)}{1 - x_{11}(t)} + \frac{\dot{x}_{21}(t)}{x_{21}(t)} - \frac{\dot{x}_{21}(t)}{1 - x_{21}(t)}$$
$$= [1 - x_{11}(t)][3 - 6x_{21}(t)] - x_{11}(t)[3 - 6x_{21}(t)]$$
$$+ [1 - x_{21}(t)][-3 + 6x_{11}(t)] - x_{21}(t)[-3 + 6x_{11}(t)]$$
$$= 0.$$

We conclude, therefore, that any interior path of the system moves along some level curve of the function ζ, i.e., a locus of states of the form $\{x = [(x_{11}, x_{12}), (x_{21}, x_{22})] \in \Delta \times \Delta : \zeta(x_{11}, x_{21}) = K\}$ for some $K \in \mathbb{R}$ given. Since these loci are one-dimensional, they must coincide with the trajectories of the system, thus confirming that the latter indeed give rise to *closed orbits*. The resulting dynamics is illustrated in Figure 10.3.

Table 10.1: *A prisonner's dilemma*

1 \ 2	C	D
C	3,3	0,4
D	4,0	1,1

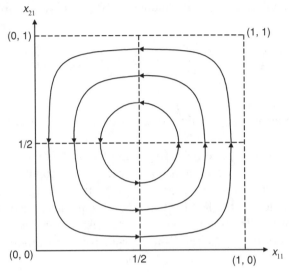

Figure 10.3: Risky trading under RD.

10.5   Evolution of cooperation: an example

To close this chapter, we provide an additional illustration that focuses on the long-standing issue of whether (and how) cooperation may consolidate in a large-population context. Both in classical and evolutionary game theory alike, this topic has attracted much attention and has been approached from a wide variety of alternative viewpoints. Here, we adopt a simple perspective and study a very stylized framework that casts the phenomenon of evolution and the notion of cooperation in its most paradigmatic forms: the RD on the one hand, and the repeated prisoner's dilemma on the other.[189]

Consider a large (continuum) population whose members are randomly matched in pairs to play a simple version of the infinitely repeated prisoner's dilemma (IRPD). Specifically, let us suppose that the *stage* game (i.e., the one-shot prisoner's dilemma) is as described by Table 10.1 and, in the infinitely repeated game, players may adopt one of only three strategies:

- Strategy C^*, which chooses action C in every stage, irrespectively of past history;
- Strategy D^*, which chooses action D in every stage, again irrespectively of past history;

[189] Most of the modeling details here are borrowed from Vega-Redondo (1996).

- Strategy *TFT* (tit-for-tat), which starts by choosing C and then mimics the action by the opponent in the previous stage.

Suppose that, over any whole string of play of the *repeated* game, the players' intertemporal payoffs are identified with the flow of stage payoffs discounted at the rate $\delta = 2/3$ and, as customary (recall Section 8.2), the corresponding discounted sum is scaled down by the factor $(1 - \delta) = 1/3$. Then, it may be easily checked that the strategic-form representation of the induced IRPD displays the following payoff matrix:

$$A = \begin{pmatrix} 3 & 0 & 3 \\ 4 & 1 & 2 \\ 3 & 2/3 & 3 \end{pmatrix},$$

where the strategies are arranged (and thus indexed by $j = 1, 2, 3$) in the same order as listed above.

As advanced, we want to study the behavior of the RD in this context. In effect, its relevant state space is two-dimensional, because the population states $x = (x_1, x_2, x_3)$ belong to the two-dimensional simplex. It is enough, therefore, to describe the law of motion of the RD for two of the frequencies involved. For concreteness, let us choose x_2 (the frequency of D^* strategists or *flat defectors*) and x_3 (that of *TFT* strategists or *reciprocators*). Their respective laws of motion are as follows:

$$\dot{x}_2(t) = x_2(t) \left\{ \begin{array}{l} 4(1 - x_2(t) - x_3(t)) + x_2(t) + 2x_3(t) \\[6pt] - \left[\begin{array}{l} 3(1 - x_2(t) - x_3(t))(1 - x_2(t)) \\ +x_2(t)(4(1 - x_2(t) - x_3(t)) + x_2(t) + 2x_3(t)) \\ +x_3(t)(3(1 - x_2(t)) + 2/3\, x_2(t)) \end{array} \right] \end{array} \right\}$$

$$\dot{x}_3(t) = x_3(t) \left\{ \begin{array}{l} 3(1 - x_2(t)) + 2/3\, x_2(t)) \\[6pt] - \left[\begin{array}{l} 3(1 - x_2(t) - x_3(t))(1 - x_2(t)) \\ +x_2(t)(4(1 - x_2(t) - x_3(t)) + x_2(t) + 2x_3(t)) \\ +x_3(t)(3(1 - x_2(t)) + 2/3\, x_2(t)) \end{array} \right] \end{array} \right\},$$

which can be simplified to

$$\dot{x}_2(t) = x_2(t) \left[1 - x_2(t) - 2x_3(t) + \frac{4}{3} x_2(t)\, x_3(t) \right] \tag{10.36}$$

$$\dot{x}_3(t) = x_3(t) \left[-\frac{1}{3} x_2(t) + \frac{4}{3} x_2(t)\, x_3(t) \right]. \tag{10.37}$$

Let us start by identifying the rest points of the system. On the one hand, of course, we have that all three *monomorphic* states are stationary. These correspond to the points $(1, 0)$, $(0, 1)$, and $(0, 0)$, where recall that the state of the system specifies only the frequencies of D^* and TFT strategists. The rest points $(0, 0)$ and $(0, 1)$ reflect configurations where there are no defectors and the *whole* population is *either* a cooperator or a reciprocator. But, clearly, not only these two latter states but also all those defector-free states in the set

$$H \equiv \{(0, x_3) : 0 \le x_3 \le 1\} \tag{10.38}$$

are rest points of the RD as well.

Finally, there is an additional rest point of the system consisting of the state $(\tilde{x}_2, \tilde{x}_3)$ where there are no cooperators (i.e., $\tilde{x}_2 + \tilde{x}_3 = 1$) and the individuals adopting D^* obtain the same payoffs as those choosing TFT. To compute this point, let $\pi(s, (x_2, x_3))$ denote the expected (or average) payoff earned by strategy $s \in \{C^*, D^*, TFT\}$ when the population state is given by (x_2, x_3). Then, to determine $(\tilde{x}_2, \tilde{x}_3)$, one must solve

$$\pi(D^*, (\tilde{x}_2, \tilde{x}_3)) = \pi(TFT, (\tilde{x}_2, \tilde{x}_3))$$

or

$$4 - 3\tilde{x}_2 - 2\tilde{x}_3 = 3 - \frac{7}{3}\tilde{x}_2, \tag{10.39}$$

which leads to $\tilde{x}_2 = 3/4, \tilde{x}_3 = 1/4$.

Let us now check the robustness (i.e., stability) of each of the aforementioned rest points. First, we note that the profile $(1, 0)$ where every individual chooses D^* is asymptotically stable. To see this observe that, if $\varepsilon > 0$ is chosen sufficiently small, any (x_2, x_3) such that $x_2 \ge 1 - \varepsilon$ satisfies

$$\pi(D^*, (x_2, x_3)) > \bar{\pi}(x_2, x_3),$$

where

$$\bar{\pi}(x_2, x_3) \equiv x\,Ax = 3 - 2x_2 - \frac{4}{3}x_2 x_3$$

stands for the average payoff earned by the *whole* population. It should be clear, therefore, that $(1, 0)$ meets the two requirements demanded for asymptotic stability in Definition 10.2.

Next, we turn to assessing the stability of the rest points in the set H, as defined in (10.38). In this case, a key role in the discussion is played by the point $(0, \hat{x}_3)$ characterized by

$$\pi(D^*, (0, \hat{x}_3)) = \bar{\pi}(0, \hat{x}_3) \tag{10.40}$$

or

$$4 - 2\hat{x}_3 = 3,$$

which implies that $\hat{x}_3 = 1/2$. At the state $(0, 1/2)$, any "infinitesimal" number of defectors that might hypothetically arise (i.e., a set of zero measure not affecting the population profile) would earn a payoff exactly equal to the population average. The frequency of reciprocators marking this state, $\hat{x}_3 = 1/2$, can be used to partition the set H into two subsets:

$$H_1 = \{(0, x_3) : x_3 \geq 1/2\} \tag{10.41}$$

$$H_2 = \{(0, x_3) : x_3 < 1/2\}. \tag{10.42}$$

As explained below, these two subsets turn out to display quite different stability properties.

On the one hand, for any given point in H_1, it can be shown that every trajectory that starts close to it remains nearby in the sense required by Liapunov stability (Condition (1) of Definition 10.2) but does not generally converge to it (i.e., its Condition (2) fails). The formal proof of this conclusion is left to the reader in Exercise 10.23. Nevertheless, the intuitive reason for it is quite clear. Suppose that a particular point in H_1 is subject to some (small) perturbation. Then, even if this perturbation brings in some defectors, the fact that the *TFT* strategists are still (roughly) no fewer than half of the whole population precludes those defectors from gaining much advantage by exploiting cooperators. In particular, their payoff must always be less than the population average and, consequently, their frequency will fall over time. In the limit, the system will return to the set H (i.e., to some state with no defectors) not far away from the point originally perturbed. In general, however, it will not return to that same point. To illustrate this claim, suppose, for example, that the contemplated perturbation introduces some new defectors but the frequency of *TFT* strategists remains unchanged. Then, the latter will enjoy some small (and decreasing) advantage against all other individuals along the ensuing trajectory, in turn leading to a slight increase in their frequency over time. In the limit, the path *cannot* return to the original point, thus violating the convergence condition required for asymptotic stability.

Polar considerations suggest that, in contrast, *no* point in the complementary subset $H_2 = H \backslash H_1$ can even be Liapunov stable. For any of these points, a perturbation that introduces some defectors will lead to a temporary *increase* in the latter's frequency that, unavoidably, will bring the limit point of the trajectory relatively far from the original point (even if it returns to the set H). In fact, the final frequency of *TFT* strategists can be seen to lie always above $1/2$, the dividing threshold between H_1 and H_2 – that is, the limit state will belong to the set H_1, the complement (in H) of the set where the path started. Again, a formal proof of this conclusion is part of Exercise 10.23.

Finally, let us consider the rest point $(\tilde{x}_2, \tilde{x}_3) = (3/4, 1/4)$. To show that this point is not asymptotically (not even Liapunov) stable, consider for example the profile $(3/4 + \zeta, 1/4 - \zeta)$ for any $\zeta > 0$. From (10.39) we readily obtain

$$\pi(D^*, (3/4 + \zeta, 1/4 - \zeta)) > \pi(TFT, (3/4 + \zeta, 1/4 - \zeta)),$$

which implies that any trajectory starting at *any* such point (i.e., a point of the form $(\tilde{x}_2 + \zeta, \tilde{x}_3 - \zeta)$) will converge to $(1, 0)$, i.e., will move away from $(\tilde{x}_2, \tilde{x}_3)$.

The above discussion focuses on issues of stability that are purely local, i.e., that pertain to how the system behaves around its rest points. Can we say something about its global dynamics, possibly far from the rest points? Certainly, the former discussion makes it apparent that there can be no *globally* absorbing state that attracts *every* possible trajectory (even if we restrict to interior ones). Initial conditions, in other words, crucially matter. Thus, in understanding the global dynamics of the system, the aim must be to partition the set of initial conditions into a number of disjoint subsets, each of them associated to a different regularity displayed by long-run behavior.

To this end, the following claim turns out to be very useful. To ascertain whether the frequency of *TFT* strategists is to increase at a particular (interior) state, the *only* relevant consideration is whether these players are in sufficient "critical mass." Or, to express it somewhat more precisely, the direction of change in the frequency of reciprocators depends only on their current frequency x_3 being above or below a certain threshold, *independently* of how the rest of the population is distributed between defectors and cooperators. To verify this claim, the RD formulation suggests focusing on the difference between the payoff earned by *TFT* strategists and the population-average payoff. This difference is readily computed as follows:

$$\pi(TFT, (x_2, x_3)) - \bar{\pi}(x_2, x_3) = \left(3 - \frac{7}{3}x_2\right) - \left(3 - 2x_2 - \frac{4}{3}x_2 x_3\right)$$

$$= -\frac{1}{3}x_2 + \frac{4}{3}x_2 x_3 \qquad (10.43)$$

and, therefore, as long as $x_2 > 0$,

$$\pi(TFT, (x_2, x_3)) - \bar{\pi}(x_2, x_3) \lessgtr 0 \Leftrightarrow x_3 \lessgtr \frac{1}{4},$$

which, as dictated by the RD, implies that the following condition must hold at interior states:

$$\forall t \geq 0, \quad \dot{x}_3(t) \lessgtr 0 \Leftrightarrow x_3(t) \lessgtr \frac{1}{4}. \qquad (10.44)$$

The above simple characterization has a sharp bearing on the global dynamics of the system. It implies, in particular, that the long-run state is a cooperative one (i.e., all defectors eventually disappear) if, and only if, the *initial* number of reciprocators is high enough. More precisely, this conclusion can be formulated as follows. Let $(x_2(\cdot), x_3(\cdot))$ be an *interior* trajectory of the RD given by (10.36) and (10.37). Then,

$$\lim_{t \to \infty} x_2(t) = 0 \Leftrightarrow x_3(0) > \frac{1}{4}. \qquad (10.45)$$

To verify (10.45), let us address in turn each of the following two (exhaustive) possibilities:

(i) $x_3(0) \leq 1/4$;
(ii) $x_3(0) > 1/4$.

In Case (i), it follows from (10.43) and (10.44) that

$$\frac{\dot{x}_3(t)}{x_3(t)} = x_2(t)\left(-\frac{1}{3} + \frac{4}{3}x_3(t)\right) \leq x_2(t)\left(-\frac{1}{3} + \frac{4}{3}x_3(0)\right) \leq 0$$

for all $t \geq 0$, i.e., the frequency of reciprocators can never increase. Thus, since *TFT* weakly dominates C^*, the frequency of cooperators cannot increase either and, consequently, $\dot{x}_2(t) \geq 0$, i.e., the frequency of flat defectors cannot fall. But then, given that the initial conditions are assumed interior, $\lim_{t \to \infty} x_2(t) \geq x_2(0) > 0$, which implies that the long-run state is not fully cooperative.

Let us now take up Case (ii). Because $x_3(0) > 1/4$, we may rely again on the fact that

$$\frac{\dot{x}_3(t)}{x_3(t)} = x_2(t) \left(-\frac{1}{3} + \frac{4}{3} x_3(t) \right)$$

to assert that

$$\frac{\dot{x}_3(t)}{x_3(t)} \geq \eta x_2(t) \tag{10.46}$$

for some given η satisfying

$$\eta \geq \frac{4}{3} \left(x_3(0) - \frac{1}{4} \right) > 0.$$

If, contrary to what is claimed, it were *not* the case that $\lim_{t \to \infty} x_2(t) = 0$, (10.46) would imply that $x_3(\cdot)$ must grow without bound, an absurdity that establishes the desired conclusion.

To sum up, expression (10.45) provides a stark manifestation of the crucial role played by reciprocating behavior in the model. Whether enough of it is present at the beginning of the process is the *sole* feature of the initial conditions that matters to predict the (un)cooperative nature of the long-run state. Initial conditions indeed matter, as it could not be otherwise given the inherent complementarities displayed by the two sorts of cooperative strategies present in our model. But they matter in an especially sharp and simple fashion, as explained above and illustrated in Figure 10.4.

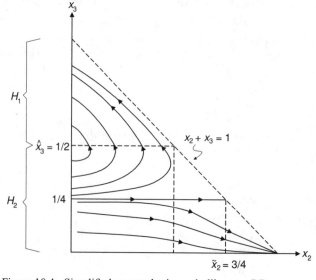

Figure 10.4: Simplified repeated prisoner's dilemma, RD.

The primary aim of this chapter has been to explore the extent to which the received notions of rationality and equilibrium that underlie classical game theory can be provided with a robust evolutionary basis. Traditionally, economists have relied on heuristic arguments to defend the idea that, under sufficiently stringent selection (e.g., "market") forces, rational behavior should be expected to prevail in the long run. To investigate this idea rigorously, we have focused on the paradigmatic context where individuals of one (or several) large population(s) are randomly matched in pairs to play a certain game. Our analysis has advanced along the following steps.

First, we have pursued a static approach, centered on the fundamental notion of evolutionarily stable strategy (ESS). This "equilibrium" concept captures the simple idea of a (single) large population that is monomorphically playing a common strategy, possibly mixed, and is able to expel (through higher payoffs) any small fraction of mutants who might threaten to invade it. We have shown that the ESS concept partially achieves the desired objective: it induces a Nash equilibrium and is therefore consistent with the classical notion of game-theoretic rationality. It is also subject, however, to important conceptual problems. Among others, it rules out by construction polymorphic situations (thus lacking a dynamic foundation that might be judged satisfactory) and is subject to serious existence problems.

Motivated by these important drawbacks, we have next undertaken an explicitly dynamic approach that allows for a population that is fully polymorphic to interact over time through different (pure) strategies. First, the focus has been on the canonical model of evolutionary dynamics that reflects Darwinian selection, i.e., the so-called replicator dynamics (RD). Again, we have found that, in a certain sense, it provides support for Nash equilibrium. Specifically, its robust (asymptotically stable) rest points give rise to population states (i.e., strategy frequencies) that match the probabilities displayed by some Nash equilibrium of the underlying game. Thus, in the language of Chapter 4, it induces a refinement of Nash equilibrium, much as the ESS was also seen to do. This begs the following question: Which of the two notions, ESS or asymptotic stability, is more "refined"? As it turns out, the ESS notion has been found to be the stricter one, since every ESS state is asymptotically stable. In this sense, therefore, the ESS concept can also be viewed as an indirect way of selecting for dynamically robust population states.

The RD is a sharp model of evolution that is useful as a canonical benchmark but it can hardly be appropriate, in general, for the study of (non-Darwinian) social evolution. To this end, one needs a more flexible framework that can accommodate a diverse number of complementary factors of strategy adjustment: imitation, dissatisfaction, population renewal, etc. This idea is captured by the abstract notion of payoff-monotonic evolutionary systems. These are general dynamical systems that respect the key qualitative requirement of payoff responsiveness that is the mark of evolutionary selection, i.e., the basic idea that higher payoff strategies should prosper at the expense of those earning lower payoffs. We have seen that this requirement is enough to guarantee much of what was shown to be true concerning the RD – in particular, every asymptotically stable state still corresponds to a Nash equilibrium of the underlying game. Furthermore, even if the analytical scope is widened to include arbitrary (possibly nonconvergent) paths, payoff monotonicity turns out to be enough to guarantee that, in the long run, the most blatant irrationalities are weeded out. For example, every strategy that is dominated (perhaps after iterative deletion) by another pure strategy must see its frequency dwindle to zero over time.

The different theoretical developments of this chapter have been illustrated by a number of classical examples in the evolutionary and economic literature, i.e., the hawk–dove and rock–scissors–paper games, as well as trading games displaying complementarities or risk. To conclude the chapter, we have turned to another example that has been repeatedly used as a test scenario for evolutionary game-theoretic ideas: the repeated prisoner's dilemma. We have considered a simplified version of it with three strategies (flat cooperation, flat defection, and tit-for-tat) and studied in this context the long-run implications of the RD. The role played by reciprocity in the rise and consolidation of cooperation has arisen very starkly. Specifically, it has been shown that there exists a knife-edge threshold for the *initial* frequency of the reciprocating tit-for-tat strategists such that cooperation will materialize in the long run if, and only if, this threshold is exceeded.

Exercises

Exercise 10.1: Recall the hawk–dove game whose payoff matrix A is given by (10.6) and suppose that $V = C$. Find all ESS under random pairwise matching.

Exercise 10.2: Consider a generalized rock–scissors–paper game with payoff matrix A as given by (10.8) except that the payoff earned when a strategy meets itself is some given $\eta \in \mathbb{R}$. Characterize the values of η for which an ESS exists in a random pairwise-matching context with a large (continuum) population.

Exercise 10.3*: Prove that, generically (cf. Footnote 66 in Chapter 4), an ESS exists in any symmetric 2×2 game under random pairwise matching.

Exercise 10.4: Let $G = \{\{1, 2\}, \{S_i\}_{i=1,2}, \{\pi_i\}_{i=1,2}\}$ be a symmetric and bilateral game that is of "pure coordination." That is, for each $i = 1, 2$, and any $s = (s_1, s_2) \in S_1 \times S_2$,

$$\pi_i(s_1, s_2) = \begin{cases} > 0 & \text{if } s_1 = s_2 \\ = 0 & \text{if } s_1 \neq s_2. \end{cases}$$

Under random pairwise matching in a continuum population, characterize (i.e., describe exhaustively) the set of ESS.

Exercise 10.5*: Let there be a large (continuum) population, composed of males and females, who are involved in the so-called *sex-ratio game*. The females are the genuine players of the game in that they are the ones who determine the sex probabilities among their offspring. Suppose there are two options (or possible strategies) in this respect. The first one, strategy s_1, involves a probability of 0.1 that any given offspring be a male (thus 0.9 that it be a female) whereas in the second one, s_2, this probability is 0.6. To produce offspring, every female needs the concourse of a male. However, independently of the characteristics of the male, all females bear the same number of offspring (independently of the latter's sex).

For each female, her payoffs are taken to be proportional to the number of *grand-children* they breed. (Of course, these grandchildren may be obtained either as the offspring of their sons or the offspring of their daughters.) Thus, in contrast with the leading context studied throughout this chapter (cf. Subsection 10.2.1), the players in the present evolutionary game (i.e., the females) *play the field*. Their interaction is *not* conducted through random matching in terms of a fixed bilateral game and, therefore, their expected payoffs are not given by a linear combination of the population frequencies.

1. Define precisely the payoff function of the game, $\pi : S \times S \to \mathbb{R}$, where $\pi(s, s')$ specifies the number of grandchildren bred by a female when her strategy is s and that of the rest of the population is, monomorphically, s'.
2. Redefine the notion of ESS presented in Definition 10.1 for the present context.
3. Show that no pure strategy can be an ESS.
4. Find the unique (mixed-strategy) ESS. Show that it induces an equal sex ratio (i.e., half males and half females) over the whole population.

Exercise 10.6: Refer to the law of motion (10.12), specified for any given $\theta \in (0, 1]$ that parametrizes the length of the relevant time period. Show that it follows from the offspring-reproduction postulate of Darwinian selection.

Exercise 10.7: Consider the (continuous-time) RD given by (10.13). Show that if $x_q(t) > 0$ for some q and $t \in \mathbb{R}_+$, then $x_q(t') > 0$ for all $t' > t$.

Exercise 10.8: Recall the property of additive invariance of payoffs introduced in Section 10.3.1. Prove that the RD verifies it.

Exercise 10.9: Consider the property of quotient dynamics presented in Section 10.3.1. Show that the RD satisfies it at all interior states. Furthermore, prove that this property in fact *characterizes* the RD in the interior of the state space.

Exercise 10.10*: Characterize fully the rest points of the RD when the underlying situation is given by some arbitrary (but finite) bilateral game G with payoff matrix A.

Exercise 10.11*: Prove Lemma 10.2.

Exercise 10.12: Consider the family of generalized rock–scissors–paper games described in Exercise 10.2, as parametrized by $\eta \in \mathbb{R}$. Within the usual random-matching context, characterize the long-run behavior of the RD, as a function of η.

Exercise 10.13: Let there be a large population whose individuals are randomly matched in pairs to play a bilateral symmetric game with the following payoff matrix:

$$A = \begin{pmatrix} 1 & 4 & 1 \\ 2 & 1 & 2 \\ 0 & 2 & 0 \end{pmatrix}.$$

Characterize the long-run behavior of the RD.

Exercise 10.14: Consider the evolutionary system for a two-population context under random matching, whose corresponding vector field $F = (F_1, F_2)$ admits the representation given in (10.22) and (10.23). However, in contrast with the specific formulation given by (10.24) and (10.25) for the adjustment flows, suppose that these inflows and outflows are determined as follows.

First, concerning the *strategy outflows*, assume that every agent abandons her strategy at the same rate, independently of the strategy and the associated payoff. (For example, one may interpret this flow as resulting from the "death" of the agent in question, every member of the population being subject to a constant and uniform death probability.)

Second, pertaining to *strategy inflows* (i.e., the dynamics of fresh strategy adoption), assume that every agent obtains a revision opportunity at the same probability rate. If this opportunity arrives, the agent observes the average payoff earned by a randomly selected strategy with some noise. More specifically, suppose she observes its corresponding average payoff plus the realization of some independent random variable, which is the same for all strategies and all times. Further suppose such a random variable displays a continuously differentiable and strictly increasing cumulative distribution function over a bounded support. Then, we postulate that the agent in question switches to the alternative strategy if the observed payoff is higher than the payoff being earned by her current strategy.

    (a) Define precisely the evolutionary system resulting from the above postulates.

    (b) Show that this evolutionary process is payoff monotonic.

Exercise 10.15*: In the context of Exercise 10.14, propose specific conditions on the revision mechanism that make the resulting evolutionary system coincide with the RD.

Exercise 10.16: Suppose the functions $g_1(\cdot)$ and $g_2(\cdot)$ that measure the extent of players' "dissatisfaction" in (10.25) as a function of their individual payoffs are linear but *not* necessarily identical. Explain the relationship between the induced evolutionary dynamics and the two-population RD.

Exercise 10.17: Derive from *primitive* Darwinian principles the two-population RD given by (10.28) and (10.29).

Exercise 10.18: Consider any *regular* evolutionary system of the form given by (10.19) and (10.20). Show that it guarantees the "dynamic invariance of simplex faces," i.e., the counterpart of the property introduced in Subsection 10.3.1 for the RD. More precisely, show that, for any path $x(\cdot)$ of the system, the following expression holds:

$$x_{kq}(0) > 0 \Leftrightarrow \forall t > 0, \ x_{kq}(t) > 0,$$

where $k = 1$ and $q = 1, 2, \ldots, n$, or $k = 2$ and $q = 1, 2, \ldots, m$.

Exercise 10.19: Prove Proposition 10.6.

Exercise 10.20: Reconsider the examples discussed in Section 10.4.3 under an evolutionary system given by the following differential equations:

$$\dot{x}_{11}(t) = \alpha \, \mathbf{sgn} \left\{ \sum_{r=1,2} a_{1r} x_{2r}(t) - \sum_{r=1,2} a_{2r} x_{2r}(t) \right\}, \qquad \alpha > 0$$

$$\dot{x}_{21}(t) = \beta \, \mathbf{sgn} \left\{ \sum_{r=1,2} b_{r1} x_{1r}(t) - \sum_{r=1,2} b_{r2} x_{1r}(t) \right\}, \qquad \beta > 0$$

where α and β are given positive parameters and $\mathbf{sgn}\{\cdot\}$ stands for the *sign function*, i.e., $\mathbf{sgn}\{x\}$ is equal to 1, -1, or 0 depending on whether x is positive, negative, or zero, respectively. (Note that any such evolutionary system is payoff-monotonic at *interior states* but not regular.) Characterize the induced dynamics both for the example that has been labeled "trading complementarities" (Subsection 10.4.3.1) and for that labeled "risky trading" (Subsection 10.4.3.2). Compare your conclusions with those obtained in the text under an RPMES.

Exercise 10.21*: Prove the analogue of Proposition 10.7 for the RD and the notion of dominance in mixed strategies. That is, show that for any path $x(\cdot)$ induced by the RD that starts at interior initial conditions, $\lim_{t \to \infty} x_{kq}(t) = 0$ for any pure strategy s_{kq} that is dominated in the sense of Definition 2.1.
Hint: Suppose that, say, population 1 has the dominated strategy s_{1q} and let σ_1 be a mixed strategy that dominates it. Define then the real function $\phi : \Delta^{n-1} \to \mathbb{R}$ given by $\phi(x_1) = \left[\sum_{r=1}^{n} \sigma_{1r} \log x_{1r} \right] - \log x_{1q}$ and determine its evolution along any path of the system by computing its time derivative.

Exercise 10.22*: Consider the (asymmetric) bilateral game whose payoff matrices are given in (10.34). Show that, from any initial conditions $x(0) = (x_{11}(0), x_{12}(0), x_{21}(0), x_{22}(0))$ with $x_{kq}(0) > 0$ for each $q, k = 1, 2$, the second strategy of population 1 (whose payoffs for this population are given by the second row of matrix A) survives in the long run – i.e., displays $\lim_{t \to \infty} x_{12}(t) > 0$.
Hint: Define the variable $z(t) \equiv 1 - x_{11}(t)/x_{21}(t)$ and show that $\lim_{t \to \infty} z(t) > 0$.

Exercise 10.23*: Refer to the sets H_1 and H_2 defined in (10.41) and (10.42). Prove that every point in the set H_1 is Liapunov stable but not asymptotically stable, whereas the points in H_2 are neither Liapunov nor asymptotically stable.

CHAPTER 11

Learning to play

11.1 Introduction

Again, as in Chapter 10, the hypothesis of *bounded rationality* underlies most of the alternative models of learning studied here. We maintain, therefore, the methodological standpoint underlying evolutionary models; i.e., players cannot readily comprehend or tackle their complex environment. However, in contrast to the "reduced-form" approach displayed by the former evolutionary framework, the present one introduces two important novelties. First, there is an *explicit* description of *how* players attempt to learn over time about the game and the behavior of others (e.g., through reinforcement, imitation, belief updating, etc.). Second, the focus is on *finite* populations, where the *interplay* among the individual adjustments undertaken by the different players generates a learning dynamics significantly richer than in the continuum case.

Naturally, the different models to be considered in this chapter must be highly dependent on the specific bounds contemplated on players' sophistication (or "rationality"). Indeed, this very same idea helps us organize our discussion, with the alternative models studied being arranged along a hierarchical ladder of players' sophistication. Thus, as this ladder is ascended, players' learning is allowed to rely on a progressively more demanding level of "reasoning" about the underlying game.

We start by studying models of learning that approach matters at the lowest level of (bounded) rationality. These are the so-called reinforcement models where players are taken to behave quite primitively, simply reacting to positive or negative stimuli in a "Pavlovian-like manner." Subsequently, the analysis turns to models where players are postulated to behave in a substantially more involved fashion, i.e., they entertain expectations on future play at every round and react optimally to them. Within such a class of models, different degrees of sophistication are still possible. They range from short-sighted players who have a "static model" of the situation (e.g., imitators or myopic best responders) to forward-looking agents who attempt to understand their environment in a genuinely dynamic fashion.

For each of these alternative scenarios, our primary aim in this chapter is to understand the dynamic implications of learning for simple yet interesting games. In particular, our concern is to identify different classes of games in which the corresponding learning processes bring about long-run convergence to some Nash equilibrium. As we shall see, many of the proposed models fare reasonably well for certain games but induce quite unsatisfactory performance for some others.

Seldom, however, can they provide a sharp and coherent rationale for equilibrium *selection* if the game in question involves several Nash equilibria. In fact, to address this important issue is the main objective of Chapter 12, where we pursue a methodological approach that is by now familiar (recall Chapter 4 or Section 10.5). Specifically, we attempt to discriminate among alternative equilibria by assessing their possibly different robustness to small perturbations.

11.2   Reinforcement learning

Reinforcement models reflect the simple "mechanistic" idea that players choose each strategy with a propensity (or disposition) that is positively related to the amount of satisfaction (or "reinforcement") historically associated with it. This approach can be traced back to the models of mathematical psychology developed in the 1950s by Bush and Mostellar (1955), which have been shown to fare quite well in simple laboratory experiments (see, e.g., Mookherjee and Sopher, 1997; Roth and Erev, 1995).

The general principle underlying the reinforcement literature can be formulated in a variety of alternative ways, with the particular modeling details sometimes being of certain significance for the induced predictions (cf. Subsections 11.2.1 and 11.2.2). Here, we focus on two alternative frameworks, each of them embodying a different version of a common underlying idea. That is, both approaches postulate that the intensity of reinforcement enjoyed by a certain strategy when played must be tailored to the difference between the payoff received and some underlying aspiration level. The aspiration level, however, is conceived differently in each case. Thus, whereas in the first framework aspirations are assumed to remain fixed and reinforcement is always positive, in the second one aspirations adjust endogenously over time and may generally lead to both positive and negative reinforcement stimuli.

11.2.1   *Positive reinforcement and fixed aspirations*

Time is measured discretely and indexed by $t = 0, 1, 2, \ldots$. For analytical simplicity, we restrict consideration to just two players, 1 and 2, who are taken to play at every t a certain finite strategic-form game $G = \{\{1, 2\}, \{S_1, S_2\}, \{\pi_1, \pi_2\}\}$. For the moment (cf. Remark 11.1), it is assumed that all payoffs are strictly positive, i.e., $\pi_i(s_{1q}, s_{2q'}) > 0$ for all $i = 1, 2$, $q = 1, 2, \ldots, r_1$, $q' = 1, 2, \ldots, r_2$ and the aspiration level held by each player is fixed at zero throughout. Under these conditions, Roth and Erev (1995) – see also Posch (1997) – propose the following reinforcement-learning model.[190]

The state of the system consists of the specification, for each player $i = 1, 2$, of a vector of (nonnegative) *propensities* $\theta_i(t) \equiv (\theta_{i1}(t), \theta_{i2}(t), \ldots, \theta_{ir_i}(t)) \in \mathbb{R}_+^{r_i}$

---

[190] There has been a recent surge of theoretical and empirical work on processes of reinforcement learning. Different specific models have been proposed and their implications compared with those of alternative models of human behavior. See, for example, Cross (1983), Borgers and Sarin (1997), Camerer and Ho (1999), and Hopkins (2002).

associated with each of her (pure) strategies at t. Assuming that the sum of the propensities is positive, this vector induces a corresponding vector of weights $\sigma_i(t) \equiv (\sigma_{i1}(t), \sigma_{i2}(t), \ldots, \sigma_{ir_i}(t))$ as follows:

$$\sigma_{iq}(t) = \frac{\theta_{iq}(t)}{\sum_{q'=1}^{r_i} \theta_{iq'}(t)}. \tag{11.1}$$

Each player i is assumed to choose each of her pure strategies at t with the probabilities reflected by the current $\sigma_i(t)$. Thus, in a natural sense, we may think of $\sigma_i(t)$ as the mixed strategy used by player i at t.

Denote by $s_i(t)$ the strategy in S_i *actually* chosen by player i at t. Then, with a slight abuse of notation, we let

$$\pi_i(t) \equiv \pi_i(s_1(t), s_2(t)) \tag{11.2}$$

be the payoff earned by each player i at t. On the other hand, for each strategy $s_{iq} \in S_i$, it is convenient to introduce the following notation:

$$\psi_{iq}(t) = \begin{cases} \pi_i(t) & \text{if } s_i(t) = s_{iq} \\ 0 & \text{otherwise.} \end{cases} \tag{11.3}$$

Thus, $\psi_{iq}(t)$ acts as a kind of payoff-scaled "indicator function" for strategy s_{iq}.

We are now in a situation to formalize the law of motion for each player's vector of propensities:

$$\theta_{iq}(t+1) = \theta_{iq}(t) + \psi_{iq}(t) \quad (i = 1, 2; \; q = 1, 2, \ldots, r_i, \; t \in \mathbb{N}). \tag{11.4}$$

The above expression embodies the following simple principle: each strategy being played receives a reinforcement equal to the payoff received. But equivalently, of course, this reinforcement can also be identified with the difference between the payoff received and the aspiration level, if one makes the supplementary assumption that this aspiration level is assumed constantly equal to zero throughout.

Our main interest is to keep track of the adjustment induced by (11.1) and (11.4) on the mixed strategies, $\sigma_1(t)$ and $\sigma_2(t)$, played by each individual at any given t. Denote by $\Theta_i(t) \equiv \sum_{q=1}^{r_i} \theta_{iq}(t)$ the sum of player i's propensities at t. Then, for each $q = 1, 2, \ldots, r_i$, we can write

$$\begin{aligned} \sigma_{iq}(t+1) &= \frac{\theta_{iq}(t+1)}{\Theta_i(t+1)} = \frac{\theta_{iq}(t) + \psi_{iq}(t)}{\Theta_i(t) + \pi_i(t)} \\ &= \frac{\theta_{iq}(t)}{\Theta_i(t)} + \frac{\psi_{iq}(t)\,\Theta_i(t) - \pi_i(t)\,\theta_{iq}(t)}{\Theta_i(t)[\Theta_i(t) + \pi_i(t)]} \\ &= \sigma_{iq}(t) + \frac{\psi_{iq}(t) - \pi_i(t)\,\sigma_{iq}(t)}{\Theta_i(t) + \pi_i(t)}. \end{aligned} \tag{11.5}$$

Simple algebraic manipulations show that

$$\frac{\psi_{iq}(t) - \pi_i(t)\sigma_{iq}(t)}{\Theta_i(t) + \pi_i(t)} = \frac{\psi_{iq}(t) - \pi_i(t)\sigma_{iq}(t)}{\Theta_i(t)} - \frac{\pi_i(t)[\psi_{iq}(t) - \pi_i(t)\sigma_{iq}(t)]}{[\Theta_i(t)]^2 + \pi_i(t)\Theta_i(t)}.$$

Therefore, for large $\Theta_i(t)$, one may approximate (11.5) as follows[191]:

$$\sigma_{iq}(t+1) = \sigma_{iq}(t) + \frac{1}{\Theta_i(t)}[\psi_{iq}(t) - \pi_i(t)\sigma_{iq}(t)] + \mathcal{O}\left(\frac{1}{[\Theta_i(t)]^2}\right),$$

(11.6)

since both $\psi_{iq}(t)$ and $\pi_i(t)$ are uniformly bounded for all i and q.

Note that, at each t, the payoff variables $\psi_{iq}(t)$ and $\pi_i(t)$ are *ex ante* random – they depend on the particular pure strategies actually chosen by both players at t. Thus, (11.6) defines a *stochastic* process whose motion cannot be predicted deterministically. For reasons to be explained below, we are interested in understanding its *expected* motion, which in turn depends on the mathematical expectation $\mathbf{E}_t[\psi_{iq}(t) - \pi_i(t)\sigma_{iq}(t)]$. In view of (11.1), (11.2), and (11.3), we have

$$\mathbf{E}_t[\psi_{iq}(t)] = \sigma_{iq}(t)\sum_{q'=1}^{r_j}\pi_i(s_{iq}, s_{jq'})\sigma_{jq'}(t)$$

$$\mathbf{E}_t[\pi_i(t)] = \sum_{q=1}^{r_i}\sum_{q'=1}^{r_j}\pi_i(s_{iq}, s_{jq'})\sigma_{iq}(t)\sigma_{jq'}(t)$$

for all $i, j = 1, 2$, $i \neq j$. Therefore,

$$\mathbf{E}_t\left[\psi_{iq}(t) - \pi_i(t)\sigma_{iq}(t)\right] = \sigma_{iq}(t)\left\{\begin{array}{l}\sum_{q'=1}^{r_j}\pi_i(s_{iq}, s_{jq'})\sigma_{jq'}(t) - \\ \sum_{q'=1}^{r_i}\sum_{q''=1}^{r_j}\pi_i(s_{iq'}, s_{jq''})\sigma_{iq'}(t)\sigma_{jq''}(t)\end{array}\right\}$$

$$\equiv F_{iq}(\sigma_1(t), \sigma_2(t)).$$

As the reader may recall (cf. (10.28) and (10.29)), the mapping $F = (F_i)_{i=1}^n$: $\Delta^{r_1-1} \times \Delta^{r_2-1} \to \mathbb{R}^{r_1+r_2}$ is simply the vector field that defines the (two-population, continuous-time) replicator dynamics (RD). Introducing it in (11.6), the system is found to display, in *expected* terms, the following law of motion:

$$\mathbf{E}_t[\sigma_{iq}(t+1) - \sigma_{iq}(t)] = \frac{1}{\Theta_i(t)}F_{iq}(\sigma_1(t), \sigma_2(t)) + \mathcal{O}\left(\frac{1}{[\Theta_i(t)]^2}\right). \quad (11.7)$$

Expression (11.7) may be provided with the following intuitive interpretation. As time grows (and, therefore, each $\Theta_i(\cdot)$ becomes arbitrarily large), the *expected direction of change* of the system can be arbitrarily well approximated (because the terms of order $[\Theta_i(t)]^{-2}$ become arbitrarily small and may be ignored) by the two-population RD.

Note that (11.7) implies that the absolute magnitude in the change per period becomes arbitrarily small as time advances. In view of this fact, one may rely on the powerful results of stochastic approximation theory[192] to aim at stronger conclusions, well beyond the mere determination of the *expected* behavior of the

---

[191] Given any variable $\xi(t)$, the notation $\mathcal{O}(\xi(t))$ stands for a term of the same order as $\xi(t)$ for large t.
[192] A classical reference for stochastic approximation theory is Kushner and Clark (1978). For more recent developments, see Benveniste *et al.* (1990) and Benaïm and Hirsch (1999).

system. Consider the continuous-time Replicator Dynamics (RD) given by

$$\dot{\sigma}_{iq}(t) = F_{iq}(\sigma_1(t), \sigma_2(t)) \quad (i = 1, 2; \; q = 1, 2, \ldots, r_i, \; t \in \mathbb{R}_+). \quad (11.8)$$

Heuristically, we may view the above ("infinitesimal-step") differential equation as a long-run approximation for the *expected* motion of (11.5). Moreover, the fact that, as the step size becomes small, the number of random (and independent) draws associated with nearby states grows unboundedly, appears to suggest the following conjecture: in the long run, the *expected* and *actual* motion of the system should become arbitrarily "close" (both to each other and to that prescribed by (11.8)), as a consequence of some suitable adaptation of large-number arguments.[193]

Indeed, this conjecture has been largely established by a recent paper of Posch (1997) for the particular case of 2×2 games (i.e., a context where $r_1 = r_2 = 2$). In this setup, he has shown the following:

(1) The stochastic learning dynamics converges, almost surely (a.s.), to a closed orbit of (11.8), i.e., a stationary point or a cycling path.
(2) If the game has some strict equilibrium, the learning dynamics converge a.s. to some strict equilibrium.
(3) If the game has no strict equilibrium, the learning algorithm displays a continuum of asymptotically cycling paths.

Point (1) provides a clear-cut sense in which the RD may be viewed as capturing the long-run behavior of our reinforcement learning dynamics: the latter's limit points are a subset of those of the former.[194] In analogy with what we learned in Subsection 10.3.2 for symmetric games (cf. Remark 10.1), it should be clear that, for general 2×2 games, the stationary points of the (two-population) RD can be of two different kinds. First, we have the pure-strategy configurations – i.e., what we called *monomorphic profiles* in the population interpretation of the RD – that are *always* stationary. On the other hand, there are also those mixed-strategy profiles where all the pure strategies displaying positive weight are payoff indifferent for the player (or population) in question. If any such profiles exist, they are also stationary for the RD. Thus, overall, we conclude from (1) that all learning paths generated by (11.5) must converge, generically, either to some pure-strategy state $\tilde{\sigma} \in \{0, 1\}^4$, a mixed-strategy Nash equilibrium in a possibly restricted subspace, or a closed (i.e., cyclical) path.

On the other hand, Points (2) and (3) elaborate on the first point by discriminating among the different limit sets of the RD on the basis of their relative robustness. Typically, some of those limit sets may be very fragile (e.g., locally unstable rest points). Consequently, not all of them should be expected to fare comparably well in

---

[193] More precisely, this is suggested by standard results of the theory of stochastic processes (cf. Karlin and Taylor, 1975) that concern the convergence of martingales, i.e., stochastic processes $\{x_t\}$ that satisfy $\mathbf{E}[x_{t+1} \mid x_0, x_1, \ldots, x_t] = x_t$ for all $t \in \mathbb{N}$. In Subsection 11.4.2, the same approach is applied to other models of learning – in particular, to the analysis of so-called fictitious play.

[194] In this respect, it is worth noting that, as established by the well-known Poincaré-Bendixon theorem (cf., e.g., Hirsch and Smale, 1974, p. 248), all limit sets of a two-dimensional dynamical system satisfying a suitable boundary condition are either stationary points or closed orbits.

Table 11.1: *A general* 2 × 2 *game*

1 ＼ 2	s_1^2	s_2^2
s_1^1	a_{11}, b_{11}	a_{12}, b_{12}
s_2^1	a_{21}, b_{21}	a_{22}, b_{22}

terms of the learning process. Since the induced dynamics remains "slightly" noisy throughout, no configuration lacking some minimum degree of local robustness should survive in the long run. This, in fact, is the essential bearing of (2) and (3), which provide us with additional criteria to select among the different limit sets of the associated RD in some salient cases.

To understand better the implications of (2) and (3), consider a typical 2 × 2 game with payoffs given by Table 11.1.

Generically,[195] the family of such 2 × 2 games can be classified in three subclasses:

(a) If $(a_{11} - a_{21})(a_{12} - a_{22}) > 0$ or $(b_{11} - b_{12})(b_{21} - b_{22}) > 0$, one of the two players has a dominant strategy and there is just one strict equilibrium.

(b) If $(a_{11} - a_{21})(a_{12} - a_{22}) < 0$, $(b_{11} - b_{12})(b_{21} - b_{22}) < 0$, and $(a_{11} - a_{21})$ $(b_{11} - b_{12}) > 0$, there are two pure-strategy (strict) equilibria and one (nonstrict) mixed-strategy equilibrium.

(c) If $(a_{11} - a_{21})(a_{12} - a_{22}) < 0$, $(b_{11} - b_{12})(b_{21} - b_{22}) < 0$, and $(a_{11} - a_{21})$ $(b_{11} - b_{12}) < 0$, there is just one (nonstrict) mixed-strategy equilibrium.

The subclass identified in (a) is particularly simple. It includes, for example, those symmetric games like the prisoner's dilemma where *both* individuals have a dominant strategy. It comprises, however, a substantially larger collection of games because (a) requires only that one player have a dominant strategy. In view of Posch's results (cf. (2) above), for any game in this class, the reinforcement learning dynamics leads to a sole robust prediction: players will end up at the unique strict equilibrium. For example, if we make $a_{11} > a_{21}$ and $b_{11} > b_{12}$, the long-run dynamics for this subclass is graphically illustrated in Figure 11.1. In this diagram, the jagged lines represent sample simulation paths of the (stochastic) reinforcement learning governed by (11.5), and the smooth lines are paths of the continuous-time (deterministic) RD given by (11.8). As explained, the former eventually approximate the latter.

For the subclass given by (b), the previous conclusion can be extended to the *two* strict equilibria: both of them are the sole limit points of the learning dynamics. In fact, it can be shown that either of them may be reached with positive prior probability, the respective magnitude of these probabilities depending on payoffs and initial conditions. Note that any game in this subclass also has a third mixed-strategy equilibrium σ^* that is highly unstable for the RD. That is, any small perturbation away from it will typically lead the RD toward one of the other two strict

---

[195] Refer to Footnote 66 for an explanation of what the requirement of genericity implies for strategic-form games. In the present case, it merely amounts to the condition that the alternative payoffs that a player may receive in the game display no ties, i.e., $a_{ik} \neq a_{jk}$ and $b_{ki} \neq b_{kj}$ for all $i, j, k = 1, 2$ with $i \neq j$.

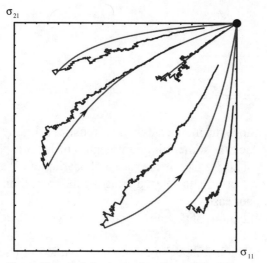

Figure 11.1: Reinforcement learning and the RD, a game with a dominant strategy.

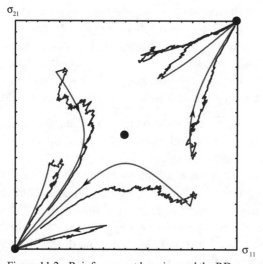

Figure 11.2: Reinforcement learning and the RD, a game with two pure-strategy equilibria.

equilibria (recall the example of this sort discussed in Subsection 10.4.3.1). In fact, it is precisely such acute instability that precludes the mixed-strategy equilibrium from becoming a possible long-run outcome of the learning dynamics. If we focus on the case where $a_{11} > a_{21}$, the long-run dynamics for this subclass are as illustrated in Figure 11.2 where, again, the smooth trajectories are paths of the RD and the jagged lines are sample simulation paths induced by reinforcement learning.

Finally, the subclass described in (c) consists of those games displaying a unique and mixed-strategy equilibrium. As explained in Subsection 10.4.3.2, any such (generic) game has the interior trajectories of the RD define closed orbits around

σ_{21}

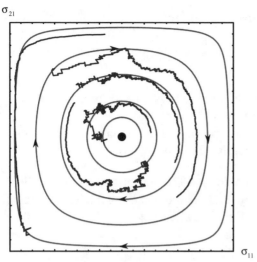

σ_{11}

Figure 11.3: Reinforcement learning and the RD, a game with a unique and mixed-strategy equilibrium.

the equilibrium point. Because these trajectories are Liapunov stable,[196] one indeed obtains the behavior asserted in (3). Namely, the long-run paths induced by the reinforcement learning dynamics cycle, asymptotically, around the Nash equilibrium along one of those closed orbits. Focusing again on the case where $a_{11} > a_{21}$, such long-run dynamics are illustrated by Figure 11.3, where jagged and smooth paths have the usual interpretation.

Remark 11.1: As formulated, the reinforcement model studied here requires that all payoffs of the game be positive (or at least nonnegative, if initial propensities are all positive). Otherwise, the combination of (11.1) and (11.4) may lead to an update of players' mixed strategies that is not well defined – it may induce negative weights. In this sense, the model displays the unappealing feature that every experience must be positively reinforcing (albeit at different degrees). Of course, if we reinterpret the postulated payoffs as "excess (net) payoffs over some given aspiration level," the proposed formulation may be viewed simply as reflecting a context in which players are rather pessimistic (or easily satisfied), never hoping for (or aiming at) a payoff higher than a very low one.

Alternatively, one could contemplate a more demanding aspiration level that allows for the possibility of negative reinforcement (i.e., payoffs falling below the aspiration level). In this case, it is not difficult to check (cf. Exercise 11.1) that, because of the additive invariance displayed by the RD (recall Subsection 10.3.1), the expected motion of the learning dynamics

---

[196] Here, we simply extend to limit sets the notion of Liapunov stability that was introduced in Part (1) of Definition 10.2 for rest points (i.e., a singleton limit cycle). Heuristically, it reflects the same idea as before: after any small perturbation away from the limit set (now, possibly, a closed orbit), the system should remain in the vicinity of it.

is not affected by what merely amounts to a "shift of origin" in the measurement of payoffs. However, the problem remains that propensities may become negative. To address this problem, one would need to transform the model so that

(a) prevailing propensities are always sure to remain positive, growing unboundedly over time[197];
(b) the probability weights prevailing at any point in the process are unaffected by the contemplated transformation.

As explained by Hopkins (1997), several natural possibilities can be proposed to guarantee (a) and (b), thus ensuring the full applicability of the above conclusions (cf. Exercise 11.2). ♦

11.2.2 *General reinforcement and flexible aspirations*

Once a certain notion of *aspirations* is introduced into the learning model, it is natural to contemplate the possibility that it may evolve endogenously on the basis of past experience. To formulate a stylized reinforcement-learning model with this important feature is the main task of the present subsection.

The model is largely inspired by Karandikar *et al.* (1998). Its underlying basic framework is as in Subsection 11.2.1, i.e., two given individuals are taken to play repeatedly over (discrete) time a strategic-form game G. To simplify matters, we postulate that agents' "propensities" to play the different strategies are given by degenerate vectors with only one positive component. Thus, in essence, we may identify the *choice* variable of each player $i = 1, 2$ at any $t = 0, 1, 2, \ldots$ with the *pure* (rather than mixed) strategy $s_i(t)$ currently adopted by this player. In the present context, where aspirations are assumed flexible, the additional state variable to be associated with each individual i is her current aspiration $y_i(t) \in \mathbb{R}$. Thus, combining both dimensions (strategies and aspirations), the state space of the system Ω is identified with some compact subset of $(S_1 \times \mathbb{R}) \times (S_2 \times \mathbb{R})$. More specifically, we make $\Omega = (S_1 \times \Lambda_1) \times (S_2 \times \Lambda_2)$, where each Λ_i is a compact real interval including both $\max_{(s_1,s_2)} \pi_i(s_1, s_2)$ and $\min_{(s_1,s_2)} \pi_i(s_1, s_2)$.

In the present context, the law of motion of the system must involve two dimensions for each player. First, concerning strategy choice, let us postulate that every player whose current payoff does *not* fall below her prevailing aspiration repeats the same action next period. In the opposite case (i.e., when the current payoff falls below the aspiration), the player is assumed to switch away from her adopted strategy with some positive probability $p \in (0, 1)$. If she does indeed abandon her former strategy, all other strategies are chosen with positive (say, equal) probability.

---

[197] In fact, the growth of aggregate propensities cannot be too fast (i.e., the system cannot slow down too early) if some of the aforementioned results are to hold. See Posch (1997) for technical details.

Formally, if $\pi_i(t)$ denotes as before the payoff earned by player $i \in \{1, 2\}$ at any t, we posit[198]:

$$\pi_i(t) \geq y_i(t) \Rightarrow s_i(t+1) = s_i(t)$$

$$\pi_i(t) < y_i(t) \Rightarrow \begin{cases} \text{with prob. } 1 - p, & s_i(t+1) = s_i(t) \\ \\ \text{with prob. } p, & s_i(t+1) \in S_i \setminus \{s_i(t)\}, \\ & \text{chosen with uniform probability.} \end{cases} \qquad (11.9)$$

It is worth stressing that, because p is taken to be strictly less than one, there is always some positive probability that a player stays with the current action despite her being dissatisfied with it. The positive magnitude $1 - p$ is conceived as an "inertia probability" and plays a useful role in our analysis.

On the other hand, each player's aspiration is taken to adjust on the basis of her own past experience.[199] Specifically, it is assumed that, at any given t, the players' aspirations prevailing in the following period are a convex combination of current aspirations and payoffs. That is,

$$y_i(t+1) = \lambda y_i(t) + (1 - \lambda)\pi_i(t) \quad (i = 1, 2, \ t = 0, 1, 2, \ldots), \qquad (11.10)$$

for some $\lambda \in (0, 1)$ that is assumed, for simplicity, common to both players. Of course, notice that (11.10) is equivalent to the following expression:

$$y_i(t+1) = \lambda^{t+1} y_i(0) + (1 - \lambda) \sum_{\tau=0}^{t} \lambda^{t-\tau} \pi_i(\tau), \qquad (11.11)$$

which simply indicates that, in the limit, aspirations become a geometric weighted average of past payoffs.

Our analysis of the reinforcement-learning dynamics defined by (11.9) and (11.10) is decomposed in two parts. First, in this subsection, we present some long-run convergence results for two interesting classes of games: prisoner's dilemma and pure-coordination games. In both cases, we show that the process converges almost surely to *some* pure-strategy configuration. Later, in Section 12.7, we enrich the model with the addition of some small stochastic noise to address the "selection issue" (i.e., which of the multiple possible outcomes is more likely to be played).

We start with the class of 2×2 games that reflect a prisoner's dilemma. In the notation of Table 11.1, this is a symmetric game, i.e.,

$$\forall i, j = 1, 2, \ a_{ij} = b_{ji} \qquad (11.12)$$

such that, if the first strategy is identified with "defection" (D) and the second with

---

[198] In general, the switching probability p could be made to depend continuously on the dissatisfaction gap $y_i(t) - \pi_i(t)$. Here, however, we abstract from this possibility since it complicates the technical analysis substantially. For a full analysis of the case with a continuous adjustment rule, the reader may refer to Karandikar *et al.* (1998).

[199] Alternatively, one could postulate that it is some aggregate (e.g., average) payoff experience that matters (cf. Palomino and Vega-Redondo, 1999). Of course, this requires that such information be available and that players should view themselves involved in a symmetric situation.

"cooperation" (C) we have

$$a_{12} > a_{22} > a_{11} > a_{21}. \tag{11.13}$$

For simplicity, let us normalize the lowest payoff a_{21} to zero. Then, denoting $a_{12} \equiv \eta$, $a_{22} \equiv \zeta$, and $a_{11} \equiv \nu$, we may write the payoff matrix as follows:

$$A = \begin{pmatrix} \nu & \eta \\ 0 & \zeta \end{pmatrix}.$$

As usual, it is assumed that

$$\frac{\eta}{2} < \zeta, \tag{11.14}$$

so that the cooperative payoff cannot be Pareto dominated by a repeated alternation between asymmetric profiles. Finally, we also find it convenient to rule out a nongeneric case (cf. Exercise 11.3) by assuming that

$$\nu \neq \frac{\eta}{2}, \tag{11.15}$$

i.e., the defection payoff is *not* exactly equal to the average of the two extreme payoffs. Under all these conditions, we have the following result.

Theorem 11.1: *Consider any 2×2 game as in Table 11.1 that satisfies (11.12)–(11.15). Then, there exists some λ_0 such that if $1 > \lambda > \lambda_0$, given any initial conditions $\omega(0) = [s_1(0), y_1(0), s_2(0), y_2(0)] \in \Omega$, the reinforcement-learning process given by (11.9) and (11.10) converges a.s. to some pure-strategy state $\omega^* = [s_1^*, y_1^*, s_2^*, y_2^*]$ with $y_i^* = \pi_i(s_1^*, s_2^*)$, $i = 1, 2$.*

Proof: It is enough to show that, at any t and every prevailing state $\omega(t) = [s_1(t), y_1(t), s_2(t), y_2(t)]$, there is positive probability, bounded away from zero, that the process converges to a pure-strategy state. Assume for simplicity that $y_i(t) > 0$ for each $i = 1, 2$ (cf. Exercise 11.4) and consider the different possibilities concerning the strategy profile $[s_1(t), s_2(t)]$.

(1) Suppose $[s_1(t), s_2(t)] = (C, D)$ – the case where (D, C) is symmetric. Consider some arbitrary open ball of radius ρ around $(0, \eta)$, $U_\rho(0, \eta)$. Given any $\rho > 0$, there is some $t' > t$ such that with positive probability $(1 - p)^{t'-t}$, by inertia, $y(t') \equiv (y_1(t'), y_2(t')) \in U_\rho(0, \eta)$ – cf. Figures 11.4 and 11.5.

Moreover, if λ_0 is large enough, there is positive probability p^2 (corresponding to player 1 first and then player 2 receiving a revision opportunity in consecutive periods) that the following events occur:
(a) $s(t') \equiv (s_1(t'), s_2(t')) = (D, D)$;
(b) $s(t' + 1) = (D, C)$;
(c) $y(t' + 1) \in U_{2\rho}(0, \eta)$.
Here, we use the fact that at t' player 1 is dissatisfied (i.e., receives a payoff below her aspiration), and at $t' + 1$ it is player 2 who is so. Now,

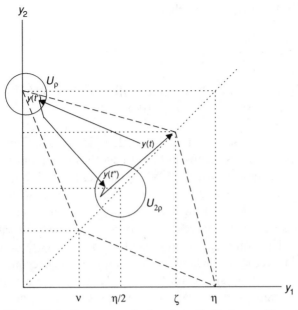

Figure 11.4: Convergence in the prisoner's dilemma, $\eta/2 > \nu$.

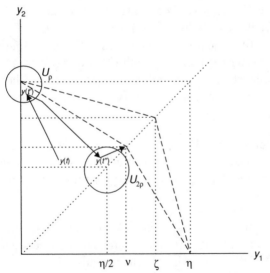

Figure 11.5: Convergence in the prisoner's dilemma, $\eta/2 < \nu$.

consider a chain of events so that at some further t'' we have

(d) $y(t'') \in U_{2\rho}(\eta/2, \eta/2)$;

(e) $s(t'') = (D, D)$;

(f) $y(t'' + 1) \in U_{2\rho}(\eta/2, \eta/2)$.

Provided λ_0 is large enough, such a chain of events has positive probability bounded below by $p(1 - p)^{\tau - t'}$ where one may choose (cf. Exercise 11.5) any τ such that:

$$\tau \geq t' + \frac{\log \frac{1}{2}}{\log \lambda}. \tag{11.16}$$

In view of (11.15), ρ may be chosen small enough so that either

  (i) $\forall i = 1, 2$, $\zeta > y_i(t'' + 1) > \nu$ (if $\nu < \eta/2$, as depicted in Figure 11.4) or

  (ii) $\forall i = 1, 2$, $y_i(t'' + 1) < \nu$ (if $\nu > \eta/2$, as depicted in Figure 11.5). In case (i), both players receive at $t'' + 1$ payoffs above their respective aspirations (i.e., they are satisfied), which ensures that the path will converge to the pure-strategy state (D, ν, D, ν). In case (ii), both players are dissatisfied at $t'' + 1$ so that, with probability p^2, we have $y(t'' + 2) = (C, C)$, after which the process converges to the pure-strategy state (C, ζ, C, ζ). This completes the argument when $[s_1(t), s_2(t)] = (C, D)$.

(2) Now, we address the case where $[s_1(t), s_2(t)] = (C, C)$. Then, we have two possibilities. If $y_i(t) \leq \zeta$ for both $i = 1, 2$, then the process converges to the pure-strategy state (C, ζ, C, ζ). Otherwise, at least one of the players is dissatisfied at t, which implies that there is positive probability no lower than $p(1 - p)$ that $[s_1(t + 1), s_2(t + 1)]$ is either (C, D) or (D, C). Hence, we can apply the argument used in (1) to conclude that there is positive probability of convergence.

(3) Finally, consider the case where $[s_1(t), s_2(t)] = (D, D)$. If $y_i(t) \leq \nu$ for both $i = 1, 2$, then the process converges to the pure-strategy state (D, ν, D, ν). Otherwise, in analogy with (2), we may assert that with probability of at least $p(1 - p)$, $[s_1(t + 1), s_2(t + 1)]$ is either (C, D) or (D, C). Applying (1) again, the desired conclusion follows as well for this case.

To summarize, combining (1)–(3), we conclude that there is positive probability, bounded above zero, that convergence occurs from any state. Thus, convergence eventually takes place with probability one, which completes the proof. ∎

Theorem 11.1 establishes long-run convergence of the reinforcement-learning dynamics defined by (11.9) and (11.10). It is an immediate consequence of the argument used in the proof of this result that, in the absence of any "noise" that could disturb the dynamics, there are alternative sets of initial conditions that univocally induce different pure-strategy states in the long run. To clarify the nature of the multiplicity problem involved, we state the following straightforward result.

Corollary 11.1: *Consider any 2×2 game as in Table 11.1 that satisfies (11.12)–(11.15). There are two open subsets of initial states, Ω_C and Ω_D, such that if $\omega(0) \in \Omega_C$ (or, alternatively, $\omega(0) \in \Omega_D$), the process defined by (11.9)–(11.10) converges to (C, ζ, C, ζ) (respectively, to (D, ν, D, ν)).*

Now, we turn our attention to the second class of bilateral games to be considered here: the so-called *pure-coordination games*. These are games $G = \{\{1, 2\}, \{S_1, S_2\}, \{\pi_1, \pi_2\}\}$ where $r_1 = r_2 = r$, players' strategies can be indexed in a way that all pure-strategy Nash equilibria are "on the diagonal," and there is a common and uniform payoff across all nonequilibrium profiles. For simplicity, let us normalize this latter payoff to zero so that, $\forall q, q' \in \{1, 2, \ldots, r\}$,

$$\pi_i(s_{1q}, s_{2q'}) > 0 \Leftrightarrow q = q'. \tag{11.17}$$

For this class of games, we provide the following convergence result of the reinforcement-learning process.

Theorem 11.2: *Consider any pure-coordination game G that satisfies (11.17). Then, given any initial conditions $\omega(0) = [s_1(0), y_1(0), s_2(0), y_2(0)] \in \Omega$, the reinforcement-learning process given by (11.9)–(11.10) converges a.s. to a pure-strategy state $\omega^* = [s_{1q}^*, y_1^*, s_{2q'}^*, y_2^*]$ with $y_i^* = \pi_i(s_{1q}^*, s_{2q'}^*)$, $i = 1, 2$. Moreover, if $y_i(0) > 0$ for some i, then one has $q = q'$, i.e., the pure-strategy state ω^* is associated with a Nash equilibrium of G.*

Proof: Consider first the case where $y_1(0) = y_2(0) = 0$. Then, if $s_1(0) = s_{1q}$ and $s_2(0) = s_{2q'}$ with $q \neq q'$, the initial state $\omega(0)$ is stationary and convergence is trivially obtained. Otherwise, if $q = q'$, then $y_i(1) > 0$ for each $i = 1, 2$ and we may analyze the long-run dynamics of the process as if the initial state had displayed both players holding a positive aspiration level.

Thus consider now the case where $y_i(0) > 0$ for some $i \in \{1, 2\}$. As in Theorem 11.1, we want to show that, from any given t where the state is $\omega(t) = [s_1(t), y_1(t), s_2(t), y_2(t)]$, there is positive probability of converging to some pure-strategy state.

(1) Suppose that

$$\pi_i(s_1(t), s_2(t)) \geq y_i(t), \quad \forall i = 1, 2, \tag{11.18}$$

and let $s_1(t) = s_{1q}$. Then, since $y_i(0) > 0$ implies that $y_i(t) > 0$ for all t, (11.18) requires that $s_2(t) = s_{2q}$, which ensures convergence to the pure-strategy state $[s_{1q}, \pi_1(s_{1q}, s_{2q}), s_{2q}, \pi_2(s_{1q}, s_{2q})]$.

(2) Next, assume that (11.18) is violated for at least one agent, say player 2. Then, with positive probability at least equal to $\min\{p^2, (1-p)^2\}$ $(\leq p(1-p))$, we have

$$s_1(t+1) = s_{1q}$$

$$s_2(t+1) = s_{2q'}$$

for some q, q' with $q' \neq q$. Thereafter, suppose that $s_1(\tau) = s_{1q}$ and $s_2(\tau) = s_{2q'}$ for all $\tau = t+2, t+3, \ldots, t'-1$, where t' is chosen large enough so that

$$y_i(t') \leq \pi_i(s_{1q}, s_{2q}), \quad \forall i = 1, 2. \tag{11.19}$$

Because $\pi_1(s_1(\tau), s_2(\tau)) = 0$ for all such τ and Ω is compact, there is a uniform bound T such that one may choose $t' \leq T$. Thus, (11.19) has positive probability bounded below by $(1 - p)^{2(T-2)}$. Then, at t', with probability $[(1 - p)p]/[r - 1]$, player 2 may switch to strategy s_{2q}, thus leading each player i to receive the payoff $\pi_i(s_{1q}, s_{2q})$. Subsequently, by (11.19), the path must converge to the pure-strategy state $[s_{1q}, \pi_1(s_{1q}, s_{2q}), s_{2q}, \pi_2(s_{1q}, s_{2q})]$. Combining the above considerations, it follows that the whole converging path may be attributed a probability bounded above zero, independently of $\omega(t)$, which is the desired conclusion.

Points (1) and (2) establish the a.s. long-run convergence of the process to some pure-strategy state. To complete the proof of the theorem, we need to show that if $y_i(0) > 0$ for some i, the limit pure-strategy state is a Nash equilibrium of G, almost surely. But this immediately follows from the fact that, under such initial conditions, player i's aspiration level $y_i(t) > 0$ for all t. Thus, the convergence to a pure-strategy state with null payoffs has prior probability no larger than $\lim_{T\to\infty}(1 - p)^T = 0$. This completes the proof. ∎

As in the case of the prisoner's dilemma, it is clear that a multiplicity of long-run states exist, whose corresponding materialization depends on the initial conditions. This is clarified by the following result, an immediate counterpart for the present scenario of Corollary 11.1.

Corollary 11.2: *Consider any pure-coordination game G that satisfies (11.17). There are open subsets of initial states, $\Omega_1, \ldots, \Omega_r$, such that if $\omega(0) \in \Omega_q$ the process defined by (11.9) and (11.10) converges to the pure-strategy state $[s_{1q}, \pi_1(s_{1q}, s_{2q}), s_{2q}, \pi_2(s_{1q}, s_{2q})]$.*

11.3   Static perceptions and myopic behavior

Proceeding along the "sophistication ladder" explained in the Introduction, now we turn to considering players whose behavior is somewhat more elaborate than the mechanical (stimulus-response) reaction to experience embodied by reinforcement learning. Implicitly, players are assumed to have a certain *model* of the situation and decide *optimally* on the basis of it. At this point, their model is still taken to be rather simple. It is of a stationary (or "static") nature, built on the idea that the (immediate) future will be like the (recent) past. Having such a perception of the world, players are then naturally postulated to behave in a "myopic" fashion, concerned only with current payoffs.

Two alternative scenarios with these characteristics will be studied in the next subsections. Each one displays different implicit assumptions on the extent of players' information and their computational abilities.

The first scenario reflects the idea that a player can only observe (or assimilate) information on the action chosen and payoff received in the preceding period by other players. Then, taking this information as descriptive of what may be expected for the future (i.e., holding static perceptions), the player is supposed to *imitate* any action that has been observed to induce a payoff higher than what she herself has obtained.[200]

The second scenario assumes instead that each player is informed of the previous strategy profile adopted by her opponents and views it as a good predictor of the *actions* to be chosen in the current period (again, displaying static perceptions of the situation). Under these expectations, she is taken to adjust her own action in a *payoff-improving* direction.

As in Section 11.2, our essential concern in what follows will be to identify interesting contexts where those two alternative learning dynamics perform satisfactorily, at least in the sense of guaranteeing long-run convergence to *some* Nash equilibrium. This leaves untackled the crucial issue of equilibrium selection, to be addressed only later in Section 12.4 within a richer (i.e., noisy) environment.

11.3.1 *The strategic framework*

Let $N = \{1, 2, \ldots, n\}$ be a certain finite population involved in a strategic-form game $G = \{N, \{S_i\}_{i=1}^n, \{\pi_i\}_{i=1}^n\}$. (Here, we are interested in going beyond the former bilateral context, because considerations pertaining to population size will turn out to be relevant for future analysis.) Sometimes, the game G is assumed symmetric, i.e., it is taken to verify the following conditions.

(i) For all $i, j = 1, 2, \ldots, n$, $S_i = S_j$, i.e., players' strategy spaces are identical.

(ii) For any permutation in player indices $\varphi : \{1, 2, \ldots, n\} \to \{1, 2, \ldots, n\}$, the following condition applies:

$$\forall s \in S, \ \forall i \in N,$$
$$\pi_i(s_1, s_2, \ldots, s_n) = \pi_{\varphi(i)}\big(s_{\varphi^{-1}(1)}, s_{\varphi^{-1}(2)}, \ldots, s_{\varphi^{-1}(n)}\big).$$

That is, the payoff functions are "anonymous," in the sense of being invariant to any relabeling of players' indices.

The above requirements of symmetry are natural ones to make if players' learning is taken to involve interagent imitation. For only if players' strategy spaces are identical (or isomorphic) and payoffs are (or at least perceived to be) essentially symmetric can players reasonably regard the experience of others as relevant for their own purposes. To fix ideas, two paradigmatic instances of the general framework serve as leading examples in much of our ensuing discussion.

- One of them is the (symmetric) model of Cournot competition first introduced in Section 3.1.1. To recall, it involves a collection of n quantity-setting firms that confront a given inverse-demand function for

---

[200] Recall that similar behavior was proposed in Section 10.4. Now, it is reconsidered in a finite-population context, where the process remains stochastic even at the aggregate level.

a homogeneous good $P(\cdot)$ and share a common cost function $C(\cdot)$. To preserve the finite nature of the game, the firms are restricted to choosing their respective quantities from a certain finite grid $\Phi = \{0, \varrho, 2\varrho, \ldots, v\varrho\}$ for some finite $v \in \mathbb{N}$ and some arbitrarily small $\varrho > 0$.

- The second particularization of the above general framework has players interact through bilateral encounters. More specifically, we focus on a so-called *round-robin* scenario where each player i meets *every* other player $j \neq i$ at every round of play. Let $A = \{a_1, a_2, \ldots, a_r\}$ stand for the set of "actions" that can be used in each encounter, with $\psi : A \times A \to \mathbb{R}$ representing the function that determines the payoff $\psi(a_q, a_{q'})$ received by a player who adopts a_q in a given encounter when her corresponding opponent plays $a_{q'}$. In this context, it is natural to assume that each player i has to choose the *same* action against every opponent. Otherwise, if a different action could be chosen in each case, a player would be facing every other player independently and no genuine population-wide interaction would take place. If we make the suggested assumption, we have $S_i = A$ and $S = A^n$. That is, the strategy space of each player in the game G coincides with the action space of the underlying bilateral game. Finally, concerning the payoffs of the overall game, these are identified with the sum of the payoffs accruing in every encounter. Hence, for any given strategy profile $(s_1, s_2, \ldots, s_n) \in S$, the payoff $\pi_i(s)$ received by player i after a complete round of play is given by

$$\pi_i(s) = \sum_{j \neq i} \psi(s_i, s_j). \tag{11.20}$$

Often, we are interested in the particular case in which the bilateral game faced by every pair of players is a *coordination game*. Generalizing the notion of *pure*-coordination game introduced in Subsection 11.2.2 (cf. (11.17)), the bilateral game is said to be one of coordination if its payoff function $\psi(\cdot)$ satisfies

$$\forall q, q' = 1, 2, \ldots, r, \ q \neq q', \ \psi(a_q, a_q) > \psi(a_{q'}, a_q). \tag{11.21}$$

11.3.2 *Learning by imitation*

We start by describing formally the imitation-learning dynamics. Time is indexed discretely, $t = 0, 1, 2, \ldots$, and the game is symmetric. At any t, the state of the system is given by the specification of the strategy profile $s(t) \equiv (s_1(t), s_2(t), \ldots, s_n(t))$ currently displayed by each of the n players. Of course, associated with $s(t)$, we have the profile $\pi(s(t)) \equiv (\pi_1(s(t)), \pi_2(s(t)), \ldots, \pi_n(s(t)))$ specifying the corresponding payoff earned by each player $i \in N$.

On the basis of $s(t)$ and $\pi(s(t))$, interagent imitation is formulated as follows. In every period, there is an independent probability $p \in (0, 1)$ that each player $i \in N$ receives a revision opportunity. In that event, player i mimics the strategy adopted by *some* other player who, in the preceding period, obtained a profit at least as high as i herself. Formally, for any player i who receives a revision opportunity at t, we postulate that

$$s_i(t) \in M_i(s(t-1)) \equiv \{s_j(t-1) : j \in N, \ \pi_j(s(t-1)) \geq \pi_i(s(t-1))\},$$

$$(11.22)$$

any choice in $M_i(s(t-1))$ being adopted with some positive probability.[201] Clearly, the above adjustment rule displays a strong built-in force toward agent homogenization (or monomorphism, in the language used in Chapter 10). In fact, such a tendency always dominates in the long run, as formally stated for future reference in the following Remark (cf. Exercise 11.6).

Remark 11.2: *Given any initial conditions, the imitation dynamics specified by (11.22) converges, a.s., to a profile $s^* = (s_1^*, s_2^*, \ldots, s_n^*) \in A^n$ with $s_i^* = s_j^*$ for all $i, j \in N$. Moreover, any such monomorphic profile is a stationary point of the imitation dynamics.* ◆

The above remark underscores the rather trivial and inconclusive range of long-run predictions to be expected, in general, from a simple-minded, unperturbed process of interagent imitation. However, this conclusion should only be viewed as a very first step in the analysis. For, as shown in Section 12.4, the different monomorphic profiles that now arise as alternative long-run candidates may well be found to respond in a very different manner when the system is subject to arbitrarily small noise.

11.3.3 *Better- and best-response adjustment*

Consider again some given set of players repeatedly interacting according to some strategic-form game $G = \{N, \{S_i\}_{i=1}^n, \{\pi_i\}_{i=1}^n\}$, not necessarily symmetric. Suppose every player continues to hold static perceptions on the evolution of any variable of the process outside her control but now has a scope of information (or a degree of sophistication) that is richer than before. Specifically, assume that, at the time of any of her revision opportunities, she is informed of the *strategy profile* that prevailed during the preceding period. Then, if she knows the payoff structure of the game (at least, as it pertains to her own payoffs), she can compute whether any contemplated adjustment would represent an "expected improvement" under the assumption that others will continue playing their preceding strategies. Any strategy that may be perceived as an improvement under such static expectations is a possible candidate for the *better-response dynamics,* as introduced below.

Formally, this dynamics is defined as follows. Time t is measured discretely and, at every $t = 0, 1, 2, \ldots$, the state of the system is given by the prevailing strategy

---

[201] Note that, for the sake of formal simplicity, player i's former strategy is included in the set of strategies to be imitated. Since $p < 1$, this is inessential. On the other hand, the fact that players are also taken to switch to any other strategy different from the status quo when both (i.e., the status quo and the alternative strategy) appear as payoff equivalent is to be viewed mostly as a convenient simplification. All our analysis is essentially maintained if one were to insist that players should perceive a strict gain to abandon their formerly chosen strategy.

profile $s(t) = (s_1(t), s_2(t), \ldots, s_n(t))$. Before play takes place in every period, there is positive probability $p \in (0, 1)$ that each player $i \in N$ independently receives a revision opportunity. In that event, she is taken to choose

$$s_i(t) \in B_i(s(t-1)) \equiv \{\tilde{s}_i \in S_i : \pi_i(\tilde{s}_i, s_{-i}(t-1)) \geq \pi_i(s(t-1))\}. \quad (11.23)$$

For simplicity, we assume that any strategy in $B_i(s(t-1))$ is chosen with positive (say, uniform) probability, although this is not strictly necessary in most cases. Note that a natural refinement of this dynamics is given by the more demanding *best-response dynamics* where (11.23) is replaced by

$$s_i(t) \in B_i^*(s(t-1)) \equiv \{\tilde{s}_i \in S_i : \pi_i(\tilde{s}_i, s_{-i}(t-1))$$
$$\geq \pi_i(s_i, s_{-i}(t-1)), \; \forall s_i \in S_i\}. \quad (11.24)$$

In this case, any player who receives a revision opportunity switches to a strategy that, given static expectations on others' behavior, induces the highest expected payoff.

For concreteness, our analysis here focuses on the better-response dynamics reflected by (11.23). As before, our central concern is to identify interesting classes of games where this dynamics may converge toward a Nash equilibrium. (Note, of course, that if convergence to a particular state occurs in the present case, that state must define a Nash equilibrium.) We start by considering the class of games that were labeled dominance-solvable in Section 2.1. Recall that these are games in which an iterative elimination of (strictly) dominated strategies by each player (undertaken in any order) leads to a unique strategy profile. As established by the next result, that strategy profile is also the unique long-run outcome induced by the better-response dynamics.[202]

Theorem 11.3: *Assume the strategic-form game G is dominance solvable, with $s^* = (s_1^*, s_2^*, \ldots, s_n^*)$ being the unique strategy profile that survives an iterative elimination of dominated strategies. Then, the better-response dynamics given by (11.23) converges a.s. to s^*.*

Proof: Consider any initial $s(0) \in S = S_1 \times S_2 \times \cdots \times S_n$ and suppose the ensuing adjustment path is such that, for each $t = i + qn$ with $i = 1, 2, \ldots, n$, $q \in \mathbb{N} \cup \{0\}$, and $t \leq M \equiv n(\sum_{i=1}^{n} r_i)$, only player i receives a revision opportunity. (Recall that $r_i = |S_i|$, i.e., the cardinality of S_i.) Obviously, this turn of events has *ex ante* probability $[p(1-p)^{n-1}]^M > 0$. Further assume that, at every such $t = i + qn$, player i chooses a *best* response to $s_{-i}(t-1)$, i.e., a strategy in $B_i^*(s(t-1))$. Since the better-response dynamics at t is postulated to have player i choose every strategy in $B_i(s(t-1)) \supseteq B_i^*(s(t-1))$ with positive probability, this combined chain of events again has positive probability that can be bounded above zero independently of $s(0)$. Let us now show that, if the described sequence of events materializes, $s(t) = s^*$ for all $t \geq M$.

---

[202] Similar results have been established by Moulin (1984) for the best-response dynamics and Milgrom and Roberts (1991) for what they call "adaptive dynamics."

Recall the sequence of pure- and mixed-strategy subsets $\{S_i^q\}_{q=1}^{\infty}$ and $\{\Sigma_i^q\}_{q=1}^{\infty}$ defined in (2.4) and (2.5) that formalize the iterative process of dominated strategies:

$$S_i^0 = S_i; \qquad \Sigma_i^0 = \Sigma_i$$

$$S_i^q = \{s_i \in S_i^{q-1} :$$

$$\left[\nexists \sigma_i \in \Sigma_i^{q-1} : \forall s_{-i} \in S_{-i}^{q-1}, \pi(\sigma_i, s_{-i}) > \pi(s_i, s_{-i}) \right] \}$$

$$\Sigma_i^q = \left\{ \sigma_i \in \Sigma_i^{q-1} : \mathbf{supp}(\sigma_i) \subseteq S_i^q \right\}.$$

We claim that the following statement applies along the M-long path described:

$$\forall t = i + (q-1)n, \ s_i(t) \in S_i^q. \tag{11.25}$$

To verify this claim, first notice that it obviously applies if $q = 1$ in (11.25). On the other hand, if $t = i + (q-1)n$ for some $i \in \{1, 2, \ldots, n\}$ and $q > 1$, the fact that $s_i(t) \in B_i^*(s(t-1))$ implies

$$\pi_i(s_i(t), s_{-i}(t-1)) \geq \pi_i(\tilde{s}_i, s_{-i}(t-1)), \ \forall \tilde{s}_i \in S_i;$$

hence

$$\nexists \sigma_i \in \Sigma_i : \ \pi(\sigma_i, s_{-i}(t-1)) > \pi(s_i(t), s_{-i}(t-1))$$

and, *a fortiori*, since $\Sigma_i^{q-1} \subset \Sigma_i$ and $s_{-i}(t-1) \in S_{-i}^{q-1}$,

$$\nexists \sigma_i \in \Sigma_i^{q-1} : \forall s_{-i} \in S_{-i}^{q-1}, \ \pi(\sigma_i, s_{-i}) > \pi(s_i(t), s_{-i}).$$

Therefore, $s_i(t) \in S_i^q$, as claimed.

Next, notice that because the game is assumed dominance solvable, we must have $s(M) = s^*$. But since s^* defines a Nash equilibrium (cf. Exercise 2.5), it is a stationary point of the better-response dynamics, i.e., $s(t) = s^*$ for all $t > M$ as well.

To complete the proof of the theorem, it is enough to realize that the above considerations apply independently of $s(0)$, the initial strategy profile. Therefore, a lower bound on their positive probability can be established independently of $s(0)$. But then, such a positive lower bound applies as well for an analogous path starting from *any* $s(t)$ at *every* t, which implies that the event $\{\exists T : s(t) = s^* \ \forall t \geq T\}$ occurs with full probability. ∎

As explained in Subsection 2.2.1, dominance solvability is indeed a very strong requirement and can hardly be expected to hold in many applications. It is of interest, therefore, to explore other kinds of games where the present learning model may lead to long-run convergence to some Nash equilibrium.

One important class is given by the so-called *potential games*, a concept introduced by Monderer and Shapley (1996a) – see also Rosenthal (1973). Any such game is defined in terms of some corresponding function $\Upsilon : S_1 \times S_2 \times \cdots \times S_n \to \mathbb{R}$, called its *potential*. In analogy with the notion of potential widely used in physics, the potential function $\Upsilon(\cdot)$ associated with some (potential) game G must satisfy that $\forall i \in N$, $\forall s_i, s_i' \in S_i$, $\forall s_{-i} \in S_{-i}$,

$$\pi_i(s_i, s_{-i}) - \pi_i(s_i', s_{-i}) = \Upsilon(s_i, s_{-i}) - \Upsilon(s_i', s_{-i}).$$

Thus, in a potential game, players may be conceived as striving to maximize a common function – the potential of the game. For our present purposes, however, it is sufficient to focus on games that satisfy the somewhat weaker requirement of displaying an *ordinal* potential. This leads to the notion of *ordinal-potential game*, which is a strategic-form game G that has a function $\Upsilon(\cdot)$ as above that satisfies the following "ordinal" property: $\forall i \in N$, $\forall s_i, s_i' \in S_i$, $\forall s_{-i} \in S_{-i}$,

$$\pi_i(s_i, s_{-i}) - \pi_i(s_i', s_{-i}) \geq 0 \Leftrightarrow \Upsilon(s_i, s_{-i}) - \Upsilon(s_i', s_{-i}) \geq 0. \tag{11.26}$$

Is the notion of (ordinal-)potential game an interesting one? At first sight, it would seem a rather restrictive notion. There is nevertheless a rather wide set of interesting games that display a potential. They include, for example, many public-good or common resource games (cf. Exercise 11.8) as well as the so-called congestion games (i.e., strategic contexts where homogeneous individuals have to choose among a finite collection of nonexclusive alternatives and their payoffs depend on how many players choose each alternative – cf. Exercise 11.9). The Cournot oligopoly described in Subsection 11.3.1 also defines a potential game if firms display constant marginal cost $c > 0$. To focus on the latter context, recall that Φ denotes the output grid (each firm's strategy space) and consider the function $\Upsilon : \Phi^n \to \mathbb{R}$ defined as follows:

$$\Upsilon(q_1, q_2, \ldots, q_n) = q_1 q_2 \ldots q_n \left[P\left(\sum_{i=1}^n q_i\right) - c \right] \tag{11.27}$$

where $P(\cdot)$ stands for the market inverse-demand function. Restricting attention to uniformly positive output profiles,[203] it is easily verified (see Exercise 11.8) that such a function $\Upsilon(\cdot)$ satisfies (11.26), i.e., it is an ordinal potential for the Cournot game.

Within the realm of potential games, the better-response dynamics always leads to equilibrium long-run behavior, as established by the following result.

Theorem 11.4: *Let G be an ordinal-potential game. Then, the better-response dynamics given by (11.23) converges a.s. to the set of Nash equilibria.*

Proof: Because the game is an ordinal-potential game, it has a function $\Upsilon : S_1 \times S_2 \times \cdots \times S_n \to \mathbb{R}$ that satisfies (11.26). Now given any t and the prevailing $s(t) \in S$, construct an ensuing sequence $\{s(\tau)\}_{\tau=t}^{t+v}$ satisfying the following two requirements. First, for each $\tau = t+1, \ldots, t+v$, only one player $i(\tau)$ changes her strategy and

$$\pi_{i(\tau)}(s_{i(\tau)}(\tau), s_{-i(\tau)}(\tau)) = \pi_{i(\tau)}(s_{i(\tau)}(\tau), s_{-i(\tau)}(\tau-1))$$

$$\geq \pi_{i(\tau)}(s(\tau-1)). \tag{11.28}$$

---

[203] This restriction has no relevance for our present purposes. In particular, the convergence result to be established in Theorem 11.4 below applies in this case because, without loss of generality, the learning process can be assumed to start at an interior state.

Second, at the end of the induced strategy path, the final strategy profile satisfies

$$\Upsilon(s(t+v)) = \arg \max_{s \in S} \Upsilon(s). \tag{11.29}$$

In view of (11.28) and the fact that the game is an ordinal-potential game, some such path exists and has prior positive probability. Moreover, since the game is finite, there is some finite $\bar{v} \in \mathbb{N}$ (independent of t and $s(t)$) such that the contemplated path may be constructed with $v \leq \bar{v}$. This path, therefore, has a positive probability bounded above zero. By an already familiar argument, we may then conclude that, with probability one, an ensuing path with these characteristics will occur at some $\hat{t}$. Thus, given (11.29) and the fact that $\Upsilon(\cdot)$ is an ordinal potential for the game, it follows that from $\hat{t} + \bar{v}$ onward some Nash equilibrium will be played. This completes the proof of the theorem. ∎

As explained, the preceding convergence result applies to one of the leading scenarios presented in Subsection 11.3.1, i.e., Cournot competition, under the assumption of constant marginal costs.[204] Next, we turn our attention to the second of the leading scenarios proposed: a round-robin setup where agents are matched to play a certain bilateral game. In this context, if the underlying bilateral game is one of coordination, better-response learning dynamics also guarantees long-run convergence to equilibrium, as established by the following result.

Theorem 11.5: *Consider a round-robin context where the payoff function satisfies (11.20) and (11.21). Then, the better-response dynamics given by (11.23) converges a.s. to some Nash equilibrium $s^* \in S$.*

Proof[205]**:** First, observe that in the coordination scenario induced by (11.20) and (11.21), all monomorphic profiles where every player adopts a common strategy are alternative pure-strategy Nash equilibria. (In fact, the reciprocal inclusion also holds, as indicated in Exercise 11.10.) Thus, suppose that, at any given t, the learning process is *not* at some such "monomorphic" rest point. Then, if we denote

$$A(t) \equiv \left\{ a_q \in A : s_i(t) = a_q \text{ for some } i \in \{1, 2, \ldots, n\} \right\},$$

it must be the case that the cardinality of this set, $|A(t)|$, is at least 2. Clearly, to prove the result, it is enough to show that, for any such t, there is positive probability (independent of $s(t)$ and t) that $|A(t+1)| < |A(t)|$.

Let a_p or a_q be two distinct strategies (or actions) in $A(t)$. For any $u, v \in \{p, q\}$ denote by $\phi_{uv}(t)$ the payoff expected at $t+1$ by an individual who chose action a_u at t if, under static expectations, she decides to switch

---

[204] Here, we implicitly assume that the Cournot-Nash equilibrium outputs lie in the grid Φ and that the grid restriction does not introduce any further Nash equilibria.

[205] The main argument here is inspired by similar analysis conducted by Bhaskar and Vega-Redondo (2001).

to the strategy a_v at $t + 1$. We have

$$\phi_{uv}(t) = \sum_{i=1}^{n} \psi(a_v, s_i(t)) - \psi(a_v, a_u).$$

Therefore, any individual i who adopted a_p at t will choose a_q at $t + 1$ with positive probability if

$$\phi_{pq}(t) - \phi_{pp}(t) = \left[\sum_{i=1}^{n} \psi(a_q, s_i(t)) - \psi(a_q, a_p)\right]$$
$$- \left[\sum_{i=1}^{n} \psi(a_p, s_i(t)) - \psi(a_p, a_p)\right] \geq 0. \tag{11.30}$$

And, similarly, any individual i who adopted a_q at t will choose a_p at $t + 1$ with positive probability if

$$\phi_{qp}(t) - \phi_{qq}(t) = \left[\sum_{i=1}^{n} \psi(a_p, s_i(t)) - \psi(a_p, a_q)\right]$$
$$- \left[\sum_{i=1}^{n} \psi(a_q, s_i(t)) - \psi(a_q, a_q)\right] \geq 0. \tag{11.31}$$

Adding (11.30) and (11.31), we find, in view of (11.21), that

$$\phi_{pq}(t) - \phi_{pp}(t) + \phi_{qp}(t) - \phi_{qq}(t) = \psi(a_p, a_p) - \psi(a_q, a_p)$$
$$+ \psi(a_q, a_q) - \psi(a_p, a_q) > 0.$$

Therefore, it follows that either (11.30) and/or (11.31) must apply. If it is the former, then with positive probability those individuals choosing a_p might receive a revision opportunity (and only them), in which case they could switch to a_q with positive probability as well. Under these circumstances, we have

$$|A(t + 1)| = |A(t)| - 1. \tag{11.32}$$

On the other hand, if it is (11.31) that applies, again we have (11.32) with positive probability, now with those individuals previously choosing a_q switching to a_p. Since the argument is independent of $s(t)$, we conclude that with probability one the process will reach a state with $|A(t')| = 1$ at some t'. This completes the proof of the result. ∎

11.4   Memory, expectations, and foresight

In Subsection 11.3.3, we identified different classes of games where myopic "better response" based on static expectations ensures long-run convergence to some Nash equilibrium of the underlying game. There are, however, many other classes of interesting games where such a learning dynamics fares quite badly. Consider, for example, any game G displaying no pure-strategy equilibrium. Then, it is clear that no strategy profile may be stationary for the better-response dynamics postulated above, thus leading to a nonconvergent process whose long-run behavior may be hard to interpret.

When such nonconvergence occurs, one may attempt to rationalize matters in a variety of alternative (but complementary) ways.

1. It can be suggested, for example, that when a player holds a static view of her environment, her memory is too short to allow for a suitable smoothening of her expectations. Consequently, the player may often overreact to current (and often just ephemeral) circumstances, preventing the learning process to settle down in many cases.

2. Alternatively, the dynamic instability can be understood as the result of non-smooth behavior, rather than as a consequence of nonsmooth expectations. Specifically, one may argue that, if players are restricted to pure strategies (as in (11.22), (11.23), and (11.24)), it is not surprising that convergence cannot materialize when the equilibrium requires some probability mixing.

3. Finally, the lack of convergence can be blamed on the fact that players are assumed unable to conceive their interaction in the appropriate intertemporal framework in which it actually takes place. It may be conjectured, for example, that if players were to choose their behavior within a complete (and therefore intertemporal) model of the situation, they should be able to learn to coordinate their expectations and play in equilibrium.

Each of these three alternative lines of attack to the problem has been pursued in the recent literature on learning in games. Concerning the first one, a noted representative is given by the classic model of learning known as "fictitious play." On the other hand, a variant of fictitious play that pursues the second approach and allows for mixed strategies is labeled "smooth fictitious play." Finally, along the third direction, the literature has developed the so-called models of "rational learning," which embed the learning process into a full-fledged intertemporal framework. Next, we present each of these alternative approaches in turn. Unfortunately, however, we shall see that none of them proves fully satisfactory.

11.4.1 *Fictitious play*

The model of dynamic adjustment known as *fictitious play* was first proposed by Brown (1951) as an algorithm for computing equilibria. Later on, it was reconsidered by others (e.g., Shapley, 1964) as an interesting model of how players might learn to play a given game.

To keep matters simple, let us restrict again to a context with just two players, $i = 1, 2$, involved in a certain strategic-form game $G = \{\{1, 2\}, \{S_1, S_2\}, \{\pi_1, \pi_2\}\}$. Fictitious play involves two parts. On the one hand, each player forms expectations about the current play of the opponent in a (naively) empiricist manner; roughly, that is, she associates subjective probabilities with the different opponent's strategies that are equal to their respective frequencies in past play. On the other hand, given the expectations formed in this fashion at each point in time, each player reacts optimally in a myopic fashion (i.e., maximizing current expected payoff).

In a sense, we may conceive this approach as an enrichment of the static-expectations framework analyzed in Subsection 11.3.3. As in that case, players

here may be conceived as having a stationary model of their environment and reacting optimally to it in a myopic fashion.[206] In contrast, however, they are currently
assumed to rely on the full length of history to form their expectations, a feature
that implicitly rules out any memory bounds.

As before, let time be measured discretely, $t \in \{0, 1, 2, \ldots\}$. Then, to define the
model formally, denote by $\eta_{iq}(t) \in \mathbb{R}_+$ the *weight* associated by player i at t to the
strategy $s_{jq} \in S_j$ of the opponent ($q = 1, 2, \ldots, r_j$, $i, j = 1, 2$, $i \neq j$). To start
the process, players attribute arbitrary initial weights

$$\eta_i(0) = (\eta_{iq}(0))_{q=1}^{r_j} \quad \text{s.t.} \quad \sum_{q=1}^{r_j} \eta_{iq}(0) > 0 \quad (q = 1, 2, \ldots, r_j,$$

$$i, j = 1, 2, \ i \neq j). \quad (11.33)$$

Thereafter, depending on the path $\{s_j(\tau)\}_{\tau=0}^{t}$ that each player i observes on the
part of her opponent up to any given t, these weights are adjusted as follows:

$$\eta_{iq}(t+1) = \begin{cases} \eta_{iq}(t) + 1 & \text{if } s_j(t) = s_{jq} \\ \eta_{iq}(t) & \text{otherwise} \end{cases} \quad \begin{array}{l} (q = 1, 2, \ldots, r_j, \\ i, j = 1, 2, \ i \neq j \end{array} \quad (11.34)$$

These weights are then used to form player i's expectations at t, $\mu_i(t) = (\mu_{iq}(t))_{q=1}^{r_j} \in \Delta^{r_j-1}$, in the following manner:

$$\mu_{iq}(t) = \frac{\eta_{iq}(t)}{\sum_{q'=1}^{r_j} \eta_{iq'}(t)} \quad (q = 1, 2, \ldots, r_j, \ i, j = 1, 2, \ i \neq j). \quad (11.35)$$

And, finally, each player is assumed to choose, at each t, a strategy that verifies

$$s_i(t) \in B_i^*(\mu_i(t)), \quad (11.36)$$

where $B_i^* : \Delta^{r_j-1} \rightrightarrows S_i$ generalizes (11.24) above as the best-response correspondence of player i, i.e.,

$$B_i^*(\mu_i) \equiv \left\{ \tilde{s}_i \in S_i : \sum_{q=1}^{r_j} \mu_{iq} \cdot \pi_i(\tilde{s}_i, s_{jq}) \geq \sum_{q=1}^{r_j} \mu_{iq} \cdot \pi_i(s_i, s_{jq}), \forall s_i \in S_i \right\}.$$

$$(11.37)$$

Note that (11.36) determines uniquely the choice of each player i except for a "thin"
subspace of her beliefs. Because this subspace has zero measure, the particular way
in which such an ambiguity is resolved through some particular selection of $B_i^*(\cdot)$
at those points is inconsequential for the analysis.

---

[206] More precisely, it can be shown that, under the hypothesis that the opponent's (mixed) strategy remains fixed
throughout, fictitious play embodies rigorous Bayesian updating if the prior distribution on the opponent's
strategy is a Dirichlet distribution (see Fudenberg and Levine, 1998, Ch. 2).

Table 11.2: *Matching-pennies game*

1 \ 2	H	T
H	1, −1	−1, 1
T	−1, 1	1, −1

It can be shown that many of the conclusions on long-run convergence to Nash equilibrium that were established in Subsection 11.3.3 for any better-response dynamics (e.g., for dominance-solvable or potential games) apply as well for fictitious play – cf. Exercise 11.12 and Monderer and Shapley (1996b). Thus, to enlarge the scope of our former analysis, let us focus on games whose Nash equilibria are in mixed strategies, such as the familiar game of matching pennies (cf. Subsection 1.2.2) whose payoffs are recalled in Table 11.2.

In this game, the unique Nash equilibrium involves each player randomizing with equal probability between both actions H and T. Since there is no pure-strategy profile defining an equilibrium, it would seem that, as for the better-response dynamics, fictitious play cannot possibly settle down in the long run. In a certain sense, this is indeed the case because, inevitably, no single pure-strategy configuration can provide the "balance" that is required for equilibrium-like behavior in this case (cf. Exercise 11.13). It can be shown, however, that even though behavior indeed cycles indefinitely when fictitious play is applied to matching pennies, the empirical frequencies (and, therefore, beliefs)[207] do converge in the long run. This convergence is, in fact, a general property displayed by any generic game that has only two strategies (as in matching pennies) or is zero sum (as is matching pennies as well). This was established by Miyasawa (1961) in the first case (2×2 games) and by Robinson (1951) in the second case (zero-sum games). Both conclusions are formally stated without proof in the following result.

Theorem 11.6 (Robinson, 1951; Miyasawa 1961): *Let G be a bilateral game in strategic form. If either*

(a) $r_1 = r_2 = 2$, or
(b) $\pi_1(s) = -\pi_2(s)$, $\forall s \in S$,

then, for generic payoffs, the following is true. Given any initial weights $\eta_i(0)$, $i = 1, 2$, there exists some $\mu_i^* \in \Delta^{r_j - 1}, j \neq i$, such that the belief sequences $\{\mu_i(t)\}_{t=0}^{\infty}$ induced by (11.33)–(11.37) satisfy a.s. that $\lim_{t \to \infty} \mu_i(t) = \mu_i^*$ for each $i = 1, 2$.

An illustration for part (a) of Theorem 11.6 is provided in Figures 11.6–11.8 for each of the three generic types of 2×2 games – recall Table 11.1 and the classification embodied in items (a)–(c) following it.

---

[207] Note that empirical frequencies and beliefs need not coincide because of the influence of the initial weights. However, the latter's influence vanishes in the long run so that empirical frequencies and beliefs approach the same limit.

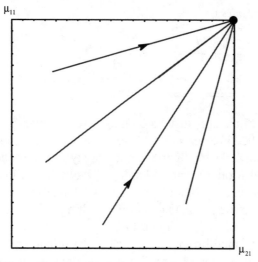

Figure 11.6: Empirical frequencies in fictitious play, a game with a dominant strategy.

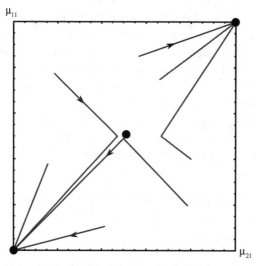

Figure 11.7: Empirical frequencies in fictitious play, a game with two pure-strategy equilibria.

By means of a famous 3×3 example where empirical frequencies do not converge in fictitious play, Shapley (1964) showed that the previous result cannot be extended to (non-zero-sum) games involving more than two strategies per player. In any case, even knowing that the convergence of empirical frequencies occurs in some interesting cases (e.g., 2×2 or zero-sum games), the question remains: What do they converge to? A clear-cut answer is provided by the following *general* result, which applies to any game where convergence materializes.

Theorem 11.7: *Let G be a bilateral game in strategic form and assume that the belief sequences $\{\mu_i(t)\}_{t=o}^{\infty}$ induced by (11.33)–(11.37) converge to*

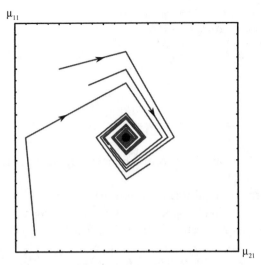

Figure 11.8: Empirical frequencies in fictitious play, a game with a unique mixed-strategy equilibrium.

some $\mu_i^* \in \Delta^{r_j-1}$, $i = 1, 2$, $j \neq i$. Then, $(\sigma_1^*, \sigma_2^*) \equiv (\mu_2^*, \mu_1^*) \in \Sigma_1 \times \Sigma_2$ defines a Nash equilibrium of G.

Proof: Suppose, for the sake of contradiction, that the limit beliefs $(\mu_2^*, \mu_1^*) \equiv (\sigma_1^*, \sigma_2^*)$ do *not* define a Nash equilibrium of G. Then, there must be at least a player i such that the following applies:

$$\exists s_{iq}, s_{iq'} \in S_i, \ s_{iq} \in \mathbf{supp}(\sigma_i^*) : \pi_i(s_{iq}, \sigma_j^*) < \pi_i(s_{iq'}, \sigma_j^*).$$

Then, since

$$\lim_{t \to \infty} \mu_i(t) = \mu_i^* = \sigma_j^*,$$

there must exist some $T \in \mathbb{N}$, such that $\forall t \geq T$,

$$\pi_i(s_{iq}, \mu_i(t)) < \pi_i(s_{iq'}, \mu_i(t)),$$

which, in view of (11.36), implies that $\forall t \geq T$,

$$\eta_{jq}(t) = \eta_{jq}(T),$$

and, therefore,

$$\mu_{jq}^* = \lim_{t \to \infty} \frac{\eta_{jq}(t)}{\sum_{q'=1}^{r_i} \eta_{jq'}(t)} = \lim_{t \to \infty} \frac{\eta_{jq}(T)}{\sum_{q'=1}^{r_i} \eta_{jq'}(T) + (t - T)} = 0,$$

contradicting that $s_{iq} \in \mathbf{supp}(\sigma_i^*) = \mathbf{supp}(\mu_j^*)$. This completes the proof. ∎

    Theorem 11.7 seems to suggest that, within the class of games where convergence of empirical frequencies is guaranteed, fictitious play should lead agents to reproduce empirically the play of some, possibly mixed-strategy, Nash equilibrium. However, this view is quite misleading, as illustrated by the following example due

Table 11.3: *A symmetric strategic-form game with two asymmetric* pure-strategy *Nash equilibria and one symmetric* mixed-strategy *Nash equilibrium*

1 \ 2	A_2	B_2
A_1	0, 0	2, 1
B_1	1, 2	0, 0

to Fudenberg and Kreps (1993). Consider two individuals playing a game whose payoffs are as indicated in Table 11.3.

This game has a mixed-strategy equilibrium where each player i chooses A_i with probability 2/3. Suppose now that these individuals start playing according to (11.33)–(11.37) with an initial weight vector $\eta_i(0) = (1, \sqrt{2})$, $i = 1, 2$. Then, both players will begin choosing $s_i(0) = A_i$. Hence, at $t = 1$, we have $\eta_i(1) = (2, \sqrt{2})$ and thus $s_i(1) = A_i$ again, for each $i = 1, 2$. Thereafter, at $t = 2$, $\eta_i(2) = (3, \sqrt{2})$, which produces a joint switch toward $s_i(2) = B_i$, $i = 1, 2$. Proceeding inductively, it is clear that, at all t,

$$\eta_1(t) = \eta_2(t)$$

and, therefore, either

$$s_i(t) = A_i$$

for both $i = 1, 2$, or

$$s_i(t) = B_i$$

for both players as well. Thus, in view of the payoffs displayed in Table 11.3, it follows that both players obtain a zero payoff *for all t*, in contrast with the payoff of at least 2/3 that they are *expecting* in every round. Given that they are consistently being frustrated in their hopes for a higher payoff, we might well ask: Shouldn't they surmise that something is wrong with their model of the world?

Despite the indefinite cyclical pattern found over time in the above example, Theorem 11.6 implies that the induced long-run empirical frequencies must coincide with the Nash equilibrium weights $(1/3, 2/3)$. Of course, this vector of weights is to be understood as the *marginal* distribution over the strategy choices made along the path by each *separate* player. However, if we focus on the induced *joint* distribution over strategy *profiles*, this distribution is far from converging to that resulting from Nash equilibrium play. Indeed, it is fully concentrated on the profiles (A_1, A_2) and (B_1, B_2), a reflection of the perfect (but perverse) correlation induced by the learning process that is at the heart of the problem illustrated by this example. The targeted equilibrium implicitly presupposes some stochastic independence that is nevertheless destroyed by the learning mechanism. Heuristically, however, one might conjecture that if players could indeed display some genuinely mixed (i.e., stochastic) behavior at some point, such an iron-clad correlation would break apart and so would its unwelcome effects. This is precisely

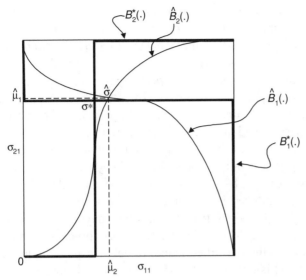

Figure 11.9: Best-response correspondences, ordinary and smooth versions.

the approach embodied by the so-called smooth fictitious play, to which we turn next.

11.4.2 *Smooth fictitious play*

Partly at least, the problems posed by (ordinary) fictitious play have to do with the highly discontinuous nature of its best-response decision rule (11.36). To understand this discontinuity and suggest natural ways of addressing the issue, it is useful to reformulate the best-response correspondence as a mapping[208]

$$B_i^* : \Delta^{r_j-1} \rightrightarrows \Delta(S_i) = \Delta^{r_i-1}$$

that associates with every possible belief the corresponding set of mixed strategies that define a best response. As explained, for almost every $\mu_i \in \Delta^{r_j-1}$, we have that $B_i^*(\mu_i) = \{e_q\}$ for some e_q, the unit vector associated with pure strategy $s_{iq} \in S_i$. Hence, with only two pure strategies, any selection of the best-response correspondence of each player i can be depicted as a step function, with a discontinuity arising at the precise beliefs $\hat{\mu}_i$ of exact indifference between the two pure strategies. This familiar construct is illustrated in Figure 11.9 for a 2×2 game with a unique (mixed-strategy) equilibrium σ^*.

Suppose now that, in contrast to the sharp changes of behavior that are typically induced by the above best-response correspondences, we suppose players react to their beliefs in a smooth fashion, i.e., they adjust their probabilities of playing each of their pure strategies in a continuous manner. Focusing on a 2×2 scenario, this is illustrated by the smoothed best-response functions labeled $\hat{B}_i(\cdot)$ in Figure 11.9.

---

[208] For simplicity, we maintain the notation formerly used for the best-response correspondence mapping on the set of pure strategies.

These smooth functions admit several interpretations. One of them is just based on the simple-minded (say, "psychological") notion that players do not switch actions abruptly but rather do so in a gradual manner. That is, close to points of indifference, they settle on one or the other possibility (i.e., pure strategy) with nondegenerate probabilities that respond monotonically to expected payoff differences.

In a theoretically more sophisticated vein, the smoothed best-response function can also be motivated along the lines of Harsanyi's approach to the "purification" of mixed strategies. As explained in Section 6.5, this approach entails constructing a suitably defined asymmetric-information game. In this game, the payoffs of each player i are perturbed stochastically through some idiosyncratic random variable $\tilde{\varepsilon}_i$ whose realization vector $\varepsilon_i \in [-1, 1]^{r_i}$ is assumed to be observed only by the player in question. In the induced Bayesian game, a *pure strategy* for player i is simply a mapping $\gamma_i : [-1, 1]^{r_i} \to S_i$ from the observed payoff perturbation to her original (pure-) strategy space. Thus, if player i adopts some such strategy at a Bayes-Nash equilibrium of the perturbed game, the choice $\gamma_i(\varepsilon_i)$ induced by the realized ε_i (observed by i) is deterministic. However, from the perspective of her uninformed opponents, her actual choice must be regarded as random, just as if player i were playing according to a genuinely mixed strategy.

If we describe the Harsanyinan construct from an *ex ante* viewpoint, the behavior of each player i may be summarized by a smooth best-response function

$$\hat{B}_i : \Delta^{r_j-1} \to \Delta^{r_i-1}, \quad i, j = 1, 2, \ i \neq j$$

that, for any belief $\mu_i \in \Delta^{r_j-1}$ held by player i, determines a "mixed strategy" $\sigma_i = \hat{B}_i(\mu_i)$ reflecting the *ex ante* probabilities with which this player chooses a pure strategy as a function of her private information ε_i (cf. Figure 11.9). Then, a Bayesian equilibrium may be simply associated with a profile $\hat{\sigma} \in \Delta^{r_1-1} \times \Delta^{r_2-1}$ that satisfies the usual rational-expectations and optimality conditions:

$$\begin{aligned} \hat{\mu}_i &= \hat{\sigma}_j, \\ \hat{\sigma}_i &= \hat{B}_i(\hat{\mu}_i), \end{aligned} \tag{11.38}$$

for each $i, j = 1, 2; \ i \neq j$. Naturally, we want to conceive the size of the perturbation induced by each $\tilde{\varepsilon}_i$ as small. For, in this case, the profile $\hat{\sigma}$ becomes arbitrarily close to the original Nash equilibrium σ^* of the unperturbed game while the smoothing implications on each $\hat{B}_i(\cdot)$ are still preserved (of course, as long as the random variables $\tilde{\varepsilon}_i$ do *not* become *fully* degenerate).

Motivated by the previous considerations, Fudenberg and Kreps (1993) – see also Benaïm and Hirsch (1999) – postulate a smoothed version of fictitious play that, in contrast to ordinary fictitious play, permits the application of the powerful techniques developed by stochastic approximation theory (recall Subsection 11.2.1). This is a consequence of the following two features:

(i) By construction, smooth fictitious play is defined through a twice continuously differentiable law of motion. More specifically, it is given by the former (unchanged) expressions (11.33), (11.34), and (11.35), while

(11.36) is replaced by

$$\sigma_i(t) = \hat{B}_i(\mu_i(t)), \tag{11.39}$$

where $\hat{B}_i : \Delta^{r_j-1} \to \Delta^{r_i-1}$ is a suitable C^2 approximation of $B_i^*(\cdot)$. For each $i = 1, 2$, and any $\mu_i(t) \in \Delta^{r_j-1}$, $\hat{B}_i(\mu_i)$ is interpreted as the probability vector (mixed strategy) with which player i chooses the different pure strategies in S_i as a function of her current beliefs. As suggested above, this formulation may be motivated by the assumption that each player i is subject to small independent payoff perturbations that are only privately observed.

(ii) Smooth fictitious play also has the property (shared with its ordinary version) that the adjustment step becomes progressively smaller with time.[209] As outlined in Subsection 11.2.1, it is precisely this increasing gradualness that allows one to conclude that, in the long run, the motion of the system can be well approximated by its *expected* direction of change.

In view of (ii), our first task is to find explicit expressions for the system's expected motion. Let $\chi_i(t) \subset \{e_1, e_2, \ldots, e_{r_i}\}$ be a random variable defined on the set of pure strategies S_i (here represented by the set of corresponding unit vectors in Δ^{r_i-1}) with

$$\Pr\{\chi_i(t) = e_q\} = \sigma_{iq}(t).$$

Smooth fictitious play, as defined by (11.33), (11.34), (11.35), and (11.39) gives rise to the following stochastic system:

$$\mu_{iq}(t+1) = \frac{\eta_{iq}(t) + \chi_{jq}(t)}{\sum_{q'=1}^{r_j} \eta_{iq'}(t) + 1} \quad (q = 1, 2, \ldots, r_j, \ i, j = 1, 2, \ i \neq j) \tag{11.40}$$

where $\chi_{jq}(t)$ is the marginal random variable induced by $\chi_j(t)$ on the qth component. Note that, for any $t \in \mathbb{N}$, we can write

$$\sum_{q'=1}^{r_j} \eta_{iq'}(t) = \sum_{q'=1}^{r_j} \eta_{iq'}(0) + t,$$

where $\sum_{q'=1}^{r_j} \eta_{iq'}(0) \equiv L_i$ is an exogenous parameter of the model. Thus, (11.40) becomes

$$\begin{aligned}
\mu_{iq}(t+1) &= \frac{\eta_{iq}(t) + \chi_{jq}(t)}{L_i + t + 1} \\
&= \frac{\eta_{iq}(t)}{L_i + t} + \frac{\chi_{jq}(t)(L_i + t) - \eta_{iq}(t)}{(L_i + t)(L_i + t + 1)} \\
&= \mu_{iq}(t) + \frac{\chi_{jq}(t) - \mu_{iq}(t)}{L_i + t + 1},
\end{aligned}$$

---

[209] In fact, the step size cannot become small "too fast" for an application of the stochastic aproximation techniques. It must hold, in particular, that if ϱ_t denotes the step size at t, $\sum_t \varrho_t = +\infty$ but $\sum_t (\varrho_t)^\alpha < +\infty$ for some $\alpha > 1$. In our case, where $\varrho_t = \mathcal{O}(1/t)$, these conditions are satisfied.

since $\mu_{iq}(t) = \eta_{iq}(t)/(L_i + t)$. Hence,

$$\mu_{iq}(t+1) - \mu_{iq}(t) = \frac{\chi_{jq}(t) - \mu_{iq}(t)}{L_i + t + 1},$$

and, by applying the expectations operator (conditional at t), we obtain

$$\mathbf{E}_t[\mu_{iq}(t+1) - \mu_{iq}(t)] = \frac{1}{L_i + t + 1}\left[\hat{B}_{jq}(\mu_j(t)) - \mu_{iq}(t)\right] \qquad (11.41)$$

because, obviously, $\mathbf{E}_t[\chi_{jq}(t)] = \hat{B}_{jq}(\mu_j(t))$.

In view of (11.41), stochastic approximation theory allows us to analyze the long-run behavior of smooth fictitious play in terms of the following system of differential equations:

$$\dot{\mu}_{iq}(t) = \hat{B}_{jq}(\mu_j(t)) - \mu_{iq}(t) \quad (q = 1, 2, \dots, r_j, \ i, j = 1, 2, \ i \neq j).$$

$$(11.42)$$

This dynamical system is simply the continuous-time version of the smoothed best-response dynamics associated to the functions $(\hat{B}_i(\cdot))_{i=1}^2$. For our purposes, the essential implication here is that, in the long run, smooth fictitious play can be guaranteed to approach *some* limit set of (11.42), almost surely. Of these limit sets, however, only those that are robust (locally stable) may have some positive probability of being reached. The heuristic reason for this important qualification was explained in Subsection 11.2.1. Since smooth fictitious play remains noisy throughout, the process will eventually escape any orbit of the approximating (deterministic) system that is "fragile" in the face of perturbations.

In general, the dynamic behavior of (11.42) can be quite complex. There is, however, a simple context where it leads to sharp limit behavior (cf. Benaïm and Hirsch, 1999). This occurs when, as in the context illustrated by Figure 11.9, each player has only two strategies. In this case, as will be recalled from Section 11.2.1, there are three generic possibilities:

(a) at least one player has a dominant strategy (and the game has a unique Nash equilibrium);

(b) players face a coordination game with two pure-strategy (and strict) Nash equilibria;

(c) the game has a unique and mixed-strategy (thus nonstrict) Nash equilibrium.

In Cases (a) and (b), it is clear that (if the payoff perturbation embodied by $(\hat{B}_i(\cdot))_{i=1}^2$ is small enough) the only robust limit sets of (11.42) are the singletons associated to the strict equilibria. These equilibria also attract the dynamics from almost every initial conditions. It follows, therefore, that smooth fictitious play settles in one of them as well, almost surely. Figures 11.10 and 11.11 illustrate such an asymptotic behavior (as given by (11.42)) in either case.

Case (c) is more complex. What are the *robust* limit sets of (11.42) in this case? As it turns out, one can show that if the (generic) game has a unique

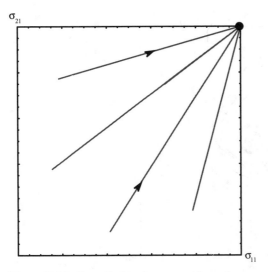

Figure 11.10: Smoothed best-response dynamics, a game with a dominant strategy.

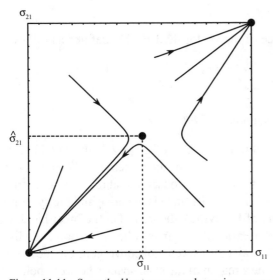

Figure 11.11: Smoothed best-response dynamics, a game with two pure-strategy equilibria.

mixed-strategy equilibrium, σ^*, all trajectories of the system converge to the profile $\hat{\sigma}$ that approximates it – cf. (11.38). To prove this claim, a convenient tool is afforded by the following well-known result in the theory of dynamical systems (cf. Arnold, 1973, p. 198):

Liouville's Theorem: Let $\dot{x}(t) = F(x(t))$ be a dynamical system defined on a certain open subset $U \subseteq \mathbb{R}^n$, where $F(\cdot)$ is a differentiable vector field. Then, if $A \subseteq U$ has a volume $V \equiv \int_A dx$, the volume $V(t)$ of the set $A(t) = \{z = x(t) : x(0) \in A\}$ satisfies

$$\dot{V}(t) = \int\limits_{A(t)} \mathbf{div}\ F(x)\ dx,$$

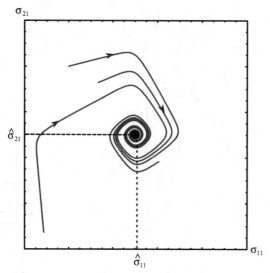

Figure 11.12: Smoothed best-response dynamics, a game with a unique mixed-strategy equilibrium.

where the divergence of the vector field $F(\cdot)$ is defined as follows:

$$\mathbf{div}\ F(x) \equiv \sum_{i=1}^{n} \frac{\partial F_i(x)}{\partial x_i},$$

i.e., the trace of the Jacobian of $F(\cdot)$.

Applying the previous result to the interior of $\Delta^1 \times \Delta^1$ (the suitable state space in this case) it follows that every trajectory of the system (11.42) must converge to its unique rest point $\hat{\sigma}$. For, on the one hand, observe that the main-diagonal entries of its Jacobian are equal to -1. Hence, its trace is negative and the system must be volume-contracting by virtue of Liouville's theorem. On the other hand, we know that every limit set of a two-dimensional system is either a rest point or a limit cycle (cf. Footnote 194). Thus, if the trajectories were not convergent and the system had a nontrivial cycle, there would be a region of the state space (the area enclosed by the corresponding closed orbit) that would not be volume-contracting. This proves that the trajectories induced by (11.42) indeed converge to $\hat{\sigma}$. Since, moreover, this point is the unique asymptotically stable state of the continuous-time system, the long-run dynamics induced by smooth fictitious play can also be guaranteed to converge to $\hat{\sigma}$, almost surely. An illustration of this conclusion is provided in Figure 11.12.

To summarize, smooth fictitious play has been shown to afford successful learning of Nash equilibrium in any generic 2×2 game. For example, the fact that players' behavior around equilibrium is always genuinely stochastic allows the process to overcome the problems of "perverse correlation" encountered in the game described in Table 11.3.[210] The general approach based on stochastic-approximation

---

[210] For a detailed analysis of these issues (in particular, the optimality properties displayed by smooth fictitious play), the reader is referred to the recent monograph by Fudenberg and Levine (1998).

arguments could be applied to any game, but the results would rarely be so sharp. In general, smoothed (continuous-time) best-response dynamics cannot be expected to display clear-cut limit behavior of the sort found above. Indeed, if the number of strategies is large (even just three) or the number of players goes beyond two, the induced long-run dynamics often happens to display rather complex (e.g., chaotic) behavior. Thus, even though the present model of learning is certainly more successful than preceding ones in dealing with important contexts (e.g., simple games with only mixed-strategy equilibria), it cannot be conceived as fully satisfactory.

In attempting to extend the range of games that allow for successful learning, the next subsection performs quite a formidable theoretical leap. It deals with agents who are essentially unbounded in what they can remember, compute, or anticipate. It is then perhaps not very surprising that, under certain conditions, they will be found capable of learning to play *some* Nash equilibria in *any* game. However, as we also discuss at some length, some delicate conceptual problems stand in the way of conceiving this learning model as a really effective one, even if we abstract from the "generous" (in a sense, nonrealistic) capabilities implicitly bestowed on the players.

11.4.3 *Rational learning*

The model of rational learning discussed here was proposed by Kalai and Lehrer (1993*a*,*b*). As advanced, players in this model (for notational simplicity, we consider just two of them) are assumed to be fully aware of the repeated-interaction framework in which they live. That is, in the language of Chapter 8, they conceive the situation as a repeated game or, more precisely, as a discounted repeated game $\mathcal{R}^\delta(W)$ over stages $t = 1, 2, \ldots$, where $\delta \in [0, 1)$ is the discount rate and $W \equiv (W_i)_i^2 : A_1 \times A_2 \to \mathbb{R}$ is the payoff function for a fixed-stage game in strategic form $G = \{N, \{A_i\}_{i \in N}, \{W_i\}_{i \in N}\}$ – recall Section 8.2.[211]

Now, rather than assuming that individuals directly play an equilibrium of the repeated game, let us postulate that each player $i \in \{1, 2\}$ has some subjective beliefs about the behavioral strategy $\gamma_j : \bigcup_{t \in \mathbb{N}} H^{t-1} \to \Delta(A_j)$ played by individual $j \neq i$. In fact, by virtue of Kuhn's theorem (recall Subsection 1.5.2), any belief by player i over j's strategy can be formally identified with a behavioral strategy of player j, $\gamma_j^i : \bigcup_{t \in \mathbb{N}} H^{t-1} \to \Delta(A_j)$, specifying player i's prediction about j's action after any possible history $h^{t-1} \in H^{t-1}$ prevailing at every t. Naturally, if we make $j = i$ in the above formulation, it must be posited that $\gamma_i^i = \gamma_i$, i.e., player i knows her own strategy.

Much of the analysis is built on the critical assumption labeled "a grain of truth." Heuristically, this assumption is *in the spirit* of asserting that player i's beliefs should be diffuse (or "cautious") enough to attribute *positive* probability to the strategy actually played by j. Precisely formulated, however, it is somewhat more general than that, as its formal statement below indicates.

---

[211] As in Chapter 8, we adopt the notational shorthand of identifying the stage game G with its corresponding payoff function W.

Let $\gamma^i = (\gamma_1^i, \gamma_2^i)$ denote the beliefs of player i, and $\gamma = (\gamma_1, \gamma_2)$ the actual strategy profile played. Each of these profiles defines probability measures μ_{γ^i} ($i = 1, 2$) and μ_γ over the set of possible plays, H^∞. We then propose the following.

Grain of Truth (GT): Let $A \subset H^\infty$ be any measurable set of plays. Then, for each $i = 1, 2$, $\mu_\gamma(A) > 0 \Rightarrow \mu_{\gamma^i}(A) > 0$.[212]

Conceptually, (GT) implies that each player's beliefs are to be such that neither of them can be "utterly surprised" by the course of play. In other words, any set of possible plays that has *ex ante* positive probability (given the strategies actually played) has to be attributed *some* positive subjective probability by both players as well.

Given any pair of beliefs that satisfy (GT), the model is completed by the natural postulate that players should choose their own strategy $\gamma_i \in \Psi_i$ to maximize expected payoffs given their beliefs. That is:

Expected Payoff Maximization (EPM): For each $i, j = 1, 2$, $i \neq j$,

$$\gamma_i \in \arg\max_{\gamma_i' \in \Psi_i} \pi_i(\gamma_i', \gamma_j^i),$$

where Ψ_i is the set of player i's admissible (behavioral) strategies and $\pi_i : \Psi_1 \times \Psi_2 \to \mathbb{R}$ is her corresponding payoff function.

For an illustrative example, suppose players are involved in a repeated prisoner's dilemma (cf. Table 1.1). Further assume they are restricted to (countable) pure-strategy sets, Ψ_1 and Ψ_2, with the following elements.

- On the one hand, each Ψ_i includes the set $\{\gamma_{i0}, \gamma_{i1}, \gamma_{i2}, \ldots\}$ of "trigger strategies" (recall Section 9.1.1), where γ_{ik} stands for the (pure) strategy that cooperates only up to period k, provided that the opponent has cooperated so far; otherwise, it defects forever.[213]
- On the other hand, suppose each Ψ_i also includes two other strategies:
  - γ_{ic}, which embodies indefinite contingent cooperation (i.e., cooperation as long as the opponent has cooperated but irreversible defection otherwise);
  - γ_{ir}, the reciprocity-minded tit-for-tat – recall that this strategy starts by cooperating and then simply matches the opponent's last action (cf. Section 8.4).

To summarize, therefore, we postulate that $\Psi_i = \{\gamma_{ic}, \gamma_{ir}\} \cup \{\gamma_{i0}, \gamma_{i1}, \gamma_{i2}, \ldots\}$.

Consider first a situation where both players choose their cooperative strategies (i.e., each of them pursues her respective γ_{ic}) and denote by $\beta_i^o = (\beta_{ik}^o)_{k=c,r,0,1,\ldots}$ the vector of initial beliefs held by player i on her opponent's strategy.[214] Assume

---

[212] In mathematical (measure-theoretic) terms, this assumption can be expressed as the requirement that the measure μ_γ be *absolutely continuous* with respect to each μ_{γ^i}.

[213] Note that, to remain consistent with the notation of Chapter 9, repeated play is taken to start at $t = 1$. Therefore, γ_{i0} stands for the strategy of continuous defection.

[214] Here, we find it convenient to use a belief formulation that, rather than mimicking the format of a behavioral strategy, specifies the weight associated with each of the opponent's pure strategies. As explained above, both approaches are equivalent in view of Kuhn's theorem.

these beliefs satisfy (GT) above and let (EPM) be satisfied as well, i.e., γ_{ic} is optimal given those beliefs. Then, it is clear that δ must be close enough to 1 and the total weight $(\beta_{ic}^o + \beta_{ir}^o)$ that each player i initially associates to the opponent's strategies being either γ_{jc} or γ_{jr} must be sufficiently large. And as play unfolds and $t \to \infty$, the posterior beliefs $\hat{\beta}_i(t)$ held by each player i at the end of each stage t converge to

$$\hat{\beta}_i(\infty) \equiv \left(\frac{\beta_{ic}^o}{1 - \sum_{k=0}^{\infty} \beta_{ik}^o}, \frac{\beta_{ir}^o}{1 - \sum_{k=0}^{\infty} \beta_{ik}^o}, 0, 0, \ldots \right).$$

Thus, in particular, as time proceeds, each player is able to predict, with near certainty, all future continuation play. Note that this fact does *not* imply that each player should be able to predict her opponent's *strategy*. For example, it could well be that, even though the sum $(\beta_{ic}^o + \beta_{ir}^o)$ is large, the *relative* weight is concentrated on γ_{jr} (i.e., $\beta_{ic}^o = 0$). Then, accurate prediction of *play* would coexist with consistently wrong prediction concerning strategies. However, this mistake would be irrelevant if all we care about is that agents' play converge to Nash equilibrium *behavior* of the repeated game.

Now, suppose initial beliefs $(\beta_i^o)_{i=1,2}$ are such that player 1 chooses (optimally, given these beliefs) strategy γ_{1k} and player 2 chooses instead $\gamma_{2k'}$ with $0 < k < k'$. Does a similar line of argument allow us to conclude that players must end up playing some Nash equilibrium of the repeated game? Indeed so, because once stage $t = k + 1$ arrives and player 1 defects, player 2's posterior beliefs $\hat{\beta}_2(k + 1)$ become concentrated on γ_{1k}, at which point both players proceed to defect from $t = k + 2$ onward.[215] This obviously defines a Nash equilibrium for the continuation game in which, as in the previous case, players are able to predict consistently the future path of play. There is, however, an asymmetry between players in this respect: whereas player 2 learns player 1's strategy, player 1 remains uninformed of the precise strategy adopted by player 2. Again, however, this is an irrelevant consideration if we insist only that agents learn to *play* in a Nash fashion.

Kalai and Lehrer (1993a,b) show that the state of affairs illustrated by the previous discussion is quite general. To present their results more precisely, we need to refer to two different ε-approximate concepts.

On the one hand, we reconsider the notion of ε-(Nash-)equilibrium (cf. Definition 8.1), as applied to the present context. As the reader may recall, it generalizes the classical notion of Nash equilibrium to allow for strategy profiles from which unilateral deviations induce expected gains no larger than ε.

On the other hand, we need a precise way to express the idea that two different probability measures on paths of play, μ and $\tilde{\mu}$, are ε-close for some $\varepsilon > 0$. Heuristically, we shall say that two such measures defined on a common space are ε-close if for some large measurable set and all of its subsets the relative measure differences according to the two alternative measures is less than ε. Formally, what is required is that, given ε, there exists a measurable set Q satisfying

---

[215] Note that the Bayesian update implicit in this statement is well defined because (GT) is assumed to hold.

(a) $\min\{\mu(Q), \tilde{\mu}(Q)\} \geq 1 - \varepsilon$, and
(b) for all measurable $A \subset Q$, $(1 - \varepsilon)\tilde{\mu}(A) \leq \mu(A) \leq (1 + \varepsilon)\tilde{\mu}(A)$.

With these two ε-concepts in hand, we can state the following result.

Theorem 11.8 (Kalai and Lehrer, 1993a,b): *Consider a repeated game as described above and assume players' beliefs $\gamma^i = (\gamma_1^i, \gamma_2^i)$, $i = 1, 2$, satisfy (GT) and (EPM). Then, for every $\varepsilon > 0$ and almost every path h^∞ (according to μ_γ), there is a time T such that, for all $t \geq T$, there is an ε-equilibrium $\tilde{\gamma}$ of the continuation game such that μ_γ and $\mu_{\tilde{\gamma}}$ are ε-close.*

A rigorous proof of the previous result goes beyond the level of mathematical competence presupposed for this book. Therefore, we simply provide a heuristic argument for the special case in which players are fully myopic (i.e., $\delta = 0$), dividing the discussion into two steps.

1. The first step concerns the issue of convergence of beliefs. Here, the main mathematical result is due to Blackwell and Dubins (1962) on the issue they called "merging of opinions." Suppose a collection of players has to learn about some *common* underlying information (in our case, the future path of the game). As they receive more information, they update their prior subjective beliefs through Bayes rule, the only mathematically consistent way of conducting these operations. Note, in particular, that because all their beliefs are assumed to contain a "grain of truth," Bayes rule is always well defined and can be used to learn over time without encountering any inconsistencies. At this point, the key observation to make is that Bayes updating makes the path of agents' beliefs (conceived as a stochastic process on the corresponding space of probability measures) a martingale (recall Footnote 193). That is, it gives rise to a process where the expected value of the next realization, contingent on past observations, coincides with the most recent realization. Why should this be the case? Heuristically, the idea is not difficult to understand. Suppose that, prior to the next observation, the mathematical *expectation* of the beliefs to be held in the ensuing period were to *differ* from the currently held beliefs. This would mean that current beliefs are not using all information available. In particular, they would be ignoring the information that might allow an agent (without any further experience) to have a belief different from that held at present. This, of course, is an absurdity, which points to the martingale property induced on the belief stochastic process by Bayes updating. (See Exercise 11.17 for an illustration.) Finally, to complete this first step in the heuristic argument, one needs to invoke an important mathematical result: the martingale convergence property, which is a deep generalization of the law of large numbers (see Karlin and Taylor, 1975). It asserts that a uniformly bounded martingale (i.e., a uniformly bounded process where no change is *expected* at each round) must eventually converge a.s. and therefore achieve stationarity in the long run.

2. The second step in the argument is much more transparent than the first one. As explained, agents' beliefs regarding the future path of the game must converge in the long run; that is, players must eventually stop learning. If this is the case (and all players indeed had a grain of truth in their initial beliefs), it must be that they are all learning an identical piece of information. But since each player certainly knows her own strategy, it follows that all of them must eventually share the same (probabilistic) prediction of future play. If we then add the consideration that players must be maximizing their expected payoff given their beliefs (not only at the beginning of the game in terms of their initial beliefs, but also later on in terms of those being updated), play must eventually approach an equilibrium, i.e., a situation where (a) everyone maximizes expected payoffs given her beliefs; and (b) all of them hold rational (i.e., accurate) expectations about future play.

The above line of reasoning is indeed a very powerful one but deals with some subtle issues in ways certain authors have found questionable. Essentially, the main quarrel that has been raised concerns (GT), the assumption that postulates a grain of truth in every agent's beliefs. This assumption would be quite reasonable if strategy spaces were finite (or even countable, as in the previous prisoner's dilemma example that restricted the set of strategies in the repeated game). Then, any *cautious* subjective beliefs that assigned positive prior probability to *every* possible strategy of the opponent would guarantee (GT). Unfortunately, the strategy spaces of a repeated game are *not* countable, at least when the stage game is nontrivial and players have at least two possible choices in every period.[216] In general, therefore, it may be impossible to define subjective beliefs (no matter how cautious or "diffuse" they are) that attribute positive probability to every possible strategy of the opponent. Then, players cannot be sure to learn how to predict the opponent's response, even as the game proceeds for an arbitrarily long stretch of time.

To illustrate the latter point, consider the following question put forward by Nachbar (1997): Is it possible for a player to have an expectation-formation rule that, as time proceeds and experience mounts, eventually becomes successful in predicting the opponent's next action? To be more concrete, suppose the opponent has only two actions in the stage game and we label the expectation rule "successful" if there exists some T such that, for all $t \geq T$, the actual action chosen by the opponent is correctly anticipated with a probability higher than an "unbiased" $1/2$. Then, the question posed has to be answered in the negative, as the following simple argument shows. Given any expectation rule, consider the opponent's

---

[216] To see that strategy spaces are uncountable, it is enough to verify that the set of infinite histories (whose cardinality cannot be larger than the set of strategy profiles that induce them univocally) is itself uncountable. And to prove the uncountability of infinite histories one may resort to the following "diagonalization" argument. Suppose the set of infinite histories H^∞ were countable. Then, a bijection could be established between the elements of H^∞ and $\mathbb{N}$. Denote by $h(k)$ the history in H^∞ associated with $k \in \mathbb{N}$ by the contemplated bijection and consider the history $\tilde{h}$ that for each k has one of the players, say 1, choose an action at $t = k$ different from $h(k)$. This procedure constructs a history that is different from any other history $h(k)$ in at least stage k, which is obviously a contradiction.

strategy that, at each t, chooses the action that is predicted with the lower probability (in case both actions are predicted with equal probability, either of them can be chosen). By construction,[217] it is clear that, when faced with such a strategy, the expectation rule in question remains unsuccessful throughout, no matter how large the available evidence becomes.

What does the previous discussion suggest about the theoretical interpretation of (GT)? In a sense, it raises the uneasy feeling that this assumption may implicitly embody a certain degree of belief (or equilibrium-like) "coordination" among the different players involved. Indeed, some such coordination seems indirectly captured by the *joint* requirement posited by (GT) on the set of individual (independent?) beliefs. Only if some such coordination is implicitly at work, one appears entitled to rule out that agents may ever become "totally surprised" (recall our previous discussion). It may be argued, therefore, that rather than postulating a grain of truth, what (GT) in fact prescribes is a "grain of equilibrium." Naturally, this may well be judged to be an inappropriate basis for a theory whose concern is understanding how players learn to play an equilibrium.

From the previous considerations, it follows that a fully satisfactory model of learning in the present context should include a theory of how (and perhaps even why) agents may come to restrict their universe of strategies under consideration. For, as explained, only under some such restriction will it be the case that cautious beliefs about the opponent's behavior can be guaranteed to attribute some positive weight to each of the opponent's strategies (in particular, therefore, to the one actually used), thus ensuring the applicability of the crucial assumption (GT). Is it possible to formulate some *ex ante* strategic restriction of this kind in a fruitful and coherent manner? Nachbar (1997) argues essentially to the contrary along the following lines.

Consider a family of repeated games of the form $\mathcal{R}^\delta(W)$, where the stage game W (recall Footnote 211) belongs to some class $\mathcal{W}$ of finite strategic-form games. For each repeated game $\mathcal{R}^\delta(\tilde{W})$, $\tilde{W} \in \mathcal{W}$, let us associate a restricted product set of repeated-game mixed strategies, $\tilde{\Psi}_1 \times \tilde{\Psi}_2$, that are labeled the *conventional strategy spaces* applicable in that case. In principle, we would like players to abide by the (tentative) label attributed to these strategy spaces and have

(a) players choose their strategies from their respective conventional spaces;
(b) players restrict their beliefs about the opponent's strategy to the latter's conventional strategy spaces.

Of course, a trivial possibility in this respect would be to postulate that, within each repeated game, the corresponding conventional sets are a pair of singletons defining a Nash equilibrium of the game. Then, if players were to have their beliefs concentrated on these singletons, no incentives to deviate from these

---

[217] Observe that the construction described here is very similar in spirit to that used in Footnote 216 to show the uncountability of the strategy spaces. In fact, this is not surprising because the unsuccesfulness of an expectation rule can be largely understood as the impossibility of using countably many finite histories to learn about a set (the opponent's strategy space) that is uncountable.

conventions would arise and, certainly, agents would immediately "learn" to play a Nash equilibrium. This underscores the point that, if the analysis is to go beyond merely trivial conclusions, one must insist that any pair of conventional sets be sufficiently rich. In particular, it should be required that these sets do *not* embody any joint restrictions embodying implicit equilibrium coordination, such as those criticized above in connection with Assumption (GT).

To ensure some minimum richness in conventional strategy spaces, Nachbar (1997) defines the notion of *neutrality*. Somewhat informally, its essential gist may be described as follows.

Neutrality (N): Given a family of stage games $\mathcal{W}$, consider any given rule that associates to each repeated game $\mathcal{R}^\delta(\tilde{W})$, $\tilde{W} \in \mathcal{W}$, the corresponding set of conventional strategy spaces $\tilde{\Psi}_1 \times \tilde{\Psi}_2$. This rule is said to be *neutral* if

    (i) It is independent of payoffs, action labels, and agent identities.
    (ii) It is consistent; i.e., any strategy that is conventional for $\mathcal{R}^\delta(\tilde{W})$ induces a conventional strategy for any other $\mathcal{R}^\delta(\hat{W})$ $(\hat{W} \in \mathcal{W}, \hat{W} \neq \tilde{W})$, provided the strategy for the former game can be suitably adapted (i.e., extended or restricted) to the latter one.[218]
    (iii) It permits pure strategies; i.e., given any mixed strategy that is postulated to be conventional, at least one of the pure strategies in its support is also conventional.

A natural way of understanding Condition (N) is as embodying a preference for simplicity that is unbiased and independent of any complexity-irrelevant considerations – note that, from the strict viewpoint of how complex it is to implement a certain strategy, entailed payoffs or action labels are to be judged irrelevant. However, as explained, the key motivation for Condition (N) is methodological: it reflects the view that learning must be understood from purely individualistic principles, without any resort to some *a priori* (but unexplained) degree of implicit coordination.

Once some notion of conventionality (that is exogenously imposed on the description of the problem) is found to satisfy neutrality, the next desideratum is that it must be a "successful" device in promoting players' learning. Specifically, what is required is that for any pair of conventional strategy spaces $\tilde{\Psi}_1 \times \tilde{\Psi}_2$ associated with a particular game $\mathcal{R}^\delta(\tilde{W})$, there should be initial *beliefs* by both players, $\beta_i^o \in \Delta(\tilde{\Psi}_j)$, $i = 1, 2$ $(i \neq j)$, that satisfy the following.

Conventional Prediction (CP): Given any strategy profile $(\gamma_1, \gamma_2) \in \tilde{\Psi}_1 \times \tilde{\Psi}_2$, long-run prediction of the path of play is eventually approached by each player.

---

[218] For example, if the action spaces of $\hat{W}$ are a subset of those of $\tilde{W}$, any strategy profile $\tilde{\gamma}$ of $\mathcal{R}^\delta(\tilde{W})$ can be taken to induce a well-defined strategy profile $\hat{\gamma}$ of $\mathcal{R}^\delta(\hat{W})$ if for all histories of the former game that are also of the latter (i.e., include only actions in $\hat{W}$) the prescribed actions are part of $\hat{W}$. The case where the action spaces of $\tilde{W}$ are a subset of those of $\hat{W}$ is analogous.

Conventional Optimization (CO): For each $i = 1, 2$, there is a strategy $\gamma_i^* \in \tilde{\Psi}_i$ that is a best response to β_i^o, even when player i is not restricted to using strategies in $\tilde{\Psi}_i$.

In view of Theorem 11.8, (CP) may be understood along the lines of Assumption (GT). Clearly, it holds if each player chooses a conventional strategy, both sets of conventional strategies are countable, and players' beliefs are "cautious" on these strategy sets.

On the other hand, (CO) requires the consistency of two key features of the model: the optimality of players' behavior and their restriction to conventional strategies. In a sense, it captures the idea that conventionality is a second-order requirement that can be expected from the players only when it does not conflict with their payoffs. For example, if we view conventionality as linked to considerations of simplicity (see above), this second condition is in line with the often-postulated notion that complexity costs are lexicographically less important than payoffs.

As advanced, Nachbar has established that, in many interesting cases, one is bound to find that the three listed conditions ((N), (CP), and (CO)) are incompatible.

Theorem 11.9 (Nachbar, 1997): *Let $\mathcal{R}^\delta(\tilde{W})$ be a repeated game where $\tilde{W}$ has no weakly dominant action. Then, there exists some $\bar{\delta} > 0$ such that if $\delta \leq \bar{\delta}$, for any conventional strategy set $\tilde{\Psi}_1 \times \tilde{\Psi}_2$ satisfying (N), there are no "conventional" prior beliefs $(\beta_1^o, \beta_2^o) \in \Delta(\tilde{\Psi}_2) \times \Delta(\tilde{\Psi}_1)$ verifying (CP) and (CO).*

The proviso on δ can be omitted for a large class[219] of stage games W that include matching pennies (cf. Table 11.2), battle of the sexes (cf. Table 1.2) or rock–scissors–paper (cf. the payoff matrix (10.8)).

Rather than providing the general argument that covers the wide range of games addressed by Theorem 11.9, we focus on the particular case in which the stage game is matching pennies. This simple context already displays the essential nature of the argument in a very clear-cut manner.

Proof (for repeated matching pennies): Suppose the stage-game payoffs are given by Table 11.2 and denote player i's conventional strategy space by $\hat{\Psi}_i$ $(i = 1, 2)$. Let γ_i be the strategy chosen by player i. By (CO), we must have that each γ_i satisfies the following:

---

[219] Formally, this class is characterized by the following condition. For each $i = 1, 2$, $i \neq j$, define

$$\tilde{a}_i(a_j) \equiv \arg\max_{a_i \in A_i} \left[\max_{a_j' \in A_j} \left(W_j(a_i, a_j') - W_j(a_i, a_j) \right) \right].$$

That is, $\tilde{a}_i(a_j)$ is the (assumed unique) action of player i that, given a_j, induces for player j a maximum "regret." Then, it is required that, if player i were to react in this j-regret-maximizing manner, the maximum payoff achievable by player j would satisfy

$$\max_{a_j \in A_j} W_j(\tilde{a}_i(a_j), a_j) < \hat{v}_j,$$

where recall from Chapter 8 that $\hat{v}_j$ denotes the stage-game minimax payoff for player j.

(i) it is conventional, i.e., $\gamma_i \in \hat{\Psi}_i$ and

(ii) it is an unrestricted best response to some beliefs $\beta_i^o \in \Delta(\hat{\Psi}_j)$.

On the other hand, from (N), we know that there is a pure strategy s_i in the support of γ_i that is also conventional, i.e., satisfies $s_i \in \hat{\Psi}_i$. Thus, by an adaptation of standard arguments, we may conclude that if player i finds strategy γ_i to be a best response to beliefs β_i^o, the pure strategy s_i in its support must also be a (conventional) best response to those beliefs. Note, however, that in the present repeated matching pennies, any pure strategy such as s_i has another pure strategy of player j associated with it, say s_j, such that (s_i, s_j) induces the minimum payoff of -1 for player i at every period. (Specifically, if we make $i = 1$ and $j = 2$, s_2 is simply the strategy that, for any given history, prescribes for player 2 the action opposite to that prescribed by s_1.) Of course, such a constant stage payoff of -1 is lower than the minimax payoff, which is equal to zero. Therefore, if s_i is to be a best response to β_i^o, it must be that $\beta_i^o(s_j) = 0$. Otherwise, it is conceivable (from the point of view of player i's *initial* beliefs) that, at some future stage, player i's *posterior* could attribute a high enough probability to player j having chosen s_j, in which case to follow s_i thereafter would not be optimal. But, if $\beta_i^o(s_j) = 0$, player i will indefinitely fail to predict the ensuing path of play if, in fact, player j chooses the strategy s_j (which is conventional, by (N)). This obviously violates (CP), thus completing the argument. ∎

The above argument is made especially simple by the fact that matching pennies is a zero-sum game. However, a similar line of reasoning can be used to prove an analogous conclusion for other simple stage games such as the battle of the sexes (cf. Exercise 11.19). Overall, the main point to be learned from Theorem 11.9 is that some of the assumptions underlying the rational-learning literature (most crucially, assumptions such as (GT) above) should be interpreted with great care. For, as the former discussion has highlighted, they may embody some questionable equilibrium-like presumptions about what players initially know about the situation that are quite at odds with the core motivation of these models.

Summary

This chapter has explored a rich variety of alternative learning models in games, with players displaying a wide range of alternative degrees of sophistication when confronting the strategic situation. In these models, agents' behavioral paradigms have moved between two poles. At one end, players have been assumed to react as rather primitive automata who respond to reinforcement stimuli (positive or negative). At the opposite extreme, they have been taken to behave as powerful Bayesian learners who have a well-specified (subjective) description of their environment and are able to learn coherently from it as play unfolds. In between, the models studied have contemplated players with intermediate levels of sophistication, an understanding of the situation that is partially distorted (e.g., stationary), and rules of behavior that are largely ad hoc. Depending on the details in this respect (e.g., the length of players' memory or their assumed knowledge on the payoff structure), a series of different learning models arise. Specifically, we have focused on those embodying imitation, myopic better (or best) response, and so-called fictitious play (smooth or not).

Such a diverse collection of alternative models suggest a rather eclectic approach to the study of learning in games. Depending on the circumstances (e.g., relative complexity of the game or players' prior experience with similar situations), quite different models should be expected to represent the best framework of analysis. Indeed, further theoretical analysis as well as available experimental evidence support such a mixed stand (see Chapter 12). In some contexts, reinforcement learning appears to be the best-suited model of learning. In other scenarios, fictitious play or even more sophisticated learning paradigms seem to be called for. This suggests the need of aiming at a richer and unified (meta-)framework where the different learning models might arise as particular cases depending on the underlying details of the environment.

Exercises

Exercise 11.1: Show that, if the payoff function is subject to a uniform (i.e., strategy-independent) additive shift, this transformation does not affect the expected direction of motion for the reinforcement learning model described by (11.1)–(11.4).

Exercise 11.2*: Propose a variation of the reinforcement model described in Subsection 11.2.1 such that, even if payoffs can be negative, one may guarantee

(a) current propensities are always sure to remain positive, growing unboundedly over time;
(b) the probability weights prevailing at any point in the process are unaffected by the contemplated transformation.

Exercise 11.3: In the reinforcement-learning model of Subsection 11.2.2 applied to the prisoner's dilemma, show that, if (11.15) is violated, there are some initial states where convergence to a pure strategy state a.s. *never* obtains.
Hint: Consider states whose aspiration vector is a convex combination of the extreme points $(\eta, 0)$ and $(0, \eta)$.

Exercise 11.4: Complete the proof of Theorem 11.1 for the case where prevailing aspiration levels $y_i(t)$ may be negative (but bounded below, since Ω is assumed compact).

Exercise 11.5: Derive the lower bound specified in (11.16).

Exercise 11.6: Prove Remark 11.2 formally.

Exercise 11.7*: Consider a strategic-form bilateral game G where iterative elimination of dominated strategies results in strategy subsets $\tilde{S}_1$ and $\tilde{S}_2$, each consisting of two different strategies.

(a) Show, by example, that the better-response dynamics given by (11.23) need not have all of its limit strategy profiles in the set $\tilde{S}_1 \times \tilde{S}_2$.

(b) Show, in your above example, that the best-response dynamics given by (11.24) must have all of its limit strategy profiles in the set $\tilde{S}_1 \times \tilde{S}_2$.

Exercise 11.8: Prove that the function Υ defined in (11.27) defines an ordinal potential for a symmetric Cournot game with linear costs when consideration is restricted to uniformly positive output profiles. Show as well that the common-pool-resource game described in Exercise 3.11 is an ordinal-potential game if the hourly cost of work effort is constant and identical across individuals.

Exercise 11.9*: Consider the following "congestion game," taken from Monderer and Shapley (1996a). There are four cities located around a lake with a single road joining them in the following clockwise order: A-B-C-D-A. There are two agents, 1 and 2, the first living in city A and the second in city B. Individual 1 wants to go to city C, whereas individual 2 wants to reach city D. The cost of travel depends on "congestion," i.e., how many individuals (one or two) use the same segment of the road joining any two adjacent cities. Costs are additive across travel segments, with $c_\xi(k)$ denoting the cost of travel segment $\xi \in \Xi \equiv \{AB, BC, CD, DA\}$ when there are k individuals using it.

Model the situation as a game where each player i has two possible strategies: "travel clockwise" or "travel counterclockwise." For any strategy profile $s = (s_1, s_2)$, define $h_\xi(s) \in \{0, 1, 2\}$ as the number of individuals using segment ξ. Moreover, define the function $\Upsilon : S \to \mathbb{R}$ as follows:

$$\Upsilon(s) = \sum_{\xi \in \Xi} \sum_{k=0}^{h_\xi(s)} c_\xi(k),$$

where we make $c_\xi(0) = 0$. Prove that $\Upsilon(\cdot)$ is a potential for the game described.

Exercise 11.10: Consider a round-robin context where the underlying bilateral game is a coordination game (cf. (11.20) and (11.21)). Show that all pure-strategy Nash equilibria are monomorphic.

Exercise 11.11*: Consider a round-robin context where the underlying bilateral game involves only two actions and displays a unique symmetric equilibrium, which is in completely mixed strategies. Let $\omega_1^* \in (0, 1)$ stand for the weight associated with the first action by the (common) mixed strategy played in this equilibrium. On the other hand, given any strategy profile $s \in S$, denote by $\upsilon_1(s)$ the fraction of individuals in the population who adopt the first action. Show that for any $\varepsilon_1, \varepsilon_2 > 0$, there exists some $\hat{n}$, $T \in \mathbb{N}$ such that the event $\{\forall t \geq T, |\upsilon_1(s(t)) - \omega_1^*| \leq \varepsilon_1\}$ has probability no smaller than $1 - \varepsilon_2$ if the population size $n \geq \hat{n}$.

Exercise 11.12*: In analogy with Theorem 11.3, show that fictitious play is globally convergent for any (bilateral) dominance-solvable game.

Exercise 11.13: Consider the matching-pennies game whose payoffs are given in Table 11.2. Suppose players behave à la fictitious play (i.e., as given by (11.33)–(11.37)), starting with initial weights $\eta_1(0) = (3/2, 2)$ and

$\eta_2(0) = (2, 3/2)$ – here, H is indexed as the first strategy. Trace the path of play for the initial 10 periods.

Exercise 11.14: Consider a process of fictitious play applied to a bilateral strategic-form game G where, at some t in the process, $s(t) = s^*$ for some $s^* = (s_1^*, s_2^*)$ that is a strict Nash equilibrium of G. Prove that $s(t') = s^*$ for all $t' > t$.

Exercise 11.15: Consider a 2×2 game with best-response correspondences as illustrated in Figure 11.9 – in particular, suppose the (unperturbed) Nash equilibrium σ^* has $\sigma_{11}^* < 1/2$ and $\sigma_{21}^* > 1/2$. Apply to this game the Harsanyian purification approach and subject each player's payoffs to independent stochastic perturbations that are symmetric around zero. Argue that the induced Bayes-Nash equilibrium $\hat{\sigma}$ is as depicted in Figure 11.9, i.e., player 1 chooses her first strategy with *ex ante* probability $\hat{\sigma}_{11} > \sigma_{11}^*$ and player 2 has $\hat{\sigma}_{21} > \sigma_{21}^*$.

Exercise 11.16*: Let there be two players involved in a game with three strategies per player, their learning process suitably modeled by a smoothed best-response dynamics in continuous time. Show that this dynamics is volume-contracting. Is it also globally convergent? Discuss your answer.

Exercise 11.17: Consider an experiment with two urns, A and B, both of which have n balls. Urn A has a white balls and $(n - a)$ black balls, while Urn B has b white balls and $(n - b)$ black balls. Consider a certain individual who is about to select randomly a ball from one of the urns without knowing which one of the two it is. A priori, she has uniform subjective probability over each urn, A or B (i.e., she attributes a subjective probability of $1/2$ to each). The agent understands and abides by Bayes rule. She also realizes that, once she has selected a ball, her subjective probability will be modified in the manner prescribed by that updating rule. Then suppose that, before undertaking the experiment, she computes the expected posterior probabilities she will hold *after* the experiment. Prove that they are $1/2$ for each urn.

Exercise 11.18*: There are two individuals playing repeatedly the game whose payoffs are as specified in Table 11.3. Player i's admissible strategies Ψ_i consist of the countable set $\{\gamma_{i1}, \gamma_{i2}, \gamma_{i3}, \ldots\} \cup \{\gamma_{i\infty}\}$ where each γ_{ik} ($k \in \mathbb{N}$) is interpreted as follows:

"Switch irreversibly to B_i at k, provided the opponent has not switched to B_j before; in the latter case, remain playing A_i for ever."

and $\gamma_{i\infty}$ is interpreted as

"Never choose B_i."

Let β_i^o stand for the initial beliefs of player i over j's strategy, with β_{iq}^o ($q = 1, 2, \ldots, \infty$) indicating the subjective probability associated with each γ_{jq}. Further assume that $\beta_{iq}^o > 0$ for each i and every $q = 2, 3, \ldots, \infty$. Within the theoretical framework proposed in Subsection 11.4.3, answer the following questions.

Table 11.4: *A pure-coordination game*

1 \ 2	A_2	B_2
A_1	1, 1	0, 0
B_1	0, 0	2, 2

(a) Does the setup described satisfy (GT)?
(b) Argue that, if (EPM) holds, some player switches to B_i at some t.
(c) Specify conditions on β_i^o guaranteeing that *both* players switch to B_i at $t = 1$.
(d) Assume that (EPM) holds. Does the process converge to Nash play for the repeated game? and for the stage game? Relate your answer to (a) and Theorem 11.8.

Exercise 11.19: Along the lines pursued in Subsection 11.4.3 for matching pennies, prove the conclusion established by Theorem 11.9 when the stage game under consideration is the battle of the sexes (cf. Table 1.2).

Exercise 11.20*: Consider two agents repeatedly playing a symmetric pure-coordination game with payoffs given in Table 11.4.

(a) Construct a space of conventional strategies $\tilde{\Psi}_i$ for each player $i = 1, 2$ that satisfies Condition (N) in Subsection 11.4.3 and is composed of exactly *three* strategies.
(b) Assume that each player i's beliefs are uniform on $\tilde{\Psi}_j$, $i, j = 1, 2, i \neq j$. Is (CP) satisfied?
(c) Given discount rate $\delta = 1/2$ and the uniform beliefs postulated in (b), determine some strategy profile consistent with (EPM). Discuss your answer in view of the conclusions established by Theorem 11.9.

CHAPTER 12

Social learning and equilibrium selection

12.1 Introduction

In this final chapter, we turn to the important issue of equilibrium selection in games, a problem that has been mostly neglected thus far. It is, however, a key issue in many game-theoretic models of economic phenomena (in particular, several of those studied in this book), which happen to display a wide multiplicity of equilibria. In those cases, one must find ways to overcome the induced "equilibrium indeterminacy" if a definite theoretical prediction is to be obtained.

The equilibrium selection problem typically is not mitigated if, rather than approaching matters statically (i.e., from an equilibrium viewpoint), a dynamic process reflecting off-equilibrium learning is postulated instead. For then, analogous considerations appear in that, often, the limit behavior of the learning process depends sharply on its initial conditions (cf. Chapter 11). Consequently, since one seldom has a convincing theory about how the initial conditions might be determined, such a dynamic approach, by itself, seldom represents a suitable solution to the problem.

To address the issue of equilibrium selection, the route to be undertaken here is reminiscent of ideas that, albeit with somewhat different motivation, have been pursued at other points in this book – e.g., concerning Nash refinements. Specifically, we conduct a robustness exercise, now applied to some of the basic learning models discussed in Chapter 11, i.e., imitation and best-response dynamics. That is, these dynamics are perturbed slightly, in the hope that such a perturbation may remove any dependence of initial conditions and thus single out a "uniquely robust" limit behavior.

For the sake of focus, most of our discussion deals with two paradigmatic scenarios. First, we consider simple coordination games, played under a variety of alternative interaction structures, i.e., global, local, centralized, or "playing the field." Second, we focus on Cournot oligopoly games, with a certain number of quantity-setting firms facing an exogenously given market demand for their homogenous product. While the study of these setups will be mostly of a theoretical nature, we shall complement the discussion with a brief summary of related experimental evidence. Finally, in the Supplementary Material (located at the end of the chapter), we turn to one of the aspiration-based scenarios considered in Chapter 11 – in particular, that concerning the prisoner's dilemma. Here, again, we compare the theoretical predictions of the model with related experimental evidence.

The mathematical analysis undertaken in this chapter requires familiarity with some key notions of the theory of stochastic processes – more specifically, those concerning (perturbed) Markov chains, as well as the techniques customarily used to characterize their long-run behavior. For the sake of completeness, Section 12.6 provides a brief tutorial of those notions and techniques. This mathematical review is also relegated to the Supplementary Material of the chapter in order not to break the continuity in the theoretical discussion of the different models. Most readers, however, are well advised to read through that material prior to entering the discussion undertaken in the main body of the chapter. Throughout this discussion, however, it should also be possible to follow the essence of the arguments without a complete understanding of the technical details.

12.2 Evolutionary games: theoretical framework

12.2.1 *Strategic setup*

The strategic scenario to be studied here is the same as that introduced in Subsection 11.3.1. It involves a finite population, $N = \{1, 2, \ldots, n\}$, playing over time the same (often symmetric[220]) strategic-form game $G = \{N, \{S_i\}_{i=1}^n, \{\pi_i\}_{i=1}^n\}$. Time t is indexed discretely, $t = 0, 1, 2, \ldots$. At every period t, each player i chooses a particular strategy, $s_i(t)$, and receives the payoff $\pi_i(s(t))$, where $s(t) = (s_1(t), s_2(t), \ldots, s_n(t))$ is the full strategy profile prevailing at t.

This framework is particularized below (Section 12.3) in a number of different directions. For each of these, the issue of equilibrium selection is tackled in the same fashion. Players are postulated to adjust their behavior according to some underlying learning dynamics, which in turn is subject to infrequent perturbations. Then, since these perturbations happen to guarantee the ergodicity of the stochastic process, the analysis is geared toward characterizing its unique long-run behavior. The alternative learning dynamics to be considered are introduced in the next subsection. Perturbations, on the other hand, are presented formally at the beginning of Section 12.4.

12.2.2 *Learning dynamics*

12.2.2.1 *General formulation.* First, we describe a general framework that accommodates each of the different kinds of learning dynamics to be considered here. Specifically, this framework will be later specialized into two of the paradigmatic formulations proposed by modern evolutionary literature: learning by imitation and best-response adjustment.

At each $t = 1, 2, \ldots$, every $i \in N$ is assumed to receive a revision opportunity with the same independent probability $p \in (0, 1)$. If such an opportunity does *not* arrive, $s_i(t) = s_i(t-1)$. Instead, if a revision opportunity does materialize, the new

---

[220] It will be remembered that the game is said to be symmetric if all players have the same (or isomorphic) strategy set and their payoff functions are invariant to any permutation of player indices.

strategy of player i is posited to satisfy

$$s_i(t) \in D_i(s(t-1)), \tag{12.1}$$

where the (nonempty) set $D_i(s(t-1))$ consists of all those strategies this player judges to be suitable fresh choices. Note that, for simplicity, the range of new possible strategies at t is postulated to depend only on the state prevailing at $t-1$.[221] If the set $D_i(s(t-1))$ is not a singleton, all strategies in it are assumed to be chosen with some positive (say, uniform) probability. Within this general formulation, different learning dynamics are simply introduced below as alternative specifications of the functions $D_i(\cdot)$.

12.2.2.2 *Learning by imitation.* Given any strategy profile $s = (s_1, s_2, \ldots, s_n)$, rely on the notation introduced in Subsection 11.3.2 and make

$$M_i(s) \equiv \{s_j : j \in N, \pi_j(s) \geq \pi_i(s)\}. \tag{12.2}$$

Then, a process of *learning by imitation* is obtained from the general formulation (12.1) by positing

$$D_i(s) \equiv M_i(s) \tag{12.3}$$

for each possible strategy profile s.

Note that, as explained in Subsection 11.3.1, the above formulation implicitly presumes that every player is in an *ex ante* symmetric situation – or at least so she conceives herself to be. For only in this case should any player view it as reasonable to evaluate her own action and payoffs in terms of what others do and obtain. Such an approach, however, is inappropriate if players are aware that their respective situation is significantly asymmetric. Then, it is natural to posit that the players should regard as relevant terms of comparison only the situation of those who face *ex ante* symmetric circumstances. An adaptation of the imitation paradigm along these lines is discussed in Subsections 12.4.2 and 12.4.3 when dealing with interaction structures that place players in asymmetric positions.

12.2.2.3 *Best-response adjustment.* Given any strategy profile $s = (s_1, s_2, \ldots, s_n)$, recall from Subsection 11.3.3 the following piece of notation:

$$B_i^*(s) \equiv \{\tilde{s}_i \in S_i : \pi_i(\tilde{s}_i, s_{-i}) \geq \pi_i(s_i, s_{-i}), \ \forall s_i \in S_i\}. \tag{12.4}$$

Then, the dynamics (12.1) is said to reflect a process of (myopic) *best-response adjustment* if

$$D_i(s) \equiv B_i^*(s). \tag{12.5}$$

---

[221] Often, one can relax this constraint substantially by allowing for counterparts of many of the commonly posited behavioral rules (e.g., imitation or better/best response) that respond to long stretches of past history or exogenous random events (see, for example, Young, 1993; Robson and Vega-Redondo, 1996).

Of course, in line with our discussion in Chapter 11, one similarly could have considered the less stringent dynamics of *better-response adjustment* given by

$$B_i(s) \equiv \{\tilde{s}_i \in S_i : \pi_i(\tilde{s}_i, s_{-i}) \geq \pi_i(s)\} \qquad (12.6)$$

and

$$D_i(s) \equiv B_i(s). \qquad (12.7)$$

Since none of our results depends on whether players pursue best- or better-response adjustment, our discussion focuses on the first option, as given by (12.4) and (12.5). In Exercise 12.11, the reader is asked to carry out a parallel analysis of the better-response dynamics (12.6) and (12.7) for one of our leading contexts.

12.3 Evolutionary games: alternative scenarios

In this section, we introduce the different strategic setups that will be explored in our subsequent discussion. First, we present a context where a simple 2×2 game of coordination is played under different interaction structures, i.e., alternative ways in which the (bilateral) encounters are organized. Second, we focus on a setup where the population continues to face a coordination problem, but one where the interaction is of the sort called "playing the field" – specifically, the *whole* population is supposed to be involved in a so-called minimum-effort game. Finally, we turn to a symmetric and discrete version of the classical Cournot setup, where we define and contrast its two benchmark outcomes: Nash and Walras equilibria.

12.3.1 *Bilateral coordination games*

As in Subsection 11.3.1, suppose players are matched in pairs every period to play a bilateral and symmetric coordination game. In fact, suppose such a coordination game is of the simplest (nontrivial) kind and allows for just two possible actions, α and β. Thus, for every bilateral encounter between any two agents, say i and j, the payoffs earned by playing the game may be described as in Table 12.1.

Since the game is assumed to be one of coordination, we must have $d > f$ and $b > e$. This makes both (α, α) and (β, β) Nash equilibria of the bilateral game. Without loss of generality, we assume as well that

$$d > b, \qquad (12.8)$$

i.e., α is the *efficient* action. Finally, we find it useful to make the following additional assumption:

$$d + e < b + f. \qquad (12.9)$$

Table 12.1: *A general 2×2 coordination game*

i \ j	α	β
α	d, d	e, f
β	f, e	b, b

The above inequality implies that β is the *risk-dominant* action, in the sense of Harsanyi and Selten (1988). Heuristically, this notion simply reflects the fact that β is the optimal (expected-payoff maximizing) choice when a player has fully unbiased (i.e., uniform) subjective beliefs about the action to be played by the opponent. In conjunction, conditions (12.8) and (12.9) indicate that there is a tension (or contradiction) between two "desirable" criteria: efficiency and risk dominance. This sets the stage for an interesting problem of equilibrium selection to arise.

Naturally, we maintain the assumption that each player must choose the same action in all of her encounters.[222] Therefore, the strategy sets of the evolutionary population game are simply taken to be $S_i = \{\alpha, \beta\}$ for each $i \in N$. To complete the description of the game, we still need to define the payoff functions $\pi_i : \{\alpha, \beta\}^n \to \mathbb{R}$, $i = 1, 2, \ldots, n$. But, to this end, we must first specify how players are bilaterally matched to play the underlying bilateral game. In general, this may be done by declaring some set $U_i \subseteq N \backslash \{i\}$ as player i's *neighborhood* and positing that every individual i plays the game with each of her neighbors, i.e., with each player in her respective U_i. Of course, for any pattern of players' neighborhoods to be well-defined, the implied "neighborhood relationship" must be symmetric, i.e.,

$$\forall i, j \in N, \quad i \in U_j \Leftrightarrow j \in U_i.$$

Denote by $\psi(a, a')$ the payoff earned by playing action a against a' in the bilateral game, as described in Table 12.1. Then, given any strategy profile $s = (s_1, s_2, \ldots, s_n) \in \{\alpha, \beta\}^n$, the payoff $\pi_i(s)$ obtained by player i in the population game is taken to be the sum of all payoffs accruing to her from the interaction with each of her neighbors $j \in U_i$, i.e.,

$$\pi_i(s) = \sum_{j \in U_i} \psi(s_i, s_j). \tag{12.10}$$

The neighborhood structure $\mathcal{U} = \{U_i\}_{i \in N}$ defines the *social network* in which the population game unfolds. Independently of the particular details of this network, it should be clear that the strategy profiles where every player chooses the same action, α or β, are both Nash equilibria of the induced population game. In general, however, one might expect the specific architecture of interaction induced by $\mathcal{U}$ to have a significant bearing on the evolutionary dynamics and the consequent equilibrium selection. To explore this idea, we focus on three paradigmatic instances of a social network: global, local, and centralized. Each of them is described in turn.

12.3.1.1 *Global interaction.* This case coincides with the round-robin setup considered in Chapter 11. Formally, it corresponds to a neighborhood structure $\mathcal{U}^g = \{U_i^g\}_{i \in N}$ where

$$U_i^g = N \backslash \{i\} \qquad (i = 1, 2, \ldots, n), \tag{12.11}$$

i.e., the neighborhood of every player $i \in N$ coincides with the rest of the population.

---

[222] Recall the discussion on this assumption conducted in Subsection 11.3.1.

12.3.1.2 *Local interaction.* In this case, players' neighborhoods are taken to display relatively small, but overlapping, ranges of interaction. For concreteness, let us posit a simple structure akin to that studied in Subsection 3.2.2 (cf. Figure 3.3). That is, players are arranged in a circle, with each player $i \in N$ placed between players $i - 1$ and $i + 1$ (recall that indices $n + 1$ and 0 are to be interpreted as 1 and n, respectively). Assuming then that each individual plays with her two adjacent players, this simply amounts to postulating a neighborhood structure $\mathcal{U}^\ell = \{U_i^\ell\}_{i \in N}$ where

$$U_i^\ell = \{i - 1, i + 1\} \qquad (i = 1, 2, \ldots, n). \tag{12.12}$$

12.3.1.3 *Centralized interaction.* Here, a particular individual, say player 1, occupies a central role in the social network. All other players are connected to (i.e., play with) her and only with her. Formally, this setup corresponds to neighborhood structure $\mathcal{U}^c = \{U_i^c\}_{i \in N}$ where

$$
\begin{aligned}
U_1^c &= N \backslash \{1\}; \\
U_i^c &= \{1\} \qquad (i = 2, 3, \ldots, n).
\end{aligned}
\tag{12.13}
$$

12.3.2 *Minimum-effort game*

Now we describe a different strategic setup that, even though it continues to reflect a coordination problem, has the population as a whole play a *single* game. Thus, in the language of Section 10.2.1, social interaction is of the playing-the-field variety. The particular game considered is the so-called *minimum-effort game,* originating from the work of Bryant (1983) – recall Section 3.4 – and then later reconsidered by a number of other authors such as van Huyck *et al.* (1990), Vega-Redondo (1993), and Robles (1997).

In the minimum-effort game, the individuals must choose simultaneously a level of effort e in the finite set $\Xi \equiv \{1, 2, \ldots, \bar{x}\}$. Effort is costly so that, for each unit of effort exerted, an individual incurs a cost $\gamma \in (0, 1)$. In return for any profile of individual efforts $(e_1, e_2, \ldots, e_n)$, the population as a whole obtains a *total* payoff equal to

$$f(e_1, e_2, \ldots, e_n) = n \cdot \min_{i \in N} e_i$$

that is assumed equally divided among all players. In the format of Subsection 12.2.1, the situation induces a strategic-form game $G = \{N, \{S_i\}_{i=1}^n, \{\pi_i\}_{i=1}^n\}$ where, for each $i \in N$, we have $S_i = \Xi$ and the payoff function $\pi_i(\cdot)$ is given by

$$\pi_i(e_1, e_2, \ldots, e_n) = \left\{ \min_{j \in N} e_j \right\} - \gamma e_i. \tag{12.14}$$

Clearly, this game has a multiplicity of *pure-strategy* Nash equilibria – indeed, every strategy profile of the form $\mathbf{x} \equiv (x, x, \ldots, x)$ for each common $x \in \Xi$ defines an equilibrium. Thus, again, one finds a tension between efficiency and safety (nonriskiness) that is analogous to that displayed by the bilateral coordination game described in Table 12.1. The unique efficient equilibrium has every player choose the highest effort $\bar{x}$. However, aiming at this equilibrium is risky for any given player (certainly, if $\bar{x}$ is large) because, if *any* other individual ends up exerting a relatively low effort, the loss (i.e., negative payoff) entailed can be substantial. Of course, this sort of risk is minimized by choosing the lowest possible effort, which guarantees to every player a positive payoff. Playing for safety in this way, however, is grossly inefficient if $\bar{x}$ (which marks the maximum payoff attainable at equilibrium) is high.

12.3.3 *Cournot oligopoly*

Recall the discretized version of the symmetric Cournot model introduced in Subsection 11.3.1. The set of players is a collection of n quantity-setting firms that confront a given (decreasing) inverse-demand function for a homogeneous good $P(\cdot)$ and share a common (increasing) cost function $C(\cdot)$. Thus, as in the coordination context presented in Subsection 12.3.2 (but unlike that introduced in Subsection 12.3.1) the firms play the field. That is, the interaction is channeled through a single population-wide game ("the market"), rather than as a series of bilateral encounters.

In this context, the strategy of each firm is identified with its respective output q_i, which is chosen simultaneously by all of them in every period. To preserve the finiteness of the model, the common strategy set S_i of each firm i is identified with an output grid $\Phi = \{0, \varrho, 2\varrho, \ldots, v\varrho\}$ where v is some (finite, but arbitrarily large) natural number and ϱ is some positive (and arbitrarily small) real number. Let $q \equiv (q_1, q_2, \ldots, q_n) \in \Phi^n$ be a strategy (output) profile. As customary, we identify the payoff earned by each firm $i \in N$ with its induced profit as given by

$$\pi_i(q) \equiv q_i P \left(\sum_{i \in N} q_i \right) - C(q_i). \tag{12.15}$$

In the strategic-form game thus defined, the following two strategy profiles represent natural benchmarks for the analysis (cf. Subsection 3.1.1):

- the (symmetric) *Cournot-Nash equilibrium*, $\mathbf{x}^c \equiv (x^c, x^c, \ldots, x^c)$, characterized by the condition

$$x^c P (n x^c) - C(x^c) \geq x P ((n-1)x^c + x) - C(x), \forall x \in \mathbb{R}_+. \tag{12.16}$$

- the (symmetric) *Walras equilibrium*, denoted by $\mathbf{x}^w \equiv (x^w, x^w, \ldots, x^w)$, which is characterized by

$$x^w P (n x^w) - C(x^w) \geq x P (n x^w) - C(x), \quad \forall x \in \mathbb{R}_+. \tag{12.17}$$

In what follows, it is assumed that the underlying data of the environment are such that these two equilibria exist and are unique,[223] and their corresponding

---

[223] Here, of course, uniqueness is assumed even when the possible output choices are restricted to belong to the grid Φ.

outputs belong to the grid Φ (cf. Exercise 12.13). Because the demand function is decreasing, they cannot coincide. However, as we shall see below, each of them is induced ("selected") by alternative evolutionary processes that differ only in their respective learning rules – imitation or myopic best response.

12.4 Stochastic stability and equilibrium selection

In view of the wide diversity of strategic environments introduced in Subsections 12.3.1 to 12.3.3, these different contexts provide a good testing ground to explore the potential and implications of evolutionary learning. Specifically, they should shed light on the long-run consequences of alternative forms of behavioral adjustment, e.g., imitation or best response, as described in Subsection 12.2.2. Indeed, to understand this contrast is one of the main concerns of the present section.

By combining those alternative strategic setups and behavioral dynamics, one arrives at different models of learning (eight possible ones), all of them describable as corresponding Markov chains on a suitable state space Ω – see Subsection 12.6.1. By relying, more or less directly, on the analysis conducted in Chapter 11, convergence to *some* stationary state from *any* initial conditions can be ensured in each of those models under quite general circumstances.[224] This fact, however, does not settle the issue of equilibrium selection. For, in general, since there are multiple stationary states, the long-run behavior of the process must depend on the initial conditions.

As advanced, to address such a multiplicity problem, we perturb the learning dynamics by allowing for some small probability that players "mutate." Such a mutation admits several interpretations. For example, a natural motivation is simply to conceive the phenomenon of mutation as embodying players' experimentation. Alternatively, it could be interpreted as formalizing the possibility that players make mistakes. Finally, a third option would be to view mutation as reflecting some extent of population renewal (i.e., a process by which some of the incumbent players are randomly replaced by fresh and uninformed newcomers).

Whatever its particular motivation, the precise formulation of mutation adopted here is as follows. In every period t, and once the learning stage is over (i.e., after all agents have completed any possible revision according to (12.1)), every player $i \in N$ is subject to some *independent* probability $\varepsilon > 0$ of *mutation*. If this event in fact materializes, the player in question is assumed to ignore her "interim" strategy choice resulting from the prior learning stage and select some strategy from S_i through a probability distribution with full support.[225] Once this mutation

---

[224] Convergence obtains with full generality for each of these models, except for the Cournot setup under best-response adjustment. In this latter case, some specific assumptions need to be made to guarantee convergence such as, for example, cost linearity – see Subsection 12.4.5 and recall Subsection 11.3.3.

[225] Many of the assumptions contemplated here may be relaxed without altering the gist of the analysis. For example, individuals could display different mutation probabilities, provided all these probabilities converge to zero at the same rate in our limiting exercise below (see Exercises 12.9 and 12.10). Or, in other respects, the probabilities with which different strategies are chosen in the case of mutation could vary across states and players, provided those probabilities satisfy the full-support requirement and are independent of the mutation rate.

stage has been thus completed, play occurs at t according to the resulting profile $s(t) = (s_1(t), s_2(t), \ldots, s_n(t))$, the individuals then obtaining their corresponding payoffs $\pi_i(s(t))$, $i = 1, 2, \ldots, n$.

Of course, the perturbed process can be modeled as a Markov chain on the same state space Ω as for the original (unperturbed) process. Furthermore, for any $\varepsilon > 0$, this perturbed Markov chain is ergodic, because every possible transition has positive probability (cf. condition (12.46) in Subsection 12.6.1). In turn, this implies that the process has a *unique* invariant distribution $\mu_\varepsilon \in \Delta(\Omega)$ that summarizes its long-run behavior, independently of initial conditions.

Naturally, we want to conceive the magnitude of the noise (i.e., the probability ε) as quite small. Or, to be more precise, we are interested in studying the long-run behavior of the process when $\varepsilon \downarrow 0$. Formally, such a long-run state of affairs (which, to repeat, is independent of initial conditions) is captured by the *limit invariant distribution*

$$\mu^* = \lim_{\varepsilon \to 0} \mu_\varepsilon.$$

The above limit can be shown to be well defined (see Subsection 12.6.3). Following Foster and Young (1990), the states in the support of the induced limit distribution μ^*, i.e., those belonging to the set

$$\Omega^* \equiv \{\omega \in \Omega : \mu^*(\omega) > 0\}$$

are called the *stochastically stable states*. They are to be conceived as the only states that are visited a significant fraction of time in the long run when $\varepsilon \downarrow 0$. They represent, therefore, the "selection" induced by the evolutionary learning process when an arbitrarily small amount of noise removes any long-run dependence of initial conditions. To characterize Ω^* is the primary aim of our analysis. As a complementary concern, we shall also be interested in assessing the rate at which such long-run states are first visited (or, relatedly, the maximum expected waiting time for the first visit). This bears on an important question that, heuristically, could be formulated as follows: How long is the long run?

12.4.1 *Bilateral coordination games under global interaction*

We start by studying the setup where individuals play a bilateral coordination game in a round-robin fashion. This was the context originally studied in the seminal work of Kandori, Mailath, and Rob (1993) – see also Foster and Young (1990) and Young (1993). It is addressed in turn under each of the two different behavioral paradigms proposed: learning by imitation and myopic best response.

12.4.1.1 *Learning by imitation.* Let (Ω, Q_ε) be the Markov chain formalizing a process of "perturbed" *learning by imitation* in a context of *global interaction* (i.e., (12.3) and (12.11) apply), with ε standing for the mutation probability and Q_ε for the transition matrix. Given the symmetric nature of the situation, it is convenient to identify the state of the process with the number of individuals who choose one of the strategies, say strategy α. That is, we simply make $\Omega = \{0, 1, \ldots, n\}$, with $\omega \in \Omega$ representing the number of players choosing strategy α (and therefore $n - \omega$ is the number of those who choose β).

As ε varies in the range $[0, 1)$, the collection of Markov chains $\{(\Omega, Q_\varepsilon)\}_{\varepsilon \in [0,1)}$ verifies the properties of the canonical evolutionary model described in Subsection 12.6.2. In particular, one can define a suitable cost function, $c : \Omega \times \Omega \to \mathbb{N} \cup \{0\}$, where, for each pair $(\omega, \omega') \in \Omega \times \Omega$, the "cost" $c(\omega, \omega')$ reflects the rate (or order) in ε at which the transition probability $Q_\varepsilon(\omega, \omega')$ converges to zero as $\varepsilon \to 0$. Next, we provide an explicit expression for this cost and show that it can be simply identified with the minimum number of *simultaneous* mutations needed to have a transition from ω to ω' across consecutive periods with positive probability.

First, we note that $c(\omega, \omega')$ is implicitly defined by the following expression (cf. (12.47)):

$$0 < \lim_{\varepsilon \to 0} \frac{Q_\varepsilon(\omega, \omega')}{\varepsilon^{c(\omega,\omega')}} < \infty,$$

which may be rewritten as follows:

$$0 < \lim_{\varepsilon \to 0} \frac{\sum_{\omega'' \in \Omega} Q_0(\omega, \omega'') M(\omega'', \omega')}{\varepsilon^{c(\omega,\omega')}} < \infty, \tag{12.18}$$

where $M(\omega'', \omega')$ denotes the probability that a transition from ω'' to ω' occurs by relying on mutation alone. As $\varepsilon \to 0$, $M(\omega'', \omega')$ satisfies

$$0 < \lim_{\varepsilon \to 0} \frac{M(\omega'', \omega')}{\varepsilon^{|\omega'' - \omega'|}} < \infty, \tag{12.19}$$

i.e., it behaves as an infinitesimal in ε of order $|\omega'' - \omega'|$. To see this, note that this absolute difference is the net change in the number of players who play strategy α (or β) in ω' and ω''. Consequently, it also corresponds to the *minimum* number of individuals who must mutate for a transition from ω'' to ω' to take place by relying on mutation *alone*. This implies that $|\omega'' - \omega'|$ is equal to the lower exponent of ε in the polynomial that defines the probability $M(\omega'', \omega')$, which in turn defines its order as an infinitesimal in ε.

In view of (12.19), the cost function $c(\cdot)$ can be uniquely defined as follows:

$$c(\omega, \omega') = \min \{|\omega'' - \omega'| : \omega'' \in \Omega, \ Q_0(\omega, \omega'') > 0\} \quad (\omega, \omega' \in \Omega), \tag{12.20}$$

since this is the only specification of the cost that is consistent with (12.18). Indeed, suppose (12.20) were violated for some $\omega, \omega' \in \Omega$, and let $\tilde{\omega}$ be a state such that

$$|\tilde{\omega} - \omega'| = \min \{|\omega'' - \omega'| : \omega'' \in \Omega, \ Q_0(\omega, \omega'') > 0\}.$$

There are two possibilities. First, if $c(\omega, \omega') - |\tilde{\omega} - \omega'| > 0$, (12.19) implies that

$$\lim_{\varepsilon \to 0} \frac{\sum_{\omega'' \in \Omega} Q_0(\omega, \omega'') M(\omega'', \omega')}{\varepsilon^{c(\omega,\omega')}} \geq \lim_{\varepsilon \to 0} \frac{Q_0(\omega, \tilde{\omega})}{\varepsilon^{c(\omega,\omega') - |\tilde{\omega} - \omega'|}} = \infty,$$

which contradicts (12.18). Conversely, if we had $c(\omega, \omega') - |\tilde{\omega} - \omega'| < 0$, it would follow that, for all $\omega'' \in \Omega$,

$$Q_0(\omega, \omega'') > 0 \Rightarrow |\omega'' - \omega'| - c(\omega, \omega') > 0,$$

and therefore, relying again on (12.19), we would have

$$\lim_{\varepsilon \to 0} \frac{\sum_{\omega'' \in \Omega} Q_0(\omega, \omega'') M(\omega'', \omega')}{\varepsilon^{c(\omega, \omega')}} = \lim_{\varepsilon \to 0} \sum_{\omega'' \in \Omega} Q_0(\omega, \omega'') \varepsilon^{|\omega'' - \omega'| - c(\omega, \omega')} = 0,$$

again contradicting (12.18). This establishes that $c(\omega, \omega')$ is to be defined by (12.20). Therefore, as claimed, it may be identified with the minimum number of (simultaneous) mutations needed to complement the unperturbed dynamics for a transition from ω to ω' to occur across consecutive periods with positive probability.

Let Ω_0 denote the *limit states* of the unperturbed process.[226] It is easy to see (cf. Remark 12.1) that no state can be stochastically stable if it is merely transient for (i.e., *not* a limit state of) the unperturbed dynamics. Thus, we must have $\Omega^* \subset \Omega_0$ and therefore a natural first step in narrowing down the search for stochastically stable states is to characterize the set Ω_0.

Clearly, both monomorphic states, denoted by $\omega_\alpha \equiv n$ and $\omega_\beta \equiv 0$, are stationary states of the unperturbed process (Ω, Q_0) and, therefore, both belong to Ω_0. In fact, there are no other states in this set. The simple reason for this is that, through common (but possibly random) access to the same set of observations, all individuals have, *ex ante,* the same range of possible choices available. Therefore, there is positive probability in *every* period that all individuals end up adopting the same action. This then leads to the conclusion that, with probability one, the process must eventually visit a monomorphic state, ω_α or ω_β. Because both states are stationary (and therefore absorb the process), each of them defines a *singleton limit set* of the unperturbed process.

The above considerations imply that $\Omega_0 = \{\omega_\alpha, \omega_\beta\}$ and, consequently, there are just two candidates for stochastic stability. To single out just one of them (i.e., to obtain a sharp selection result), we conduct our discussion in terms of an instrumental process derived from the original one with the following two features:

- First, the derived process "records" the situation only when one of the two states in Ω_0 is visited.
- Second, it relies on the perturbation only to exit a state in Ω_0. Thereafter, just the unperturbed dynamics operates.

As explained in Subsection 12.6.4.2, such a derived evolutionary model, $\{(\Omega_0, \hat{Q}_\varepsilon)\}_{\varepsilon \in [0,1)}$, is obtained from the original one, $\{(\Omega, Q_\varepsilon)\}_{\varepsilon \in [0,1)}$, by composing a *single* step according Q_ε with an ensuing (potentially indefinite) operation of the unperturbed process according to Q_0. The derived model displays the properties required from the canonical evolutionary model and therefore has a well-defined cost function $\hat{c} : \Omega_0 \times \Omega_0 \to \mathbb{N} \cup \{0\}$. Along the lines explained above for the original model, the induced cost may be interpreted as the minimum number of

---

[226] Refer to (12.49) for a formal definition of Ω_0.

simultaneous mutations (from either state ω_α or ω_β) that are needed to produce the contemplated transition (to ω_β or ω_α, respectively) by a subsequent operation of the unperturbed dynamics alone. More precisely, it can be shown (cf. Exercise 12.2) that, for each pair $(\omega, \omega') \in \Omega_0 \times \Omega_0$, we have

$$\hat{c}(\omega, \omega') = \min \{c(\omega, \omega'') : \omega'' \in \Omega, \ (Q_0)^k(\omega'', \omega') > 0 \text{ for some } k \in \mathbb{N}\}.$$
(12.21)

Or, if we let[227]

$$B(\omega') \equiv \{\omega'' \in \Omega : (Q_0)^k(\omega'', \omega') > 0 \text{ for some } k \in \mathbb{N}\}$$

stand for the *basin of attraction* of ω' (i.e., the set of states from which the *unperturbed* process can reach ω' with positive probability), we may rewrite (12.21) in the following more compact fashion:

$$\hat{c}(\omega, \omega') = \min \{|\omega - \omega''| : \omega'' \in B(\omega')\}.$$

That is, $\hat{c}(\omega, \omega')$ simply coincides with the minimum number of mutations that must simultaneously occur at ω to enter the basin of attraction of ω'.

Now, we want to apply Proposition 12.3 in Subsection 12.6.4.3, which relies on the concepts of radius and co-radius (Definitions 12.2 and 12.3). Specifically, our objective is to show that, if the population size is large enough,

$$R(\omega_\beta) > CR(\omega_\beta),$$
(12.22)

i.e., the radius of the singleton limit set $\{\omega_\beta\}$ is larger than its co-radius. By virtue of the aforementioned proposition, this implies that $\Omega^* = \{\omega_\beta\}$.

Let us first determine $R(\omega_\beta)$. Applying Definition 12.2, we obtain

$$R(\omega_\beta) = \hat{c}(\omega_\beta, \omega_\alpha)$$

where, as explained, $\hat{c}(\omega_\beta, \omega_\alpha)$ stands for the *mutation cost* of the transition from ω_β to ω_α in the evolutionary model $\{(\Omega_0, \hat{Q}_\varepsilon)\}_{\varepsilon \in [0,1)}$. To compute $\hat{c}(\omega_\beta, \omega_\alpha)$, we need to identify the minimum number of mutations at state ω_β that lead the mutant (who chooses α) to obtain a payoff at least as high as those who did not mutate (who continue choosing β). Denoting by $\pi_a(\omega)$ the payoff earned by an individual who chooses action $a \in \{\alpha, \beta\}$ when the state is ω, such a number of mutations is the minimum integer k for which

$$\pi_\alpha(k) \geq \pi_\beta(k).$$

If (and only if) no fewer than these k mutations occur, the payoff to action α is at least as large as that of β. Therefore, in (and only in) that case can the contemplated transition take place through imitation alone. This then readily leads to the following expression:

$$\hat{c}(\omega_\beta, \omega_\alpha) = \min\{k : k \in B(n)\} = \min\{k : \pi_\alpha(k) \geq \pi_\beta(k)\}.$$

---

[227] The matrix $(Q_0)^k$ (i.e., the application of the matrix Q_0 repeatedly, k times) simply embodies the transition probabilities resulting from k-step transitions – cf. Subsection 12.6.1.

In terms of the payoffs specified in Table 12.1, the inequality $\pi_\alpha(k) \geq \pi_\beta(k)$ can be written as follows:

$$(k-1)d + (n-k)e \geq kf + (n-k-1)b,$$

which implies that

$$k \geq \frac{b-e}{b-e+d-f}n + \frac{d-b}{b-e+d-f} \equiv H_{\beta\alpha}(n).$$

Therefore, if we denote by $\lceil x \rceil$ the smallest integer that is at least as large as x, integer (or "player indivisibility") considerations indicate that

$$R(\omega_\beta) = \lceil H_{\beta\alpha}(n) \rceil. \tag{12.23}$$

Now, we proceed reciprocally and determine the co-radius of ω_β. From Definition 12.3, it is given by

$$CR(\omega_\beta) = \hat{c}(\omega_\alpha, \omega_\beta).$$

To compute the mutation cost $\hat{c}(\omega_\alpha, \omega_\beta)$, we need to identify the minimum number of mutations from state ω_α that are needed to launch a transition, through the operation of the unperturbed dynamics alone, away from state ω_α and into state ω_β. By considerations analogous to those explained above for the converse transition, $\hat{c}(\omega_\alpha, \omega_\beta)$ is the minimum integer r (i.e., number of mutations from state ω_α) that satisfies

$$\pi_\beta(n-r) \geq \pi_\alpha(n-r).$$

From Table 12.1, we can write the above inequality as follows:

$$(n-r)f + (r-1)b \geq (n-r-1)d + re,$$

which implies

$$r \geq \frac{d-f}{b-e+d-f}n + \frac{b-d}{b-e+d-f} \equiv H_{\alpha\beta}(n). \tag{12.24}$$

Thus, again due to integer considerations, we have

$$CR(\omega_\beta) = \lceil H_{\alpha\beta}(n) \rceil. \tag{12.25}$$

From (12.23) and (12.25), to confirm the desired conclusion (i.e., the inequality (12.22)), it is enough to show that, for large enough n, we have

$$\lceil H_{\beta\alpha}(n) \rceil - \lceil H_{\alpha\beta}(n) \rceil > 0. \tag{12.26}$$

But this easily follows from the fact that, by the assumed risk dominance of the β action (cf. (12.9)), we have that

$$\frac{b-e}{b-e+d-f} > \frac{d-f}{b-e+d-f}$$

and, therefore, for large n,

$$\left(\frac{b-e}{b-e+d-f} - \frac{d-f}{b-e+d-f}\right) n > 2,$$

which allows one to ignore integer considerations in guaranteeing the strict inequality in (12.26). That is, even allowing for "player indivisibility" (which never requires increasing by more than one the typically fractional number of mutants prescribed by $H_{\beta\alpha}(n)$ and $H_{\alpha\beta}(n)$), the desired positive difference arises.

The above derivations show that $\Omega^* = \{\omega_\beta\}$, i.e., the monomorphic situation in which everyone plays the risk-dominant (but inefficient) action β is the unique stochastically stable state. Thus, it follows from the standard theory of Markov chains (cf. Subsection 12.6.1) that ω_β is the state at which the process spends "most of the time" in the long run when ε is very small. This, of course, raises the issue of how fast is the convergence to such a long-run outcome. If this question is posed in terms of the *maximum expected waiting time* for visiting the stochastically stable state ω_β, denoted by $\eta_\varepsilon(\omega_\beta)$, the answer is also found in Proposition 12.3. Specifically, we may invoke this result to conclude that, as $\varepsilon \to 0$,

$$\eta_\varepsilon(\omega_\beta) \sim (1/\varepsilon)^{CR(\omega_\beta)}.$$

That is, $\eta_\varepsilon(\omega_\beta)$ grows with $(1/\varepsilon)$ at a power rate equal to the co-radius of ω_β.

How fast then, intuitively speaking, is the induced rate of convergence? In effect, it is quite slow if, as implicitly supposed, the population size n is large. Notice from (12.24) and (12.25) that $CR(\omega_\beta)$ is essentially proportional to population size. Thus, as n grows, the maximum expected waiting time of transiting from ω_α (the alternative absorbing state of the unperturbed learning dynamics) to the stochastically stable state ω_β grows very fast. To obtain some intuitive feeling of the magnitudes involved, suppose that, by chance, the process had settled initially in the state where α is monomorphically played. Further assume, to fix ideas, that mutation occurs at the moderately small rate $\varepsilon = 0.01$, the population consists of only 100 players (i.e., $n = 100$) and, say, $d = 4$, $b = 3$, $f = 2$, $e = 0$. Then, the expected waiting time for the process to *first* visit ω_β is of order 10^{80}, a mind-boggling figure!

In view of such sluggish rates of convergence, one may naturally feel inclined to dispute the real significance of the long-run predictions embodied by the notion of stochastic stability. It turns out, however, that the extremely slow convergence noted here is crucially dependent (an artifact, one might even say) of a vastly unrealistic feature of the present model – namely, the assumption that there is *global* interaction among *all* players in the population. In real-world setups (certainly, if the population is large) one can hardly expect that each individual ends up playing with everyone else. Instead, social networks typically display a less encompassing structure (local, centralized, etc.). This, in turn, is a feature that, intuitively, would seem to work in the direction of improving substantially the speed of long-run convergence. Indeed, a stark confirmation of this conjecture is found in Subsections 12.4.2 and 12.4.3.

12.4.1.2 *Best-response adjustment.* Let us now reconsider the evolutionary learning model studied in the former subsection under the assumption that behavioral adjustment is conducted under myopic best response. That is, we consider the context of global interaction presented in Subsection 12.3.1.1 with (12.5) substituting (12.3).

Let $\{(\Omega, Q_\varepsilon)\}_{\varepsilon \in [0,1)}$ stand for the collection of Markov chains formalizing the induced learning dynamics, as parametrized by the mutation probability ε. Again, the requirements of our canonical evolutionary model are satisfied. Thus, the steps to be undertaken by the analysis are quite parallel to those of the previous case. First, we want to identify the limit states of the unperturbed dynamics. It follows from a ready adaptation of the arguments used in Subsection 11.3.3 that $\Omega_0 = \{\omega_\alpha, \omega_\beta\}$, each separate state defining by itself a singleton limit set (cf. Exercise 12.1).

Next, we show that, just as in the former imitation scenario, we still have that

$$R(\omega_\beta) > CR(\omega_\beta), \tag{12.27}$$

provided the population is large enough. Thus, by invoking Proposition 12.3, we conclude that $\Omega^* = \{\omega_\beta\}$. That is, the present learning dynamics continues to select the risk-dominant action.

To establish (12.27), we first determine $R(\omega_\beta)$. As before, it equals $\hat{c}(\omega_\beta, \omega_\alpha)$, which in turn has an analogous interpretation. Namely, it is to be conceived as the minimum number of simultaneous mutations from state ω_β that are needed to trigger a transition toward ω_α through the ensuing operation of the best-response dynamics alone. Now, however, to carry out the counterpart derivations, it is useful to introduce the following variation on former notation. Given any state $\omega \in \Omega$, $\pi_a(a', \omega)$ will denote the payoff perceived by an individual who

- is choosing action $a \in \{\alpha, \beta\}$ in the prevailing state ω,
- holds static expectations on the behavior of others, and
- currently considers revising her choice toward action a' (possibly equal to a).

Then, it should be clear that, for any given number of mutations k from state ω_β to trigger a transition toward ω_α, a necessary condition is that the following expression holds:

$$\pi_\beta(\alpha, k) \geq \pi_\beta(\beta, k), \tag{12.28}$$

which, in view of Table 12.1, can be rewritten as follows:

$$kd + (n - k - 1)e \geq kf + (n - k - 1)b \tag{12.29}$$

or, equivalently,

$$k \geq \frac{b - e}{b - e + d - f}(n - 1).$$

The above inequality embodies a lower bound on the number of mutations that must *necessarily* occur at state ω_β if a transition toward ω_α may take place via the unperturbed dynamics. Once we allow for integer considerations, this amounts to a lower bound on $R(\omega_\beta)$ – i.e., $\hat{c}(\omega_\beta, \omega_\alpha)$ – as follows:

$$R(\omega_\beta) \geq \left\lceil \frac{b-e}{b-e+d-f}(n-1) \right\rceil, \tag{12.30}$$

where recall that $\lceil x \rceil$ denotes the smallest integer that is at least as large as x.

Now, we turn to computing $CR(\omega_\beta)$. In this case, we are interested in finding the minimum number of mutations at state ω_α that are *sufficient* to produce a transition toward ω_β through the unperturbed dynamics alone. Using the above notation, it should be clear that, for such a transition to occur with positive probability, it is enough that the number r of mutations satisfy[228]

$$\pi_\alpha(\beta, n-r) \geq \pi_\alpha(\alpha, n-r),$$

which can be written as:

$$(n-r-1)f + rb \geq (n-r-1)d + re,$$

or

$$r \geq \frac{d-f}{b-e+d-f}(n-1).$$

Therefore, we may assert that

$$CR(\omega_\beta) = \hat{c}(\omega_\alpha, \omega_\beta) \leq \left\lceil \frac{d-f}{b-e+d-f}(n-1) \right\rceil. \tag{12.31}$$

By the assumed risk dominance of β,

$$\frac{b-e}{b-e+d-f} > \frac{d-f}{b-e+d-f};$$

hence, if n is large enough,

$$\left\lceil \frac{b-e}{b-e+d-f}(n-1) \right\rceil > \left\lceil \frac{d-f}{b-e+d-f}(n-1) \right\rceil,$$

which, in view of (12.30) and (12.31), implies, as claimed, that

$$R(\omega_\beta) > CR(\omega_\beta).$$

Thus, to repeat, the same long-run selection is obtained here as in the case when players learn through imitation. We also arrive, on the other hand, at an analogous result concerning rates of convergence. It is easy to see (cf. Exercise 12.3) that the inequality displayed in (12.31) can be reversed, i.e.,

$$CR(\omega_\beta) = \hat{c}(\omega_\alpha, \omega_\beta) \geq \left\lceil \frac{d-f}{b-e+d-f}(n-1) \right\rceil, \tag{12.32}$$

---

[228] Note that, after those r mutations have occurred, the best-response dynamics allows with positive probability that those players who have mutated do *not* receive a revision opportunity. Thus, it is enough to check the incentives to revise toward β for those who have not mutated (and therefore are still playing α).

so that, in fact, $CR(\omega_\beta) = \lceil [(d-f)/(b-e+d-f)](n-1) \rceil$. This implies that, just as in the former imitation context (recall (12.25)), the co-radius of ω_β happens to be roughly proportional to n, the population size. Again, therefore, the convergence turns out to be extremely slow when the population is moderately large. The same voice of concern is thus pertinent here, and so is our former discussion about the role played in this respect by the (unrealistic) assumption of global interaction.

12.4.2 *Bilateral coordination games under local interaction*

Now we turn to a context in which the bilateral coordination game is played on a social network that displays the *local* interaction structure described in (12.12). In principle, this context could be analyzed under each of the two learning dynamics we have proposed: imitation and best-response adjustment. Concerning imitation, however, the fact that local interaction induces significant *asymmetries* among the different players suggests modifying the behavioral rule accordingly. Specifically, it seems natural to relax the strong symmetry displayed by (12.2), which implies that players should treat all observations equivalently. Instead, one might postulate, for example, that any given player views the experience of her direct neighbors (who are in a position relatively similar to hers) as the only relevant piece of information in guiding her imitation.

A variation of the imitation process along these lines is proposed in Exercise 12.4, where the reader is also asked to contrast it with our leading (symmetric and global) imitation rule (12.3). In fact, both of these approaches to imitation, global and local, happen to lead to essentially the same selection result, which in turn also coincides with that induced by myopic best-response adjustment. Here, therefore, our ensuing discussion of the local interaction framework focuses alone on the model with best-response dynamics, as first studied by Ellison (1983).

Under local interaction, a purely anonymous description of the situation no longer qualifies as a sufficient state of the system. Therefore, the state space Ω is now identified with $S_1 \times S_2 \times \cdots \times S_n$, the space of (player-indexed) strategy profiles. Let (Ω, Q_ε) be the Markov chain on such a state space that models, for some $\varepsilon > 0$, the perturbed process of best-response dynamics in this case (cf. (12.4) and (12.5)). In characterizing its long-run behavior for small ε, much of the analysis is quite akin to that conducted before for the global-interaction scenario. Our discussion, therefore, will dispense with, or simply sketch, those steps that are analogous, devoting special attention only to the genuinely novel aspects. As we shall explain, these new considerations essentially pertain to the much faster rate of long-run convergence that is now attained.

First, we characterize the limit states of the unperturbed process. It is straightforward to see that, again, the two monomorphic states (which, by a slight abuse of notation, we continue to denote by ω_α and ω_β) are the sole singleton limit sets. Thus, to settle the issue of long-run selection it is enough to show that, as was the case under global interaction, we have

$$R(\omega_\beta) > CR(\omega_\beta), \tag{12.33}$$

provided the population is large enough.

To establish the above inequality, our first step is to prove that $CR(\omega_\beta) = 1$. This, in turn, follows from the fact that if one player mutates to action β from state ω_α, there is positive probability that the best-response dynamics brings the process to state ω_β. Suppose, for concreteness, that the mutant in question is player 1. Then, there is positive probability that, in the next period, player 1 does *not* receive a revision opportunity but at least player 2 does. In this event, by the assumed risk dominance of β (cf. (12.9)), player 2 must change her action to β. (Note that the payoff of a player is maximized by choosing β if at least one of her neighbors chooses β.) Now suppose that, thereafter, only the best-response dynamics is at work. In that case, neither player 1 nor 2 will ever want to change her action. However, as that dynamics unfolds, their neighbors (players n and 3 first, then players $n - 1$ and 4, etc.) will in turn change their action to β if given a revision opportunity. Hence, we may conclude that, after players 1 and 2 have switched to action β (the first by mutation and the second by best-response adjustment), all others will eventually do so as well in finite time, with probability one.

Similar considerations, on the other hand, imply that $R(\omega_\beta) > 1$ if $n \geq 3$. To see this, simply note that, starting from state ω_β, just one mutation to action α by any player will *not* induce any further move toward β on the basis of best-response adjustment (again, this follows from the risk-dominance condition on β). Therefore, if just a single mutation occurs from state ω_β, the unperturbed dynamics will lead the process back to ω_β with probability one. This implies that two or more mutations are needed for a transition away from ω_β (into ω_α), which finally establishes (12.33).

The previous argument shows that, under local interaction, (perturbed) best-response adjustment selects exactly the same outcome as with global (round-robin) interaction. That is, $\Omega^* = \{\omega_\beta\}$ and therefore the unique stochastically stable state has all players choosing the risk-dominant action. In the present case, however, the predictive relevance of this conclusion is much enhanced by the fact that $CR(\omega_\beta) = 1$, i.e., the co-radius of ω_β is minimal. This implies that the maximum expected waiting time for observing ω_β grows linearly with $(1/\varepsilon)$, *independently of population size*. More specifically, one can show (cf. Exercise 12.5) that such a waiting time, denoted $\eta_\varepsilon(\omega_\beta)$, can be bounded for small ε as follows:

$$\eta_\varepsilon(\omega_\beta) \leq \frac{n-2}{p} + \frac{1}{p(1-p)}(1/\varepsilon), \tag{12.34}$$

where recall that $p \in (0, 1)$ is the independent probability with which every player receives a revision opportunity in each period. To stress the difference between this conclusion and that obtained under global interaction, let us return to the simple illustration discussed at the end of Subsection 12.4.1.1. That is, suppose $\varepsilon = 0.01$ and $n = 100$, the specific payoff magnitudes (i.e., b, d, e, and f) being irrelevant in the present case as long as (12.9) is satisfied. Then, if the process were to start at state ω_α and, say, $p = 1/3$, the expected waiting time for a *first* visit to ω_β is computed from (12.34) to be at most 744 periods, in sharp contrast with the state of affairs prevailing in the global-interaction setup.

12.4.3 *Bilateral coordination games under centralized interaction*

We close our discussion of bilateral coordination games by studying a social network displaying centralized interaction of the kind given by (12.13). As we argued in the case of local interaction, when the social network embodies significant asymmetries among the players, the imitation rule should be required to reflect (at least partially) those asymmetries as well. In essence, the idea here is that a player can be expected to view as relevant only those observations that are obtained from players who, *ex ante,* are in circumstances similar to those of herself.

In a centralized social network, one may rely on these considerations to propose an imitation process undertaken only by (and among) the peripheral players, all of whom occupy symmetric *ex ante* roles in the interaction structure. Imitation, however, does not represent a useful basis to model the behavior of the central agent, whose position in the network has no counterpart. Thus, let us build on such a center-periphery asymmetry to enrich what thus far has been our standard practice (i.e., assume a homogeneous kind of learning for all players), positing instead an eclectic evolutionary model that includes two different types of behavioral rules.[229] On the one hand, assume the peripheral players are relatively unsophisticated and thus behave as imitators among themselves – they are implicitly supposed, therefore, to be aware of the different roles played by any of them and the central player. This amounts to postulating that, for each $i = 2, 3, \ldots, n$,

$$D_i(s) = \check{M}_i(s) \equiv \{s_j : j = 2, \ldots, n, \ \pi_j(s) \geq \pi_i(s)\}, \tag{12.35}$$

which modifies (12.2) by restricting the set of players under consideration to the peripheral ones alone. On the other hand, the central player (player 1), who has no reason to imitate other players, is assumed sophisticated enough to be capable of determining her myopic best response to the current situation. Thus, for this player we suppose, as in (12.5), that

$$D_1(s) \equiv B_1^*(s). \tag{12.36}$$

Let $\{(\Omega, Q_\varepsilon)\}_{\varepsilon \in [0,1)}$ stand for the collection of Markov chains modeling the (perturbed) evolutionary dynamics in the present centralized setup under the above behavioral rules, (12.35) and (12.36). As before, the state space Ω is identified with $S_1 \times S_2 \times \cdots \times S_n$, the space of (player-indexed) strategy profiles. For the unperturbed process, it is straightforward to see that the set Ω_0 of limit states continues to be $\{\omega_\alpha, \omega_\beta\}$, each of its constituent states defining by itself a separate singleton limit set. As usual, we are interested in narrowing down such a multiplicity by identifying the subset Ω^* of stochastically stable states.

As a first approach (later proven to be unsuccessful), we attempt to follow the route pursued in former cases. That is, we focus on one of the monomorphic states, say ω_β, and determine its radius and co-radius. First, to obtain the co-radius $CR(\omega_\beta)$, we have to compute $\hat{c}(\omega_\alpha, \omega_\beta)$, whose interpretation here is as usual, i.e., the minimum number of simultaneous mutations that are required at ω_α to produce

---

[229] See Exercise 12.6 for some other specifications.

an ensuing transition to ω_β according to the unperturbed process. If n is large enough, it is clear that just one mutation is unable to do so. If this mutation toward β affects player 1 (the central player), then since all peripheral players continue playing α, imitation among themselves will not lead them to change their action. Thus, eventually, with probability one, the central player must switch back to α, which restores state ω_α. On the other hand, if any of the peripheral players mutates, neither the central nor the other peripheral players will change their actions if n is large enough (cf. Exercise 12.7). That is, the central player will continue to find α a best response to the resulting state. And, this being the case, the payoff received by the mutant is lower than that of the rest of the peripheral players, which implies that the latter players will continue to play α as well. Thus, eventually, the mutant will return to α, restoring the state ω_α.

We conclude, therefore, that at least two mutations are required for a transition from ω_α to ω_β. But are two mutations enough? Indeed they are, as the following argument shows. Suppose both the central player and any *one* peripheral player mutate toward β. Now assume that, subsequently, the central player does *not* receive a revision opportunity but *all* peripheral players do so. Given that the mutant peripheral player is receiving a higher payoff than the others (because she is "well coordinated" with the central player), all the other peripheral players must change to action β. This leads the process to state ω_β, as desired.

The above considerations imply that

$$C R(\omega_\beta) = R(\omega_\alpha) = \hat{c}(\omega_\alpha, \omega_\beta) = 2. \tag{12.37}$$

But note that the argument can be reproduced mimetically for the converse transition from ω_β to ω_α. Therefore, we also have

$$C R(\omega_\alpha) = R(\omega_\beta) = \hat{c}(\omega_\beta, \omega_\alpha) = 2. \tag{12.38}$$

Combining (12.37) and (12.38), one concludes that, concerning their radii and co-radii, the situation is fully symmetric between states ω_α and ω_β. This prevents us from relying on Proposition 12.3 to achieve a clear-cut long-run selection, because the hypotheses contemplated by this result are not satisfied for any of those two states. We need to resort, therefore, to more "fundamental" tools of analysis to characterize the stochastically stable states. This is precisely the objective afforded by the graph-theoretic techniques described in Subsection 12.6.4.1, later applied in Subsection 12.6.4.2 to the derived evolutionary model $\{(\Omega_0, \hat{Q}_\varepsilon)\}_{\varepsilon \in [0,1)}$ that is obtained from the original one in the usual fashion.

To apply those techniques, we first need to find for each of the two states in Ω_0, ω_α and ω_β, the minimal-cost ω-trees arising in the derived model (cf. Definition 12.1 for the concept of ω-tree). In general, finding minimal-cost trees can be quite involved. Here, however, it is extremely simple because there is just one such tree for either state. That is, the unique ω_α-tree in Ω_0, say Y_α, consists of the arrow $(\omega_\beta, \omega_\alpha)$ and the unique ω_β-tree in Ω_0, say Y_β, is the arrow $(\omega_\alpha, \omega_\beta)$. From (12.37) and (12.38), we know that

$$\hat{c}(Y_\alpha) = \hat{c}(Y_\beta) = 2$$

and therefore, by virtue of Proposition 12.2, we conclude that

$$\Omega^* = \{\omega_\alpha, \omega_\beta\},$$

i.e., both ω_α and ω_β are stochastically stable. Heuristically, this conclusion is simply a reflection of the following intuitive idea. If transitions across the two limit states of the unperturbed process require the same (minimum) number of mutations, both of them should be expected to arise a comparable fraction of time (not necessarily the same, of course) in the long run. Thus, in the long run, we do not obtain any sharp selection result beyond that imperfect one contained in the set Ω_0 – see, however, Exercise 12.8.

12.4.4 *Minimum-effort game*

Consider now the strategic setup described in Subsection 12.3.2. As in many other *symmetric* coordination contexts, the analysis in the present case is unaffected by whether players are either postulated to learn by imitation or their behavior is adjusted through myopic best (or better) responses – cf. Exercise 12.11. Thus, for concreteness, we focus in what follows on the former possibility and suppose that players' behavioral dynamics is governed by imitation. The analysis largely builds on Robles (1997).

Let $\{(\Omega, Q_\varepsilon)\}_{\varepsilon \in [0,1)}$ stand for the collection of Markov chains modeling the perturbed evolutionary dynamics under the imitation rule (12.3) and the payoff structure (12.14). The state space is chosen as follows:

$$\Omega = S_1 \times \cdots \times S_n = \Xi^n,$$

where recall that $\Xi \equiv \{1, 2, \ldots, \bar{x}\}$ represents the finite set of possible effort levels. First, we observe that the limit states of the corresponding unperturbed dynamics (Ω, Q_0) coincide with the monomorphic states. That is,

$$\Omega_0 = \{\mathbf{x} \equiv (x, x, \ldots, x) : x \in \Xi\}.$$

The reason should be familiar by now. Given that all players are exposed to the same "pool of information," there is positive probability that all may end up making the same choice. That is, there is positive probability that the learning process should lead to a monomorphic state. In view of this fact, one can guarantee that, with probability one, the unperturbed dynamics must eventually visit some monomorphic state $\mathbf{x}$. Since any such state is obviously absorbing (i.e., stationary), it follows that Ω_0 consists of all those states and, moreover, each of them defines a singleton limit set.

To select among the different states in Ω_0, we ask which of these are stochastically stable. Relying back again on the notions of radius and co-radius, we next show that

$$R(\mathbf{1}) > CR(\mathbf{1}), \tag{12.39}$$

where $\mathbf{1} \equiv (1, \ldots, 1)$. Thus, in view of Proposition 12.3, we have

$$\Omega^* = \{\mathbf{1}\},$$

i.e., the lowest-effort equilibrium is the unique long-run selection of the perturbed evolutionary process.

To prove (12.39), let us first compute the co-radius of **1**. From Definition 12.3, it is to be determined as follows:

$$CR(\mathbf{1}) = \max_{\mathbf{x} \in \Omega_0 \backslash \{\mathbf{1}\}} \hat{c}(\mathbf{x}, \mathbf{1}),$$

where the function $\hat{c}(\cdot, \cdot)$ has the usual interpretation, i.e., it specifies the mutation *cost* of the contemplated transition in terms of the derived evolutionary model $\{(\Omega_0, \hat{Q}_\varepsilon)\}_{\varepsilon \in [0,1)}$. We now claim that $\hat{c}(\mathbf{x}, \mathbf{1}) = 1$ for every $\mathbf{x} \in \Omega_0 \backslash \{\mathbf{1}\}$. To see this, simply note that if any *single* individual mutates at some such $\mathbf{x}$, there is positive probability that this mutation may lead her to choosing the lowest effort level of 1. In this event, of course, the mutant player ends up receiving a higher payoff than the rest (cf. (12.14)). Therefore, with positive probability (i.e., if all players, possibly including the mutant, receive a revision opportunity), the subsequent state has everyone choosing an effort level equal to 1. That is, the process is led to state **1**.

The previous argument indicates that $CR(\mathbf{1}) = 1$. Thus, to establish (12.39), it is enough to show that

$$R(\mathbf{1}) = \min_{\mathbf{x} \in \Omega_0 \backslash \{\mathbf{1}\}} \hat{c}(\mathbf{1}, \mathbf{x}) > 1.$$

To prove this inequality, let the process start at state **1** and allow any single individual to mutate to some effort level higher than 1. Clearly, no matter what this particular level might be, the mutant then receives a lower payoff than the rest. Consequently, not only will she have no imitators but, eventually, she will switch back to the original effort level with probability one. No single mutation, therefore, is able to trigger a transition away from state **1** through the unperturbed dynamics alone. We thus conclude that $R(\mathbf{1}) > 1$, as claimed.

In the minimum-effort game, we encounter again, in a modified form, the tension between risk dominance (or safety) and efficiency that arose quite starkly in bilateral coordination games under a variety of social networks. And, as it was also the case under either *global* or *local* interaction (recall Subsections 12.4.1 and 12.4.2), we find it here as well that safety predominates over efficiency as the long-run selection criterion. In the present context, however, players' interaction is of the playing-the-field kind, which in turn has forceful effects on the speed of convergence. Specifically, the fact that the state **1** has the smallest possible co-radius of one implies, by virtue of Proposition 12.3, that $\eta_\varepsilon(\mathbf{1})$ grows linearly with $1/\varepsilon$. Thus, by contrast with the situation prevailing under global interaction in bilateral coordination games, the long-run convergence is now very fast, even if the population size is large.

12.4.5 *Cournot oligopoly*

We now focus on a discretized version of the Cournot oligopoly setup, as presented in Subsection 12.3.3. In this context, we follow Vega-Redondo (1997) in contrasting the long-run implications of the two alternative behavioral paradigms introduced in

Subsection 12.2.2: learning by imitation and best-response adjustment. And, unlike what hitherto has been the case, we find sharp and very significant differences in the predictions induced by each of these alternative learning dynamics. Thus, while in the former case the Walrasian outcome prevails in the long run, the second learning dynamics leads to a Cournot-Nash equilibrium of the oligopoly game.

12.4.5.1 *Learning by imitation.* Let $\{(\Omega, Q_\varepsilon)\}_{\varepsilon \in [0,1)}$ stand for the collection of Markov chains modeling the perturbed evolutionary dynamics in the present oligopolistic context, with payoffs given by (12.15) and players adjusting their behavior as prescribed by the imitation learning rule (12.3). We make $\Omega = \Phi^n$, where recall that $\Phi = \{0, \varrho, 2\varrho, \ldots, v\varrho\}$ is the finite grid of admissible outputs ($v \in \mathbb{N}$ and $\varrho \in \mathbb{R}$ are arbitrary parameters). For convenience, it is assumed that the outputs x^c and x^w defining the symmetric Cournot-Nash and Walras equilibria both belong to Φ.

First, as usual, we are interested in identifying the set Ω_0 consisting of the limit states of the unperturbed process. Just as explained in other cases (cf. Subsection 12.4.1.1), the fact that firms' imitation operates on common information eventually leads, a.s., to a monomorphic state of the form $\mathbf{x} \equiv (x, x, \ldots, x)$ where every firm chooses the same $x \in \Phi$. Thus, since every such configuration is an absorbing state of the unperturbed process (Ω, Q_0), we have

$$\Omega_0 = \{\mathbf{x} \equiv (x, x, \ldots, x) \in \Omega : x \in \Phi\}.$$

Next, we show that the unique state in Ω_0 that qualifies as stochastically stable is the one where the Walrasian output x^w is played by all firms (recall Subsection 12.3.3). To establish this claim, it is enough to show that

$$R(\mathbf{x}^w) > CR(\mathbf{x}^w) \tag{12.40}$$

where, as usual, $R(\cdot)$ and $CR(\cdot)$ stand for the radius and co-radius of the state in question. The essential step in proving this inequality is provided by the following Lemma.

Lemma 12.1: *Let $x \in \Phi$ with $x \neq x^w$ and consider any m such that $1 \leq m \leq n - 1$. Then,*

$$x^w P(m x^w + (n - m)x) - C(x^w)$$
$$> x P(m x^w + (n - m)x) - C(x).$$

Proof: Consider any x and m as indicated. The fact that the inverse-demand function is assumed decreasing implies

$$[P(n x^w) - P(m x^w + (n - m)x)] x^w$$
$$< [P(n x^w) - P(m x^w + (n - m)x)] x,$$

which, by subtracting the production costs $C(x^w)$ and $C(x)$ to both sides, may be rewritten as follows:

$$[P(n\,x^w)\,x^w - C(x^w)] - [P(n\,x^w)\,x - C(x)] <$$
$$[P\,(m\,x^w + (n - m)x)\,x^w - C(x^w)] - [P\,(m\,x^w + (n - m)x)\,x - C(x)].$$

$$\tag{12.41}$$

Now note that, by the definition of Walras equilibrium in this setup (cf. (12.17)), we have

$$[P(n\,x^w)\,x^w - C(x^w)] - [P(n\,x^w)\,x - C(x)] \geq 0,$$

which, in view of (12.41), implies

$$[P\,(m\,x^w + (n - m)x)\,x^w - C(x^w)]$$
$$- [P(m\,x^w + (n - m)x)\,x - C(x)] > 0,$$

which is the desired conclusion. ∎

By making $m = 1$ in the above Lemma, we first argue that, starting at any $\mathbf{x} = (x, x, \ldots, x) \in \Omega_0$ with $x \neq x^w$, a single mutation by *any* firm to x^w may lead the unperturbed dynamics toward $\mathbf{x}^w$ with positive probability. To see this, simply note that, right after such a mutation, one has that the mutant earns higher profit than the rest of $n - 1$ nonmutants. Thus, by imitation alone, the process may undertake a transition to $\mathbf{x}^w$ and therefore

$$C\,R(\mathbf{x}^w) = \max_{\mathbf{x} \in \Omega_0 \backslash \{\mathbf{x}^w\}} \hat{c}(\mathbf{x}, \mathbf{x}^w) = 1, \tag{12.42}$$

where the function $\hat{c}(\cdot, \cdot)$ determines the *mutation costs* resulting from the evolutionary model $\{(\Omega_0, \hat{Q}_\varepsilon)\}_{\varepsilon \in [0,1)}$.

But, reciprocally, by making $m = n - 1$ in Lemma 12.1, it follows that after just *one* mutation at state $\mathbf{x}^w$, the unperturbed (imitation) dynamics must lead the process back to state $\mathbf{x}^w$ with probability one. Consequently,

$$R(\mathbf{x}^w) = \min_{\mathbf{x} \in \Omega_0 \backslash \{\mathbf{x}^w\}} \hat{c}(\mathbf{x}^w, \mathbf{x}) > 1, \tag{12.43}$$

which in combination with (12.42) leads to the desired inequality (12.40). This finally establishes that, as advanced,

$$\Omega^* = \{\mathbf{x}^w\},$$

i.e., the Walrasian monomorphic state is the unique stochastically stable state of the evolutionary process.

12.4.5.2 *Best-response adjustment.* Now we turn to studying the Cournot setup under the assumption that the firms adjust their behavior through myopic best response, as given by (12.5). Our first task concerns the characterization of the limit states of induced unperturbed process (Ω, Q_0). To simplify matters in this respect, let us make the convenient assumption that firms display linear costs so that their (common) cost function $C(\cdot)$ is of the following form:

$$C(q_i) = c\, q_i$$

for some (constant) marginal cost $c > 0$.

In this case, it was shown in Subsection 11.3.3 that the Cournot oligopoly game exhibits a well-defined potential (cf. (11.27)) and thus qualifies as a potential game. Thus, by a straightforward adaptation of Theorem 11.4, it follows that the best-response dynamics converges a.s. to the (assumed unique) Cournot-Nash equilibrium $\mathbf{x}^c \equiv (x^c, x^c, \ldots, x^c)$ defined in (12.16).[230] This implies that

$$\Omega_0 = \{\mathbf{x}^c\}$$

and, therefore, since

$$\emptyset \neq \Omega^* \subset \Omega_0$$

(cf. (12.50)), we have

$$\Omega^* = \{\mathbf{x}^c\};$$

i.e., the unique stochastically stable state corresponds to the Cournot-Nash equilibrium.

The acute contrast between the present conclusion and that obtained in Subsection 12.4.5.1 illustrates the crucially different implications of alternative behavioral rules. In general, the long-run dynamics of best-response adjustment must always gravitate toward a Nash equilibrium of the game (provided, of course, it converges). This simply reflects the fact that players' unilateral change of strategy is then guided alone by their own individual payoffs. Instead, if players' adjustment is based on imitation, the players' behavior responds to relative payoffs. Naturally, this is a feature that happens to exacerbate the "competitive" features of players' interaction in many cases (e.g., in the Cournot setup studied here).

12.5   Experimental evidence

Following the theoretical analysis conducted in the previous section, our present objective is to contrast the essential implications derived from it with related experimental evidence. For concreteness, our attention is directed toward two of the scenarios studied above. First, we consider coordination games and focus, specifically, on the minimum-effort game studied in Subsection 12.4.4. Second, we turn to the oligopoly Cournot games analyzed in Subsection 12.4.5.

---

[230] The statement of Theorem 11.4 concerned the better-response dynamics but it should be apparent that the logic of the proof applies unchanged to the best-response dynamics as well.

12.5.1 *Minimum-effort game*

In a very influential paper, van Huyck, Battalio, and Beil (1990) – henceforth labeled VHBB – conducted an experimental investigation of the minimum-effort game.[231] Given the stark coordination dilemma posed by this game (i.e., the acute conflict between efficiency and safety), it represents a particularly well-suited scenario to shed light on the important issue of coordination failure.

The experimental setup designed by these authors may be outlined as follows. A collection of university undergraduate students were divided into seven disjoint groups composed of 14 to 16 subjects. Each of these groups was made to play the minimum-effort game for a range of efforts $\Xi \equiv \{1, 2, \ldots, 7\}$ and a (scaled)[232] value of $\gamma = 1/2$ in (12.14). In a first experimental treatment, labeled A, every group of individuals played the game over 10 consecutive rounds. Thereafter, the *same* groups were subject to a second treatment, B, consisting of 5 rounds in which the payoff function was changed to $\gamma = 0$. Finally, there was a third treatment called A', which was played under the same conditions as the initial treatment A (i.e., with the original value of $\gamma = 1/2$) for another 5 consecutive rounds.

The experimental results obtained by VHBB were surprisingly sharp. In treatment A, almost all subjects in every group started by playing suboptimal responses to the initial behavior of others, with a relatively wide initial dispersion in their effort choices. As the game was repeated, intragroup miscoordination decreased steeply, but at the expense of having players adjust their behavior toward the minimum effort level. By the last period of treatment A, 72% of the subjects were choosing the lowest effort level of 1, and this was also the minimum effort level displayed by every group.

The results reported for treatment A could be attributed, at least in part, to the strategic uncertainty induced by the initially wide distribution of effort levels. Since players' expectations were not suitably "coordinated" at the beginning of play, it may be argued that the move toward safety observed thereafter is intuitively justified. The role of the intermediate treatment B was precisely to explore the validity of this explanation by attempting to impinge on players' expectation. Note that, because this treatment has $\gamma = 0$, the highest effort of 7 is a weakly dominant strategy in this case. Thus, one would expect that players should then adjust their behavior toward the efficient equilibrium as play proceeds in this treatment. Indeed, this is what VHBB observe in their experiments. By the end of treatment B (i.e., after just 5 rounds), 84% of the subjects adopted effort 7 and this was also the minimum effort found in most groups.

Having thus achieved a strong focalization of players' expectations on the highest effort by round 15 of the overall experiment (i.e., at the end of treatment B), the ensuing treatment A' was conducted under the original conditions ($\gamma = 1/2$). To

---

[231] See also van Huyck, Battalio, and Beil (1991), where these authors extend the analysis of coordination failure to other related contexts such as the so-called average-opinion games.

[232] In fact, the cost coefficient multiplying individual effort was chosen equal to 0.1 and the coefficient multiplying gross payoff (itself equal to the overall minimum effort) was made equal to 0.2.

repeat, this was intended to assess the validity of the aforementioned explanation of the learning dynamics observed in the first treatment A. Was such earlier dynamics to be understood as a consequence of the initially mismatched expectations? The evidence observed throughout treatment A' suggests the contrary. Even though at round 16 (the first one of treatment A'), a significant fraction of players chose an effort level of 7 (25% of them), many others did choose the lowest effort. Eventually, this reverted the population back to a widespread low effort by the end of treatment A'. Specifically, at round 20 (the last one), 84% of the subjects chose an effort of 1, even a larger proportion than that observed at the end of treatment A.

The experiments conducted by VHBB support the idea that safety considerations are indeed a very strong determinant of choice in the minimum-effort game. In this sense, therefore, they are in accordance with the theoretical analysis of Subsection 12.4.4, where we showed that the inefficient equilibrium where everyone chooses the lowest effort level is the only robust one in the presence of noise. In essence, this is the message delivered by the above experiments. For, even if players' expectations are "manipulated" through the intermediate treatment B so that they focus on the high-effort equilibrium, this turns out to have only very short-lived consequences. Once the original conditions of the minimum-effort game are restored, so is the strong tendency of players to adjust their choices toward the risk-minimizing action, i.e., the lowest effort level.

12.5.2 *Cournot oligopoly*

Despite the central role played by the Cournot model as the canonical framework to study oligopolistic competition, it is surprising that one can find few cases in the literature where it has been carefully analyzed in laboratory experiments (cf. Holt, 1995; Davis, 1999; Rassenti *et al.*, 2000; Offerman *et al.*, 2002). Here, we focus on recent experimental work by Huck, Normann, and Oechssler (1999) – henceforth referred to as HNO – whose approach is very well suited for an empirical assessment of the different learning models studied in Subsection 12.4.5.

The experimental setup designed by HNO was particularly simple. Every treatment involved six *fixed* and *independent* groups of just four subjects ("firms"), all 24 of them playing repeatedly within their respective group under unchanged conditions. Each group faced the same linear demand function and every subject displayed a constant and identical marginal cost. One of the primary objectives of the experiments was to study the long-run implications of different behavioral rules – in particular, imitation and best-response adjustment. This led HNO to vary the information provided to the subjects across different treatments, with the aim of inducing their use of alternative behavioral rules. In real-world markets, the information available to the agents can be seen largely as a reflection of the relative complexity of the environment and/or, relatedly, the ability of these agents to comprehend it. In this light, the consideration of different informational scenarios in the HNO experimental setup can be conceived as a way of addressing what, in their real-world counterparts, would be alternative environmental conditions (e.g., concerning complexity).

In all the experimental setups studied by HNO, the subjects knew they were involved in a market game and that their decisions were to be regarded as output choices. Beyond this basic information, provided in all their experiments, the authors considered five different informational scenarios (or treatments). In two of them (labeled BEST and FULL), subjects were completely aware of market and cost conditions, i.e., they knew the demand and cost functions. Furthermore, each subject was also informed, after every round, of the market price just realized and the corresponding *aggregate* quantity.[233] While such a general information was common to both BEST and FULL, these scenarios differed in the individualized information made available to the subjects. Thus, whereas in BEST they were just informed of their *own* profits, in FULL they were also informed of the *complete* array of all individual quantities.

Two other treatments (labeled NOIN and IMIT) provided subjects with much less information. In NOIN, they knew virtually nothing but their *own* past profits. Instead, in IMIT, each subject was informed after every round of what had been the *array* of individual quantities chosen *and* the corresponding profits associated with all of them. In either case, however, subjects were *not* informed of precise market or cost conditions and even ignored whether the underlying circumstances remained unchanged throughout.

Finally, the treatment IMIT+ was as IMIT above, except that in it subjects were informed of some essential *qualitative* features of their environment. Specifically, they knew the scenario would remain constant throughout each treatment and that *all* firms would face exactly symmetric (cost and demand) conditions.

Not surprisingly, the experimental evidence varied quite significantly across different treatments. All these treatments involved a series of 40 consecutive rounds. In BEST and FULL, subjects eventually approximated[234] a total quantity that exceeded the Cournot outcome but was nevertheless substantially lower than the competitive (i.e., Walrasian) level – more so in BEST than in FULL. In both cases, standard deviations were around 10% of average quantities. This evidence stands in rough accord with the customary prediction of the Cournot model, even though there is the indicated upward deviation from its Nash equilibrium.

In contrast, treatments NOIN and IMIT displayed much larger total quantities. Specifically, in NOIN these quantities were slightly below the competitive level, while in IMIT they were nearly 50% larger than it. However, the standard deviations in each case were quite significant: around 25% in NOIN, and nearly 30% in IMIT. As the authors explain, it appeared that in these cases (mostly in the latter one) subjects experienced substantial "problems understanding the situation as they made losses in almost all periods."

In view of the fact that IMIT conditions failed to provide players with a sufficient basis for a systematic and convergent analysis of the situation, IMIT+ was

---

[233] Of course, this information involves redundancies: if subjects know the demand function, they can compute the total quantity associated with any given price. An analogous comment applies to other cases below, e.g., concerning the information about one's own profit.

[234] All our statements here pertain to averages and standard deviations associated with the last 20 rounds of each treatment.

introduced as a richer imitation-inducing treatment. As explained above, in it subjects were further endowed with some qualitative, but important, information about the environment. They turned out to use this additional information effectively since, compared to IMIT, both total quantities and their standard deviations fell drastically in IMIT+. Specifically, it was found that, in treatment IMIT+, subjects approximated the Walrasian outcome quite closely. That is, average quantities remained within less than 3% of the competitive level and the standard deviations lay around 15% of the average magnitudes. Thus, even though the standard deviations were still significant, they were substantially lower than those arising in the treatments IMIT and NOIN.

Overall, the evidence reported by HNO seems to provide a reasonably good empirical basis for the theoretical predictions obtained in Subsection 12.4.5. Thus, when players have the information/sophistication required to adjust their behavior as a best response to what others do, they appear to do so and long-run behavior is reasonably well described by the Cournot-Nash equilibrium. On the other hand, if players can only imitate (and they know the strategic situation is symmetric and stable), they tend to mimic successful behavior and the long-run outcome is roughly competitive (or Walrasian). Indeed, this interpretation of the results is reinforced by the assessment conducted by HNO on the "weight" to be attributed to the different behavioral rules in each scenario. In this respect, they found that the predominant rule in BEST and FULL was best-response adjustment, while in both IMIT and IMIT+ the most common rule was that based on imitation.

Supplementary material

12.6   Perturbed Markov processes: basic concepts and techniques

12.6.1   *Markov chains*

A *Markov chain* is simply a stochastic dynamical system on a certain state space (for the moment, assumed finite),[235] with time being measured discretely, $t = 0, 1, 2, \ldots$. Formally, it is given by a pair (Ω, Q), where Ω is the state space and $Q : \Omega \times \Omega \to [0, 1]$ is the transition rule (or law of motion) specifying the probabilities $Q(\omega, \omega')$ for a transition to occur, at *any* given point in time t, from a certain state ω to some state ω'. Sometimes, we find it useful to represent Q as a transition matrix, $Q = (q_{ij})_{i,j=1,2,\ldots,n}$, with the states in Ω indexed as $\omega_1, \omega_2, \ldots, \omega_n$ and $q_{ij} \equiv Q(\omega_i, \omega_j)$. Naturally, the matrix Q is to be a so-called stochastic matrix; i.e., all entries should be nonnegative and the sum of them along any given row, $\sum_{j=1}^{n} q_{ij}$, must equal unity.

Let $\Delta(\Omega)$ be the set of probability vectors (measures) in Ω. Denote a typical such vector by $\mu \equiv (\mu(\omega_1), \mu(\omega_2), \ldots, \mu(\omega_n))$ and assume the initial state of the process is chosen through a certain $\mu_0 \in \Delta(\Omega)$. Then, we may ask: What is the probability the process ends up in each of the possible states at $t = 1$? If the vector

---

[235] Often, the term "Markov chain" is reserved for the case in which the state space is either finite or countably infinite. When the state has the cardinality of the continuum (as in Section 12.7), one simply speaks of a (general) Markov process.

of such probabilities is denoted by $\mu_1 \equiv (\mu_1(\omega_1), \mu_1(\omega_2), \ldots, \mu_1(\omega_n))$, we may simply compute

$$\mu_1 = \mu_0 \, Q.$$

That is, for each $\omega_i \in \Omega$,

$$\mu_1(\omega_i) = \sum_{j=1}^{n} \mu_0(\omega_j) \, q_{ji}.$$

Of course, these considerations can be repeated any finite number of times, thus yielding the vector of probabilities corresponding to any future t:

$$\mu_t = \mu_{t-1} \, Q = \mu_{t-2} \, Q^2 = \cdots = \mu_0 \, Q^t.$$

In fact, one can show that, under mild regularity conditions,[236] the limit defined by

$$\tilde{\mu} = \lim_{t \to \infty} \mu_0 \, Q^t \tag{12.44}$$

is well defined. The probability distribution $\tilde{\mu}$ thus obtained captures the long-run behavior of the process in the following sense: for each state $\omega \in \Omega$, the probability that the process is at this state converges to $\tilde{\mu}(\omega)$ as $t \to \infty$. Of course, the fact these probabilities are taken to converge implies that

$$\tilde{\mu} = \tilde{\mu} \, Q, \tag{12.45}$$

i.e., $\tilde{\mu}$ is an *invariant distribution* of the process.

In general, however, the invariant distribution eventually attained in the limit may depend on the initial μ_0 used to select the state at time $t = 0$. As a stark illustration of this possibility, simply suppose Q is the identity matrix, i.e., $Q = I$. Then, it obviously follows that $\tilde{\mu} = \mu_0$, which indicates that long-run probabilities are exactly equal to initial ones.[237]

In contrast, there are also cases where the long-run probabilities are independent of the initial conditions. To focus again on a particularly simple illustration, consider the case where Q has some specific column (say, the first one) with all its entries equal to one, whereas all remaining entries in the matrix are uniformly zero. Clearly, this implies that, for any initial μ_0,

$$\mu_0 \, Q = \mu_1 = \mu_1 \, Q = (1, 0, \ldots, 0).$$

This indicates that, independently of initial conditions, the process switches to state ω_1 and stays there, from period $t = 1$ onward. Consequently, we have $\tilde{\mu} = (1, 0, \ldots, 0)$, independently of μ_0.

When the long-run behavior of the process (as given by (12.44)) is well defined and independent of initial conditions, the Markov chain is said to be *ergodic*. The theory of stochastic processes has contemplated a variety of different assumptions

---

[236] Heuristically, what is required is that the process does not allow for periodic behavior (see, e.g., Karlin and Taylor, 1975).

[237] Note that, if $Q = I$, any probabilistic uncertainty displayed by μ_0 as to the choice of the initial state at $t = 0$ is fully resolved from $t = 1$ onward; i.e., the state initially selected remains unchanged forever after. From an *ex ante* viewpoint, however, the long-run distribution $\tilde{\mu}$ exactly inherits the uncertainty reflected by μ_0.

that guarantee such an ergodicity (see Karlin and Taylor, 1975; Meyn and Tweedie, 1993). Here, it is enough for our purposes to focus on the following condition:

$$\forall i, j = 1, 2, \ldots, n, \quad q_{ij} > 0. \tag{12.46}$$

This condition simply expresses the requirement that all possible transitions should occur with some positive (possibly very small) probability. Then, it can be shown that the Markov chain must display a unique invariant distribution that "summarizes" the long-run behavior of the process, independently of initial conditions. In fact, such a long-run summary is not only *probabilistic* in the sense indicated above (i.e., in the sense of embodying limit probabilities for any given state). By a suitable adaptation of the law of large numbers, one may also make the following assertion. If the process is ergodic, the *frequency* of any particular state along a sample path of the process will converge (with probability one) to its corresponding weight in the (unique) invariant distribution. Thus, from this "frequentist" viewpoint, the invariant distribution of an ergodic Markov chain can be viewed as an almost sure description of the empirical frequencies displayed by any sufficiently long path (again, independently of initial conditions).

12.6.2 *A canonical model*

Following Young (1993) and Ellison (2000), we now propose a certain canonical model for the analysis of perturbed Markov chains. This general framework accommodates all the different evolutionary models studied in the main body of this chapter (Subsections 12.4.1 to 12.4.5) but is not directly applicable (because the state space is a continuum) to the reinforcement-learning model studied in Section 12.7. For the latter case, however, we shall argue that the special simplicity of its theoretical setup allows an intuitive adaptation of the essential ideas presented here.

Our *canonical evolutionary model* consists of a family of Markov chains parametrized by ε, $\{(\Omega, Q_\varepsilon)\}_{\varepsilon \in [0,1)}$, where

- Ω is a common (and finite) state space.
- For each $\varepsilon \in [0, 1)$, Q_ε is a transition matrix; if, in particular, $\varepsilon = 0$, the corresponding Q_0 is called the *unperturbed* transition matrix.
- As a function of ε, the transition probability $Q_\varepsilon(\omega, \omega')$ associated with any given pair of states (ω, ω') is continuous at all $\varepsilon \in [0, 1)$.
- For each $\varepsilon \in (0, 1)$, (Ω, Q_ε) defines an ergodic Markov chain, with its unique invariant distribution denoted by μ_ε.
- There exists a *cost function*, $c : \Omega \times \Omega \to \mathbb{N} \cup \{0\}$, such that, for all pairs $(\omega, \omega') \in \Omega \times \Omega$,

$$0 < \lim_{\varepsilon \to 0} \frac{Q_\varepsilon(\omega, \omega')}{\varepsilon^{c(\omega,\omega')}} < \infty, \tag{12.47}$$

i.e., $Q_\varepsilon(\omega, \omega')$ and $\varepsilon^{c(\omega,\omega')}$ are infinitesimals in ε of the same order.

The above theoretical construct is provided with the following interpretation. The family $\{(\Omega, Q_\varepsilon)\}_{\varepsilon \in [0,1)}$ is a collection of evolutionary processes subject to underlying noise, with $\varepsilon \in [0, 1)$ parameterizing the magnitude of this noise. Typically, the parameter ε is identified with the independent probability with which individuals mutate, experiment, or make mistakes (cf. Section 12.4). In the presence of noise (i.e., when $\varepsilon > 0$), the induced perturbed process is taken to be ergodic and thus exhibits a unique long-run distribution. However, when $\varepsilon = 0$ and no noise interferes with agents' behavior/adjustment, the evolution of the process is exclusively governed by purposeful (or payoff-responsive) considerations and ergodicity may be lost; i.e., initial conditions generally determine the limit behavior.

A key property of the canonical model concerns the existence of a cost function $c(\cdot)$ that satisfies (12.47). To clarify its implications, consider the transition across any given pair of states, say from ω to ω', and suppose first that $Q_0(\omega, \omega') = 0$. This implies that the unperturbed dynamics alone is unable to perform this transition. Thus, even though the transition must be possible through a "perturbation,"[238] the corresponding probability $Q_\varepsilon(\omega, \omega')$ has to converge to zero as $\varepsilon \downarrow 0$. (Here, we rely on the assumed continuity of transition probabilities with respect to ε.) Furthermore, it follows from (12.47) that the rate in ε at which this convergence takes place is precisely given by $c(\omega, \omega')$.

Alternatively, suppose the transition from ω to ω' has $Q_0(\omega, \omega') > 0$. Then, (12.47) implies that one must have $c(\omega, \omega') = 0$. This, of course, is now simply a reflection of the fact that no perturbation needs to be invoked for the contemplated transition to occur with positive probability.

12.6.3 *Stochastic stability and long-run dynamics*

As explained and motivated in Section 12.4, our analysis of evolutionary models (that is, stochastic models consistent with the above canonical framework) focuses on the *limit invariant distribution* given by $\mu^* \equiv \lim_{\varepsilon \to 0} \mu_\varepsilon$. More specifically, our main concern is the characterization of the set $\Omega^* \equiv \{\omega \in \Omega : \mu^*(\omega) > 0\}$, the support of μ^*, whose elements are called the *stochastically stable states*.

First note that the limit operation underlying μ^* is well defined because, by virtue of (12.47), each of the transition probabilities $Q_\varepsilon(\cdot, \cdot)$ behaves, asymptotically, as a polynomial in ε. Thus, by the invariant property (12.45) displayed by μ_ε for each $\varepsilon > 0$, the weight associated with any given state simply turns out to be a ratio of polynomials in ε, whose limit always exists as $\varepsilon \downarrow 0$.

Next, to clarify some further important issues concerning the set Ω^*, it is useful to organize the ensuing discussion in two separate remarks. First Remark 12.1 makes the simple point that every stochastically stable state must be a limit state of the unperturbed dynamics. Besides its theoretical import, this suggests that, in characterizing Ω^*, a natural first step should be to characterize the limit states of the unperturbed dynamics. Second, Remark 12.2 raises the question of convergence rates, an essential consideration in assessing the true relevance of the *long-run* predictions embodied by the set Ω^*.

---

[238] The present canonical model implicitly assumes that every perturbed process displays some positive probability for any possible transition. This condition, however, could be relaxed as long as the ergodicity of the perturbed processes is preserved. Then, one could simply associate an "infinite cost" with a transition that can never occur, even in the presence of a perturbation.

Remark 12.1: *Stochastic stability and limit behavior of the unperturbed dynamics*

For every $\varepsilon > 0$, the corresponding invariant distribution μ_ε must satisfy (cf. (12.45))

$$\mu_\varepsilon = \mu_\varepsilon Q_\varepsilon,$$

which implies

$$\lim_{\varepsilon \to 0} \mu_\varepsilon = \lim_{\varepsilon \to 0} \mu_\varepsilon Q_\varepsilon$$

or

$$\mu^* = \mu^* \lim_{\varepsilon \to 0} Q_\varepsilon.$$

Therefore, by the continuity of Q_ε in ε, we have

$$\mu^* = \mu^* Q_0; \tag{12.48}$$

i.e., μ^* is an invariant distribution of the unperturbed process.

A direct consequence of (12.48) is that every stochastically stable state must be a *limit state* of the unperturbed process. That is, for any $\omega \in \Omega^*$, one must have

$$\left[\lim_{t \to \infty} \mu^* (Q_0)^t \right] (\omega) = \mu^* (\omega) > 0,$$

which implies that the long-run probability of visiting state ω is positive when the initial state is chosen according to μ^*. Consequently, if we denote[239]

$$\Omega_0 \equiv \left\{ \omega \in \Omega : \left[\lim_{t \to \infty} \mu(Q_0)^t \right] (\omega) > 0 \text{ for some } \mu \in \Delta(\Omega) \right\} \tag{12.49}$$

as the set of the limit states of (Ω, Q_0), one obviously has

$$\Omega^* \subset \Omega_0. \tag{12.50}$$

If a state is not a limit state, then it is *transient*, i.e., eventually (with probability one), the process escapes that state and never returns to it. In this light, the reason for the inclusion (12.50) is quite transparent: if a state is transient for the unperturbed dynamics, it cannot be observed any *significant* fraction of the time in the long run when the perturbation probability ε is very small. For, in this case, the unperturbed dynamics operates *alone* most of the time and therefore will have the evolutionary process be at limit states of this dynamics almost always.

To formulate matters somewhat more precisely, it is useful to introduce the concept of *limit set* of the unperturbed dynamics (Ω, Q_0). Heuristically, a limit set is simply a *minimal* subset of Ω satisfying that, once the process visits *any* of its states, it never leaves this set again. Formally, set $A \subset \Omega$

---

[239] We implicitly assume throughout that the unperturbed dynamics is such that limit probabilities are always well defined for any initial conditions (cf. Footnote 236).

is a limit set of the unperturbed process if $\forall \omega \in \Omega$, $\forall \mu \in \Delta(\Omega)$ with $\mathbf{supp}(\mu) \subset A$,

$$\left[\lim_{t \to \infty} \mu(Q_0)^t \right](\omega) > 0 \Leftrightarrow \omega \in A.$$

Denote the collection of limit sets of (Ω_0, Q_0) by $\mathcal{L}$. Then, along the lines of our former discussion, it is easy to strengthen (12.50) as follows:

$$\exists \mathcal{V} \subset \mathcal{L} : \Omega^* = \bigcup_{A \in \mathcal{V}} A. \tag{12.51}$$

That is, the set of stochastically stable states can be written as the union of limit sets. ◆

Remark 12.2: *Speed of convergence*

The conclusion that, for any $\varepsilon > 0$, the sequence of distributions $\{\mu_t : \mu_t = \mu_0(Q_\varepsilon)^t\}_{t=1}^{\infty}$ converges (for any initial μ_0) toward the unique invariant distribution of the process is silent on an important issue: How "long" is the long run? That is, how fast is the convergence to the invariant distribution? Even though it can be shown that, for Markov chains, such a convergence is always exponentially fast, the question of how high the (exponential) rate is still remains open. If very low, the unique long-run predictions following from ergodicity may be of little practical relevance.

A related way of addressing this issue involves focusing on expected waiting times. Specifically, one may ask what is the *maximum* expected time one must wait before the process visits some particular stochastically stable state (or a subset of these) after starting at *any* other state. Naturally, in the context of the canonical evolutionary framework, such expected waiting time must be tailored to the noise parameter ε. For example, the maximum expected waiting time for visiting *some* state in Ω^*, which we denote by $\eta_\varepsilon(\Omega^*)$, must grow to infinity as ε approaches zero whenever there are several limit sets of the unperturbed dynamics. This is simply a consequence of the fact that, to move across different limit sets, the process has to rely on some perturbation (whose probability is of a certain positive order in ε). In general, therefore, a key issue of concern in the analysis of the model bears on the order at which such $\eta_\varepsilon(\Omega^*)$ grows as $\varepsilon \downarrow 0$. For only if this growth is not too fast may one view the predictions embodied by Ω^* as a relevant description of the dynamic behavior of the process for low ε. Indeed, as we shall explain, one of the aims of the analytical methods discussed in the following subsections is to provide a quantitative assessment of these speed-of-convergence considerations. ◆

12.6.4 *Stochastic stability: mathematical techniques*

Now, we outline (without proof) the main mathematical techniques that have been developed to analyze stochastic evolutionary models. The early literature relied on suitable adaptations of the graph-theoretic techniques proposed by Freidlin and

Wentzell (1984), as first used by Kandori, Mailath, and Rob (1993) or Young (1993), the latter usefully simplifying the approach. These techniques are described in Subsections 12.6.4.1 and 12.6.4.2 below. They *characterize* the set of stochastically stable states as those that minimize a certain measure of cost or "potential." More recently, Ellison (2000) proposed a somewhat different route that is described in Subsection 12.6.4.3. Because the latter approach is based on exclusively local comparisons, it often turns out to be significantly simpler than the former graph-theoretic techniques. However, the drawback is that, sometimes (cf. Subsection 12.4.3), it fails to provide a full characterization.

12.6.4.1 *Freidlin-Wentzell's approach.* Consider a canonical evolutionary model as described above, with $\{(\Omega, Q_\varepsilon)\}_{\varepsilon \in [0,1)}$ being the constituent collection of Markov chains and $c(\cdot)$ the corresponding cost function. First, we introduce the notion of an ω-tree.

Definition 12.1: *Let $\omega \in \Omega$. An ω-tree Y is a directed graph on Ω such that*

1. *Every state $\omega' \in \Omega \setminus \{\omega\}$ is the initial point of exactly one arrow (ω', ω'').*
2. *For every state $\omega' \in \Omega \setminus \{\omega\}$, there is a path linking ω' to ω, i.e., there is a sequence of arrows $\{(\omega_1, \omega_2), (\omega_2, \omega_3), \ldots, (\omega_{n-1}, \omega_n)\}$ with $\omega_1 = \omega'$ and $\omega_n = \omega$.*

Given any $\omega \in \Omega$, let $\mathcal{Y}_\omega$ denote the set of all the corresponding ω-trees. Then, associated with every tree $Y \in \mathcal{Y}_\omega$, we can define its total cost

$$C(Y) = \sum_{(\omega', \omega'') \in Y} c(\omega', \omega''),$$

where $c(\cdot, \cdot)$ is as defined in Subsection 12.6.2. With these notions in place, the analysis of Freidlin and Wentzell (1984, Lemma 3.1, p. 177) leads to the following characterization result of Ω^*, the set of stochastically stable states.

Proposition 12.1: *A state ω is stochastically stable if, and only if, there exists some $Y \in \mathcal{Y}_\omega$ such that $C(Y) \leq C(Y')$ for every $Y' \in \mathcal{Y}_{\omega'}$ and any $\omega' \in \Omega$.*

An intuitive way to understand the previous result is by introducing the notion of *stochastic potential*. It is given by a function $\psi : \Omega \to \mathbb{R}$ defined as follows:

$$\psi(\omega) = \min_{Y \in \mathcal{Y}_\omega} C(Y).$$

For each state ω, its stochastic potential $\psi(\omega)$ may be conceived as the *minimum total cost* involved in implementing transitions to this state from *every* other one. Then, in view of Proposition 12.1, the stochastically stable states can be simply characterized as those that display a minimum stochastic potential, i.e., $\Omega^* = \arg \min_{\omega \in \Omega} \psi(\omega)$.

12.6.4.2 *Young's approach.* As explained in Remark 12.1 (cf. (12.50)), only the limit sets of (Ω, Q_0) are candidates to being stochastically stable. Building on this observation, Young (1993) simplified the previous approach as follows – see also Kandori and Rob (1995).

First, consider the dynamics resulting from an *indefinite* iteration of the *unperturbed* process and define the "limit transition matrix" $Q^\infty : \Omega \times \Omega \to [0, 1]$ by

$$Q^\infty(\omega, \omega') = \left[\lim_{k \to \infty} (Q_0)^k \right](\omega, \omega')$$

for each $\omega, \omega' \in \Omega$. The transition matrix Q^∞ simply specifies the probabilities of converging to any given ω' from every possible ω through the operation of the unperturbed dynamics alone. Obviously, $Q^\infty(\omega, \omega') = 0$ for all $\omega \in \Omega$ and $\omega' \notin \Omega_0$. This allows one to define an associated "perturbed process" restricted to Ω_0, say $(\Omega_0, \hat{Q}_\varepsilon)$, where the transition matrix $\hat{Q}_\varepsilon : \Omega_0 \times \Omega_0 \to [0, 1]$ is given by $\hat{Q}_\varepsilon = Q_\varepsilon Q^\infty$. That is, for each $\omega, \omega' \in \Omega$, we have

$$\hat{Q}_\varepsilon(\omega, \omega') = \sum_{\omega'' \in \Omega} Q_\varepsilon(\omega, \omega'') Q^\infty(\omega'', \omega') \tag{12.52}$$

where $Q_\varepsilon(\cdot, \cdot)$ are the transition probabilities contemplated by the original model. The above construction induces a well-defined transition matrix in Ω_0. Intuitively, this transition matrix $\hat{Q}_\varepsilon(\cdot, \cdot)$ captures the probability of a transition between two different limit states through the *concatenation* of the original perturbed process (applied once) and the ensuing indefinite operation of the original unperturbed dynamics.

It may be verified (Exercise 12.17) that the family of Markov chains $\{(\Omega_0, \hat{Q}_\varepsilon)\}_{\varepsilon \in [0,1)}$ just defined displays all the properties of the canonical evolutionary model (now restricted to the set Ω_0) – thus, in particular, it induces a suitable cost function $\hat{c} : \Omega_0 \times \Omega_0 \to \mathbb{N} \cup \{0\}$. Therefore, one can proceed in parallel with our discussion in Subsection 12.6.4.1 and define ω-trees for every $\omega \in \Omega_0$, with $\hat{\mathcal{Y}}_\omega$ denoting the set of those trees and $\hat{C}(\cdot)$ the associated total-cost functions. On the basis of these constructs, the following counterpart of Proposition 12.1 can be established.

Proposition 12.2: *A state, $\omega \in \Omega_0$, is stochastically stable if, and only if, there exists some $Y \in \hat{\mathcal{Y}}_\omega$ such that $\hat{C}(Y) \le \hat{C}(Y')$ for every $Y' \in \hat{\mathcal{Y}}_{\omega'}$ and any $\omega' \in \Omega_0$.*

12.6.4.3 *Ellison's approach.* Finally, we describe the approach proposed by Ellison (2000) that, as explained, often proves simpler to use in many applications. It also has the additional benefit of addressing the important issue of long-run convergence rates by providing an explicit assessment of expected waiting times (recall Remark 12.1). In part, the advantages of Ellison's techniques derive from the fact that they embody an essentially *local* test. This feature, however, also has the drawback already advanced, i.e., the conditions involved may sometimes be insufficient to attain a full characterization of the set Ω^*.

First, we introduce the notions of radius and co-radius, which play a central role in the present approach. Since these concepts pertain to unions of limit sets for the unperturbed process (recall Remark 12.1), the original definitions may be reformulated in terms of the simplified framework proposed by Young (1993). That is, they may be cast in terms of the derived canonical model $\{(\Omega_0, \hat{Q}_\varepsilon)\}_{\varepsilon \in [0,1)}$ and the corresponding cost function $\hat{c}(\cdot)$.

Definition 12.2: *Let V be a union of limit sets of the unperturbed process, i.e., $V = \bigcup_{A \in \mathcal{V}} A$ for some $\mathcal{V} \subset \mathcal{L}$.[240] The radius of V is given by*

$$R(V) \equiv \min_{(\omega, \omega') \in V \times (\Omega_0 \setminus V)} \hat{c}(\omega, \omega').$$

Definition 12.3: *Let V be a union of limit sets of the unperturbed process. The co-radius of V is given by*

$$CR(V) \equiv \max_{\omega \in \Omega_0 \setminus V} \min_{\omega' \in V} \hat{c}(\omega, \omega').$$

Heuristically, the radius of any set V as indicated is the minimum cost involved in moving out of it; reciprocally, its co-radius is the maximum cost required to move into this set from some limit state not included in it. Based on these intuitive notions, we have the following result.

Proposition 12.3: *Let V be a union of limit sets of the unperturbed process. Then, if $R(V) > CR(V)$, $\Omega^* \subset V$. On the other hand, as $\varepsilon \to 0$, the maximum expected waiting time of visiting the set V, $\eta_\varepsilon(V)$, grows at the same order as $\varepsilon^{-CR(V)}$, i.e.,*

$$0 < \lim_{\varepsilon \to 0} \frac{\eta_\varepsilon(V)}{\varepsilon^{-CR(V)}} < \infty. \tag{12.53}$$

In many evolutionary models, one is able to circumscribe to some small subset of Ω_0 the verification of the hypothesis contemplated by the above proposition. That is, one often finds a small subset of Ω_0 whose radius exceeds its co-radius. This then provides a narrow delimitation of the set of stochastically stable states (cf. Exercise 12.18), which may even represent a unique selection – and thus a full characterization[241] – if the subset in question is a singleton. On the other hand, (12.53) indicates that one may also pinpoint the order (in $1/\varepsilon$) at which the expected times grow. Quite sharply, it turns out that, for any subset V for which the required hypothesis applies, the maximum expected waiting time $\eta_\varepsilon(V)$ grows as reflected by its co-radius, i.e., grows at the same rate as $(1/\varepsilon)^{CR(V)}$ when $\varepsilon \downarrow 0$. Recalling the considerations explained in Remark 12.2, this is indeed an important feature contributed by the present approach.

12.7   Reinforcement learning with flexible aspirations

The theoretical analysis conducted in Subsections 12.4.1–12.4.5 has focused on population games where, implicitly, it has been assumed that every player is aware

---

[240] Recall (12.51), which indicates that the set Ω^* always consists of a union of limit sets.

[241] Even if the subset V in question is *not* a singleton, one can be sure it provides a full characterization of the set Ω^* (i.e., $V = \Omega^*$) if V encompasses by itself a *single* limit set of the unperturbed dynamics. This follows directly from (12.51).

of the interactive (and symmetric) nature of the situation in which she is involved. Thus, depending on their information and/or sophistication, players' behavioral adjustment – by imitation or best response – builds on some relevant *population-wide* information.

In contrast, a quite different model of learning was proposed in Subsection 11.2.2. In this model, players are supposed to react to their own experience alone and need not even know they are involved in an interactive situation (i.e., a game). More specifically, it is postulated that every player reacts to a comparison of her current payoff and an aspiration level that is endogenously shaped by past experience. If the former is at least as high as the latter, the player is declared "satisfied" and consequently is supposed to continue doing what she currently does. Instead, if her current payoff is lower than the aspiration level, she is assumed "dissatisfied" and thus is taken to abandon her current action with some probability – in that event, she chooses some other action randomly, any of the available ones with some positive probability.

Formally, the model proposed in Subsection 11.2.2 involved just two players,[242] with each player's strategy adjustment and aspiration updating captured, respectively, by (11.9) and (11.10). For convenience, let us recall these two laws of motion.

- First, strategy adjustment is formulated as follows:

$$\pi_i(t) \geq y_i(t) \Rightarrow s_i(t+1) = s_i(t)$$

$$\pi_i(t) < y_i(t) \Rightarrow \begin{cases} \text{with prob. } 1-p, & s_i(t+1) = s_i(t) \\ \text{with prob. } p, & s_i(t+1) \in S_i \setminus \{s_i(t)\}, \text{ full support,} \end{cases}$$

$$(12.54)$$

where, at every time t, $y_i(t)$ denotes player i's current aspiration level, $s_i(t)$ stands for her strategy choice and $\pi_i(t) \equiv \pi_i(s_1(t), s_2(t))$ represents the payoff she earns. (As usual, payoffs are given by real functions of the form $\pi_i : S_1 \times S_2 \to \mathbb{R}$, where S_i is player i's strategy space.)

- On the other hand, aspiration updating is given by

$$y_i(t+1) = \lambda y_i(t) + (1-\lambda)\pi_i(t) \qquad (i = 1, 2, \ t = 0, 1, 2, \ldots),$$

$$(12.55)$$

where $\lambda \in (0, 1)$ is a (common) parameter measuring the speed of aspiration adjustment. That is, each player sets her new aspiration as a convex combination of the previous level and her latest payoff.

In mathematical terms, the reinforcement-learning process induced by (12.54) and (12.55) can be formulated as a Markov process with a continuum state space. Specifically, we may choose as its state space the set $\Omega = (S_1 \times \Lambda_1) \times (S_2 \times \Lambda_2)$ where, for each $i = 1, 2$, the set Λ_i is taken to be a compact real interval that

---

[242] See Exercise 12.22 for an extended setup where a possibly large (but finite) population of individuals is randomly matched to play the game.

encompasses the possible range of player i's aspirations and includes both her maximum and minimum possible payoffs. Despite the compactness of the state space Ω, this set is *not* finite (aspiration levels vary in a continuum). This prevents us from using directly the framework and techniques presented in Section 12.6, which presume a finite state space. It turns out, however, that the present context can be suitably studied by relying on notions and tools that are the natural counterparts of those introduced before. Thus, based on these parallelisms, we carry out a heuristic, and hopefully instructive, discussion of the model along the lines pursued before. For a more detailed and completely rigorous analysis, the reader is referred to Karandikar *et al.* (1998).

First we note that, in this case, the transition probabilities must be given by some transition probability function of the form

$$Q_0 : \Omega \times \mathcal{B} \to [0, 1],$$

where $\mathcal{B}$ is a suitable measure space on Ω – in particular, we choose the collection of Borel subsets of Ω.[243] This function is the analogue of the transition matrix in finite Markov chains (cf. Subsection 12.6.1). For each state $\omega \in \Omega$ and every $B \in \mathcal{B}$, $Q_0(\omega, B)$ specifies the probability the process undertakes a one-step transition from ω to *some* $\omega' \in B$.

As illustrated in Subsection 11.2.2 (cf. Theorems 11.1 and 11.2), the Markov process (Ω, Q_0) is generally nonergodic; i.e., its long-run behavior strongly depends on the initial conditions. Here again we aim at tackling such multiplicity by perturbing the process "slightly." Now, however, there are two possible dimensions in which an agent may be perturbed: her action and her aspiration. For simplicity, in what follows we choose to restrict perturbations to the aspiration dimension alone, while in Exercise 12.21 the reader is asked to explore the alternative possibility of perturbing action choice.

To proceed formally, let $\varepsilon \in (0, 1)$ parametrize the size of the perturbation. Then, the dynamics of the process at any given t is specified as follows.

- At every t and for each player $i = 1, 2$, there is independent probability $(1 - \varepsilon)$ that the transition from state $\omega(t) = [s_1(t), y_1(t), s_2(t), y_2(t)]$ to the ensuing action–aspiration pair of this player, $(s_i(t + 1), y_i(t + 1))$, occurs as prescribed by the *unperturbed process* (Ω, Q_0).[244]
- On the other hand, with the complementary probability ε, each player i experiences at every t a perturbation on her aspiration adjustment process. This perturbation does not affect action choice and, therefore, her choice of

---

[243] A probability measure is defined on a σ-algebra, which is simply a collection of subsets that is closed under countable unions and complementation. The smallest σ-algebra containing the open subsets of Ω (with the usual topology) is the collection of Borel subsets and is known as the Borel σ-algebra. See, for example, Wheeden and Zygmund (1977, Chapter 3).

[244] Given the prevailing state $\omega(t)$, the transition is performed in a stochastically independent fashion by each player $i = 1, 2$. Therefore, there is probability $(1 - \varepsilon)^2$ that the *whole* transition, as it applies to both players, occurs *via* the unperturbed process.

new action is still governed by (12.54). Her new aspiration level, however, is obtained through the following modified version of (12.55):

$$y_i(t+1) = \lambda y_i(t) + (1 - \lambda)\pi_i(t) + \rho_i(t), \tag{12.56}$$

where $\rho_i(t)$ is the realization of a random variable, independent across players and with continuous density. In general, the random variable $\rho_i(t)$ may depend on $y_i(t)$ and $\pi_i(t)$, although its support is assumed to be a nondegenerate interval around zero (truncated, if necessary, to have the induced aspirations remain in Λ_i). This perturbation, nevertheless, is always "local" in the sense that its magnitude (i.e., the length of the aforementioned interval) is uniformly bounded above by some suitable $\vartheta > 0$, i.e.,

$$|\rho_i(t)| \leq \vartheta \qquad (i = 1, 2, \ t = 0, 1, 2, \ldots). \tag{12.57}$$

Given any $\varepsilon > 0$, denote by $Q_\varepsilon : \Omega \times \mathcal{B} \to [0, 1]$ the transition probability function reflecting the perturbed process of reinforcement learning just described. As usual, we are interested in characterizing the long-run behavior of this process for small $\varepsilon > 0$. Next, we address this issue in turn for each of the two different strategic setups studied in Chapter 11: prisoner's dilemma and pure-coordination games.

12.7.1 *Prisoner's dilemma*

Consider a general prisoner's dilemma game whose payoffs are recalled in Table 12.2. As in Subsection 11.2.2, we assume that $\eta > \zeta > v > 0$ and $\zeta > \eta/2 \ (\neq v)$.

Let the learning dynamics of each of the two individuals be as described above, i.e., it is given by the Markov process (Ω, Q_ε) induced by (12.54)–(12.56), where $\varepsilon > 0$ stands for the perturbation probability. It is easy to see (cf. Exercise 12.19) that, through repeated operation of the perturbation, the process can visit any open subset of the state space from any given initial state. That is, for any open subset $U \subset \Omega$ and any $\omega \in \Omega$, we have

$$\sum_{t=1}^{\infty} (Q_\varepsilon)^t(\omega, U) > 0. \tag{12.58}$$

This is enough to guarantee that the process is ergodic (cf. Meyn and Tweedie, 1993), so that there is a unique invariant distribution $\mu_\varepsilon \in \Delta(\Omega)$ that summarizes

Table 12.2: *A general prisoner's dilemma game*

1 \ 2	C	D
C	ζ, ζ	$0, \eta$
D	$\eta, 0$	v, v

uniquely (independently of initial conditions) the long-run behavior of the process.[245]

As usual, our interest centers on the limit invariant distribution $\mu^* \equiv \lim_{\varepsilon \to 0} \mu_\varepsilon$. More specifically, we aim at characterizing the support of μ^* – a set that we still denote by Ω^* and continue to call the set of *stochastically stable states*. To achieve such a characterization, Karandikar *et al.* (1998) show that one can proceed along natural counterparts of the steps pursued in the analysis of finite-state perturbed Markov chains.

Thus, first, we want to identify the limit states of the unperturbed process (Ω, Q_0). Under the assumption that λ is large enough, this readily follows from Theorem 11.1, which guarantees that the process (Ω, Q_0) converges a.s. to some *pure-strategy state* $\omega^* = [s_1^*, y_1^*, s_2^*, y_2^*]$ with $y_i^* = \pi_i(s_1^*, s_2^*)$, $i = 1, 2$. We have, therefore, that

$$\Omega_0 = \{(C, \zeta, C, \zeta), (D, \nu, D, \nu), (C, 0, D, \eta), (D, \eta, C, 0)\},$$

each of these states defining a singleton limit set of the unperturbed process.

Next, we turn to studying the "derived process" resulting from the concatenation of a one-step transition according to the perturbed stochastic process and an indefinite operation of the unperturbed dynamics. This gives rise to the *transition probability function* $\hat{Q}_\varepsilon : \Omega_0 \times \mathcal{B} \to [0, 1]$, which is the analogue of the transition matrix defined in (12.52). In terms of the process $(\Omega_0, \hat{Q}_\varepsilon)$ thus induced, the key question underlying the present selection exercise may be posed as follows: How "costly" is it (as measured by the number of simultaneous perturbations required) to perform each of the possible transitions across the different states in Ω_0?

In answering this question, two different payoff scenarios have to be distinguished. The first one corresponds to the case where $\eta/2 > \nu$ and therefore joint defection is the worst possible *symmetric* outcome (i.e., it is Pareto dominated by every other possible outcome where players receive the same payoff). In fact, such a Pareto domination occurs in this case even if one considers those payoff vectors that could be obtained on average over time by a suitable sequence of play. Graphically, this scenario is illustrated in Figure 12.1 below, where the convex hull of the four different payoff vectors attainable at pure-strategy states displays a "diamond" shape. Alternatively, we have the scenario where $\eta/2 < \nu$ and, therefore, the payoff vector (ν, ν) obtained from joint defection is *not* the worst possible symmetric configuration in the convex hull of payoffs. In this case, for example, it dominates the payoff vector that could be obtained, on average, through a repeated alternation of the two extreme and asymmetric payoff configurations, $(\eta, 0)$ and $(0, \eta)$. This scenario is illustrated in Figure 12.2 below.

In the first scenario ($\eta/2 > \nu$), the unique stochastically stable state turns out to be $\omega_C \equiv (C, \zeta, C, \zeta)$, provided ϑ (which bounds the support of the perturbation) is small enough and λ (which controls the speed of aspiration adjustment) is

---

[245] In the present case, $\Delta(\Omega)$ represents the probability measures on Ω defined on the set $\mathcal{B}$, i.e., the set of Borel probability measures on Ω.

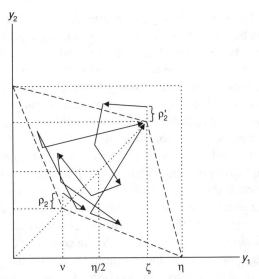

Figure 12.1: Convergence to aspirations (ζ, ζ) after any *single* perturbation to player 2 (i.e., ρ_2 or ρ_2') when $\eta/2 > \nu$.

sufficiently large.[246] The key basis for this conclusion is grounded on the following twofold observation.

(i) From any limit state $\omega \in \Omega_0 \setminus \{\omega_C\}$ there is a single perturbation that, by subsequently relying on the unperturbed dynamics alone, has the process converge to ω_C in the long run.

(ii) Conversely, no single perturbation from ω_C may induce the unperturbed process to converge with positive probability to any other limit state – in this case, therefore, the unperturbed process converges a.s. back to ω_C.

To understand intuitively the essential logic underlying these two observations refer to Figure 12.1. For concreteness, we focus on the state $\omega_D \equiv (D, \nu, D, \nu)$ as the sole alternative to ω_C. Then, we simply have to evaluate the "relative difficulty" (mutation-wise) of the transitions across these two states. First, concerning the transition from ω_D to ω_C, suppose a perturbation such as ρ_2 occurs at some t that brings the aspiration pair $(y_1(t), y_2(t))$ to the *interior* of the convex hull of payoffs given by

$$\mathcal{P} \equiv \left\{ \begin{array}{c} y = (y_1, y_2) \in \Lambda_1 \times \Lambda_2 : y = \alpha_1(\zeta, \zeta) + \alpha_2(\nu, \nu) \\ + \alpha_3(\eta, 0) + \alpha_4(0, \eta), \alpha_i \geq 0, \sum_{i=1}^{4} \alpha_i = 1 \end{array} \right\}.$$

Once this mutation has occurred, it is clear that the *unperturbed* process cannot bring the players' aspirations out of **int**$(\mathcal{P})$, the interior of the set $\mathcal{P}$. Thus, because at any point in **int**$(\mathcal{P})$ both players can be satisfied only if they are both cooperating

---

[246] As explained, the upper bound on ϑ is required to ensure that perturbations are genuinely local. On the other hand, the lower bound on λ is geared toward guaranteeing the convergence of the unperturbed process (cf. Subsection 11.2.2).

(and their aspirations are both below ζ), it follows from arguments used in proving Theorem 11.1 that the unperturbed process must eventually converge, a.s., to ω_C.

But, by a similar token, we may also argue that, after a perturbation such as ρ_2' takes place at ω_C, the only state to which the unperturbed process may converge is ω_C itself. Again, the simple reason here is that, along the ensuing path, the only case in which both players may be satisfied is when both are cooperating and their aspiration is below ζ. This continues to guarantee that, eventually, the unperturbed process must converge to the state ω_C with probability one.

The former two observations easily extend to all other possible transitions in Ω_0 (cf. Exercise 12.20). Specifically, one finds that, while just one perturbation is enough to have the unperturbed dynamics bring the system from any state in $\Omega_0 \setminus \{\omega_C\}$ to ω_C, any of the opposite transitions cannot be triggered by a single perturbation. Thus, in the language used in the analysis of finite-state models (recall Subsection 12.6.4.3), one may heuristically say that while the co-radius of $\{\omega_C\}$ is equal to one, its radius is unambiguously larger. Indeed, this is the essential logic that, rigorously formalized, may be used to establish that ω_C is the unique stochastically stable state in the present case.

Let us now turn to the second payoff scenario where $\eta/2 < \nu$. Then, as illustrated in Figure 12.2, it is easy to see that just a *single* perturbation from either ω_C or ω_D may have the unperturbed process converge to the other state, ω_D or ω_C, respectively, with positive probability. By contrast, concerning the other two states in Ω_0, no path can converge to either $(C, 0, D, \eta)$ or $(D, \eta, C, 0)$ from any initial state where both players have a positive aspiration level. This implies, in particular, that no (small) perturbation at ω_C or ω_D may have the unperturbed process converge to $(C, 0, D, \eta)$ or $(D, \eta, C, 0)$ – that is, the process must return a.s. to either ω_C or ω_D (both with positive probability).

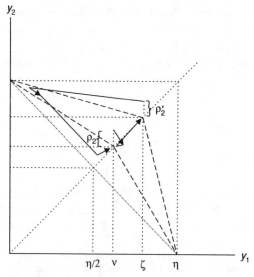

Figure 12.2: Reciprocal convergence across aspiration levels (ν, ν) and (ζ, ζ) after a *single* perturbation (i.e., ρ_2 and ρ_2', respectively) when $\eta/2 < \nu$.

The former considerations can be succinctly summarized as follows. While ω_C and ω_D are *both* reachable by the unperturbed dynamics after a single perturbation from any other state in Ω_0, neither of the two other states in Ω_0, $(C, 0, D, \eta)$ or $(D, \eta, C, 0)$, can be reached with positive probability from ω_C and ω_D. Overall, this allows us to build on the customary logic and intuition to conclude that, in this second scenario,[247]

$$\Omega^* = \{\omega_C, \omega_D\}, \tag{12.59}$$

i.e., both ω_C and ω_D are stochastically stable.

As it stands, of course, (12.59) does not fully solve the equilibrium multiplicity problem because the support of μ^* fails to be a singleton. This means both of the states in Ω^*, ω_C and ω_D, will be visited a nonnegligible fraction of time by the (perturbed) learning process, even as $\varepsilon \to 0$. To refine this conclusion, it is natural to turn our attention toward the other key parameter of the model, i.e., the rate λ at which aspiration levels adjust on the basis of past experience. Clearly, the precise weights displayed by the limit invariant distribution (not the support) have to depend on it. To reflect such a dependence, let us refer to the limit invariant distribution as μ_λ^*. Then, we now argue that, as the aspiration adjustment becomes very gradual (i.e., as λ approaches unity), we have

$$\lim_{\lambda \to 1} \mu^*(\omega_C) = 1, \tag{12.60}$$

i.e., almost all weight of the limit invariant distribution is concentrated in the cooperative state ω_C.

To grasp the intuition underlying (12.60), the key point to understand concerns the different nature of the paths that may lead from ω_C to ω_D and those that must underlie the reciprocal transition. Even though both of them just require a single perturbation, they are not comparably "easy" (or likely). Consider, on the one hand, the transition from ω_D to ω_C after a perturbation such as ρ_2 in Figure 12.2. This transition may be done through the following sample chain of events. First, player 2 may switch to C (since she is dissatisfied with a payoff of ν once her aspiration has risen to $\nu + \rho_2$). Next period, she may switch again (to D) because she is obtaining a zero payoff that is still below her aspiration. Then, both players would become dissatisfied in the following period, which implies that both could switch to C with positive probability. If the aforementioned events in fact occur after the perturbation, both players end up cooperating, being satisfied with their current payoffs, and continue with this same state of affairs as they converge to the state ω_C from below in aspirations.

Consider now the opposite transition from ω_C to ω_D after a single perturbation, ρ_2', a typical case being depicted in Figure 12.2. Note that, after such a perturbation, the convergence of the unperturbed process to ω_D requires that the aspiration levels become sufficiently low so that their path may approach (ν, ν) from below. But this can conceivably happen only if players are subject to substantial inertia in

---

[247] Of course, our conclusions still depend on the proviso that ϑ be small enough and λ sufficiently large – recall Footnote 246.

their choice adjustment. As the players adjust their aspiration downward, they are permanently dissatisfied and would therefore revise their current action if given the opportunity. If they do not carry out this revision, it must be because the process does not "allow" them to do so, an event that happens for each player with independent probability $(1 - p) > 0$ every period (cf. (12.54)). But, of course, an *uninterrupted* chain of these events is more unlikely the longer it is. As λ approaches one, the length of this chain (i.e., the required number of consecutive periods at which both players must be subject to adjustment inertia) grows unboundedly. Therefore, the probability that some such path in fact occurs after a perturbation at ω_C becomes progressively more unlikely, tending to zero, as $\lambda \uparrow 1$.

The above considerations suggest that, as indicated, the relative weights displayed by μ^* must be sharply biased toward the cooperative state ω_C if players update their aspirations very gradually. In essence, the main insight obtained in this respect can be described as follows. When players react to endogenously determined aspirations, upward adjustment – which "rides on satisfaction" – is so much more likely than the opposite one that must struggle in an "uphill battle" against dissatisfaction. As we discuss next, these considerations also play an important role in pure-coordination games, where the same asymmetry between upward and downward aspiration adjustment leads to long-run selection of the efficient equilibrium.

12.7.2 *Pure-coordination games*

Now, we focus on bilateral pure-coordination games, the second strategic context studied in Subsection 11.2.2 under reinforcement learning. Recall that a strategic-form bilateral game $G = \{\{1, 2\}, \{S_1, S_2\}, \{\pi_1, \pi_2\}\}$ is said to be of *pure coordination* if payoffs are nonnegative, $|S_1| = |S_2| = r$, and $\forall q, q' \in \{1, 2, \ldots, r\}$,

$$\pi_i(s_{1q}, s_{2q'}) > 0 \Leftrightarrow q = q'. \tag{12.61}$$

In this context, consider a reinforcement-learning model with flexible aspirations (as given by (12.54)–(12.56)) and let (Ω, Q_ε) stand for the induced Markov process. The analysis of this process is only outlined here, because the main considerations involved are parallel to those explained in detail for the prisoner's dilemma. The essential points of the discussion can be organized as follows (cf. Exercise 12.23).

(a) First, we note from Theorem 11.2 that the unperturbed learning dynamics converges a.s. to some pure-strategy state $\omega^* = [s_{1q}^*, y_1^*, s_{2q'}^*, y_2^*]$ with $y_i^* = \pi_i(s_{1q}^*, s_{2q'}^*)$ for some $q, q' \in \{1, 2, \ldots, r\}$. Therefore, the set of limit states of the unperturbed dynamics Ω_0 coincides with the set of pure-strategy states and each of these states defines a singleton limit set of the dynamics.

(b) Theorem 11.2 also establishes that, if the initial aspiration of at least one of the players is positive ($y_i(0) > 0$ for some $i \in \{1, 2\}$), the unperturbed dynamics converges a.s. to a Nash equilibrium of the game, i.e., a pure-strategy state $\omega^* = [s_{1q}^*, y_1^*, s_{2q}^*, y_2^*]$ for some $q \in \{1, 2, \ldots, r\}$, common for both players. Let Ω_e denote the set of such equilibrium states. Then, the former conclusion can be strengthened as follows. If the initial state $\omega(0) \notin \Omega_e$ and $y_i(0) > 0$ for at least one $i \in \{1, 2\}$, there is positive probability that the unperturbed process converges to *any* particular $\omega \in \Omega_e$.

(c) Now consider the process $(\Omega_0, \hat{Q}_\varepsilon)$ resulting from the concatenation of a one-step transition according to the perturbed stochastic process and an indefinite operation of the unperturbed dynamics. Then, if the value ϑ that bounds the magnitude of the perturbation is small (recall (12.57)), items (a) and (b) above jointly imply the following conclusions:

(c.1) $\hat{Q}_\varepsilon(\omega, \omega') > 0$ for all $\omega \in \Omega_0$, and every $\omega' \in \Omega_e$.

(c.2) $\hat{Q}_\varepsilon(\omega, \omega') = 0$ for all $\omega \in \Omega_e$ and every $\omega' \in \Omega_0 \backslash \Omega_e$.

(d) In view of (c), we must have $\Omega^* \subset \Omega_e$. But, on the other hand, because just a single perturbation is required for the transitions contemplated in (c.1) – cf. the last part of (b) – the converse inclusion also holds. Therefore, we have $\Omega^* = \Omega_e$.

(e) Assume there is a pure-strategy Nash equilibrium of the game G, which Pareto-dominates all others. Without loss of generality, suppose this equilibrium is (s_{1r}, s_{2r}) so that, for each $i = 1, 2$,

$$\pi_i(s_{1r}, s_{2r}) > \pi_i(s_{1q}, s_{2q}) \qquad (q = 1, 2, \ldots, r - 1).$$

Then, the same considerations explained in Subsection 12.7.1 for the prisoner's dilemma suggest that, as $\lambda \to 1$, the limit invariant distribution becomes concentrated on the state $\omega_{rr} \equiv [s_{1r}, \pi_1(s_{1r}, s_{2r}), s_{2r}, \pi_2(s_{1r}, s_{2r})]$. That is, we have

$$\lim_{\lambda \to 1} \mu_\lambda^*(\omega_{rr}) = 1,$$

where μ_λ^* stands for the limit invariant distribution, as parametrized by λ.

The main insights obtained in the present pure-coordination scenario are quite akin to those obtained for the prisoner's dilemma under reinforcement learning. At the risk of some redundancy, they can be summarized as follows. First, we find that, as for the prisoner's dilemma, all stochastically stable states are symmetric strategy profiles and vice versa. Thus, in this case, the concepts of stochastic stability and Nash equilibrium yield equivalent implications. To attain a sharper selection result, we resort to an additional limit exercise (beyond the usual one on perturbation) that focuses on the rate at which aspirations are updated. This leads to the conclusion that, if aspiration updating is sufficiently gradual, the "doubly limiting" invariant distribution induced (first the limit is taken in ε, then in λ) becomes concentrated in the efficient (equilibrium) profile. In essence, this result reflects the same considerations already explained at the end of Subsection 12.7.1: upward adjustment of aspirations is so much easier than a downward one, because the latter has to struggle against the dissatisfaction pressure working to derail it.

12.7.3 *Experimental evidence: prisoner's dilemma*

Since the very early days of game theory, the prisoner's dilemma has been one of the paradigmatic setups used for an experimental assessment of various behavioral hypotheses concerning rationality and equilibrium. In fact, this game was first proposed as the basis for a series of experiments, which were conducted by Melvin Dresher and Merrill Flood at the Rand Corporation in 1950 – see Flood (1958).[248] Springing from that original work, a large body of research on this game, both theoretical and experimental, has developed along a wide range of directions.

In recent times, most of the experimental interest on the prisoner's dilemma has focused on the finitely repeated version of it. Specifically, the experimental designs have been geared toward shedding light on the issue of backward induction (recall Sections 8.1 and 8.5.2), asking the following questions: Do players eventually learn to behave "rationally" and abide by the backward-induction logic? Or do they, alternatively, eschew the implications of this logic in their quest of earning higher "cooperative" payoffs? Two of the most influential papers addressing these questions are those by Selten and Stoecker (1986) and Andreoni and Miller (1993), both of which we briefly discuss below.

In contrast, most of the earlier experimental literature on the prisoner's dilemma did *not* focus on the strategic considerations induced by *repeated* interaction. Instead, the experiments were designed with the objective of having players regard the repeated play of the prisoner's dilemma as a concatenation of *one-shot* games. This, of course, reflects a perspective on the game that is quite different from that induced by its repeated interaction. In particular, it raises the issue of whether bounded-rationality considerations may bring about cooperation when players may adjust their behavior over time. As a representative instance of this early experimental literature, our subsequent discussion focuses on the work of Lave (1962).

Each of the three different papers mentioned above highlights a different aspect of the repeated prisoner's dilemma. Thus, the experiments by Selten and Stoecker (1986) underscore the tension between the reluctance of players (even experienced ones) to play as the Nash equilibrium prescribes and the internal inconsistency of attempting to do otherwise. On the other hand, the experimental setup studied by Andreoni and Miller (1993) aims at understanding the possible rise of cooperation in the finitely repeated prisoner's dilemma along the lines of the incomplete-information (reputation-building) model of Kreps *et al.* (1982) – recall Sections 8.4 and 8.6. Finally, the experimental results reported by Lave (1962) suggest that the forces at work in the simple reinforcement-learning model studied in Subsection 12.7.1 may lead to cooperation when players ignore repeated-game considerations. In what follows, we briefly outline these three papers.

In the experimental setup designed by Selten and Stoecker, subjects played 25 repeated games (or rounds), each of these rounds consisting of 10 consecutive repetitions of the prisoner's dilemma with the same partner. Subjects were made to believe they could never play in two different rounds with the same player. The

---

[248] This experiment was first reported by Flood (1952).

main regularities observed can be summarized as follows.

(1) Once players had gained some experience (roughly, after the first 12 rounds had been completed), play mostly consisted of what the authors call "cooperative play." This kind of play is characterized by the following threefold requirement:

(a) There is some m, $4 \leq m < 10$, such that in the first m periods both players cooperate.

(b) In period $m + 1$, at least one of the players defects.

(c) For all periods $j = m + 2, \ldots, 10$, both players jointly defect.

(2) Among "experienced" players (i.e., roughly in the last 13 rounds, as explained above), the intended deviation period where players target their first defection displays a gradual but clear-cut tendency to move forward (i.e., earlier in the repeated game).

Somewhat informally, the above two observations can be summarized as follows. On the one hand, there is a first phase of the experiment consisting of its early rounds when individuals learn how to support cooperation in the game by relying on reciprocating (trigger-like) strategies. Then, once this learning has been largely achieved, there is a second phase when players turn to realizing the force of the backward-induction logic and the consequent risk of being "exploited" by their partners. This gives rise to *end effects* that, as players gain experience, materialize at earlier stages in the repeated game.

Next, we turn to the experiments of Andreoni and Miller (1993). As advanced, the aim of these authors was to assess the empirical basis for the incomplete-information approach proposed by Kreps *et al.* (1982) to resolve the "prisoner's dilemma paradox." The experimental design was as follows. Different groups of 14 subjects played 20 rounds of a 10-stage repetition of a prisoner's dilemma. There were a number of distinct treatments performed under different conditions, with each subject participating in only one of them. An important point to emphasize, however, is that the 20 rounds of each treatment were conducted among the same 14 individuals, all of whom were randomly paired afresh at the beginning of each round.

We concentrate our discussion on just two of the treatments considered by Andreoni and Miller. One of them – labeled *Partners* – refers to the ordinary version of the repeated game, with no particular "noise" added to it. For this case, the authors report an average level of cooperation across different rounds that decreases steadily as the repeated game moves forward. Thus, in the early stages of the different repeated games, around 40% of the subject pairs cooperate, while this fraction eventually fell well below 10% by the last stage. The authors attribute the observation that some significant amount of cooperation materializes at the beginning of many repeated games to the fact that the same pool of 14 players is rematched in every round. This, they argue, makes some subjects entertain the conjecture (indeed a correct one) that some of their partners in the (fixed) population behave altruistically. This conjecture leads those subjects to trying to build for themselves an altruistic reputation in any given repeated game, with the hope that such a reputation may succeed in supporting some early cooperation.

In a different treatment – labeled *Computer50* – Andreoni and Miller introduced *explicitly* the possibility of reputation buildup into the design of the experiment. Specifically, players were informed that, at the beginning of each round, there would be a 50% chance their partner might be a nonhuman (i.e., a computer) that played the following tit-for-tat strategy (cf. Section 8.4):

> "At each t, cooperate if the partner chose C in the preceding period; otherwise, defect."

As one would expect, this had a strong effect in enhancing the reputation-building incentives of players and therefore induced a large increase in average cooperation. Specifically, it was observed that quite a large fraction of subject pairs (around 60%) maintained joint cooperation in an almost stable (i.e., constant) manner up to the very last two periods. This represents a rather sharp confirmation that, under incomplete information of the sort posited by Kreps *et al.* (1982) in the finitely repeated prisoner's dilemma, players' incentives to build up a "useful reputation" may indeed support cooperative behavior.

Finally, we turn to the experiments of Lave (1962). As advanced, his approach was not designed to study repeated-game effects but focused instead on how players learn to play the prisoner's dilemma over a large number of repetitions of the one-shot game. In general, the issue of whether the experimental setup can be effectively controlled so that the subjects indeed view the situation as intended (i.e., as a sequence of one-shot games) is highly controversial. We argue, however, that some of the features of Lave's experimental design as well as the main regularities observed can be regarded as indirect support for this standpoint.

Lave reports on four different series of experiments, each conducted at different times and with different subjects. All these experiments consisted of several protracted runs of play of the same prisoner's dilemma conducted in a parallel and independent manner. Every run was played between a fixed pair of subjects and this was known to the individuals involved. In three of the series, there were at least 100 repetitions.[249] And while in one of these the number of repetitions was fixed, in the other two series there was an independent probability of ending the game once it had reached the 100th iteration. Finally, it is important to stress that, in every case, the players were fully informed about all the details of the situation (i.e., number of repetitions, ending probability, etc.)

In view of the substantial length displayed by the experimental runs, end effects (when present) affected only an insignificant fraction of the total observations. For the most part, behavior in any given run was governed by other considerations. The main regularities observed across the different series of experiments can be summarized as follows. Along each run, the average fraction of cooperating subject pairs displayed a clear upward trend. It moved from a rough 20% at the early stages

---

[249] A fourth series of experiments had only 50 iterations *per* run and is ignored in our discussion. Its qualitative behavior, however, is not different in any essential way from the other three series.

to over 80% by the 80th stage. The situations in which the individuals in a given pair chose a different action were very short-lived and rare. In contrast, the cooperating pairs tended to display a rather strong steadiness in their actions. Despite that the aforementioned trend appeared very clearly, the growth of cooperation was not always monotone. That is, relatively short relapses were observed where overall cooperation decreased for a few rounds, just to see it regain its previous level along the underlying trend.

The former regularities are largely consistent with the model discussed in Subsection 12.7.1. Indeed, this model predicts that, as time proceeds, a progressively larger fraction of (independent) subject pairs must have been successful in implementing a transition to the cooperative outcome. Once there, of course, any of these pairs may still return to joint defection thereafter (hence producing occasional reversals on the frequency of cooperation). However, the fact that this opposite transition is much less likely should still lead one to observe that an upward trend does hold in the overall population.

Summary

In this final chapter, our objective has been to complement the learning models studied in Chapter 11 with a "robustness" analysis tailored to tackling the key issue of equilibrium selection in games. To this end, we have focused on behavioral rules that, along the sophistication ladder used to organize them, embody relatively more stringent bounds on players' reasoning and perception abilities. Specifically, these rules have ranged from best- (or better-) response adjustment to interplayer imitation or reinforcement learning with flexible aspirations. In each case, the methodological approach has been the same. The learning dynamics has been perturbed with some stochastic noise, which may be interpreted as the outcome of individual "mutation" or experimentation. This perturbation renders the induced stochastic process ergodic and thus leads to a unique pattern of long-run behavior, as captured by its (unique) invariant distribution. Our primary interest has then been to characterize this limit invariant distribution (or, more specifically, its support) when the magnitude of the underlying noise becomes arbitrarily small.

This approach has been applied to a variety of strategic setups: bilateral coordination games, the minimum-effort game, Cournot oligopoly, and the prisoner's dilemma. In some of these cases, we have contrasted the implications of alternative interaction setups (e.g., local versus global interaction) and/or different learning dynamics (best-response adjustment versus imitation). The overall message that transpires from this exercise can be summarized as follows. In general, the details of the interaction setup and the nature of the learning dynamics may have drastic effects on the theoretical predictions of the model, both concerning the long-run outcomes selected as well as the rates of convergence. This, of course, may be seen as a word of warning to be heeded in specific applications. On the other hand, it is also suggestive of the theoretical richness of the approach, which responds to what often should be regarded as relevant details of the environment. In fact, we have provided some empirical support to the latter viewpoint by briefly reviewing some relevant experimental evidence. In this evidence, many of the key insights derived from the theoretical analysis appear largely corroborated. In particular, we have observed that considerations of strategic risk are an important determinant of choice in coordination games or that imitation and best-response adjustment induce the contrasting implications predicted by our learning models in Cournot setups.

Exercises

Exercise 12.1: Recall the global-interaction coordination framework studied in Subsection 12.4.1. Show that the best-response dynamics given by (12.4) and (12.5) converges, almost surely, to one of the two monomorphic states ω_α or ω_β.

Exercise 12.2: Show that, in the round-robin coordination context played under imitation, the cost function $\hat{c}(\cdot)$ for the derived model $\{(\Omega_0, \hat{Q}_\varepsilon)\}_{\varepsilon \in [0,1)}$ is given by (12.21).

Exercise 12.3: Prove that, in the round-robin coordination context played under best-response adjustment, the co-radius of the state ω_β satisfies the lower bound displayed in (12.32).

Exercise 12.4*:

(i) Reconsider the coordination setup with local interaction studied in Subsection 12.4.2 and study the long-run performance of the learning model induced by the imitation rule given by (12.2) and (12.3) – specifically, characterize the stochastically stable states and provide upper bounds on their expected waiting times.

(ii) Now reformulate the model studied in (i) above under a "local" imitation rule that replaces (12.2) by

$$\tilde{M}_i(s) \equiv \{s_j : j \in U_i^\ell, \ \pi_j(s) \geq \pi_i(s)\},$$

where $\mathcal{U}^\ell = \{U_i^\ell\}_{i \in N}$ is the social network given in (12.12). Characterize the stochastically stable states.

Exercise 12.5: Derive the upper bound (12.34) on expected waiting times arising in the model of local interaction studied in Subsection 12.4.2.

Exercise 12.6*: Recall the evolutionary setup with centralized interaction that is postulated in Subsection 12.4.3 and consider two alternative variants of it. In the first one, all players adjust their behavior through myopic best response. In the second one, the peripheral players learn by imitation among themselves, but the central player never adjusts her behavior (except by mutation) since she has no similarly positioned player to imitate. Characterize the set of stochastically stable states.

Exercise 12.7: In the context with centralized interaction studied in Subsection 12.4.3, provide an explicit lower bound on n (the size of the population) that is required for the conclusions specified in the text to hold. How is the analysis affected if this lower bound is not met? Characterize the stochastically stable states in the latter case.

Exercise 12.8*: Consider again the centralized-interaction setup studied in Subsection 12.4.3. We have shown that, in this context, the limit invariant distribution attributes positive weight to each of the states in Ω_0, i.e., both $\mu^*(\omega_\alpha) > 0$ and $\mu^*(\omega_\beta) > 0$. Can you suggest what the relative magnitudes of each of these weights should be? Attempt to provide a precise answer or, alternatively, at least a heuristic one.

Exercise 12.9*: Generalize the evolutionary approach introduced at the beginning of Section 12.4 as follows. Suppose each player $i \in N$ mutates with respective (idiosyncratic) probabilities ε_i, which are determined by corresponding smooth functions $\phi_i : [0, 1) \to [0, 1)$, $\varepsilon_i = \phi_i(\varepsilon)$, where ε is the common base parameter reflecting the "overall level of noise" in the system. Further suppose that $\phi_i(0) = 0$ and

$$0 < \lim_{\varepsilon \to 0} \frac{\phi_i(\varepsilon)}{\phi_j(\varepsilon)} < \infty \qquad (i, j = 1, 2, \ldots, n). \tag{12.62}$$

It can be shown that the techniques presented in Section 12.6 can be used to obtain the same results as in the text for each of the different strategic setups considered. Prove it in detail for the case in which the population plays a bilateral coordination game under global interaction.

Exercise 12.10*:

(i) In a spirit similar to that of Exercise 12.9, now assume that the mutation probabilities may depend on the prevailing state so that there is some smooth function $\phi : [0, 1) \times \Omega \to [0, 1)$, where $\varepsilon_\omega = \phi(\varepsilon, \omega)$ is the mutation probability at state ω when the base parameter reflecting the overall noise of the system is ε. (For simplicity, assume all players mutate with the same probability.) Further suppose that $\phi(0, \cdot) = 0$ and, as the counterpart of (12.62), we have that

$$0 < \lim_{\varepsilon \to 0} \frac{\phi(\varepsilon, \omega)}{\phi(\varepsilon, \omega')} < \infty \tag{12.63}$$

for each $\omega, \omega' \in \Omega$. Focus on the context in which the population plays a bilateral coordination game under global interaction and show that the results established in the text are not affected by the proposed variation.

(ii) Now consider a situation such as the one described in (i) above but, instead of (12.63), suppose $\phi(\varepsilon, \omega) = \varepsilon$ for all $\omega \neq \omega_\alpha$ but

$$\phi(\varepsilon, \omega_\alpha) = \varepsilon^r$$

for some $r \in \mathbb{N}$. Given n (the population size), characterize the values of r that lead to the same selection result (i.e., the same stochastically stable state) as in the text. What happens for other values of r?

Exercise 12.11:

   (i) Recall the evolutionary model of Subsection 12.4.1 where agents play a bilateral coordination game under global interaction. Reformulate it under the assumption that players adjust their actions on the basis of the *better-response* rule given by (12.6) and (12.7). Characterize the stochastically stable states.

   (ii) Consider the same behavioral assumption contemplated in (i) above for the case in which players are involved in the minimum-effort game (cf. Section 12.4.4).

Exercise 12.12: Suppose the payoff function of the minimum-effort game (cf. (12.14)) is changed to that of a "maximum-effort game" as follows:

$$\pi_i(e_1, e_2, \ldots, e_n) = \left\{ \max_{j \in N} e_j \right\} - \gamma e_i \qquad (i = 1, 2, \ldots, n),$$

where $\gamma \in (0, 1)$. Let players be involved in a (perturbed) evolutionary process where they adjust their behavior through imitation (i.e., (12.2) and (12.3) applies). Characterize the stochastically stable states and compare them with the Nash equilibria of the game. Contrast your conclusions with those of the minimum-effort game analyzed in the text.

Exercise 12.13:

   (i) Propose conditions on the demand and cost functions of the Cournot model described in Subsection 12.3.3 that guarantee that both the Cournot and Walras symmetric equilibria exist and are unique.

   (ii) Show that if a Walras symmetric equilibrium exists, it is always unique, provided that the law of demand is satisfied (i.e., the demand function is decreasing). Is the analogous statement true for Cournot equilibrium?

Exercise 12.14*: Consider the Cournot context presented in Subsection 12.3.3 and suppose that not only the demand function but also the firms' (common) cost function are both decreasing. Determine the stochastically stable states obtained in the evolutionary model where all firms are imitators (i.e., adjust their behavior according to (12.2) and (12.3)). Compare your conclusions with those obtained in the text and discuss the formal and conceptual differences.

Exercise 12.15*: Reconsider the Cournot evolutionary model under imitation studied in Subsection 12.4.5.1 but introduce the following variation on the original model: when a firm is subject to mutation, it changes its prior output x to one of the two neighboring outputs in Φ (i.e., $\max \{x - \varrho, 0\}$ or $\min \{x + \varrho, v\varrho\}$), each of them chosen with equal probability. Using the Kandori-Rob techniques described in Subsection 12.6.4.2, characterize the set of stochastically stable states of the corresponding (perturbed) evolutionary process.

Exercise 12.16: Recall the hybrid behavioral dynamics contemplated in Subsection 12.4.3 for the context in which a bilateral coordination game is played under centralized interaction. There, player 1 was postulated to adjust her behavior through myopic best response (i.e., according to (12.36)), whereas players 2 through n were assumed imitators among themselves (i.e., behave as in (12.35)). Apply the same behavioral mixture to the Cournot context described in Subsection 12.4.5.1; i.e., suppose firm 1 behaves according to (12.5) and firms 2 through n behave according to (12.3). Characterize the stochastically stable states of the (perturbed) evolutionary process thus induced.

Exercise 12.17: Show that the derived family of Markov chains $\{(\Omega_0, \hat{Q}_\varepsilon)\}_{\varepsilon \in [0,1)}$ constructed in Subsection 12.6.4.2 from the original canonical model defines by itself a proper canonical evolutionary model.

Exercise 12.18: Let $A \subset \Omega_0$ satisfy $R(A) > CR(A)$. Show *directly* (i.e., not merely invoking Proposition 12.3) that *no* other set $B \subset \Omega_0 \backslash A$ may satisfy $R(B) > CR(B)$.

Exercise 12.19: Let (Ω, Q_ε) stand for the perturbed stochastic process modeling reinforcement learning in the prisoner's dilemma (cf. Subsection 12.7.1). Show that the sufficient condition (12.58) invoked to guarantee the ergodicity of the process holds in this case.

Exercise 12.20: Recall the argument spelled out in Subsection 12.7.1 concerning the stochastic stability of ω_C in the prisoner's dilemma when $\eta/2 > \nu$. This argument was restricted to transitions across the symmetric states ω_C and ω_D. Extend it to the transitions involving the other two limit states $(C, 0, D, \eta)$ and $(D, \eta, C, 0)$.

Exercise 12.21*: Consider a reinforcement-learning model such as the one described in Section 12.7 but now postulate that, if an individual is subject to a perturbation, the following events occur: (i) her aspiration adjustment rule is unaffected (i.e., aspirations are still modified according to (12.55)); (ii) her action is chosen afresh, all of those possible selected with equal probability. Use this alternative model to study the prisoner's dilemma when $\eta/2 > \nu$ and argue that a line of argument analogous to that used in the text leaves our main conclusions unchanged, i.e., the unique stochastically stable state displays joint cooperation.

Exercise 12.22*: Assume there are $2n$ players who learn through (perturbed) reinforcement learning, as described in Section 12.7. Every period, they are randomly matched in pairs to play (only once) a prisoner's dilemma. Model the social dynamics as a Markov process and extend the reasoning used in the text to conclude that, if $\eta/2 > \nu$, the unique stochastically stable state must involve full cooperation by every player. What happens if $\eta/2 < \nu$?

Exercise 12.23: Recall the itemized discussion of Subsection 12.7.2 pertaining to the long-run behavior of a reinforcement-learning process in pure-coordination games. Prove in detail the items labeled (b) and (c).

Bibliography

Abreu, D. (1986): "Extremal equilibria of oligopolistic supergames," *Journal of Economic Theory* **39**, 191–228.

Akerlof, G. (1970): "The market for lemons: quality uncertainty and the market mechanism," *Quarterly Journal of Economics* **84**, 488–500.

Alós-Ferrer, C. (1999): "Dynamical systems with a continuum of randomly matched agents," *Journal of Economic Theory* **86**, 245–67.

Andreoni, J. and J.H. Miller (1993): "Rational cooperation in the finitely repeated Prisoner's Dilemma: experimental evidence," *The Economic Journal* **103**, 570–85.

Arnold, V.I. (1973): *Ordinary Differential Equations*, Cambridge: MIT Press.

Aumann, R. (1959): "Acceptable points in general cooperative *n*-person games," in A.W. Tucker and R.D. Luce (eds.), *Contributions to the Theory of Games IV*, Princeton: Princeton University Press.

Aumann, R. (1974): "Subjectivity and correlation in randomized strategies," *Journal of Mathematical Economics* **1**, 67–96.

Aumann, R. (1976): "Agreeing to disagree," *Annals of Statistics* **4**, 1236–9.

Aumann, R. (1987): "Correlated equilibrium as an expression of Bayesian rationality," *Econometrica* **55**, 1–18.

Aumann, R. and L. Shapley (1976): "Long-term competition: a game-theoretic analysis," mimeo.

Benaïm, M. and M.W. Hirsch (1999): "Mixed equilibria and dynamical systems arising from fictitious play in perturbed games," *Games and Economic Behavior* **29**, 36–72.

Benoit, J.P. and V. Krishna (1985): "Finitely repeated games," *Econometrica* **53**, 890–904.

Benoit, J.P. and V. Krishna (1987): "Nash equilibria of finitely repeated games," *International Journal of Game Theory* **16**, 197–204.

Benoit, J.P. and V. Krishna (1988): "Renegotiation in finitely repeated games," *Econometrica* **61**, 303–24.

Ben-Porath, E. and E. Dekel (1992): "Signalling future actions and the potential for self-sacrifice," *Journal of Economic Theory* **57**, 36–51.

Benveniste, A., M. Metivier, and P. Priouret (1990): *Adaptive Algorithms and Stochastic Approximations*, Berlin: Springer Verlag.

Bernheim, B.D. (1984): "Rationalizable strategic behavior," *Econometrica* **52**, 1007–28.

Bernheim, B.D., B. Peleg, and M.D. Whinston (1987): "Coalition-proof Nash equilibria I: concepts," *Journal of Economic Theory* **42**, 1–12.

Bertrand, J. (1883): "Théorie mathématique de la richesse sociale," *Journal des Savants*, 449–58.

Bhaskar, V. and F. Vega-Redondo (2001): "Migration and the evolution of conventions," *Journal of Economic Behavior and Organization*, in Press.

Binmore, K.G. (1987, 1988): "Modelling rational players I and II," *Economics and Philosophy* **3**, 179–214; **4**, 9–55.

Binmore, K.G. and A. Brandenburger (1990): "Common knowledge and game theory," in K.G. Binmore (ed.), *Essays on the Foundations of Game Theory*, Oxford: Blackwell.

Blackwell, D. and L. Dubins (1962): "Merging of opinions with increasing information," *Annals of Mathematical Statistics* **38**, 882–6.

Bomze, I.M. (1986): "Non-cooperative, two-person games in biology: a classification," *International Journal of Game Theory* **15**, 31–57.

Border, K.C. (1985): *Fixed Point Theorems with Applications to Economics and Game Theory*, Cambridge: Cambridge University Press.

Borgers, T. and R. Sarin (1997): "Learning through reinforcement," *Journal of Economic Theory* **77**, 1–14.

Brown, G. W. (1951): "Iterative solutions of games by fictitious play," in T. C. Koopmans (ed.), *Activity Analysis of Production and Allocation*, New York: Wiley.

Bryant, J. (1983): "A simple rational expectations Keynes-type model," *The Quarterly Journal of Economics*, **98**, 525–8.

Bryant, J. (1994): "Coordination theory, the Stag Hunt, and macroeconomics," in J. Friedman (ed.), *Problems of Coordination in Economic Activity*, Boston: Kluwer Academic Publishers.

Burguet, R. (2000): "Auction Theory: a guided tour," *Investigaciones Económicas* **24**, 3–50.

Bush, R. and R. Mostellar (1955): *Stochastic Models of Learning*, New York: Wiley.

Camerer, C. and T.-H. Ho (1999): "Experience-weighted attraction learning in normal-form games," *Econometrica* **67**, 827–74.

Chatterjee, K. and W. Samuelson (1983): "Bargaining under incomplete information," *Operations Research* **31**, 835–51.

Cho, I.-K. (1987): "A refinement of sequential equilibria," *Econometrica* **55**, 1367–90.

Cho, I.-K. and D. Kreps (1987): "Signalling games and stable equilibria," *Quarterly Journal of Economics* **102**, 179–221.

Cooper, R. and A. John (1988): "Coordinating coordination failures in Keynesian models," *Quarterly Journal of Economics* **103**, 441–63.

Cournot, A. (1838): *Recherches sur les Principes Mathématiques de la Théorie des Richesses*, Paris: Hachette.

Crawford, V.P. (1991): "An 'evolutionary' interpretation of van Huyck, Battalio, and Beil's experimental results on coordination," *Games and Economic Behavior* **3**, 25–59.

Cross, J. (1983): *A Theory of Adaptive Behavior*, Cambridge: Cambridge University Press.

Dasgupta, P. and E. Maskin (1986a): "The existence of equilibrium in discontinuous economic games, I: theory," *Review of Economic Studies* **46**, 1–26.

Dasgupta, P. and E. Maskin (1986b): "The existence of equilibrium in discontinuous economic games, II: applications," *Review of Economic Studies* **46**, 27–41.

Dastidar, K.G. (1997): "Comparing Cournot and Bertrand in a homogeneous product market," *Journal of Economic Theory* **75**, 205–12.

Davis, D. (1999): "Advance production and Cournot outcomes: an experimental investigation," *Journal of Economic Behavior and Organization* **40**, 59–79.

Debreu, G. (1952): "A social equilibrium existence theorem," *Proceedings of the National Academy of Sciences* **38**, 886–93.

Diamond, P. A. (1982): "Aggregate-demand management in search equilibrium," *Journal of Political Economy* **4**, 881–94.

Edgeworth, F. (1897): "La teoria pura del monopolio," *Giornale degli Economisti* **40**, 13–31. Translated as "The theory of monopoly" in *Papers Relating to Political Economy*, vol. 1, 111–42, London: Macmillan, 1925.

Ellison, G. (1983): "Learning, local interaction and coordination," *Econometrica* **61**, 1047–71.

Ellison, G. (2000): "Basins of attraction, long-run stochastic stability, and the speed of step-by-step evolution," *Review of Economic Studies* **67**, 17–45.

Fan, K. (1952): "Fixed points and minimax theorems in locally convex topological linear spaces," *Proceedings of the National Academy of Sciences* **38**, 121–6.

Farrell, J. and E. Maskin (1989): "Renegotiation in repeated games," *Games and Economic Behavior* **1**, 327–60.

Feldman, M. and C. Gilles (1985): "An expository note on individual risk without aggregate uncertainty," *Journal of Economic Theory* **35**, 26–32.

Flood, M.M. (1952): "Some experimental games," Research Memorandum RM-789, Santa Monica, Ca., RAND Corporation, June.

Flood, M.M. (1958): "Some experimental games," *Management Science* **5**, 5–26.

Foster, D. and P. Young (1990): "Stochastic evolutionary game dynamics," *Theoretical Population Biology* **38**, 19–32.

Freidlin, M. and A. Wentzell (1984): *Random Perturbations of Dynamical Systems*, New York: Springer-Verlag.

Friedman, D. (1991): "Evolutionary games in economics," *Econometrica* **59**, 637–66.

Friedman, J. (1971): "A non-cooperative equilibrium for supergames," *Review of Economic Studies* **38**, 1–12.

Friedman, M. (1953): "The methodology of positive economics," in *Essays in Positive Economics*, Chicago: University of Chicago Press.

Fudenberg, D. and D. Kreps (1993): "Learning mixed equilibria," *Games and Economic Behavior* **5**, 320–67.

Fudenberg, D. and D.K. Levine (1992): "Maintaining a reputation when strategies are imperfectly observed," *Review of Economic Studies* **57**, 555–73.

Fudenberg, D. and D.K. Levine (1998): *Theory of Learning in Games*, Cambridge: MIT Press.

Fudenberg, D. and E. Maskin (1986): "The folk theorem in repeated games with discounting or with incomplete information," *Econometrica* **54**, 533–56.

Fudenberg, D. and J. Tirole (1991): "Perfect Bayesian equilibrium and sequential equilibrium," *Journal of Economic Theory* **53**, 236–60.

Gale, D. (1987): "Limit theorems for markets with sequential bargaining," *Journal of Economic Theory* **43**, 20–54.

Gibbons, R. (1992): *Game Theory for Applied Economists*, Princeton: Princeton University Press.

Glazer, J. and A. Ma (1989): "Efficient allocation of a 'prize' – King Solomon's Dilemma," *Games and Economic Behavior* **1**, 222–33.

Glicksberg, I.L. (1952): "A further generalization of the Kakutani fixed point theorem with application to Nash equilibrium points," *Proceedings of the National Academy of Sciences* **38**, 170–4.

Green, E. and R. Porter (1984): "Non-cooperative collusion under imperfect information," *Econometrica* **52**, 87–100.

Hammerstein, P. and R. Selten (1992). "Evolutionary game theory," in R. Aumann and S. Hart (eds.), *Handbook of Game Theory*, Amsterdam: North Holland.

Harsanyi, J.C. (1967–68): "Games with incomplete information played by 'Bayesian' players," *Management Science* **14**, 159–82, 320–34, 486–502.

Harsanyi, J.C. (1973): "Games with randomly disturbed payoffs: a new rationale for mixed-strategy equilibrium points," *International Journal of Game Theory* **2**, 1–23.

Harsanyi, J.C. and R. Selten (1988): *A General Theory of Equilibrium Selection*, Cambridge: MIT Press.

Heller, W. (1986): "Coordination failure in complete markets with applications to effective demand," in W. Heller *et al.* (eds.), *Equilibrium Analysis: Essays in Honor of Kenneth Arrow, vol. 2*, Cambridge: Cambridge University Press.

Hellwig, M. (1986): "Some recent developments in the theory of competition in markets," mimeo, Universität Bonn.

Hines, W.G.S. (1980): "Strategy stability in complex populations," *Journal of Applied Probability* **17**, 600–10.

Hirsch, M. and S. Smale (1974): *Differential Equations, Dynamical Systems, and Linear Algebra*, New York: Academic Press.

Hofbauer, J. and K. Sigmund (1988): *Dynamical Systems and the Theory of Evolution*, Cambridge: Cambridge University Press.

Hofbauer, J., P. Schuster, and K. Sigmund (1979): "A note on evolutionary stable strategies and game dynamics," *Journal of Theoretical Biology*, **81**, 609–12.

Holt, C. (1995): "Industrial organization: a survey of the results of laboratory experiments," in J. Kagel and A. Roth (eds.), *The Handbook of Experimental Economics*, Princeton: Princeton University Press.

Hopkins, E. (1997): "Modelling how people play games: some analytic results," mimeo, University of Edinburgh.

Hopkins, E. (2002): "Two competing models of how people learn in games," *Econometrica*, **70**, 2141–66.

Hotelling, H. (1929): "Stability in competition," *Economic Journal* **39**, 41–57.

Huck, S., H.-T. Normann, and J. Oechssler (1999): "Learning in Cournot oligopoly: an experiment," *Economic Journal* **109**, 80–95.

Hurwicz, L. (1972): "On informationally decentralized systems," in R. Radner and C.B. McGuire (eds.), *Decision and Organization*, Amsterdam: North Holland.

Hurwicz, L. (1979): "Outcome functions yielding Walrasian and Lindahl allocations at Nash equilibrium points," *Review of Economic Studies* **46**, 217–25.

Judd, K.L. (1985): "The Law of Large Numbers with a continuum of IID random variables," *Journal of Economic Theory* **35**, 19–25.

Kalai, E. and E. Lehrer (1993*a*): "Rational learning leads to Nash equilibrium," *Econometrica* **61**, 1019–45.

Kalai, E. and E. Lehrer (1993*b*): "Subjective equilibrium in repeated games," *Econometrica* **61**, 1231–40.

Kandori, M. and R. Rob (1995): "Evolution of equilibria in the long run: a general theory and applications," *Journal of Economic Theory* **65**, 383–414.

Kandori, M., G. Mailath, and R. Rob (1993): "Learning, mutation, and long-run equilibria in games," *Econometrica* **61**, 29–56.

Karandikar, R., D. Mookherjee, D. Ray, and F. Vega-Redondo (1998): "Evolving aspirations and cooperation," *Journal of Economic Theory* **80**, 292–332.

Karlin, S. and H.M. Taylor (1975): *A First Course in Stochastic Processes*, London: Academic Press.

Kohlberg, E. and J.-F. Mertens (1986): "On the strategic stability of equilibria," *Econometrica* **54**, 1003–37.

Kreps, D. (1987): "Out of equilibrium beliefs and out of equilibrium behavior," mimeo, Stanford University.

Kreps, D. (1990): *A Course in Microeconomic Theory*, New York: Harvester Wheatsheaf.

Kreps, D. and J. Scheinkman (1983): "Quantity precommitment and Bertrand competition yield Cournot outcomes," *Rand Journal of Economics* **14**, 326–37.

Kreps, D. and R. Wilson (1982*a*): "Sequential equilibria," *Econometrica* **50**, 863–94.

Kreps, D. and R. Wilson (1982*b*): "Reputation and imperfect information," *Journal of Economic Theory* **27**, 253–379.

Kreps, D., P. Milgrom, J. Roberts, and R. Wilson (1982): "Rational cooperation in the finitely repeated prisoner's dilemma," *Journal of Economic Theory* **27**, 245–52.

Kuhn, H.W. (1953): "Extensive games and the problem of information," in H.W. Kuhn and A.W. Tucker (eds.), *Contributions to the Theory of Games II*, Princeton: Princeton University Press.

Kushner, H. J. and D. S. Clark (1978): *Stochastic Approximation Methods for Constrained and Unconstrained Systems*, Berlin: Springer Verlag.

Lave, L.B. (1962): "An empirical approach to the Prisoner's Dilemma game," *Quarterly Journal of Economics* **76**, 424–36.

Mas-Colell, A., M. Whinston, and J. Green (1995): *Microeconomic Theory*, Oxford: Oxford University Press.

Maskin, E. (1977): "Nash equilibrium and welfare optimality," mimeo, MIT.

Maskin, E. (1999): "Nash equilibrium and welfare optimality," *Review of Economic Studies* **66**, 23–38.

Maynard Smith, J. (1982): *Evolution and the Theory of Games*, Cambridge: Cambridge University Press.

Maynard Smith, J. and G.R. Price (1973): "The logic of animal conflict," *Nature* **246**, 15–21.

Meyn, S.P. and R.L. Tweedie (1993): *Markov Chains and Stochastic Stability*, London: Springer-Verlag.

Milgrom, P. and J. Roberts (1982): "Predation, reputation, and entry deterrence," *Journal of Economic Theory* **27**, 280–312.

Milgrom, P. and J. Roberts (1991): "Adaptive and sophisticated learning in normal-form games," *Games and Economic Behavior* **3**, 82–100.

Miyasawa, K. (1961): "On the convergence of learning processes in a 2×2 non-zero two-person game," Research Memorandum no. 33, Economic Research Program, Princeton University.

Monderer, D. and L. Shapley (1996*a*): "Potential games," *Games and Economic Behavior* **14**, 124–43.

Monderer, D. and L. Shapley (1996*b*): "Fictitious play for games with identical interests," *Journal of Economic Theory* **68**, 258–65.

Mookherjee, D. and B. Sopher (1997): "Learning and decision costs in experimental constant-sum games," *Games and Economic Behavior* **19**, 97–132.

Moore, J. and R. Repullo (1988): "Subgame perfect implementation," *Econometrica* **56**, 1191–220.

Moreno, D. and J. Wooders (1996): "Coalition-proof equilibrium," *Games and Economic Behavior* **17**, 80–112.

Moulin, H. (1984): "Dominance solvability and Cournot stability," *Mathematical Social Sciences* **7**, 83–102.

Munkres, J.R. (1974): *Topology: A First Course*, Englewood Cliffs, NJ: Prentice Hall.

Myerson, R. (1978): "Refinements of the Nash equilibrium concept," *International Journal of Game Theory* **7**, 73–80.

Myerson, R. (1979): "Incentive compatibility and the bargaining problem," *Econometrica* **47**, 61–73.

Myerson, R. (1981): "Optimal auction design," *Mathematics of Operation Research* **6**, 58–73.

Myerson, R. (1991): *Game Theory: Analysis of Conflict*, Cambridge: Harvard University Press.

Myerson, R. and M.A. Satterthwaite (1983): "Efficient mechanisms for bilateral trading," *Journal of Economic Theory* **29**, 265–81.

Nachbar J. (1990): "Evolutionary selection in dynamic games," *International Journal of Game Theory* **19**, 59–90.

Nachbar, J.H. (1997): "Prediction, optimization, and learning in repeated games," *Econometrica* **65**, 275–309.

Nash, J. (1951): "Non-cooperative games," *Annals of Mathematics* **54**, 286–95.

Offerman, J. Potters and J. Sonnemans (2002): "Imitation and belief learning in an oligopoly experiment," *Review of Economic Studies*, **69**, 973–97.

Palfrey, T.R. and S. Srivastava (1991): "Nash implementation using undominated strategies," *Econometrica* **59**, 479–501.

Palomino, F. and F. Vega-Redondo: (1999) "Convergence of aspirations and (partial) cooperation in the Prisoner's Dilemma," *International Journal of Game Theory* **28**, 465–88.

Pearce, D. (1984): "Rationalizable strategic behavior and the problem of perfection," *Econometrica* **52**, 1029–50.

Porter, R. (1983): "Optimal cartel trigger-price strategies," *Journal of Economic Theory* **29**, 313–38.

Posch, M. (1997): "Cycling in a stochastic learning algorithm for normal-form games," *Journal of Evolutionary Economics* **7**, 193–207.

Radner, R. (1980): "Collusive behavior in non-cooperative epsilon equilibria of oligopolies with long but finite lives," *Journal of Economic Theory* **22**, 136–54.

Rassenti, S., S. Reynolds, V. Smith, and F. Szidarovsky (2000): "Adaptation and convergence of behavior in repeated experimental Cournot games," *Journal of Economic Behavior and Organization* **41**, 117–46.

Reny, P.J. (1999): "On the existence of pure and mixed strategy Nash equilibria in discontinuous games," *Econometrica* **67**, 1029–56.

Repullo, R. (1987): "A simple proof of Maskin's Theorem on Nash implementation," *Social Choice and Welfare* **4**, 39–41.

Riley, J.G. (1979a): "Informational equilibrium," *Econometrica* **47**, 331–59.

Riley, J.G. (1979b): "Evolutionary equilibrium strategies," *Journal of Theoretical Biology*, **76**, 109–23.

Ritzberger, K. (2002): *Foundations of Non-Cooperative Game Theory*, New York: Oxford University Press.

Robinson, J. (1951): "An iterative method of solving a game," *Annals of Mathematics* **54**, 296–301.

Robles, J. (1997): "Evolution and long run equilibria in coordination games with summary statistic payoff technologies," *Journal of Economic Theory* **75**, 180–93.

Robson, A. and F. Vega-Redondo (1996): "Efficient equilibrium selection in evolutionary games with random matching," *Journal of Economic Theory* **70**, 65–92.

Rosenthal, R. (1973): "A class of games possessing pure-strategy Nash equilibria," *International Journal of Game Theory* **2**, 65–7.

Rosenthal, R. (1981): "Games of perfect information, predatory pricing, and the chain store paradox," *Journal of Economic Theory* **25**, 92–100.

Roth, A.E. and I. Erev (1995): "Learning in extensive-form games: experimental data and simple dynamic models in the intermediate term," *Games and Economic Behavior* **8**, 164–212.

Rotschild, M. and J. Stiglitz (1976): "Equilibrium in competitive insurance markets: an essay on the economics of imperfect information," *Quarterly Journal of Economics* **90**, 629–49.

Rubinstein, A. (1982): "Perfect equilibrium in a bargaining model," *Econometrica* **50**, 97–110.

Rubinstein, A. and A. Wolinsky (1985): "Equilibrium in a market with sequential bargaining," *Econometrica* **53**, 1133–50.

Rubinstein, A. and A. Wolinsky (1990): "Decentralized trading, strategic behaviour and the Walrasian outcome," *Review of Economic Studies* **57**, 63–78.

Rudin, W. (1976): *Principles of Mathematical Analysis*, New York: McGraw-Hill.

Samuelson, L. and J. Zhang (1992): "Evolutionary stability in asymmetric games," *Journal of Economic Theory* **57**, 363–91.

Savage, L.J. (1954): *The Foundations of Statistics*, New York: John Wiley and Sons.

Schaffer, M.E. (1988): "Evolutionary stable strategies for a finite population and a variable contest size," *Journal of Theoretical Biology*, **132**, 469–78.

Schmidt, K. (1993): "Reputation and equilibrium characterization in repeated games with conflicting interests," *Econometrica* **61**, 325–52.

Selten, R. (1965): "Spieltheoretische behandlung eines oligopolmodells mit nachfragetragheit," *Zeitschrift für die gesampte Staatswissenschaft* **12**, 301–24.

Selten, R. (1975): "Re-examination of the perfecteness concept for equilibrium points in extensive games," *International Journal of Game Theory* **4**, 25–55.

Selten, R. (1978): "The chain-store paradox," *Theory and Decision* **9**, 127–59.

Selten, R. and R. Stoecker (1986): "End behavior in sequences of finite Prisoner Dilemmas's supergames," *Journal of Economic Behavior and Organization* **7**, 47–70.

Shaked, A. and J. Sutton (1984): "Involuntary unemployment as a perfect equilibrium in a bargaining game," *Econometrica* **52**, 1351–64.

Shapiro, C. and J. Stiglitz (1984): "Equilibrium unemployment as a worker discipline device," *American Economic Review* **74**, 433–44.

Shapley, L.S. (1964): "Some topics in two-person games," in M. Dresher, L.S. Shapley, and A.W. Tucker (eds.), *Advances in Game Theory*, Princeton: Princeton University Press.

Spence, M. (1973): "Job market signalling," *Quarterly Journal of Economics* **87**, 355–74.

Spence, M. (1974): *Market Signalling*, Cambridge: Harvard University Press.

Stahl, I. (1972): *Bargaining Theory*, Stockholm: Economics Research Institute at the Stockholm School of Economics.

Tan, T. and S. Werlang (1988): "The Bayesian foundations of solution concepts of games," *Journal of Economic Theory* **45**, 370–91.

Úbeda, L. (1997): "The inefficiency of trade with asymmetry of information. A reconsideration," mimeo, MIT.

van Damme, E. (1987): *Stability and Perfection of Nash Equilibria*, Berlin: Springer-Verlag.

van Huyck, J., R. Battalio, and R. Beil (1990): "Tacit coordination games, strategic uncertainty, and coordination failure," *American Economic Review* **80**, 234–48.

van Huyck, J., R. Battalio, and R. Beil (1991): "Strategic uncertainty, equilibrium selection principles, and coordination failure in average opinion games," *Quarterly Journal of Economics* **106**, 885–911.

Varian, H. (1992): *Microeconomic Analysis* (3rd edition), New York: W.W. Norton and Company.

Vega-Redondo, F. (1993): "Competition and culture in an evolutionary process of equilibrium selection: a simple example," *Games and Economic Behavior* **5**, 618–31.

Vega-Redondo, F. (1996): *Evolution, Games, and Economic Behavior*, Oxford: Oxford University Press.

Vega-Redondo, F. (1997): "The evolution of Walrasian behavior," *Econometrica* **65**, 375–84.

von Neumann, J. (1928): "Zur Theorie der Gesellschaftsspiele," *Mathematische Annalen* **100**, 295–320.

von Stackelberg, H. (1934): *Marktform und Gleichgewicht*, Vienna: Julius Springer.

Walker, M. (1981): "A simple incentive compatible mechanism for attaining Lindahl allocations," *Econometrica* **49**, 65–73.

Weibull, J. (1995): *Evolutionary Game Theory*, Cambridge: MIT Press.

Wheeden, R.L. and A. Zygmund (1977): *Measure and Integral: An Introduction to Real Analysis*, New York: Marcel Dekker.

Wilson, R. (1977): "A model of insurance markets with incomplete information," *Journal of Economic Theory* **16**, 167–207.

Young, P. (1993): "The evolution of conventions," *Econometrica* **61**, 29–56.

Index